Special Feature: Political Science PRACTICES

American Government

Stories of a Nation
For the AP® Course

Scott F. Abernathy
University of Minnesota

Karen Waples
Holy Family High School, Colorado

bedford, freeman & worth
high school publishers

Boston | New York

Vice President, Social Sciences: Charles Linsmeier
Senior Publisher High School: Ann Heath
Executive Program Manager: Nathan Odell
Senior Development Editor: Donald Gecewicz

Assistant Editor: Corrina Santos
Editorial Assistant: Carla Duval
Senior Marketing Manager: Janie Pierce-Bratcher
Marketing Assistant: Tiffani Tang
Media Editor: Kim Morte
Executive Media Producer: Keri deManigold
Senior Media Project Manager: Michelle Camisa
Director of Design, Content Management: Diana Blume
Senior Cover Designer: William Boardman
Interior Designer: Lumina Datamatics, Inc.
Director, Content Management Enhancement: Tracey Kuehn
Senior Managing Editor: Michael Granger
Content Project Manager: Louis C. Bruno Jr.
Manager of Publishing Services: Andrea Cava
Senior Workflow Project Supervisor: Joe Ford
Production Supervisor: Robin Besofsky
Illustrations: Troutt Visual Services
Senior Photo Editor: Cecilia Varas
Photo Researcher: Julie Tesser/Lumina Datamatics, Inc.
Art Manager: Matthew McAdams
Director of Rights and Permissions: Hilary Newman
Composition: Lumina Datamatics, Inc.
Printing and Binding: Transcontinental Printing
Cover photo: Tristan Eaton, photo by Rey Rosa/The L.I.S.A. Project NYC

Library of Congress Control Number: 2018949837

ISBN-13: 978-1-319-19536-6
ISBN-10: 1-319-19536-6

© 2019 by Bedford/St. Martin's

Printed in Canada

4   5   6   7   23   22   21   20   19

W. H. Freeman and Company
Bedford, Freeman & Worth
One New York Plaza
Suite 4500
New York, NY 10004-1562
highschool.bfwpub.com/AmGov1e

Brief Contents

Unit 1   Democracy and the Constitution

BasSlabbers/Getty Images

Unit 2   The Branches of the Federal Government

Chris Hondros/Getty Images

Unit 3   Civil Rights and Civil Liberties

Wang Ying/Xinhua/Alamy Live News

Sarah Hussain/Red Dirt Report

Ariel Skelley/Getty Images

Detailed Contents

Unit 1
Democracy and the Constitution

BasSlabbers/Getty Images

Chapter 1 American Government and Politics
The Stories of Our Nation

Chapter 2 The Constitution
A New Vision of Government

Chapter 3 Federalism
Dividing Power between the National Government and the States 63

Unit 2
The Branches of the Federal Government

Chris Hondros/Getty Images

Chapter 4 Congress
Representation, Organization, and Legislation   106

Chapter 5 The American Presidency

Individuals, Institutions, and Executive Power

Chapter 6 The Federal Judiciary

Politics, Power, and the "Least Dangerous" Branch

Chapter 7 The Federal Bureaucracy
Putting the Nation's Laws into Effect

Wang Ying/Xinhua/Alamy Live News

Unit 3
Civil Rights and Civil Liberties

Unit 4
American Political Ideologies and Beliefs

Sarah Hussain/Red Dirt Report

Chapter 10 American Political Culture
What Americans Believe

Chapter 11 Public Opinion

Measuring Americans' Opinions

Chapter 12 Political Ideology

How Beliefs Shape Our Choices

Chapter 15 Interest Groups and Social Movements

Chapter 16 The Media

Acknowledgments

A number of instructors helped to guide the development of the college edition of *American Government: Stories of a Nation* and its resources. We appreciate the time and thoughts the reviewers of the college edition put into their feedback, which helped author Scott Abernathy to refine the material and ensure that the content is useful to both instructors and students.

Reviewers of the College Edition

Richard A. Almeida, Francis Marion University

John A. Aughenbaugh, Virginia Commonwealth University

Madelyn P. Bowman, Tarrant County College, South Campus

Marla Brettschneider, University of New Hampshire

Mark A. Cichock, University of Texas at Arlington

Amy Colon, SUNY Sullivan

Victoria Cordova, Sam Houston State University

Kevin Davis, North Central Texas College

Michael J. Faber, Texas State University

Terry Filicko, Clark State Community College

Patrick Gilbert, Lone Star College

Andrew Green, Central College

Sally Hansen, Daytona State College

Alyx D. Mark, North Central College

David F. McClendon, Tyler Junior College

Michael P. McConachie, Collin College

Patrick Moore, Richland College

Tracy Osborn, University of Iowa

Carl Palmer, Illinois State University

Melodie Pickett, Tarleton State University

Daniel E. Ponder, Drury University

Nicholas L. Pyeatt, Penn State Altoona

Paul Rozycki, Mott Community College

Deron T. Schreck, Moraine Valley Community College

Justin S. Vaughn, Boise State University

Tony Wohlers, Cameron University

In writing the edition for the AP® course, author Karen Waples has relied on three special reviewers for accuracy checking, advice about presentation, and suggestions for making the content conform better to the AP® course and to the needs of high-school students. She would like to thank Prof. Stanley Luger, University of Northern Colorado, Jeff Reiman, Grandview High School, Aurora, Colorado, and Benwari Singh, Cherry Creek High School, Greenwood Village, Colorado. (And a tip of the hat to Greg Snoad for his work on the practice exam.)

Reviewers of the Edition for the AP® Course

These reviewers participated in many ways in shaping the content of the textbook. They reviewed chapters, gave advice on student assessments, and participated in an early survey about the book and the AP® course that it serves.

Richard L. Andres Jr., North Tonawanda High School, New York

Carlene Baurichter, Bangor High School, Bangor, Wisconsin

Lee Boyer, Sylvania Southview High School, Sylvania, Ohio

Carlos Caldwell, Santa Fe High, Santa Fe, New Mexico

Matthew Desjarlais, Allatoona High School, Acworth, Georgia

Lorraine Dumerer, R.L. Turner High School, Carrollton, Texas

Allison Echlin, Northville High School, Northville, Michigan

Bob Fenster, Hillsborough High School, Hillsborough, New Jersey

Bonnie Herzog, Tampa, Florida

Jessica Hunsberger, Sleepy Hollow High School, Sleepy Hollow, New York

Bonnie Monteleone, Brecksville-Broadview Heights High School, Broadview Heights, Ohio

Mark Oglesby, The Episcopal School of Dallas, Dallas, Texas

Michael Vieira, Bishop Connolly High School, Fall River, Massachusetts

Edward Williams, Austin Preparatory School, Reading, Massachusetts

We also thank the nearly 200 teachers of AP® U.S. Government and Politics who participated in an initial survey to help the author and editors to shape this program to the AP® course.

Courtesy of Scott Abernathy

Scott F. Abernathy

University of Minnesota

After working as an on-street counselor for homeless adolescents in Boston, Scott received a master of curriculum and instruction and taught fourth and seventh grades in Wisconsin public schools. Hoping to learn more about the underlying systems that drove educational outcomes, Scott completed an M.P.A in domestic policy and then a Ph.D. in Politics from Princeton University.

Scott is now an associate professor of political science and a University Distinguished Teaching Professor at the University of Minnesota. He is also the author of *School Choice and the Future of American Democracy* and *No Child Left Behind and the Public Schools*, both from University of Michigan Press.

Alex Nelson, Cherry Creek Schools

Karen Waples

Holy Family High School, Colorado

Formerly a trial attorney, Karen Waples has taught since 1999 and currently teaches AP® Comparative Government and College Prep Government at Holy Family High School in Broomfield, Colorado. Karen has served as a reader for the AP® U.S. Government and Politics, as well as the AP® U.S. History exams, and she was the 2018 exam leader for the AP® Comparative Government and Politics exam. She is an endorsed consultant for the College Board® and conducts AP® U.S. Government and Politics workshops and institutes throughout the country. Karen was the chair of the College Board® Social Science Academic Advisory Committee and was a member of the Curriculum Redesign Committee for AP® U.S. Government and Politics. She received the Colorado Governor's Award for Excellence in Education in 1997 and was recognized as a Cherry Creek High School Teacher of the Year in 2002.

To the Student

Understanding U.S. Government and Politics: Tackling This Fun and Challenging Course

Dear AP® student:

Recently, there were some big changes in the AP® U.S. Government and Politics course. These changes give you an opportunity to gain the knowledge, skills, and reasoning practices that will help you to understand and participate in government and politics throughout your life. This class doesn't focus on memorization. It's about thinking and doing. This textbook, *American Government: Stories of a Nation for the AP® Course*, was written specifically for you as a high school student.

At the end of the course, you will take the AP® Exam. The new AP® Exam focuses on disciplinary practices and reasoning processes that require you to think like a political scientist. This redesigned exam will ask you to apply what you have learned to real-world scenarios. The exam provides you with a chance to demonstrate your ability to understand and interpret data, graphs, speeches, and debates about laws and policies. AP® Tips throughout the book help you navigate the new exam. Watch for them.

Here are some parts of the book designed to help you:

Each chapter in *American Government: Stories of a Nation for the AP® Course* begins with a story showing citizens in action and their impact on laws and government. As an author and teacher, I want to demonstrate how real people have made a difference through political actions. These stories create a vivid context that will help you better understand the content in each chapter.

The new course includes nine foundational documents, such as the Declaration of Independence. The course also includes fifteen required Supreme Court cases—decisions that have had a big effect on constitutional law and American life. This book explains each of these required readings and helps you to understand their nuances, in language you can understand, without overly simplifying their meaning. Look for the bright boxes about required cases and required documents that I put in the text to summarize what you should know.

Each chapter also contains two AP® Political Sciences Practices features that explain how to write an essay question better, how to assess data, and how to analyze photographs and political cartoons. Read them carefully so that you can apply the content in new ways and begin thinking like a political scientist.

I'm a high school teacher, and I get to work with students like you every day. I am proud of this book and believe it can help you achieve success on the AP® exam. More important, I believe this book will help you think deeply about important issues and encourage you to become a citizen actively engaged in your community and nation.

Sincerely,
Karen Waples
Co-Author of *American Government: Stories of a Nation for the AP® Course*
Teacher, Holy Family High School, Colorado

Tips for Taking the AP® Exam

The Exam for the AP® U.S. Politics and Government course consists of fifty-five multiple-choice questions and four free-response questions.

Multiple-Choice Questions

You will have an hour and twenty minutes to complete this part of the exam. This amounts to eighty minutes to answer fifty-five questions. Budget your time wisely. If you get stuck on a question, mark it in the exam booklet, bubble in a random answer, move to the next one, and come back to the question later, if you have time.

The multiple-choice exam has six different kinds of questions:

1. **Quantitative Analysis**   Interpreting tables, charts, graphs, maps, and infographics
2. **Qualitative Analysis**   Interpreting readings from primary and secondary sources
3. **Visual Analysis**   Interpreting cartoons, maps, and infographics
4. **Concept Application**   Applying political concepts to scenarios
5. **Comparison**   Explaining similarities and differences in the concepts learned in the course
6. **Knowledge**   Identifying and defining important terms and concepts in government and politics

Each multiple-choice question has four answer choices. You will earn one point for each correct answer, and there is no penalty for guessing, so answer every question. The multiple-choice portion makes up half of your score on the exam.

Free-Response Questions

You will answer four written questions in an hour and forty minutes.

Question 1: **Concept Application** (suggested time: 20 minutes)
Read a scenario and explain how it relates to what you have learned about government and politics.

Question 2: **Quantitative Analysis** (suggested time: 20 minutes)
Analyze data, identify a trend, or draw a conclusion from a table, chart, graph, map, or infographic and explain how it relates to the course content.

Question 3: **Supreme Court Comparison** (suggested time: 20 minutes)
Read about a nonrequired Supreme Court case and compare it with one of the fifteen required Supreme Court cases. The nonrequired case will be described in enough detail to give you the information that you need to answer the question. The required Supreme Court case will be identified in the question.

Question 4: **Argumentation Question** (suggested time: 40 minutes)
Write an essay with a thesis that develops an argument about a topic.

- You must use at least one of the nine foundational documents as a piece of evidence to support your argument.
- The question will contain a list of the foundational documents that you may use in your response.
- You must also use a second piece of evidence to support your argument, which may be a foundational document or something else you learned in the course.
- You will also have to provide an alternative perspective and respond to that alternative perspective using refutation, rebuttal, or concession.

The free-response section makes up half of your score on the exam. Each free-response question is worth 12.5 percent, which means the questions are evenly weighted, even though the argumentation question will take you longer to write. Again, budget your time carefully.

American Government: What's Inside

Meticulously Aligned to the Redesigned AP® U.S. Government and Politics Course

From the Big Ideas to the Essential Knowledge statements, this book has been painstakingly aligned to the concepts of the course. Each book unit corresponds to the same unit in the course framework. We've kept the coverage brief and targeted to make the book and, thus, the course more manageable for you and your students.

Simple Unit Structure

Unit 1   Democracy and the Constitution
Unit 2   The Branches of the Federal Government
Unit 3   Civil Rights and Civil Liberties
Unit 4   American Political Ideologies and Beliefs
Unit 5   Political Participation

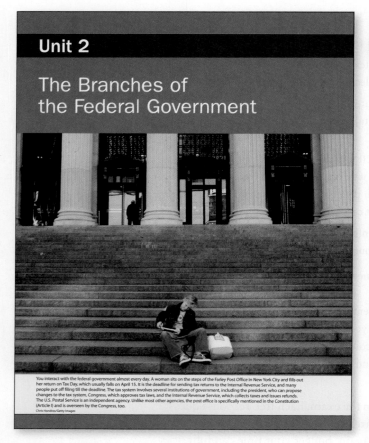

Unit 2

The Branches of the Federal Government

You interact with the federal government almost every day. A woman sits on the steps of the Farley Post Office in New York City and fills out her return on Tax Day, which usually falls on April 15. It is the deadline for sending tax returns to the Internal Revenue Service, and many people put off filing till the deadline. The tax system involves several institutions of government, including the president, who can propose changes to the tax system. Congress, which approves tax laws, and the Internal Revenue Service, which collects taxes and issues refunds. The U.S. Postal Service is an independent agency. Unlike most other agencies, the post office is specifically mentioned in the Constitution (Article I) and is overseen by the Congress, too.
Chris Hondros/Getty Images

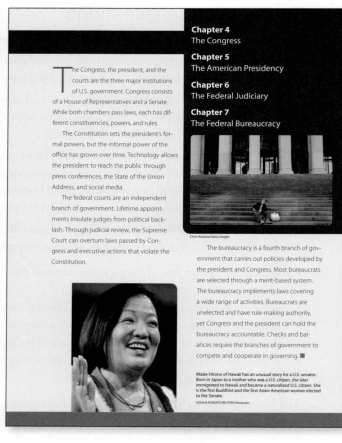

The Congress, the president, and the courts are the three major institutions of U.S. government. Congress consists of a House of Representatives and a Senate. While both chambers pass laws, each has different constituencies, powers, and rules.

The Constitution sets the president's formal powers, but the informal power of the office has grown over time. Technology allows the president to reach the public through press conferences, the State of the Union Address, and social media.

The federal courts are an independent branch of government. Lifetime appointments insulate judges from political backlash. Through judicial review, the Supreme Court can overturn laws passed by Congress and executive actions that violate the Constitution.

Chapter 4
The Congress

Chapter 5
The American Presidency

Chapter 6
The Federal Judiciary

Chapter 7
The Federal Bureaucracy

Chris Hondros/Getty Images

The bureaucracy is a fourth branch of government that carries out policies developed by the president and Congress. Most bureaucrats are selected through a merit-based system. The bureaucracy implements laws covering a wide range of activities. Bureaucrats are unelected and have rule-making authority, yet Congress and the president can hold the bureaucracy accountable. Checks and balances require the branches of government to compete and cooperate in governing. ■

Mazie Hirono of Hawaii has an unusual story for a U.S. senator. Born in Japan to a mother who was a U.S. citizen, she later immigrated to Hawaii and became a naturalized U.S. citizen. She is the first Buddhist and the first Asian-American woman elected to the Senate.
JOSHUA ROBERTS/REUTERS/Newscom

Easy-to-Use Organization

Pacing your AP® U.S. Government and Politics course can be challenging because there are so many concepts and skills to teach, usually in only a single semester. To help, we have segmented chapters into sixty-eight sections guided by learning targets. Each section is just enough for a single day's lesson to deliver content, skills, assignments, and assessments in a brief and easy-to-use "chunk." Whether you are a novice or veteran teacher, these modules will save you hours of planning time.

Integrated AP® Political Science Practices Features

Each chapter includes two or three special features to enhance students' mastery of the course's Disciplinary Practices and Reasoning Processes. Each includes instruction, modeling, and practice in the AP® style.

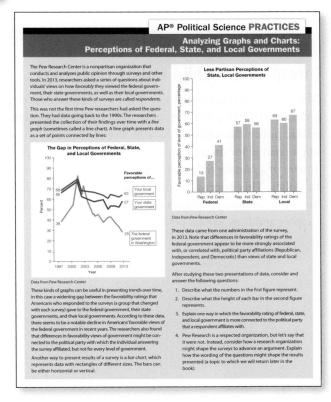

Meaningful, Focused Work on the Required Court Cases

The College Board chose fifteen required U.S. Supreme Court cases to highlight the role of the U.S. Supreme Court in interpreting the Constitution and Bill of Rights. In *American Government: Stories of a Nation for the AP® Course*, chapters that align with particular cases introduce a deep reading of the case, point out the importance of the case to the AP® course, and assess students' knowledge. Argumentation questions introduce pertinent cases and ask students to articulate a thesis, use the cases as evidence, and write an essay.

Integrated Public Policy Coverage

Most traditional books relegate public policy to discrete, separate chapters, but the new AP® course integrates public policy throughout. As you would expect from a book created for the new course, *American Government: Stories of a Nation for the AP® Course* incorporates public policy. This approach emphasizes how public policy functions as the application of principles taught in each chapter and how public policies are implemented.

▆ 7.3 The Bureaucracy and Policymaking

The bureaucracy carries out executive actions and laws passed by Congress, and it is the key institution responsible for implementing policy. Making public policy involves a series of steps. The entire process is fluid, constantly changing, and, above all else, political. The American political system is designed to have multiple points of access and debate throughout the process.[18]

Defining the Problem and Getting Congress to Act

What may seem like the most simple—and nonpolitical—part of policymaking may be the most significant and the most consequential: defining the problem. (See Figure 7.5.) There are different ways of looking at an issue. Having one's definition of the problem accepted is an effective exercise of power in the policy process.

Getting on the policy agenda—the set of issues on which policymakers focus their attention—is a crucial goal of anyone who wants to influence the policymaking process. Getting on the agenda, or keeping an idea off it, is also an effective exercise of political power. The science of getting on the agenda remains somewhat *un*scientific because the ability to get one's concerns considered depends not only on the merits of the issue but also on the political and economic contexts in which the ideas are offered and on the ways in which the public views the issue at the time.

Getting a policy proposal on the agenda is only the beginning. The policies have to be debated and passed by the Congress and signed into law by the president. Financing an

FIGURE 7.5

The Policymaking Process

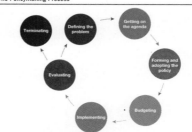

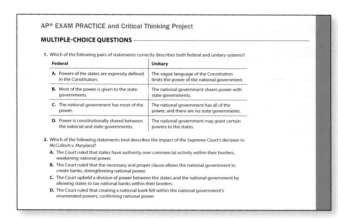

Integrated AP® Exam Practice

At the end of every section, chapter, and unit, you will find AP®-style practice items—multiple-choice questions, free-response questions, and argumentation questions—that conform to the rewritten AP® exam. These questions were written and vetted by AP® teachers deeply familiar with the format of the new exam.

Deeper Understanding of the Foundational Documents

The revised course focuses on foundational documents like the Declaration of Independence and the U.S. Constitution. This book leads students carefully through those foundational documents, quoting them extensively and summarizing their arguments. Besides practice with multiple choice and free response questions, students will also learn how to use the foundational documents as evidence in the model argumentation questions where they can practice writing an essay in the style of the revised AP® Exam. A supplemental document reader containing required foundational documents and court cases is also available. (More on the **Reader** below.)

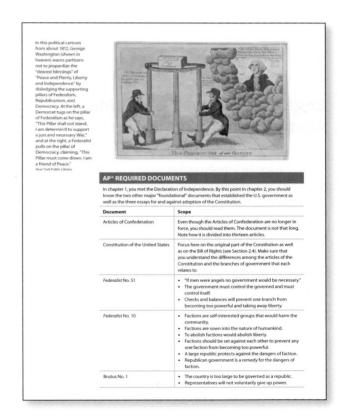

In this political cartoon from about 1812, George Washington (shown in heaven) warns partisans not to jeopardize the "dearest blessings" of "Peace and Plenty, Liberty and Independence" by dislodging the supporting pillars of Federalism, Republicanism, and Democracy. At the left, a Democrat tugs on the pillar of Federalism as he says, "This Pillar shall not stand. I am determin'd to support a just and necessary War," and at the right, a Federalist pulls on the pillar of Democracy, claiming, "This Pillar must come down. I am a friend of Peace."
New York Public Library

AP® REQUIRED DOCUMENTS

In chapter 1, you met the Declaration of Independence. By this point in chapter 2, you should know the two other major "foundational" documents that established the U.S. government as well as the three essays for and against adoption of the Constitution.

Document	Scope
Articles of Confederation	Even though the Articles of Confederation are no longer in force, you should read them. The document is not that long. Note how it is divided into thirteen articles.
Constitution of the United States	Focus here on the original part of the Constitution as well as on the Bill of Rights (see Section 2.4). Make sure that you understand the differences among the articles of the Constitution and the branches of government that each relates to.
Federalist No. 51	• "If men were angels no government would be necessary." • The government must control the governed and must control itself. • Checks and balances will prevent one branch from becoming too powerful and taking away liberty.
Federalist No. 10	• Factions are self-interested groups that would harm the community. • Factions are sown into the nature of humankind. • To abolish factions would abolish liberty. • Factions should be set against each other to prevent any one faction from becoming too powerful. • A large republic protects against the dangers of faction. • Republican government is a remedy for the dangers of faction.
Brutus No. 1	• The country is too large to be governed as a republic. • Representatives will not voluntarily give up power.

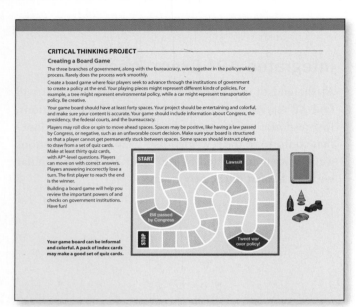

Critical Thinking Projects to Extend Learning

To add some fun and interesting ideas for taking your class beyond the exam, this book includes Critical Thinking Projects at the end of each chapter and unit to prompt students to engage with the course concepts in novel and creative ways.

Engaging Stories That Bring Abstract Concepts to Life

American Government: Stories of a Nation for the AP® Course puts an emphasis on practical applications by framing each chapter with a story from the real world showing how the principles of government have real effects that impact real people. For example, to understand political participation and political formation, we follow the story of an AP® U.S. Government student in Colorado who volunteered for a Republican congressional campaign and became increasingly involved in electoral politics.

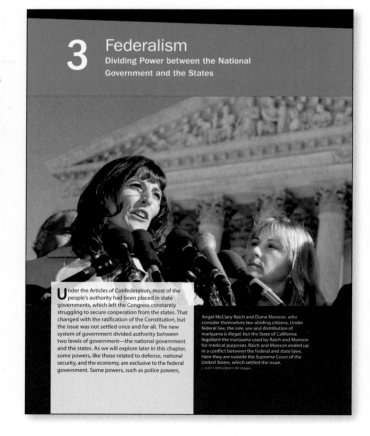

3 Federalism
Dividing Power between the National Government and the States

U nder the Articles of Confederation, most of the people's authority had been placed in state governments, which left the Congress constantly struggling to secure cooperation from the states. That changed with the ratification of the Constitution, but the issue was not settled once and for all. The new system of government divided authority between two levels of government—the national government and the states. As we will explore later in this chapter, some powers, like those related to defense, national security, and the economy, are exclusive to the federal government. Some powers, such as police powers,

Angel McClary Raich and Diane Monson, who consider themselves law-abiding citizens. Under federal law, the sale, use and distribution of marijuana is illegal, but the State of California legalized the marijuana used by Raich and Monson for medical purposes. Raich and Monson ended up in a conflict between the federal and state laws. Here they are outside the Supreme Court of the United States, which settled the issue.
J. SCOTT APPLEWHITE/AP Images

Complete Package to Support Teachers and Students

Support for Teachers

This book comes with a wraparound **Teacher's Edition**, written by veteran AP® teachers and College Board® consultants who know the course and know the students. Full of creative and insightful ideas about teaching, pacing, and planning this redesigned course, this Teacher's Edition is an indispensable tool for new and experienced teachers alike.

The **Teacher's Resource Materials** include everything you need to support your teaching and your students' learning. From handouts to lesson plans, you'll find it all in the TRM (available as a flash drive, or as resources in the e-book).

Student Support: A Document Reader Tailored to the Redesigned Course

The **Foundational Documents and Court Cases Reader** includes all of the documents and cases required by the College Board®, as well as some frequently taught works that go beyond the course framework. Each document is accompanied by commentary and guided questions to help students understand these complex texts.

Supplements to Suit Your Classroom Needs

 *American Government: Stories of a Nation for the AP® Course* is available in a range of e-book platforms, including our fully interactive **LaunchPad e-book**. In LaunchPad, every question in the book is assignable. This means that students can respond directly in the e-book and have their work report to your gradebook. The e-book includes integrated Teacher's Resource Materials and Learning-Curve adaptive quizzing, and it works on any device. To find the e-book that's right for you, contact your Bedford, Freeman & Worth sales representative.

LearningCurve Our **LearningCurve** adaptive quizzing engine will guide students to mastery of the course content. This first-ever LearningCurve for AP® U.S. Government is specifically designed to build understanding of the revised AP® course concepts.

TURNING technologies EXAMVIEW® ASSESSMENT SUITE The **ExamView® Assessment Suite** includes more than a thousand AP®-style multiple-choice, free-response, and argumentation questions to help students prepare for the AP® Exam. The ExamView Test Generator lets you quickly create paper, internet, and LAN-based tests. Tests can be created in minutes, and the platform is fully customizable, allowing you to enter your own questions, edit existing questions, set time limits, and incorporate multimedia. To discourage plagiarism and cheating, the test bank can scramble answers and change the order of questions. Detailed result reports feed into a gradebook.

Unit 1

Democracy and the Constitution

The American Revolution was based on the idea that sovereignty comes from the people and government is limited. People immigrate to the United States in search of the American dream of freedom and equality.

BasSlabbers/Getty Images

Our voices matter. The Constitution is based on the idea that sovereignty comes from the people and government is limited. The Constitution balances individual freedom, order, and equality of opportunity.

Our first form of government, the Articles of Confederation, failed to create a stable nation, and the founding fathers created a new system that gave more power to the national government. Power is divided among the president, a two-house legislature, and the courts. Each branch of government checks the others to prevent one branch from becoming too powerful.

Power is also divided between the national government and the states. This causes continuing controversy over how much power the states should have compared to the national government. Ratification of the Constitution did not end the controversy over how power is shared in America, and we continue to debate how to best protect property, order, liberty, and equality. ■

BasSlabbers/Getty Images

Syrian refugees Molham, Mohammed, and Ebrahim Kayali (left to right) pose at Emporia State University in Kansas. They have fled their native country and seek to continue their educations in the United States. The American dream is discussed in chapter 1.

Orlin Wagner/AP Images

1 American Government and Politics
The Stories of Our Nation

College and high school students march in Baltimore, Maryland, in 2015 in protest of the death of Freddie Gray while in police custody. Their protest is part of the American political story: people claiming their constitutional rights and demanding to be heard.
Andrew Burton/Getty Images

This book uses stories to help sharpen your ability to interpret the political world around you. Stories in each chapter will illustrate important concepts in the study of American politics. They are meant to make those ideas come to life—to help you understand that American government is not something that exists apart from you.

Hardly any of the stories have tidy endings. And because they are *real* stories, in all their messy, complicated glory, they will urge you and your classmates to think in ways that don't amount to either/or. Stories are a way to learn to walk in the shoes of people whose circumstances, experiences, and opinions differ from yours.

Read the stories. Absorb the nuts-and-bolts facts and concepts that you are studying. Most important, however, connect the facts to concepts. Use the stories to more deeply understand the complexity of American politics. Use them to understand the many voices that are a part of the national conversation. Use the stories to make your own arguments stronger, better formed, more politically savvy, and more effective.

The stories told in this book illustrate how big questions are resolved and revisited through **politics**, the process of influencing the actions and policies of a **government**. Politics and government are closely connected, but they are not the same. Politics describes processes; government describes the rules and institutions that make up the system of policymaking within a country. Throughout the book, we'll hear from people who have engaged with those institutions and who have taken part in those processes.

politics
the process of influencing the actions and policies of government.

government
the rules and institutions that make up that system of policymaking.

We will begin with two stories about schools: one about a young woman in Nebraska who fought for the right to start a Bible study group, the other about a group of Kentucky students who wanted to establish a Gay-Straight Alliance.

We will witness the efforts of many kinds of people who have wrestled with the meaning of fundamental rights in American democracy and see how they, as individuals and groups, have fought for their rights.

By connecting to those stories about the foundations of American government, you will be able to

1.1 Describe the balance between governmental power and individual rights.

1.2 Describe American political culture.

1.3 Explain and compare models of representative democracy.

1.4 Describe a constitutional republic.

LEARNING TARGETS

■ 1.1 The Fight for Students' Rights

Bridget Mergens walked into the office of her school principal in Omaha, Nebraska, with a request. She wanted to start a student group—a Christian Bible study club. Mergens's high school sponsored many other extracurricular clubs, including a photography club and a scuba diving club. Her principal and her local school board denied her request, claiming that the religious club she proposed was different from the other approved clubs. To Mergens, the school board's arguments were flawed.

Mergens was represented by a Christian advocacy group, the National Legal Foundation. The legal basis of Mergens's claim was a national law, the Equal Access Act

Liz Loverde, a sophomore at Wantagh Senior High School on Long Island, New York, in 2014. Loverde successfully pressured her school to allow a Bible study club, following in the footsteps of others, such as Bridget Mergens, in claiming rights under the Equal Access Act of 1984.

The Liberty Institute

of 1984 (EAA).[1] The law's main intent was to restrict the ability of public high schools to exclude religious extracurricular clubs.

In 1981, before the act's passage, the Supreme Court had already affirmed these rights for students at public colleges and universities, but it had not yet done so for those in public high schools. One consideration was whether high school students are mature enough to distinguish between their school's efforts to provide an open forum and the possibility that the school endorsed the club members' religious beliefs.

In June 1990, five years after Bridget Mergens tried to start the Bible study club, the Supreme Court ruled in her favor. The Court upheld high school students' rights to have the same access for their faith-based extracurricular clubs as that granted to other student groups. It also upheld the constitutionality of the EAA. In her majority opinion in *Board of Education of Westside Community Schools v. Mergens*, Supreme Court justice Sandra Day O'Connor wrote, "High school students are mature enough and are likely to understand that a school does not endorse or support student speech that it merely permits on a nondiscriminatory basis."[2]

Others, including some of the justices of the Supreme Court, worried that the free-speech provisions of the EAA might also guarantee access for student groups with much more controversial agendas. It was this possibility that had especially worried school administrators. Omaha principal James Findley recounted, "I didn't have a concern about the five or six kids having a Bible study club. I was concerned about what and who it opens the doors to. I've had students say they'll start a Satanist club or a skinheads group."[3]

As it turned out, other groups of high school students *did* test the system, including a group of high school students in Boyd County, Kentucky, who circulated a petition to start a Gay-Straight Alliance (GSA). In 2002, school officials turned down the students' request to form the GSA. Of twenty-one student group applications, theirs was the only one denied. Requests from groups such as the Future Business Leaders of America and the Fellowship of Christian Athletes were approved.[4] The students then contacted the American Civil Liberties Union (ACLU) for help. One month after the ACLU sent a letter to the school board that referred to the Equal Access Act, the board reversed itself and approved the formation of the GSA.[5]

But that didn't fully settle the matter. Back at Boyd County High School, at the first official meeting of the GSA, a crowd "directly confronted the GSA supporters 'with facial expressions, hand gestures . . . some very uncivil body language . . . people were using loud voices and angry voices.'"[6] Two days later, a group of students protesting outside the school "shouted at [GSA] students as they arrived, 'We don't want something like that in our school.'"[7]

In an emergency meeting held in December, the school board suspended all non-curricular clubs for the remainder of the 2002–03 school year.[8] Members of the GSA stopped meeting at the school, but other groups, including the school's drama and Bible study clubs, continued to use the high school's facilities. The members of the GSA went to court.

In 2004, the ACLU announced a settlement with the Boyd County public schools: "The settlement requires that the district treat all student clubs equally and conduct an

Decades after both the *Mergens* and the *Boyd County* cases, Jennifer Villasana, president of the Gay-Straight Alliance at Richland High School, holds a badge that she wears at the White House LGBT Conference on Safe Schools and Communities held at the University of Texas at Arlington, Texas, on Tuesday, March 20, 2012.
Rodger Mallison/Fort Worth Star-Telegram/MCT via Getty Images

anti-harassment training for all district staff as well as all students in high school and middle school."[9]

The efforts of these students highlight the ways in which individuals have used the political tools available to them to secure their rights. In filing her lawsuit and pursuing her claims, Bridget Mergens had help from the National Legal Foundation, a Christian public interest law firm.[10] The Boyd County High School GSA had the help of the ACLU. Both Mergens and the members of the Boyd County High School GSA based their claims on the same federal law, the Equal Access Act. With help, they harnessed the power of the American judicial system to realize their goals.

Equal Access Act
• Bible Study Club
• GSA

Both groups' efforts demonstrate how to use tactics effectively in the political process. In this book, we will consider those dynamics in detail. We will also dive into the stories of many other individuals and groups who have sought to assert their rights and reshape the laws. Whether the others whose stories you will read "won" or "lost" is not the most important consideration. By adding their voices to the American conversation, they mattered.

AP® Political Science PRACTICES

Exam Task Verbs

The AP® U.S. Government and Politics exam contains three free-response questions and one argumentation question. Task verbs tell you how to write your response. These task verbs appear on the exam:

Identify: To name a factor, person, power, or other term.

Example: *Identify* the tactic used by Bridget Mergens to assert her rights.

Answer: Mergens filed a lawsuit.

Describe: To state the meaning of a term or concept.

Example: *Describe* the Equal Access Act of 1984.

Answer: The EAA protects the right of students to form religious clubs in public high schools.

Explain: To give a cause or reason. Explanations usually include the word *because*.

Example: *Explain* how the Equal Access Act of 1984 causes tension between liberty and order.

Answer: The EEAA demonstrates tension between liberty and order because when students form controversial clubs, school officials worry that the controversy will cause protest and disorder within the school.

This chapter's main ideas are reflected in the Learning Targets. By reviewing after each section, you should be able to

—**Remember** the key points,

—**Know** terms that are central to the topic, and

—**Think** critically about these questions.

1.1 Describe the balance between governmental power and individual rights.

REMEMBER   The American system of government is complex and balances competing rights.

KNOW
- *politics*: the process of influencing the actions and policies of government. (p. 5)
- *government*: the rules and institutions that make up the system of policymaking. (p. 5)

THINK   How do the actions of the students and school officials featured in this story demonstrate the balance between protecting liberty and establishing order?

1.1 Review Question: Free Response

The Equal Access Act of 1984 (EAA) states, "It shall be unlawful for any public secondary school which receives Federal financial assistance . . . to deny equal access or a fair opportunity to, or discriminate against, any students who wish to conduct a meeting . . . on the basis of the religious, political, philosophical, or other content of the speech at such meetings."[11]

After reading the passage, please respond to parts A, B, and C.

A.   Describe the purpose of the EAA.

B.   Describe how Bridget Mergens and the Gay-Straight Alliance (GSA) at Boyd County High School used the EAA to assert their rights.

C.   Explain one way in which the efforts of Bridget Mergens and the GSA, and the actions of officials at their schools, illustrate the tension between protecting liberty and establishing order.

■ 1.2 American Political Culture

When they asserted their rights, Bridget Mergens and members of the Boyd County High School GSA did so on the basis of a handful of ideas that form the foundation of the American Republic. Indeed, these ideas were affirmed in the Declaration of Independence in 1776, making them part of the country's basic DNA: "We hold these truths to be self-evident, that all men are created equal, that they are endowed by their Creator with certain unalienable Rights, that among these are Life, Liberty, and the pursuit of Happiness." These were revolutionary ideas, but they were not original ones.

The Declaration of Independence

In drafting the Declaration of Independence, Thomas Jefferson drew upon ideas about liberty and government that were widely known in the colonies and Great Britain—ideas Jefferson wanted to convey so persuasively that they would launch a revolution. From the histories and philosophical works of ancient Greece and Rome came the idea of **democracy** (from the Greek *demos*, meaning "people," and *kratos*, "power"), in which power is held by the people.

democracy
a system of government where power is held by the people.

The would-be revolutionaries also borrowed from English Enlightenment philosopher John Locke, who had argued against a divine, or God-given, right of kings to rule with absolute power. Locke argued that people are born with **natural rights** that kings cannot give or take away.[12] These rights include life, liberty, and property. According to Locke, government is based on a **social contract**, in which people give to their governments the ability to rule over them to ensure an orderly and functioning society. If a government breaks that social contract by violating people's natural rights, then the people have the right to replace that unjust government with a just one.

From the French Enlightenment, Jefferson drew on the works of the Baron de Montesquieu,[13] who proposed that power in government should be divided between different branches so that no one branch could become too powerful. Jefferson also relied on Scottish Enlightenment thinkers such as David Hume.[14] Noticing the tendency of leaders throughout history to abuse political power, Hume believed a just government should be carefully designed to keep the greedy and ambitious from using political power to their own advantage.

Today, the ideas of liberty, equality, and rights shape the shared set of beliefs, customs, traditions, and values that define the relationship of Americans to their government. We call those shared beliefs **American political culture**. Rodgers Smith, a contemporary political scientist, argues that there are multiple, often contradictory, political traditions.[15] Republicanism, with its roots in ancient Greece, emphasized participatory rights and a focus on the common good, even as a hierarchical tradition has embraced racial and gender hierarchies and inequality, where some people had more rights than others.[16]

The Declaration of Independence contains five parts. In the preamble, Jefferson wrote, "When in the Course of human events, it becomes necessary for one people to dissolve the political bands which have connected them with another . . ." This set the stage for the argument that the British government was no longer legitimate. Next, Jefferson defined citizens' rights as "Life, Liberty and the pursuit of Happiness." Jefferson deviated from John Locke in this statement of rights, replacing "property" with "happiness." The longest part of the Declaration is a list of grievances against the King of England, including charges that the colonists were not being represented in government, justice was obstructed, standing armies threatened colonists, and unfair taxes were imposed, along with a long list of other complaints. The Declaration ends with a statement separating the colonies from Great Britain and with a pledge by the signers to each other to protect "our Lives, our Fortunes, and our Sacred Honor."

On July 4, 1776, Congress approved Thomas Jefferson's Declaration of Independence, which became the first formal document establishing the basic principles of American democracy.

Popular Sovereignty and Republicanism

Sovereignty is the right of a government to rule. It can derive from many sources, such as monarchy, a divine right given by a god, or the leadership of an elite group. American political culture is based on the principle of **popular sovereignty**—the idea that the government's right to rule comes from the people. As stated in the Declaration's preamble, all of the government's power comes from the citizens, and when the citizens are unhappy, they can replace the government through regular, free, and fair elections.

American political culture is also based on the concept of **republicanism**, which means that the authority of the government comes from the people. Long gone are the days of the

natural rights
the right to life, liberty, and property, which government cannot take away.

social contract
people allow their governments to rule over them to ensure an orderly and functioning society.

John Locke

American political culture
the set of beliefs, customs, traditions, and values that Americans share.

AP® TIP

Vocabulary matters!
The AP® U.S. Government and Politics exam assesses knowledge of important concepts. Pay attention to the bold terms in the textbook. Understanding key concepts means much more than just memorizing words. It's crucial to understand why each concept is important and to be able to apply it to new scenarios.

popular sovereignty
the idea that the government's right to rule comes from the people.

republicanism
a system in which the government's authority comes from the people.

direct democracy practiced in ancient Greece, where eligible male citizens met to vote on policy issues. Representative government is much more practical and efficient than asking Americans to vote on every issue facing the nation. In representative government, citizens can choose representatives to assert their interests in the national policymaking process. Furthermore, representatives are held accountable in free and fair elections that take place at frequent and regular intervals. Members of the U.S. House of Representative stand for election every two years, and the term of a U.S. senator is six years. Presidential elections happen every four years.

Inalienable Rights

inalienable rights
rights the government cannot take away.

The thinking behind the Declaration of Independence is that some rights are *self-evident*. These are called **inalienable rights** in the sense that government may not take them away. The rights of life, liberty, and the pursuit of happiness are among those inherent, self-evident rights. A just system of political rule must be constructed to protect these rights and their expression. The desire to safeguard individuals' rights led to the complex structure of American political institutions in the Constitution, which we will explore in the next chapter.

Two Visions of Liberty

liberty
social, political, and economic freedoms.

Another foundational American ideal expressed in the Declaration is a commitment to **liberty**—to social, political, and economic freedoms. Liberty may mean freedom *from* interference by a government or a freedom *to* pursue one's dreams. There is often a tension between these two visions of liberty. In the case of the Bridget Mergens's Bible study club, the tension between these two freedoms came into sharp focus. Mergens and her fellow students claimed the freedom *to* explore their faith in an extracurricular club. By allowing the group, however, Omaha public school officials risked violating other students' freedoms *from* having a government endorse a particular religious faith or endorse religious over nonreligious beliefs.

The Pursuit of Happiness and the American Dream

When Thomas Jefferson wrote about "the pursuit of Happiness," he was tapping into another core American political value: the belief that individuals should be able to achieve their goals through hard work, sacrifice, and their own talents. Throughout U.S. history, there have been debates about what it means to "pursue" happiness and the American Dream.

Religion and American Political Culture

Religious traditions have also helped shape American political culture. Religion has played a more influential role in America than it has in many modern democratic governments. Some of the first British colonies were founded by groups fleeing religious persecution. While the diversity of religious belief represented in American society continues to expand, America is a nation partly defined by religious faith and expression. In this book, we will continue to explore how the government balances religious freedom with other important interests.

The state of the American dream in the twenty-first century is something that we can study. Words are not the only way to tell stories, nor are images and videos. Data can tell political stories as well. In this book, we will investigate data—numbers, statistics, observations, and survey results—as well as the stories that political actors and reporters construct around the numbers. Stories told by data can be used for political ends, too. This book includes Political Science Practices features that require you to analyze data. The goal of these features is twofold: to help you become more capable and confident at interpreting data and to help you gain the skills to critically examine the narratives constructed around data.

We start with what at first glance seems like a simple data story—one taken from the results of a survey by the social-services and relief agency, Oxfam. In the 2013 survey, Oxfam asked low-wage workers whether most people can get ahead if they work hard.[17] The results of the survey are shown.

1. Identify the most common belief about the American Dream based on the pie chart.

2. Describe one limitation of the pie chart in measuring beliefs about the American Dream.

3. Explain one way in which a politician might use the results of the survey in advocating for or against social programs to assist low-wage workers.

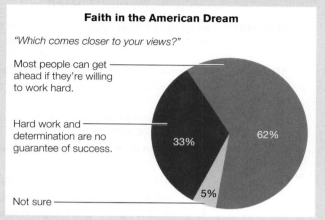

Faith in the American Dream

"Which comes closer to your views?"

Most people can get ahead if they're willing to work hard.

Hard work and determination are no guarantee of success. — 33%

62%

5%

Not sure

Data from Oxfam

You may think that low-wage workers have given up on the American dream, but in the survey, 62 percent of low-wage workers believed that most people can advance with enough hard work. However, that's not the end of the story. It's important to know what groups were surveyed, how the survey was taken, and what questions were asked.

AP® REQUIRED DOCUMENTS

In chapter 1, you have just met the first required document in the AP® U.S. Government and Politics course, the Declaration of Independence. In chapter 2, you will encounter the Articles of Confederation, the Constitution, and three other required foundational documents that were written during the period when the Constitution was ratified.

Document	Scope
Declaration of Independence	• You are required to read and understand the entire Declaration of Independence. • The Declaration has five sections: the Preamble, the Statement of Human Rights, Charges against Human Rights, Charges against the King and Parliament, and the Statement of Separation. • The Declaration of Independence is a statement of political philosophy and not a governing document.

1.2 Describe American political culture.

REMEMBER   American political culture consists of the beliefs, customs, traditions, and values that Americans share. American political culture values popular sovereignty, natural rights, and republicanism.

KNOW
- *democracy*: a system of government where power is held by the people. (p. 8)
- *natural rights*: the right to life, liberty, and property, which government cannot take away. (p. 9)
- *social contract*: people allow their governments to rule over them to ensure an orderly and functioning society. (p. 9)
- *American political culture*: the set of beliefs, customs, traditions, and values that Americans share. (p. 9)
- *popular sovereignty*: the idea that the government's right to rule comes from the people. (p. 9)
- *republicanism*: a system in which the government's authority comes from the people. (p. 9)
- *inalienable rights*: rights the government cannot take away. (p. 10)
- *liberty*: social, political, and economic freedoms. (p. 10)

THINK   How might changing values influence American political culture in the future?

1.2   Review Question: Free Response

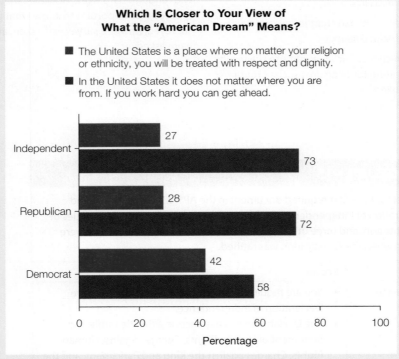

Which Is Closer to Your View of What the "American Dream" Means?

- ■ The United States is a place where no matter your religion or ethnicity, you will be treated with respect and dignity.
- ■ In the United States it does not matter where you are from. If you work hard you can get ahead.

Data from Ipsos

Use the information in the bar chart to answer parts A, B, and C.

A.   Identify the most common belief about the American dream shown in the bar chart.

B.   Describe difference of opinion shown in the bar chart, based on political ideology.

C.   Explain one reason why it is difficult to measure beliefs about the American dream.

1.3 Competing Theories of Democracy

Not everyone agrees about how power and influence are distributed in American democracy. Some theorists believe that political participation drives our system, others think that groups have the most influence, and some believe that most of the power is held by the elite.

Participatory Democratic Theory

Widespread participation in politics is the key to **participatory democracy**. This includes joining **civil society groups**, independent associations outside the government's control. Those who believe in the theory of participatory democracy emphasize the importance of citizen involvement. In *Bowling Alone: The Collapse and Revival of the American Community*,[18] author Robert Putnam laments the decline of civil society in America. The book's title refers to the fact that the same number of Americans go bowling as they did in the past, but fewer Americans are joining bowling leagues. This means more Americans are bowling with like-minded friends, instead of joining bowling leagues where they would meet a diverse group of individuals. Putnam argues that fewer Americans are participating in civil society, which is a cornerstone of participatory democracy. When people join groups, they meet others from their communities, develop new perspectives, and are more likely to work for the common good. Critics of Putnam's argument point out that many people, especially young people, are actively involved in their communities. While they may not be joining traditional organizations, like bowling leagues, they are finding new ways to organize and interact for the common good.[19]

participatory democracy a theory that widespread political participation is essential for democratic government.

civil society groups independent associations outside the government's control.

Pluralist Theory

One of the best ways to influence the political process is by joining a group of like-minded citizens. In the 1830s, French writer Alexis de Tocqueville noted something distinctive about U.S. culture, "Americans of all ages, all conditions, all minds constantly unite."[20] From this observation comes the expression, "a nation of joiners." **Pluralist theory** emphasizes the role of groups in the policymaking process. Bridget Mergens relied on the National Legal Foundation, a group that advocates for Christians' beliefs and protects their interests. The GSA at Boyd County High School got help from the ACLU, an organization that defends and protects civil rights and liberties. There are thousands of interest groups in America, each advocating for its own interests, such as the National Rifle Association (NRA) and the American Association of Retired Persons (AARP).

pluralist theory a theory of democracy that emphasizes the role of groups in the policymaking process.

Those who believe in pluralist theory point out that thousands of groups are competing in the political process.[21] Therefore, it is impossible for one of them to win all of the time. Groups have many ways to influence the government, including contacting government officials, donating to campaigns, and filing lawsuits. Pluralists argue that groups weak in one resource, like money, still have other resources, like a large number of members or a smart legal team. According to pluralists, policymaking is complex and results from bargaining and compromise.

Elitist Theory

Some people are less optimistic about how American democracy works. According to **elitist theory**, a small minority with most of the economic power controls government

elitist theory a theory of democracy that the elites have a disproportionate amount of influence in the policymaking process.

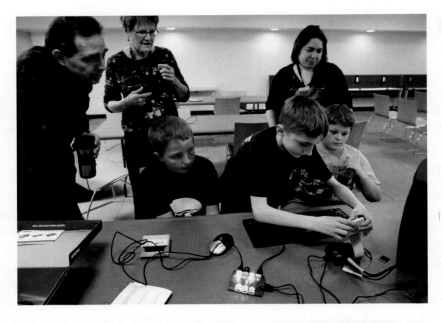

While traditional associations like bowling leagues may be in decline, new groups are forming. The photo shows a Raspberry Pi computer club, an effort that stresses build-it-yourself computing and coding. Other groups that have recently arisen include yarn bombing and forms of "craftivism" that involve decoration of public spaces, as shown by these yarn-bombed trees in California.

(top) AP Photo/Daily Herald, George LeClaire; (bottom) All Access Photo/Splash News/Los Angeles/USA

and politics, and elected officials are too heavily influenced by wealthy interest groups. Those who support elitist theory point out that some groups have more money, and more influence, than others.[22] They argue that groups representing big businesses have much more sway than smaller public interest groups.

Elite theorists are concerned with the growing income gap in America, and they believe that the top 1 percent of wealth holders have too much control over policymaking. While poor Americans may benefit from social programs like Medicaid, which provides medical assistance to low-income individuals, rich people and businesses, elites argue, get far more benefits from tax exemptions and lax government regulations. Critics of elitist theory argue that groups with less money can still participate in the political process through other effective methods, like filing lawsuits and encouraging their members to vote.

1.3 Explain and compare models of American democracy.

REMEMBER   The participatory, pluralist, and elitist models differ in their description of how American democracy functions.

KNOW
- *participatory democracy*: a theory that widespread participation is essential for democratic government. (p. 13)
- *civil society groups*: independent associations outside the government's control. (p. 13)
- *pluralist theory*: a theory of democracy that emphasizes the role of groups in the policymaking process. (p. 13)
- *elitist theory*: a theory of democracy that the elites have a disproportionate amount of influence in the policymaking process. (p. 13)

THINK   Bridget Mergens used a law firm to assert her rights. Does her story best represent pluralism, elitism, or participatory democracy?

1.3 Review Question: Free Response

Our politicians have aggressively pursued a policy of globalization—moving our jobs, our wealth, and our factories to Mexico and overseas. Globalization has made . . . politicians very wealthy. But it has left millions of our workers with nothing but poverty and heartache.
—Donald Trump, excerpts from campaign speech in Monessen, Pennsylvania, June 28, 2016.[23]

Three models of representative democracy—participatory, pluralist, and elite—have been used to describe American democracy. After reading the quotation, please respond to parts A, B, and C.

A. Describe the model of democracy that is best represented in the quotation.

B. Describe a different model of democracy from the model you described in part A.

C. Explain one reason why civil society is a cornerstone of the participatory and pluralist models of democracy.

▬ 1.4 Institutions, Systems, and Power

In devising a system of government, two basic questions need to be resolved: how much power government will have, and how political power will be distributed. Different forms of governments distribute power in very different ways. Totalitarian governments have no limitations on their own power. Similarly, authoritarian governments suppress the voices of their citizens to maintain a grip on power. Unlike totalitarian systems, however, authoritarian systems may have some economic or social institutions not under governmental control that may serve to moderate the government's power, and the government does not exert total control over citizens' lives.

The United States Constitution forms the basis of the nation's government and establishes the framework of **political institutions**, including the executive, legislative, and judicial branches. To protect Americans' fundamental rights, it limits the power of the national government. The first seven words of the Preamble, "We the People of the United States," establish that sovereignty comes from the citizens.

political institutions
the structure of government, including the executive, legislature, and judiciary.

Americans have tried to create institutions that balance order and security with freedom and prosperity. Giving the national government the power to maintain order runs the risk that it will use its power to oppress citizens. The United States of America is a **constitutional republic**. Americans elect representatives to make most of the laws and policies in the nation, rather than voting on them directly, which would be unwieldy in a nation of more than 300 million people. Further, and crucially, limits are placed on the power of government to prevent it from infringing on people's rights. The Constitution is the supreme law of the nation.

constitutional republic
a democratic system with elected representatives in which the Constitution is the supreme law.

Our Nation and Your Story

American government and politics are all about real people and their choices. This book will not try to persuade you to adopt a particular point of view. The goal instead is to help you sharpen your skills in analyzing and dealing with the governmental decisions that influence your life and with the political challenges our nation faces.

Should you choose to act in American politics—should you choose to stake your own claims for your rights—you should be well informed, both about your own positions on critical issues and the positions of those with whom you disagree. You have to develop your skills in analyzing the words, images, and data that will serve as tools along the way.

People like you matter. And your stories matter as well, even if nobody ever retells them in a book.

Section Review

1.4 Describe a constitutional republic.

REMEMBER A constitutional republic is a democracy in which people elect representatives to carry out their interests and the Constitution is the supreme law of the land.

KNOW
- *political institutions*: the structure of government, including the executive, legislature, and judiciary. (p. 15)
- *constitutional republic*: a democratic system with elected representatives in which the Constitution is the supreme law. (p. 15)

THINK Are the three models of democracy the best way to describe our system? Why or why not?

1.4 Review Question: Free Response

Types of Governments

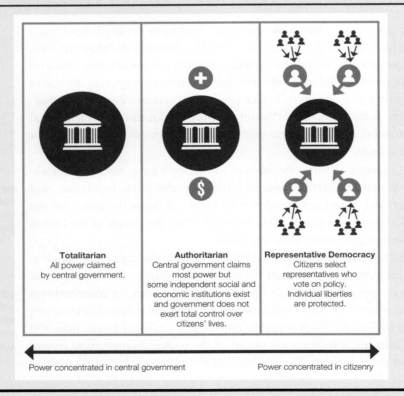

Totalitarian
All power claimed by central government.

Authoritarian
Central government claims most power but some independent social and economic institutions exist and government does not exert total control over citizens' lives.

Representative Democracy
Citizens select representatives who vote on policy. Individual liberties are protected.

Power concentrated in central government   Power concentrated in citizenry

Use the graphic and your knowledge of U.S. Government and Politics to answer parts A, B, and C.

A. Define constitutional republic.

B. Describe how the Preamble of the Declaration of Independence illustrates the concept of natural rights.

C. Explain one way in which the national government's role in establishing order creates tension with its role in protecting fundamental rights.

HOW TO USE This Book

This book teaches American government and politics with stories. When a high school student tries to start a Christian Bible study club, or a group of high school students tries to start a Gay-Straight Alliance, their schools and the government must respond in a way that reflects our Constitution and American values. The stories told in this book and, most important, your engagement with them, have the potential to bring several important concepts to life:

- American political institutions did not fall out of the sky. They were created through conscious actions.

- In American government and politics, there is rarely, if ever, an either/or solution to major problems but instead a complex interplay among ideals, actions, time, and place.

- The development of American government and politics has always involved the experiences of real people, with important stories.

- People matter, even if they do not always succeed.

- Your own opinions, thoughtfully constructed and respectfully offered, matter, too. You can make a difference.

Tristan Eaton, photo by Rey Rosa/The L.I.S.A Project NYC

Chapter 1 Review

AP® KEY CONCEPTS

- *politics* (p. 5)
- *government* (p. 5)
- *democracy* (p. 8)
- *natural rights* (p. 9)
- *social contract* (p. 9)
- *American political culture* (p. 9)

- *popular sovereignty* (p. 9)
- *republicanism* (p. 9)
- *inalienable rights* (p. 10)
- *liberty* (p. 10)
- *participatory democracy* (p. 13)
- *civil society groups* (p. 13)

- *pluralist theory* (p. 13)
- *elitist theory* (p. 13)
- *political institutions* (p. 15)
- *constitutional republic* (p. 15)

AP® EXAM PRACTICE and Critical Thinking Project

MULTIPLE-CHOICE QUESTIONS

1. John Locke's concept of natural rights and the social contract emphasizes which pair of concepts and definitions?

Key concept	Definition
A. Republicanism	Representatives chosen by citizens
B. Civil society	Broad citizen involvement
C. Limited government	Confiscation of private property
D. Popular sovereignty	Political equality among citizens

Gustavo Rodriguez/www.cartoonstock.com

2. The cartoon expresses which of the following viewpoints?

   A. American political culture consists of shared beliefs and customs.

   B. Political ideology consists of an individual's set of beliefs.

   C. Many Americans are not well informed and hold conflicting views about the role of government.

   D. Americans become more conservative as they age.

   _____

3. We should remember that the Declaration of Independence is not merely a historical document. It is an explicit recognition that our rights derive not from the King of England, not from the judiciary, not from government at all, but from God.

   —Mark Levin[24]

   The quotation best represents which concept?

   A. Natural rights

   B. Constitutional democracy

   C. Republicanism

   D. Participatory democracy

Ronaldo Dias/Cartoon Stock

4. Which of the following statements best describes the viewpoint of American culture expressed in the cartoon?

A. The United States offers equality of opportunity.

B. Citizens are more interested in playing games than in politics.

C. Inequality makes it difficult for African Americans to achieve the American dream.

D. Individualism is a core American value, and it's up to each person to take steps to advance.

———————————

5. Which of the following best describes a constitutional democracy?

A. The power of government is clearly specified in the Constitution.

B. The powers of government are both described and limited by the Constitution.

C. Representatives are elected to carry out the will of the people.

D. Citizens have the opportunity to vote directly on policies.

Question 6 refers to the following graph.

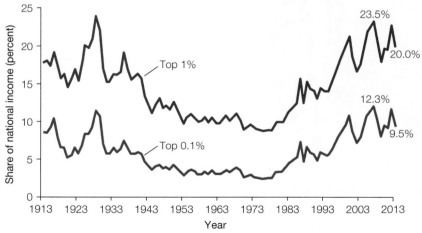

U.S. Income Shares of Top 1 Percent and Top 0.1 Percent of Households, Including Capital Gains, 1913–2013

Data from Piketty and Saez, January 2015.

6. The graph supports which of the following conclusions?

A. Income in the United States is unduly low, because it consistently falls below 50 percent.

B. Over the past four decades, America's wealthiest individuals have been earning a larger share of America's national income.

C. America had more wealth in 1925 and 2005 than in any other year.

D. People in the top 1% of American households are wealthier than people in the top 0.1%.

[O]ur ancestors, who first settled these colonies, were at the time of their emigration from the mother country, entitled to all the rights, liberties, and immunities of free and natural-born subjects, within the realm of England. . . . By such emigration they by no means forfeited, surrendered, or lost any of those rights, but that they were, and their descendants now are, entitled to the exercise and enjoyment of all such of them, as their local and other circumstances enable them to exercise and enjoy. . . . The foundation of English liberty, and of all free government, is a right in the people to participate in their legislative council: and as the English colonists are not represented, and from their local and other circumstances, cannot properly be represented in the British parliament, they are entitled to a free and exclusive power of legislation in their several provincial legislatures, where their right of representation can alone be preserved, in all cases of taxation and internal polity. . . .[25]

7. The quote makes which of the following arguments?

A. England was the mother country of the American colonists.

B. The British parliament must continue to have the exclusive power to make laws.

C. The colonists were entitled to the rights of English subjects.

D. The right to emigrate must remain the foundation of English liberty.

8. What political philosophy set forth in the quote was incorporated two years later into the Declaration of Independence?

A. A theocracy is the best form of government because God created humans and endowed them with unalienable rights.

B. Taxation inherently destroys the natural rights of life, liberty, and the pursuit of happiness.

C. Direct democracy is a more legitimate form of government than indirect democracy.

D. People have the right to elect representatives to the legislatures that govern them.

Question 9 refers to the following cartoon.

"I'm not so sure about this 'life, liberty and pursuit of happiness' bit. Whaddya say we look at some polling numbers first?"

Tim O'Brien/CARTOONSTOCK.com

9. The cartoon expresses which of the following viewpoints?

A. Politicians tend to be more focused on public opinion than policy.

B. It's hard to define "life, liberty, and pursuit of happiness."

C. The members of the Continental Congress were old and feeble.

D. Sometimes even wealthy and educated individuals don't know the best course of action.

10. Which of the following arguments would a proponent of the pluralist system of political participation most likely make?

   A. American democracy is furthered when groups representing all points of view help make public policy.

   B. Gridlock results when too many groups seek to influence the policymaking process.

   C. Although many groups participate in policymaking, wealthy groups have the most influence.

   D. American society should return to a rugged frontier philosophy and reliance on the individual.

FREE-RESPONSE QUESTIONS

1. In 2014, a deadly strain of the Ebola virus killed a large number of people in West Africa, mainly in the countries of Sierra Leone, Liberia, and Guinea. Many American doctors and nurses traveled to those countries to assist the victims of that virus. Shortly afterwards, some governors in the United States issued orders that anyone who visited those three countries must be quarantined in their homes for 21 days on returning to the United States. Then-governor of Maine, Paul LePage, justified his quarantine order by saying, "While we certainly respect the rights of one individual, we must be vigilant in protecting 1.3 million Mainers, as well as anyone who visits our great state."[26] In response, American nurse Kaci Hickox refused to follow that quarantine order, saying, "So many states have started enacting these policies that I think are just completely not evidence-based. They don't do a good job of balancing the risks and benefits when thinking about taking away an individual's rights."[27]

Use the scenario and your knowledge of U.S. Government and Politics to answer parts A, B, and C.

   A. Describe natural rights philosophy.

   B. Describe one way in which the scenario relates to the concept of natural rights.

   C. Explain one way in which the quarantine illustrates the government's role of balancing individual liberty with social order.

2. Examine the following table and answer the question.

Largest Political Contributions by Interest Group Sector, 2013–2014

Rank	Sector	Amount contributed	Amount directly contributed to parties and candidates	% Contributed to Democrats	% Contributed to Republicans
1	Finance/insurance/real estate	$464,350,782	$321,830,419	38	62
2	Ideology/single issue	$335,668,041	$221,691,858	51	49
3	Miscellaneous business	$215,657,965	$173,315,418	39	61
4	Lawyers/lobbyists	$145,087,918	$134,658,060	65	35
5	Health	$134,548,323	$125,439,915	43	57
6	Labor	$132,584,959	$58,441,510	89	11
7	Communications/ electronics	$107,564,564	$85,126,768	60	40
8	Energy/natural resources	$103,972,928	$82,923,250	22	78
9	Agribusiness	$70,881,926	$61,003,885	25	75
10	Construction	$62,589,150	$55,400,717	29	71

Data from www.opensecrets.org

Use the data from the table and your knowledge of U.S. Government and Politics to answer parts A, B, and C.

    A. Identify the interest group most likely to contribute to the Democratic Party and the interest group most likely to contribute to the Republican Party.

    B. Explain one reason why an interest group might contribute money to a political party.

    C. Explain one way in which the data in the chart support the theory of pluralist democracy.

ARGUMENTATION QUESTION

NOTE TO STUDENTS: The following is designed to resemble an argumentation essay prompt that you will see on the AP® Exam. Argumentation questions will usually refer to more than one required document or Supreme Court case.

But at this point in the textbook, you've only had a chance to examine one of those foundational documents, the Declaration of Independence. (You'll examine the rest of them later in this textbook.) For that reason, this argumentation question will give you practice at developing an argument in the form of the essay you'll write during the AP® Exam, while still focusing on the one foundational document you've already seen.

But one hundred years later, the Negro still is not free. One hundred years later, the life of the Negro is still sadly crippled by the manacles of segregation and the chains of discrimination. One hundred years later, the Negro lives on a lonely island of poverty in the midst of a vast ocean of material prosperity.

. . . [W]e have come to our nation's capital to cash a check. When the architects of our republic wrote the magnificent words of the Constitution and the Declaration of Independence, they were signing a promissory note to which every American was to fall heir.

                                        —Martin Luther King, "I Have a Dream . . ." Speech[28]

Should the Declaration of Independence be interpreted as a promise that the government will protect the natural rights of all of its citizens?

In your essay:

- Articulate a claim or thesis that responds to the prompt, and use a line of reasoning to defend it.
- Use the Declaration of Independence to support your claim.
- Use reasoning to explain why the evidence you provided supports your claim or thesis.
- Use refutation, concession, or rebuttal to respond to an opposing or alternative perspective.

CRITICAL THINKING PROJECT

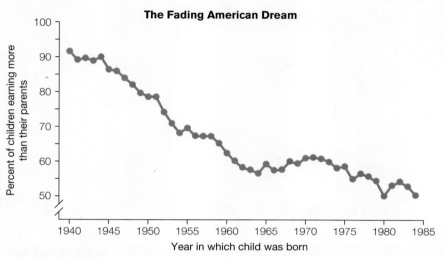

The Fading American Dream

Data from Stanford Center on Poverty and Inequality

Does the graph prove that the American dream is fading? To reach your conclusion, answer the following questions:

1. Describe the trend shown in the data. Provide a specific example from the data in describing the trend.

2. Explain the political conclusion the author of the graph is trying to prove.

3. Describe one limitation of the data provided.

4. Write a paragraph explaining whether or not the graph proves that the American dream is fading. Support your conclusion with two distinct arguments.

2 The Constitution
A New Vision of Government

"We the People of the United States . . ." Perhaps no seven words are as important in American political history as these.

The delegates to the Constitutional Convention drafted a blueprint for a new government, although the delegates themselves were often divided about what this government should be, how it should be structured, and how much power it should have. In spite of all of these divisions

Volunteers help to roll up a giant banner printed with the Preamble to the Constitution of the United States during a demonstration at the Lincoln Memorial in Washington, D.C., against a ruling by the Supreme Court in 2010 that allowed unlimited campaign contributions by associations of individuals and corporations.
Chip Somodevilla/Getty Images

and challenges, they produced a **constitution**, a document that sets out the fundamental principles of governance and establishes the institutions of government.

In this chapter, we will explore the stories of the events leading up to the Constitutional Convention, the political debates within the convention, and the debates surrounding the ratification process. We will focus mainly on one person: James Madison of Virginia. Although not the most powerful political figure of the time, Madison and his well-thought-out efforts were instrumental in shaping the Constitution of the United States.

LEARNING TARGETS

After reading this chapter, you will be able to

2.1 Explain how weaknesses in the Articles of Confederation led to the proposal for a new, stronger national government.

2.2 Describe how the Constitution was shaped by negotiation and compromise.

2.3 Describe checks and balances, and explain the impact of checks and balances on the political system.

2.4 Compare and contrast the arguments put forth by the Federalists and Antifederalists during the ratification debates.

■ James Madison: Clear-Eyed Visionary

In the spring of 1786, thirty-five-year-old James Madison Jr. settled into the house on his plantation, called Montpelier, in the town of Orange, Virginia. Madison was one of America's first political scientists, an engineer as well as a philosopher, and an avid researcher of the most pressing political questions of his era. Kingdoms and empires had endured, sometimes for centuries, under the rule of monarchs and emperors. But **republics**, governments ruled by representatives of the people, without exception had eventually died. Madison wanted to know how people could create a republic that lasted—a republic that could avoid being taken over by a small group of men or descending into civil war or anarchy. Madison poured himself into this project systematically, scientifically, and with a great deal of energy.

republic
a government ruled by representatives of the people.

In the tumultuous years that followed American independence, economic disruption, the threat of European powers, and the threat of rebellion within the thirteen states gave ammunition to those who wanted change. Madison's research played a critical role in designing a new American government, selling it to a skeptical public,.and laying out the logic of the constitutional republic for subsequent generations of Americans.[1]

Madison's preparation, intellect, and understated political skill played the leading role in the creation of the Constitution of the United States. The American Republic that he helped shape was based on the premise that liberty is something with which people are born, something that cannot be given or taken away by governments.

Madison had the artist Charles Willson Peale create the portrait as a pin, along with its fine case, as a gift to a woman he was courting named Catherine Floyd. As was the custom of the time, he sent a lock of his hair, which is braided and glued to the back of the portrait.
Library of Congress

A portrait of American statesman and political theorist James Madison at the age of thirty-two, while he was serving in the Congress of the Confederation, representing Virginia. Only four years later, he would attend the Constitutional Convention.
Library of Congress

Articles of Confederation and Perpetual Union
a governing document that created a union of thirteen sovereign states in which the states, not the national government, were supreme.

▰ 2.1 The Articles of Confederation

The government that James Madison wanted to change was formed under the **Articles of Confederation and Perpetual Union**. Adopted by the Second Continental Congress in 1777 and formally ratified in 1781, the articles created a union of sovereign states in which the states, not the national government, were supreme. While they had successfully guided the country through war and the accompanying economic and material devastation, the articles established a weak national government with few structures to make member states work together. By 1786, the American confederation was facing serious problems.

A Firm League of Friendship

When they created the Articles of Confederation, the delegates to the Second Continental Congress had to confront two related issues. Citizens in one state did not always trust the motives of the governments of the other states. They also did not trust any government that would rule over them from far away, whether it be that of Great Britain before the war or of the new American nation after victory had been achieved. Mistrust of other states crystallized in conflicts over land, representation, and sovereignty.

The Articles of Confederation created a "league of friendship"[2] among states. It provided states with protections against the possibility of any other state claiming disputed territory on its own, without the approval of the confederal government. In the face of the prospect of large, populous, and ever-growing neighbors, smaller states demanded, and received, equal representation in the new government. Each state had one vote in the new Congress. The Confederal Congress was unicameral, meaning it had only one chamber.[3] States selected their representatives to the legislature and could choose the number of representatives that they sent, though each state received only one vote. Finally, states and not the national government would be sovereign, a right that was firmly established in the document: "Each state retains its sovereignty, freedom, and independence, and every Power, Jurisdiction, and right, which is not by this confederation expressly delegated to the United States, in Congress assembled."[4] Table 2.1 summarizes the Articles of Confederation and shows how it differs from the structure and scope of the U.S Constitution.

TABLE 2.1 Key Provisions of the Articles of Confederation and Constitution

Article	Articles of Confederation	U.S. Constitution
Preamble		Sovereignty comes from the people, and the Constitution will create a "more perfect Union."
I	Names the Union as "The United States of America."	Creates a bicameral legislature, establishes requirements for serving in the House of Representatives and Senate, lists expressed powers of Congress, and allows for implied powers.
II	Provides that states retain sovereignty not delegated to the national government.	Creates the presidency, establishes requirements for office, lists expressed powers of the executive.
III	Creates a "league of friendship" for defense and security.	Creates a Supreme Court and provides that Congress may establish lower federal courts.
IV	Protects equal treatment and freedom of movement for citizens.	Sets forth the relationships between states.
V	Allocates one vote in Congress for each state.	Establishes the process for amending the Constitution.
VI	Gives the national government the power to declare war.	Establishes that the Constitution, federal laws, and treaties are the supreme law of the land.
VII	Gives states the power to assign military ranks.	Describes how the Constitution will be ratified.
VIII	Expenditures by the United States will be paid with funds raised by state legislatures.	
IX	Gives Congress the power to declare war and peace, appoint tribunals for crimes on the seas, regulate the post office, appoint a president, and request requisitions from the states. Nine states are required to consent to declare war.	
X	Allows a "committee of the states" to exercise the powers of Congress when Congress is not in session.	
XI	Provides that Canada may join the Union.	
XII	Provides that the Confederation accepts the war debt.	
XIII	Provides that amendments require approval of all state legislatures.	

Limitations on the Power of the Confederal Government

The national government under the Articles of Confederation was intentionally weak, and state legislatures had most of the power. Citizens had experienced the tyranny of British rule, and they did not want to re-create it in an American version. The confederal government could not force states to carry out its policies. The power to raise an army and navy were among the few powers of the national government, but the Confederation Congress did not have the money to pay for the military. Under Article VIII of the Articles of Confederation,

> All charges of war, and all other expenses that shall be incurred for the common defense or general welfare, and allowed by the United States in Congress assembled, shall be defrayed

out of a common treasury, which shall be supplied by the several States in proportion to the value of all land within each State, granted or surveyed for any person, as such land and the buildings and improvements thereon shall be estimated according to such mode as the United States in Congress assembled, shall from time to time direct and appoint. The taxes for paying that proportion shall be laid and levied by the authority and direction of the legislatures of the several States within the time agreed upon by the United States in Congress assembled.

Because it lacked taxation power, the national government had to ask the states for money. States usually refused to send money, hampering the country's ability to pay its debts. The national government printed worthless currency in an attempt to cover its debts. Congress sold western lands to raise funds for the national government.

States retained most of their sovereignty, complicating foreign policy. Article IX of the Articles of Confederation illustrates the tension between the national government and the states in conducting foreign affairs. It provides, "The United States in Congress assembled, shall have the sole and exclusive right and power of determining on peace and war, except in the cases mentioned in the sixth article—of sending and receiving ambassadors— entering into treaties and alliances." However, the next clause of Article IX allows states to impose tariffs: "no treaty of commerce shall be made whereby the legislative power of the respective States shall be restrained from imposing such imposts and duties on foreigners, as their own people are subjected to, or from prohibiting the exportation or importation of any species of goods or commodities whatsoever . . ."

State control over trade also hindered the domestic economy. Congress did not have the power to regulate interstate commerce, and states placed trade restrictions on one another, which made it difficult to cultivate a national economy.

Article V of the Articles of Confederation created a **unicameral** (one-house) legislature. States could send up to seven delegates to serve in the legislature, but each state was only given one vote on legislation. States could recall their representatives at will, and limits were placed on how long a representative could serve.[5]

There was no independent judicial branch. The judiciary existed to resolve differences between states but had no way of enforcing its decisions. The Articles of Confederation placed a tall hurdle in the path of potential reformers: Article XIII required the approval of all thirteen of the states to amend the articles.[6] The president of the Confederation Congress served mostly to keep order and count votes. There was no separate executive branch.

The Articles of Confederation created a weak government in a time of crisis, when the new nation was struggling to survive. The national government was ineffective and did not have the power to resolve brewing economic, political, and social unrest.

The Annapolis Convention

The Annapolis Convention was called in the fall of 1786 to address trade and navigation disputes among states. Unofficially, at least in the minds of Madison and those who shared his views, the hope was that the outcome of the

unicameral
a one-house legislature.

A United States continental currency $65 banknote from 1779. The collapse in the value of the currency caused severe economic disruption and unrest in the years leading up to the Constitutional Convention. One result was Shays's Rebellion, based in economic grievances and led by veterans of the Revolution.
Granger/Granger

The Maryland State House, where the Annapolis Convention took place in 1786. Only five of the thirteen states sent representatives, including James Madison. Despite the poor attendance, delegates to the convention enlivened the movement for reform by calling for a convention in Philadelphia in the spring of 1787 to discuss how to make the U.S. government more effective.
MPI/Getty Images

convention might lead to significant changes in the fundamental structure of the government of the United States. Although Madison wanted to see major reforms, he was not optimistic about the prospect for real change. "Tho' my wishes are in favor of such an event," he wrote to Thomas Jefferson in August, "yet I despair so much of its accomplishment at the present crisis that I do not extend my views beyond a Commercial Reform. To speak the truth I almost despair even of this."[7]

Madison's lack of optimism turned out to be well founded. Participation at the convention was weak. Only five of the thirteen states sent representatives. The other states either did not appoint anyone or did not do so in time to make it to the meeting. Maryland itself did not send any delegates, even though the convention was in Annapolis and the state was directly involved in the trade disputes. Despite the poor attendance, delegates to the convention increased the chances of reform by calling for a convention in Philadelphia the following spring to discuss how to make the American government more effective in dealing with issues of trade and other pressing needs of the nation.

Unrest and the Danger of Rebellion

In spite of what many saw as problems with the articles, many Americans did not want to amend, much less replace, them. Some in the southern states feared that slavery would be restricted or outlawed. Citizens of smaller states feared losing equal representation in Congress and seeing it replaced by representation based on population, a change that would drastically weaken their position.

When a small group of people takes it upon themselves to overturn a political order, there is no guarantee that what they create will not be worse, maybe much worse, than what came before. Many were also still nervous about the idea of a strong national government.

Shays's Rebellion, named after Daniel Shays, one of its military leaders, was a grassroots popular uprising against a state government. The rebellion took place in Massachusetts, but the conditions that caused it and the popular anger that fueled it were also present in other states. This crisis added to the sense of urgency in the American confederation, and it provided ammunition to those who tried to replace the structure of government under the Articles. Some, like James Madison, wanted a stronger union, a different kind of republic than had ever been tried before.

Shays's Rebellion
a popular uprising against the government of Massachusetts.

Debt and Economic Crisis in Post-Revolutionary America

The roots of Shays's Rebellion were both economic and political. In the difficult economic times that followed the Revolutionary War, there was a shortage of "hard money," of gold and silver as well as money backed by gold and silver. What there was no shortage of was debt. Citizens and governments throughout the confederation found themselves unable to pay debts that had been incurred during the war or during the tough economic times that followed. Shopkeepers demanded that their customers pay debts in hard currency. Cash-strapped state governments raised taxes and demanded hard money from their citizens to pay their own sizable debts. Foreclosures—the taking of property to pay outstanding debts backed by that property—were widespread.

Civil Unrest and Military Conflict

Many of the members of Shays's Rebellion were veterans of the Revolutionary War with sufficient military skills and popular support to offer a genuine challenge to the Massachusetts government. The rebels organized themselves by town and family, and they made a point of trying not to antagonize the local population. Instead, they focused on the courts,

Consider these two depictions of Shays's Rebellion. Although they aim to depict the same broad set of events, they do so in different ways. This image comes from an edition of *Harper's Monthly* published in January 1884—late in the nineteenth century. It was originally a painting by U.S. illustrator Howard Pyle and is entitled *Shays's Mob in Possession of a Court-House*. The courthouse depicted is in the town of Great Barrington in western Massachusetts. There is a time gap, however, of about one hundred years between the rebellion and this depiction of events.

This engraving is likely to be the earlier of the two. A wood engraving from the middle of the nineteenth century, it shows the participants in Shays's Rebellion as middle class. Note their clothing. The rebellion took place mainly in western Massachusetts, where money was tight and debts could not be paid off. The gap in time between event and its depiction is not as long. Yet would this image be more accurate than the accompanying one by Pyle?

closing them down in the hopes of stalling the foreclosure process until a solution to the debt crisis could be achieved in the state legislature.

The Massachusetts government clamped down, which only riled the population more. In October 1786, the Massachusetts legislature passed the Riot Act,[8] which absolved sheriffs and other officials from prosecution for killing rioters.

The Massachusetts state militia was unable to put down the rebellion. Many militia members, themselves Revolutionary War veterans, sided with the rebels. The government of the United States, the Confederal Congress, could not raise an army; its requests to the states for money were refused by every state except Virginia. The wealthy elites in Boston ultimately paid for an army on their own, lending money to Massachusetts for the purposes of suppressing the rebellion.

Shays's Rebellion: Crisis and Reconciliation

Major General William Shepard, commanding the newly raised state militia, defeated Shays and the rebels, who were forced to withdraw. Two rebel leaders were hanged, yet most of the other rebels eventually returned to their farms and towns. Shays escaped to Vermont and was later pardoned, though he never returned to Massachusetts.[9]

Shays's Rebellion convinced George Washington to return to public life. After the Revolutionary War, Washington had, as promised, returned to civilian life and his plantation, Mount Vernon, to focus on agriculture and breeding animals. Madison wrote a letter to Washington, hoping that Shays's Rebellion would be enough to lure Washington out of retirement and align his unequalled status among Americans with the effort to create a new political order. Although reluctant at first to attend the Philadelphia conference, Washington eventually agreed. The Philadelphia Convention would have the most famous and respected American there to give it legitimacy.[10]

AP® Political Science PRACTICES
Analyzing Primary Sources

Primary sources are documents created at the time an event occurred. The same event can have different interpretations, depending on an individual's point of view. The quotes refer to Shays's Rebellion:

> "Even this evil is productive of good. It prevents the degeneracy of government and nourishes a general attention to the public affairs. I hold it that a little rebellion now and then is a good thing, and as necessary in the political world as storms in the physical. Unsuccessful rebellions, indeed, generally establish the encroachments on the rights of the people which have produced them. An observation of this truth should render honest republican governors so mild in their punishment of rebellions as not to discourage them too much. It is a medicine necessary for the sound health of government."
>
> Thomas Jefferson, letter to James Madison, January 30, 1787, written from Paris.[12]

> "... if three years ago any person had told me that at this day, I should see such a formidable rebellion against the laws & constitutions of our own making as now appears I should have thought him a bedlamite — a fit subject for a mad house. [If the government] shrinks, or is unable to enforce its laws ... anarchy & confusion must prevail."
>
> George Washington, letter to Henry Knox, February 3, 1787[13]

1. Describe one similarity in the way the letters portray Shays's Rebellion.

2. Describe one difference in the way the letters portray Shays's Rebellion.

3. Explain two reasons why primary sources might have different interpretations about the political consequences of the same event.

Rebellion was not the only worry among the new states. Great Britain had been defeated but hardly destroyed. The nation had merely been pushed back into Canada, and that was only due to the help of Great Britain's other rivals, like France, who might not always be helpful to the young United States. According to political scientist Keith Dougherty, "By the summer of 1787, the federal government had no funds to protect American shipping from the Barbary [North African] states, it couldn't dislodge the British from their garrisons along the Canadian border, and it could not breach the Spanish blockade of the Mississippi—let alone suppress a domestic insurrection."[11] As states sent their delegates to Philadelphia in the spring of 1787, the world powers were watching, expecting, and perhaps hoping for, failure.

Section Review

This chapter's main ideas are reflected in the Learning Targets. By reviewing after each section, you should be able to

—**Remember** the key points,

—**Know** terms that are central to the topic, and

—**Think** critically about these questions.

2.1 Explain how weaknesses in the Articles of Confederation led to the proposal for a new, stronger national government.

REMEMBER
- The Articles of Confederation created a government in which the states had more power than the national government.
- Under the Articles of Confederation, the national government could not tax citizens or provide for the national defense.

KNOW
- *constitution*: a document that sets out the fundamental principles of governance and establishes the institutions of government. (p. 25)
- *republic*: a government ruled by representatives of the people. (p. 25)
- *Articles of Confederation and Perpetual Union*: a governing document that created a union of thirteen sovereign states in which the states, not the union, were supreme. (p. 26)
- *unicameral*: a one-house legislature. (p. 28)
- *Shays's Rebellion*: a popular uprising against the government of Massachusetts. (p. 29)

THINK
Why would some Americans worry about replacing the Articles of Confederation even though most people believed they were ineffective?

2.1 Review Question: Free Response

In a letter to James Madison in November of 1786, George Washington wrote,

What stronger evidence can be given of the want of energy in our government than these disorders? If there exists not a power to check them, what security has a man of life, liberty, or property? To you, I am sure I need not add aught on this subject, the consequences of a lax, or inefficient government, are too obvious to be dwelt on. Thirteen sovereignties pulling against each other, and all tugging at the foederal head will soon bring ruin to the whole; whereas a liberal, and energetic Constitution, well guarded & closely watched, to prevent incroachments, might restore us to that degree of respectability & consequence, to which we had fair claim, & the brightest prospect of attaining.[14]

After reading the passage, use your knowledge of U.S. Government and Politics to respond to parts A, B, and C.

A. In the context of the passage, describe George Washington's main concern regarding the Articles of Confederation.

B. Describe one way in which the Articles of Confederation distributed power between the states and the national government.

C. Explain one reason why the drafters of the Articles of Confederation were worried about creating too much power in a central government.

2.2 The Constitutional Convention

In May 1787, fifty-five delegates from twelve of the thirteen states began to arrive at the **Constitutional Convention**, a meeting held to fix the Articles of Confederation. Rhode Island refused to participate because leaders there were opposed to a stronger central government that they believed, correctly, would result from the new Constitution. It was a hot, humid summer, typical of Philadelphia.

Constitutional Convention
a meeting attended by state delegates in 1787 to fix the Articles of Confederation.

James Madison was the first delegate to arrive. Although he would become perhaps the most influential person at the convention, Madison was not the only delegate who shaped the final document. George Washington served as the president of the proceedings. Most delegates expected that he would be the leader of whatever government emerged. Once in Philadelphia, the tall and handsome Washington found no shortage of requests for his presence at tea with prominent ladies in the city. His first call, though, was to his friend Benjamin Franklin. Because of Franklin's poor health, four prisoners from a city jail carried him through the streets of Philadelphia in a chair on his way to and from the convention. He remained a shrewd politician, however, and used his many skills at important moments in the debate. Other delegates, many of whom had done their own reading and study in preparation for the proceedings, also guided and shaped the debates and outcomes. Alexander Hamilton, who had served as Washington's aide in the war, emerged as one of the leading proponents of a strong national government.

The delegates who assembled in Philadelphia certainly did not represent a snapshot of the people living in the thirteen states. All were men. Most were well educated. Roughly one-third owned slaves. Not all were wealthy, but they were all members of the elite. Most of the founders had previous practical political experience to guide them and temper their revolutionary ideals, Madison included. The solutions that the delegates came up with were pragmatic, political, and strategic.

Two Big Issues: Representation and Power

The first order of business was to unanimously select Washington as president of the convention. Madison sat up front and became the informal reporter for the convention.[15] Much of what we know about what happened in Philadelphia comes from his notes.

The delegates adopted a set of rules. They called for absolute secrecy, "that nothing spoken in the House be printed, or otherwise published, or communicated without leave of the House."[16] They knew that the enormous task of creating a new government would be harder if the details of their discussions were leaked, either deliberately or unintentionally.

With an overall goal of creating a stronger fiscal and military state, the two biggest issues were the representation of states in the national government and the powers of the national government. Most debates centered on practicalities. With some important exceptions, speeches and discussions about slavery in the convention focused not on its immorality but on how it would affect representation of states and the power of the national government over trade and commerce.

Individual Rights

The founding fathers created a limited government, which would protect individual freedoms. Power was distributed between different branches of government and between the national government and the states, preventing one branch or level of government from becoming too powerful and taking away the rights of citizens. There are few individual rights protected in the original Constitution. However, the Constitution does protect some individual freedoms. Article VI prohibits a religious test as a condition for holding office in the federal government.

writ of habeas corpus
the right of people detained by the government to know the charges against them.

bills of attainder
when the legislature declares someone guilty without a trial.

ex post facto laws
laws punishing people for acts that were not crimes at the time they were committed.

The Constitution provides some protection for those accused of crimes. Article I, Section 9 forbids the suspension of the **writ of habeas corpus**, except during rebellion or invasion. A writ of habeas corpus allows people detained by the government to know why they are being held. A judge may order them released if the government does not provide reasons for the detention. Article I, Section 9 also prohibits Congress and the states from passing **bills of attainder**, when the legislature declares someone guilty without a trial. The same article prohibits **ex post facto laws** punishing people for acts that were not crimes at the time they were committed. Article III, Section 2 provides the right to a trial by jury in criminal cases.

The founding fathers were sensitive about the crime of treason, because they would have faced execution by the British government if the American Revolution had failed. Treason is defined as giving aid to the enemy or plotting the overthrow of the government. Article III, Section 3 requires two witnesses to the same overt act of treason or a confession in front of a judge.

Representation in Congress

States with small populations worried that they would not be fairly represented in the legislature. Big states were also worried. If each state received one or two representatives in Congress, then citizens of big states, like Virginia, would be underrepresented compared to small states, like Delaware.

The **Virginia Plan**, devised by James Madison, created a three-branch government with a bicameral national legislature, that is, with two houses. Members of the lower house would be elected directly by the people. The upper house would consist of representatives nominated by state legislatures and chosen by members of the lower house. More populous states would have more members in both houses of the legislature.

Delegates from smaller states reacted immediately and strongly to the Virginia Plan's suggestion of representation by population. Under the Virginia Plan, Virginia would have sixteen votes to South Carolina's one. New Jersey's William Paterson flatly stated, according to Madison's notes, that New Jersey would be "swallowed up" and would never submit to "such a fate."

Within days of its introduction, several provisions of the Virginia Plan—a government of three branches and a bicameral legislature—had already been approved, but the question of representation in Congress remained.

The New Jersey Plan

Paterson presented the small states' response to the Virginia Plan. Known as the **New Jersey Plan**, it proposed a unicameral legislature where each state delegation (chosen by state legislatures) would get one equal vote in that legislature. That legislature would get new powers, mostly over taxation and the economy, though it would still depend on the states for some revenue.

Madison and James Wilson grew frustrated over the less populous states' objections to the Virginia Plan. To allow equal representation in Congress for states would allow the political divisions between and within states to infect national politics. Delegates from smaller states did not see it this way. To them, equal representation was not open for negotiation; it was essential to their sovereignty.

The Great Compromise

With the issue of how states would be represented threatening to break apart the convention, the question was sent to a **Grand Committee**. The committee responded with a proposal to give something to each side. On July 16, by a vote of 5–4, the delegates agreed to what would be called the **Great (Connecticut) Compromise**.[17] Under Article I, Section 1, the national legislature would be **bicameral**. Under Article I,

A profile portrait of Irish-born American jurist William Paterson. Paterson presented what became known as the New Jersey Plan, which preserved most of the structure of the government as established under the Articles of Confederation. Other members of the Constitutional Convention who were immigrants included Alexander Hamilton of New York and Robert Morris of Pennsylvania.
Stock Montage/Getty Images

Virginia Plan
a plan of government calling for a three-branch government with a bicameral legislature, where more populous states would have more representation in Congress.

New Jersey Plan
a plan of government that provided for a unicameral legislature with equal votes for each states.

Grand Committee
a committee at the Constitutional Convention that worked out the compromise on representation.

Great (Connecticut) Compromise
an agreement for a plan of government that drew upon both the Virginia and New Jersey Plans; it settled issues of state representation by calling for a bicameral legislature with a House of Representatives apportioned proportionately and a Senate apportioned equally.

bicameral
a two-house legislature.

TABLE 2.2 Legislative Structures under the Virginia Plan, New Jersey Plan, and the Great Compromise

	Virginia Plan	New Jersey Plan	Great Compromise
Structure of Legislature	Bicameral (two chamber)	Unicameral (single chamber)	Bicameral (two chamber)
Apportionment	**Lower House** • Number of seats apportioned by state population. • Members directly elected by citizens. **Upper House** • Number of seats apportioned by state population. • Members elected by lower house (from list supplied by state legislatures).	**Legislature** • Equal representation for states regardless of state population. • Members appointed by the states.	**House of Representatives** • States represented according to population. • Members directly elected by citizens. **Senate** • States represented equally (two senators per state). • Members appointed by state legislatures.
Powers	• Legislature has strong powers, including the ability to veto state laws.	• Legislature has similar power as under the Articles of Confederation but can also levy taxes and regulate commerce.	• Legislature has broad powers over commerce and the ability to make laws as necessary. • House of Representatives has the "power of the purse" to levy taxes.

Section 2, the number of members from each state in the House of Representatives would be chosen according to state populations. The people would directly elect these representatives. Under Article I, Section 3, states would be represented equally in the upper chamber, the Senate. Two senators would be chosen from each state by their state legislatures. Table 2.2 summarizes the two plans and the Great Compromise.

Having secured equal representation in the Senate, small states offered less opposition to a strong national government. They were now less afraid of Congress, even seeing it as a defense against the power of their larger neighbors. The Constitution was the result of compromise. One of the most important of these consequences dealt with an issue that later divided the nation—that of slavery.

Slavery: A Fateful Compromise

At the time of the convention, nearly one out of every six individuals living in the thirteen states was a slave. Most, but not all, lived in the southern states. About one-third of the delegates to the convention, including Madison and Washington, were slave owners.

Southern plantation owners, many of whom were politically powerful in their state legislatures and some of whom were delegates to the Philadelphia convention, had no intention of seeing slavery outlawed or heavily regulated. A few others, however, saw the preservation of slavery as a moral failure and spoke out at the convention about the hypocrisy of trying to preserve liberty in a document that allowed slavery.

Slavery was an issue that could have easily torn apart the convention—or the country—at the time. It invoked the core values of a people who were trying to constitute themselves in a republic. In spite of a few speeches on the floor of the convention, however, the question of slavery was not generally debated in terms of morality or of liberty but rather in terms of states' representation, the same issue that affected so many others at the convention. In the end, the question of slavery was settled not according to high ideals but on practical, political considerations.

The final document dealt with slavery in three ways. The word *slavery* never appears—a minor tactical victory for those who did not want the Constitution to appear to approve of it. One question was how slaves would be counted for purposes of representation in the House of Representatives. In Article I, Section 2, the **Three-Fifths Compromise** determined that a slave—called an "other person" in the Constitution—would count as three-fifths of a person for the purpose of calculating a state's representation.[18] Slaves could not vote, but their numbers would boost the influence of the slave states. Because slaves were counted among the population, slave-holding states would be allotted more members of Congress and, as a result, in the Electoral College. This gave Southern states more clout in the House of Representatives and more say in selecting the president than they would have had otherwise.

Article I, Section 9 sets forth the **Compromise on Importation**. Congress would not be allowed to restrict the slave trade until 1808 at the earliest. Third, under Article IV, slaves who had successfully escaped would have to be returned to their owners, regardless of the laws of individual states.

The Three-Fifths Compromise merely postponed the inevitable conflict over slavery, which was settled by the Civil War.

There are several reasons why the delegates agreed to preserve slavery even though it went against the very idea of natural rights upon which the Constitution is based. The first reason is that slave owners threatened to leave the convention unless slavery was protected. Had the southern states pulled out, the Articles of Confederation, which contained no restrictions on slavery, would have remained the law of the land. Politics during the convention also played a large role. The question of slavery had been handed to the Committee of Detail, chaired by John Rutledge of South Carolina. Not surprisingly, Rutledge's committee proposed to give the slave states everything that they demanded.

Regardless of the reasons, the question of slavery was temporarily handled but fundamentally unsettled. Not until the country was torn apart in the Civil War eighty years later would the issue of slavery be decided. Even today, the question of whether Americans are all truly equal in the Republic endures.

James Madison on Slavery

Although his views on slavery evolved over time, James Madison, a slave owner throughout his life, was never able to completely resolve the contradictions inherent in a Constitution

Three-Fifths Compromise an agreement reached by delegates at the Constitutional Convention that a slave would count as three-fifths of a person in calculating a state's representation.

Compromise on Importation Congress could not restrict the slave trade until 1808.

Montpelier, the residence in Orange County, Virginia, of James Madison, was home to over one hundred slaves whose labor supported the plantation.
GRANGER / GRANGER-All Rights Reserved

One of the most important compromises between the states during the Constitutional Convention was on the issue of slavery.

Figure A shows the percentage of each state's population that was enslaved in 1790, three years after the drafting of the Constitution. The divisions between northern and southern states are striking.

Figure B presents the same data, but it does so in a way that breaks down the population — free, slave, and total — of each state and the two regions. Note the bars that represent the total population of the states and regions.

FIGURE A

Percentage Slave Population by State

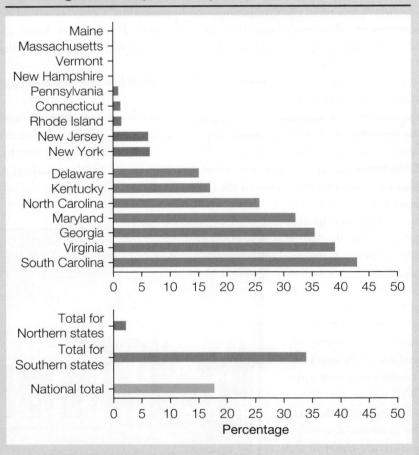

and government that, although based on natural rights and liberties, permitted slavery. In an essay published following the drafting of the Constitution, Madison acknowledges this contradiction, raising a hypothetical argument with which he later agrees:

> But we must deny the fact, that slaves are considered merely as property, and in no respect whatsoever as persons. The true state of the case is, that they partake of both of these qualities; being considered by our laws, in some respects, as persons, and in other respects as property. In being compelled to labour, not for himself, but for a master; in

FIGURE B

Free and Slave Population Totals by State

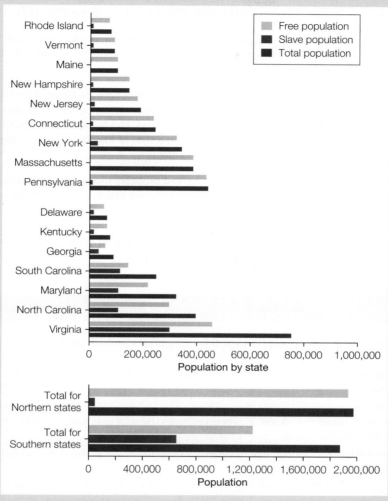

Data from U.S. Census Bureau

1. Describe one major difference between the data shown in Figure A and the data shown in Figure B.

2. Explain how the data in Figure B relate to the reason for the Three-Fifths Compromise.

3. Explain whether the data in Figure A or Figure B would be more useful to a political scientist in understanding the reasons for the Three-Fifths Compromise.

being vendible [able to be sold] by one master to another master; and in being subject at all times to be restrained in his liberty, and chastised in his body, by the capricious will of another, the slave may appear to be degraded from the human rank, and classed with those irrational animals which fall under the legal denomination of property. In being protected, on the other hand, in his life and in his limbs, against the violence of all others, even the master of his labour and his liberty; and in being punishable himself for all violence committed against others; the slave is no less evidently regarded by the law as a member of society.[19]

In a letter to a colleague later in his life, Madison discussed a plan for ending slavery that involved a separate treatment for African Americans, whether in returning freed slaves to Africa or settling them in the Western territories:

Sir,—I have rec. [received] your letter of the 3d instant, requesting such hints as may have occurred to me on the subject of an eventual extinguishment of slavery in the U.S.

A general emancipation of slaves ought to be 1. gradual. 2. equitable & satisfactory for the individuals immediately concerned. 3. consistent with the existing & durable prejudices of the nation.

To be equitable & satisfactory, the consent of both the Master & the slave should be obtained. That of the Master will require a provision in the plan for compensating a loss of what he held as property guarantied by the laws, and recognized by the Constitution. That of the slave, requires that his condition in a state of freedom, be preferable in his own estimation, to his actual one in a state of bondage.

To be consistent with existing and probably unalterable prejudices in the U. S. the freed blacks ought to be permanently removed beyond the region occupied by or allotted to a White population.[20]

Madison never did free his own slaves or provide for their freedom upon his death, as his colleague George Washington would do.

Section Review

2.2 Describe how the Constitution was shaped by negotiation and compromise.

REMEMBER The delegates at the Constitutional Convention reached compromises on the key issues of representation and slavery.

KNOW
- *Constitutional Convention*: a meeting attended by state delegates in 1787 to fix the Articles of Confederation. (p. 33)
- *writ of habeas corpus*: the right of people detained by the government to know the charges against them. (p. 34)
- *bills of attainder*: when the legislature declares someone guilty without a trial. (p. 34)
- *ex post facto laws*: laws punishing people for acts that were not crimes at the time they were committed. (p. 34)
- *Virginia Plan*: a plan of government calling for a three-branch government with a bicameral legislature, where more populous states would have more representation in Congress. (p. 35)
- *New Jersey Plan*: a plan of government that provided for a unicameral legislature with equal votes for each states. (p. 35)
- *bicameral*: a two-house legislature. (p. 35)
- *Grand Committee*: a committee at the Constitutional Convention that worked out the compromise on representation. (p. 35)
- *Great (Connecticut) Compromise*: an agreement for a plan of government that drew upon both the Virginia and New Jersey Plans; it settled issues of state representation by calling for a bicameral legislature with a House of Representatives apportioned proportionately and a Senate apportioned equally. (p. 35)
- *Three-Fifths Compromise*: an agreement reached by delegates at the Constitutional Convention that a slave would count as three-fifths of a person in calculating a state's representation. (p. 37)
- *Compromise on Importation*: Congress could not restrict the slave trade until 1808. (p. 37)

THINK How did the compromises at the Constitutional Convention pave the way for conflict in the future?

Percentage Slave Population by State

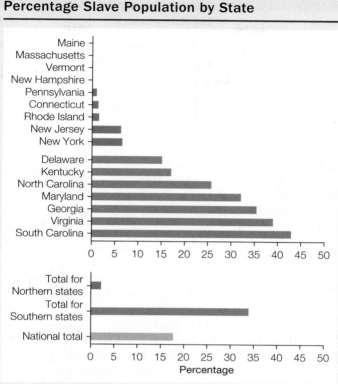

Data from U.S. Census Bureau

Use the information in the graph and your knowledge of U.S. Government and Politics to answer parts A, B, and C.

A. Describe one similarity between northern and southern states shown by the data in the figure.

B. Describe one difference between northern and southern states shown by the data in the figure.

C. Explain how the data in the figure relate to the Great Compromise.

■ 2.3 Branches of Government

With the bicameral legislature having resolved the first and largest issue of the convention—the distribution of power between the states and the citizens in the legislature—the convention moved on to the structure of the rest of the government and the specific powers of each branch.

Separation of Powers

The delegates tried to make sure that no one branch can become too powerful on its own. The idea of **separation of powers** was widely supported by delegates at the convention and well known to those who had studied the writings of the Baron de Montesquieu. Under this system, branches are not meant to preside over their own spheres. Rather, a system

> **AP® TIP**
>
> Know the expressed powers of each branch of government! AP® exam questions often focus on these enumerated constitutional powers and on how each branch checks the others.

separation of powers
a design of government that distributes powers across institutions in order to avoid making one branch too powerful on its own.

TABLE 2.3 Separated Institutions Sharing Powers

	POWERS OF EACH BRANCH		
	Executive Branch	**Legislative Branch**	**Judicial Branch**
Lawmaking Authority	• Executes laws. • Works to shape legislative agenda. • Has power to veto legislation. • Nominates judges to the federal judiciary. • Nominates key executive branch officials. • Gives State of the Union Address.	• Writes nation's laws. • Can override a presidential veto. • Determines number of Supreme Court justices. • Creates lower courts.	• Interprets contested laws. • Can declare both federal and state laws unconstitutional.
National Security and Foreign Policy Responsibilities	• President acts as commander in chief of the military. • Sets foreign policy agenda. • Negotiates treaties.	• Declares war. • Senate ratifies treaties.	
Oversight Responsibilities	• Oversees federal bureaucracy.	• House issues articles of impeachment; Senate holds impeachment trials (over president, executive branch officials, and federal judges). • Budget authority and oversight over executive branch agencies. • Senate confirms judicial nominees. • Senate confirms key executive branch officials.	• May declare executive branch actions in conflict with the Constitution.

checks and balances
a design of government in which each branch has powers that can prevent the other branches from making policy.

of "separated institutions *sharing* powers" was created.[21] Under the system of **checks and balances**, each branch has powers that can prevent the other branches from making policy. For example, while the president has the power to negotiate treaties under Article II, Section 2, the Senate has the power to ratify them under Article I, Section 3. (See Table 2.3). The founding fathers feared too much concentration of power in a single executive. One of the most important checks on the executive is Congress's power to impeach and remove a president who commits bribery, treason, or other high crimes or misdemeanors, under Article I, Section 3. The power of impeachment will be discussed in more detail in chapters 4 and 5.

federalism
the sharing of power between the national government and the states.

To divide power further, the Constitution creates a system of **federalism**, the sharing of power between the national government and the states. Federalism is as central to American government as checks and balances, and it has been the source of much conflict and controversy.

Separation of powers and federalism create multiple access points for citizens to influence government policies. For example, in the 1950s civil rights advocates were unable to get Congress to pass legislation to prohibit race discrimination, so they filed lawsuits instead. Gay rights activists who wanted gay marriage legalized started at the state level before bringing their cause to the Supreme Court. Because there are multiple branches and levels of government, citizens have many ways to access policymakers.

The Legislative Branch

legislative branch
the institution responsible for making laws.

As the **legislative branch** of government, Congress's purpose is to legislate—to make laws. Both houses have to work together to pass laws, but because of how congressional members are chosen, each house had a slightly different purpose. Members of the House of Representatives are elected directly by the people and have to run for reelection every two years. They were meant to be more responsive to the people, to directly represent their constituents. Senators, who were originally chosen by state legislatures and serve six-year terms, represent the states and check the passions of the people. Senators' terms are staggered in two-year shifts so that only about a third of senators are up for reelection in any given election year, making it more difficult for any swift change in mood among citizens to quickly affect national policy.

Congress was granted more power than the unicameral legislature under the Articles of Confederation, especially with regard to issues of money and the economy. The specific powers given directly to Congress in Article I of the Constitution are **expressed** or **enumerated powers**. For example, Congress is given the power to borrow money, collect taxes, and "regulate Commerce with foreign Nations, and among the several states." The commerce clause has enabled Congress to become involved in large areas of the American economy, even within states. Debates over the power of and limits to the commerce clause continue today, especially between states and the federal government.

To preserve its flexibility, Article I, Section 8 contains the **necessary and proper** or **elastic clause** giving Congress the ability "to make all Laws which shall be necessary and proper for carrying into Execution the foregoing Powers, and all the other Powers vested by this Constitution in the Government of the United States." Powers of the federal government that go beyond the expressed powers under the necessary and proper clause are called **implied powers**. As we will see in chapter 3, the necessary and proper clause, combined with the commerce clause, paved the way for a dramatic expansion in Congress's implied power over national policy in the centuries following ratification.

expressed or enumerated powers
authority specifically granted to a branch of the government in the Constitution.

necessary and proper or elastic clause
language in Article I, Section 8, granting Congress the powers necessary to carry out its enumerated powers.

implied powers
authority of the federal government that goes beyond its expressed powers.

The Executive Branch

The delegates settled on a single executive—a president—who would serve a four-year term. As head of the **executive branch**, the president is there to "execute," or carry out, the laws that had been passed by Congress. The president is given some, but not unlimited, power over Congress with the ability to veto a piece of legislation that Congress has passed. Congress can, however, override the veto with a two-thirds vote in each of the two houses. The president is commander in chief of the army and navy. Again, though, power is shared. Congress, not the president, has the power to declare (and raise money for) war. Presidents oversee the people working in the executive branch, which has led to the growth of a large and influential federal bureaucracy. Finally, the president has the power to make foreign policy, although this responsibility is shared with the Senate.

executive branch
the institution responsible for carrying out laws passed by the legislative branch.

Shown here arriving at Congress Hall in Philadelphia on March 4, 1793, for his second inauguration, George Washington chose to retire after his second term despite the fact that the Constitution would have permitted him to run for reelection for an unlimited number of terms.
GRANGER / GRANGER-All Rights Reserved

Citizens do not vote directly for the president. Instead, an Electoral College, consisting of electors awarded to states based on their representation in Congress, selects the president. Every state receives two electors (because each has two senators) plus one elector for each member of the House of Representatives.

The Judiciary

The Constitution is not very specific about the **judicial branch**, the system of federal courts. The Supreme Court is the highest in the land and the Constitution allows for a system of lower federal courts whose structure and composition would be determined by Congress. The federal courts have jurisdiction—the authority to hear and decide cases—over all disputes between states and the national government, between two or more states, and between citizens of different states. Combined with the **supremacy clause** in Article VI, Clause 2 of the Constitution, which declares that national treaties and laws "shall be the supreme law of the Land," the federal courts emerged as superior to state courts and laws.

The Constitution does not expressly provide for judicial review, the power of the Supreme Court to overturn a law or executive action that violates the Constitution. The Supreme Court established the principle of judicial review later in *Marbury v. Madison* (1803).[22] We will examine the concept of judicial review in much more detail in chapter 6 on the judiciary. The power of judicial review, combined with the supremacy clause, became crucial in later battles to protect civil liberties and secure civil rights.

As with the other two branches, the judiciary does not exist in isolation. Congress has the authority to create the lower federal courts. Congress determines the number of Supreme Court justices, and the Senate has the power to confirm justices (by majority vote). Justices are nominated by the president.

Making Changes to the Constitution

By making provisions for changing the Constitution through a process of **amendment** laid out in Article V, the framers acknowledged that it would always be unfinished, that it had to be adaptable if it were to endure. The founders purposely designed a system for amending the Constitution that makes change slow and difficult to achieve.

Amending the document is a two-stage process, with two possible routes to completion of each stage. First, the amendment has to be officially proposed, which can happen in two ways: (1) passage by a two-thirds vote in both the House and the Senate, or (2) passage in a national convention called at the request of two-thirds of the states. After formal proposal, the amendment must be ratified, either by (1) a majority vote in three-fourths of the state legislatures, or (2) acceptance by ratifying conventions in three-fourths of the states. The second method for ratification has only been used once. See Figure 2.1.

Of the thousands of suggestions for amending the Constitution presented in Congress since its founding, only twenty-seven amendments have been ratified. The first ten of these, which make up the Bill of Rights, became part of the debate over ratification of the Constitution itself and, for some, were a condition of ratification. Two others—an amendment prohibiting the sale and consumption of alcoholic beverages and one repealing that prohibition—cancel each other out. Since the passage of the Bill of Rights, therefore, the Constitution has only had fifteen lasting changes. Although the Constitution has seldom been amended, some scholars argue that important decisions by the Supreme Court and major changes in how the American people view their rights have at critical times in history led to changes in government just as significant as formal amendments.[23]

FIGURE 2.1

How to Amend the U.S. Constitution

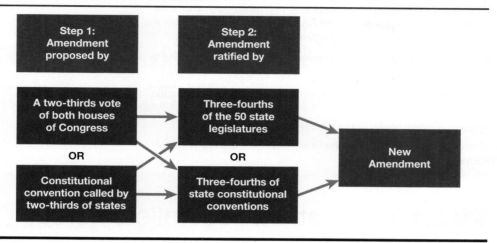

An Uncertain Future

The delegates also used a bit of trickery to get around another issue. The Articles of Confederation required that any amendments had to have the approval of all thirteen state delegations in Congress. The members of the Constitutional Convention knew that achieving unanimity was going to be very difficult. So the delegates decided that the Constitution would become law if ratifying conventions in nine of the thirteen states approved it, bypassing the state legislatures. Even with this somewhat unconventional ploy, it was still far from certain that the Constitution would be adopted.

Section Review

2.3 Describe checks and balances and explain the impact of checks and balances on the political system.

REMEMBER   The Constitution separates power among three branches of government, and each branch is given checks over the others.

KNOW
- *separation of powers*: a design of government that distributes powers across institutions in order to avoid making one branch too powerful on its own. (p. 41)
- *checks and balances*: a design of government in which each branch has powers that can prevent the other branches from making policy. (p. 42)
- *federalism*: the sharing of power between the national government and the states. (p. 42)
- *legislative branch*: the institution responsible for making laws. (p. 42)
- *expressed or enumerated powers*: authority specifically granted to a branch of the government in the Constitution. (p. 43)
- *necessary and proper or elastic clause*: language in Article I, Section 8 granting Congress the powers necessary to carry out its enumerated powers. (p. 43)
- *implied powers*: authority of the federal government that goes beyond its expressed powers. (p. 43)
- *executive branch*: the institution responsible for carrying out laws passed by the legislative branch. (p. 43)
- *judicial branch*: the institution responsible for hearing and deciding cases through the federal courts. (p. 44)
- *supremacy clause*: constitutional provision declaring that the Constitution and all federal laws and treaties are the supreme law of the land. (p. 44)
- *amendment*: the process by which changes may be made to the Constitution. (p. 44)

THINK   How did the Constitution allow the executive and judicial branches to become more powerful over time?

In 2017, President Trump and Republicans in Congress tried to repeal the Affordable Care Act (Obamacare). Among other things, this law requires Americans to purchase health insurance or pay a fine. Although President Trump is a member of the Republican Party, and Republicans controlled both houses of Congress, they were unable to repeal the Affordable Care Act.

After reading the passage, use your knowledge of U.S. Government and Politics to respond to A, B, and C.

A. Describe an expressed constitutional power Congress could use to address the situation described above.

B. Describe an expressed constitutional power of the president.

C. Explain how the division of powers between Congress and the president influences the situation described above.

2.4 Ratification: Federalists Versus Antifederalists

It was America's first national political campaign. The fate of the Constitution would be decided in the state ratifying conventions. Nine of the thirteen states had to ratify for the Constitution to take effect. The proposed new Constitution was the subject of intense debates everywhere—in homes, taverns, coffeehouses, and newspapers.

It was also its first *negative* national political campaign. The fight between those in favor of the Constitution and those opposed to it was characterized by dire premonitions of what might happen if the Constitution was or was not ratified. The debate was carried out through the printing presses, which had become widespread enough to allow both sides to carry their messages to the people. Some wrote under their own names. Others adopted the names of Roman figures or used simple descriptors such as "landowner." Both sides flooded the country with pamphlets and letters to newspapers. The campaign was sometimes personal, with attacks on the character of members of the other side.

Supporters of the proposed Constitution claimed the name **Federalists**. Those arguing against the document would be tagged as **Antifederalists**. Both Federalists and Antifederalists were interested in a politically and economically secure nation, but they differed in how they thought that would best be achieved.

For the Antifederalists, part of the negativity associated with their name and their political campaign was perhaps inevitable. They were forced to argue against a proposal, and basing their argument on the merits of the Articles of Confederation was a tough sell. So they turned negative. They raised fears about what this new change in the government would bring. Mostly, they argued, it would trample on the rights of the people and the states, perhaps not immediately, but at some point in the nation's future.

The Federalists also campaigned partly on fear. They pointed to the problems that plagued the government under the Articles—the inability to deal with foreign powers, economic challenges, and, especially, the threat of anarchy—and warned citizens that the only way to avoid these dangers was through the new Constitution. The Federalists had celebrity on their side in the figures of Washington and Franklin. A personal appeal by Washington in which he argued, "There is *no Alternative* between the *Adoption* of it [the Constitution] and *Anarchy*," was reprinted fifty-one times during the campaign.[24]

In some ways, the Federalists and Antifederalists split along distinctions of class. Many wealthy merchants favored the strong economic policy that the Constitution would allow,

Federalists
supporters of the proposed Constitution, who called for a strong national government.

Antifederalists
those opposed to the proposed Constitution, who favored stronger state governments.

TABLE 2.4 Federalists and Antifederalists

Differed in Terms of...	Federalists	Antifederalists
View of proposed Constitution	Supporters	Opponents
Proponents of...	A strong national government	Stronger state governments
Concerned about...	The tyranny of the majority	Oppression of the rights of the states and the people
Supporters included...	More wealthy merchants and southern plantation owners George Washington, Benjamin Franklin, Alexander Hamilton, James Madison, John Jay	More people in rural areas, more farmers and shopkeepers Fewer well-known supporters, but leadership included educated elites, Revolutionary War heroes, and convention delegates Patrick Henry, Samuel Adams, George Clinton
Required documents for AP® U.S. Government and Politics	*Federalist* No. 10 *Federalist* No. 51	Brutus No. 1

and many wealthy southern plantation owners supported the agreements that had been reached at the Constitutional Convention. On the other side, a large number of Antifederalists came from rural areas and mistrusted powerful elites. To say that the Federalists were wealthy elites and the Antifederalists small farmers and shopkeepers is, however, too strong a simplification. Many Antifederalist leaders were part of educated elites; some of the most prominent had been heroes in the Revolutionary War, delegates to the convention itself, or important members in state politics. See Table 2.4, which highlights the differences.

Although the Federalists tried to associate the threat of anarchy and Shays's Rebellion with their opponents, the Antifederalists were just as concerned as their opponents with securing a stable future for the country. Three main issues divided the Antifederalists and the Federalists: (1) the feasibility of republican government in such a large nation, (2) the relative power of states and the national government, and (3) the lack of a bill of rights in the Constitution.

The Federalists used a positive approach in their campaign. They had to explain to skeptical Americans that a large republic could be constructed in a way that would prevent it from growing so self-interested and powerful that it would trample on the rights of states and their citizens. The Federalists made their case in a collection of eighty-five essays written for New York newspapers from the fall of 1787 to the spring of 1788. Published under the collective name "Publius," these **Federalist Papers** were written by Alexander Hamilton, James Madison, and John Jay. The *Federalist Papers* were intended to influence the ratification debate, especially in the contested state of New York. Hamilton had the "idea of laying down this propaganda barrage on the still undecided minds of New Yorkers."[39] The *Federalist Papers* were an example of political propaganda—the framing and discussion of a political issue in a way that tries to influence people's views of that issue.

Many of Madison's essays are now considered to be the most important in the collection. Two essays in particular, **Federalist No. 51** and **No. 10**, tackle the Antifederalist critiques by laying out the reasons behind the proposed constitutional republic. The *Federalist Papers* are now considered some of the most important writings in American political history.

Federalist Papers
a series of eighty-five essays written by Alexander Hamilton, James Madison, and John Jay and published between 1787 and 1788 that lay out the theory behind the Constitution.

Federalist No. 51
an essay in which Madison argues that separation of powers and federalism will prevent tyranny.

Federalist No. 10: Blunting the Power of Factions

The danger to the republic was not only that people would act according to their self-interest. They might work together with others who had the same motives, trampling the rights of others in the process. According to Madison, a **faction** is a group of self-interested individuals who form groups to use the government to get what they want, trampling on the rights of others. Madison believed factions would present the most dangerous challenge to a republic.

In ***Federalist* No. 10**, he describes the problem of faction and explains how the Constitution provides a solution. "By faction," Madison wrote, "I understand a number of citizens, whether amounting to a majority or minority of the whole, who are united and actuated by a common impulse of passion, or of interest, adverse to the rights of other citizens, or to the permanent and aggregate interests of the community."[25] Madison identifies inequality of wealth as the main cause of faction asserting that "those who hold and those who are without property have ever formed distinct interests in society."[26]

The cause of factions could be eliminated but, Madison argued, only through unacceptable means. A tyrannical government that suppressed the liberties of its citizens could prevent factions from organizing. "Liberty," Madison argued, "is to faction what air is to fire."[27] Suppress liberty, and factions cannot survive. Factions also cannot form or survive in societies where everyone has "the same opinions, the same passions, and the same interests."[28] This second preventive measure is as unrealistic as the first is unthinkable, especially in a large republic like the United States. Therefore, Madison concludes that a nation cannot avoid the problem of faction, only try to check its dangers.

Madison argues that a republican form of government protects against small factions: "If a faction consists of less than a majority, relief is supplied by the republican principle, which enables the majority to defeat its sinister views by regular vote. It may clog the administration, it may convulse the society; but it will be unable to execute and mask its violence under the forms of the Constitution."[29]

Factions are more difficult to control when they are made up of a majority. According to Madison,

> When a majority is included in a faction, the form of popular government, on the other hand, enables it to sacrifice to its ruling passion or interest both the public good and the rights of other citizens. To secure the public good and private rights against the danger of such a faction, and at the same time to preserve the spirit and the form of popular government, is then the great object to which our inquiries are directed.

There are two ways to mitigate the dangers of a faction of a majority. The first is republican government. According to Madison,

> as each representative will be chosen by a greater number of citizens in the large than in the small republic, it will be more difficult for unworthy candidates to practice with success the vicious arts by which elections are too often carried; and the suffrages of the people being more free, will be more likely to centre in men who possess the most attractive merit and the most diffusive and established characters.

The second way to prevent the dangers of a faction of a majority is the large size of the republic: "The influence of factious leaders may kindle a flame within their particular States, but will be unable to spread a general conflagration through the other States."

American history has proven Madison correct. The American republic has had factions since its origin. Political parties can be thought of as factions, as can interest groups.

The best way to check the power of factions, Madison argued in *Federalist* No. 10, is through a republic so large and diverse, with so many factions vying for power, that no one faction is able to assert its will over all of the others. Tactically, this was a clever argument. With it, Madison countered the Antifederalist charge that the American republic would be too large to govern effectively by arguing that the only solution to the dangers of faction was precisely to have such a large republic.

Tyranny of the Majority, Tyranny of the Minority

Both the Federalists and the Antifederalists acknowledged that tyranny could take two forms. In a tyranny of the minority, a small number of citizens tramples on the rights of the rest of the larger population. In a tyranny of the majority, a large number of citizens uses the power of their majority to trample on the rights of a smaller group. The two sides disagreed on which was the greater danger and, therefore, on how a republic should be structured.

The Antifederalists focused more on the dangers of a tyranny of the minority. They feared the government would become disconnected from the majority and controlled by the wealthy elites. While acknowledging the dangers of tyranny of the minority, Madison and the Federalists focused more on the dangers of majority rule. A majority of people may use their power to oppress a minority of citizens. Given the panic associated with Shays's Rebellion, the Federalists feared that a majority of poor people would use their power to take land away from the rich.

In *Federalist* No. 10, Madison argued against direct democracy, in which citizens vote directly on policies. Viewing direct democracies throughout history as "spectacles of turbulence and contention . . . incompatible with personal security or the rights of property," Madison argued for republican government as the remedy to the dangers of tyranny.[30] We will revisit *Federalist* No. 10 in our study of interest groups in chapter 15.

In a republic, people delegate their power to representatives. In *Federalist* No. 51, Madison sketched out such a structure. Separation of powers is the guiding principle, with power divided between the national government and the states, among the three branches of the national government, and within each branch.

The Power of the National Government and the States

Debates over the relative power of the states and the national government were central to the political battles over ratification of the Constitution. The Federalists tried to convince American citizens that the proposed form of government was necessary to preserve their rights and liberties. The Antifederalists argued against the proposed increase in national power and warned Americans that the Constitution might allow the national government to infringe on the authority of the states.

Brutus No. 1: Antifederalist Suspicion of Power

The Antifederalists feared a radical increase in national power, not only in the proposed Constitution but in how the government might evolve over time. The Antifederalists understood that the government under the Articles of Confederation was too weak. According to **Brutus No. 1**, written by the Anti-Federalist Robert Yates from New York in 1787,[31] "We have felt the feebleness of the ties by which these United-States are held together, and the want of sufficient energy in our present confederation, to manage, in some instances, our general concerns." Despite the concession that the national government was ineffectual,

Brutus No. 1
an Antifederalist Paper arguing that the country was too large to be governed as a republic and that the Constitution gave too much power to the national government.

the Antifederalists worried that representation of the people's interests could not be maintained as the country grew in size, population, and power: "a free republic cannot succeed over a country of such immense extent, containing such a number of inhabitants, and increasing in such rapid progression. . . ."

They feared that, once elected and comfortable in their jobs, the representatives would not relinquish power. Brutus No. 1 states, "Many instances can be produced in which the people have voluntarily increased the powers of their rulers; but few, if any, in which rulers have willingly abridged their authority."[32] Furthermore, being some distance away from their congressional district would alienate the representatives from their constituents' wishes.

The economic power of the national government to tax and to regulate interstate commerce was one of the Antifederalists' greatest worries, and it was only made worse by the necessary and proper clause of the proposed Constitution. According to Brutus No. 1, "this power, given [to] the federal legislature, directly annihilates all the powers of the state legislatures."[33] Over time, when individual states attempted to reassert their authority, "it will be found that the power retained by individual states, small as is it is, will be a clog upon the wheels of government of the United States; the latter therefore will be naturally inclined to remove it out of the way."[34]

The Antifederalists were also concerned that the federal government's control over the military could be used to destroy liberty: "It might be here shewn, that the power in the federal legislative, to raise and support armies at pleasure, as well in peace as in war, and their controul over the militia, tend, not only to a consolidation of the government, but the destruction of liberty."[35] Brutus No. 1 also discusses the dangers of a standing army: "In despotic governments, as well as in all the monarchies of Europe, standing armies are kept up to execute the commands of the prince or the magistrate, and are employed for this purpose when occasion requires: But they have always proved the destruction of liberty. . . ."[36]

Brutus No. 1 also expresses concern that the powers of the states under the system of federalism would eventually be overtaken by the federal government:

> it is a truth confirmed by the unerring experience of ages, that every man, and every body of men, invested with power, are ever disposed to increase it, and to acquire a superiority over every thing that stands in their way. This disposition, which is implanted in human nature, will operate in the federal legislature to lessen and ultimately to subvert the state authority, and having such advantages, will most certainly succeed, if the federal government succeeds at all.[37]

Brutus No. 1 ends with a plea to reject the proposed Constitution:

> Though I am of opinion, that it is a sufficient objection to this government, to reject it, that it creates the whole union into one government, under the form of a republic, yet if this objection was obviated, there are exceptions to it, which are so material and fundamental, that they ought to determine every man, who is a friend to the liberty and happiness of mankind, not to adopt it.[38]

Federalist No. 51: Sharing Power to Prevent Tyranny

The factions for and against the Constitution disagreed on the very possibility of a republic in a country as large as the United States. Many of the Enlightenment writers had argued that republics had to remain small to work properly, and everyone expected the United States to grow even larger over time, worsening the challenges to a republican government. The Antifederalists argued that the national government would grow more distant from the people over time and would eventually begin to oppress them. Congress having the power to tax would only make this danger greater, they claimed. As the national government grew more powerful and more distant from the citizens, states would grow weaker and provide citizens with fewer checks on the power of the national government. The Antifederalists asserted that more restrictions had to be placed on the national government while it was still possible.

Madison studied human nature. He knew that people are self-interested, putting their own needs before what is best for the nation. He proposed that the American republic must be constructed to account for self-interest and selfish motives. In *Federalist* No. 51, he wrote, "If men were angels, no government would be necessary. If angels were to govern men, neither external nor internal controls on government would be necessary. In framing a government which is to be administered by men over men, the great difficulty lies in this: you must first enable the government to control the governed; and in the next place oblige it to control itself."[40]

Madison argued that the key to preventing tyranny was to provide a system of separation of powers within the national government to prevent any one branch from trampling on the rights of citizens: "it is evident that each department should have a will of its own; and consequently should be so constituted that the members of each should have as little agency as possible in the appointment of the members of the others."

Like the separation of powers, bicameralism prevents too much power from accumulating in a single branch: "In republican government, the legislative authority necessarily predominates. The remedy for this inconveniency is to divide the legislature into different branches; and to render them, by different modes of election and different principles of action, as little connected with each other as the nature of their common functions and their common dependence on the society will admit."

Furthermore, a federal system, in which power is separated between the national government and the states, would provide an important defense against the dangers of tyranny:

> In the compound republic of America, the power surrendered by the people, is first divided between two distinct governments, and then the portion allotted to each subdivided among the distinct and separate departments. Hence a double security arises to the rights of the people. The different governments will control each other, at the same time that each will be controlled by itself.[41]

In *Federalist* No. 51, Madison returns to the argument he made in *Federalist* No. 10 about the importance of having multiple factions compete in the policymaking process:

> In a free government the security for civil rights must be the same as that for religious rights. It consists in the one case in the multiplicity of interests, and in the other in the multiplicity of sects. The degree of security in both cases will depend on the number of interests and sects; and this may be presumed to depend on the extent of country and number of people comprehended under the same government.

We will revisit *Federalist* No. 51 in chapter 4, when we continue our study of the institutions of government.

A Bill of Rights

Strategically, the most effective Antifederalist charge against the Constitution was that it lacked a bill of rights—a list of rights and liberties that governments cannot take away. Many state constitutions already had them, and the idea of inserting a statement

In this political cartoon from about 1812, George Washington (shown in heaven) warns partisans not to jeopardize the "dearest blessings" of "Peace and Plenty, Liberty and Independence" by dislodging the supporting pillars of Federalism, Republicanism, and Democracy. At the left, a Democrat tugs on the pillar of Federalism as he says, "This Pillar shall not stand. I am determin'd to support a just and necessary War," and at the right, a Federalist pulls on the pillar of Democracy, claiming, "This Pillar must come down. I am a friend of Peace."

New York Public Library

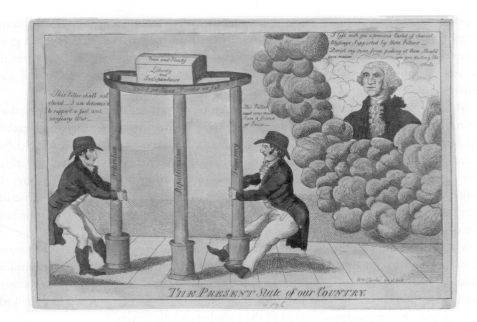

AP® REQUIRED DOCUMENTS

In chapter 1, you met the Declaration of Independence. By this point in chapter 2, you should know the two other major "foundational" documents that established the U.S. government as well as the three essays for and against adoption of the Constitution.

Document	Scope
Articles of Confederation	Even though the Articles of Confederation are no longer in force, you should read them. The document is not that long. Note how it is divided into thirteen articles.
Constitution of the United States	Focus here on the original part of the Constitution as well as on the Bill of Rights (see Section 2.4). Make sure that you understand the differences among the articles of the Constitution and the branches of government that each relates to.
Federalist No. 51	• "If men were angels no government would be necessary." • The government must control the governed and must control itself. • Checks and balances will prevent one branch from becoming too powerful and taking away liberty.
Federalist No. 10	• Factions are self-interested groups that would harm the community. • Factions are sown into the nature of humankind. • To abolish factions would abolish liberty. • Factions should be set against each other to prevent any one faction from becoming too powerful. • A large republic protects against the dangers of faction. • Republican government is a remedy for the dangers of faction.
Brutus No. 1	• The country is too large to be governed as a republic. • Representatives will not voluntarily give up power.

protecting specific rights and liberties into the Constitution had come up during the convention. To Madison and other opponents of a bill of rights, a statement of rights was not necessary. Under the Constitution, the people were already sovereign, and the government was already limited. Some worried that a bill of rights could limit liberty because the government might not respect those rights not expressly listed.

Some however, both during the convention and after, remained strongly in favor of a bill of rights. A bill of rights, they argued, was necessary to check the tendency of government to infringe on the rights and liberties of citizens over time. The Antifederalists argued that a bill of rights would serve to remind citizens of their natural rights and remind them to assert those rights when governments might try to take them away.

As it turned out, the lack of a bill of rights proved to be the most effective argument that the Antifederalists would make in the ratification campaign. Many Americans were suspicious of centralized power and wanted specific protections against it.

In February 1788, the Federalists won a narrow victory in Massachusetts, but only after the pro-constitutional forces agreed to propose a bill of rights once the original document had been ratified. On June 21, 1788, New Hampshire became the ninth state to ratify the Constitution, which would become the supreme law of the land the following year. James Madison continued to worry. If Virginia and New York failed to ratify, it might lead to deep divisions within the new country. Virginia ratified in June, and New York followed in July, each by a narrow margin. During the ratification campaign, sensing the realities of the political landscape, Madison shifted course and promised to introduce a bill of rights as proposed amendments during the first session of the new Congress once the Constitution had been ratified. Madison kept his word, and in 1791, ten of the amendments that he proposed became part of the Constitution.

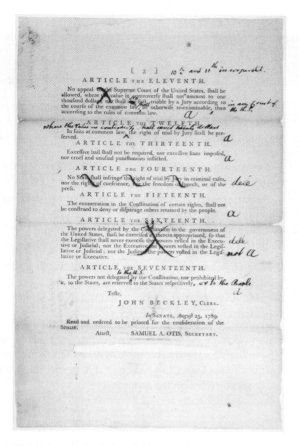

Shown is a draft of the Bill of Rights from September 9, 1789.

The Founders' Motives

The stories surrounding the framers' efforts have shifted over time. The founders of the American republic have been described as being guided by their own privilege and accused of crafting a government that preserved distinctions of wealth and class.

According to Charles Beard, wealthy elites supported the proposed Constitution because it would protect private property from attempts at redistribution and confiscation.[42] He argued that the Constitution was written to increase the personal wealth of the founding fathers. Most of the founding fathers held property and were from the upper class. According to Beard, they wanted to protect their interests from the majority of citizens who did not own property.[43] Furthermore, they held bonds and other investments that would likely increase in value if the Constitution was ratified.

Under Article VI, the U.S. government assumed all of the debts incurred under the Articles of Confederation. Many of the founding fathers were debt holders who had purchased bonds at a discount, but under the Constitution, they would be paid in full. These men certainly *did* consider their own financial futures, though the argument

The AP® U.S. Government and Politics exam contains an argumentation question that requires you to use the skills of refutation, concession, and rebuttal.

— **Refutation** is using evidence to prove that an opponent's contention is false.

— **Rebuttal** means discrediting an argument by offering a differing point of view.

— **Concession** means acknowledging a point and demonstrating an understanding of a differing viewpoint.

Read the following excerpts from *Federalist* No. 10, and using your knowledge of the arguments in *Brutus* No. 1, decide if each statement represents refutation, rebuttal, or concession.

Statement A:
"The influence of factious leaders may kindle a flame within their particular States, but will be unable to spread a general conflagration through the other States."

Statement B:
"Extend the sphere, and you take in a greater variety of parties and interest; you make it less probable that a majority of the whole will have a common motive to invade the rights of other citizens . . ."

Statement C:
"By enlarging too much the number of [representatives], you render the representatives too little acquainted with all of their local circumstances . . ."

1. Restate the argument made in Statement A in your own words. Explain whether Statement A represents refutation, rebuttal, or concession. Why?

2. Restate the argument made in Statement B in your own words. Explain whether Statement B represents refutation, rebuttal, or concession. Why?

3. Restate the argument made in Statement C in your own words. Explain whether Statement C represents refutation, rebuttal, or concession. Why?

---

against them focuses more on protecting elite interests in general than enriching any one individual.

Not all of the founding fathers were wealthy. Some had to sell off property, several of them died bankrupt, and the estates of more than one had to sell off property to pay off debt after their deaths. Near the end of his life, Madison himself was distracted by serious financial problems.

The founders have also been accused of being antidemocratic.[44] This was certainly true of most of the men at the convention. They saw pure democracy as dangerous. The mistrust of pure democracy was not a controversial opinion at the time. The founders had watched democratic state legislatures with unease. These institutions had often trampled on the rights of minorities, especially members of religious minorities and former supporters of Great Britain, whose wealth they eyed. The

New York City celebrates the ratification of the Constitution on July 23, 1788, with a Federal Procession, including a miniature ship called the *Hamilton*. After the Federal Procession, a banquet was served at ten tables, each 440 feet long, for the 5,000 people who participated.
Sarin Images / GRANGER-All Rights Reserved

framers intentionally placed obstacles in the path of those who would use the government to give into unrestrained popular demands.

The distrust of democracy is shown in the way officials were selected to hold office. Under Article I, Section 2, only members of the House of Representatives were directly elected, and their terms were a short two years. Until ratification of the Seventeenth Amendment in 1913, senators were chosen by state legislatures for six-year terms. Under Article II, Section 1, the president is selected by an Electoral College, which allows the elite, rather than average citizens, to choose the executive.

No one of these explanations likely accounts for the motives of all of the framers as they sought to create a new government. Many probably had mixed motives. Regardless of their motives, the framers of the Constitution created a flexible document that changed with the times.

The founders of the American Republic were practical men. They understood short-term political tactics and long-term strategies for governing a large, diverse republic. The Constitution they created had enormous consequences for people's lives, then and now. Disagreement continues over the role of the national government, the powers of state governments, and the rights of individuals. The philosophies of the founding fathers and the Constitution continue to serve as our guide as we navigate in the twenty-first century.

Section Review

2.4 Compare and contrast the arguments put forth by the Federalists and Antifederalists during the ratification debates.

REMEMBER
- The proposed Constitution had to be ratified by nine of the thirteen states in order to replace the Articles of Confederation.
- Proponents and opponents of the Constitution tried to rally others to their side and convince individuals of their position.

KNOW
- *Federalists*: supporters of the proposed Constitution, who called for a strong national government. (p. 46)
- *Antifederalists*: those opposed to the proposed Constitution, who favored stronger state governments. (p. 46)
- *Federalist Papers*: a series of eighty-five essays written by Alexander Hamilton, James Madison, and John Jay and published between 1787 and 1788 that lay out the theory behind the Constitution. (p. 47)
- *Federalist No. 51*: an essay in which Madison argues that separation of powers and federalism will prevent tyranny. (p. 47)
- *faction*: a group of self-interested people who use the government to get what they want, trampling the rights of others in the process. (p. 48)
- *Federalist No. 10*: an essay in which Madison argues that the dangers of faction can be mitigated by a large republic and republican government. (p. 48)
- *Brutus No. 1*: an Antifederalist Paper arguing that the country was too large to be governed as a republic and that the Constitution gave too much power to the national government. (p. 49)

THINK
- What were the primary points of disagreement between the Federalists and Antifederalists?
- Which side eventually prevailed?
- Why did the arguments of the Federalists eventually prevail over the arguments of the Antifederalists?

2.4 Review Question: Argumentation

Some historians believe the founding fathers wrote the Constitution to protect the interests of the wealthy elite. Others contend that the founding fathers wrote the Constitution to create a republican form of government based on compromise so that no one group can obtain too much power.

Choose the position that best achieves the goals of the founding fathers of ensuring a stable government. Defend your position with relevant evidence or reasoning from at least one required foundational document from the list below, as well as your knowledge from the study of U.S. government and politics. Describe at least one argument that an advocate of the other side of the argument might make, and explain why that argument is not as convincing.

- Declaration of Independence
- Constitution of the United States
- Brutus No. 1
- *Federalist* No. 10
- *Federalist* No. 51

In your response, be sure to

- Clearly state your thesis.
- Support your thesis with two pieces of relevant evidence.
- Organize your evidence using reasoning and analysis.
- Use refutation, concession, or rebuttal to respond to the opposing viewpoint.

Chapter 2 Review

AP® KEY CONCEPTS

- constitution (p. 25)
- republic (p. 25)
- Articles of Confederation and Perpetual Union (p. 26)
- unicameral (p. 28)
- Shays's Rebellion (p. 29)
- Constitutional Convention (p. 33)
- writ of habeas corpus (p. 34)
- bills of attainder (p. 34)
- ex post facto laws (p. 34)
- Virginia Plan (p. 35)
- New Jersey Plan (p. 35)

- Grand Committee (p. 35)
- Great (Connecticut) Compromise (p. 35)
- bicameral (p. 35)
- Three-Fifths Compromise (p. 37)
- Compromise on Importation (p. 37)
- separation of powers (p. 41)
- checks and balances (p. 42)
- federalism (p. 42)
- legislative branch (p. 42)
- expressed or enumerated powers (p. 43)
- necessary and proper or elastic clause (p. 43)

- implied powers (p. 43)
- executive branch (p. 43)
- judicial branch (p. 44)
- supremacy clause (p. 44)
- amendment (p. 44)
- Federalists (p. 46)
- Antifederalists (p. 46)
- Federalist Papers (p. 47)
- Federalist No. 51 (p. 47)
- faction (p. 48)
- Federalist No. 10 (p. 48)
- Brutus No. 1 (p. 49)

AP® EXAM PRACTICE and Critical Thinking Project

MULTIPLE-CHOICE QUESTIONS

Sydney Harris/www.cartoonstock.com

1. According to the cartoon, the founding fathers wrote the Constitution to achieve which goal?

   A. balance liberty with the protection of social order

   B. prevent the elite from holding too much power

   C. establish republican government

   D. prevent one branch of government from becoming too powerful

Question 2 refers to the following quote.

The powers reserved to the several States will extend to all the objects which, in the ordinary course of affairs, concern the lives, liberties, and properties of the people, and the internal order, improvement, and prosperity of the State. The operations of the federal government will be most extensive and important in times of war and danger; those of the State governments, in times of peace and security. As the former periods will probably bear a small proportion to the latter, the State governments will here enjoy another advantage over the federal government. The more adequate, indeed, the federal powers may be rendered to the national defense, the less frequent will be those scenes of danger which might favor their ascendancy over the governments of the particular States.

          —James Madison, *Federalist* No. 45

2. Which of the following best summarizes Madison's argument in *Federalist* No. 45?

   A. States do not have the resources to defend the nation.

   B. The national government should have more power than the states because the country will face frequent danger.

   C. State power is protected by a strong national defense.

   D. State governments should have advantages over the national government because they do not have to pay for their own militias.

3. Which of the following constitutional provisions gives Congress and the president expressed power over the national defense?

   A. Article VI

   B. Articles I and II

   C. Article VII

   D. the Preamble

Question 4 refers to the following quote.

The Congress, whenever two thirds of both houses shall deem it necessary, shall propose amendments to this Constitution, or, on the application of the legislatures of two thirds of the several states, shall call a convention for proposing amendments, which, in either case, shall be valid to all intents and purposes, as part of this Constitution, when ratified by the legislatures of three fourths of the several states, or by conventions in three fourths thereof, as the one or the other mode of ratification may be proposed by the Congress; provided that no amendment which may be made prior to the year one thousand eight hundred and eight shall in any manner affect the first and fourth clauses in the ninth section of the first article; and that no state, without its consent, shall be deprived of its equal suffrage in the Senate.

—**United States Constitution, Article V**

4. Which of the following principles is reflected in Article V?

   A. checks and balances

   B. separation of powers

   C. federalism

   D. popular sovereignty

Christopher Weyant/Cagle Cartoons, Inc.

5. The cartoon demonstrates which viewpoint about the founding fathers?

   A. They did not trust the average American citizen to make important political decisions.

   B. They trusted Americans to use good judgment in interpreting the Constitution in the future.

   C. They wanted to protect the right to bear arms.

   D. They did not foresee the development of automatic weapons.

6. Which of the following concepts was not included in the original Constitution as drafted in 1787 and ratified in 1788?

   A. The new central government must have more power than its predecessor had.

   B. We hold these truths to be self-evident, that all men are created equal.

   C. Congress has implied powers to carry out its expressed powers.

   D. The Supreme Court should have the right to overturn laws passed by Congress.

Question 7 refers to the following table.

State Ratification of the U.S. Constitution

State	Date of Ratification	Vote at the Ratifying Convention	Estimated State Population (and ranking among the 13 states)
Delaware	Dec. 7, 1787	30–0	60,000 (13/13)
Pennsylvania	Dec. 12, 1787	46–23	434,000 (3/13)
New Jersey	Dec. 18, 1787	38–0	184,000 (9/13)
Georgia	Dec. 31, 1787	26–0	83,000 (11/13)
Connecticut	Jan. 9, 1788	128–40	238,000 (8/13)
Massachusetts	Feb. 6, 1788	187–168	475,000 (2/13)
Maryland	Apr. 26, 1788	63–11	320,000 (7/13)
South Carolina	May 23, 1788	149–73	250,000 (5/13)
New Hampshire	June 21, 1788	57–47	142,000 (10/13)
Virginia	June 25, 1788	89–79	821,000 (1/13)
New York	July 26, 1788	30–27	340,000 (6/13)
North Carolina	Nov. 21, 1789	194–77	429,000 (4/13)
Rhode Island	May 29, 1790	34–32	69,000 (12/13)

Data from teachingamericanhistory.org

7. The table supports which of the following statements?

   A. States with the three largest populations also had the three closest ratification margins.

   B. States with large slave populations were quicker to ratify the Constitution than states that had outlawed slavery.

   C. New Jersey ratified the Constitution before Virginia because the delegates to the Constitutional Convention ratified the New Jersey Plan and rejected the Virginia Plan.

   D. The first four states that ratified the Constitution did so by wider margins than did the final four.

———————————

8. No man is allowed to be a judge in his *own cause*, because his interest would certainly bias his judgment, and, not improbably, corrupt his integrity. With equal, nay with greater reason, a body of men are unfit to be both judges and parties at the same time.

—*Federalist* No. 10

Which of the following principles is reflected in the quote?

   A. Popular sovereignty

   B. The danger of factions

   C. Checks and balances

   D. Federalism

The States are every day giving proofs that separate regulations are more likely to set them by the ears, than to attain the common object. When Massachusetts set on foot a retaliation of the policy of Great Britain, Connecticut declared her ports free. New Jersey served New York in the same way. And Delaware I am told has lately followed the example in opposition to the commercial plans of Pennsylvania. A miscarriage of this attempt to unite the States in some effectual plan will have another effect of a serious nature. . . . I almost despair of success.[45]

9. Which of the following best describes the author's perspective and reasoning?
   A. International and interstate trade must be regulated by the central government.
   B. Revolution against Great Britain is the only logical course.
   C. The Articles of Confederation properly permit separate regulations to attain a common object.
   D. The states are capable of agreeing among themselves towards a common trade policy.

10. Which provision in the Constitution most specifically addresses the problems described in the excerpt?
    A. Senatorial power to ratify treaties with foreign governments
    B. Three-Fifths Compromise
    C. Commerce clause
    D. Great Compromise

FREE-RESPONSE QUESTIONS

1. In *Myers v. United States* (1926),[46] the U.S. Supreme Court analyzed the constitutionality of an 1876 congressional statute requiring the president to obtain the Senate's consent before removing a postmaster whose nomination had been confirmed by the Senate. In analyzing that issue, Justice Louis Brandeis wrote in his dissent:

The doctrine of the separation of powers was adopted by the convention of 1787 not to promote efficiency, but to preclude the exercise of arbitrary power. The purpose was not to avoid friction but, by means of the inevitable friction incident to the distribution of the governmental powers among three departments, to save the people from autocracy.[47]

Use the quote and your knowledge of U.S. Government and Politics to respond to parts A, B, and C.
   A. Describe the doctrine of separation of powers.
   B. Describe one way in which the Supreme Court's decision in *Myers v. United States* illustrates the doctrine of separation of powers.
   C. Explain how the doctrine of separation of powers is designed "to save the people from autocracy."

2. In his essay "Framing the Constitution," historian Charles A. Beard described the Constitutional Convention as follows:

It was a truly remarkable assembly of men that gathered in Philadelphia on May 17, 1787, to undertake the work of reconstructing the American system of government. . . . The makers of the Constitution represented the solid, conservative, commercial and financial interests of the country. . . . [T]he members of that assembly were not seeking to realize any fine notions about democracy and equality, but were striving with all the resources of political wisdom at their command to set up a system of government that would be stable and efficient, safeguarded on the one hand against the possibilities of despotism and on the other against the onslaught of majorities. . . . Madison doubtless summed up in a brief sentence the general opinion of the convention when he said that to secure private rights against minority factions, and at the same time to preserve the spirit and form of popular government, was the great object to which their inquiries had been directed. They were anxious above everything else to safeguard the rights of private property against any leveling tendencies on the part of the propertyless masses.[48]

Use the quote and your knowledge of U.S. Government and Politics to respond to parts A, B, and C.

A. Describe the author's opinion of the founding fathers' goal in drafting the Constitution.

B. Identify one constitutional provision that could be used to support the author's opinion, and explain how it could be used to support the author's opinion.

C. Identify one constitutional provision that could be used to refute the author's opinion, and explain how it could be used to refute the author's opinion.

ARGUMENTATION QUESTION

Your sentiments, that our affairs are drawing rapidly to a crisis, accord with my own. What the event will be is also beyond the reach of my foresight. We have errors to correct. We have probably had too good an opinion of human nature in forming our confederation. Experience has taught us, that men will not adopt & carry into execution, measures the best calculated for their own good without the intervention of a coercive power. I do not conceive we can exist long as a nation, without having lodged somewhere a power which will pervade the whole Union in as energetic a manner, as the authority of the different state governments extends over the several States. To be fearful of vesting Congress, constituted as that body is, with ample authorities for national purposes, appears to me the very climax of popular absurdity and madness. . . . We must take human nature as we find it. Perfection falls not to the share of mortals.

—Letter from George Washington to John Jay, August 1, 1786[49]

Is the Constitution an adequate remedy for the fears expressed by George Washington in the quote? Why or why not?

Defend your position using relevant evidence from at least one foundational document from the list below, as well as your knowledge of the Constitution. Identify at least one argument that would be made by an advocate for a differing viewpoint and explain why that argument is less convincing.

- Articles of Confederation and Perpetual Union
- United States Constitution
- *Federalist* No. 10
- *Federalist* No. 51
- Brutus No. 1

In your response, be sure to:

- Articulate a defensible thesis that responds to the prompt.
- Support your thesis with at least two pieces of accurate and relevant evidence.
- Use reasoning to organize your evidence.
- Respond to an alternative perspective using refutation, concession, or rebuttal.

CRITICAL THINKING PROJECT

Proposing an Amendment

Several proposals have been made to amend the Constitution, including:

—Providing equal rights for women

—Prohibiting flag burning

—Requiring Congress to balance the budget

—Imposing term limits on members of Congress

—Electing federal judges directly

—Eliminating the Electoral College

—Allowing naturalized citizens to serve as president

—Making it easier to amend the Constitution

—Making it easier to impeach the president

Pick one of the issues above, or select another important issue, with your teacher's approval. Research your issue, reading at least one credible source on both sides of the issue.

Drafting and Defending Your Own Amendment

    A. Write an introductory paragraph that explains the issue and ends with your proposed new constitutional amendment.

    B. Write two paragraphs, each containing a separate argument in favor of your proposed amendment. Each of your arguments should be supported with evidence from the article(s) you read.

    C. Write a paragraph explaining the best argument against your amendment, supported with evidence from the article(s) you read.

    D. Write a rebuttal paragraph demonstrating that the argument in favor of your proposed amendment is stronger than the argument against it. Conclude your paper with a statement about why your proposed amendment should be adopted.

Citations and Bibliography

Cite sources throughout the paper using MLA format. *If you got information from an article, you must cite the article, even if you do not quote the article directly.*

Attach a bibliography of the sources you used in researching the topic. The sources listed in your bibliography must be cited at least once in your paper.

3 Federalism
Dividing Power between the National Government and the States

Under the Articles of Confederation, most of the people's authority had been placed in state governments, which left the Congress constantly struggling to secure cooperation from the states. That changed with the ratification of the Constitution, but the issue was not settled once and for all. The new system of government divided authority between two levels of government—the national government and the states. As we will explore later in this chapter, some powers, like those related to defense, national security, and the economy, are exclusive to the federal government. Some powers, such as police powers,

Angel McClary Raich and Diane Monson, who consider themselves law-abiding citizens. Under federal law, the sale, use and distribution of marijuana is illegal, but the State of California legalized the marijuana used by Raich and Monson for medical purposes. Raich and Monson ended up in a conflict between the federal and state laws. Here they are outside the Supreme Court of the United States, which settled the issue.
J. SCOTT APPLEWHITE/AP Images

federalism
a system that divides power
between the national and
state governments.

are under the authority of the states. Some powers, like the power of taxation, are shared, and some powers, like those that would take away the rights of citizens, are denied to both levels. This system is called **federalism**.

The Constitution created a basic framework for our federal system but did not define the boundaries sharply between the specific powers of the national and state governments. Many of the most important and controversial issues in our representative democracy involve difficult questions of American federalism.

In this chapter, we will explore federalism through the stories of Angel Raich and Diane Monson, who use medical marijuana. In doing so, we will explore the tensions inherent in American federalism, how federalism has changed over time, and where it stands now.

LEARNING TARGETS

After reading this chapter, you will be able to

3.1 Explain the tension in American federalism between state and federal laws.

3.2 Describe how the Constitution divides power between the national and state governments.

3.3 Describe the development of American federalism over time.

3.4 Explain how federalism changed in the twentieth and twenty-first centuries.

3.5 Discuss the current status of American federalism and how it might continue to evolve.

3.1 Conflict over Medical Marijuana

In 2002, Angel McClary Raich and Diane Monson filed law suits in a California federal court against the U.S. government. They argued that their use of medical marijuana, which was legal under the laws of California but illegal under federal law, was protected by the laws of their state and by the Constitution of the United States.

"I am not a criminal," Raich declared. "I do not deserve to be behind bars."[1] Both women were trying to cope with significant health issues and they wanted to use cannabis as part of their treatment. Raich described her illnesses as an "inoperable brain tumor, seizures, endometriosis, scoliosis and a wasting disorder. She [weighed] only 97 pounds and claimed that without marijuana she'd starve to death."[2] Diane Monson used marijuana as part of her treatment for chronic back pain and spasms and grew her own plants.

Both women were using marijuana under the supervision of their doctors and in compliance with a California state law, the Compassionate Use Act of 1996. This act made the use and cultivation of marijuana for medical purposes legal if undertaken under the supervision of a licensed physician and in accordance with state regulations. However, Raich and Monson feared that the federal government might restrict their access to medical marijuana. The use, cultivation, or possession of marijuana is illegal under a federal law, the

Controlled Substances Act of 1970 (CSA).[3] Under that law, marijuana is classified as a Schedule I drug, among the most dangerous substances, such as heroin and LSD. The Controlled Substances Act of 1970 was enacted under Congress's constitutional authority to regulate interstate commerce. Raich and Monson were caught between the laws of their state and those of the nation. They found themselves front and center in one of the most enduring debates in American political life—that of federalism.

In August 2002, county deputy sheriffs and agents from the federal Drug Enforcement Administration (DEA) came to Monson's home. The county officials concluded that her cultivation and use of marijuana were permitted under California law. After a three-hour standoff, though, the federal agents seized and destroyed the six marijuana plants that she was growing. Monson alleged that the DEA's actions violated her civil rights and her rights under California law.

Many states have lessened penalties for use of marijuana. Several states have legalized medical and/or recreational use. The changes made by the states have produced dispensaries and retail outlets for marijuana, along the lines of another controlled substance, alcohol. How do sales at this store in California create tension with the power of the Congress to regulate interstate commerce?

ZUMA Press, Inc. /Alamy

The two women filed suit, and an appeals court ruled in their favor. U.S. Attorney General Alberto Gonzales appealed, and the Supreme Court agreed to hear the case. Raich and Monson based their claims upon the laws of California and the Constitution of the United States. The Attorney General and the DEA countered that they were rightfully upholding federal law and federal authority. "Everything we're doing is according to the law," said Richard Meyer, a San Francisco–based DEA spokesman.[4] By enforcing federal law, however, the DEA agents were restricting actions that were legal under California state laws. The Supreme Court was asked to decide whether the Controlled Substances Act prevailed over the California law that legalized medical marijuana.[5]

Raich and Monson's legal challenge centered on a question fundamental to our system of government: Where is the boundary between the powers of the federal government and those of the states?

Section Review

This chapter's main ideas are reflected in the Learning Targets. By reviewing after each section, you should be able to

—**Remember** the key points,

—**Know** terms that are central to the topic, and

—**Think** critically about these questions.

3.1 Explain the tension in American federalism between state and federal laws.

REMEMBER	Political authority is divided between two levels of government: the national government and the states.
KNOW	*federalism*: a system that divides power between the national and state governments. (p. 64)
THINK	Explain how the conflict between California's Compassionate Use Act and the federal Controlled Substances Act reflects tensions between the national and state governments.

3.1 Review Question: Free Response

Twenty-nine states and the District of Columbia currently have laws broadly legalizing marijuana in some form. Nine states and the District of Columbia have adopted the most expansive laws legalizing marijuana for recreational use. Recently, California, Massachusetts, Maine, and Nevada legalized recreational marijuana. California's recently passed Proposition 64 measure allows adults twenty-one and older to possess up to one ounce of marijuana and grow up to six plants in their homes. Other tax and licensing provisions of the law will not take effect until January 2018.

After reading the passage, use your knowledge of U.S. Government and Politics to respond to parts A, B, and C.

A. Define federalism.

B. Describe one way in which the Controlled Substances Act of 1970 impacts the situation described in the scenario.

C. In the context of the scenario, explain how federalism causes tension between the national and state governments.

◼ 3.2 Federalism and the Constitution

The conflict between California's marijuana law and the Controlled Substances Act demonstrates tensions within our federal system of government.

Systems of Government

There are three ways of dividing power between the national government and the states. (See Figure 3.1.) In **unitary systems**, one central government exercises authority over the subnational governments (such as states). The national government may delegate (devolve) certain powers to subnational governments, but it has the authority to take back any powers it delegates. The United Kingdom, China, and Iran are unitary systems. The United Kingdom has devolved some of the powers of the national government to regional assemblies in Scotland, Northern Ireland, and Wales. However, Parliament still has the final authority over policy making. Most countries have a unitary system. Strong central governments often are hesitant to disperse power.

At the opposite end of the spectrum are **confederal systems** in which the subnational governments, such as states, have more power than the national government. In confederal systems, national governments are heavily dependent upon the states to carry out

unitary system
a system where the central government has all of the power over subnational governments.

confederal system
a system where the subnational governments have most of the power.

FIGURE 3.1

The Division of Power under Different Systems of Government

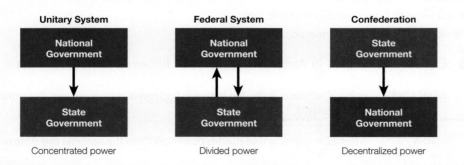

and pay for public policies. The United States under the Articles of Confederation was an example of a confederal system. Switzerland is organized as a confederal system.

Federalism is one of the most important innovations of the Constitution. In **federal systems**, power is divided between the states and the national government. Each level of government retains some exclusive powers and has some powers denied to it. Federal systems have constitutional protections for each level against encroachment on its powers by the other levels. The United States, Mexico, Nigeria, and Russia are examples of countries with federal systems.

federal system
a system where power is divided between the national and state governments.

National and State Powers

In general, the powers of the national government are explicitly listed and described by the Constitution. **Enumerated** or **expressed powers** refer to those powers granted to the national government in the Constitution, and especially to Congress. These include the **exclusive powers** that only the national government may exercise, such as the power to coin money, declare war, raise and support an army and navy, make treaties, provide for the naturalization of American citizens, and regulate interstate and foreign commerce. Most of the enumerated powers in the Constitution are granted to the legislative branch in Article I, Section 8.

Implied powers are not specifically granted to the federal government. Under the necessary and proper clause, in Article I, Section 8, however, Congress can make laws to carry out its enumerated powers. For example, the Constitution does not give the national government the authority to create an air force (though the first hot-air balloon had taken flight in 1783, before the drafting of the Constitution, and some may have anticipated combat in the air). That authority, however, is a necessary part of its power to raise and support a military.

enumerated or expressed powers
powers explicitly granted to the national government through the Constitution; also called expressed powers.

exclusive powers
powers only the national government may exercise.

implied powers
powers not granted specifically to the national government but considered necessary to carry out the enumerated powers.

Besides describing the enumerated and implied powers, the Constitution denies certain powers to the national government. Although the original Constitution did not protect many civil liberties, the federal government was prohibited from violating some rights. The Constitution prohibits bills of attainder, when the legislature declares someone guilty without a trial. Congress may not pass ex post facto laws, which punish actions that were legal when they occurred. Finally, the national government may not suspend the writ of habeas corpus, giving defendants the right to be informed of the charges and evidence against them. The national government may not admit new states to the union, nor can it change state boundaries without the consent of the state's citizens. It also cannot impose taxes on goods and services exported and imported between states. (Refer back to chapter 2 for more information on powers denied to the national government.)

Graduation celebrations at the United States Air Force Academy in 2015. The Constitution gives the national government the implied power to create the U.S. Air Force as part of its power to raise and support a military. The U.S. Air Force became a separate uniformed service in 1947. What expressed powers do the president and Congress have over the armed forces?
RJ Sangosti/Getty Images

The Commerce, Necessary and Proper, and Supremacy Clauses

The Constitution contains a set of provisions—the commerce, necessary and proper, and supremacy clauses and the Tenth Amendment—that shape the relative authority of the state and national governments. At the same time, however, it does not outline just how the system of federalism would work.

commerce clause
grants Congress the authority to regulate interstate business and commercial activity.

The **commerce clause** strongly influences modern American federalism. It grants Congress the power to "regulate Commerce with foreign Nations, and among the several States, and with the Indian Tribes."[6] By using the commerce clause—in combination with the necessary and proper and supremacy clauses—Congress has claimed the authority to define nearly any productive activity as commerce. For example, even though Diane Monson's homegrown marijuana was never sold and did not leave her home state, the federal government claimed the authority to regulate it as interstate commerce.

necessary and proper clause
grants the federal government the authority to pass laws required to carry out its enumerated powers. Also called the elastic clause.

The **necessary and proper clause** gives Congress the power to "make all Laws which shall be necessary and proper for carrying into Execution . . . Powers vested by this Constitution in the Government of the United States."[7] Also called the elastic clause, the necessary and proper clause is a critical source of power for the national government, granting Congress the authority to legislate as necessary for carrying out its constitutionally granted powers.

supremacy clause
establishes the Constitution and the laws of the federal government passed under its authority as the highest laws of the land.

One of the Constitution's most important statements about the power of the national government is the **supremacy clause**, which reads, "This Constitution, and the Laws of the United States . . . shall be the supreme Law of the Land."[8] The supremacy clause means that the states must abide by the laws passed by Congress, even if state constitutional provisions conflict with them. States must abide by national treaties, and state courts must follow the Constitution.

Powers of the State Governments

The Constitution does not specifically use the word *federalism* and is much less specific about powers allocated to the states. Much of the protection for state authority comes from the **Tenth Amendment**, which states, "The powers not delegated to the United States by the Constitution, nor prohibited by it to the States, are reserved to the States respectively, or to the people."[9] Those who advocate for more state authority argue that the Tenth Amendment limits the federal government to the power enumerated in the Constitution and that the states and the people have superior power over all remaining issues. However in *United States v. Darby* (1941), the Supreme Court labeled that interpretation of the Tenth Amendment as a "truism," meaning that it was not supposed to give the states and people powers that supersede those of the national government.[10] The Supreme Court's decision in *Garcia v. San Antonio Metropolitan Transit Authority* (1985)[11] involved whether or not the San Antonio Metropolitan Transit Authority had to comply with the Fair Labor Standards Act in paying its workers. The Supreme Court ruled, in effect, that Congress could decide when to regulate activities by state and local governments.[12]

Tenth Amendment
reserves powers not delegated to the national government to the states and the people; the basis of federalism.

reserved powers
powers not given to the national government, which are retained by the states and the people.

Reserved powers were not given to the national government and are, therefore, retained by the states. Among the most important of these are police powers, which state governments use to protect residents and provide for their safety, health, and general welfare. States are also authorized to conduct elections, including those for national office.[13] States have the power to establish local, town, county, and regional governmental bodies. Article V gives states the final say about whether an amendment will become part of the Constitution. The Constitution cannot be amended without the consent of three-fourths of the states, either by their legislatures or by ratification conventions in the states.[14]

concurrent powers
powers granted to both states and the federal government in the Constitution.

Finally, both the national government and states are given the authority to act in certain areas of public policy. These **concurrent powers** allow national and state authority to overlap. The power to tax is shared by the national and state governments. Both levels are allowed to borrow money, although many states place more restrictions on their ability to go into debt than does the federal government. Both may pass and enforce laws, create and operate a system of courts, and charter banks and corporations (see Figure 3.2).

FIGURE 3.2

Enumerated, Concurrent, and Reserved Powers in American Federalism

POWERS GRANTED

Federal **Enumerated and implied powers**	**Shared** **Concurrent powers**	**State** **Reserved powers**
Coin money	Levy taxes	Provide police and fire protection
Declare war	Borrow money	Conduct elections
Raise and support armed forces	Regulate interstate commerce	Amendments approved by 3/4 of the states
Make treaties	Regulate banks	Establish local, town, county, and regional bodies
Provide for the naturalization of citizens	Create and operate court systems	Regulate intra state commerce
Regulate interstate and foreign trade and trade with Indian tribes	Determine voting qualifications	

POWERS DENIED

The federal government may not:

- Violate rights and liberties outlined in the Bill of Rights
- Admit new states without the consent of the territory's residents
- Change state boundaries without consent of its residents
- Impose taxes on goods and services exported and imported within state boundaries

States may not:

- Enter into treaties with foreign governments
- Print money
- Tax imports or exports
- Declare war

Regional and Local Governments Rely on the States

The Constitution does not describe the powers of the levels of government below the states—cities, towns, counties, and districts. Generally, relationships between states and local governments are unitary, with the authority of the smaller units dependent upon and subordinate to the power and authority of the state. States can disband local governments because their power and sovereignty depend on the state. States can also set rules that local governments must follow. For example, state governments can set rules governing public utilities or change the boundaries of school districts or combine two school districts into one larger one.

Therefore, while we often talk about three levels of government in the United States—national, state, and local—from the point of view of American federalism there are only two—national and state. Dependence upon state authority is often a source of frustration for mayors, school board members, and other local officials.

Relationships between States Federalism does not just involve the relationship between the national government and the states. States also interact with each other. Article IV of the Constitution outlines the obligations between states. The **full faith and credit clause** requires states to recognize the public acts, records, and civil court proceedings from

full faith and credit clause constitutional clause requiring states to recognize the public acts, records, and civil court proceedings from another state.

another state. This means that a couple married in Vermont is still married when their family relocates to South Carolina, even though the requirements for getting a marriage license may differ between states. When a couple divorces, a child-support order issued in one state is enforceable in another state.

There are limits to the full faith and credit clause. If you drive through Missouri on your way to college, Missouri must recognize your driver's license. But if you move to Missouri, the state can compel you to obtain a new driver's license.[15]

Someone who commits a crime in one state may flee to another state in an attempt to avoid prosecution. **Extradition** is the requirement that officials in one state return a defendant to another state where a crime was allegedly committed. Most states are happy to comply with extradition because they don't want to harbor criminals.

The **privileges and immunities clause** prevents states from discriminating against people from out of state. For example, Florida cannot charge a higher sales tax for tourists at Disney World, or anywhere else in the state, than it charges for in-state residents.[16] You might wonder why state-funded universities can charge more for out-of-state than in-state college students. As a taxpayer of the state in which you live, you and your parents have already subsidized your state's colleges. As a general rule, the more fundamental the right, the more it is protected from discrimination under the privileges and immunities clause.

extradition
the requirement that officials in one state return a defendant to another state where a crime was committed.

privileges and immunities clause
constitutional clause that prevents states from discriminating against people from out of state.

Section Review

3.2 Describe how the Constitution divides power between the national and state governments.

REMEMBER The Constitution lays out much of the framework of American federalism. The supremacy, necessary and proper, and commerce clauses define federal powers.

KNOW
- *unitary system:* a system where the central government has all of the power over subnational governments. (p. 66)
- *confederal system:* a system where the subnational governments have most of the power. (p. 66)
- *federal system:* a system where power is divided between the national and state governments. (p. 67)
- *enumerated or expressed powers:* powers explicitly granted to the national government through the Constitution; (p. 67)
- *exclusive powers:* powers only the national government may exercise. (p. 67)
- *implied powers:* powers not granted specifically to the national government but considered necessary to carry out the enumerated powers. (p. 67)
- *commerce clause:* grants Congress the authority to regulate interstate business and commercial activity. (p. 68)
- *necessary and proper clause:* grants the federal government the authority to pass laws required to carry out its enumerated powers. Also called the elastic clause. (p. 68)
- *supremacy clause:* establishes the Constitution and the laws of the federal government passed under its authority as the highest laws of the land. (p. 68)
- *Tenth Amendment:* reserves powers not delegated to the national government to the states and the people; the basis of federalism. (p. 68)
- *reserved powers:* powers not given to the national government, which are retained by the states and the people. (p. 68)
- *concurrent powers:* powers granted to both states and the federal government in the Constitution. (p. 68)
- *full faith and credit clause:* constitutional clause requiring states to recognize the public acts, records, and civil court proceedings from another state. (p. 69)
- *extradition:* the requirement that officials in one state return a defendant to another state where a crime was committed. (p. 70)
- *privileges and immunities clause:* constitutional clause that prevents states from discriminating against people from out of state. (p. 70)

THINK How does federalism create tensions between the states and the national government?

In *Texas v. Johnson* (1989), the Supreme Court overturned a Texas state law banning flag burning as a violation of the First Amendment's protection of free speech. According to an article by the *Washington Post,*

Polls show that most Americans want flag desecration outlawed . . . They said that burning a U.S. flag in public—while rare these days—is a reprehensible insult to the nation's founders and a dishonor to the Americans who died fighting tyranny.
—Charles Babington, "Senate Rejects Flag Desecration Amendment," *Washington Post,* June 28, 2006

After reading the scenario, use your knowledge of U.S. Government and Politics to respond to parts A, B, and C.

A. In the context of the scenario, explain why federalism makes it difficult for states to address an issue like flag burning, even though most Americans want flag desecration outlawed.

B. Explain how the process for amending the Constitution reflects federalism.

C. Explain why it was difficult to pass a constitutional amendment banning flag burning, even though most Americans wanted to outlaw flag desecration.

3.3 The Dynamic Nature of Federalism

Federalism changes over time. Defining the relative power of the national and state governments happens through a dynamic political process. In this section, we will look at federalism through the early twentieth century. Perhaps the most important figure in shaping federalism after the ratification of the Constitution was John Marshall, chief justice of the Supreme Court from 1801 to 1835, and the longest-serving chief justice in American history. During his tenure, Marshall issued several of the most important decisions that define American federalism.

The Marshall Court: Expanding National Power

The first of the major federalism case decided by the Marshall Court was *McCulloch v. Maryland* (1819).[17] The case centered on the Second Bank of the United States, a national bank chartered by Congress, whose charter had been left to expire amid a "debate about its constitutionality."[18] Many questioned if Congress had the authority to charter a national bank.

Several states, including Maryland, passed laws to tax the Second Bank of the United States. Bank officials in Maryland refused to pay the state tax, and the dispute went to the U.S. Supreme Court.

The case centered on two questions: Did Congress have the authority to establish the bank in the first place? And did individual states have the authority to tax its branches operating within their borders? Chief Justice John Marshall's opinion on both questions, speaking for a unanimous Supreme Court, came down firmly on the side of the authority of the national government. The decision emphasizes that the states and people ceded some of their sovereignty to the national government in ratifying the Constitution. The decision states,

> The assent of the States in their sovereign capacity is implied in calling a convention, and thus submitting that instrument to the people. But the people were at perfect liberty to accept or reject it, and their act was final. It required not the affirmance, and could not be negatived, by the State Governments. The Constitution, when thus adopted, was of complete obligation, and bound the State sovereignties.[19]

AP® TIP

Students are required to be familiar with fifteen required Supreme Court cases on the AP® exam. Other Supreme Court cases may appear on the exam, and students will be given enough information about those cases to analyze them.

In this book and in your course, you will be asked to interpret, analyze, and apply key U.S. Supreme Court cases. To do so, it will be important to become familiar with the format and components of Supreme Court decisions, as well as how to study them.

General Tips in Approaching These Key Cases

- Reading cases takes time, especially at first, because a legal decision is a specific kind of writing. Be sure to give yourself plenty of time.

- Supreme Court cases are usually organized using a four-part formula:

  - **First, the Court gives an overview of the facts of the case.** Become familiar with what happened in the case—who was involved, and how the case rose through the court system.

  - **Second, the Court explains the issue it was asked to resolve.** In the fifteen required Supreme Court cases, the fundamental issue always involves the Constitution. Therefore, be sure that you understand the particular clause or amendment that the Supreme Court is being asked to interpret.

  - **Third, the Court announces who won the case.** This is simply a decision about which party won.

  - **Fourth, and most important, the Court explains the reasons for its decision.** Sometimes, the Court will have several reasons for its decision, and these are usually explained in separate sections or paragraphs.

Make sure you understand each reason for the Court's decision and the logic behind it.

- Try to gain a deeper understanding of the *context* of the case, which may include the larger political climate in which the case was decided.

- Generally, do not worry too much about details. Think about the big picture, especially the implications of the decision for constitutional law and public policy. Consider how the case sets a precedent to be applied in future cases.

- Be sure to practice comparing different cases. Sometimes, one decision will build on others. Sometimes, a previous decision may be overturned.

Key Terms and Concepts in Reading Supreme Court Decisions

- **Majority Opinion:** The decision and legal reasoning of the majority of justices. A majority opinion may be unanimous.

- **Concurring Opinion (concurrence):** There may be no concurrences, or many. These are opinions written by justices who voted with the majority but have different or additional reasons for their decision. Concurring opinions do not serve as precedent for future cases, although they may contain reasoning that the Supreme Court might use in the future.

- **Dissenting Opinion (dissent):** There may be no dissents or several. These are opinions written by justices who voted with the minority. Though they do not serve as precedent for future cases, they may lay down the logic of the other side should the Court decide to reevaluate precedent in future cases.

Citing the necessary and proper clause of the Constitution, Marshall affirmed the right of Congress to establish the bank, arguing, "Let the end be legitimate, let it be within the scope of the Constitution, and all means which are appropriate, which are plainly adapted to that end, which are not prohibited, but consist with the letter and spirit of the Constitution, are Constitutional."[20] Marshall argues against a strict, literal view of the Constitution in stating,

> The subject is the execution of those great powers on which the welfare of a Nation essentially depends. It must have been the intention of those who gave these powers to insure, so far as human prudence could insure, their beneficial execution. This could not be done by confiding the choice of means to such narrow limits as not to leave it in the power of Congress to adopt any which might be appropriate, and which were conducive to the end.[21]

A constitution, he argued, cannot contain the "prolixity of a legal code. Its nature, therefore, requires that only its great outlines should be marked."[22] The right to establish the bank was, according to Marshall's logic, a valid *implied power* of Congress, even though the right to create a national bank is not explicitly given in the text of the Constitution. The opinion states, "Among the enumerated powers, we do not find that of establishing a bank or creating a corporation. But there is no phrase in the instrument which, like the Articles of Confederation, excludes incidental or implied powers and which requires that everything granted shall be expressly and minutely described."[23]

This means that Congress is not limited by its expressed powers. Under the necessary and proper clause, it has the implied authority to take actions needed to carry out its expressed powers.

On the second question—of the authority of individual states to tax the branches of the Second Bank—Marshall and the Court also came down on the side of the national government. Maryland and other states did not have the authority to tax the bank's state branches. Arguing "the power to tax involves the power to destroy," the Court ruled, "State governments have no right to tax any of the constitutional means employed by the Government of the Union to execute its constitutional powers."[24]

Having reaffirmed the constitutionality of *implied powers* under the *necessary and proper clause* in *McCulloch v. Maryland*, the Marshall Court next turned its attention to other sources of national power.

In *Gibbons v. Ogden* (1824), the Marshall Court weighed in on the powers of Congress under the commerce clause of the Constitution.[25] As with the *McCulloch* decision, the Court in *Gibbons* affirmed national power. Known as the "steamboat monopoly case," *Gibbons v. Ogden* arose from a battle between two powerful businessmen in the steamboat business in New York and New Jersey. Aaron Ogden had been granted a monopoly by a New York state law that protected his routes within New York and between New York and New Jersey. Thomas Gibbons was a steamboat operator who had been granted a license by the federal government to operate on the same route. Gibbons filed suit to block the monopoly that the State of New York had granted Ogden.

Marshall's decision in the case reaffirmed national power using a different part of the Constitution. While *McCulloch* involved the necessary and proper clause, *Gibbons* focused on the power of Congress to regulate trade "among the several States" as part of its authority under the commerce clause. Marshall also cited the power of the national government under the supremacy clause. The Court, again unanimously, struck down the steamboat monopoly between the two states and the part of the New York law that had made the monopoly possible. In doing so, Marshall affirmed the exclusive authority of Congress to regulate interstate commerce, defining commerce "among the several States" as including "the deep streams which penetrate our country in every direction [and] pass through the interior of almost every state in the Union."[26]

Lurking in the background during this time were the interconnected and unresolved problems of slavery, states' rights, and American federalism.

Even today, Chief Justice John Marshall's decisions are among the most important in shaping the powers and limits in U.S. federalism. Robert Sully painted this portrait in 1830, when Marshall was in his seventies, near the end of his long career in politics and as the fourth chief justice of the Supreme Court.
GRANGER /GRANGER-All rights reserved.

The Thirteenth, Fourteenth, and Fifteenth Amendments

Following the Civil War, three amendments were ratified that reduced the power of the states. The **Thirteenth Amendment** outlawed slavery. The **Fourteenth Amendment** contains several clauses that place limits on state actions. The first section of the Fourteenth Amendment provides that all persons born in the United States are citizens. The effect of this section meant that Southern states could not deny citizenship to former slaves. Under the Equal Protection

Thirteenth Amendment constitutional amendment that outlaws slavery.

Fourteenth Amendment constitutional amendment that provides that persons born in the United States are citizens and prohibits states from denying persons due process or equal protection under the law.

Clause, states may not deny persons equal protection under the laws. The Due Process Clause prevents states from denying persons due process under the law. The **Fifteenth Amendment** gave African Americans the right to vote. These three amendments were passed to limit the ability of states to discriminate against their citizens. We will study these amendments in more depth in chapter 5.

Following the Civil War, the Supreme Court did not strongly support African American civil rights, a move that would have provided uniform protection for African Americans at the national level. Instead, it affirmed a vision of federalism that recognized state authority, even if that authority was used to restrict the rights of citizens based only on their racial identity.

Plessy v. Ferguson (1896) was a landmark case in restricting the rights of African Americans following the Civil War and asserting states' rights. In this case, the Supreme Court upheld the constitutionality of legalized racial segregation (the separation of individuals based on their racial identity) and the ability of states to pass such laws.[27] *Plessy* was a test case, organized by the African American community in New Orleans to challenge Louisiana's segregation laws. Homer Plessy, "a light-skinned man who described himself as 'seven-eighths Caucasian,'" had been arrested and fined for violating a state law requiring separate railroad facilities for whites and African Americans.[28]

In the decision in *Plessy*, Justice Henry Billings Brown declared that Louisiana's law did not violate the Fourteenth Amendment. Arguing that "[s]ocial prejudices cannot be overcome by legislation," Brown upheld Plessy's conviction and declared that "separate but equal" did not violate the Constitution.

Justice John Marshall Harlan, the lone dissenter on the Court, countered, "Our Constitution is color-blind, and neither knows nor tolerates classes among citizens. In respect of civil rights, all citizens are equal before the law." Harlan, correctly, as it would turn out, saw *Plessy* as a dangerous and damaging ruling. Brown's majority opinion, however, set policy. The ruling that racial segregation could be constitutionally permissible endured for almost sixty years. We will explore the efforts—first in the states, later in the Supreme Court—of individuals to overturn this doctrine in detail in chapter 9.

Shifting from Dual to Cooperative Federalism

For much of the history of the American republic, the model of the relationship between states and nation was one of **dual federalism**, which presumes a distinct, though not complete, separation between the federal and state governments, as if both operate side by side with relatively little interaction between the two. Dual federalism, according to an observer of American government in 1888, "is like a great factory wherein two sets of machinery are at work, their revolving wheels apparently intermixed, their bands crossing one another, yet each set doing its own work without touching or hampering the other."[29] (See Figure 3.3.)

The Supreme Court drew a similar image of two separate systems in the nineteenth century: "The government of the United States and the government of a state are distinct and independent of each other within their respective spheres of action, although existing and exercising their powers within the same territorial limits. Neither government can intrude within the jurisdiction, or authorize any interference therein by its judicial officers with the action of the other."[30] In fact, however, the division of authority between states and national government has never been clean and neat. Even in areas of public policy that have

FIGURE 3.3

Dual Federalism

For much of the history of the American republic, state and federal governments operated under an arrangement of dual federalism. In this model, federal and state governments have distinct powers and function independently of one another, addressing their own areas of policy, something like separate layers of the same cake. Here, a red-white-and-blue layer cake depicting dual federalism was made by students in Minnesota to celebrate federalism.

Erik Anderson @MrAndersonGov · 3 Feb 2017
Federalism cake day today in #APGov! Great (and tasty) examples of cooperative and dual federalism! #vvmsgov

Erik Anderson

been traditionally handled by the states, such as education, the federal government has been involved.[31]

As America industrialized, the states and the national government attempted to regulate wages, working conditions, and the right to unionize. However, the Supreme Court struck down many of these efforts, including initial efforts to regulate child labor. The Court ruled that such efforts violated the Constitution's protection of the liberty of contract. Some legal scholars have labeled this time as the Lochner Era after the case *Lochner v. New York* (1905),[32] in which the state tried to limit the working hours of bakers to 60 hours per week.

In 1925, the Supreme Court weighed in on the rights states must provide their citizens. As will be discussed in chapter 4, *Gitlow v. New York*[33] began the process of **selective incorporation**, by which fundamental liberties in the Bill of Rights are applied to the states on a case-by-case basis. This is done through Section 1 of the Fourteenth Amendment, which provides, "nor shall any State deprive any person of life, liberty, or property, without due process of law; nor deny to any person within its jurisdiction the equal protection of the laws."

In the *Gitlow* case, the Court ruled that freedom of speech and the press are fundamental liberties protected by the due process clause from violations by the states. This limited states' actions in taking away the personal freedoms guaranteed in the First Amendment. Over time, on a case-by-case basis, the Supreme Court has applied the Fourteenth Amendment to prevent states from taking away most of the liberties provided in the Bill of Rights.

During the latter part of the nineteenth century and the early decades of the twentieth, states and the national government moved away from dual federalism toward a system of **cooperative federalism**, in which both levels work together in the same areas of public policy. Under this type of federalism, the two levels do not generally play the same roles.

selective incorporation
the process through which the Supreme Court applies fundamental rights in the Bill of Rights to the states on a case-by-case basis.

cooperative federalism
a form of American federalism in which the states and the national government work together to shape public policy.

FIGURE 3.4

Cooperative Federalism

Beginning in the late nineteenth century and extending into the early twentieth, state and federal governments forged a relationship of cooperative federalism in which they worked together to shape public policy. Marble cake is often used to show the mixing in the new relationship—this cake was enjoyed by students at Centerville High School in Fairfax, Virginia. Notice that in cooperative federalism the colors (and functions) are less distinct.

Catherine Ruffing

Instead, the national government tends to be "responsible for raising revenues and setting standards," while state and local governments remain "primarily responsible for administering the programs."[34] (See Figure 3.4.)

The Great Depression and Changes in American Federalism

The Great Depression, and the inability of state governments to cope with the crisis, increased the power of the national government and changed the nature of federalism. The crisis of the Great Depression strained American federalism. During the boom times of the 1920s, states increased their spending, especially to expand the highways for the nation's growing fleet of automobiles. To do so, states borrowed large amounts of money. When the economic crisis took hold, many state governments faced shortfalls and were unable to respond to their residents' needs. Local governments also were overwhelmed, unable

Franklin Delano Roosevelt's inaugural address, March 4, 1933. In the address, President Roosevelt asserted, "This great Nation will endure as it has endured, will revive and will prosper. So, first of all, let me assert my firm belief that the only thing we have to fear is fear itself—nameless, unreasoning, unjustified terror which paralyzes needed efforts to convert retreat into advance." How did Roosevelt's response to the Great Depression re-shape federalism?
Franklin D. Roosevelt Presidential Library & Museum

to care for millions of unemployed workers. Faced with challenges that they could not meet and citizens whose needs they could not assist, state and local governments appealed to the national government for help.

Roosevelt Greatly Expanded the Role of the National Government   At his inaugural address in 1933, President Franklin Delano Roosevelt made it clear that he was prepared to bring the full power of the executive branch to bear on the Great Depression. Should Congress not take proper action to assist, he said "I shall ask Congress for . . . broad Executive power to wage a war against the emergency, as great as the power that would be given to me if we were in fact invaded by a foreign foe."[35]

Roosevelt was a savvy politician who, as a former governor, exerted a powerful influence on the country in a short span of time. Roosevelt knew that state governments did not have the resources to handle the urgent problems they faced. They were in no position to refuse the big sums of federal aid that Roosevelt offered, even if accepting financial aid meant trading away some state authority. This dynamic fundamentally changed the relationship between the states and the national government, dramatically strengthening the role of the national government in the economy.

The expansion of national power under Roosevelt's New Deal—especially Congress's authority to regulate interstate commerce—permanently altered the relationship between the states and the national government. Cooperative federalism, in which both levels of government are involved in setting policy, firmly replaced earlier models of dual federalism and made the national government at least a coequal in many areas of public policy traditionally handled by the states.

Many programs that define modern cooperative federalism originated in Roosevelt's New Deal. For example, the Social Security Act of 1935 created a set of programs to support vulnerable groups of Americans.[36] It established unemployment insurance for American workers. It set up old-age insurance and old-age assistance programs, later supplemented with disability insurance. The Works Progress Administration (WPA) was the largest of the New Deal public works programs.[37] It was created to provide jobs for the thousands of people who were unemployed during Great Depression. By 1943, the WPA had brought 8.5 million Americans into the workforce.[38] The WPA projects built infrastructure projects to benefit the pubic, such as bridges, airports, schools, parks, and utilities.[39] In addition, the program supported theater, music, and visual arts projects. Other programs funded research, historic preservation, and public libraries.[40]

The revolution in federalism was made possible by the severe economic crisis facing the nation and the inability of states to handle its fallout. States were desperate for help in handling the impact of the Great Depression, and the Roosevelt administration drastically increased the role of the federal government as a result.

A poster from 1935 informing Americans aged sixty-five and older of their benefits under the Social Security program and how to obtain them.

GraphicaArtis/Getty Images

3.3 Describe the development of American federalism over time.

REMEMBER
- The boundaries between the authority of national and state governments have changed over time.
- Many of these changes have come about as a result of Supreme Court decisions in interpreting the Constitution.
- The New Deal fundamentally reshaped American federalism.

KNOW
- *Thirteenth Amendment:* constitutional amendment that outlaws slavery. (p. 73)
- *Fourteenth Amendment:* constitutional amendment that provides that persons born in the United States are citizens and prohibits states from denying persons due process or equal protection under the law. (p. 73)
- *Fifteenth Amendment:* constitutional amendment that gave African Americans the right to vote. (p. 74)
- *dual federalism:* a form of American federalism in which the states and the national government operate independently in their own areas of public policy. (p. 74)
- *selective incorporation:* the process through which the Supreme Court applies fundamental rights in the Bill of Rights to the states on a case-by-case basis. (p. 75)
- *cooperative federalism:* a form of American federalism in which the states and the national government work together to shape public policy. (p. 75)

THINK
- How has American federalism changed and developed? What factors have helped to drive this change?
- How did nineteenth-century interpretations of American federalism deny some Americans their fundamental rights?
- How did the New Deal impact the relationship between the national government and the states?
- Given the dynamic nature of federalism, what kinds of events might cause federalism to change in the future?

3.3 Review Question: Free Response

Carol Ann Bond learned that her husband was having an affair with her friend, Myrlinda Haynes, who became pregnant. Bond stole and purchased chemicals, which she put on Haynes's doorknobs and car handle, causing burns. Bond was changed with violating the Chemical Weapons Convention Implementation Act of 1998, a federal law, which makes it a crime to use certain chemicals with the intent to harm others.

In *Bond v. United States* (572 U.S. ___ (2014)), the Supreme Court ruled that Congress exceeded its authority in passing the Chemical Weapons Convention Implementation Act because the law infringed on the traditional police powers of the states.

After reading the scenario, use your knowledge of U.S. Government and Politics to respond to parts A, B, and C.

A. Identify the constitutional provision that is common to both *McCulloch v. Maryland* (1819) and *Bond v. United States.*

B. Based on the constitutional provision identified in part A, explain how the facts of *Bond v. United States* lead to a different holding than in *McCulloch v. Maryland.*

C. Explain how another clause of the Constitution supports the ruling in *Bond v. United States.*

▰ 3.4 Modern American Federalism

During the second half of the twentieth century, the federal government expanded its role in the economy. Many federal agencies created during the New Deal stayed in place, and some grew larger. The dual federalism of the nineteenth and early twentieth centuries was long gone. Cooperative federalism remained the dominant model.

Grants-in-Aid and the Expansion of Cooperative Federalism

One of the primary tools that the federal government has used to achieve its policy objectives within the states is **grants-in-aid**, money provided to states by the federal government to carry out a policy that the national government has decided is important. This is known as **fiscal federalism**. **Categorical grants** provide money to states or to local or regional governments for specific policy objectives and with certain conditions attached to receiving or spending the funds. These conditions may involve the requirement that the state, local, or regional authority provide matching funds to receive the federal monies. They may also include specific instructions on how the grant funds are to be used. Sometimes categorical grants are awarded based on formulas that allocate federal money according to factors such as population, income, and need.

A political cartoon depicts the politically perilous relationship between state governments and the federal government with regard to grants. States need federal aid, often urgently, but they don't care for the increased weight of federal authority that comes with the funds.

Dave Granlund/Cagle Cartoons

Categorical grants-in-aid are an important source of national power. Though state, local, and regional governmental authorities are often not required to accept these funds, once they do so, they accept the national regulation that goes along with taking the money. Once a state establishes a program based on the receipt of a categorical grant-in-aid, it depends on the continued provision of those funds by the national government to avoid disruption of the provision of services to its citizens and residents.

Categorical grants act as both a carrot—to encourage states to carry out national policy objectives—and as a stick—to threaten states with the withholding of funds if they fail to carry out the federal government's policy objectives. According to critics of expanded national power, categorical grants pose several problems for the states. They may act as "bribes to induce subnational governments to execute national policies" at the expense of their own authority.[41] For example, most states raised the drinking age to twenty-one as a result of the National Minimum Age Drinking Act, a condition of a block grant that provided transportation funds from the national government to the states. Officials and citizens of wealthier states worry that their taxes are used to subsidize states that spend less money.[42] The uncertainty surrounding the continued provision of the grants can make it harder for states to plan their own budgets. Finally, the administration of these programs requires a further expansion of the size of both national and state governments.

Sometimes, the federal government requires states to pay for programs without providing funds. Such requirements are called **unfunded mandates**. The Americans with Disabilities Act of 1990 is an example. It required states to change existing public buildings to make them accessible to those with disabilities.[43] In passing this law, Congress championed the rights of disabled individuals. It did so, however, at a cost to state budgets.

Those who favor the use of categorical grants as a tool of national policymaking emphasize that redistributing money between states can reduce inequality among the states. Also, these monies can help state, local, and regional governments improve the lives of their citizens in ways that may not be possible without the help of the federal government.[44]

Social welfare involves health, safety, education, and opportunities for citizens. Under the old system of dual federalism, social welfare policies were mostly under state control.

grants-in-aid
federal money provided to states to implement public policy objectives.

fiscal federalism
the federal government's use of grants-in-aid to influence policies in the states.

categorical grants
grants-in-aid provided to states with specific provisions on their use.

unfunded mandate
federal requirements that states must follow without being provided with funding.

Political scientists use data to explain patterns. A trend is a pattern of data that appears over time, demonstrating that a topic being measured is moving in a certain direction. Trends can be short-term, appearing over a period of days, or months. Long-term trends can appear over several years.

1. Describe what the graph measures.

2. Identify two trends shown in the graph. Use specific years and data points in your response. For example, your

response might state, "From [year] to [year] the [describe the data being measured] went from [numerical value] to [numerical value].

3. Explain one reason for a trend you identified in part 2.

4. Explain one reason why it is difficult to draw conclusions about the reasons for a trend using only the data.

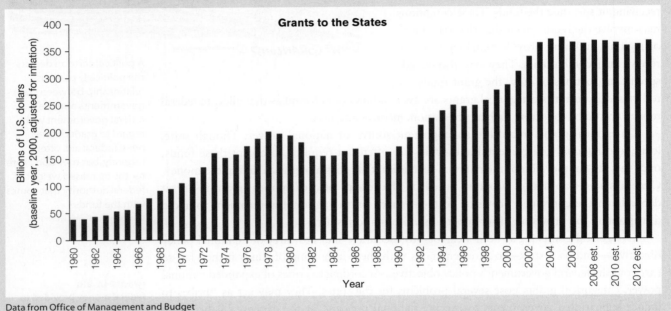

Data from Office of Management and Budget

Lyndon Johnson's Great Society program in the mid-1960s expanded the federal government's role in social welfare policy in part to ensure that states used these funds as intended and did not discriminate against minorities.

The Medicaid program (1965) provided health-care assistance to low-income individuals receiving other forms of aid as well as to those "who were medically indigent but not on welfare."[45] As with many Great Society programs, Medicaid was funded partly by the federal government and partly by the states. The Elementary and Secondary Education Act of 1965 (ESEA) "provided for the first time, general federal support for public elementary and secondary education."[46] Title I of the ESEA provided federal assistance to children from low-income families in both public and private schools.

Devolution and Block Grants

block grant
a type of grant-in-aid that gives state officials more authority in the disbursement of federal funds.

When Richard Nixon was elected president in 1968, he promised to roll back the expansion of national authority and return at least some of the power to the states. One of Nixon's main tactics to reduce national authority was the **block grant**. Though they are still a type of grant-in-aid, block grants provide federal money for public policies in a way

that tries to increase state, local, and regional authority in how that money is spent and lessen federal influence.

Efforts to restore more authority to the states continued under the presidency of Ronald Reagan, who, in his speech accepting the Republican Party's nomination in 1980, promised, "Everything that can be run more effectively by state and local government we shall turn over to state and local government, along with the funding sources to pay for it."[47] As part of his program, Reagan increased the use of block grants for social welfare programs. Block grants help fund a variety of programs.[48] The Department of Health and Human Services provides block grants to set up programs to treat those with drug and alcohol addictions. Another block grant provides assistance to those struggling with mental illness. The U.S. Department of Energy provides block grants to help state and local government reduce energy use, rely less on oil and gas, and improve energy efficiency.

Revenue sharing occurs when the federal government apportions tax money to the states with no strings attached. States can use these federal funds for any governmental purpose. Federal revenue sharing ended in 1986.[49] Mounting federal deficits will likely prevent revenue sharing in the near future.

Devolution returns authority for federal programs to the states. Devolution increases states' autonomy in economic and social policy by decentralizing control and administration of programs. One of the most important of these efforts focused on social welfare policies. Democratic president Bill Clinton signed the Personal Responsibility and Work Opportunity Reconciliation Act of 1996 (PRWORA), which devolved social welfare programs to the states.[50] PRWORA replaced Aid to Families with Dependent Children (AFDC)—a legacy of Roosevelt's New Deal—with Temporary Assistance for Needy Families (TANF), which placed time limits on receipt of welfare assistance and added work requirements. Block grants gave states more authority in setting and enforcing the rules of welfare programs.

Pediatrician Lanre Falusi examining an infant patient in a Maryland community health clinic in 2015. With powerful lobbying efforts behind them, members of the American Medical Association pressured Congress to revamp physician reimbursement under Medicare.

Andrew Harrer/Bloomberg/Getty Images

revenue sharing when the federal government apportions tax money to the states with no strings attached.

devolution returning more authority to state or local governments.

Federalism and Public Policy: Education

In 1965, as part of Lyndon Johnson's Great Society, the Elementary and Secondary Education Act was passed in an effort to provide equal educational opportunities, particularly for students living in low-income areas.[51] The Act provided federal grant money for the states to create programs that would reduce dropout rates and improve schools. The ESEA Act was reauthorized in 2002, with the passage of the No Child Left Behind Act (NCLB).[52] This controversial law provided states with grant money, if they agreed to give standardized assessment tests to students at certain grade levels. The wave of testing that followed was often criticized by school districts, teachers, parents, and, of course, students. In 2015, NCLB was replaced with the Every Student Succeeds Act (ESSA).[53] ESSA gave states more latitude in setting educational standards but retained mandatory standardized testing.

Advocates of state control over education argue that the federal government has overstepped its bounds in asserting control over what has traditionally been a state issue. On the other hand, advocates for federal education policy argue that students should not be

Analyzing Graphs and Charts:
Perceptions of Federal, State, and Local Governments

The Pew Research Center is a nonpartisan organization that conducts and analyzes public opinion through surveys and other tools. In 2013, researchers asked a series of questions about individuals' views on how *favorably* they viewed the federal government, their state governments, as well as their local governments. Those who answer these kinds of surveys are called *respondents*.

This was not the first time Pew researchers had asked the question. They had data going back to the 1990s. The researchers presented the collection of their findings over time with a *line graph* (sometimes called a line chart). A line graph presents data as a set of points connected by lines:

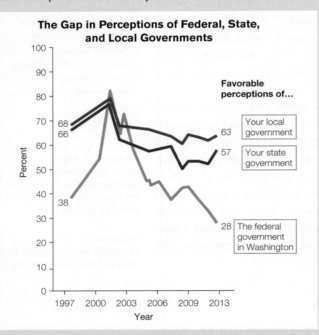

Data from Pew Research Center

These kinds of graphs can be useful in presenting trends over time, in this case a widening gap between the favorability ratings that Americans who responded to the surveys (a group that changed with each survey) gave to the federal government, their state governments, and their local governments. According to these data, there seems to be a notable decline in Americans' favorable views of the federal government in recent years. The researchers also found that differences in favorability views of government might be connected to the political party with which the individual answering the survey affiliated, but not for every level of government.

Another way to present results of a survey is a *bar chart*, which represents data with rectangles of different sizes. The bars can be either horizontal or vertical.

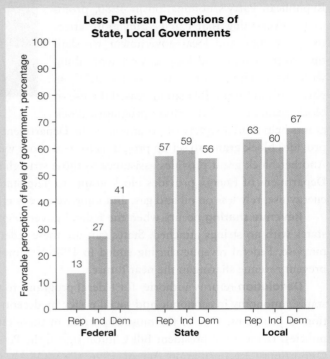

Data from Pew Research Center

These data came from one administration of the survey, in 2013. Note that differences in favorability ratings of the federal government appear to be more strongly associated with, or *correlated* with, political party affiliations (Republican, Independent, and Democratic) than views of state and local governments.

After studying these two presentations of data, consider and answer the following questions:

1. Describe what the numbers in the first figure represent.

2. Describe what the height of each bar in the second figure represents.

3. Explain one way in which the favorability rating of federal, state, and local government is more connected to the political party that a respondent affiliates with.

4. Pew Research is a respected organization, but let's say that it were not. Instead, consider how a research organization might shape the *surveys* to advance an argument. Explain how the wording of the questions might shape the results presented (a topic to which we will return later in the book).

FIGURE 3.5

Per-Pupil Spending in Public Elementary-Secondary School Systems, by State: Fiscal Year 2013

The map shows spending per pupil across the states for grades pre-K through 12. The key highlights big differences in levels of spending. Education traditionally was controlled by the states and local school districts. Many changes in funding happened in response to desegregation and to Great Society programs. Looking at the color variations, is it possible to discern a source of tension in a federal system—how much some states "subsidize" other states?

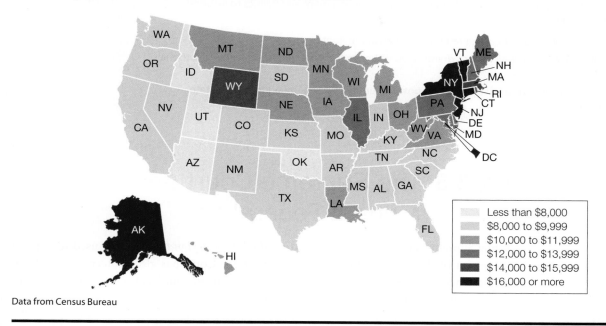

Data from Census Bureau

educationally disadvantaged based on the state in which they live. See Figure 3.5 for differences in funding of schools. In the meantime, teachers, parents, and students are caught in the middle as education policy continues to evolve.

Section Review

3.4 Explain how federalism changed in the twentieth and twenty-first centuries.

REMEMBER
- The federal government influences state policies through grants-in-aid.
- Ronald Reagan favored devolution, which returns some policymaking authority to the states.

KNOW
- *grants-in-aid:* federal money provided to states to implement public policy objectives. (p. 79)
- *fiscal federalism:* the federal government's use of grants-in-aid to influence policies in the states. (p. 79)
- *categorical grants:* grant-in-aid provided to states with specific provisions on their use. (p. 79)
- *unfunded mandate:* federal requirements the states must follow, without being provided with funding. (p. 79)
- *block grant:* a type of grant-in-aid that gives state officials more authority in the disbursement of the federal funds. (p. 80)
- *revenue sharing:* when the federal government apportions tax money to the states with no strings attached. (p. 81)
- *devolution:* returning more authority to state or local governments. (p. 81)

THINK
Under what circumstances should the national government transfer more authority in policymaking back to the states and local governments?

3.4 • Modern American Federalism   **83**

Everything that can be run more effectively by state and local government we shall turn over to state and local government, along with the funding sources to pay for it. We are going to put an end to the money merry-go-round where our money becomes Washington's money, to be spent by the states and cities exactly the way the federal bureaucrats tell them to.[54]　　—Ronald Reagan, Presidential Nomination Acceptance Speech

After reading the passage, use your knowledge of U.S. Government and Politics to respond to parts A, B, and C.

A. Describe the argument about federalism given in the quote.

B. Explain one way in which block grants devolve power from the national government to the states.

C. Explain one way in which the national government uses grants-in-aid to control state policies.

▌ 3.5 The Supreme Court and Modern Federalism

While Supreme Court cases, such as *McCulloch v. Maryland,* have been used to expand the power of the national government, the Supreme Court has also protected states from further encroachment on their power. The Tenth Amendment has become a more prominent tool in asserting state authority in recent decades.

United States v. Lopez: Preserving States' Authority

On March 10, 1992, Alfonso Lopez Jr. began yet another day of his senior year at Edison High School in San Antonio, Texas. However, this day he entered his high school with an unloaded .38 special revolver and five cartridges he kept in his pocket. He planned to deliver the revolver and ammunition to another student, in exchange for $44. Through anonymous sources, school authorities were made aware that Lopez was carrying an unloaded revolver and confronted Lopez about these accusations. After admitting that he was carrying a firearm and ammunition, Lopez was charged under a Texas state law, which prohibited firearms in schools. The state charges were dropped, and Lopez was then charged with violating the federal Gun-Free School Zones Act of 1990.[55]

Lopez moved to dismiss the charges, claiming that the act was unconstitutional because Congress did not have the power to regulate public schools. The trial court denied the motion, claiming that the Gun-Free School Zones Act was within the powers enumerated to Congress under the Constitution, because activities within elementary, middle, and high schools are related to interstate commerce.

After being tried and convicted, Lopez appealed to the U.S. Court of Appeals for the Fifth Circuit, in hopes of reversing the decision by the trial court. Lopez and his lawyers thought that Congress overstepped the enumerated powers granted in the commerce clause in passing the Gun-Free School Zones Act. The Fifth Circuit agreed and the conviction was reversed. The United States appealed the Fifth Circuit's ruling, and the Supreme Court agreed to hear the case. The U.S. government was required to prove that the Gun-Free School Zones Act was constitutional under the commerce clause and that the law regulated an activity that was substantially related to interstate commerce.

The question presented to the Supreme Court was, "Is the 1990 Gun-Free School Zones Act, forbidding individuals from knowingly carrying a gun in a school zone, unconstitutional because it exceeds the power of Congress to legislate under the Commerce Clause?"[56]

The federal government argued that guns in schools increase violent crime, which impacts the national economy. The government argued that crime is expensive, and insurance spreads the cost of crime throughout the nation. The government also argued that businesses would not want to relocate to high crime areas, which impacts interstate commerce.

In a 5–4 decision, the Supreme Court upheld the ruling of the Fifth Circuit, finding, "The possession of a gun in a local school zone is in no sense an economic activity that might . . . substantially affect any sort of interstate commerce."[57] Chief Justice William Rehnquist delivered the majority opinion, with concurring opinions delivered by Justice Anthony Kennedy and Justice Clarence Thomas. The majority opinion used a "slippery slope" argument, stating that according to the government's argument, "any activity could be looked upon as commercial."

According to the majority opinion, if the Court were to rule that bringing a gun to a local high school is interstate commerce,

> Congress could regulate any activity that it found was related to the economic productivity of individual citizens: family law (including marriage, divorce, and child custody), for example. Under the theories that the Government presents . . . it is difficult to perceive any limitation on federal power, even in areas such as criminal law enforcement or education where States historically have been sovereign. Thus, if we were to accept the Government's arguments, we are hard pressed to posit any activity by an individual that Congress is without power to regulate.[58]

Under the government's argument, the Court said, everything would be commerce, and nothing would be left to the states.[59]

The Court reaffirmed that the Tenth Amendment creates a federal system, which protects state power. In the concluding paragraph of the opinion, the Supreme Court stated,

> To uphold the Government's contentions here, we would have to pile inference upon inference in a manner that would bid fair to convert congressional authority under the Commerce Clause to a general police power of the sort retained by the States . . . and that there never will be a distinction between what is truly national and what is truly local . . . This we are unwilling to do.[60]

Justice Stephen Breyer delivered the main dissenting opinion in which he concluded that gun violence could influence interstate commerce and education. He reasoned that a court should not examine a lone isolated case of regulation but rather the overarching effect of firearms on education. He described the problem of gun violence as "widespread and serious," using statistics to demonstrate that thousands of children are impacted by violence in or near their schools nationwide. Justice Breyer concluded that Congress could have reasonably concluded that guns in schools undermine educational opportunities, impairing commerce nationwide. Although education is more than economics, Justice Breyer asserted that education "has long been inextricably intertwined with the Nation's economy."

The Supreme Court's decision in *United States v. Lopez* is important because it reverses the trend toward expanding national power and reaffirms state police powers under the Tenth Amendment. In 1997, in *Printz v. United States*, the Court again cited the Tenth Amendment when it struck down portions of a federal law that required local law enforcement officers to perform background checks on prospective handgun purchasers.[61] These court decisions reversed a trend of broadening the power of the national government and reasserted states' authority.

By this point in chapter 3, you have met the first two of the required cases in the U.S. Government and Politics course. Keep in mind that you have to know the facts of each case, the question the Supreme Court was asked to decide, who won, the reasoning used by the Supreme Court in reaching the majority decision, and the logic put forth in the dissenting opinion. It's also important to be able to explain how the decision affects the interpretation of the U.S. Constitution.

Document	Scope
McCulloch v. Maryland	The *McCulloch* case established that Congress has the implied power to charter a bank under the necessary and proper clause, and states may not tax the federal government.
United States v. Lopez	The *Lopez* case involves the Tenth Amendment. It limits the federal government's ability to pass legislation under the commerce clause and gives more power to the states.

Same-Sex Marriage

States issue marriage licenses, and they have traditionally set the requirements for getting married. However, marriage also involves civil rights. For example, in *Loving v. Virginia* (1967),[62] the Supreme Court overturned a Virginia law prohibiting interracial marriage. Similar to the issue of interracial marriage in the 1960s, the more recent issue of same-sex marriage highlighted the tension between states' rights under the system of federalism and the national protection of civil rights. In 2009, Edith Windsor's wife, Thea C. Spyer, passed away. They were married in Canada two years before, and their same-sex marriage had been recognized as valid by New York, their state of residence at the time of Spyer's death.

Windsor and Spyer's marriage, however, was not considered legal under federal law. After her wife died, Windsor was not entitled to the same federal tax provisions granted to surviving spouses in opposite-sex marriages. Windsor had to pay more than $350,000 in federal estate taxes. With help, especially from the Lesbian, Gay, Bisexual, and Transgender (LGBT) Community Center in New York City, she sued the federal government, claiming her right to have her marriage recognized as legal under federal law and to "the equal protection principles that the Court has found in the Fifth Amendment's Due Process clause."[63]

Windsor's case challenged the constitutionality of the Defense of Marriage Act (DOMA), passed by Congress during the presidency of Bill Clinton in 1996 by proponents of traditional marriage. DOMA had two substantive sections. One section stated that for purposes of federal law, marriage meant a legal union between a man and a woman: "In determining the meaning of any Act of Congress, or of any ruling, regulation, or interpretation of the various administrative bureaus and agencies of the United States, the word 'marriage' means

The same-sex marriage of Thea Spyer, left, and Edie Windsor, right, was legally recognized by the State of New York but not by the federal government. After the death of her wife, Windsor successfully fought to overturn a portion of a federal law that defined marriage as only between opposite-sex couples.

Neville Elder/Corbis via Getty Images

only a legal union between one man and one woman as husband and wife, and the word 'spouse' refers only to a person of the opposite sex who is a husband or a wife."[64]

Another section reaffirmed the power of the states to make their own decisions about marriage: "No State, territory, or possession of the United States, or Indian tribe, shall be required to give effect to any public act, record, or judicial proceeding of any other State, territory, possession, or tribe respecting a relationship between persons of the same sex that is treated as a marriage under the laws of such other State, territory, possession, or tribe, or a right or claim arising from such relationship."[65] This section of DOMA made clear that same-sex marriage did not fall under the protection of the full faith and credit clause, which states, "Full faith and credit shall be given in each state to the public acts, records, and judicial proceedings of every other state. And the Congress may by general laws prescribe the manner in which such acts, records, and proceedings shall be proved, and the effect thereof."[66] Under the full faith and credit clause, a state is required to recognize and honor the public laws of other states unless those laws are contrary to the strong public policy of that state. Full faith and credit is why, for example, you only have to obtain a driver's license from one state.

In a 5–4 decision in *United States v. Windsor* (2013), the Supreme Court ruled that the section of DOMA classifying only opposite-sex marriages as legal under federal law was unconstitutional.[67] In his majority opinion, Justice Anthony Kennedy denounced the intent of DOMA, stating, "The history of DOMA's enactment and its own text demonstrate that interference with the equal dignity of same-sex marriages, a dignity conferred by the States in the exercise of their sovereign power, was more than an incidental effect of the federal statute. It was its essence."[68] In his dissent, Justice Samuel Alito, joined in part by Justice Clarence Thomas, challenged the foundations of the majority's logic, claiming, "Same-sex marriage presents a highly emotional and important question of public policy—but not a difficult question of constitutional law. The Constitution does not guarantee the right to enter into a same-sex marriage."[69]

While the Supreme Court in *Windsor* validated state-recognized same-sex marriages for *federal* purposes, it did not strike down the other substantive clause of DOMA, which allowed states to reject same-sex marriage licenses from other states. Same-sex marriage was legal in some states but not in others.

Windsor's victory in court spurred James Obergefell and John Arthur to action. In July 2013, after a decades-long commitment to each other, Obergefell married Arthur on the tarmac of a Maryland airport. The two men lived in Ohio, which did not recognize same-sex marriage, so they flew to Maryland, which did. Arthur was struggling with amyotrophic lateral sclerosis (ALS), a progressive neurological degenerative disease. The disease has no known cure.[70]

The two men had flown to Maryland in a medical transport plane, seeking to get married while they still could. In an interview with BuzzFeed News a few months before the Court's decision in his case, Obergefell described their ceremony: "We landed at Baltimore, sat on the tarmac for a little bit, said 'I do,' and 10 minutes later were in the air on the way home."[71] John Arthur died in October 2013, three months after their wedding.

Ohio law did not permit Obergefell to be listed as the surviving spouse on Arthur's death certificate. Rather than accept Ohio's refusal to recognize their marriage, Obergefell sued. "This case," he said, "was another way to take care of him and to respect him and to respect our relationship."[72]

In 2015, in its decision in *Obergefell v. Hodges*, the Supreme Court affirmed the legality of Obergefell and Arthur's marriage and guaranteed the right of all couples to marry in yet another 5–4 vote. Citing constitutional protections of fundamental civil liberties

James Obergefell in 2015, two and a half months before the Supreme Court decision that would guarantee marriage equality for all Americans.

Maddie McGarvey/The Washington Post/Getty Images

and the right to privacy, Justice Kennedy, in his majority opinion, affirmed that "the right to marry is a fundamental right inherent in the liberty of the person."[73] The *Obergefell* case legalized same-sex marriage nationwide.

Reflecting on his case in an interview with *USA Today* two months before the Court's decision, Obergefell recalled how he felt about having to fly, given his husband's serious medical issues, to another state just to get married: "All I thought was, 'This isn't right . . .'"[74]

Gonzales v. Raich: The Supreme Court Decides

As Angel Raich and Diane Monson pursued their claims for the use of medical marijuana through the American legal system, they did so against a politically murky background. The boundaries between state power and national power were not definitively settled. Local governments were caught in the middle because the laws in their states conflicted with federal law.

In 2004, the U.S. Supreme Court took up the case of Angel Raich and Diane Monson. The issue was whether the power of the federal government to ban marijuana under the Controlled Substances Act superseded California's legalization of medical marijuana.

In skeptical questioning of the women's attorneys, Justice Antonin Scalia, a conservative, challenged their assertion that growing and distributing cannabis—even if it stayed within California's borders—would not contribute to the national market for marijuana. Justice Breyer, considered one of the liberal members of the Court, suggested that a better course of action for medical cannabis advocates was to change federal law itself.

In *Gonzales v. Raich* (2005), the Court ruled against Raich and Monson by a 6–3 vote. The Court sided with the authority of the federal government—and that of Congress under the commerce and supremacy clauses of the Constitution. The Supreme Court distinguished this situation from the *Lopez* case by stating, "the CSA regulates quintessentially economic activities: the production, distribution, and consumption of commodities for which there is an established, and lucrative, interstate market."[75] The Supreme Court determined that it did not matter whether Raich and Monson were personally involved in interstate commerce because Congress had a rational basis for concluding that the market for marijuana as a whole substantially impacted interstate commerce.

If marijuana grown at home for private use can be considered interstate commerce, then what *can't* be? In the debates over American federalism, defining the proper limits of the commerce clause remains a hotly contested issue.

Today, the landscape has changed from the time of *Gonzales v. Raich*. More than half of the states have passed laws allowing the use of marijuana for certain medical conditions. Others have decriminalized the possession of small amounts of marijuana, substituting civil fines for criminal penalties. In addition, nine states and the District of Columbia have legalized marijuana for recreational use. (See Figure 3.6.) Federal law, however, has not changed, and marijuana is still illegal under federal law.

State laws allowing marijuana use have put recent presidential administrations in a tight spot. During President Barack Obama's term in office, fully enforcing the Controlled Substances Act in the states had become very difficult. In December 2015, in a federal suit brought by neighboring states against Colorado (one of the four states in which recreational

FIGURE 3.6

Marijuana Legalization Today

State law related to marijuana varies, as this map shows. Some recent changes to state laws are still being phased in.

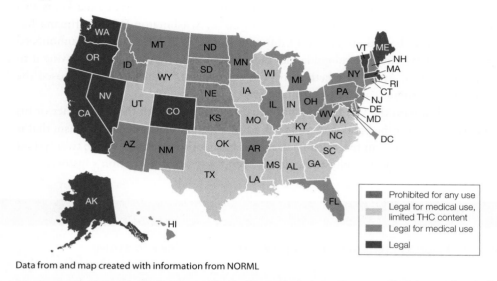

Data from and map created with information from NORML

use had been made legal), Obama's solicitor general argued in a brief presented to the Supreme Court that it should not decide to hear the case. To some observers, the administration's position implied "that marijuana should be federally legalized—even for recreational use."[76] The Justice Department, under the president's direction, however, retained authority to prosecute under the CSA, though it was to focus on drug trafficking and not on prosecuting "individuals who were in 'unambiguous compliance with existing state laws.'"[77]

The boundary between state and federal laws governing medical and recreational marijuana use remains unsettled. According to the Office of National Drug Control Policy, "It is important to recognize that these state marijuana laws do not change the fact that using marijuana continues to be an offense under federal law."[78]

By 2016, it had become harder for the federal government to enforce the Controlled Substances Act because strict enforcement would have meant putting more than a million, perhaps millions, of state-law-abiding citizens in federal prison, not to mention the political fallout from fully executing the law.[79] In a 2013 memo, the Department of Justice under President Obama affirmed the legality and supremacy of the Act but also acknowledged the impossibility of complete enforcement of the law in the states. The memo stated, "The Department is also committed to using its limited investigative and executorial resources to address the most significant threats in the most effective, consistent and rational way."[80] In the memo, the Justice Department declared that instead it would focus on preventing access to marijuana by youth, transport of marijuana from a state in which it is legal to states in which it is not, and the use of firearms in connection with the production or distribution of marijuana.

With the election of Republican Donald Trump as president in 2016, many observers thought that federal policy might shift toward letting the states regulate medical and recreational marijuana use, possibly reclassifying or even removing marijuana from the list of controlled substances under the federal law. With the confirmation of Jefferson

Sessions as Attorney General, however, that possibility became unlikely because Sessions expressed strong opposition to relaxing federal enforcement. In a letter written by Attorney General Sessions on July 24, 2017, he responded to concerns expressed by the Governor of Washington Jay Inslee and the state attorney general. Attorney General Sessions stated: "Congress has determined that marijuana is a dangerous drug and that the illegal distribution and sale of marijuana is a crime. The 'recreational licensed' marijuana market is also incompletely regulated . . . Since legalization in 2012, Washington State marijuana has been found to have been destined for 43 different states."[81] In 2018, Sessions announced that he was withdrawing federal guidelines that limited federal prosecutions, leaving it to each individual U.S. Attorney whether to prosecute or not.[82] This decision exposed the conflict between federal and state marijuana laws.

How to deal with the fact that an individual may comply with the laws of her or his state but at the same time break federal law is a fundamental question of federalism that is still unanswered. American federalism has always been loosely defined. In the twenty-first century, it remains as hotly contested as it has been for most of the nation's history.

Section Review

3.5 Discuss the current status of American federalism and how it might continue to evolve.

REMEMBER • In *United States v. Lopez,* the Supreme Court reaffirmed states' rights under the Tenth Amendment.

THINK • What issues are likely to challenge the balance of power between the national and state governments in the rest of the twenty-first century?
• Will the power of the national government grow or will states successfully reassert their powers in the twenty-first century?

3.5 Review Question: Argumentation

Under the Every Student Succeeds Act (ESSA) of 2015, states are required to test students in reading and mathematics once a year in grades 3 through 8, as well as once in high school. They must also test kids once in science in grade school, middle school, and high school. States that fail to comply with the ESSA lose federal educational funds.

Make an argument that the ESSA is either constitutional or unconstitutional.

In your essay:

• Articulate a claim or thesis that responds to the prompt, and use a line of reasoning to defend it.
• Use at least TWO pieces of relevant and accurate evidence to support your claim.
• At least ONE piece of evidence must be from one of the listed foundational documents:
Constitution of the United States
Federalist No. 10
• Use a second piece of evidence from another foundational document from the list or from your study of federalism.
• Use reasoning to explain why the evidence you provided supports your claim or thesis.
• Use refutation, concession, or rebuttal to respond to an opposing or alternative perspective.

Chapter 3 Review

AP® KEY CONCEPTS

- federalism (p. 64)
- unitary system (p. 66)
- confederal system (p. 66)
- federal system (p. 67)
- enumerated or expressed powers (p. 67)
- exclusive powers (p. 67)
- implied powers (p. 67)
- commerce clause (p. 68)
- necessary and proper clause (p. 68)
- supremacy clause (p. 68)

- Tenth Amendment (p. 68)
- reserved powers (p. 68)
- concurrent powers (p. 68)
- full faith and credit clause (p. 69)
- extradition (p. 70)
- privileges and immunities clause (p. 70)
- Thirteenth Amendment (p. 73)
- Fourteenth Amendment (p. 73)
- Fifteenth Amendment (p. 74)

- dual federalism (p. 74)
- selective incorporation (p. 75)
- cooperative federalism (p. 75)
- grants-in-aid (p. 79)
- fiscal federalism (p. 79)
- categorical grants (p. 79)
- unfunded mandate (p. 79)
- block grant (p. 80)
- revenue sharing (p. 81)
- devolution (p. 81)

AP® EXAM PRACTICE and Critical Thinking Project

MULTIPLE-CHOICE QUESTIONS

1. Which of the following pairs of statements correctly describes both federal and unitary systems?

Federal	Unitary
A. Powers of the states are expressly defined in the Constitution.	The vague language of the Constitution limits the power of the national government.
B. Most of the power is given to the state governments.	The national government shares power with state governments.
C. The national government has most of the power.	The national government has all of the power, and there are no state governments.
D. Power is constitutionally shared between the national and state governments.	The national government may grant certain powers to the states.

2. Which of the following statements best describes the impact of the Supreme Court's decision in *McCulloch v. Maryland*?

- **A.** The Court ruled that states have authority over commercial activity within their borders, weakening national power.
- **B.** The Court ruled that the necessary and proper clause allows the national government to create banks, strengthening national power.
- **C.** The Court upheld a division of power between the states and the national government by allowing states to tax national banks within their borders.
- **D.** The Court ruled that creating a national bank fell within the national government's enumerated powers, confirming national power.

3. By holding that Congress may regulate activity that is neither interstate nor commerce under the Interstate Commerce Clause, the Court abandons any attempt to enforce the Constitution's limits on federal power . . .   —Justice Clarence Thomas, dissenting opinion,
Gonzales v. Raich

Which of the following statements best describes the viewpoint conveyed in the quotation?

A. The federal government's authority under the commerce clause applies to interstate and commercial activity.

B. The commerce clause allows the federal government to regulate commercial activity within each state.

C. The Tenth Amendment established a federal system of government where powers are reserved to the states.

D. The system of federalism is threatened by the national government's expansion of power under the commerce clause.

4. Federal nutrition guidelines require public schools to serve healthy lunches to students and limit the amount of "junk food" available in vending machines. A state seeking to challenge these nutrition rules should cite which of the following cases?

A. *McCulloch v. Maryland*

B. *United States v. Lopez*

C. *Gibbons v. Ogden*

D. None of these cases could serve as precedent.

Glenn Foden/The Daily Signal

5. Which of the following statements best describes the viewpoint expressed in the political cartoon?

A. States should have the authority to make policy over moral issues, such as abortion and same-sex marriage.

B. The Supreme Court makes controversial decisions.

C. Supreme Court decisions do not resolve long-standing disagreements over social policy issues.

D. The Supreme Court should not make decisions involving the division of power between the national government and the states.

6. In 1993, Congress enacted the Brady Handgun Violence Prevention Act,[83] mandating that anyone seeking to buy a firearm must first undergo a federal background check. One provision in that act required state law enforcement officials to conduct those background checks. In *Printz v. United States* (1997),[84] the Supreme Court declared that portion of the act to be unconstitutional, reasoning, "The Federal Government may not compel the States to enact or administer a federal regulatory program." Which constitutional provision most logically and directly supports the Court's conclusion in the quoted language?

   A. Supremacy clause

   B. Necessary and proper clause

   C. Second Amendment

   D. Tenth Amendment

Questions 7 and 8 refer to the graph.

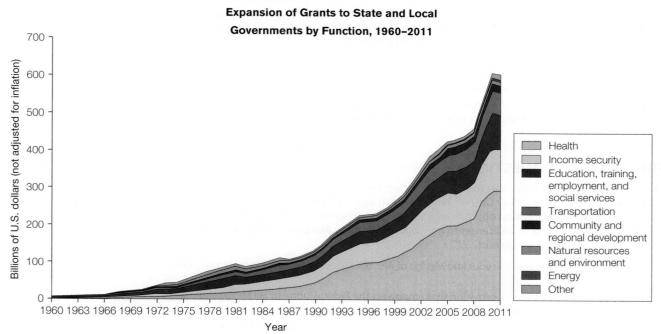

Expansion of Grants to State and Local Governments by Function, 1960–2011

Data from Office of Management and Budget

7. Which inference is most clearly drawn from the graph?

   A. More federal grant money goes to "Other" than to all specifically identified categories combined.

   B. During the period 2000–2010, "Transportation" funding grew by a greater percentage than "Income security" funding.

   C. The category receiving the largest federal funding has shifted over time from "Education, training, employment, and social services" in 1975 to "Health" in 2011.

   D. The same amount of funding has been allocated to "Community and regional development" each year since 1978.

8. What is the significance of the data on the graph, and how do the data relate to American government and politics?

   A. For over fifty years, the federal government has become increasingly involved in state and local governmental affairs.

   B. The federal government has forced the states to devote a larger share of their budgets to health and income security.

   C. Federal spending on items such as defense and border security has decreased since 1960.

   D. The federal government is no longer subject to the checks and balances that were established in the original Constitution.

The idea of a [unitary] government involves in it, not only an authority over the individual citizens, but an indefinite supremacy over all persons and things, so far as they are objects of lawful government. . . . In [that] case, all local authorities are subordinate to the supreme; and may be controlled, directed, or abolished by it at pleasure. In [a federal system], the [regional] authorities form distinct and independent portions of the supremacy, no more subject, within their respective spheres, to the general authority, than the general authority is subject to them, within its own sphere.

—James Madison, *Federalist* No. 39

9. Which of the following statements best describes the author's perspective and reasoning?

    A. The U.S. Constitution should be ratified because a unitary government is preferable to the Articles of Confederation.

    B. The powers that the Constitution would grant to the national government will not intrude upon the power of state governments.

    C. The supremacy clause will subordinate state governments to the federal sphere.

    D. Lawful government has the authority to make any laws it deems necessary and proper for effectuating a peaceful society.

10. Which constitutional concept is best reflected in the passage?

    A. Cooperative federalism

    B. Constitutional supremacy

    C. Dual federalism

    D. Separation of powers

FREE-RESPONSE QUESTIONS

1. On September 3, 2015, the *New York Times* reported the following, in an article entitled "Clerk in Kentucky Chooses Jail Over Deal on Same-Sex Marriage": "A Kentucky county clerk who has become a symbol of religious opposition to same-sex marriage was jailed Thursday after defying a federal court order to issue licenses to gay couples. The clerk, Kim Davis of Rowan County, Ky., was [jailed] for contempt of court. . . ."[85]

After reading the passage, use your knowledge of AP® U.S. Government and Politics to respond to parts A, B, and C.

    A. Identify the constitutional provision that empowers the federal judge to jail Ms. Davis under this scenario for her failure to follow the Supreme Court's ruling.

    B. Explain how the constitutional provision you identified in part A relates to the concept of federalism.

    C. Explain how the federal and state governments both play a role in policymaking regarding marriage.

2. Use the information in the table to answer parts A, B, and C.

Federal Versus State Share of Medicaid Spending, 1960–2010

Spending in billions of dollars (and percentage share borne by each government)

	1960	1970	1980	1990	2000	2010
Total Medicaid spending	0	5.3	26.0	73.7	200.3	397.2
Federal government's share of total Medicaid spending	0	2.8 (53%)	14.5 (56%)	42.6 (58%)	116.8 (58%)	266.4 (67%)
State governments' share of total Medicaid spending	0	2.5 (47%)	11.5 (44%)	31.1 (42%)	83.5 (42%)	130.9 (33%)

Data from Centers for Medicare and Medicaid Services

A. Describe two trends that can be seen from the chart over the period 1960–2010.
B. Explain how the principles of dual and cooperative federalism differ from one another.
C. Explain how the principles of dual and cooperative federalism can be inferred from the data in the chart.

ARGUMENTATION QUESTION

During the ratification debate, Federalists and Antifederalists disagreed over the scope and meaning of the necessary and proper clause appearing in Article I, Section 8, Clause 18 of the Constitution. In particular, the two sides debated whether that clause would lead either to eliminating state governments entirely or at least rendering them powerless. Does the past 230 years of constitutional history prove the arguments of the Federalists? Or does it prove the arguments of the Antifederalists?

In your essay:

- Articulate a claim or thesis that responds to the prompt, and use a line of reasoning to defend it.
- Use at least TWO pieces of relevant and accurate evidence to support your claim.
- At least ONE piece of evidence must be from one of the listed foundational documents:
  Articles of Confederation
  Constitution of the United States
  Brutus No. 1
  Federalist No. 51
- Use a second piece of evidence from another foundational document from the list or from your study of federalism.
- Use reasoning to explain why the evidence you provided supports your claim or thesis.
- Use refutation, concession, or rebuttal to respond to an opposing or alternative perspective.

Writing a Letter to the Editor on a Controversial Issue

Read the following excerpt from a news article.

Supreme Court denies Oklahoma and Nebraska challenge to Colorado pot

By **JOHN INGOLD** | jingold@denverpost.com and
RICARDO BACA | rbaca@denverpost.com | The Denver Post
PUBLISHED: March 21, 2016 at 2:34 am | UPDATED: October 2, 2016 at 4:08 pm

The U.S. Supreme Court on Monday declined to hear Nebraska and Oklahoma's proposed lawsuit against Colorado's legal marijuana laws.

The 6-2 vote means the nation's highest court will not rule on the interstate dispute, and Colorado's legal cannabis market is safe — for now.

"Since Colorado voters overwhelming passed legal recreational marijuana in 2012, we have worked diligently to put in place a regulatory framework — the first in the world — that allows this new industry to operate while protecting public health and safety," Colorado Gov. John Hickenlooper said in a statement Monday. "With today's Supreme Court ruling, the work we've completed so far remains intact." . . .

Nebraska Attorney General Doug Peterson said he was disappointed, but that he is working with partners in Oklahoma "and other states" to figure out their next steps "toward vindicating the rule of law," according to a statement. "Today, the Supreme Court has not held that Colorado's unconstitutional facilitation of marijuana industrialization is legal," Peterson said in the statement, "and the Court's decision does not bar additional challenges to Colorado's scheme in federal district court."

Oklahoma Attorney General Scott Pruitt added: "The fact remains — Colorado marijuana continues to flow into Oklahoma, in direct violation of federal and state law. Colorado should do the right thing and stop refusing to take reasonable steps to prevent the flow of marijuana outside of its border. And the Obama administration should do its job under the Constitution and enforce the Controlled Substances Act. Until they do, Oklahoma will continue to utilize every law enforcement tool available to it to ensure that the flow of illegal drugs into our state is stopped."

Colorado Attorney General Cynthia H. Coffman celebrated the victory but also acknowledged that Nebraska and Oklahoma's concerns won't disappear with the court's ruling.

"Although we've had victories in several federal lawsuits over the last month, the legal questions surrounding Amendment 64 still require stronger leadership from Washington," Coffman said in the statement.

While the attorneys general were all hoping for more federal guidance, legal experts aren't surprised they got so little.

Nebraska and Oklahoma filed the proposed lawsuit more than a year ago, and it specifically challenges Colorado's ability to license and regulate marijuana businesses. The two states say Colorado's system impermissibly conflicts with federal law and creates burdens for them by increasing the amount of pot coming across their borders.

Because the matter involves a dispute between states, it was filed directly to the Supreme Court. The first step in the lawsuit was for the justices to decide whether they even wanted to consider it. When the Supreme Court does accept such cases, the subsequent litigation can go on for years or even decades.

Attorneys for both the state of Colorado and the Obama administration had urged the court not to take up the lawsuit, while a group of former leaders of the Drug Enforcement Administration sided with Nebraska and Oklahoma and asked the court to accept the case.

In 2012, Colorado voters legalized possession of small amounts of marijuana and also authorized the creation of state-administered rules that would allow stores to sell marijuana to anyone over 21 years old. Those stores opened in 2014, and since then, Nebraska and Oklahoma say they have seen an increased number of people bringing marijuana into their states, in violation of both their state laws and federal law.

The Supreme Court justices spent more than a year pondering whether to take the case. The proposed lawsuit was scheduled and rescheduled five times for a closed-door conference, where the justices would debate the merits of taking the case.

Write a letter to the editor of *The Denver Post* taking a position on the Supreme Court's decision not to take the case brought by Nebraska and Oklahoma.

1. Your letter should articulate a clear, defensible claim.
2. Support your letter with evidence from this chapter.
3. Refute, concede, or rebut the opposing perspective.
4. Focus on the principles of federalism, and not on the perceived benefits or harms associated with legalizing marijuana.
5. Limit your letter to a single, double-spaced page.

Source: From "Supreme Court denies Oklahoma and Nebraska challenge to Colorado pot," by John Ingold and Ricardo Baca, *The Denver Post*, October 2, 2016.

UNIT 1 REVIEW

AP® EXAM PRACTICE and Critical Thinking Project

MULTIPLE-CHOICE QUESTIONS

1. Tax protest groups have been organized throughout the United States. Some of these groups claim the tax system unfairly benefits the wealthy. Others oppose local property taxes. Some groups want a flat tax, in which everyone would pay the same percentage of income. These groups are an example of:
   A. American political culture
   B. Republicanism
   C. Civil society
   D. Popular sovereignty

Questions 2 and 3 are based on the political cartoon.

Polyp.org

2. The cartoon from Europe also represents which theory of American democracy?
   A. Elitism
   B. Pluralism
   C. Participatory democracy
   D. Republicanism

3. The protests shown in the cartoon are an example of
   A. Elite democracy
   B. Republican government
   C. Pluralist democracy
   D. Popular sovereignty

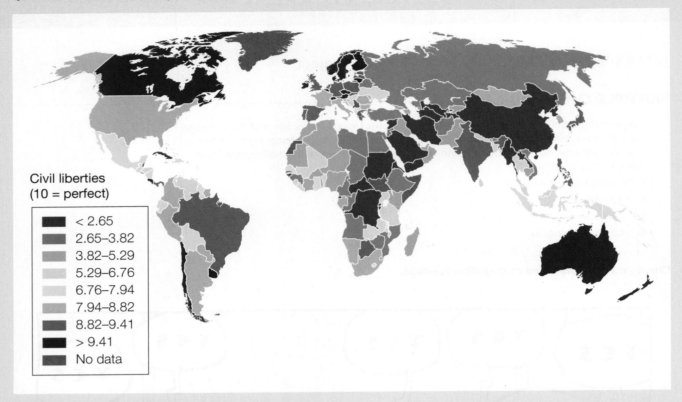

Civil liberties
(10 = perfect)

- ■ < 2.65
- ■ 2.65–3.82
- ■ 3.82–5.29
- ■ 5.29–6.76
- ■ 6.76–7.94
- ■ 7.94–8.82
- ■ 8.82–9.41
- ■ > 9.41
- ■ No data

Data from Economist Intelligence Unit

4. Which of the following conclusions is supported by the map?
   A. The United States is the most democratic country in the world.
   B. The United States has a comparatively high level of civil liberties.
   C. Civil liberties are increasing worldwide.
   D. North America is more democratic than Western Europe.

   _____

5. Why did Shays's Rebellion cause concern about the effectiveness of the Articles of Confederation?
   A. It demonstrated the weakness of state legislatures.
   B. It demonstrated the financial insecurity of the national government.
   C. It raised fears about tyranny of the minority.
   D. It raised fears about tyranny of the majority.

Questions 6–8 are based on the quotation.

He has the power of receiving ambassadors from, and a great influence on their appointments to foreign courts; as also to make treaties, leagues, and alliances with foreign states, assisted by the Senate, which when made becomes the supreme law of land. He is a constituent part of the legislative power, for every bill which shall pass the House of Representatives and Senate is to be presented to him for approbation. If he approves of it he is to sign it, if he disapproves he is to return it with objections, which in many cases will amount to a complete negative; and in this view he will have a great share in the power of making peace, coining money, etc., and all the various objects of legislation, expressed or implied in this Constitution. —Antifederalist Paper 67

6. Which of the following statements summarizes the argument made in Antifederalist Paper 67?
   A. The Constitution creates an executive with too much power.
   B. Checks and balances make it too difficult to pass laws.
   C. Treaties will become the supreme law of the land.
   D. The Constitution makes the president a member of the legislature.

7. Which of the following constitutional provisions best supports the arguments made in Antifederalist Paper 67?
   A. Article I, Section 8
   B. Article II, Section 1
   C. Article III
   D. The supremacy clause

8. Which of the following statements in *Federalist* No. 51 directly addresses the arguments made in Antifederalist Paper 67?
   A. "A dependence on the People is, no doubt, the primary control on the government."
   B. "Different interests necessarily exist in different classes of citizens."
   C. "Each department should have a will of its own."
   D. "The society itself will be broken into so many parts . . . that the rights of individuals . . . will be in little danger."

9. How do separation of powers and federalism impact civil society?
   A. The reserved powers of the states protect the rights of assembly and free speech, ensuring a lively civil society.
   B. The Constitution prevents the formation of civil society groups that operate as factions.
   C. Wealthy groups have more access to policymakers.
   D. There are multiple access points for civil society groups to influence policymaking.

Bradford Veley/Cartoonstock

10. Which of the following best describes the viewpoint in the cartoon?
    A. The Constitution creates a republican form of government.
    B. The Constitution is a living document that changes with the times.
    C. Checks and balances prevent one branch of government from becoming too powerful.
    D. The Constitution provides strong protections against foreign powers.

11. Which of the following best describes the impact of the Three-Fifths Compromise?
    A. Southern states received more representation in the House of Representatives.
    B. Southern states received more representation in the Senate.
    C. It expanded the rights of African Americans.
    D. It increased the political power of state governments in the South.

12. Which of the following best describes the argument made in *Federalist* No. 10?

    A. Factions can be eliminated through a system of checks and balances.

    B. Factions are healthy because they represent different political viewpoints.

    C. Factions are inevitable, but republican government can control them.

    D. Factions are necessary to protect the minority from tyranny of the majority.

Questions 13 and 14 are based on *the quotation*.

In *United States v. Morrison* (2000),[1] the Supreme Court struck down the Violence Against Women Act of 1994, stating:

> Gender-motivated crimes of violence are not, in any sense of the phrase, economic activity. While we need not adopt a categorical rule against aggregating the effects of any noneconomic activity in order to decide these cases, thus far in our Nation's history our cases have upheld Commerce Clause regulation of intrastate activity only where that activity is economic in nature.

13. Which of the following cases best serves as precedent for the decision in *United States v. Morrison*?

    A. *Marbury v. Madison* (1803)

    B. *United States v. Lopez* (1994)

    C. *McCulloch v. Maryland* (1819)

    D. None of these cases could serve as precedent.

14. Which of the following steps could Congress take to encourage states to enact higher penalties for domestic violence?

    A. Pass legislation overturning *United States v. Morrison*.

    B. Pass another version of the Violence Against Women Act, using the necessary and proper clause.

    C. Use a grant-in-aid to influence state policies regarding domestic violence.

    D. Ignore the Supreme Court's decision in *United States v. Morrison*.

Questions 15 and 16 are based on the map.

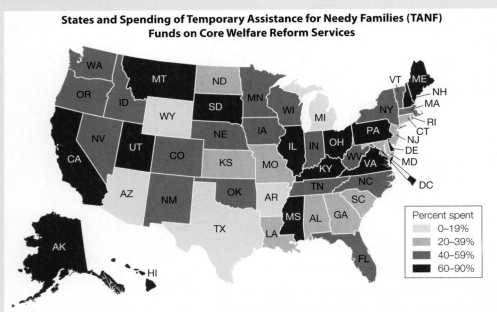

States and Spending of Temporary Assistance for Needy Families (TANF) Funds on Core Welfare Reform Services

Percent spent
- 0–19%
- 20–39%
- 40–59%
- 60–90%

Data from Department of Health and Human Services

15. The map supports which of the following statements?

    A. Welfare spending has increased in some states by 60–90 percent.

    B. The amount of welfare money each state receives from the national government varies.

    C. States in the South are more likely to spend TANF funds on core welfare reform services than states in the North.

    D. States have discretion in how to spend welfare funds they receive from the federal government.

16. Which of the following type of grants-in-aid is most likely to lead to the result shown in the map?

    A. Block grants

    B. Categorical grants

    C. Unfunded mandates

    D. Formula grants

Questions 17 and 18 are based on the quotation.

Schools won't have to cut the salt in meals just yet and they can serve kids fewer whole grains, under changes to federal nutrition standards announced Monday. The move by the Trump administration rolls back rules championed by former first lady Michelle Obama as part of her healthy eating initiative.   —*U.S. News and World Report*, May 2, 2017

17. Which of the following best describes the trend explained in the passage?

A. Devolution of power

B. The use of grants-in-aid to influence state policies

C. Executive oversight

D. Congressional authority under the commerce clause

18. Which part of the Constitution would states use to challenge federal nutrition guidelines?

A. The Tenth Amendment

B. The necessary and proper clause

C. The enumerated powers in Article I, Section 8

D. The supremacy clause

19. What was the trend in the decisions of the Supreme Court under Chief Justice John Marshall?

A. The commerce clause was used to expand the power of state governments.

B. The Tenth Amendment was used to expand the power of state governments.

C. The national government gained power in comparison to the states.

D. The necessary and proper clause was used to expand the power of the executive.

Nick Anderson Editorial Cartoon used with the permission of Nick Anderson, the Washington Post Writers Group and the Cartoonist Group. All rights reserved.

20. Choose the pair that best represents the symbolism in the cartoon.

Californian	Elephant
A. Popular sovereignty	Increased states' rights
B. Natural rights	Separation of powers
C. Devolution of power	Supremacy clause
D. Republicanism	Civil liberties

Jimmy Margulies/Cagle Cartoons, Inc.

1. Use the cartoon and your knowledge of U.S. Government and Politics to answer parts A, B, and C.

    A. Identify the viewpoint expressed in the cartoon.

    B. Describe whether the cartoon represents participatory, pluralist, or elitist democracy.

    C. Explain how the cartoon relates to American political culture.

When Democrats couldn't pass their carbon cap-and-trade plan, the Obama administration instituted a power plan that outstripped the legal authority Congress had afforded the Environmental Protection Agency. If Trump is successful in rescinding these onerous regulations, he will be reinstituting boundaries on the regulatory state. If your goal is inhibiting energy production, then elect members of Congress to pass legislation that does so.[2]

—David Harsanyi

2. Use the excerpt and your knowledge of U.S. Government and Politics to answer parts A, B, and C.

    A. Describe the viewpoint expressed in the excerpt.

    B. Describe two ways in which the Constitution prevents one branch of government from becoming too powerful.

    C. Explain two reasons why the founding fathers created a system of checks and balances.

ARGUMENTATION QUESTION

The Brady Handgun Violence Prevention Act, enacted in 1993, required a national system to instantly run a background check on people who wanted to purchase handguns. Montana and Arizona challenged the part of the law that required state officials to conduct the background checks.[3]

Construct an argument that the provision of the Brady Act requiring state officials to conduct background checks is constitutional or unconstitutional.

In your essay:

- Articulate a claim or thesis that responds to the prompt, and use a line of reasoning to defend it.
- Use at least TWO pieces of relevant and accurate evidence to support your claim.
- At least ONE piece of evidence must be from one of the listed foundational documents:

  Constitution of the United States

  Federalist No. 10

- Use a second piece of evidence from another foundational document from the list or from your study of federalism.
- Use reasoning to explain why the evidence you provided supports your claim or thesis.
- Use refutation, concession, or rebuttal to respond to an opposing or alternative perspective.

CRITICAL THINKING PROJECT

Constitution Art Project

This project takes you beyond the AP® Exam to think critically and creatively about the Constitution and federalism. Create an artistic analogy that represents the U.S. system of government and label the following parts:

- Citizens
- The Congress
  - **At least one** of the following powers
  - Makes laws
  - Overrides presidential vetoes
  - Budgetary authority
  - Senate confirms appointments
  - Senate ratifies treaties

- The President
  - **At least one** of the following powers
  - Veto of laws
  - Commander-in-chief
  - Appointment power
  - Signs treaties

- The Supreme Court
  - Judicial review
- The bureaucracy
  - Implements laws
- The states
- Local governments
  - Police powers

Use poster paper, and make your artwork colorful. Your artwork can be drawn by hand, or you may create a collage. Your goal is to illustrate how the institutions and levels of government work together.

Example:

In an American Government League baseball game, the constitution is the home plate. The pitcher represents Congress, and the baseball represents a law. When a law misses the home plate, the umpire, representing the Supreme Court, calls an out. When the batter, representing the president, hits a home run, he scores. The bureaucracy carries out its task of putting the run on the scoreboard, as the citizens cheer.

An umpire calls Chase Hedley out at the plate. In the analogy, this resembles the Supreme Court exercising the power of judicial review.

Denis Poroy/Getty Images

Unit 2

The Branches of
the Federal Government

You interact with the federal government almost every day. A woman sits on the steps of the Farley Post Office in New York City and fills out her return on Tax Day, which usually falls on April 15. It is the deadline for sending tax returns to the Internal Revenue Service, and many people put off filing till the deadline. The tax system involves several institutions of government, including the president, who can propose changes to the tax system, Congress, which approves tax laws, and the Internal Revenue Service, which collects taxes and issues refunds. The U.S. Postal Service is an independent agency. Unlike most other agencies, the post office is specifically mentioned in the Constitution (Article I) and is overseen by the Congress, too.

The Congress, the president, and the courts are the three major institutions of U.S. government. Congress consists of a House of Representatives and a Senate. While both chambers pass laws, each has different constituencies, powers, and rules.

The Constitution sets the president's formal powers, but the informal power of the office has grown over time. Technology allows the president to reach the public through press conferences, the State of the Union Address, and social media.

The federal courts are an independent branch of government. Lifetime appointments insulate judges from political backlash. Through judicial review, the Supreme Court can overturn laws passed by Congress and executive actions that violate the Constitution.

Chris Hondros/Getty Images

The bureaucracy is a fourth branch of government that carries out policies developed by the president and Congress. Most bureaucrats are selected through a merit-based system. The bureaucracy implements laws covering a wide range of activities. Bureaucrats are unelected and have rule-making authority, yet Congress and the president can hold the bureaucracy accountable. Checks and balances require the branches of government to compete and cooperate in governing. ■

Mazie Hirono of Hawaii has an unusual story for a U.S. senator. Born in Japan to a mother who was a U.S. citizen, she later immigrated to Hawaii and became a naturalized U.S. citizen. She is the first Buddhist and the first Asian-American woman elected to the Senate.

JOSHUA ROBERTS/REUTERS/Newscom

4 Congress
Representation, Organization, and Legislation

The Constitution divides the legislature into two chambers: the House of Representatives and the Senate. They are divided along lines of political partisanship. They sort themselves into a host of committees and subcommittees to do the work of their institution. In spite of all of their divisions and differences, however, all members of the U.S. Congress share one thing in common. They are there to represent the interests of the voters who sent them.[1] Americans elect people to make the laws, raise and spend the nation's money, and watch over other institutions in the federal government, along with a host of activities that shape American public policy.

Congress is idealized as a place where the voice of the people is heard and great debates over policy are held, but the halls of Congress can make citizens feel like outsiders looking in.
Jonathan Ernst/Reuters

In this chapter, we will focus on congressional organization, action, and representation. This chapter explores what representation means in American democracy, what has been accomplished, and what is still under construction.

After reading this chapter, you will be able to:

4.1 Describe the differences between the House of Representatives and the Senate, the functions of each chamber, and how Congress operates within a system of check and balances.

4.2 Describe congressional elections.

4.3 Compare the authority and rules affecting the policymaking process in the House of Representatives and the Senate.

4.4 Explain the lawmaking process.

4.5 Describe how Congress creates a budget that addresses discretionary and mandatory spending.

4.6 Explain how constituency, partisanship, and divided government influence Congress.

Secret Invitation to the Map Room

Like most states, Wisconsin has a partisan process for redistricting in which the legislature draws the boundaries for election districts. In 2011, Wisconsin's Republican state legislators, one by one, were invited to the "map room" in the office of a law firm hired by party officials to orchestrate the process, and done to maximize the newly elected majority's advantage. No Democrat was invited. Each was asked to sign a pledge of secrecy such as Dale Schulze, who was then a state legislator.

In *Baldus v. Brennan*,[2] one of the first challenges to the map, Peter Earle, a civil-rights lawyer from Milwaukee, and Doug Poland, a commercial litigator from Madison, managed to extract some unexpected evidence from that law firm. "Among the documents were the secrecy pledges Republican senators signed to review their district maps, strict rules for anyone entering the map room and talking points about the significance of the redrawn maps. There was also a print-out of a spreadsheet showing the partisan effect of the final map," according to an article in the *Wisconsin State Journal*.[3]

In 2012, the first election in Wisconsin with the new district boundaries, Republicans won 47 percent of the vote, but captured sixty out of ninety-nine seats in the State Assembly; in 2014 they won 57 percent of the vote, but sixty-four seats, and in 2016 they won 53 percent of the vote and sixty-four seats. Wisconsin was not alone. Overall, in the seventeen states where Republicans drew the maps, 53 percent of voters cast their ballots for Republican candidates for the U.S. House of Representatives, but Republicans won 72 percent of the seats. Meanwhile, in the six states where Democrats controlled the process, their candidates received 56 percent of the vote but won 71 percent of the

Two lawyers who brought a suit against gerrymandering. At right, Doug Poland. At left, Peter Earle, who summed up the evidence: "You have a piece of the jigsaw puzzle in your hand, but imagine you can't see clearly the boundaries of it and where it fits with the other pieces. You can't create the whole picture."

Courtesy Ruth Greenwood

seats. By 2017, Schulze was lamenting that "reapportionment is a moment of opportunity for the ruling party" and is now co-chair of a group calling for nonpartisan redistricting.[4]

With modern computer technology, this process of distorting the reapportionment process is now done with scientific precision, so that elected officials are now able to pick their constituents rather than voters picking their representatives. In the fall of 2017, the U.S. Supreme Court heard arguments in *Gill v. Whitford*,[5] a case concerning whether Wisconsin's 2011 redistricting process was so extreme as to effectively deny full voting rights to its residents. In the past, the Supreme Court has weighed in on the principle of one person, one vote—where legislative districts had to have equal numbers of people—and has overturned districts that packed black voters together to dilute their voting strength in other districts. The Supreme Court was expected to decide if the redistricting plan lacked legitimate justification. Yet when the Court announced its decision in *Gill* in June 2018, it didn't settle the matter. It sent the case back to the lower courts, and litigation will continue.

■ 4.1 The Constitution and Congress

In the Constitution, Congress is dealt with first. Article I, which describes Congress, is longer than the articles dealing with the executive and judicial branches.[6] The powers of Congress are described in more detail than the other branches.

Key Differences between the Chambers

One of the results of compromise between the more populous and less populous states at the Constitutional Convention was the creation of a bicameral legislature composed of two chambers, the House of Representatives and the Senate. While both the House and the Senate make laws, the framers of the Constitution envisioned different roles for them. The founders designed these differences partly to add checks and balances *within* Congress and not just between Congress and the other branches. A bicameral legislature, according to James Madison in the *Federalist Papers*, "doubles the security to the people, by requiring the concurrence of two distinct bodies in schemes of usurpation and perfidy."[7] By "usurpation and perfidy," Madison was referring to the dangers of faction, in which a group of individuals, whether constituting a majority of citizens or a minority of them, could damage the rights and liberties of others or the interests of the Republic.[8] Federalism and the separation of powers among the three branches were two ways in which the framers tried to contain the dangers of faction. Separating legislative authority within Congress itself was yet another. (See Figure 4.1 to compare the two chambers.)

The House of Representatives

Directly elected by the eligible voters in their districts, members of the House of Representatives are meant to be close to the people and their wishes. Representatives serve

TABLE 4.1 The House of Representatives and the Senate Compared

	House of Representatives	Senate
Requirements for Membership	At least twenty-five years old	At least thirty years old
	Seven years of citizenship	Nine years of citizenship
	Resident of the state	Resident of the state
Service	Two-year terms, with unlimited number of terms	Six-year terms, divided into three classes, with unlimited number of terms
Constituency	District, apportioned to states by population	Entire state
Organization	More governed by rules, more formally structured, more power to individual leadership positions	Less governed by rules, more power to individual members, more informal
Goals	To be closer to voters' preferences	To be more insulated from voters' preferences

two-year terms. A brief term would keep them close and accountable to the people while also giving them enough time to become competent in their work and familiar with what Madison called "The great theatre of the United States."[9]

A Representative must be at least twenty-five years old, a resident of his or her state, and a citizen of the United States for seven years.[10] While the Constitution did not bar women from holding office, the states did, excluding all but a few (generally widows with property) from participating in public life. Madison argued that the House of Representatives would be inclusive: "the door of this part of the federal government is open to merit of every description, whether native or adoptive, whether young or old, and without regard to poverty or wealth, or to any particular profession of religious faith."[11] In reality, however, when Madison wrote these words, there were property qualifications set by the states for voting and for holding office. (Figure 4.1 on page 110 shows the backgrounds and professions of the First Congress and the current Congress.)

The Senate

Senators are more insulated from the public and any "passions" that might sweep through the populace, adding stability to the legislative branch. Elected for six-year terms, the election of senators is staggered so that a third are up for reelection every two years. Since its members do not have to run for reelection every two years, the Senate, Madison argued, should serve "as a defense to the people against their own temporary errors and delusions."[12]

With Shays's Rebellion fresh in their minds, many of the delegates to the Constitutional Convention were concerned about the ability of the poor majority to take away the property of the wealthy. Many framers also had deep concerns about the voters themselves. They worried that the passions and prejudices of voters were ripe for manipulation and that factions could easily shape Americans' political opinions. The framers constructed the Senate to set up roadblocks to prevent an American electorate from too quickly voting its wishes into policy.

Senatorial candidates must be older than representatives—at least thirty years old—and citizens for at least nine years, and they must live in the state that they seek to represent. The Constitution does not limit the number of terms a given representative or senator may serve.

AP® TIP

Differences between the selection process and term lengths of members of the House of Representatives and the Senate are important and may appear on the AP® Exam.

FIGURE 4.1

The Makeup of the First Federal Congress Compared to Today

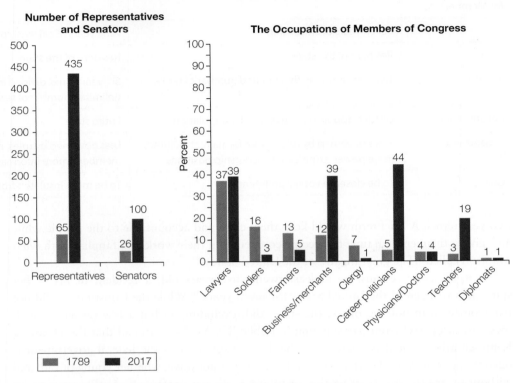

Note: Only one profession was listed for each member of the First Congress. Percentages do not total to one hundred, though, because of rounding. For the 115th Congress, members were allowed to list more than one job or profession in their careers. Percentages for the 115th Congress will not total to one hundred.

Data from the National Constitution Center, U.S. Census Bureau, *Congressional Quarterly*, and the Congressional Research Service.

In the original Constitution, state legislatures elected senators. The Seventeenth Amendment (1913) replaced the indirect election of senators by state legislatures with direct popular election by a state's eligible voters.

The Powers of Congress

The powers of Congress generally fall into three broad areas: lawmaking, budgeting, and exercising oversight of the federal bureaucracy and other public officials.

Legislative Authority

The most important power of Congress is its ability to pass laws in areas of national policy. In the next three chapters, you will also learn about other types of dictates and actions that carry the force of law: presidential executive orders, constitutional law as defined by courts, and administrative regulations established by bureaucratic agencies.

The list of the enumerated powers of Congress is substantial. Congress is authorized to legislate in economic policy, national security, foreign policy, and other policy areas[13] (Table 4.2).

TABLE 4.2 Legislative Powers of Congress in the Constitution

The Constitution grants Congress the power to legislate in the following areas. Unless otherwise noted, these powers are laid out in Article I, Section 8.

	Both Chambers	House	Senate
Enumerated Powers			
Economic Policy	Create and collect taxes, coin money, borrow money, regulate the value of currency, and regulate interstate and foreign commerce. Power to create laws "necessary and proper" to carry out enumerated powers.	All bills to raise revenue must be generated in the House.	Propose budgetary amendments. In practice, the Senate has become a coequal partner in setting national revenue policy.
Foreign Policy	Regulate trade with other nations.		Confirm ambassadors with a majority vote and ratify treaties entered into by a president through a two-thirds vote.
National Security	Declare war, raise and support armies and a naval force, power to call up the military "to execute the laws of the Union, suppress Insurrections, and repel Invasions," define and punish piracies and felonies committed on the high seas.		
Other Powers Involving the Executive Branch		Issue articles of impeachment against the president, vice president, and other executive branch officers (Article I, Section 2 and Article II, Section 4).	Confirms presidential nominations of executive branch officers with a majority vote (Article II, Section 2) and convicts impeached officials with a 2/3 vote (Article I, Section 3 and Article II, Section 4).
Powers Involving the Judicial Branch	Create levels of the judicial branch below the Supreme Court, establish the number of Supreme Court justices (Article III, Section 1).	Issues articles of impeachment against members of the federal judiciary (Article I, Section 2).	Confirms nominees to the federal judiciary by a majority vote (Article II, Section 2). Senate tries members of the federal judiciary who have been impeached (Article I, Section 3).
Through the Necessary and Proper Clause			
	"To make all Laws which shall be necessary and proper for carrying into Execution the foregoing Powers, and all other Powers vested by this Constitution in the Government of the United States." (Article I, Section 8, Clause 18)		
Through Subsequent Amendments			
	Individual amendments (such as the Thirteenth, Fourteenth, and Fifteenth) grant Congress "the power to enforce, by appropriate legislation," those amendments.		

The Budgeting Process

Congress sets a federal budget. Because Congress appropriates funds for agencies and programs, it has substantial power over policymaking. Congress can impede the president's proposals by refusing to fund them. Congress's budgetary powers also have an impact on the bureaucracy. Creating a bureaucratic agency requires two steps: First, congressional action authorizes the department or agency. Second, through the process of appropriation, Congress funds the agency's activities.[14] The Congressional Budget Office (CBO) provides information and estimates of the likely budgetary consequences of funding the agencies and programs created by Congress.

pork barrel spending
legislation that directs specific funds to projects within districts or states.

One of the more controversial ways in which members of Congress have been involved in the budgetary process has been the inclusion of **pork barrel spending** through earmarks to proposed legislation, through which members allocate and direct monies to projects or groups within their districts or states. Often popular with constituents, pork barrel spending has been criticized for putting narrow interests ahead of those of the nation's voters. Members of Congress may vote for earmarks in another state to get their own earmarks passed. This process is called **logrolling**. In 2011, the House of Representatives, led by Republicans, banned earmarks.

logrolling
trading of votes on legislation by members of Congress to get their earmarks passed into legislation.

In Defense of Earmarks

Earmarks—the allocation of money to specific projects in states or congressional districts—are often popular with those who receive them and with the senators and representatives who can claim credit for bringing the money home. Others, however, have criticized them as putting the needs of a few beneficiaries ahead of the needs of the nation as a whole. In the wake of the House's ban on earmarks in 2011, two former members of Congress, Martin Frost (D-TX) and Tom Davis (R-VA), offered their defense of earmarks:

> First, without them, Congress delegates the authority to allocate vast sums of discretionary federal spending to the executive branch. The president submits a budget at the beginning of each year and then Congress decides how much money each department and agency will get for its programs. But then someone in the federal bureaucracy decides which communities and states actually get those dollars. Earmarks reclaim a portion of that power for Congress. . . .
>
> Second, eliminating earmarks takes away the incentive for the parties to cooperate to pass appropriations bills on time. Instead, for weeks and months after the start of each fiscal year on October 1, much of the government is left operating on a continuing resolution. When a number of representatives and senators have "skin in the game," they'll make sure a spending bill gets passed. . . .
>
> Third, taking away earmarks removes nearly all the leverage that party leaders have to make Congress run. Already the two parties show little inclination to pass laws simply because they are in the national interest. Removing earmarks took one more arrow out of the party leaders' quivers.[15]
>
> Reproduced with permission of Tom Davis and Martin Frost.

oversight
efforts by Congress to ensure that executive branch agencies, bureaus, and cabinet departments, as well as their officials, are acting legally and in accordance with congressional goals.

Oversight

Congress uses its **oversight** authority to ensure that laws are implemented in the way that Congress intended or to investigate the president or members of the executive branch for wrongdoing. Given the growth in the size and complexity of the federal government, this is not an easy task. Congress has oversight responsibilities over the federal bureaucracy as well as over other branches of government and elected and appointed officials.

Congressional committees and subcommittees may conduct hearings and investigations into the actions of the federal bureaucracy to ensure that funds appropriated for programs are being spent efficiently, legally, and in accordance with the law's intent. While many committee hearings are routine, some may be called in the event of a perceived breakdown or failure by an executive branch agency, such as the widely criticized federal response to the devastating effects of Hurricane Katrina in New Orleans and the Gulf Coast in 2005.

Exercising Checks and Balances

In the Constitution's system of checks and balances, each of the branches shares authority with the other branches over some aspects of governance. Congress is given the authority to declare war, and the Senate to ratify treaties, thus forcing the executive and legislative branches to work together in important aspects of foreign and national security policy.

Congress also has a role in the nation's judicial system as it has the power "to constitute Tribunals inferior to [below] the Supreme Court" (Article I, Section 8) and sets the number of justices on the Supreme Court. The Senate—using its power of advice and consent—confirms presidential nominees to the federal courts by a simple majority.

In addition to the confirmation of presidential nominees to the federal judiciary, the Senate also exercises the same role of advice and consent in the confirmation of most presidential nominees to important posts in the federal bureaucracy, like cabinet secretaries.

Congress has the power to remove federal officials—including the president, vice president, members of the bureaucracy, and federal judges—through the process of impeachment. The House of Representatives may issue articles of impeachment. The standard for impeachment is whether an official has committed "Treason, Bribery, or other high Crimes and Misdemeanors" (Article II, Section 4). The vagueness of this language has resulted in debates about just what constitutes an impeachable offense.

If a majority of the members of the House votes to impeach, the trial takes place in the Senate, with a two-thirds majority needed to convict (Article I, Section 3).[16] Two presidents have faced successful House resolutions to impeach, but neither was removed from office. Andrew Johnson—impeached during the Reconstruction era following the Civil War—survived by a single vote in the Senate. Bill Clinton—charged with lying and obstructing an investigation into his relationship with intern Monica Lewinsky—was acquitted by a vote of 55–45. Richard Nixon resigned before proceedings reached the full House of Representatives for an impeachment vote.

AP® TIP

It's important to know how Congress can check the president, bureaucracy, and courts. Make sure you understand the constitutional and informal powers that Congress can use to influence the other branches of government.

Section Review

This chapter's main ideas are reflected in the Learning Targets. By reviewing after each section, you should be able to

—**Remember** the key points,

—**Know** terms that are central to the topic, and

—**Think** critically about these questions.

4.1 Describe the differences between the House of Representatives and the Senate, the functions of each chamber, and how Congress operates within a system of checks and balances.

REMEMBER
- The Constitution created a bicameral legislature divided between the House of Representatives and the Senate to establish checks and balances within Congress.
- Members of the House are meant to be closer to the people. Shorter terms and looser eligibility requirements open the doors wider to potential representatives.

- Senators are more insulated from the public to ensure greater stability. Longer terms and stricter eligibility requirements make the bar higher for candidates.
- Both the House and Senate have legislative authority as well as budgetary and oversight powers. They have the power to tax, coin money, regulate currency, establish a system of uniform weights and measures, regulate trade domestically and with foreign nations, declare war, and create lower courts.
- The House may introduce bills to raise revenue and impeach members of the executive and judicial branches.
- The Senate has the power to ratify treaties with a two-thirds vote and confirm executive branch officers and federal judges with a majority vote. It also tries members of the executive and judicial branches impeached by the House.

KNOW
- *pork barrel spending*: legislation that directs specific funds to projects within districts or states. (p. 112)
- *logrolling*: trading of votes on legislation by members of Congress to get their earmarks passed into legislation. (p. 112)
- *oversight*: efforts by Congress to ensure that executive branch agencies, bureaus, and cabinet departments, as well as their officials, are acting legally and in accordance with congressional goals. (p. 112)

THINK
- What are the advantages and disadvantages of having a bicameral Congress?
- Why did the founding fathers give Congress a long list of enumerated powers in the Constitution?

4.1 Review Question: Free Response

In 2017, Congress considered several proposals to repeal the Patient Protection and Affordable Care Act (Obamacare). Although President Trump is a Republican and the Republican Party controlled both houses of Congress, the proposals to repeal Obamacare failed.

Use the scenario and your knowledge of U.S. Government and Politics to answer parts A, B, and C.

A. Identify one difference between members of the House of Representatives and senators.

B. Explain one reason why the structure of Congress made it difficult to repeal the Affordable Care Act.

C. Describe one power, other than the power to make laws, that Congress could use to influence healthcare policy.

◼ 4.2 Politics of Congressional Elections

The Constitution sets the framework for the boundaries of constituencies. Would-be senators hope to represent the voters of their states. Candidates for the House strive to win the votes of the constituents in their congressional districts. House districts change with fluctuations in population, and a very political redistricting process changes district boundaries. Redistricting is done by each individual state, as the story about the Wisconsin legislature demonstrates.

Constituency: The Boundaries of Representation

constituency
a body of voters in a given area who elect a representative or senator.

At the most basic level, the rules governing the division of voters into **constituencies**—bodies of voters in an area who elect a representative or senator—are laid out in the Constitution. However, the process of this division, especially for the House of Representatives, is often political and controversial. The Constitution is silent on the issue of House of Representatives districting. The 1842 Apportionment Act mandated single-member districts.[17] The ways in which incumbent members of Congress use their incumbency to enhance their chances of getting reelected have significant effects on the behavior of all candidates in an election. Finally, every election is unique. Local, state, and national conditions during a given election matter as well, and there are always unanticipated events that can powerfully shape a candidate's electoral chances.

Constituency and the Senate

The Senate is composed of one hundred members, two from each state. To stagger the elections of senators, no two Senate seats from the same state will be up for grabs in the same election, unless a retirement or other event has opened up one of the seats. The Senate represents the states. The result of equal *state* representation is that individual *voters* are unequally represented in the Senate. The 586,107 citizens of Wyoming get two senators; so do the 39,144,818 citizens of California. (See Figure 4.2.)

FIGURE 4.2

The Representational Consequences of the Great Compromise

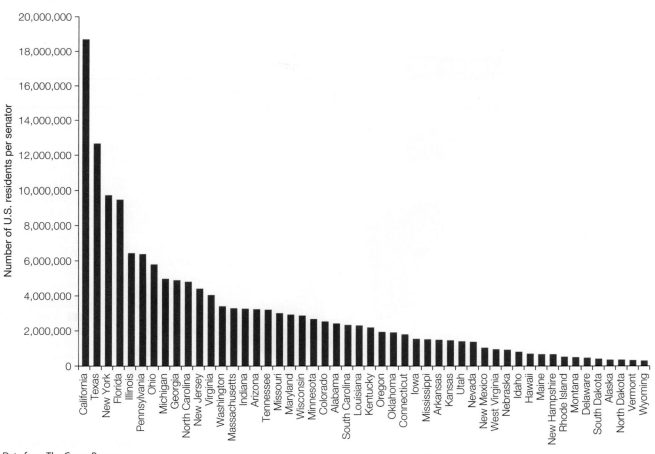

Data from The Green Papers

Apportionment in the House of Representatives

Since 1929, the House of Representatives has been set at 435 members.[18] The size of a state's representation in the House depends upon its population. The process of determining the number of representatives for each state is called **apportionment**. Through this process the number of representatives is allocated based on the results of the census that is conducted every ten years. (See Figure 4.3.) Each state is divided into one or more congressional districts, with one seat in the House representing each district and each state guaranteed one representative, no matter how small its population.

Given that the size of the House is capped, changes in population can produce "winners and losers" among the states following each census. Trends in population growth and distribution in recent decades have produced a clear pattern of gains in House seats for states in the South and West and losses for states in the Northeast and Midwest.

Redistricting and Gerrymandering

While the process of apportionment has important consequences for the representation of states in the House, it also has important consequences for the boundaries of constituency. Following each census, **redistricting** occurs, in which states redraw the boundaries of the electoral districts. Seven states have only one representative, so their district boundaries are the same as the boundaries of the state. Some states have undertaken redistricting *between* censuses, especially when a political party gains control over the state's legislative

apportionment
the process of determining the number of representatives for each state using census data.

redistricting
states' redrawing of boundaries of electoral districts following each census.

FIGURE 4.3

Apportionment Gains and Losses after the 2010 Census

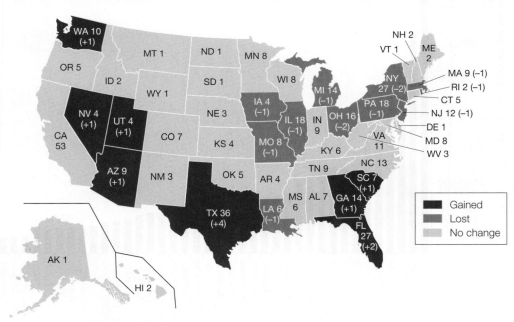

Note: Numbers to the right of the state names show the total number of representatives allocated to the state. Numbers between parentheses show the change as either a gain (+) or a loss (–).

Data from the U.S. Census Bureau

---

and executive branches, although many states have constitutional or legislative prohibitions against this practice.

The stakes involved in redistricting are high, and the process is often highly political and controversial. Redistricting can put incumbents at risk by changing the composition of their constituencies or by forcing two incumbents to run for the same seat. In most states, the legislature draws the district boundaries.[19] In others, a bipartisan or nonpartisan commission handles the process to try to make it less political, although the state legislatures typically approve these plans.

The intentional use of redistricting to benefit a specific interest or group of voters is referred to as **gerrymandering**. The term comes from state legislative districts that were oddly drawn in 1812 under Massachusetts governor Elbridge Gerry to benefit his Democratic-Republican Party. Federalists complained that one district looked like a monster or a salamander, and the term created by the fusion of salamander with the governor's last name stuck.

gerrymandering
the intentional use of redistricting to benefit a specific interest or group of voters.

Partisan Gerrymandering

Partisan gerrymandering aims to increase the representation of one political party at the expense of another. The idea is to concentrate the opposing party's supporters in a small number of districts, which that party will win easily. The party in control then tries to maximize the number of districts that its candidates will win comfortably yet not by huge margins. By doing so, the party in charge of redistricting is able to "waste" many of the votes of its opposition because there is no more of an advantage—in terms of the number of House seats a party has—in winning 90 percent of the votes in any one district than there is by winning just one more vote than your opponent.

Partisan gerrymandering is drawing district boundaries into strange shapes to benefit a political party. The word *gerrymandering* comes from a famous 1812 cartoon of a senate district in Massachusetts created under Governor Elbridge Gerry. Compare the cartoon to Figure 4.4. Does the shape look familiar?

partisan gerrymandering
drawing of district boundaries into strange shapes to benefit a political party.

Partisan gerrymandering is not the only reason congressional districts are packed with voters who support one party. More and more people are moving to communities with those who are like-minded.[20] Some states, like Arizona and California, are using independent commissions to draw boundaries and make districts more competitive.[21] By some estimates, only about forty seats in the House of Representatives are competitive.[22] For the vast majority of members of Congress, the danger of losing an election is remote unless an incumbent is challenged in a primary by someone from the same party. People who vote in primaries are more ideologically extreme and less representative of the electorate as a whole. As a result, voting behavior in Congress has become more polarized, partly because members of Congress worry about primary voters and large donors.[23]

THE GERRY-MANDER.

"The Gerry-Mander. A new species of Monster which appeared in Essex South District in Jan. 1812." The cartoon was published originally in the *Boston Gazette* in March 1812 and is still widely circulated.
Bettmann/Getty Images

Racial and Ethnic Gerrymandering

A second form of gerrymandering aims to increase the likelihood of electing members of racial and ethnic minorities as representatives by concentrating voters of minority ethnicity within specific congressional districts. Racial and ethnic gerrymandering results in **majority-minority districts**, in which voters of *minority* ethnicity constitute an electoral *majority* within the electoral district. Racial and ethnic gerrymandering has led to some oddly-shaped congressional districts, some of the most notable of which were drawn after the 1990 census. The Twelfth District of North Carolina, for example, "stitched together African American communities in several of the state's larger cities, using Interstate 85 . . . as the thread."[24]

Not all scholars agree that creating majority-minority districts increases the repetitive representation of minorities in Congress. Political scientist Carol Swain has argued that while creating such districts increases the probability of electing African Americans within those districts, it may not lead to improving representation of African Americans repetitive. According to her, "More black faces in political office (that is, more descriptive representation for African Americans) will not necessarily lead to more representation of the tangible interests of blacks."[25] Swain argues that it may be better to have a larger number of legislators who have to consider the views of their African American constituents than a small number of descriptively representative legislators who lack enough votes collectively to advance their positions.

The Supreme Court and Congressional District Boundaries

Until the 1960s, the drawing of district boundaries had generally been left up to the states. Drawing congressional district boundaries is a political process, and parties use the opportunity to draw boundaries that will give their party the highest possible number of representatives.

In *Baker v. Carr* (1962),[26] a registered Republican challenged Tennessee's congressional district boundaries, which had not been changed since 1901. As a result, some districts contained ten times the population of other districts. Tennessee argued that drawing congressional boundaries was a political question that should be left to the states. The Supreme Court disagreed, requiring Tennessee to redraw congressional district boundaries so that each district would have roughly the same number of constituents. This lead to the principle of "one person, one vote" articulated in *Gray v. Sanders* (1963)[27] and *Reynolds v. Sims* (1964).[28] **Malapportionment**—where the population is distributed in uneven numbers between legislative districts—is unconstitutional because it violates the equal protection clause of the Fourteenth Amendment.[29] Justices in a dissenting opinion argued that voters were not denied their right to vote, and all votes were counted. The dissenting justices argued that drawing district boundaries was a state issue and that the Supreme Court overstepped its bounds in ordering redistricting.

The Court has also weighed in on the proper role of racial and ethnic considerations in drawing district boundaries. In *Shaw v. Reno* (1993), the Court rejected a North Carolina reapportionment plan designed to produce majority-minority districts because it resulted in a bizarrely shaped district and used race to such a degree in drawing these boundaries that it could "only be understood as an effort to segregate voters into separate districts on the basis of race."[30] (See Figure 4.4.) The dissenting opinion emphasized that the racial redistricting plan was meant to provide representation for African Americans, the group the Fourteenth Amendment was originally written to protect. The dissent argued that the Equal Protection Clause should not have been used to block an effort to create a district

majority-minority district
a district in which voters of a minority ethnicity constitute an electoral majority within that electoral district.

malapportionment
the uneven distribution of the population among legislative districts.

FIGURE 4.4

Gerrymandering and *Shaw v. Reno*

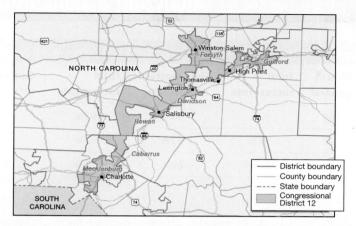

The Twelfth Congressional District of North Carolina was put in place for the 1992 elections and was one of the main districts at issue in *Shaw v. Reno*. It was designed with the aid of computer technology to merge predominantly African American communities. Known as the "I-85 district," the Twelfth stretched 160 miles across the central Piedmont region of the state. For part of its length, the district was no wider than the freeway right-of-way.

that was mostly African American. Since *Shaw v. Reno*, states are allowed to use race as a consideration, but not as the main factor, in drawing district boundaries.

Institutional Factors: The Advantages of Congressional Incumbents

Incumbency—running for reelection as opposed to running for the first time—strongly affects the outcomes of congressional elections. Incumbents usually win. Congressional incumbents possess so many advantages, such as media coverage, a record of providing benefits and legislation to a state or district, an established donor network, and name recognition, that qualified challengers often rationally wait until they can run in an open seat election after an incumbent has retired or moved on to another office.

The **incumbency advantage** is greater in the House of Representatives than in the Senate. House members run for reelection every two years, so their names are fresh in the minds of voters. House incumbents often represent safe districts, where their political party dominates the electorate. House districts are smaller than an entire state, making it easier for House members to conduct town hall meetings and provide constituent service.

Senators have longer terms, which means they may lose touch with the state residents. It is harder for them to reach constituents, because they represent large numbers of people. States are much more politically diverse than House districts, making it more difficult for senators to please voters.

Sometimes incumbents lose. A scandal might tarnish an incumbent's reelection campaign. Poor economic conditions may spark calls to "throw the bums out" among voters. House incumbents can be redistricted out of their former district, forcing them to compete against another incumbent. Redistricting may make a district more politically diverse and competitive.

incumbency
being already in office as opposed to running for the first time.

incumbency advantage
institutional advantages held by those already in office who are trying to fend off challengers in an election.

AP® TIP

The incumbency advantage is important. Know why it exists and the reasons why the advantage is greater for members of the House of Representatives than for senators.

Experience and Money

Above all else, challengers need experience and money. Experience is hard earned, usually gained by moving up through the layers of local and state politics and becoming professional, polished, and respected. Congressional elections are no place for amateurs, who

Office	Incumbents in 2016						Post-WWII Period	
	Sought reelection	Lost in Primary	Lost in general	Won in general	Total success rate	Gen. election success rate	Total success rate	Gen. election success rate
House	393	5	8	380	97%	98%	93%	94%
Senate	29	0	2	27	93%	93%	80%	84%
Governor	5	0	1	4	80%	80%	73%	78%

Data from Larry Sabato's Crystal Ball

1. Describe the incumbency advantage.

2. Describe two differences in the incumbency advantages between the House of Representatives, Senate, and governors.

3. Describe the difference between the incumbency rates in the post-WWII period and incumbency rates in 2016, and explain one reason why the rates have changed.

often lack the knowledge, political organization, and well-honed political skills to succeed in a high-stakes national campaign.

Incumbent representatives and senators possess many advantages over any candidate who may challenge them. This incumbency advantage is very strong, and it has only grown stronger in recent decades.

The vast majority of congressional incumbents who seek reelection succeed. Even in years noted for a major change in Congress, 85 or even 90 percent of House incumbents are successful. Reelection rates for incumbent senators, although lower than for the House, are still commonly at or above 80 percent.

Money matters as well. It buys more airtime, advertising, and campaign events, which are important in getting a new candidate's message out. Money also buys information. By hiring pollsters, a candidate can better understand her or his constituents' preferences. Money, especially early in a campaign, is also a weapon to scare off potential opponents and a signal to potential donors that the campaign has a shot at success.

Challengers face a difficult "chicken and egg problem." To be taken seriously, they need money, but to get money, they have to show that they are serious challengers to incumbents. Campaigns continue to get more and more expensive. In 2016, for example, the total cost of congressional races was $4 billion, while just eight years earlier it was $2.5 billion. The average cost of running for the Senate reached $1.5 million, while on average it cost a half million dollars to run for a House seat. In 2016, $59 million was spent altogether in the most expensive Senate race.[31] The fact is that most challengers lack the financial resources to wage effective campaigns.[32]

Maximizing the Advantage

Political scientist David Mayhew explained how incumbents use their advantages to maximize their chances of reelection.[33] These advantages include advertising their efforts on behalf of their constituents; this is made easier and cheaper by the franking privilege, which is free use of the mail for communication with constituents. Incumbents usually enjoy higher levels of name recognition than their challengers, which is increased by more media coverage than potential challengers. In media coverage and public events, incumbents will claim credit for what they have done in Washington and announce their positions on key pieces of legislation of interest to their constituents.[34] Finally, incumbents perform casework for individual constituents, especially in helping them deal with the federal and state bureaucracy.

Incumbents maximize their resources to try to ensure that they will not face qualified challengers. Knowing the odds, strong challengers often wait for their chance to run in an open seat election, in which there is no incumbent to face: "Experienced candidates are much more likely to be found in races for open seats, regardless of the election year."[35]

AP® REQUIRED CASES

In this chapter, you work with two Supreme Court cases related to voting rights and drawing of voting districts. The following two cases are required for the AP® U.S. Government and Politics course:

Case	Effect of the decision
Baker v. Carr (1961)	The equal protection clause requires legislative district boundaries to be drawn to have roughly the same number of constituents under the principle of "one man, one vote."
Shaw v. Reno (1993)	The Supreme Court overturned the race-conscious drawing of a strangely shaped legislative district.

Section Review

4.2 Describe congressional elections.

REMEMBER
- Factors that contribute to winning a seat in Congress include understanding one's constituency, experience, and money.
- Incumbents enjoy an easier path to reelection, whereas challengers typically try to wait for the right circumstances to make a bid.

KNOW
- *constituency*: a body of voters in a given area who elect a representative or senator. (p. 114)
- *apportionment*: the process of determining the number of representatives for each state using census data. (p. 116)
- *redistricting*: states' redrawing of boundaries of electoral districts following each census. (p. 116)
- *gerrymandering*: the intentional use of redistricting to benefit a specific interest or group of voters. (p. 117)
- *partisan gerrymandering*: drawing of district boundaries into strange shapes to benefit a political party. (p. 117)
- *majority-minority district*: a district in which voters of a minority ethnicity constitute an electoral majority within that electoral district. (p. 118)
- *malapportionment*: the uneven distribution of the population among legislative districts. (p. 118)
- *incumbency*: being already in office as opposed to running for the first time. (p. 119)
- *incumbency advantage*: institutional advantages held by those already in office who are trying to fend off challengers in an election. (p. 119)

THINK
What are the benefits and drawbacks of an election system that results in large advantages for incumbents?

Jeff Parker, Florida Today/Cagle Cartoons, Inc

Use the cartoon and your knowledge of U.S. Government and Politics to answer parts A, B, and C.

A. Describe the viewpoint expressed in the cartoon.

B. Explain why gerrymandering increases the incumbency advantage in the House of Representatives.

C. Explain one reason, other than gerrymandering, why incumbents in the House of Representatives are reelected at higher rates than incumbents in the Senate.

▰ **4.3** The Organization of Congress

The Constitution does not describe most of the day-to-day procedures of Congress, and each chamber has created and modified its own rules. Political parties, party leaders, and the committee system shape much of what happens in the House and Senate. Congressional staff and the congressional bureaucracy are involved as well. Informally, behavioral expectations and traditional ways of doing things also play a role.

Political Parties in Congress

Much of the formal structure of Congress revolves around the role of political parties and party leaders. The majority party, which is the party with the most members in each chamber, and the minority party, which has the second-highest number of members, each control important leadership positions and organize congressional behavior—both to advocate for their preferred policies and to help individual members in their reelection efforts.

Compared to many other representative democracies, party discipline in the United States has traditionally been weak. Party leaders in Congress often struggle to make sure that their own members vote in support of party positions, especially when preferences of a member's constituents clash with those of the member's political party. Leaders, however, are not powerless and have a variety of carrots and sticks with which to steer their members toward the party's goals. Party leaders work with their members to set legislative goals, choose leaders, assign members to committees, and try to present a unified message to the U.S. electorate through the media. In recent years, straight party line voting has dramatically increased.

Party Leadership in the House of Representatives

The House of Representatives has 435 members. By necessity, the House is more formally structured than the Senate, with rank-and-file House members individually less powerful than their Senate colleagues. The **Speaker of the House**—the only House leadership position described in the Constitution[36]—wields a considerable amount of power.

At the beginning of each new Congress (every two years), members of the House elect the Speaker, who has almost always been a member of the majority party. A long history of successful service in the House is usually a prerequisite. Increasingly, the ability to raise money for other members of one's party is considered in selecting a Speaker. The leadership is supported by **political action committees (PACs)**. These leadership PACs "are designed for two things: to make money and to make friends," and representatives use that money to assist fellow party members' campaigns.[37] The Speaker is second in the line of succession (behind the vice president) to the presidency in the event of death, resignation, removal from office, or inability to conduct the office's duties. The Speaker has considerable power over the House agenda and committee assignments.

Assisting the Speaker are the **House majority leader**, who is the second-in-command, and the majority **whip**. The whip collects collect information about how individual members are planning to vote, corralling their support on key votes and setting party strategy in Congress. The House **minority leader** has far less influence in the House than the Speaker but works to coordinate minority party activity, opposition to the majority party, and overall strategy. House minority party leadership also includes its own whips.

Party Leadership in the Senate

Constitutionally, the official leader of the Senate is the vice president of the United States,[38] though he or she can only cast a vote in the event of a tie. The president pro tempore presides over the chamber's proceedings when the vice president is not present (which is almost all of the time) but wields no real power. Typically, junior senators fill in to oversee the day-to-day proceedings.

The most powerful position in the Senate is the **Senate majority leader**, who is chosen from the majority party. Individual senators retain more power than their colleagues in the House, and the Senate majority leader is not as powerful as the Speaker of the House. However, he or she plays a key role in shaping the legislative agenda. The Senate minority leader acts as the leader of the opposition in the Senate. Assisting both party leaders are party whips and leadership committees.

The Committee System

Congress deals with weighty and complex issues. There is no way any one member can be involved directly in each piece of legislation. To divide the workload, both the House and the Senate have established a system of committees and subcommittees that do most of the work of Congress. Writing about congressional government in 1885, Princeton professor of politics and future president Woodrow Wilson observed, "It is not far from the truth to say that Congress in session is Congress on public exhibition, whilst Congress in its committee-rooms is Congress at work."[39]

Speaker of the House
the leader of the House of Representatives, chosen by an election of its members.

political action committee (PAC)
an organization that raises money for candidates and campaigns.

House majority leader
the person who is the second in command of the House of Representatives.

whip
a member of Congress, chosen by his or her party members, whose job is to ensure party unity and discipline.

minority leader
the head of the party with the second-highest number of seats in Congress, chosen by the party's members.

Senate majority leader
the person who has the most power in the Senate and is the head of the party with the most seats.

Committee Membership and Leadership

committee chair
leader of a congressional committee who has authority over the committee's agenda.

Committee membership is determined by party leaders and generally reflects the ratio of party membership in each chamber. **Committee chairs** have considerable influence over committee processes, especially in setting the committee's agenda. Because of the differences in the size of the chambers, House committees tend to have more members than Senate committees, while individual senators tend to serve on more committees than their colleagues in the House. Since 1995, when Republicans took control of the House for the first time in forty years, seniority is no longer used to determine who chairs a committee, as it had been since 1911. Party leaders now have the say in who is selected. Meanwhile, Republicans have placed term limits on chairs. With both of these changes, the party leaders, not committee chairs, have exerted greater control over the legislative business.[40]

New representatives and senators often try to get appointed to committees that deal with issues of interest to their constituents or that provide benefits to their districts and states. This adds to their incumbency advantage. Requests for committee membership may be driven by genuine policy interests on the part of members of Congress.[41] Other factors also shape committee assignments. In 2017, Rep. Ken Buck (R-CO) wrote that for freshman lawmakers to get good committee assignments they were charged dues, money that would go to the party. For a good committee, such as Judiciary, the fund-raising requirement was $220,000, while for the powerful Ways and Means Committee the price was $450,000. The cost of chairing committees is even higher. Senator Buck reports, for example, that chairing top committees requires dues of $1.2 million. To be the Speaker of the House, the dues rose to $20 million.[42]

Types of Committees

Congress has four types of committees: standing, joint, conference, and select. Standing committees are where most of the work of Congress gets done. They are permanent and divided by policy area, and members tend to serve on them for multiple terms, developing expertise (See Table 4.3.) Standing committees consider legislation and exercise oversight of bureaucratic agencies, usually recommending funding levels for them. Standing committees are divided into subcommittees, which specialize even further, usually considering parts of legislation under instructions from their parent committees.

Joint committees contain members of both the House and the Senate. They focus public attention on an issue, gather information for Congress, or help party leaders speed things along in the legislative process.

The conference committee is a temporary joint committee that resolves differences between the House and Senate versions of a bill, which is required by the Constitution before a president can sign the bill into law. Party leaders determine conference committee membership, though members who have been centrally involved in a bill are usually included.

The fourth type of committee is the select or special committee. These temporary bodies are usually called upon to investigate an issue, sometimes in response to a crisis or a scandal.

Congressional Staff and the Congressional Bureaucracy

Congressional staff assists representatives and senators in providing casework and gives members information about policies, legislation, and constituent preferences. Staff often works closely with members in drafting bills. As the size of the American republic and the complexity of issues before Congress have both grown, so has the size of the congressional staff.

TABLE 4.3 Standing Committees in the 115th Congress

House of Representatives	Senate
Agriculture	Agriculture, Nutrition, and Forestry
Appropriations	Appropriations
Armed Services	Armed Services
Budget	Banking, Housing, and Urban Affairs
Education and Workforce	Budget
Energy and Commerce	Commerce, Science, and Transportation
Financial Services	Energy and Natural Resources
Foreign Affairs	Environment and Public Works
Homeland Security	Finance
House Administration	Foreign Relations
Judiciary	Health, Education, Labor, and Pensions
Natural Resources	Homeland Security and Governmental Affairs
Rules	Judiciary
Science, Space, and Technology	Rules and Administration
Small Business	Small Business and Entrepreneurship
Transportation and Infrastructure	Veterans' Affairs
Veterans' Affairs	
Ways and Means	

Note: Does not include joint and select committees.

Norms of Behavior

Norms are unwritten expectations of how members are supposed to act and contribute to the smooth functioning of the Congress. Members are expected to be respectful toward their colleagues, to reciprocate help from other members, and to specialize in one or more policy areas to assist the overall level of information and expertise in Congress. Animosity between members of the two political parties has grown, which challenges the traditional norms of behavior in Congress, making compromise harder to achieve.

Section Review

4.3 Compare the authority and roles affecting the policymaking process in the House of Representatives and the Senate.

REMEMBER
- Political parties exert a good deal of influence in Congress. Both the majority and minority parties in Congress control key leadership positions and work to advance policy goals and get members reelected. The Speaker of the House is especially powerful, and the Senate majority leader also plays a key role.
- Congressional committees do most of the work of Congress and are divided into types specializing in different subject areas.
- A large congressional staff assists with casework, researching and drafting policy and legislation, and constituent preferences.

KNOW

- *Speaker of the House*: the leader of the House of Representatives, chosen by an election of its members. (p. 123)
- *political action committee (PAC)*: an organization that raises money for candidates and campaigns. (p. 123)
- *House majority leader*: the person who is the second in command of the House of Representatives. (p. 123)
- *whip*: a member of Congress, chosen by his or her party members, whose job is to ensure party unity and discipline. (p. 123)
- *minority leader*: the head of the party with the second-highest number of seats in Congress, chosen by the party's members. (p. 123)
- *Senate majority leader*: the person who has the most power in the Senate and is the head of the party with the most seats. (p. 123)
- *committee chair*: leader of a congressional committee who has authority over the committee's agenda. (p. 124)

THINK

- How is Congress organized to make policy efficiently?
- How is Congress organized to make effective policy?

4.3 Review Question: Free Response

Congressional leadership and the committee system play a large role in how Congress functions.

Use the scenario and your knowledge of U.S. Government and Politics to answer parts A, B, and C.

A. Describe one way in which the committee system impacts legislation.

B. Describe one difference between the role played by party leaders in the House and the role played by party leaders in the Senate.

C. Explain one reason why it is difficult for party leaders to control the way the members of their party vote on legislation.

◼◼ 4.4 "I'm Just a Bill"

One of the classic *Schoolhouse Rock!* animated educational videos that aired on ABC on Saturday mornings in the 1970s and 1980s was "I'm Just a Bill," the story of a "sad little scrap of paper" sitting on the steps of Capitol Hill hoping to become a law someday. Happily, our little cartoon legislative friend, Bill, succeeds in his dream, announcing triumphantly, "Oh! Yes!" when told that the president had just signed him into law.[43]

Although there was much useful information in that short cartoon, it could have been more realistic. Bill could have been "surrounded by ninety or so expired comrades scattered about the steps of Capitol Hill."[44]

Bill, star of the classic *Schoolhouse Rock!* video, sits on the shoulder of a smiling congressperson, sporting his new medal "Law." In the real world, Bill would have faced frustration. Most bills do not make it through the legislative process to become laws.
Kari Rene Hall/Getty Images

The Legislative Process

By design, the legislative process is complicated and multi-stepped, with each stage offering another chance to kill a prospective law. The framers of the Constitution—having seen the passions of the people sweep through state legislatures and sometimes trample on minority rights—intentionally placed many hurdles in the path of legislation. (See Figure 4.5 on the next page for the many steps in the legislative process.)

The First Step: Introduction

The first stage of the legislative process is the formal introduction of a bill in either the House or the Senate. Only members of Congress may introduce a bill. In practice, however, interest groups often play a role in shaping a bill or encouraging a member to introduce it. Presidents can encourage members of either chamber to get a major piece of legislation on the national legislative agenda, whether through discussions with party leaders or though appeals to the American public.

For a bill to become law, it must pass in both the House of Representatives and the Senate. Formally, only the House may introduce revenue bills. In practice, however, both chambers often act at the same time on similar policies, with frequent communication between party leaders of each chamber.

The vast majority of bills never become law, and members realize these odds. According to political scientist Barbara Sinclair, members may introduce legislation for a variety of reasons. They may want to placate a persistent interest group in their home state. Sometimes members of Congress introduce legislation to call attention to a problem that has been ignored or to propose an innovative approach to an acknowledged problem. Members may not want or expect some of their bills to pass.[45]

Referral to Committee

Because committees are so important to the ultimate success or failure of a bill, assignment to committee involves strategic political calculations. Bills may be assigned to more than one committee—a process called multiple-referral—especially if the bill is large and complex.

Committees and Subcommittees in Action

Once referred to one or more committees, legislation is usually sent to one or more subcommittees—more narrowly focused groups of legislators operating under the guidance of a parent committee. Committees and subcommittees hold hearings to gather information about a bill. Individuals outside of Congress may be brought in to testify and offer their expertise. The markup session allows committee members to make changes to a bill before the committee reports it to the floor. The committee report follows the bill from committee to the floor. It acts as a history of the bill and offers guidance to administrative agencies and (if necessary) courts about the committee's intent regarding the bill. Sometimes early cost estimates of the bill's provisions are included in the conference report.

The number of congressional hearings has declined by more than 50 percent since the mid-1970s, while the number of staff members has also declined.[46] As a result, members of Congress rely more and more on interest groups for analysis and information.

Congressional committees are the graveyards of most bills. Had our cartoon friend, Bill, wanted to visit his deceased comrades to pay his animated respects, congressional committees are the battlegrounds on which he would have found most of their parchment

FIGURE 4.5

The Legislative Process

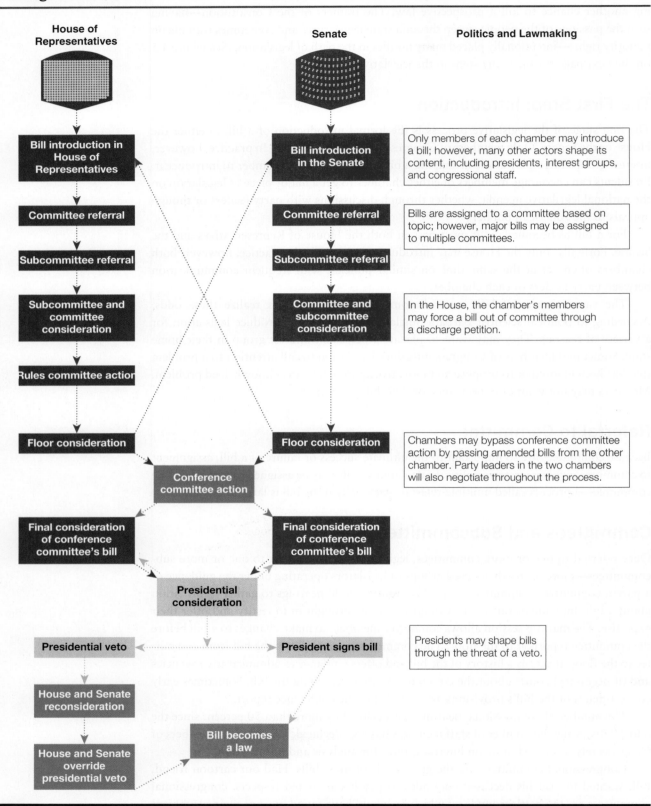

House of Representatives

Senate

Politics and Lawmaking

Bill introduction in House of Representatives

Bill introduction in the Senate

Only members of each chamber may introduce a bill; however, many other actors shape its content, including presidents, interest groups, and congressional staff.

Committee referral

Committee referral

Bills are assigned to a committee based on topic; however, major bills may be assigned to multiple committees.

Subcommittee referral

Subcommittee referral

Subcommittee and committee consideration

Committee and subcommittee consideration

In the House, the chamber's members may force a bill out of committee through a discharge petition.

Rules committee action

Floor consideration

Floor consideration

Chambers may bypass conference committee action by passing amended bills from the other chamber. Party leaders in the two chambers will also negotiate throughout the process.

Conference committee action

Final consideration of conference committee's bill

Final consideration of conference committee's bill

Presidential consideration

Presidential veto

President signs bill

Presidents may shape bills through the threat of a veto.

House and Senate reconsideration

House and Senate override presidential veto

Bill becomes a law

FIGURE 4.6

Congressional Workdays: On the Decline

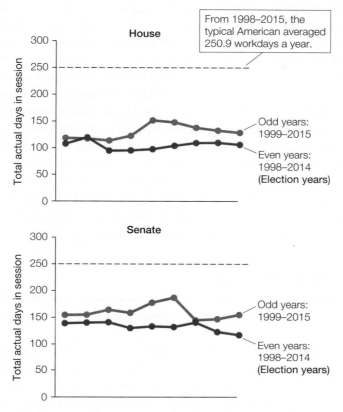

In 2015, the first year of a two-year Congress, the U.S. House of Representatives put in 130 working days. That number has steadily declined since 2007, when the House worked 153 days. The Senate was also down to 156 days from a high of 188 days in 2009.

Data from Reuters

---

remains. In committee, bills can die from a committee's refusal to report the bill to the full chamber, changes made to them to make them impassable on the House or Senate floor, or simple neglect.

The committee may reject the bill by vote, or it may table the bill with no further action. In the House, a member may file a **discharge petition** to free a bill from an unfriendly committee and move it to the House floor for a vote if a majority of representatives agrees. Discharge efforts are rarely successful, but they can serve to "pressure a committee and the majority party leadership to bring to the floor measures that they would rather not consider."[47]

In recent years, Congress has been in session fewer days, held fewer hearings, and passed fewer bills. (See Figure 4.6.) Major bills, such as the 2017 effort to repeal the Patient Protection and Affordable Care Act (Obamacare), largely bypassed the committee process, with almost no hearings or analysis by non-partisan staff before votes were held.[48]

discharge petition
a motion filed by a member of Congress to move a bill out of committee and onto the floor of the House of Representatives for a vote.

Floor Consideration

Once they have successfully passed out of committee, bills proceed to consideration on the floors of the House and the Senate.

Consideration in the House of Representatives

House Rules Committee
a powerful committee that determines when a bill will be subject to debate and vote on the House floor, how long the debate will last, and whether amendments will be allowed on the floor.

Committee of the Whole
consists of all members of the House and meets in the House chamber but is governed by different rules, making it easier to consider complex and controversial legislation.

An important difference between the House and the Senate is the role of the **House Rules Committee**. A majority of the House Rules Committee's members is chosen by the Speaker. This committee determines when a bill will be subject to debate and vote on the House floor, how long the debate will last, and whether amendments will be allowed on the floor. These special rules can play a major role in whether the bill passes the House or not. The **Committee of the Whole** consists of all members of the House of Representatives and meets in the House chamber, but it is governed by different rules of procedure than when the House of Representatives normally meets. Only one hundred members are needed for a quorum. The Committee of the Whole gives the House a faster means for considering the complex and often controversial legislation referred to it. The House resolves itself into a new Committee of the Whole to consider a particular bill. A specific Committee of the Whole is dissolved when it reports with a recommendation to the House.[49]

A roll-call vote is a vote in which each member of the chamber debating a bill indicates "yea," "nay," or "present." In the House, most votes are electronic. Interest groups keep track of key votes on issues relevant to them, scoring individual members on how friendly or unfriendly their votes have been to that interest group.

Consideration in the Senate

hold
a delay placed on legislation by a senator who objects to a bill.

unanimous consent agreement
an agreement in the Senate that sets the terms for consideration of a bill.

filibuster
a tactic through which an individual senator may use the right of unlimited debate to delay a motion or postpone action on a piece of legislation.

cloture
a procedure through which senators can end debate on a bill and proceed to action, provided 60 senators agree to it.

Individual senators have more ability to shape outcomes on the floor than their House colleagues. Party leadership still matters, however, and the Senate majority leaders schedule the agenda.

If a senator objects to a bill or part of a bill, that senator may place a **hold** on the legislation and communicate to the majority leader her or his reservations about the bill. The ability to place holds, offer amendments, and debate issues allows a senator to consume Congress's scarcest resource: time. As political scientist Barbara Sinclair reports, "A single dissatisfied senator, even if she is junior and a minority party member, can cause a great deal of trouble."[50] While the majority leader does not have to honor the hold request, a hold indicates the possibility of a filibuster on the bill. **Unanimous consent agreements** set terms for the consideration of a specified bill. The majority leader or floor manager of the measure usually proposes these agreements, and they reflect negotiations among interested senators. These agreements may limit the time available for debate. Some agreements permit only specified amendments. Unanimous consent agreements may contain other provisions, such as allowing the majority leader to call up the measure at will.[51]

The Senate operates on the principle of unlimited debate. A **filibuster** is the power of an individual senator to talk and talk and talk to delay a motion or vote on the floor.[52] The senator leading the filibuster can read from Harry Potter or a cookbook, as long as he or she keeps talking. Only a successful vote of **cloture**, which requires three-fifths of senators (60), can shut down debate and end a filibuster, allowing the Senate to move on to a vote. Therefore, a determined minority party, provided they have at least forty-one seats and maintain party unity, can use a filibuster to delay or kill legislation. Filibusters are not mentioned in the Constitution but are simply part of the rules the Senate has adopted. Until the early twentieth century, there was no way to stop a filibuster. The Senate changed its rules and provided that if two-thirds of the Senate agreed, a filibuster would be ended. In the 1970s, the threshold for a vote of cloture was lowered to 60. Filibusters were rare until very recently. From the 1970s to the past ten years, there were only about two or three a month. Beginning in 2006, and increasing with the election of Barack Obama, the number rose to two per week.[53]

The placing of holds and threats of a filibuster have become more common in a closely split and deeply divided Senate. Because of the increased use of threats of a filibuster, votes of cloture have become much more numerous as well. In spite of frequent calls to eliminate or reform the filibuster, doing so would require changing the rules of the Senate. Further, individual senators may be reluctant to give up a power that can result in favors for their home states during negotiations to avoid a threatened filibuster.

Senators may not only threaten to filibuster a bill that they object to. They may also hold up an unrelated vote or confirmation of a presidential nominee to extract concessions, a process referred to as hostage-taking.[54] In March 2013, Rand Paul (R-KY) held up the confirmation of John Brennan as director of the Central Intelligence Agency to push the Obama administration to clarify in writing that drone strikes would not be carried out on Americans on U.S. soil in the absence of an imminent threat. Senator Paul was concerned that drone strikes violated several constitutional liberties, including the right to be informed of charges and a trial by jury.[55] During

The filibuster by Senator Rand Paul (R-KY) of John Brennan's nomination as CIA director was surpassed in length by Senator Chris Murphy (D-CT). This photo shows Sen. Murphy concluding his speech by showing a photo of a boy killed through gun violence at Sandy Hook School, which happened in Sen. Murphy's home state.
C-Span

the filibuster, one tweet wryly commented, "It turns out that people all over the political spectrum strongly favor the idea of not being murdered by flying robots."[56] Senator Paul ended his filibuster after nearly thirteen hours—by his own account, defeated by biological necessity.[57] He had, however, used the power of an individual senator to force a discussion about the issue of drone strikes, and he also earned himself national public attention. In June 2016, Chris Murphy (D-CT) filibustered for fifteen hours to call attention to gun violence, ending his speech with a photo of Dylan Hockley, a six-year-old boy who was killed in the shooting at Sandy Hook Elementary School.[58]

Resolution of Differences between House and Senate Bills

Conference committees reconcile differences between two versions of a bill. On minor bills, or when the differences are small, one chamber may avoid going to conference by simply accepting the other chamber's version of the bill. This especially happens late in a session when time is scarce and can be used by the political opposition as a weapon.[59] Sometimes the bill goes through the process of reconciliation, where the bill is sent to a committee to adjust spending, taxing, or the debt limit to meet the final budget resolution. The budget resolution is the total amount of revenue and expenditures in that year's budget.

Once differences between the two versions have been resolved, the single bill goes back to each chamber for reconsideration, without the possibility of amendment. By this point, on major bills, party leaders have already engaged in lengthy negotiations with their counterparts in the other chamber to avoid any surprises.

Presidential Action

Following successful passage in each chamber, the bill goes to the president for action. Under Article I, Section 7, the president then has three choices for each bill that lands on

veto
the power of a president to reject a bill passed by Congress, sending it back to the originating branch with objections.

her or his desk. The president may sign it, in which case the bill becomes a law. He may **veto** it, sending it back to Congress with his objections. The president may allow a bill to become law through inaction. A bill automatically becomes law if the president doesn't sign it within ten days while Congress is in session.[60] Bills that are vetoed can still become law if two-thirds of both chambers vote to override the president's veto. Veto overrides are not common and signal a deep disconnect between a president and Congress.

Section Review

4.4 Explain the lawmaking process.

REMEMBER
- Before they can become law, bills must be passed by both the House and Senate and then approved by the president. They are first introduced in either chamber, then referred to committee. The committee and/or subcommittee may take various actions, such as holding hearings, marking up the bill, or voting on the bill. The bill might be sent to a committee for reconciliation. The bill then proceeds to the House or Senate floor for a vote. Finally, the bill moves on to the president for consideration.
- Some bills go to multiple committees. Bills can be forced out of committees through discharge petition. Presidents have the ability to shape bills through the threat of a veto vote.
- Actors other than members of Congress may play a role in influencing whether a bill gets introduced.
- Most bills are never passed.

KNOW
- *discharge petition*: a motion filed by a member of Congress to move a bill out of committee and onto the floor of the House of Representatives for a vote. (p. 129)
- *House Rules Committee*: a powerful committee that determines when a bill will be subject to debate and vote on the House floor, how long the debate will last, and whether amendments will be allowed on the floor. (p. 130)
- *Committee of the Whole*: Consists of all members of the House and meets in the House chamber but is governed by different rules, making it easier to consider complex and controversial legislation. (p. 130)
- *hold*: a delay placed on legislation by a senator who objects to a bill. (p. 130)
- *unanimous consent agreement*: an agreement in the Senate that sets the terms for consideration of a bill. (p. 130)
- *filibuster*: a tactic through which an individual senator may use the right of unlimited debate to delay a motion or postpone action on a piece of legislation. (p. 130)
- *cloture*: a procedure through which senators can end debate on a bill and proceed to action, provided 60 senators agree to it. (p. 130)
- *veto*: the power of a president to reject a bill passed by Congress, sending it back to the originating branch with objections. (p. 132)

THINK
Should the lawmaking process be simplified to reduce gridlock? How?

4.4 Review Question: Free Response

One of the most cherished safeguards of liberty in our government [is]—the right of a political minority to have a voice. Until now, this has always been the defining characteristic of the Senate. That's why all senators have traditionally defended the Senate as an institution, because they knew that the Senate was the last legislative check for political minorities and small states against the kind of raw exercise of power large states and majority parties have always been tempted to wield.

—Senator Mitch McConnell[61]

Use the quote and your knowledge of U.S. Government and Politics to answer parts A, B, and C.

A. Describe the viewpoint expressed in the quote.

B. Describe one advantage of the filibuster in the lawmaking process.

C. Explain two reasons why the filibuster has been criticized.

4.5 Congress and the Budget

The Budget and Accounting Act of 1921 established the basis of modern federal budgeting processes, particularly with its incorporation of the president as a key part of the process. In 1970, the **Office of Management and Budget (OMB)** was established to assist the president in setting national spending priorities.

Setting the Federal Budget

As with other kinds of lawmaking we have covered in this book, setting the federal budget occurs in several stages. In setting the national budget, the federal government operates in some ways like an American household, considering money coming in and money going out.

Step 1: The President's Proposed Budget

The Congressional Budget and Impoundment and Control Act of 1974[62] modified the process of setting the federal budget, requiring that the president's proposed budget be reviewed by congressional committees. The committees are assisted by advice and research from the Congressional Budget Office (CBO). The federal government's fiscal year begins in October, and the president is expected to submit a proposed budget to Congress in February of that year. The president's proposal carries no constitutional weight, but it does carry a great deal of political weight.

The majority of any fiscal year's federal budget has already been allocated or promised. **Entitlement programs** provide benefits to those who qualify for them by law. Entitlement programs include Social Security and Medicare, and they consume the bulk of yearly federal spending. Because this spending is "locked in," it is referred to as **mandatory spending**. The amount available for **discretionary spending**—spending for programs and policies at the discretion of Congress and the president, including defense spending—constitutes a much smaller slice of the pie.

Step 2: Congress Acts

In response to a president's proposals, Congress is expected to produce a budget resolution that provides broad outlines for federal spending. The real action, however, happens in the House and Senate appropriations committees, which set the budgets for departments, agencies, and bureaus. These committees then submit budget resolutions that are passed from Congress to the president for approval.

The budgeting process influences both the total amount of money the national government plans to spend and the ways in which that money is allocated. It also sends a signal to other nations and their economic policymakers as well as the international financial markets about the soundness of American economic policy.

Taxation, Deficits, and Debts

The federal government taxes citizens to pay for spending. Aside from a brief period during the Civil War, individual incomes were not taxed until 1913 and the ratification of the Sixteenth Amendment,[63] which instituted a national income tax.[64]

Office of Management and Budget (OMB)
the executive branch office that assists the president in setting national spending priorities.

entitlement program
a program that provides benefits for those who qualify under the law, regardless of income.

mandatory spending
spending required by existing laws that is "locked in" the budget.

discretionary spending
spending for programs and policies at the discretion of Congress and the president.

FIGURE 4.7

Federal Budget Deficits, Historical and Projected

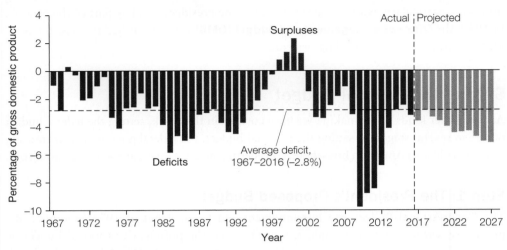

Data from Congressional Budget Office

Federal taxation policies, as complicated as they may seem to individual taxpayers, determine the amount of money that the federal government takes in to pay for its fiscal policies. If the federal government takes in more money than it spends, it runs a **budget surplus**. If not, it runs a **budget deficit**, forcing it to borrow. On this issue, one thing is clear: The federal government will be borrowing for the foreseeable future. (See Figure 4.7.) For the federal government, incurring deficits to meet immediate needs or to finance investment in the American economy that will produce higher tax revenues in the future can be a rational choice. Deficit spending, though, shows no signs of abating.

The **national debt** continues to grow and was roughly $20.5 trillion in November 2017.[65] According to data from the Bureau of Economic Analysis of the U.S. Department of Commerce, the estimate of American GDP was about $19.5 trillion, meaning that the federal government owes more than a year's production of the entire national economy.[66]

Congress and Public Policy: Social Insurance

The budget is a reflection of public policy. Social Security, for example, is a program that continues to impact the federal budget. The Social Security Act of 1935 created a set of programs to support vulnerable groups of Americans. It established unemployment insurance for workers and set up the Old Age Insurance and Old Age Assistance programs, which were later supplemented with disability insurance.[67] Social Security was designed to be self-funding so as not to force the government to raise taxes and further depress the economy. Its ability to be sustained in the twenty-first century—when life spans are significantly longer than when the program was first enacted—is the subject of much current debate in American politics. While the Social Security Act created several types of

budget surplus
the amount of money remaining when the government takes in more than it spends.

budget deficit
the shortfall when a government takes in less money than it spends.

national debt
the total amount of money owed by the federal government.

insurance, the term *Social Security* is generally used to refer to old-age insurance, which protects against the loss of income in an individual's later years.

Social Security is an example of an entitlement program because it is financed by current payroll taxes paid by individuals and does not have income-based requirements to receive its benefits. Those who meet the requirements, such as age or a minimum number of years of payroll contributions, are entitled to receive the benefits, regardless of income. The level of benefits received depends upon one's contributions during his or her working years, or the contributions of one's spouse in the case of survivorship. As of January 2017, the average monthly benefit was $1,360 a month, with a maximum monthly benefit of $2,687. Each recipient's benefit depends upon his or her earnings history.[68]

Americans do not have individual accounts like a savings account at a bank. Instead, payments to current recipients come from current payees. In 2017, about 62 million Americans were receiving a total of $1 trillion in Social Security benefits. The majority received retirement benefits, although disabled workers and survivors also constituted a significant percentage of recipients.[69]

Due to an increase in life expectancies in recent decades, the adjustment of benefits to account for inflation, and the tens of millions of Americans born in the years following the end of World War II (often called "baby boomers") reaching their retirement years, the system has come under severe financial stress. According to the Office of Social Security, "In 1940, the life expectancy of a 65-year-old was almost 14 additional years; today it is about 20. By 2033, the number of older Americans will increase from 46.6 million today to over 77 million. There are currently 2.8 workers for each Social Security beneficiary. By 2033, there will be 2.1 workers for each beneficiary."[70]

If no changes to the law are made, current projections indicate that three-quarters of promised benefits will be paid.[71] Fixing the shortfall is not just a problem of mathematics; it is also a problem of politics. Reducing benefits to current recipients would produce a backlash from a large group of politically active Americans who would mobilize to ensure the continuation of the program. Raising the payroll tax on current workers is another possibility, though, again, one with significant political risk for lawmakers if enacted.

Another solution that has been proposed is allowing individuals to invest some of their funds in privately directed investment accounts under the logic that individuals will be more careful and skillful in seeking higher returns on "their" money. Others counter that such a plan would create too much personal risk and leave individuals at the mercy of market corrections or poor investing strategies.

FIRST PENSION RECIPIENT
FIRST TO GET AID INCREASE
LUDLOW, Vt., Oct. 3 (P).—Miss Ida M. Fuller, 76, first person in the United States to receive an old-age insurance check, today was the first in the nation to receive her increased benefit check under the new Social Security law.
Miss Fuller received serial check 00-000-001 Jan. 17, 1940

In January 1940, Ida May Fuller of Ludlow, Vermont, became the first beneficiary under the Social Security system. She is shown here holding her first check.
GRANGER/Granger, NYC

4.5 Describe how Congress creates a budget that addresses discretionary and mandatory spending.

REMEMBER
- The president proposes a budget for each federal fiscal year, and the Congress votes on the president's proposals, typically after amending the budget.
- The budget covers discretionary spending (money that can be allocated for any purpose) and mandatory spending (the majority of outlays, which are required to be paid).
- The federal budget may result in a surplus or a deficit, although deficit spending is more common in recent years.
- Social Security is the largest social program of the U.S. government and is an entitlement program that most Americans participate in.

KNOW
- *Office of Management and Budget (OMB)*: the executive branch office that assists the president in setting national spending priorities. (p. 133)
- *entitlement program*: a program that provides benefits for those who qualify under the law, regardless of income. (p. 133)
- *mandatory spending*: spending required by existing laws that is "locked in" the budget. (p. 133)
- *discretionary spending*: spending for programs and policies at the discretion of Congress and the president. (p. 133)
- *budget surplus*: the amount of money remaining when the government takes in more than it spends. (p. 134)
- *budget deficit*: the shortfall when a government takes in less money than it spends. (p. 134)
- *national debt*: the total amount of money owed by the federal government. (p. 134)

THINK   What factors make it difficult for Congress to control the budget?

4.5 Review Question: Free Response

Mandatory and Discretionary Spending in the 2015 Budget

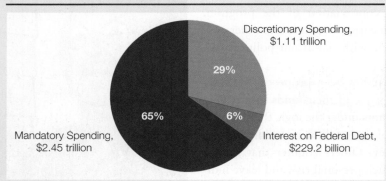

Data from Office of Management and Budget and the National Priorities Project

A. Use the pie chart and your knowledge of U.S. Government and Politics to explain why it is difficult for Congress to create new programs.

B. Explain how the Social Security program makes it difficult for Congress to control spending.

C. Explain why it is difficult to make changes to the Social Security program.

■■ 4.6 Challenges of Representation

Voters select representatives who may or may not share their policy preferences, identities, interests, and experiences. Constituents expect their representatives to add their voices to the debates and deliberations in Congress. Voters want their representatives to be effective in Washington, which takes them away from home. However, voters also want members of Congress to come home and explain what they have been up to and what they plan to accomplish.[72] More time at home connects representatives and senators to their constituents, yet effective representation means spending time operating in the intricate machinery of Congress.

Acting in Congress

Passing laws is Congress's most important task, and it is easy for constituents to learn how their representatives voted on an issue. However, the process of legislation involves many stages and many less visible acts, such as committee work, bill sponsorship, and negotiation that can pose a challenge to constituents trying to keep tabs on their elected representatives.

Legislators' Voting Decisions

Members of Congress consider several factors when voting on a law.[73] First, they must consider their constituents' interests. Though a senator or representative may ultimately decide to vote against the wishes of their constituents, no member can ignore voters repeatedly without facing a backlash. If, however, a senator or representative has earned a level of trust from constituents—from long and successful service to them—then she or he may be more willing to act against constituent interests if it feels like the right course of action.[74]

A member's political party also influences how that member will vote. Members may seek input from their colleagues, especially if those colleagues are policy specialists with expertise relevant to a bill. Input from a member's congressional staff may play a role, as may signals from interest groups, especially if people from the interest groups can convince the representative that his or her constituents agree with the group's position. Campaign donors also influence the voting decisions of members of Congress. Political scientists have measured how members of Congress vote and compared these votes to their constituents' opinions and found that the preferences of average voters do not count as much as upper-income voters and donors. Still, members of Congress must balance these interests to remain in office.[75] Finally, the president may try to persuade representatives to vote a certain way, especially if they are in the same political party.

Representing Constituents

Members of Congress may play three roles. The **delegate role** emphasizes that the main duty of members of Congress is to carry out their constituents' wishes. Working as **trustees**, members of Congress make decisions using their knowledge and judgment, and voters rely on the judgment of the member in policymaking. The **politico role** emphasizes that Congress is a politicized body, and its members must balance their choices with the interests of constituents and their political party.

Elections are the main method voters have to shape the actions of their elected representatives, whether by extracting promises from candidates during the election campaign or by the threat of backlash in the future if those promises are not kept.[76] Both of these mechanisms, however, require basic information from constituents and representatives.

delegate role
the idea that the main duty of a member of Congress is to carry out constituents' wishes.

trustee role
the idea that members of Congress should act as trustees, making decisions based on their knowledge and judgment.

politico role
representation where members of Congress balance their choices with the interests of their constituents and parties in making decisions.

Just a few days before a Senate vote in July 2017 to repeal the Patient Protection and Affordable Care Act (Obamacare), eighty-year-old Senator John McCain announced that he had a form of brain cancer. McCain's personal experience and his long career in the Senate shaped how he approached a bill that he considered poorly written and forced through the chamber. "Ultimately, I think a lot of it comes down to the unique nature of Sen. McCain as a person and a legislator," Greg Vigdor, president of the Arizona Hospital and Healthcare Association, said. "He really believes in the Senate as the great bastion of debate and deliberate consideration."[79] McCain is shown here leaving the Senate chamber after the repeal vote failed.

Justin Sullivan/Getty Images

Constituents must have policy preferences to begin with and must communicate those preferences to their representatives. Constituents must also have basic information about the actions of their representatives in Congress to know whether to reward or punish those representatives in the next election.

Unfortunately, a long tradition of research in political science has shown that on most issues the majority of constituents is poorly informed, has little interest, or lacks coherent policy preferences. It's hard to keep track of every issue, even for those who are actively interested in politics. Some constituents are far better informed than others, especially if they are part of an interest group for the purpose of influencing congressional action. This inequality of information runs the risk of tilting Congress in the direction favored by the most informed and involved constituents to the detriment of the majority of uninformed ones.

Incumbents cannot afford to ignore uninformed voters. Interest groups may act on the behalf of less informed and less aware voters.[77] Congressional challengers may bring up issues in a campaign that incumbents incorporate into their own agendas.[78] Even the most secure incumbents worry about an issue that may cause their constituents alarm. Successful incumbents plan ahead to ward off problems.

The Problem of Partisanship

Political scientists, congressional observers, and some members of Congress have become increasingly concerned about trends in partisan polarization in which members of parties vote and act strongly with their own party and become less likely to cross the aisle and cooperate with each other. While scholars disagree about the causes of polarization in Congress, voting records on the House and Senate floor show a clear trend away from **bipartisanship**, where the parties work together to pass legislation.[80]

Intense partisanship can lead to acrimony between members. It may also contribute to **gridlock**, when Congress's ability to legislate is slowed or stopped by its inability to overcome divisions, especially those based on partisanship. Gridlock is made more likely in a period of **divided government**, which occurs when control of the presidency and one or both chambers of Congress is split between the two major parties. Partisanship may also result in presidential initiatives and nominees being blocked by the opposing party,

bipartisanship
agreement between the parties to work together in Congress to pass legislation.

gridlock
a slowdown or halt in Congress's ability to legislate and overcome divisions, especially those based on partisanship.

divided government
control of the presidency and one or both chambers of Congress split between the two major parties.

Analyzing Visual Data: How to Visualize Partisan Polarization

In this dot-distribution map, each dot represents a data point. These maps can be visually appealing, but they have drawbacks.

1. Describe what the map shows about partisan polarization.

2. Describe one advantage of a dot distribution map in visualizing partisan polarization.

3. Describe two drawbacks of using dot distribution maps in analyzing data.

Data from Clio Andris et al., "The Rise of Partisanship and Super-Cooperators in the U.S. House of Representatives," *PloS One* 10, no. 4 (2015)
© 2015 Andris et al.

especially when a president who has not been reelected or is leaving office is in a **lame duck period** near the end of the presidential term.

lame duck period period at the end of a presidential term when Congress may block presidential initiatives and nominees.

The Roles of a Member of Congress

Many of the framers expected that Congress would be a reflection of the people of the republic, although the definition of who had the right to be represented was highly restricted. Several challenges arise when attempting to view Congress as a portrait of America. No single member can represent each of his or her constituents' diverse identities, experiences, and interests. People expect members of Congress to know more about politics than the average voter.

Descriptive Representation: Reflecting Constituents' Characteristics

When scholars talk about making Congress a more accurate reflection of America, they are referring to descriptive representation, in which members of Congress "mirror some of the more frequent experiences and outward manifestations of belonging to the group."[81] Usually a focus on increasing descriptive representation in Congress aims to increase the membership of a particular group, like women and ethnic minorities, who remain underrepresented in proportion to their share of the population.[82]

Members of Congress today do not come close to mirroring the American electorate. As a whole, members of Congress tend to be older, whiter, wealthier, and more educated than the American electorate.

Although Congress remains descriptively unrepresentative, there has been improvement in recent elections. As with all data stories told with graphs, how one draws the *scale* of the chart, the vertical or *y*-axis here, can leave the viewer with different impressions of the same data. Consider this graph of the percentages of women in the Senate over the past twenty-five Congresses (fifty years).

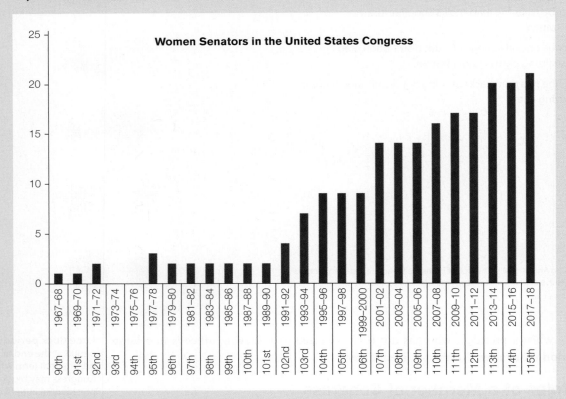

Women Senators in the United States Congress

In this bar chart, the gains made by women in recent elections look quite impressive. Notice, however, that the *y*-axis (the vertical one) does not go from 0 to 100—the number of senators—but from 1 to 25. Consider the same data but with the scale of the *y*-axis showing the full range of the number of senators, from 0 to 100.

This presentation of the same data in the second graph gives a different impression. With the full scale corrected to a range from 0 to 100, recent gains in the descriptive representation of women in the Senate do not look so impressive. The tactic of cutting off the scale of a graph can be used to either draw a pessimistic or an optimistic portrait, depending on the storyteller's

While Congress has grown more descriptively representative in recent years, women; lower-income Americans; members of racial and ethnic minorities; union members; members of certain religious faiths; and gay, lesbian, and transgendered Americans remain underrepresented in proportion to their percentage of the American voting-age population.

Substantive Representation: Doing What Constituents Want

While it may be important for American voters to believe that Congress is an accurate portrait of the nation, what really matters, according to Hanna Pitkin, is "the nature of the

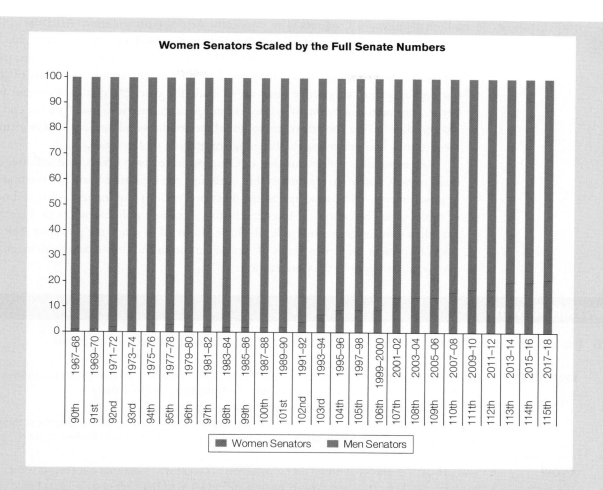

Women Senators Scaled by the Full Senate Numbers

Legend: Women Senators, Men Senators

objective. In the first presentation of the data, the election of 1992 appears to mark the beginning of a major wave of change. Looking at the same data in the second figure, however, tells a somewhat different story. There were gains, but much less dramatic ones.

When reading a graph and the story it's telling, pay attention to the ways in which different presentations of the same set of data—in this case the scale—can portray the facts depending on which story about the data someone seeks to tell.

1. Describe the difference in how the data are presented in the first and second figures.

2. Explain how the y-axis of each bar chart might influence the opinion of a person viewing that bar chart.

3. Pick the bar chart that is more accurate in conveying information about the growth of the number of women in the Senate, and explain why that bar chart is more accurate than the other bar chart.

activity itself, what goes on during representation, the substance or the content of acting for others."[83] Pitkin calls this substantive representation.

Substantive representation happens when members of Congress represent the interests and policy preferences of their constituents. It may facilitate representation across geographical and partisan boundaries.

In any session of Congress, only so many issues can be dealt with as part of the legislative agenda. Some issues seem to rocket to the top of the agenda, and others to languish at the bottom. In times of national crisis, some concerns are more urgent than others.

By bringing unconsidered issues to the foreground, legislators who act on behalf of underrepresented constituents may enlarge Congress's agenda. Presenting information to fellow members of Congress is an important part of representation. After the 2000 election, a reporter asked Senator Kay Bailey Hutchinson (R-TX), "Why can't a male senator do everything a woman senator can do?" Hutchinson's reply was, "Sometimes, from our experience there are issues that men just haven't thought about. . . . Most of the time our colleagues are supportive once we've made the case."[84] Equally important is going beyond just getting a "woman's issue" or an "African American issue" on the congressional agenda—having enough voices to reveal the conflicts and tensions *within* members of these groups and presenting the full range of opinion on the issues.

Representation and lawmaking in Congress have always been, and still are, complicated, messy, and often uncomfortable. Although the legislative branch is the first branch of government—and considered as the most powerful by the framers—it is still only one of three. Over the course of American history, strategic political actors in the other two branches—the executive and judicial—have also tried to shape the power of their institutions, to present their own views of representation in the United States, to stand for the people, and to uphold the Constitution.

Section Review

4.6 Explain how constituency, partisanship, and divided government influence Congress.

REMEMBER
- Members of Congress must consider several factors in making policy, including how to consider the preferences of their constituents, their donors, their judgment, and their party.
- Members of Congress may act as delegates, trustees, or politicos.
- Descriptive representation means that representatives are similar demographically to those they represent. Substantive representation means putting forth policies that constituents support.

KNOW
- *delegate role*: the idea that the main duty of a member of Congress is to carry out constituents' wishes. (p. 137)
- *trustee role*: the idea that members of Congress should act as trustees, making decisions based on their knowledge and judgment. (p. 137)
- *politico role*: representation where members of Congress balance their choices with the interests of their constituents and parties in making decisions. (p. 137)
- *bipartisanship*: agreement between the parties to work together in Congress to pass legislation. (p. 138)
- *gridlock*: a slowdown or halt in Congress's ability to legislate and overcome divisions, especially those based on partisanship. (p. 138)
- *divided government*: control of the presidency and one or both chambers of Congress split between the two major parties. (p. 138)
- *lame duck period*: period at the end of a presidential term when Congress may block presidential initiatives and nominees. (p. 139)

THINK
What is more important in policy making—descriptive or substantive representation? Why?

4.6 Review Question: Free Response

John Adams wrote that Congress "should be a portrait, in miniature, of the people at large, as it should think, feel, reason and act like them."[85]

Use the scenario and your knowledge of U.S. Government and Politics to answer parts A, B, and C.

A. Describe the view of representation conveyed in the quote.

B. Explain one reason why it is difficult for members of Congress to carry out the view of representation conveyed in the quote.

C. Describe a view of representation that differs from the view conveyed in the quote.

Chapter 4 Review

AP® KEY CONCEPTS

- *pork barrel spending* (p. 112)
- *logrolling* (p. 112)
- *oversight* (p. 112)
- *constituency* (p. 114)
- *apportionment* (p. 116)
- *redistricting* (p. 116)
- *gerrymandering* (p. 117)
- *partisan gerrymandering* (p. 117)
- *majority-minority districts* (p. 118)
- *malapportionment* (p. 118)
- *incumbency* (p. 119)
- *incumbency advantage* (p. 119)
- *Speaker of the House* (p. 123)
- *political action committee (PAC)* (p. 123)
- *House majority leader* (p. 123)
- *whip* (p. 123)
- *minority leader* (p. 123)
- *Senate majority leader* (p. 123)
- *committee chair* (p. 124)
- *discharge petition* (p. 129)
- *House Rules Committee* (p. 130)
- *Committee of the Whole* (p. 130)
- *hold* (p. 130)
- *unanimous consent agreement* (p. 130)
- *filibuster* (p. 130)
- *cloture* (p. 130)
- *veto* (p. 132)
- *Office of Management and Budget (OMB)* (p. 133)
- *entitlement program* (p. 133)
- *mandatory spending* (p. 133)
- *discretionary spending* (p. 133)
- *budget surplus* (p. 134)
- *budget deficit* (p. 134)
- *national debt* (p. 134)
- *delegate role* (p. 137)
- *trustee role* (p. 137)
- *politico role* (p. 137)
- *bipartisanship* (p. 138)
- *gridlock* (p. 138)
- *divided government* (p. 138)
- *lame duck period* (p. 139)

AP® EXAM PRACTICE and Critical Thinking Project

MULTIPLE-CHOICE QUESTIONS

The house of representatives . . . can make no law which will not have its full operation on themselves and their friends, as well as the great mass of society. This has always been deemed one of the strongest bonds by which human policy can connect the rulers and the people together . . . but without which every government degenerates into tyranny.[86]

—James Madison, *Federalist* No. 57

1. Which of the following statements best describes the viewpoint in the quote?
   A. The House of Representatives was created to directly represent the citizens.
   B. The Constitution creates rule of law, and elected officials are not above the law.
   C. Congress is bicameral, which means the House of Representatives cannot make laws independently.
   D. Congress must rely on other branches of government to carry out the laws.

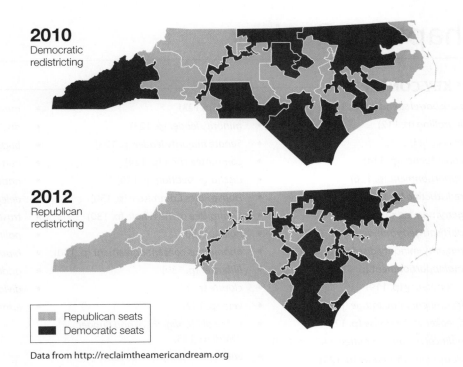

2010
Democratic
redistricting

2012
Republican
redistricting

Republican seats
Democratic seats

Data from http://reclaimtheamericandream.org

2. What do the maps illustrate?
   A. partisan gerrymandering
   B. demographic shifts within a congressional district
   C. increase in electoral support for the Republican Party
   D. the process of reapportionment

3. Select the pair of answers that best explains why the incumbency advantage is higher in the House of Representatives than it is in the Senate.

House of Representatives	Senate
A. Frequent reelection	Ability to filibuster bills
B. Partisan districts	Exclusive use of franking privileges
C. More name recognition	Fewer opportunities for media coverage
D. Smaller districts	Represents entire state

How to fix Congress...

DAVE GRANLUND © www.davegranlund.com

Dave Granlund/Cagle Cartoons

4. Which of the following is most likely to lead to the situation shown in the cartoon?

A. legislative deliberation

B. divided government

C. bipartisanship

D. substantive representation

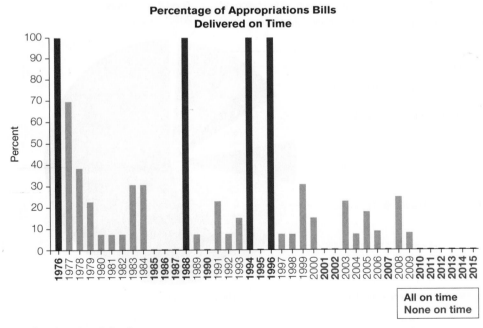

Percentage of Appropriations Bills Delivered on Time

All on time
None on time

Data from Bipartisan Policy Center

5. Which of the following best explains the trend shown in the graph?

A. During periods of divided government, the president and Congress are forced to compromise.

B. Increased partisanship makes it more difficult for Congress to pass spending bills.

C. Budgetary bills must start in the House of Representatives, and the House Rules Committee places limitations on spending bills.

D. Discharge petitions cannot be used on spending bills, making it difficult to appropriate funds.

Question 6 refers to this excerpt from a newspaper article.

Two conservative Republicans booted from House budget panel

By David Lawder

Two of the most conservative Republicans in the House of Representatives have been kicked off the House Budget Committee, a rare move that could make it easier for the panel to advance a deal with Democrats to cut fiscal deficits.

Representatives Tim Heulskamp of Kansas and Justin Amash of Michigan—both favorites of the anti-tax Tea Party movement—are among those Republicans voting most often against House Speaker John Boehner. . . .

Heulskamp and Amash cast the only House Budget Committee votes against [Chairman Paul] Ryan's budget plan earlier this year.[87]

6. Which of the following inferences can be drawn from the excerpt?
   A. Members of Congress usually support the policies favored by their party.
   B. Members of Congress who defy their party's leadership face political consequences.
   C. The Tea Party movement seeks to advance deal making with the Democratic Party.
   D. Conservative members of Congress are unwelcome on the Budget Committee.

Questions 7 and 8 refer to these two graphs:

Graph 1

Discretionary Spending, 2015

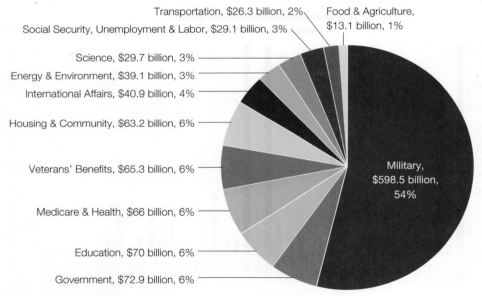

Transportation, $26.3 billion, 2%

Food & Agriculture, $13.1 billion, 1%

Social Security, Unemployment & Labor, $29.1 billion, 3%

Science, $29.7 billion, 3%

Energy & Environment, $39.1 billion, 3%

International Affairs, $40.9 billion, 4%

Housing & Community, $63.2 billion, 6%

Veterans' Benefits, $65.3 billion, 6%

Medicare & Health, $66 billion, 6%

Education, $70 billion, 6%

Government, $72.9 billion, 6%

Military, $598.5 billion, 54%

Data from the Office of Management and Budget and the National Priorities Project

Graph 2

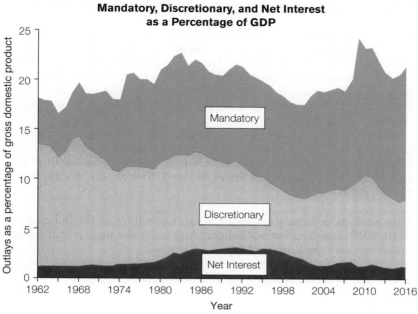

Mandatory, Discretionary, and Net Interest as a Percentage of GDP

Data from the Congressional Research Service and the Office of Management and Budget

7. In examining the data found in Graphs 1 and 2, what pattern or trend would you most likely predict for the anticipated budget for fiscal year 2035?

   A. The United States will devote a larger share of the budget to the military.

   B. Payments for new interest on the debt will be eliminated.

   C. Discretionary expenditures will consume a decreasing share of the federal budget.

   D. The percentage of America's GDP devoted to federal spending will continue its downward trend.

8. What is the most likely explanation for the pattern or trend described in your answer to Question 7?

   A. the aging of the Baby Boomer generation

   B. the increasing diversity of the American population

   C. additional pork barrel spending

   D. renewed fiscal discipline

RESOLVED: That the President is requested, and the Attorney General of the United States is directed, to transmit, respectively (in a manner appropriate to classified information, if the President or Attorney General determines appropriate), to the House of Representatives, not later than 14 days after the date of the adoption of this resolution, copies of any document, record, memo, correspondence, or other communication in their possession, or any portion of any such communication, that refers or relates to the following:

(1) Any meeting or communication that occurred between Senator Jeff Sessions and any representative of the Russian government, including his meetings with the Russian Ambassador to the United States, Sergey I. Kislyak, on July 18, 2016, and September 8, 2016.

(2) Senator Sessions' testimony before the Senate Committee on the Judiciary on January 10, 2017, including but not limited to his statement that he "did not have communications with the Russians."[88]

9. What congressional power was used in passing this resolution?

- **A.** law making
- **B.** treaty ratification
- **C.** appropriations
- **D.** legislative oversight

10. Select the response that matches the most likely motivation of the resolution's sponsor and the most likely outcome of the resolution, given the fact of a Republican majority on the House Judiciary Committee.

	Motivation	Outcome
A.	To learn embarrassing information about the president and attorney general for partisan purposes	Defeat of the resolution along strict party lines
B.	To gain further insight into how best to negotiate with the Russian government	Request to the president and the attorney general for additional information
C.	To waive the protections given to classified information	Request of the Supreme Court for guidance as to how best to proceed
D.	To begin impeachment proceedings against the president and his top aides	Support for the resolution to require the president and attorney general to testify before Congress

FREE-RESPONSE QUESTIONS

1. In 2008, $147,660 was proposed by Rep. Peter King (R-NY) for the plush de Seversky Center Mansion in Old Westbury, New York, which "brings together Gatsby-era opulence, modern convenience, and highly personalized service" for corporate events and weddings. Wedding-spot.com calls the facility "one of the premier event and wedding venues in the New York area" and cites the average wedding cost "at between $73,015 and $86,737 for a ceremony & reception for 150 guests."[89]

    —Citizens Against Government Waste

    Use your knowledge of U.S. Government and Politics to answer parts A, B, and C.

    A. Identify the type of legislation described in the quote.

    B. Explain one reason why the type of legislation described in the quote has been criticized.

    C. Describe two benefits of the type of legislation described in the quote.

2. On November 13, 2015, a series of terrorist attacks in Paris, France, killed 130 people. Days later, a bill was introduced in the House of Representatives entitled the American Security Against Foreign Enemies Act of 2015 or the American SAFE Act. The bill would require that any resident of Iraq or Syria seeking refugee status in the United States must first be certified by the director of the Federal Bureau of Investigation (FBI), secretary of Department of Homeland Security (DHS), and director of National Intelligence (DNI) as being "not a threat to the security of the United States." The following is the substance of the legislative history of that bill.

    Legislative progress of H.R. 4038, the American SAFE Act of 2015, as reported in the Congressional Record[90]

Date	Legislative action
November 17, 2015	Introduced in the House
November 17, 2015	Referred to the House Judiciary Committee
November 17, 2015	Referred to the House Judiciary Subcommittee on Immigration and Border Security
November 18, 2015	Referred to House Rules Committee
November 18, 2015	Rules Committee adopts rule that "provides for consideration of H.R. 4038 with 1 hour of general debate. . . . Bill is closed to amendments."
November 19, 2015	H.R. 4038: "passed by recorded vote of 289-137"
November 19, 2015	H.R. 4038 "received in the Senate"
January 20, 2016	Motion seeking "cloture on the motion to proceed" in the Senate: Yea – 55 votes Nay – 43 votes

The progress of the American SAFE Act through the House of Representatives and the Senate reflects the differing lawmaking rules adopted by those two chambers consistent with their powers set forth in Article I, Section 5, of the U.S. Constitution.

Use the table and your knowledge of U.S. Government and Politics to answer parts A, B, and C.

A. Describe one lawmaking rule of the House of Representatives that affected the progress of the American SAFE Act in that chamber, and explain how the rule affected that bill's progress.

B. Describe one lawmaking rule of the Senate, and explain how that rule affected the progress of the American SAFE Act in the Senate.

C. From the data appearing in the table, describe whether the bill entitled the American SAFE Act passed the Congress, and explain the basis for your conclusion.

ARGUMENTATION QUESTION

Three models—delegate, trustee, and politico—describe representation in Congress. Develop an argument that explains which model you think best achieves the founders' intent when they designed Congress.

In your essay:

- Articulate a claim or thesis that responds to the prompt, and use a line of reasoning to defend it.
- Use at least TWO pieces of relevant and accurate evidence to support your claim.
- At least ONE piece of evidence must be from one of the listed foundational documents:
  - Constitution of the United States
  - *Federalist* No. 10
  - *Federalist* No. 51
- Use a second piece of evidence from another foundational document from the list or from your study of Congress.
- Use reasoning to explain why the evidence you provided supports your claim or thesis.
- Use refutation, concession, or rebuttal to respond to an opposing or alternative perspective.

CRITICAL THINKING PROJECT

Send an E-Mail Message to Your Representative

Most Americans are not familiar with the positions and voting records of the members of Congress who represent them. Members of Congress want to hear from the constituents so that they can effectively represent their interests.

  A. Go to https://www.house.gov and find your representative using the zip code lookup feature.
  B. Click on the name of your representative, and then click "on the issues."
  C. Research your representative's stance on an issue that matters to you.
  D. Write a draft of a message to your representative.
    1. Your e-mail message should begin with "Dear Representative [name]" as the salutation.
    2. Tell the representative who you are and why you are writing.
    3. Explain why the issue is important to you and why you support or oppose your representative's stance on the issue. Be factual and respectful.
    4. Get to the point. Limit your message to one typed, double-spaced page.
    5. Ask your teacher to review and critique your e-mail message.
    6. Send your e-mail message, and evaluate your representative's response in deciding whether or not to vote for him or her in the next election.

Donald Trump is sworn in on January 20, 2017, as the forty-fifth president of the United States.
Richard Ellis/Alamy Stock Photo

It is, without question, one of the most powerful positions in the world—perhaps *the* most powerful. If you want to understand the weight of the American presidency, compare photographs of a new president's inauguration to those taken in the final days before leaving office. You will observe that each person has aged, often dramatically.

The president must work with the other branches of government, as the framers of the Constitution intended. The president sits atop a massive collection of departments and agencies. He or she must contend with a Congress whose members have their own political goals, even if the majority of those members are from the president's own political party. If the majority of one or both chambers in Congress is not from the president's party, things get even tougher. And then there are the American people, to whom a president speaks directly. With the American people on his or her side, a president can be powerful, especially when dealing with members of Congress. Without this support, presidents are vulnerable. In the American political system, the president acts as the head of the **executive branch** of government, which is charged with executing the laws of the nation.

executive branch
the branch of government charged with putting the nation's laws into effect.

Presidents act to shape policy in all areas—economic, social, domestic, and foreign. Yet the stories in this chapter focus mainly on one aspect of presidential power: war making. Although Congress has the power to declare war, the president is the commander in chief. By engaging with the stories of presidential decisions to imprison or kill citizens suspected of terrorism, you will gain a deeper understanding of the American presidency.

LEARNING TARGETS

After reading this chapter, you will be able to

5.1 Explain how presidents have used their powers in the fight against terrorism.

5.2 Describe the powers of the presidency and ways in which the president influences the bureaucracy.

5.3 Describe the ways in which Congress and the Supreme Court may check presidential powers.

5.4 Explain how modern presidents interact with the bureaucracy, Congress, and the public.

5.5 Evaluate how presidents have exercised their powers in the war on terror.

■ 5.1 Presidential Power and the War on Terror

On September 11, 2001, terrorists associated with Osama bin Laden's Al Qaeda organization hijacked four U.S. passenger planes. Two of the planes flew into the twin towers of the World Trade Center in New York City, and one hit the Pentagon. Passengers in the fourth plane overtook the terrorists, and the plane crashed into a field in rural southwestern Pennsylvania. Following the 9/11 attacks, President George W. Bush issued a series of executive orders in response to the national security crisis. Within weeks of the attacks,

Chief of Staff Andrew Card whispers into the ear of President George W. Bush on the morning of the September 11, 2001, attacks, which took place while President Bush was on a visit to an elementary school in Sarasota, Florida.
DOUG MILLS/AP Images

Bush had, through the issuance of executive orders, called members of the Ready Reserve of the Armed Forces to active duty, seized financial assets, and blocked financial transactions with persons and organizations suspected of aiding terrorism, and established the Office of Homeland Security.[1]

The Capture of Yaser Hamdi

In fall 2001, the Northern Alliance, a local militia that was giving support to the U.S. military operation in Afghanistan, captured Yaser Hamdi. Hamdi was an American citizen, born in Baton Rouge, Louisiana, although his parents moved back to Saudi Arabia with him about a year after his birth. Hamdi was accused of aiding the Taliban in operations against the U.S. military in Afghanistan. Hamdi was moved to a series of U.S. military facilities where he was held as an "enemy combatant" without an attorney or the right to challenge his detention in U.S. courts.

Yaser Hamdi's father, Esam Fouad Hamdi, filed a petition for a writ of habeas corpus on behalf of his son in June 2002, arguing that his son's detention "violated and continue[d] to violate the Fifth and Fourteenth Amendments to the United States Constitution."[2] A writ of habeas corpus is a court order requiring the government to describe the charges and produce the evidence against someone charged with a crime. Esam Hamdi asserted that his twenty-year-old son traveled to Afghanistan to do "relief work" and would not have had time to receive military training because he had arrived in the country only months before the 9/11 attacks.[3] Attorneys for the Bush administration argued that "the Executive possesses plenary authority to detain pursuant to Article II of the Constitution" as part of the office's constitutional warmaking authority.[4]

Ten years later, the war on terror continued, and President Obama continued to use executive actions to target suspected terrorists. On a September morning in 2011, a group of men had just finished eating breakfast in a remote desert in Yemen. One of them was Anwar al-Awlaki, an American citizen who was, to counterterrorism officials, "a rock star propagandist for al-Qaeda's arm in Yemen who recruited followers over the Internet. He posted fiery sermons in idiomatic English and called on all who listened to attack the West."[5] Patrolling the skies above Yemen that day were American drones launched from an airstrip in Saudi Arabia and piloted from far way. Noticing the drones, the men "scrambled to get to their trucks."[6]

They were too late. Two Predator drones marked the men's trucks with lasers, and larger Reaper drones launched three Hellfire missiles. Al-Awlaki's vehicle "was totally torn up into pieces," according to reports from unidentified witnesses to the strike. The missiles "left nothing of the target but small human parts, which were later collected together and buried in one tomb."[7] Also killed in the strike was another American citizen named Samir Khan, "who had moved to Yemen from North Carolina and was the creative force behind *Inspire*, the militant group's English-language magazine."[8]

For more than a year and a half following the strike, the administration of President Barack Obama remained officially silent about the targets. Under pressure from members of Congress, including some key Democrats, Attorney General Eric Holder formally acknowledged in May 2013 that the 2011 strike had targeted an American citizen: al-Awlaki. According to the *New York Times*, "For what was apparently the first time since the Civil War, the United States government had carried out the deliberate killing of an American citizen as a wartime enemy and without a trial."[9] Al-Awlaki's name had been placed at the top of the Central Intelligence Agency's (CIA) list of individuals to be captured if possible, or killed, if not. Many of the details about how individuals made this list were secret. One journalist reported that "officials said that every name added to the list underwent a careful, if secret, legal review. Because of Mr. Awlaki's [U.S.] citizenship, the decision to add him to the target list was approved by the National Security Council as well."[10]

The administration's secret decision to target al-Awlaki made many uncomfortable. In a speech in 2012, Obama's top counterterrorism adviser, John Brennan, reassured his audience that individuals, including Americans, were only targeted for killing if capture was not a realistic option and only after a careful and thorough review. "Of course," he added, "how we identify an individual naturally involves intelligence sources and methods, which I will not discuss."[11]

Two weeks after the killing of al-Awlaki, "his 16-year-old son, Abdulrahman—also an American citizen, who had gone to the Yemeni desert in search of his father—was killed in a drone strike meant for someone else. That strike was similarly unacknowledged, although a senior administration official privately characterized it as a 'mis-

U.S. citizen and Muslim cleric Anwar al-Awlaki poses for a photo at Dar al Hijrah Mosque in October 2001 in Falls Church, Virginia. There is yet no clear answer to the question of how al-Awlaki, who preached peace following the 9/11 attacks, came to wage war on the country of his birth. Ten years later, al-Awlaki was killed in a targeted drone strike by the United States in Yemen.
Linda Spillers/The New York Time/Redux Pictures

take.'"[12] The target, a senior al-Qaeda official, was not in the area at the time of the strike. Abdulrahman, who "liked sports and music and kept his Facebook page regularly updated," was apparently an unintended casualty of the war on terror.[13] In less than a month, the United States government had killed three American citizens with drone strikes on foreign soil, though the death of one, the younger al-Awlaki, was likely unintentional.

The Obama administration argued that the targeted killing of al-Awlaki was the only option to protect national security. Under the Authorization for Use of Military Force Act of 2001 (AUMF),[14] passed in the aftermath of the attacks of September 11, 2001, presidents have the authority to use military force against terrorists and their associates. According to officials, Al-Awlaki had become a clear and present danger to the United States. In 2010, an anonymous counterterrorism official in the Obama administration told the *New York Times*, "American citizenship doesn't give you carte blanche to wage war against your own country."[15] The AUMF was passed in response to the terrorist attacks of September 11, 2001, and yet was still being used to conduct drone strikes more than ten years later. Some in Congress, including Representative Barbara Lee from California, worried that the AUMF gives presidents a blank check to wage war without congressional approval.[16]

This chapter's main ideas are reflected in the Learning Targets. By reviewing after each section, you should be able to

—**Remember** the key points,

—**Know** terms that are central to the topic, and

—**Think** critically about the role of the executive branch within a system of check and balances.

5.1 Explain how presidents have used their power in the fight against terrorism.

REMEMBER	Yaser Hamdi is an American citizen who challenged his detention as an enemy combatant. President Obama used drone strikes to target terrorists.
KNOW	*executive branch*: the branch of government charged with putting the nation's laws into effect. (p. 152)
THINK	How does the War on Terror expand presidential power?

5.1 Review Question: Free Response

Al-Awlaki was a radical advocate for terrorism. . . . But the summary execution of a citizen, based on evidence that is being withheld from the public because of security implications, has been described by a commentator … as "abandoning our own values" in the pursuit of the war against terror.

—Azeem Ibrahim[17]

Use the quote and your knowledge of U.S. Government and Politics to respond to parts A, B, and C.

A. Describe the viewpoint expressed in the quote.

B. Describe one power that enables the president to conduct drone strikes.

C. Explain two reasons why some people believe that the power to conduct drone strikes gives the president too much power.

5.2 The Constitution and the American Presidency

While the framers of the Constitution knew that the executive needed to be powerful enough to lead, they also feared that the office might become too powerful. They were in no mood to re-create the tyranny of the British monarchy with an elected one.

Selection, Qualifications for Office, and Length of Terms

Once the delegates to the Constitutional Convention settled on a single president, the most contentious issues facing them were how this person was going to be selected, the term of office, and the powers of the executive. The debate between less populous and more populous states that had resulted in the bicameral Congress reared its head once again. Less populous states feared that direct popular election of the president would see their states' interests swallowed up by their more populous neighbors. Most delegates assumed that voters would pick candidates from their own states. Many delegates also mistrusted giving Americans the means of directly electing a president. In the end, the delegates agreed to a complicated method of presidential selection, instead of a direct popular election. Electors, apportioned to states based on congressional representation and chosen by state legislatures, would choose the president.

The delegates settled on a term of four years with the possibility of reelection. During their deliberations, Hamilton proposed that presidents and senators, once selected, serve for life, akin to the term for federal judges, but was rebuffed. No limits were placed on the number of times a person could be elected president. The nation's first president, George Washington (1789–1797), chose not to seek a third term, however, establishing a precedent that held until Franklin Roosevelt (1933–1945) was elected four times.[18] Proposed and ratified largely in response to Roosevelt's multiple terms, the Twenty-Second Amendment (1951) prohibits presidents from being elected more than twice, and only once if that person had assumed the office (due to a death, impairment, resignation, or impeachment) more than two years before the end of a partial term.

The delegates stipulated that presidents have to be "a natural born Citizen, or a Citizen of the United States at the time of the Adoption of this Constitution" as well as having "attained to the Age of thirty-five years, and been fourteen years a Resident within the United States" (Article II, Section 1). The Constitution did not explicitly prohibit women from holding the office. At the time of ratification, though, women were generally denied the right to vote or hold political office within their states.[19]

Federalist No. 70

Alexander Hamilton was aware of the concerns that the Constitution created a single executive with too much power, and he addressed the issue in *Federalist* No. 70. Hamilton's essay focused on the importance of having a single energetic executive, stating, "Energy in the Executive is a leading character in the definition of good government. It is essential to the protection of the community against foreign attacks; it is not less essential to the steady administration of the laws; to the protection of property against those irregular and high-handed combinations which sometimes interrupt the ordinary course of justice; to the security of liberty against the enterprises and assaults of ambition, of faction, and of anarchy."

Hamilton argued that having more than one executive decreases the ability to protect the nation and weakens the ability to take strong, decisive action, "Decision, activity, secrecy, and despatch will generally characterize the proceedings of one man in a much more eminent degree than the proceedings of any greater number; and in proportion as the number is increased, these qualities will be diminished." Hamilton argue that countries with dual executives often face dissension and disagreement, which deprives citizens of the faithful execution of executive duties. He concludes by pointing out that it is easier for the public to keep watch over a single executive.

AP® REQUIRED DOCUMENTS

Federalist No. 70 is one of the nine foundational documents required in AP® U.S. Government and Politics. Make sure you read it carefully and understand why Hamilton argues in favor of a strong executive.

Document	Scope
Federalist No. 70	Hamilton argues that an energetic single executive will protect against foreign attacks, provide for the administration of laws, and protect liberty and property.

Presidential Powers and Roles

The expectation that Washington, trusted and admired throughout the nation, would be the first president may have lessened delegates' concerns about the powerful office they were creating. The Constitutional Convention settled on the simple name of President of the United States, and Washington preferred to be called "Mr. President." John Adams, though, had proposed, "His High Mightiness, the President of the United States and Protector of their Liberties."[20] Jefferson called that title "the most superlatively ridiculous thing I ever heard of."[21]

When the delegates hammered out the framework of the American presidency, they created an institution that had never been seen on a national scale. In some ways there is still no exact equivalent to its scope and complexity in modern democracies. The president has both formal and informal powers. **Formal (or enumerated) powers** are those given to the president explicitly in the Constitution. **Informal powers**, though not laid out in the text, are necessary to carry out the expressed powers. In wielding these two kinds of powers, the American president assumes a variety of roles.[22] Political scientists have identified five key roles of the president: chief executive, chief diplomat, commander in chief, legislative leader, and party leader.

A portrait of George Washington, circa 1796, near the end of his second term. That Washington was so respected a figure may have calmed fears that the executive would become too powerful. Note how Washington presents himself in this painting: His black coat indicates sobriety and restraint. His desk is covered with books and a scroll, a sign of scholarship. The leg of the desk has carvings of eagles that evoke the Roman Republic—as well as bundled rods, an ancient symbol of strength through unity.
UniversalImagesGroup/Getty Images

Chief Executive

As the head of the executive branch, the president carries out the laws of the nation. The president oversees a large and complex system of agencies and bureaucracies. The Constitution, however, does not offer many specifics as to what it means to execute the laws. Article II, which is devoted to the presidency, begins, "The executive Power shall be vested in a President of the United States of America."[23] When taking the oath of office, the president promises to "faithfully execute the Office of the President of the United States" and is later instructed to "take Care that the Laws be faithfully executed."[24] Other than that, the Constitution does not give much detail on *how* the president is supposed to run the federal government.

The president's cabinet consists of the heads of the fifteen major executive branch departments, the vice president, and the heads of other agencies that the president wishes to assign cabinet-level status. Besides leading their agencies, cabinet department heads, most of whom are called secretaries, advise the president and act as the link between the president and the bureaucracy. Unlike the majority of people who work for the federal bureaucracy, heads of the executive branch departments typically come and go with each new administration. (Figure 5.1 on the next page shows the organization of the Cabinet.)

In choosing cabinet members, presidents have to juggle several considerations. The Senate confirms cabinet heads. Assertive cabinet secretaries, who often have their own bases of power, can challenge the president or drag their heels if they disagree with a policy. Presidents must also consider politics and public opinion in their choices. Cabinet

formal or enumerated powers
powers expressly granted in the Constitution.

informal powers
powers not laid out in the Constitution but used to carry out presidential duties.

department heads with ties to important interest groups—members of the business community, for example—can help a president be informed of the concerns of those groups as policy is shaped. Finally, having a diverse cabinet is seen by many as demonstrating a commitment to representing all Americans and their interests.

The president influences the federal bureaucracy by appointing cabinet and agency heads who will carry out the policies he favors. The president can issue an executive order instructing the bureaucracy how to implement policy. For example, in April 2017, President Trump signed an executive order directing Secretary of Education Betsy DeVos to identify those policies and practices that overreach to ensure that the federal government does not "obstruct the ability of states, local governments, teachers, and most importantly, parents, to make the best decisions for their students and, in many cases, for their children."[25] The president can use the budget to reward or punish agencies, depending on whether or not they have implemented policies according to his wishes. Despite these tools, presidents often have trouble controlling the bureaucracy. The bureaucracy is vast and complex, and it's hard to keep tabs on its actions. Agency heads and employees may pursue their own goals, hindering the president's agenda.

Presidents *are* given some guidance, however. They are authorized to "require the Opinion, in writing, of the principal Office in each of the executive Departments, upon any Subject relating to the Duties of their respective Offices."[26] Though not mentioned by name in the Constitution, the president's cabinet has evolved into a powerful source of

FIGURE 5.1

The Organization of the Cabinet

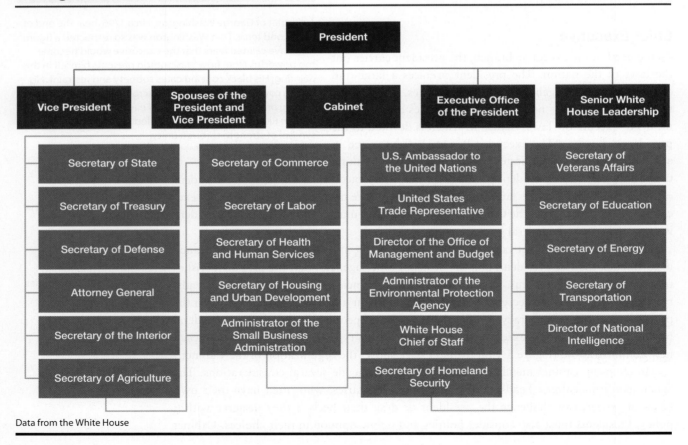

Data from the White House

information and control over the nation's sprawling federal bureaucracy. It also provides a way to reward individuals and members of important interest groups for past and future support through their appointment to positions within the cabinet.

Modern presidents have the authority to appoint individuals to thousands of administrative positions, from closest advisors and heads of large agencies to lower-level administrative staff. Roughly one thousand of these appointments require Senate confirmation. Presidents also nominate individuals to serve as judges in the federal judiciary, with each nomination also requiring Senate confirmation.

Chief Diplomat

The president is also responsible for guiding U.S. foreign policy and interacting with the heads of other nations. The president is authorized "to make **Treaties**," to "appoint Ambassadors," and to "receive Ambassadors and other public Ministers,"[27] subject to a two-thirds ratification vote in the Senate. The power of diplomacy is partly symbolic and ceremonial. Diplomacy can involve elaborate state dinners and parties and, in the case of President Obama's reception of British Prime Minister David Cameron in 2012, courtside seats to the NCAA men's basketball tournament.

The diplomatic power of the president also helps shape U.S. foreign policy. Congress, particularly the Senate, plays a major role in foreign affairs, yet the president is a single person—and not 100 or 435, as is the case for the Senate and House—which gives him or her an advantage over Congress. The president can act quickly and decisively on the international stage. As Clinton Rossiter put it, "Secrecy, dispatch, unity, continuity, and access to information—the ingredients of successful diplomacy—are properties of his office, and Congress . . . possesses none of them."[28]

treaty
an agreement with a foreign government negotiated by the president and requiring a two-thirds vote in the Senate to ratify.

Chief Legislator

In devising a system in which power has to be shared among three branches, the framers gave the president a limited and mostly negative role in the legislative process. However, this role has been expanded substantially.

Article II, section 3, of the Constitution directs the president to "from time to time give Congress Information of the State of the Union." Modern presidents use the opportunity provided by the **State of the Union Address** to speak live on television before Congress, members of the Supreme Court, the military, and, most important, the entire nation. In the address, a president often encourages or cajoles Congress to pass key pieces of his or her legislative agenda. The real audience, however, is the American people, and presidents use the address to try to mobilize public support and pressure members of Congress to act. Speaking before a joint session of Congress is a relatively new tradition. The presidents from Thomas Jefferson until Woodrow Wilson did not come before Congress, but instead they simply sent a written report. Jimmy Carter also did not appear before Congress in 1981 as he was about to leave office.

The president is also expected to "recommend to their [Congress's] Consideration such Measures as he shall judge necessary and expedient."[29] While, as we saw in Chapter 4, only members of Congress can formally introduce bills, presidents work with party leaders in both chambers to shape the legislative agenda. Finally, the president is given the power to **veto** legislation, although this veto is subject to a potential override by a two-thirds vote in both chambers. A **pocket veto** occurs when a president does not sign a piece of legislation within ten days, during a period when Congress has adjourned at the end of a session. Individual presidents have varied considerably in the use of the veto.

State of the Union Address
the annual speech from the president to Congress updating that branch on the state of national affairs.

veto
formal rejection by the president of a bill that has passed both houses of Congress.

pocket veto
an informal veto caused when the president chooses not to sign a bill within ten days, during a time when Congress has adjourned at the end of a session.

Both familiarity and formality are involved in presidential diplomacy. President Donald Trump chats with British Prime Minister Theresa May during her official visit to Washington, D.C., in January 2017.
BRENDAN SMIALOWSKI/Getty Images

In the second photo, Prime Minister May and President Trump hold a joint press conference. Why is one photo informal while the other is formal? What do the photos indicate about the president's various roles?
Pablo Martinez Monsivais/AP Images

Congressional overrides of vetoes seldom happen. Marshaling the required two-thirds vote in both chambers usually is hard to do. The mere threat of a presidential veto is often enough to shape a piece of legislation more to a president's liking.[30] Vetoes are more likely during periods of divided government, when one or both chambers of Congress are under the control of a party other than that of the president.

Commander in Chief

Perhaps the most fateful role that the Constitution creates for the president is his or her authority as "Commander in Chief of the Army and Navy of the United States, and of the Militia of the several States."[31] The president is at the top of the entire military chain of command, including the strategic nuclear forces of the nation. No president is ever intentionally far from the so-called nuclear football. The contents of this heavy briefcase are classified but have traditionally included communications equipment and strategic plans and codes to launch nuclear missiles. It is an awe-inspiring responsibility. Every president "is never for one day allowed to forget that he will be held accountable by people, Congress, and history for the nation's readiness to meet an enemy assault."[32]

The framers of the Constitution limited the war-making power of the presidency but designed it so the president could efficiently lead the American armed forces to protect the nation. Congress has the power to declare war, but the nation might be unable to respond quickly to threats when Congress is not in session. Therefore, the president was also given a role in national war making.

Pardons

The Constitution gives the president the power to issue a **presidential pardon**. The "Power to grant Reprieves and Pardons for Offenses against the United States, except in Cases of Impeachment," allows the president to release individuals convicted of federal crimes from all legal consequences and restore their benefits of citizenship.[33] A reprieve is a temporary release due to extenuating circumstances, such as medical necessity. Presidents often grant pardons in the final days and weeks of office. In cases when it appears that pardoned individuals have close personal or professional ties to the president, this practice can be quite controversial.

Unilateral Presidential Action

Presidents sometimes act unilaterally to influence both domestic and foreign policy with few or no constraints by Congress or the judiciary. Individual presidents have often tried to defend the power of their office or even enlarge the boundaries of that power. Yet the scope and frequency of unilateral presidential action in recent administrations has raised questions about the degree to which powers truly remain separated among the three branches of government.

Presidents attempt to exercise independent control over information through the assertion of **executive privilege**, in which they try to shield from Congress, the judiciary, and ultimately the public, the details of debates, discussions, memos, and emails surrounding presidential decisions and actions. Since the administration of George Washington, presidents have asserted that their ability to control information is central to maintaining their effectiveness.[34]

In the area of foreign policy, presidents may sign **executive agreements** with foreign nations without going to the Senate for ratification, unlike treaties, which required a two-thirds vote for ratification.[35] Although they are not binding on future presidents in the way that treaties are, executive agreements can give a president a way to shape foreign policy that bypasses the Senate's role of advice and consent. Their details are often kept secret from the public and Congress for reasons of national security.

In the president's role in the legislative process, the use of **signing statements** has gained increased attention recently. When a president signs a bill into law, he or she may add written comments that convey instructions to the various agencies that will carry out the law. Sometimes signing statements are added to build a public record of support for an issue, to call attention to an issue, or to offer a slightly different interpretation of a law that a president otherwise supports. If the president either interprets the law differently from

In this 2016 photo, a U.S. military aide carries the president's nuclear arsenal command briefcase (larger bag, at right) as then-President Barack Obama returns to the White House from a trip.
OLIVIER DOULIERY/Getty Images

presidential pardon
presidential authority to release individuals convicted of a crime from legal consequences and set aside punishment for a crime.

executive privilege
a right claimed by presidents to keep certain conversations, records, and transcripts confidential from outside scrutiny, especially that of Congress.

executive agreement
an agreement between a president and another nation that does not have the same durability in the American system as a treaty but does not require Senate ratification.

signing statement
written comments issued by presidents while signing a bill into law that usually consist of political statements or reasons for signing the bill but that may also include a president's interpretation of the law itself.

STEPHEN JAFFE/Getty Images

President George W. Bush delivers a speech aboard the aircraft carrier U.S.S. *Abraham Lincoln* on May 1, 2003. The president's speech declared an end to major combat operations in Iraq. Behind him is a banner reading "Mission Accomplished." Critics of the war and the Bush administration pointed to the photo opportunity as an indication of the president's optimism about the challenges of a war that would go on for eight more years.

A "photo op" is a picture carefully staged by a politician to convey a positive message. Consider the following in analyzing the photo:

1. Describe the purpose of the photo.

2. Describe two factors presidents should consider before posing for photo ops.

3. Explain one reason why a photo op might be successful in conveying a positive image of the president to the public. Explain one reason why a photo op might not succeed in conveying a positive image of the president to the public.

the way Congress intended or instructs agencies to execute it selectively or differently, however, concerns arise that the president is encroaching on the lawmaking authority of Congress.

executive order
policy directives issued by presidents that do not require congressional approval.

Executive orders are policy directives issued by presidents that do not require congressional approval. (See Figure 5.2.) Most executive orders are issued under congressional authorization and constitute a set of instructions given by the president to the executive branch agencies informing them of how they should go about implementing a law or policy. Often, they deal with routine administrative procedures. Presidents have used executive orders, however, to make major changes in public policy.[36] Following President Roosevelt's Executive Order 9066, more than 130,000 Japanese American citizens were relocated to internment camps during World War II.

While you have read mainly about unilateral presidential action in the area of national security, questions about unilateral action extend to many other political fields. As political

FIGURE 5.2

Executive Orders, Washington to Trump

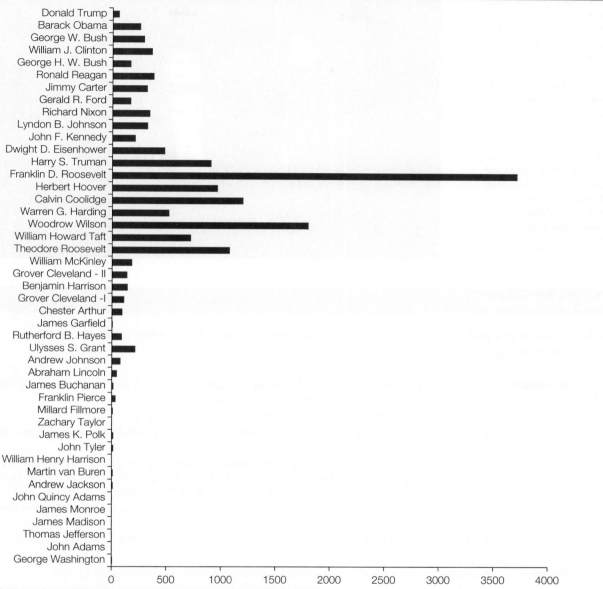

Note: Data for the Trump administration are current through the end of November 2017.

Data from Gerhard Peters, "Executive Orders," in *The American Presidency Project*, ed. John T. Woolley and Gerhard Peters (Santa Barbara: University of California, 1999–2016).

scientist William Howell has examined, presidents may act first and alone across a wide variety of policy areas, often by issuing directives to the vast federal bureaucracy without waiting for Congress to clarify the laws that it has passed (see Chapter 7). In doing so, "the president moves policy first and thereby places upon Congress and the courts the burden of revising a new political landscape."[37] Acting first and acting alone may force the other two branches to react.

George Takei stars in a musical play titled *Allegiance*, based in part on his own family's history of internment in camps during World War II simply for being of Japanese descent. This photo from a performance also shows co-stars Telly Leung and Lea Salonga. Salonga was involved in the show from the first reading of an early draft. Since its premiere at the Old Globe Theater in San Diego, the play has been performed throughout the country, including a Broadway production in 2015.
Photo courtesy of Allegiance Broadway and Sing OutLouise Productions

Section Review

5.2 Describe the powers of the presidency and ways in which the president influences the bureaucracy.

REMEMBER
- The framers called for a single executive, the president, with enough power to lead successfully but not so much power as to make the office susceptible to tyranny.
- The president serves a four-year term with the possibility of reelection.
- Candidates must be natural-born citizens, at least thirty-five years old, and a resident of the nation for fourteen years.
- The office of the presidency is granted a set of formal and informal powers, including the power to carry out the laws of the nation, guide foreign policy and relations with foreign leaders, make policy recommendations to Congress, veto legislation, act as commander in chief of the military, and grant pardons.
- Presidents have expanded their informal powers through executive agreements, executive orders, and signing statements.
- Executive power is constitutionally limited by powers granted to Congress and the judiciary.

KNOW
- *formal (or enumerated) powers*: powers expressly granted in the Constitution. (p. 157)
- *informal powers*: powers not laid out in the Constitution but used to carry out presidential duties. (p. 157)
- *treaty*: an agreement with a foreign government negotiated by the president and requiring a two-thirds vote in the Senate to ratify. (p. 159)
- *State of the Union Address*: the annual speech from the president to Congress updating that branch on the state of national affairs. (p. 159)
- *veto*: formal rejection by the president of a bill that has passed both houses of Congress. (p. 159)
- *pocket veto*: an informal veto caused when the president chooses not to sign a bill within ten days, during a time when Congress has adjourned at the end of a session. (p. 159)
- *presidential pardon*: presidential authority to release individuals convicted from a crime of legal consequences and forgive an individual and set aside punishment for a crime. (p. 161)
- *executive privilege*: a right claimed by presidents to keep certain conversations, records, and transcripts confidential from outside scrutiny, especially that of Congress. (p. 161)
- *executive agreement*: an agreement between a president and another nation that does not have the same durability in the American system as a treaty but does not require Senate ratification. (p. 161)

- *signing statement*: written comments issued by presidents while signing a bill into law that usually consist of political statements or reasons for signing the bill but that may also include a president's interpretation of the law itself. (p. 161)
- *executive order*: policy directives issued by presidents that do not require congressional approval. (p. 162)

THINK
- Why is it often difficult for Congress to check the power of the president, despite the formal checks provided in the Constitution?
- How have presidents used executive agreements, executive orders, and signing statements to expand their power?

5.2 Review Question: Free Response

Though the president, during the sitting of the legislature, is assisted by the senate, yet he is without a constitutional council in their recess—he will therefore be unsupported by proper information and advice, and will generally be directed by minions and favorites, or a council of state will grow out of the principal officers of the great departments, the most dangerous council in a free country.

—Antifederalist Papers, Cato IV[38]

Use the quote and your knowledge of U.S. Government and Politics to respond to parts A, B, and C.

A. Describe the viewpoint expressed in the quote.

B. Describe two arguments in *Federalist* No. 70 that address the concerns expressed in the quote.

C. Explain how two different provisions in Constitution were designed to prevent the concerns expressed in the quote.

◼◼ 5.3 Limits on Presidential Power

The framers limited the power of the president by granting specific powers to Congress and the federal judiciary.[39] (See Table 5.1.) Presidents cannot accomplish most of their objectives without Congress, as the Constitution gives Congress several negative checks

TABLE 5.1 Division of Powers between the President and Congress

Presidential Powers	Congressional Powers
Execute the nation's laws.	Investigate or impeach the president.
Submit the annual federal budget.	Pass the budget.
Appoint and seek the advice of cabinet departments.	Confirm, delay, or block nominations.
Shape foreign policy by negotiating treaties, appointing ambassadors, and conducting diplomacy.	Ratify treaties and confirm ambassadors.
Make policy recommendations to Congress; veto congressional legislation.	Override vetoes.
Act as commander in chief of the armed forces.	Declare war and fund the armed forces.
Deliver pardons.	Congress retains the power to impeach officials who have been pardoned, but neither the legislature nor the judiciary may override a pardon.

on presidential action. Presidents must have majority support in Congress to pass the laws and create and fund the programs. The president must obtain majority approval in the Senate to confirm appointments to the federal judiciary as well as cabinet secretaries and the heads of many executive branch offices. Ratification of a treaty requires a two-thirds vote in the Senate.[40] With a two-thirds vote in each chamber, Congress can override a presidential veto, although veto overrides do not happen often, given the high number of votes required to succeed. Through the power of judicial review, the Supreme Court can overturn executive orders and other presidential actions that violate the Constitution.

The War Powers Resolution

The **War Powers Resolution** (1973), which passed despite President Nixon's veto, has been one of the most enduring and controversial legacies of his presidency.[41] The resolution is credited by some scholars as being "the high-water mark of congressional reassertion in national security affairs."[42] The resolution was the product of widespread public and congressional dissatisfaction with the expansion of the Vietnam conflict as well as unilateral presidential actions carried out by Presidents Lyndon Johnson and Nixon.

Under the terms of the War Powers Resolution, a president may only introduce armed forces into conflict or likely conflict if one of the three following conditions is present:

1. "A declaration of war [by Congress],"
2. a "specific statutory authorization [by Congress]," or
3. "a national emergency created by an attack on the United States, its territories or possessions, or its armed forces."[43]

Once introduced, the president is required to notify Congress within 48 hours of "the circumstances necessitating the introduction of United States Armed Forces; . . . the constitutional and legislative authority under which such introduction took place; and . . . the estimated scope and duration of the hostilities or involvement."[44] Unless Congress has declared war, passed specific authorization, extended the notification deadline, or is physically unable to meet, the president must withdraw forces within sixty days, with a thirty-day extension if necessary to withdraw those forces safely.[45]

The last war officially declared by Congress was World War II in 1941. Since that time, American armed forces have been stationed in more than one hundred countries, though many of these are allies or military partners. Presidents have asserted that the War Powers Resolution unconstitutionally restricts their power as commander in chief.[46]

Impeachment

Congress has the power to impeach the president (as well as "the Vice President and all civil Officers of the United States") for the vaguely defined transgressions of "Treason, Bribery, or other high Crimes and Misdemeanors."[47] A majority vote in the House is required to pass articles of **impeachment**, which list the charges against the officeholder. Once an officeholder is impeached, the trial takes place in the Senate. The chief justice of the Supreme Court presides over a presidential impeachment and a two-thirds vote is necessary to convict and remove from office.[48] Impeachment and removal are not the same as a criminal conviction. A person who has been impeached and removed from office remains subject to potential criminal charges.

Court Decisions

The Supreme Court can check presidential power by overturning executive actions. During the investigation of President Nixon and his role in the Watergate affair, Nixon refused

War Powers Resolution
a law passed over President Nixon's veto that restricts the power of the president to maintain troops in combat for more than sixty days without congressional authorization.

AP® TIP

The War Powers Resolution is important because it was an attempt by Congress to limit the power of the president as commander in chief. It is likely to appear on the AP® exam.

impeachment
the process of removing a president from office, with articles of impeachment issued by a majority vote in the House of Representatives, followed by a trial in the Senate, with a two-thirds vote necessary to convict and remove.

to hand over to a special prosecutor audio recordings of his conversations with senior aides as well as other documents relating to the investigation, citing executive privilege. In *United States v. Nixon* (1974), the Supreme Court affirmed the power of executive privilege, finding that "a President and those who assist him must be free to explore alternatives in the process of shaping policies and making decisions, and to do so in a way many would be unwilling to express except privately."[49] However, the Court also demanded that the president hand over the recordings and documents, balancing the need for executive privilege with the need for the rule of law in criminal investigations.

Recent executive orders have faced court challenges. When President Obama issued an executive order that would have allowed four million undocumented immigrants to apply for citizenship, the Supreme Court deadlocked in reaching a decision, effectively blocking the order.[50] President Trump issued a travel ban on immigrants from seven predominantly Muslim countries. The Supreme Court upheld parts of the ban, and blocked others.[51] In response, the Trump administration revised the travel restrictions, dropping Iraq from the ban, and eliminating language that expressed a preference for certain religious groups.[52]

Section Review

5.3 Describe the ways in which Congress and the Supreme Court may check presidential power.

REMEMBER
- Congress checks executive power through its budgetary powers and its power to override vetoes.
- The Senate checks the president by confirming nominations to the cabinet and federal judiciary with a majority vote and ratifying treaties with a two-thirds vote.
- Congress has the power to declare war. It passed the War Powers Resolution in an attempt to restrict the president's ability to commit troops.
- The House has the power to impeach a president for high crimes or misdemeanors, and the Senate has the power to convict and remove an impeached president with a two-thirds vote.
- The Supreme Court may check the president by overturning executive actions.

KNOW
- *War Powers Resolution*: a law passed over President Nixon's veto that restricts the power of the president to maintain troops in combat for more than sixty days without congressional authorization. (p. 166)
- *impeachment*: the process of removing a president from office, with articles of impeachment issued by a majority vote in the House of Representatives, followed by a trial in the Senate, with a two-thirds vote necessary to convict and remove. (p. 166)

THINK
- Why is Congress often more successful in checking the president's domestic agenda than in blocking his actions in foreign affairs?
- Why do presidents issue executive orders that might be blocked by the Supreme Court?

5.3 Review Question: Free Response

In April 2016, U.S. spy agencies recorded each step of a chemical weapons attack against Syrian civilians, from the extensive preparations to the launching of rockets to the after-action assessments by Syrian officials. On April 6, 2017, President Trump ordered a series of missile strikes on Syria, in response to the use of chemical weapons against Syrian civilians.[53]

Use the excerpt and your knowledge of U.S. Government and Politics to respond to parts A, B, and C.

A. Identify the power used by President Trump in ordering the airstrike in Syria.

B. Describe two ways in which Congress can check the president's actions in foreign affairs.

C. Explain one reason why it is difficult for Congress to check the president's powers over foreign affairs.

5.4 The Modern Presidency in Context

While the American presidency is based on the actions of a single person, no president truly acts alone. The president oversees a large executive office. However, the size and complexity of the federal bureaucracy can act as a powerful brake on presidential initiatives, particularly since most lower-level federal bureaucrats keep their jobs long after any one president has come and gone. Congress and the opinions of the public also influence presidential decision making.

The Vice Presidency

While the Constitution's vague language created an ultimately powerful presidency, it also created a very weak vice president. Under the original constitution, the person with the most votes in the Electoral College became president and the next highest vote-getter became vice president. A tie vote between Aaron Burr and Thomas Jefferson following the election of 1800 led to a constitutional crisis resulting in the ratification of the Twelfth Amendment. Under the Twelfth Amendment, instead of casting two votes for a presidential candidate, members of the Electoral College cast two separate votes: one for the president and the other for the vice president.

Constitutionally, the vice president has two jobs. He or she is "President of the Senate, but shall have no Vote, unless they be equally divided."[54] Rarely does the vice president preside over the Senate. Instead the president pro tempore of the Senate usually presides officially, but as discussed in chapter 4, junior senators routinely fill this role.

Second, the vice president assumes the office of the presidency should a sitting president vacate the office due to death, impairment, resignation, or impeachment. The Twenty-Fifth Amendment (1967) sets the modern rules of succession and also establishes a process for replacing a vice president who leaves office during his or her term. Under Section 2, the vice president takes over temporarily when the president voluntarily removes himself from office. This occurs when the president undergoes routine medical procedures requiring sedation. Sections 3 and 4 of the Twenty-Fifth Amendment provide for the permanent replacement of a president who is no longer able to discharge the powers and duties of office. In this process, the president nominates a replacement and approval is required "by a majority vote of both Houses of Congress."

In 1973 Gerald R. Ford, who was serving in Congress at the time, was approved as vice president in the Nixon administration after the resignation of Spiro T. Agnew because of criminal charges surrounding a bribery scandal when Agnew had been governor of Maryland. The following year, Ford became president after Nixon's resignation because of the Watergate scandal, and Congress approved Ford's nominee for vice president, Nelson Rockefeller. From 1974 to 1977, therefore, neither the president nor the vice president had been elected by the people.

The Twenty-Fifth Amendment also established a procedure through which the vice president may temporarily assume the role of acting president in the event "that the President is unable to discharge the powers and duties of his office." The vice president knows that he or she is a heartbeat away from one of the most powerful positions in the world.

In calling for the abolition of the institution of the vice presidency, Arthur M. Schlesinger Jr. once argued, "The Vice President has only one serious thing to do: that is, to wait around for the President to die. This is hardly the basis for a cordial and enduring friendship."[55] In the nation's history, eight vice presidents have assumed the office of the presidency on the death of the serving president and one upon the president's resignation.

In the past, most vice presidents had little impact on national policy, but it has recently become more common for vice presidents to have a larger role in White House deliberations. Other than being ready to take over, the main job of the vice president is to help the president get elected. Vice presidential nominees are often selected to "balance the ticket" with respect to geographical representation, connections to important blocs of voters, or experience.

The First Spouse

The wife or husband of a president occupies no formal role in an administration but is in a unique position to act as an advisor to the president. The first spouse also is a personal link between the president and the people.

Edith Bolling Galt Wilson, President Woodrow Wilson's wife, was probably the most powerful first lady. She helped organize and run the White House after her husband suffered a serious stroke in 1919. Eleanor Roosevelt was an outspoken critic of race discrimination. Modern first spouses often choose one or more policy areas and use their influence and visibility to call attention to issues in those areas and promote solutions. Michelle Obama, for example, focused on obesity, nutrition, and physical fitness among young people. Melania Trump has announced plans to bring awareness to the problem of bullying and other issues facing children with her "Be Best" initiative.

The Executive Office of the President

In response to the Great Depression and World War II, the office of the presidency was fundamentally transformed. Previously, there had been strong presidents, such as Abraham Lincoln, but for the most part presidents in the nineteenth century were subordinate to Congress. All of this changed during the presidency of Franklin D. Roosevelt. Since that time the presidency has become the dominating office of the national government. Presidential scholar Fred Greenstein argued that the changes in the office of the presidency, and its relationship to Congress and to the public, have been so significant as to warrant a new label: The Modern Presidency.[56] For Greenstein, there are four main features of the modern presidency: (1) the president now regularly initiates legislation; (2) many unilateral powers have been delegated to the presidency by Congress, including greater authority over trade policy and war; (3) the president is now the focus of public attention; (4) and there is a large staff directly working for the president housed in the **Executive Office of the President (EOP)**, which contains the president's closest advisors.

Executive Office of the President (EOP)
a collection of offices within the White House organization designed mainly to provide information to the president.

First Lady Melania Trump shares a moment with a young boy while visiting a school in Riyadh, Saudi Arabia. Should First Ladies avoid controversy, or should they advocate for policies?
GIUSEPPE CACACE/Getty Images

FIGURE 5.3

The Organization of the Executive Office

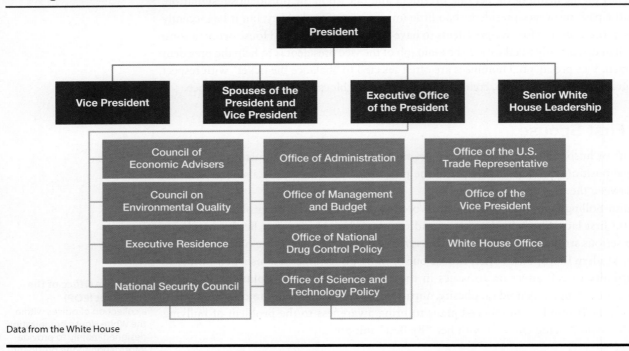

Data from the White House

With greater demands placed upon the federal government during the Great Depression. FDR needed help, and in 1939 the Executive Office of the President was created. Today there are between 2000–2500 staffers serving within the EOP who have policy-making responsibilities. The offices within the EOP touch upon all the key aspects of national responsibility, including the Office of Management and Budget (OMB), the National Security Council, and the Council of Economic Advisors, together the most important offices within the White House. (See Figure 5.3). The OMB is responsible for developing budget priorities, and each year the president submits his budget proposals to Congress. The National Security Council was formed in 1947 in response to the Cold War and the greater need for coordination of foreign policy, while the Council of Economic Advisors was formed in 1946 to aid the president in carrying out the responsibility of steering the economy to ensure stable economic growth.

The White House Office (part of the EOP) has grown into an important bureaucracy itself, and its most important members share offices near the president's. In choosing the members of the White House staff, presidents value political skill and loyalty. Many times staff members are individuals who were involved in the campaign or with the president in previous roles. Directors and deputy directors of communication ensure that the president's message is clearly and coherently presented to the American people. The White House press secretary acts as the president's spokesperson to the media and conducts daily press briefings, partly to inform but also partly to shape the national conversation in a way that helps the president achieve his policy goals.

The President and a Partisan Congress

The role that the president plays as "chief of party" is not mentioned in the Constitution. The framers worried about the dangers of faction, and political parties were viewed as particularly dangerous. Parties, however, are nearly as old as the republic. Divisions between President Washington's closest advisors gave rise to the nation's first political parties.

Modern presidents serve as the unofficial leaders of their political parties. They often choose the official leadership of their party, or at least have a major say in it. Presidents must contend with partisan politics in Congress, especially if they serve during a period of divided government with the opposing political party controlling one or both chambers of Congress. Periods of divided government are often associated with legislative gridlock, in which Congress's ability to pass laws is diminished or grinds to a halt completely.[57]

Presidents expect to have to battle and negotiate with members of the opposing party in Congress. However, support from their own party members can never be taken for granted. Presidents and members of Congress serve different constituencies. Presidents use **bargaining and persuasion** in dealing with Congress. This may take the form of personal phone calls to members of his or her party in Congress urging them to support the president's agenda. It may include a promise by a popular president to support the reelection campaign of an incumbent member of Congress. The president may approach members of the opposing party to convince them that his or her proposals will benefit their constituents.

bargaining and persuasion
an informal tool used by the president to persuade members of Congress to support his or her policy initiatives.

The American people demand that presidents keep them safe and prosperous. Demands on senators and representatives are often more local and address the unique

AP® Political Science PRACTICES

Analyzing Trends: The First One Hundred Days

Many commentators and historians use a president's first hundred days in office as a gauge of effectiveness. They look in particular at the passage of major legislation as a signal of the future success of a presidency. Is using the first one hundred days to assess a presidency a wise decision?

This bar chart gives a sense of how the first one hundred days of the first administrations of Bill Clinton, George W. Bush, Barack Obama, and Donald Trump compare.

1. Describe one trend shown on the bar chart.

2. Describe two factors that enable a president to pass major legislation during his first hundred days in office.

3. Explain one reason why the number of bills passed during the first hundred days in office may not indicate that the president will be successful in passing bills later in his presidency.

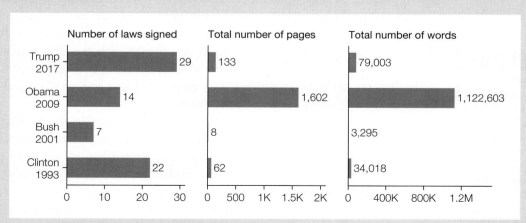

Data from Newsweek and from FiveThirtyEight.com

characteristics and needs of their states or districts. No member of Congress can ignore the wishes of her or his constituents without risk, even if the president requests it. Skillful presidents are fully aware of these tensions and—working with party leaders in Congress—often try to accommodate individual defections by members of their own party with the expectation that loyalty will be shown on less locally contentious votes somewhere down the line.

The President and Public Opinion

As the power of the American presidency has evolved, so has the president's relationship to the nation's citizens. Public opinion plays an important role in expanding or constraining the president's power. Public opinion is a powerful weapon in battles with Congress, the judiciary, and members of a president's own political party. If it is poorly mobilized or understood, however, the unfortunate president, in the words of Clinton Rossiter, "will find himself exposed to all those enemies who multiply like mosquitoes in a [New] Jersey August."[58]

Modern communications technologies and ease of travel have significantly contributed to connecting the president to the American public. Modern presidents attempt to make full use of communications technologies and public appearances to mobilize American public opinion in support of their own goals and policies. Presidents use the **bully pulpit** to appeal to the public to pressure other branches of government to support their policies. Political scientist Samuel Kernell used the term **going public** to describe "a strategy whereby a president promotes himself and his policies in Washington by appealing directly to the American public for support."[59] The State of the Union Address, press conferences, major speeches, and statements on social media platforms like Twitter all provide an opportunity for presidents to go public. Yet presidents have to be careful of what they say. Public opinion can turn against a president powerfully and quickly.

Americans' Evaluations of Presidential Performance

Since Franklin Roosevelt's presidency, pollsters have periodically taken the national pulse on Americans' views of how well their presidents are doing. These presidential approval ratings provide more than just a snapshot of the public's views. A president with high approval ratings is in a more powerful position in relation to Congress than one with low or sinking ratings. Sometimes unanticipated events—and the president's response to them—can produce dramatic changes in presidential approval. A national economic or military crisis, if handled successfully in the eyes of the American public, can produce a surge in presidential approval. In the months after the 9/11 attacks, President George W. Bush's approval rating rose to 90 percent, the highest ever recorded, but it later declined as the public became increasingly skeptical of his handling of the war in Iraq and as the nation's economy went into a recession.

Some patterns of presidential approval are more predictable. A president—especially after a convincing first-term victory—often enjoys a period of strong public approval, called a honeymoon period. For this reason, presidents often try to secure major legislative victories early in their first terms to capture public support and build momentum for future battles with Congress. Presidential approval usually declines over time as the American public begins to assign blame to the president for things that are not going well, whether this is deserved or not. There is also typically some recovery in presidential approval as the term draws to a close.[60] (See Figure 5.4.)

bully pulpit
presidential appeals to the public to pressure other branches of government to support his or her policies.

going public
a tactic through which presidents reach out directly to the American people with the hope that the people will, in turn, put pressure upon their representatives and senators to press for a president's policy goals.

FIGURE 5.4

Looking at Presidential Approval Ratings

Historical Average Job Approval Statistics

	Dates in office	Average approval rating %
Harry Truman	April 1945–January 1953	45.4
Dwight Eisenhower	January 1953–January 1961	65.0
John Kennedy	January 1961–November 1963	70.1
Lyndon Johnson	November 1963–January 1969	55.1
Richard Nixon	January 1969–August 1974	49.0
Gerald Ford	August 1974–January 1977	47.2
Jimmy Carter	January 1977–January 1981	45.5
Ronald Reagan	January 1981–January 1989	52.8
George H. W. Bush	January 1989–January 1993	60.9
Bill Clinton	January 1993–January 2001	55.1
George W. Bush	January 2001–January 2009	49.4
Barack Obama	January 2009–January 2017	47.9

Data from Gallup

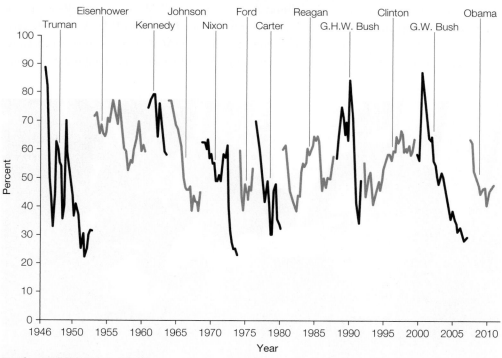

Historical Presidential Approval Ratings

Data from Wall Street Journal On-Line

Gallup has compiled average approval ratings for the presidents since the end of World War II. Terms in office vary. Eisenhower, Reagan, Clinton, George W. Bush, and Obama served two full terms. The graph uses polling data to show changes in approval ratings over the course of the presidents' terms in office. Why are average presidential approval ratings usually around 50 percent?

The President and Public Policy: The Dream Act

In 2012 President Obama issued an executive order creating the Deferred Action for Childhood Arrivals Program, or DACA.[61] Under DACA, undocumented individuals who came to the United States before the age of sixteen and who were in, or recently graduated from, school could seek a deferment on their deportation.

According to public opinion polls, most Americans believe that undocumented immigrants living in the United States who meet certain requirements should be allowed to stay in the country legally, but more Democrats support that position than Republicans, making the issue a partisan one.[62] As part of a broader effort at immigration reform, DACA was aimed at protecting a group of people who seemed to be both the most vulnerable and least controversial from a policy perspective—the children of undocumented immigrants. As one report put it, "DACA is an important tool for expanding economic and civic contributions from these individuals. Ultimately, these . . . initiatives will benefit places, not just individuals and families."[63]

With the arrival of the administration of President Donald Trump in 2017, however, many expected that DACA would be rescinded. A spokesperson for the Federation for American Immigration Reform, a group that supports reduced immigration, noted, "This was the crown jewel of illegal executive orders—amnesty for illegal aliens. It doesn't get any more blatant than that."[64] Many Republicans criticized President Obama's executive orders on immigration, along with other issues, as a way of sidestepping the Republican-controlled Senate and House.

Many state government officials tried to force the president's hand: "Texas Attorney General Ken Paxton was joined by his counterparts in nine other states in a letter . . . warning [federal] Attorney General Jeff Sessions that if the Trump administration does not move to end the Deferred Action for Childhood Arrivals, they will file a court challenge to the program."[65] In September 2017, President Trump rescinded Obama's DACA order effective March 2018 unless Congress acted to address this issue. DACA remains in effect, because the Supreme Court refused to hear a case challenging a ruling that extended the program.[66]

Abby, who is twenty-six, holds her ticket after being first in line among other Deferred Action for Childhood Arrivals (DACA) recipients waiting at the Coalition for Humane Immigrant Rights (CHIRLA) office in Los Angeles on September 30, 2017. Volunteer lawyers were on hand to offer assistance on the final weekend before the October 5, 2017, deadline when more than 154,000 DACA recipients had to renew their work permits before the program was scheduled to end in March 2018. The deadline was extended when the Supreme Court refused to hear an appeal of a ruling, which resulted in the DACA program continuing.
FREDERIC J. BROWN/Getty Images

5.4 Explain how modern presidents interact with the executive branch, Congress, and the public.

REMEMBER
- The vice president assumes the office of the presidency should a serving president vacate the office due to death, infirmity, resignation, or impeachment.
- The Twenty-Fifth Amendment sets the modern rules of succession and also establishes a process for replacing a vice president who leaves office during his or her term.
- The first spouse typically chooses a policy area to focus on and uses her influence and visibility to call attention to the issue and promote solutions.
- The Executive Office of the President is a collection of agencies and offices that assist the president in both an advisory and policymaking capacity.
- Public opinion plays an important role in expanding or constraining the power of individual presidents.
- A president's approval ratings tend to decline over time.

KNOW
- *Executive Office of the President*: a collection of offices within the White House organization designed mainly to provide information to the president. (p. 169)
- *bargaining and persuasion*: informal tool used by the president to persuade members of Congress to support his policy initiatives. (p. 171)
- *bully pulpit*: presidential appeals to the public to pressure other branches of government to support his policies. (p. 172)
- *going public*: a tactic through which presidents reach out directly to the American people with the hope that the people will, in turn, put pressure upon their representatives and senators to press for a president's policy goals. (p. 172)

THINK
- Should presidents use public approval ratings in making difficult policy decisions?
- Do presidents have an obligation to make difficult decisions, even when the public does not support those decisions?

5.4 Review Question: Free Response

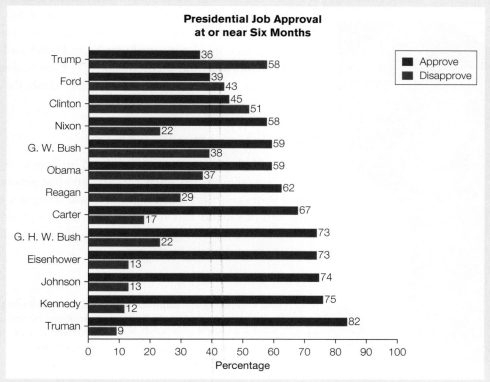

Presidential Job Approval at or near Six Months

	Approve	Disapprove
Trump	36	58
Ford	39	43
Clinton	45	51
Nixon	58	22
G. W. Bush	59	38
Obama	59	37
Reagan	62	29
Carter	67	17
G. H. W. Bush	73	22
Eisenhower	73	13
Johnson	74	13
Kennedy	75	12
Truman	82	9

Data from ABC News / Washington Post and Gallup polls

Use the bar chart and your knowledge of U.S. Government and Politics to answer parts A, B and C.

A. Describe presidential job approval ratings at or near six months.

B. Define *presidential honeymoon period* and describe two reasons for the honeymoon period.

C. Explain one reason why presidential approval ratings tend to be lower at the end of a term than they are in the beginning of a term.

 **5.5** The War on Terror and Presidential Power

In the twenty-first century, with the nation involved in combating threats to national security arising from multiple terrorist networks without defined geographic and political boundaries, the question of presidential power has only grown more complex, more relevant, and more controversial. In times of crisis, especially economic or military crises, no single actor in the American political system is able to react to the demands of the situation as quickly and decisively as the president. As political scientist Lester G. Seligman put it, "Under crisis conditions the political system undergoes a drastic change. The White House becomes a command post, Congress and interest groups assume minor roles, the public becomes acutely aware of the threat and looks fervently to the president for authoritative guidance."[67] The ability to act first and act alone is a tool unique to the president. Its power is only magnified during times of threat and crisis.

The Supreme Court Restricts Presidential Power

In *Hamdi v. Rumsfeld* (2002), the Supreme Court considered the petition by Yaser Hamdi's father, challenging his son's detention in Guantanamo Bay. Sandra Day O'Connor delivered the Court's opinion, concluding that "a state of war is not a blank check for the President when it comes to the rights of the Nation's citizens." The decision also asserted that Yaser Hamdi had the right to a hearing "before a neutral decision maker."[68] Even in times of war, the president may not act unilaterally if doing so violates the constitutional rights of American citizens.

The Paradox of Power

No writ of habeas corpus was ever issued for Anwar al-Awlaki. After the U.S. government had acted, there was no live person to bring to a United States court for a hearing. There was likely not even an intact body. Barack Obama was not the first American president to authorize a drone strike that resulted in the death of an American citizen.

Yaser Hamdi in captivity at Guantanamo Bay in 2002. Hamdi's father petitioned for a writ of habeas corpus, but the Bush administration claimed to have the wartime power to hold Hamdi indefinitely without trial. Should citizens accused of terrorism be granted more rights than noncitizens? Why?
United States Navy

Evaluating an Argument: Attorney General Eric Holder on the Use of Lethal Force against U.S. Citizens Abroad

Pressured by members of Congress to disclose more information about the use of lethal force against Americans abroad without trial and away from active combat operations, on May 22, 2013, President Obama's attorney general, Eric H. Holder Jr., released a memorandum to key congressional leaders justifying the administration's actions in the killing of four Americans.

Although Holder's memo did not explicitly state that any of the four Americans were killed by pilotless drone aircraft, it was widely reported in the media that at least one, Anwar al-Awlaki, had in fact been killed by a drone strike. Holder's memo focused largely on laying out the justification for killing al-Awlaki. In it, Holder stated,

> Since 2009, the United States, in the conduct of U.S. counterterrorism operations against al-Qa'ida and its associated forces outside of areas of active hostilities, has specifically targeted and killed one U.S. citizen, Anwar al-Aulaqi. The United States is further aware of three other U.S. citizens who have been killed in such U.S. counterterrorism operations over that same time period. . . .
>
> Al-Aulaqi was a senior operational leader of al-Qa'ida in the Arabian Peninsula (AQAP), the most dangerous regional affiliate of al-Qa'ida and a group that has committed numerous terrorist attacks overseas and attempted multiple times to conduct terrorist attacks against the U.S. homeland. Anwar al-Aulaqi was not just a senior leader of AQAP—he was the group's chief of external operations, intimately involved in detailed planning and putting in place plots against U.S. persons.
>
> Moreover, information that remains classified to protect sensitive sources and methods evidences al-Aulaqi's involvement in the planning of numerous *other* plots against U.S. and Western interests and makes clear he was continuing to plot attacks when killed.

Former U.S. Attorney General Eric H. Holder Jr.
PAUL J. RICHARDS/Getty Images

> The decision to use lethal force is one of the gravest that our government, at every level, can face. The operation to target Anwar al-Aulaqi was thus subjected to an exceptionally rigorous interagency review. . . . When capture is not feasible, the policy provides that lethal force may be used only when a terrorist target poses a continuing, imminent threat to Americans, and when certain other preconditions, including a requirement that no other reasonable alternatives exist to effectively address the threat, are satisfied.[69]

Speeches are given to persuade an audience to accept a point of view. In evaluating Attorney General Holder's speech discuss the following:

1. Describe the point of view conveyed in the memo.

2. Describe two pieces of factual evidence cited by Attorney General Holder in support of his position.

3. Explain one reason why some people criticize allowing the president to use deadly force against citizens accused of terrorism.

In 2002, under the administration of President George W. Bush, "the C.I.A. struck a car carrying a group of suspected militants, including an American citizen, who were believed to have Qaeda ties."[70]

The power of the American presidency is not easily defined, nor are its roots and sources easily traced or separated. Many factors—constitutional provisions, institutional and political contexts, individual personality and skill, and responses to crises—have all played a role in its development. As scholars have observed, the office of the presidency is full of paradoxes.[71] The framers wanted a strong and decisive office, yet they were wary of creating an elected monarch. Americans often look to their presidents for leadership above the fray of partisan politics, yet the position is, by design, political and embedded in a system of checks and balances. Americans look to their presidents for leadership yet expect them to follow the Constitution and the will of the people.

Section Review

5.5. Evaluate how presidents have used their powers in the war on terror.

REMEMBER
- In *Hamdi v. Rumsfeld*, the Supreme Court held that American citizens accused of terrorism have the right to a hearing.
- The president can act more quickly than other branches in responding to threats.
- The need to respond quickly to modern threats has expanded the power of the president.

THINK
- What factors may lead to an expansion of presidential power in the future?
- Has the presidency become too powerful, given our system of checks and balances?

5.5 Review Question: Free Response

Today, our nation saw evil, the very worst of human nature, and we responded with the best of America—with the daring of our rescue workers, with the caring for strangers and neighbors who came to give blood and help in any way they could. Immediately following the first attack, I implemented our government's emergency response plans. Our military is powerful, and it's prepared. Our emergency teams are working in New York City and Washington, D.C., to help with local rescue efforts.

—President George W. Bush, September 11, 2001[72]

Use the excerpt and your knowledge of U.S. Government and Politics to answer parts A, B, and C.

A. Describe one power used by President Bush on September 11, 2001.

B. Explain one reason why the founding fathers gave the president substantial powers over national defense.

C. Explain two reasons why issues involving national defense have led to the expansion of power in the twenty-first century.

Chapter 5 Review

AP® KEY CONCEPTS

- *executive branch* (p. 152)
- *formal (or enumerated) powers* (p. 157)
- *informal powers* (p. 157)
- *treaty* (p. 159)
- *State of the Union Address* (p. 159)
- *veto* (p. 159)

- *pocket veto* (p. 159)
- *presidential pardon* (p. 161)
- *executive privilege* (p. 161)
- *executive agreement* (p. 161)
- *signing statement* (p. 161)
- *executive order* (p. 162)

- *War Powers Resolution* (p. 166)
- *impeachment* (p. 166)
- *Executive Office of the President* (p. 169)
- *bargaining and persuasion* (p. 171)
- *bully pulpit* (p. 172)
- *going public* (p. 172)

AP® EXAM PRACTICE and Critical Thinking Project

MULTIPLE-CHOICE QUESTIONS

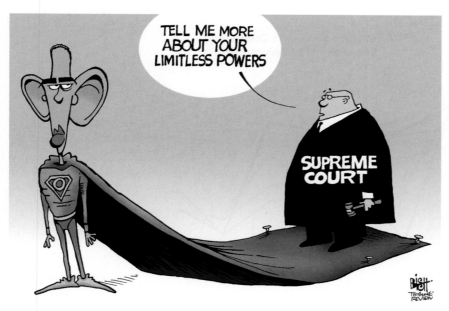

Cagle Cartoons, Inc.

1. Which of the following best describes the viewpoint shown in the cartoon?
   A. Presidents believe they have superpowers.
   B. The Supreme Court unfairly blocks presidential initiatives.
   C. Executive orders are unconstitutional.
   D. Other branches of government check the president.

Use the information in this passage to answer questions 2 and 3.

On November 20, 2014, President Obama issued a statement removing the threat of deportation for approximately five million undocumented parents and permanent residents who lived in the country for at least five years.

2. Which of the following powers did President Obama use in in the scenario?
   A. The informal power to issue an executive order
   B. The formal power as commander in chief
   C. The formal power as chief diplomat
   D. The informal power to issue an executive agreement

3. Which of the following is the best argument that President Obama exceeded his authority in the situation described?
   A. The president should have used an executive agreement because other countries are involved in the issue of immigration.
   B. The action expands presidential power beyond its constitutional limits.
   C. Under the system of federalism, the national government must work with the states in setting immigration policy.
   D. The president infringed on the authority of the Immigration and Naturalization Service, which was created to set immigration policies.

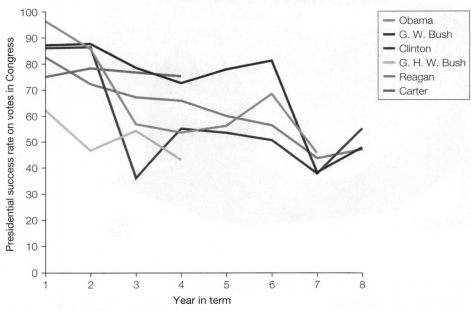

Presidents' Success in Congress: Better earlier in their terms

Data from Congressional Quarterly

4. Which of the following best explains the trend shown in the graph?
   A. Presidents rarely face divided government at the beginning of a term.
   B. Newly elected presidents take advantage of a "honeymoon" period with Congress to get their policies passed.
   C. Presidents often win elections by large margins, making them popular at the beginning of their terms.
   D. Members of Congress rely on the president for electoral support, making them more likely to support presidential initiatives.

5. Select the pair of examples that matches the presidential role with the correct enumerated constitutional power.

Presidential role	Enumerated constitutional power
A. Commander in chief	Declare war
B. Chief diplomat	Ratifies treaties
C. Chief legislator	Gives the State of the Union Address
D. Chief executive	Issues executive orders

6. President Smith begins slurring her words and speaking incoherently about dropping nuclear bombs on Russia. What is the most expeditious way under the Constitution to avert disaster?

   A. The president can be removed at the end of her term of office when a new president is sworn in.

   B. The president can be removed when the vice president and a majority of the cabinet advise the Congress that the president is unfit.

   C. The president can be removed when the Supreme Court declares the president unfit upon application of the surgeon general.

   D. The president can be removed via impeachment and removal proceedings in the House and Senate.

Questions 7 and 8 refer to the quote.

On July 10, 1832, President Andrew Jackson sent the following message to the United States Senate:

> The bill "to modify and continue" the act entitled "An act to incorporate the subscribers to the Bank of the United States" was presented to me on the 4th July instant. Having considered it with that solemn regard to the principles of the Constitution which the day was calculated to inspire, and come to the conclusion that it ought not to become a law, I herewith return it to the Senate, in which it originated, with my objections. A bank of the United States is in many respects convenient for the Government and useful to the people. . . . [D]eeply impressed with the belief that some of the powers and privileges possessed by the existing bank are unauthorized by the Constitution, subversive of the rights of the States, and dangerous to the liberties of the people, I felt it my duty at an early period of my Administration to call the attention of Congress to the practicability of organizing an institution combining all its advantages and obviating these objections.[73]

7. What is President Jackson's perspective in the quote?

   A. A bank of the United States is useful to the people and should be established.

   B. The Constitution is subversive of the rights of the states.

   C. Congress cannot establish a bank of the United States.

   D. The Constitution does not protect the liberties of the people.

8. Which of the following terms describes Jackson's message?

   A. veto

   B. signing statement

   C. executive order

   D. State of the Union message

Questions 9 and 10 refer to the bar chart.

Presidential Judicial Nominees, 1977–2018

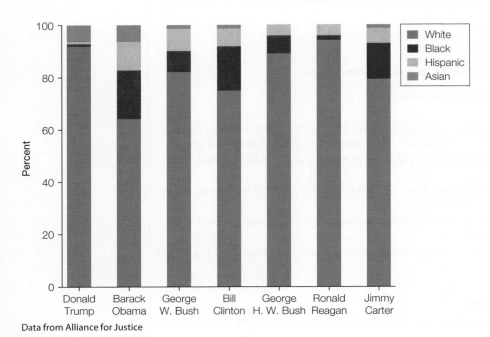

Data from Alliance for Justice

9. The bar chart supports which of the following inferences?
   A. President Donald Trump has nominated more white federal judges than any president since Ronald Reagan.
   B. President Jimmy Carter nominated more African American judges than any other president.
   C. The president who nominated the most Asian American judges also nominated the fewest Hispanic judges.
   D. A consistent trend has emerged over the decades favoring the nomination of an increasing number of judges from minority backgrounds.

10. What is the most logical explanation for the data on the bar chart?
   A. Republican presidents are more interested than Democratic presidents in leaving a judicial legacy that extends beyond their term in office.
   B. Republican presidents are unwilling to nominate minority candidates for judicial office.
   C. Minority judges are more likely to be confirmed during periods of economic uncertainty.
   D. Presidents tend to nominate judges who match the demographics of their political supporters.

FREE-RESPONSE QUESTIONS

1. In 1994, President Clinton deployed troops to Haiti, without congressional approval, to fight against atrocities perpetrated by Haiti's former leaders and to oversee a transition to democracy.

   Use the scenario and your knowledge of U.S. Government and Politics to respond to parts A, B, and C.

   A. Describe a power of the president used in the scenario.
   B. Explain one way in which the War Powers Resolution might affect the scenario.
   C. Explain one reason why it is difficult for Congress to check the power of the president to commit troops despite the War Powers Resolution.

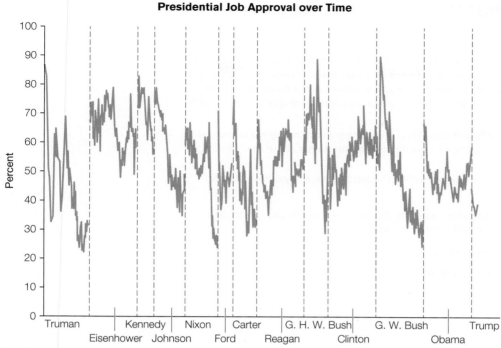

Presidential Job Approval over Time

Data from Gallup

2. Use the information in the graph and your knowledge of U.S. Government and Politics to respond to parts A, B, and C.

A. Describe one trend shown in the graph.

B. Describe two ways in which public approval ratings might impact the president's success in getting his initiatives passed in Congress.

C. Describe two factors, other than public approval ratings, that might impact the president's legislative success.

ARGUMENTATION QUESTION

In a 1973 book, historian Arthur Schlesinger analyzed whether the president of the United States has become overly powerful and was no longer subject to constitutional checks and balances. Schlesinger made his argument following the Watergate scandal stating, "The expansion and abuse of presidential power constitute the underlying issue, the issue that Watergate has raised to the surface, dramatized, and made politically accessible."[74] Take a position on whether or not Schlesinger's argument that the presidency has become too powerful is true today. In your essay,

- Articulate a claim or thesis that addresses the issue raised by Schlesinger, and use a line of reasoning to defend it.
- Use at least TWO pieces of relevant and accurate evidence to support your claim or thesis.
- At least ONE piece of evidence must be from one of the foundational documents listed below:
  - Constitution of the United States
  - *Federalist* No. 51
  - *Federalist* No. 70
  - Brutus No. 1
- Use a second piece of evidence from another foundational document listed above or from your study of the American presidency.
- Use reasoning to explain why the evidence you provided supports your claim or thesis.
- Use refutation, concession, or rebuttal to respond to an opposing or alternative perspective.

CRITICAL THINKING PROJECT

Analyzing a White House Press Briefing

The White House press secretary is a direct connection between the president, the media, and the public. The press secretary gives a daily briefing, presenting a prepared statement and responding to questions from reporters assigned to cover the president, known as the White House Press Corps. White House press briefings are located at: https://www.whitehouse.gov/briefing-room/press-briefings.

Pretend you are a member of the White House Press Office. The press secretary has asked you to review a press briefing given in the last two weeks and give advice to her about the following:

1. Was her prepared statement clear and well written? Support your analysis with specific examples.

2. Did she answer the questions reporters asked, or did she avoid directly answering their questions? Support your analysis with specific examples.

3. What went well during the press briefing?

4. What suggestions do you have to improve press briefings in the future?

6 The Federal Judiciary
Politics, Power, and the "Least Dangerous" Branch

The **federal judiciary** is one of the three branches of the nation's government. Its role is to interpret and apply the laws of the nation. In *Federalist* No. 78, Alexander Hamilton described the federal judiciary as "least dangerous to the political rights of the Constitution."[1] Sitting atop the federal judiciary is the **Supreme Court**, which was established in Article III of the Constitution and serves as the highest court in the nation.

As we have explored, both Congress and the president have the power to shape national public policy. Congress writes the laws, and it has the

Acting Chief Justice Brent Benjamin, left, and Judge Fred Fox listen to arguments before the Supreme Court of Appeals of West Virginia in a rehearing of a judgment awarded to Harman Mining against Massey Energy. The rehearing was required by the Supreme Court of the United States, after a case that involved conflicts of interest and their effects on judicial independence.
Bob Bird/AP Images

federal judiciary
the branch of the federal government that interprets the laws of the nation.

Supreme Court
the highest level of the federal judiciary, which was established in Article III of the Constitution and serves as the highest court in the nation.

power to tax and to fund programs. The president executes the laws of the nation and is the commander in chief of the armed forces. Congress and the president are perceived as the political branches of the government, with elected officers.

Judges are not elected, but they pass judgment on issues that have political implications. Federal judges serve for life, so they don't face political consequences at the ballot box. The degree to which the federal judiciary chooses to involve itself in political controversies, however, can impair its legitimacy with the American public.

In this chapter, you will engage with the stories of John Marshall's establishment of judicial review and the confirmation of Sonia Sotomayor to the Supreme Court. The story of Chief Justice John Marshall and how he led the Court to establish judicial review is the story of the Court itself—the framing tale about how the Supreme Court assumed the place it holds in U.S. society. Justice Sonia Sotomayor brings a unique perspective as the first Latina justice on the Supreme Court. The story of her confirmation demonstrates the role of politics in the appointment process.

First, though, we will examine a tale with some twists. In this story, you will read about how the Supreme Court of the United States oversees behavior within the court system and uses the Constitution to make sure judges provide everyone with equal access to the court system.

LEARNING TARGETS

After reading this chapter, you will be able to

6.1 Explain why federal court justices are appointed, rather than elected.

6.2 Describe how the Constitution structures the federal judiciary.

6.3 Define judicial review and explain how it checks the power of Congress, the president, and the states.

6.4 Explain how the life tenure of justices, coupled with the power of judicial review, leads to controversy over Supreme Court nominations.

6.5 Describe the Supreme Court's role in policymaking and how Congress and the president may limit the powers of the Supreme Court.

■ 6.1 Judicial Independence from Money and Politics

Alexander Hamilton, in *Federalist* No. 78, argued that an independent judiciary was essential for preserving liberty and upholding the checks and balances of the constitution. To accomplish this goal, he argued that federal judges should be appointed for life, and their salaries protected. And that practice still stands today.

Money, Politics, and How the Supreme Court Preserves Judicial Independence

Federal judges are appointed. At the state level, however, beginning in the nineteenth century, populist reformers feared that legislators and governors were too close to appointed judges, undermining judicial independence. Reformers pushed for the election of state judges. For these reformers, judicial independence meant insulation from partisan patronage in appointments.[2] Today, the United States is the only country in the world that elects judges,[3] and almost 90 percent of state judges have to face the voters.[4] Thirty-eight states elect their supreme court justices.

In recent years, as more and more money has flooded into state judicial election campaigns by special interests seeking to shape the courts, concerns have been raised that judicial independence is threatened. Former U.S. Supreme Court Justice Sandra Day O'Connor, for example, has written: "We expect all judges to be accountable to the law rather than political supporters or special interests. . . . This crisis of confidence in the impartiality of the judiciary is real and growing. Left unaddressed, the perception that justice is for sale will undermine the rule of law that the courts are supposed to uphold."[5]

The flood of money into judicial campaigns is apparent when comparing the 1990s to the decade after. During the 1990s, $83 million was raised in state supreme court races, but between 2000 and 2009, this figure more than doubled to $207 million.[6] In 2016, spending by outside groups for TV ads broke all previous records, with most of the money from so-called dark money donations, which comes from donors whose identities are not disclosed. Dark money will be discussed in more detail in Chapter 13.[7] During the 2015–16 election cycle, thirty-three states held supreme court elections for seventy-six seats, and an estimated $69 million was spent.[8]

In 2009, the U.S. Supreme Court weighed in on the question of campaign contributions and undue influence in the case of *Caperton v. Massey Coal Co.*[9] The case hinged on the role that Don Blankenship, the head of Massey Coal, played in the election of one of the justices of the Supreme Court of Appeals of West Virginia, the state's highest court, because after the election Blankenship's case went before the court.

Hugh Caperton was president of Harmon Mining, which had been put out of business due to the fraudulent practices of Massey Coal. After a jury awarded Caperton $50 million in damages in 2002, Blankenship appealed to overturn this judgment. With the 2004 election on the horizon and Justice Warren McGraw up for reelection, Blankenship spent $3 million to help the campaign of McGraw's opponent, Brent Benjamin. With this support, Benjamin won by a margin of 53–47 percent of the 700,000 votes cast. Benjamin cast the deciding vote in the Caperton appeal, ruling in favor of Blankenship.

When the West Virginia Supreme Court heard the case, Caperton argued that Blankenship's contributions made it impossible for Benjamin to be impartial and requested that Benjamin recuse himself, as had another justice on the court who was personal friends and vacationed with Blankenship. Benjamin refused, and in 2007, he was the pivotal vote in overturning the $50 million verdict.

Although there were no allegations that Blankenship's money amounted to an actual bribe, Caperton argued that it created a debt of gratitude. The U.S. Supreme Court ruled that the appearance of a conflict of interest due to the extraordinary campaign contributions made by Donald Blankenship required Justice Brent Benjamin to recuse himself from hearing the case.[10] The failure to do so violated the due process clause of the Fourteenth Amendment.[11]

In ruling that Benjamin should have recused himself, the U.S. Supreme Court "concluded there is a serious risk of actual bias—based on objective and reasonable perceptions—when a person with a personal stake in a particular case had a significant and disproportionate influence in placing the judge on the case by raising funds or directing the judge's election campaign when the case was pending or imminent."[12] Thus, the U.S. Supreme Court reversed the judgment of the West Virginia Supreme Court.

This decision upheld the importance of judicial independence because conflicts of interest, or the appearance of a conflict of interest, go to heart of the legitimacy of any court proceeding. The U.S. Supreme Court's majority stated that West Virginia's own judicial code of conduct required that a judge "disqualify himself or herself in a proceeding in which the judge's impartiality might reasonably be questioned."[13] The extraordinary role that Blankenship played in the election of Brent Benjamin threatened judicial independence, making a fair hearing impossible.

The *Caperton* case emphasizes that a properly designed judicial system is supposed to be above politics, and that the Supreme Court is the ultimate arbiter of the Constitution. The Supreme Court in *Caperton* found Blankenship's political contributions to have at least potentially weighed on Benjamin's judicial decision. As the Caperton case demonstrates, Supreme Court decisions can be viewed through a political lens, and therefore, federal judges risk being drawn into the political fray.

Sotomayor's Appointment to the Supreme Court

The Constitution requires that all federal judges be appointed by the president and confirmed by the Senate. This process is meant to insulate federal judges from the kind of politics involved in the Blankenship case. Nevertheless, the appointment of federal judges remains political.

In May 2009, President Barack Obama was presented with his first opportunity to nominate an individual to the U.S. Supreme Court. Although the retiring justice, David H. Souter, had been appointed by a Republican president (George H. W. Bush), his votes on the Court had generally placed him in the liberal bloc of justices. Obama's appointment, therefore, was not likely to shift the ideological balance of the Court. In the partisan world of the modern federal government, preserving the Court's ideological balance lessened tensions surrounding the nomination. Even so, observers and insiders expected an intensely political battle because justices on the Supreme Court are appointed for life.

President Obama nominated Sonia Sotomayor, the daughter of parents who moved to New York from Puerto Rico, a graduate of Yale Law School, a former prosecutor and litigator, and—at the time—a judge with the U.S. Court of Appeals for the Second Circuit. She was, however, according to the *Washington Post*, the "riskiest choice" of the likely nominees, largely because of public remarks that she had made on the importance of identity and personal history in approaching judicial decision making.[14]

Republicans in the Senate were prepared to criticize Sotomayor as a justice who would be "willing to expand constitutional rights beyond the text of the Constitution."[15] Given a popular president and a Senate under Democratic control, though, defeating Sotomayor was unlikely.

Speaking in 2001, Sotomayor, then an appellate court judge, had highlighted the role that her identity as a Latina and life experiences had played and would continue to play in her judicial career—a perspective that, in her opinion, helped her make just decisions, especially in cases involving equality and discrimination. These remarks by Sotomayor at a public lecture received particular scrutiny from Republicans during the confirmation proceedings.

Republicans in the Senate hoped to use the confirmation proceedings to increase their support among conservative voters.[16] With their opposition, however, Republicans risked

This undated family photograph shows Judge Sonia Sotomayor as a child with her mother Celina Sotomayor, left, and father Juan Luis Sotomayor, right. Her parents came to the mainland from Puerto Rico during World War II. Sonia Sotomayor was born and raised in New York. She has spoken about her experiences and the role of identity in judicial decision making.

The White House/Getty Images

alienating female voters and Hispanics. Hispanic voters make up the fastest growing group of Americans, and their political importance is increasing.

When the Senate Judiciary Committee began its proceedings on the nomination in mid-July 2009, Republicans promised to avoid personal attacks. Sotomayor rehearsed her testimony and her answers to expected questions in the week before the hearings.

In the end, the vote in the Senate Judiciary Committee went off without drama or surprise. In a 13–6 vote, with one Republican joining the unanimous Democrats, the committee approved her nomination and sent it to the full Senate. Shortly thereafter, the Senate confirmed Sotomayor's appointment to the Supreme Court by a vote of 68–31.

Sotomayor took the judicial oath of office, promising to "administer justice without respect to persons, and do equal right to the poor and the rich" as the nation's newest member of the Supreme Court. As a Supreme Court justice, Sotomayor carries the hopes and aspirations of many Americans on her shoulders. She also joins an institution that is designed to act independently of politics and the other branches of government in protecting the Constitution.

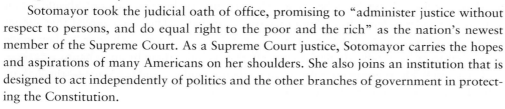

Section Review

This chapter's main ideas are reflected in the Learning Targets. By reviewing after each section, you should be able to

—**Remember** the key points,

—**Know** terms that are central to the topic, and

—**Think** critically about these questions.

6.1 Explain why federal court justices are appointed, rather than elected.

REMEMBER	• Many states elect judges, and politics influences their selection.
	• Federal judges are appointed by the president and confirmed by the Senate in an effort to make them independent from politics and from the other branches of government.
KNOW	• *federal judiciary*: the branch of the federal government that interprets and applies the laws of the nation. (p. 186)
	• *Supreme Court*: the highest level of the federal judiciary, which was established in Article III of the Constitution and serves as the highest court in the nation. (p. 186)
THINK	• What are the disadvantages of electing judges at the state level?
	• Are unelected federal judges, who serve for life, a threat to representative democracy?

6.2 The Constitution and the Federal Judiciary

The delegates to the Constitutional Convention spent much less time debating the structure and powers of the federal judiciary than they did hammering out the design of the legislative and executive branches. The delegates agreed that the judiciary should retain a degree of independence from the other two branches.[17] They also agreed that judges should be allowed lifetime tenure, with the condition of "good behavior." They made provisions to protect judicial salaries from efforts to reduce them by an unhappy or vengeful Congress.[18] The president would nominate federal judges, and the Senate—through its role of advice and consent—would confirm the nominations.[19]

Article III: The Federal Judiciary in the Constitution

In the Constitution, the judiciary (Article III) comes in third, behind Congress (Article I) and the executive branch (Article II), both in terms of placement and in amount of coverage. Only the highest level of the federal judiciary—the Supreme Court—is described in the document, leaving the establishment of lower federal courts in the hands of Congress: "The judicial Power of the United States, shall be vested in one supreme Court, and in such inferior Courts as the Congress may from time ordain and establish."[20]

The Constitution was clear that the federal judiciary, and the Supreme Court in particular, was to be the highest judicial power in the land: "The judicial power shall extend to all Cases, in Law and Equity, arising under this Constitution, the laws of the United States, and Treaties made, or which shall be made, under their Authority."[21] This judicial power, combined with the supremacy clause of the Constitution, which declared the "Constitution, and the Laws of the United States" to be "the supreme Law of the Land" establishes the supremacy of the federal judiciary over matters involving the Constitution and federal law.[22]

original jurisdiction
the authority of a court to act as the first court to hear a case, which includes the finding of facts in the case.

appellate jurisdiction
the authority of a court to hear and review decisions made by lower courts in that system.

The Constitution also briefly describes the federal courts' jurisdiction, or authority to decide specific cases.[23] If a court has **original jurisdiction** in a case, that court has the authority to hear the case first, act as a finder of facts, and decide the case. Courts with original jurisdiction are commonly referred to as trial courts. A court with **appellate jurisdiction** has the authority to review the decision of a lower court to overturn or revise

Analyzing Visual Information:
The Presentation of the Supreme Court

Periodically, members of the Supreme Court pose for a "class photo," which is posted on the Court's official Web site. In the second photo, Justice Clarence Thomas, a conservative, interacts with Justice Stephen Breyer, a liberal.

1. Describe the mood conveyed in the first photo. Explain how the photographer conveys this mood.

2. Describe the mood conveyed in the second photo. Describe the elements of the photo that convey this mood.

3. Compare the photos. Explain how each photo conveys an image about the role of the Supreme Court in the political process.

The justices of the Supreme Court gather for an official group portrait to include new Associate Justice Neil Gorsuch, top row, far right, on June 1, 2017, at the Supreme Court Building in Washington. Seated, from left are Ruth Bader Ginsburg, Anthony Kennedy, Chief Justice John Roberts, Clarence Thomas, and Stephen Breyer. Standing, from left: Elena Kagan, Samuel Alito Jr., Sonia Sotomayor, and Gorsuch.

Olivier Douliery/Picture Alliance/Washington/District ofColumbia/US

Supreme Court justices Stephen Breyer, left, and Clarence Thomas.

AP Photo/Manuel Balce Ceneta

that decision. Courts operating under appellate jurisdiction generally focus on the lower courts' actions and procedures, without finding facts on their own.

Ratification: Antifederalist Concerns and the Federalist Response

During the ratification debates, opponents of the Constitution raised concerns about potential abuses of power by the proposed federal judiciary. The Antifederalists feared that the growth of the national government through an increasingly powerful judiciary would diminish the rights of states and individuals. An Antifederalist essay, Brutus No. 11, published in a New York newspaper in January 1788, warned against this very possibility. In granting the power to overturn legislation to the Supreme Court, "Brutus" argued that the nation would run the risk of unconstrained justices imposing their own views of what is constitutional and what is not. He cautioned, "They will give the sense of every article of the constitution that may from time to time come before them. And in their decisions they will not confine themselves to any fixed or established rules, but will determine, according to what appears to them, the reason and spirit of the constitution. The opinions of the supreme court, whatever they may be, will have the force of law, because there is no power provided in the constitution that can correct their errors or control their adjudications."[24]

In **Federalist No. 78**, Alexander Hamilton sought to reassure skeptical Antifederalists and others that the federal judiciary would not trample upon their rights and liberties. Hamilton argued, members of the federal judiciary—because of the process of their selection and their lifetime tenure—would stand apart from politics and be able to "secure a steady, upright, and impartial administration of the laws."[25] Compared to the power of the sword and the purse, Hamilton reassured, the federal judiciary—exercising only the power of judgment and located outside the arena of political struggle—did not pose a threat to liberty. He argued that the judiciary needed protection from encroachment on its limited powers by the other two branches.

Federalist No. 78 argument by Alexander Hamilton that the federal judiciary would be unlikely to infringe upon rights and liberties but would serve as a check on the other two branches.

AP® Political Science PRACTICES
Interpreting Foundational Documents

Whoever attentively considers the different departments of power must perceive that, in a government in which they are separated from each other, the judiciary, from the nature of its functions, will always be the least dangerous to the political rights of the constitution; because it will be least in a capacity to annoy or injure them. The executive not only dispenses the honours, but holds the sword of the community; the legislature not only commands the purse, but prescribes the rules by which the duties and rights of every citizen are to be regulated; the judiciary, on the contrary, has no influence over either the sword or the purse; no direction either of the strength or of the wealth of the society; and can take no active resolution whatever. It may truly be said to have neither

FORCE nor WILL, but merely judgment; and it must ultimately depend upon the aid of the executive arm even for the efficacy of its judgments.[26]
—Alexander Hamilton, *Federalist* No. 78

1. Describe Hamilton's view of the power held by the executive.

2. Describe Hamilton's view of the power held by the legislature.

3. Explain why, according to Hamilton, the judiciary is not as powerful as the executive or legislature.

4. Identify a power of the judiciary Hamilton omits from the quote, and explain why Hamilton omits this power in making his argument.

Congress Builds the Judiciary

The first Congress passed the Judiciary Act of 1789 to flesh out "the nature and the organization" of the court system.[27] Only the chief justice of the Supreme Court is mentioned in the Constitution; the document does not specify the number of justices in the Court, instead leaving that decision to Congress. The Judiciary Act added five associate judges to the Supreme Court, bringing the total number of justices to six. Although the number of justices has varied throughout the nation's history, it has been set at nine since 1869. The act also established two lower tiers to the federal judiciary because only the Supreme Court had been set out in the Constitution, although changes have been made to their organization since. (See Figure 6.1.)

FIGURE 6.1

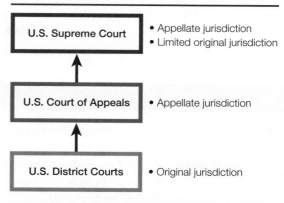

How the Federal Judiciary Is Structured

U.S. Supreme Court
- Appellate jurisdiction
- Limited original jurisdiction

U.S. Court of Appeals
- Appellate jurisdiction

U.S. District Courts
- Original jurisdiction

Appointment to the Federal Judiciary

Federal judges must be nominated by the president and confirmed by a majority vote in the Senate. Because federal judges are appointed for life—on the condition of "good behavior"—successfully placing individuals on the federal bench is a way for a president to have an enduring influence on the government and on public policy long after the end of a president's time in office.

While most district court nominees are approved, confirmations of appellate and Supreme Court judges have become more contentious and affected by partisan political battles in recent years. Part of the reason that things tend to run more smoothly at the district court level is the custom of senatorial courtesy, in which presidents consult with senators from the state in which the vacant district judgeship is located, especially if those senators are from the president's political party.

While most Supreme Court nominees are confirmed, in recent years their confirmation hearings often involve intense scrutiny. Recent confirmation votes in the Senate have tended to be closer than those in earlier decades. As with other presidential nominees, subject to Senate approval, federal judicial nominees have sometimes found their paths blocked by a filibuster. In November 2013, a majority of senators voted to change the filibuster rules to allow the closure of debate over executive nominees to the lower courts by a simple majority vote rather than the previous requirement of sixty votes.[28] In April 2017, Senate Republicans voted to lower the threshold for advancing Supreme Court nominees from sixty to a simple majority, paving the way for the confirmation of Neil Gorsuch.[29]

Politics and Supreme Court Nominations

The Constitution imposes no qualifications to become a federal judge. Judges do not even have to be lawyers. When vacancies occur on the Supreme Court, presidents are presented with an important opportunity to shape policy for years to come. When the position of chief justice is vacant, a president may nominate a sitting member of the Court or the president may nominate an individual from outside the Court.

Because they are such high-profile appointments, nominees to the Court have to be considered carefully. Presidents have to balance both legal and political considerations. Experience, ethical integrity, and legal accomplishment are extremely important factors and can help smooth the confirmation process. Modern Court nominees will have typically already served in the federal judiciary or another high-level position.

Presidents strive to nominate individuals who share their judicial philosophies and approach to constitutional interpretation. Once justices are confirmed, presidents have no control over their behavior. More than one president has successfully nominated an individual only to be surprised by some of that justice's later decisions. Political calculations come into play as well. Nominees who are considered outspoken on contentious political issues are likely to face careful scrutiny and intense questioning by senators.

Section Review

6.2 Describe how the Constitution structures the federal judiciary.

REMEMBER
- The Constitution contains less detail about the judiciary than about the legislative or executive branches.
- Article III, along with the supremacy clause, establishes the supremacy of the Supreme Court over matters involving the Constitution and federal law.
- The Supreme Court is described in Article III, and it is the highest court in the nation. However, the establishment of lower courts was left to Congress.
- The Constitution also clarified the jurisdiction of the courts—what authority they have to hear and decide on specific cases.
- The Judiciary Act of 1789 allowed Congress to flesh out the organization of the court system.
- All federal judges must be nominated by the president and confirmed by a majority vote in the Senate. Most district court nominees are approved, but appellate and Supreme Court appointment processes can be more contentious.
- The Constitution places no requirements on the necessary qualifications to serve in the federal judiciary, but experience, ethical integrity, and legal accomplishment are important factors and can help smooth the confirmation process.
- Presidents tend to nominate individuals with whom they share similar philosophies and approaches to constitutional interpretation, but there is no guarantee that justice will behave as expected once confirmed.

KNOW
- *original jurisdiction*: the authority of a court to act as the first court to hear a case, which includes the finding of facts in the case. (p. 190)
- *appellate jurisdiction*: the authority of a court to hear and review decisions made by lower courts in that system. (p. 190)
- *Federalist No. 78*: argument by Alexander Hamilton that the federal judiciary would be unlikely to infringe upon rights and liberties but would serve as a check on the other two branches. (p. 192)

THINK
- Why do you think the founding fathers wanted the federal judiciary to be the most independent branch of government?
- Why did the founding fathers give the judiciary less power than the other branches?

6.2 Review Question: Free Response

It is easy to see, that in the common course of things, these courts will eclipse the dignity, and take away from the respectability, of the state courts. These courts will be, in themselves, totally independent of the states, deriving their authority from the United States, and receiving from them fixed salaries; and in the course of human events it is to be expected, that they will swallow up all the powers of the courts in the respective states.[30]

—Brutus No. 1

Use the quote and your knowledge of U.S. Government and Politics to respond to parts A, B, and C.

A. Describe the argument made about the judiciary in Brutus No. 1.

B. Describe two arguments made in *Federalist* No. 78 in response to the concerns raised in the quote.

C. Explain two reasons why the Supreme Court is insulated from politics.

■■ 6.3 John Marshall and the Power of the Supreme Court

In 1803, John Marshall faced a difficult test. He was chief justice of the U.S. Supreme Court, the highest court in the federal judiciary. Marshall's Court was hearing a case that on its surface might have seemed to be a small one. It was brought by four men who felt that they had been cheated out of their jobs.

Like so many other seemingly "small" cases in the history of the Supreme Court, this one turned out to be much, much bigger. Marshall's handling of it had profound effects on the power and prestige of the federal judiciary. The case was about politics. It placed front and center the question of what this third branch of the federal government really was, or might become.

The Election of 1800

It started with a national election, one of the nastiest in American history. In 1800, incumbent president John Adams and his Federalist Party squared off against Thomas Jefferson and the Republican Party.[31]

By 1800, with the parties well-formed and organized, many Americans were fed up with President Adams and the Federalist Party.[32] The Republicans accused Adams and the Federalists of trying to bring a British-style monarchy to America. The Federalists accused Jefferson and his fellow Republicans of being too close to France and pointed to the chaos that had unfolded in that country in the wake of the French Revolution.

Under the rules of the Constitution at the time, each elector would cast two votes for President. Assuming a majority of electors voted for a single candidate, that person was elected president, and the person with the second largest number of votes (assuming no tie) became the vice president. In the case of a tie, or if no candidate received a majority vote by the electors, the election of the president went to the House of Representatives, with each state delegation receiving one vote. A majority vote was required to secure the presidency.[33]

CHIEF-JUSTICE MARSHALL IN THE LIBRARY OF CONGRESS.

The early republic was known for its rambunctious politics. Here, a cartoon satirizes John Marshall, who has had a mishap with some heavy volumes in the Library of Congress. The Library of Congress is still technically the library for the use of the Congress, although it also serves as the national library. It was officially founded in 1800.
Sarin Images / GRANGER–All Rights Reserved

Jefferson and Burr each got the same number of electoral votes, and thus tied in the electoral college because every Democratic-Republican elector cast his two votes for Jefferson and Burr as provided in Article II of the original Constitution, even though Burr was intended to be, and ran as, Jefferson's vice president. After tying with his running mate, Aaron Burr, in the House of Representatives, Thomas Jefferson was finally elected president by the House of Representatives on the thirty-sixth ballot. The Twelfth Amendment to the Constitution (ratified in 1804) changed the presidential election rules by separating the votes for president and vice president.[34] The House would continue to settle presidential elections if there was not a majority vote for one candidate by the electors, and the Senate would choose the vice president. The last election decided by the House of Representatives was in 1824.

The election of 1800 had far-reaching implications. John Adams lost the election, and the Federalist Party unraveled. Friendships and political alliances were fractured. Aaron Burr and Alexander Hamilton continued their bitter rivalry. Here, Burr shoots and kills Hamilton in a duel.

Sarin Images / GRANGER-All Rights Reserved

The Judiciary Act of 1801: Appointments Signed, Sealed, but Not Delivered

Trying to preserve their influence within the national government, the Federalists turned to the federal judiciary, the one branch where they might endure. Federal judges are shielded by lifetime appointment, providing they do not commit an impeachable offense.[35] In the waning weeks of John Adams's administration, the Federalists sought to cement their position within the federal judiciary by passing the Judiciary Act of 1801, expanding the number of federal judges.[36]

With the Judiciary Act of 1801, the Federalists changed the Supreme Court's schedule, reduced the size of the Court from six to five justices, and reorganized the lower federal courts in such a way as to create sixteen vacancies that were promptly filled by Adams's administration. Adams's last-minute appointments have been called "the midnight judges" because of the hasty nature of their nomination and confirmation. In the scramble to complete the paperwork before the Republicans took the reins of government, some of the commissions signed by Adams, including one for William Marbury, were not delivered and were still sitting on Secretary of State John Marshall's desk when Adams's term expired at midnight.

While President Jefferson did deliver the commissions to some of the midnight appointees after he took office, William Marbury and several others did not receive theirs. Marbury, along with three other men, brought suit against James Madison, Jefferson's Secretary of State, requesting that the Court issue a writ of mandamus, a kind of court order, requiring Madison to deliver their commissions as justices of the peace of the District of Columbia.[37] The men argued that all of the required steps in their appointments had been properly taken: President Adams had nominated them, the Senate had confirmed their nominations, and the commissions had been signed and affixed with the presidential seal. Madison's failure to deliver the commissions, they insisted, constituted a serious breach of etiquette and tradition.

Politics and the Power of the Supreme Court

Less than two weeks before Adams signed the Judiciary Act of 1801 into law, the Senate confirmed the president's appointment of his Secretary of State, John Marshall, to be the new chief justice of the Supreme Court.[38] Marshall was a Federalist. He was also an experienced politician. He had been a supporter of the Constitution at Virginia's ratifying convention and was considered "a gregarious [sociable] individual, someone who valued good company, good food, and good wine."[39] Marshall served as chief justice of the Supreme Court from 1801 to 1835 and remains the longest-serving chief justice in American history. Over the course of his service as chief justice, Marshall worked to strengthen the power of the national government and the independence of the judicial branch.

Chief Justice Marshall had to consider the political implications of his decision. He also had to reflect on how his decision would affect the overall power of the judiciary, as a coequal branch of government. If the Supreme Court waded into the political battle—by ordering

Jefferson's administration to deliver the commissions—he risked being ignored by the president or even impeached by the Republican-controlled Congress. Marshall could deny Marbury's petition, thus preventing a confrontation with Jefferson and his Republicans. However, to do so might send a message that the judiciary was weak in the face of powerful political forces, which could deal a blow to its power, prestige, and independence. The way in which Marshall dealt with this dilemma continues to shape the role of the Supreme Court in American political life to this day.

Marbury v. Madison and the Establishment of Judicial Review

Marshall broke the decision before him into three separate questions. First, the chief justice asked if the men were entitled to their commissions. To this first question, Marshall, in his opinion, answered "yes." The president had signed the commissions. Presidential signing of such commissions is the last formal act, and that had been done. Delivery of the commissions, Marshall noted, "is a practice directed by convenience, but not by law."[40] Once this part of the decision was established, Marshall considered whether or not a legal remedy involving the courts was available to Marbury and his fellow plaintiffs. To this second question, Marshall also answered in the affirmative, arguing that "the individual who considers himself [so] injured has a right to resort to the laws of the country for a remedy."[41]

Marshall presented a third question for his Court to consider: Were Marbury and the other plaintiffs entitled to the remedy that they sought—the writs of mandamus? To this question, Marshall answered "no." The power to issue these kinds of writs in this particular instance, he declared, had been improperly given to the Court by a section of the Judiciary Act of 1789.[42] Marshall argued that when Congress granted the Court the authority "to issue writs of mandamus to public officers," it was attempting to expand the scope of the original jurisdiction of the Court, which Congress cannot do. Article III of the Constitution limits the Supreme Court's original jurisdiction to a few, specifically defined cases. The power to issue a writ of mandamus is not mentioned in Article III's discussion of original jurisdiction. Therefore, the Court did not have the power to give Marbury the remedy he sought. In the end, William Marbury and his fellow job seekers never received their commissions.

Marshall held that the part of the Judiciary Act that tried to give his Court such power was in violation of the Constitution and, therefore, invalid: "[A] law repugnant to the Constitution is void, and that courts, as well as other departments, are bound by that instrument."[43] In this statement, Marshall established that the Supreme Court has the power of **judicial review**, which is the authority of a court to strike down a law passed by Congress or an executive action if they are in conflict with the Constitution.

The Implications of Marshall's Decision

In establishing the power of judicial review, Marshall expanded the Court's power to interpret the Constitution. In exercising judicial review, according to Marshall's logic, the Court does not place itself above the other two branches; it is coequal to them, and the Constitution is supreme to all three.

Marshall did not invent the idea of judicial review. He drew on constitutional principles that were already understood.[44] In *Federalist* No. 78, Alexander Hamilton had discussed the ability of the courts to "pronounce legislative acts void" as necessary to

Judicial nominee William Marbury, whose suit against James Madison in *Marbury v. Madison* established judicial review of federal law.
Sarin Images/GRANGER

Marbury v. Madison (1803)
a Supreme Court decision that established judicial review over federal laws.

judicial review
the authority of the Supreme Court to strike down a law or executive action if it conflicts with the Constitution.

AP® TIP

Marbury v. Madison is a required case. Make sure you understand its importance because judicial review is likely to appear on the AP® Exam.

preserving the Constitution. Hamilton also made it clear that "whenever a particular statute contravenes the constitution, it will be the duty of the judicial tribunals to adhere to the latter and disregard the former." Yet Hamilton cautioned, "Nor does this conclusion by any means suppose a superiority of the judicial to the legislative power. It only supposes that the power of the people is superior to both."[45]

Under the decades-long tenure of Marshall, the Supreme Court used judicial review to weigh in on the constitutionality of several state laws, declaring some invalid. It was not until 1857 that the Court struck down another federal statute as unconstitutional in the infamous case of *Dred Scott v. Sanford,* which will be further discussed in Chapter 9.[46] Often ranked as one of the worst decisions in Supreme Court history, *Dred Scott* further exacerbated the tensions over slavery by striking down legislation that was intended to balance free and slave states. The Court ruled that former slaves taken into free states did not have standing to sue for their freedom because they were not citizens under the Constitution. The role of the Court in constitutional interpretation remains controversial.

AP® REQUIRED FOUNDATIONAL DOCUMENTS AND SUPREME COURT CASES

Federalist No. 78 is one of the nine foundational documents required in AP® U.S. Government and Politics. *Marbury v. Madison* is the earliest of the required Supreme Court cases.

Document	Scope
Federalist No. 78	Hamilton argues that the judiciary will act impartially and is insulated from politics. He also argues that the judiciary is the weakest branch.
Marbury v. Madison (1803)	Supreme Court decision establishing judicial review, which is the power of the Court to overturn executive, legislative, or state actions that violate the Constitution. This power makes the judiciary a coequal branch of government.

Section Review

6.3 Define judicial review and explain how it checks the power of Congress, the president, and the states.

REMEMBER
- In *Marbury v. Madison*, Chief Justice Marshall found that part of the law that Marbury was basing his claim on, the Federal Judiciary Act of 1789, was unconstitutional and thus unenforceable.
- *Marbury v. Madison* established the power of judicial review, which is the power to review laws and actions of other branches and levels of government to decide if they are in conflict with the Constitution.

KNOW
- *Marbury v. Madison* (1803): a Supreme Court decision that established judicial review over federal laws. (p. 197)
- *judicial review*: the authority of the Supreme Court to strike down a law or executive action if it conflicts with the Constitution. (p. 197)

THINK
- How does the power of judicial review make the Supreme Court a coequal branch of government?
- Did the Supreme Court overstep its bounds in assuming the power of judicial review?

Popularity makes no law invulnerable to invalidation. Americans accept judicial supervision of their democracy—judicial review of popular but possibly unconstitutional statutes—because they know that if the Constitution is truly to constitute the nation, it must trump some majority preferences.

—George Will[47]

Use the excerpt and your knowledge of U.S. Government and Politics to respond to parts A, B, and C.

A. Define judicial review.

B. Describe the viewpoint expressed in the quote above.

C. Explain how the decision in *Marbury v. Madison* insulates the judiciary from public opinion.

6.4 Organization of the Federal Judiciary

Each of the two levels in the federal system—the national and the state level—operates its own system of courts. There is a single federal judiciary for the nation and there are separate state judiciaries in each of the fifty states.

Criminal and Civil Cases

Both state and federal courts have jurisdiction over two categories of law, criminal and civil.[48] **Criminal law** covers actions that harm the community, such as committing an act of violence against another person.[49] In a criminal case, the state or federal government acts as the prosecutor and tries to prove the guilt of the defendant, the party accused of a crime. Although many acts (such as murder or assault) are criminal offenses in all of the states, some acts (such as gambling or recreational use of marijuana) are legal in some states but not in others. As of 2017, for example, an adult in several states could lawfully use marijuana recreationally according to state law (subject to certain restrictions) but in doing so be in violation of federal law, presenting a tricky issue for American federalism.[50] States may also vary in the punishments handed out for those convicted of similar crimes.

> **criminal law**
> a category of law covering actions determined to harm the community.

Defendants in criminal cases are guaranteed a set of constitutional protections, including the right not to be forced to testify (Fifth Amendment), the right to a speedy and public trial by an impartial jury, the right to confront witnesses, and the right to be represented by an attorney (Sixth Amendment).[51] If found by a jury to be "not guilty," criminal defendants are protected from being tried for the same crime by the double jeopardy clause (Fifth Amendment).[52] However, a defendant may be tried more than once for the same actions if more than one law has been broken.

Being convicted under a criminal statute leads to some form of punishment, such as a fine, imprisonment, or, in some cases, the death penalty.[53]

Civil law covers cases involving private rights and relationships between individuals and groups. In a civil case, the plaintiff is the party who argues that she or he has been wronged, and the defendant is the party accused of violating a person's rights or breaking an agreement. In civil cases the plaintiff may be a government or an individual. A jury or a judge might decide civil cases.

> **civil law**
> a category of law covering cases involving private rights and relationships between individuals and groups.

FIGURE 6.2

The Modern Court System

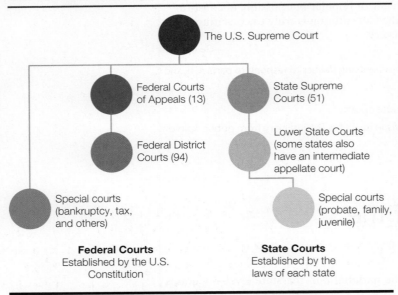

The U.S. Supreme Court

Federal Courts of Appeals (13)

State Supreme Courts (51)

Federal District Courts (94)

Lower State Courts (some states also have an intermediate appellate court)

Special courts (bankruptcy, tax, and others)

Special courts (probate, family, juvenile)

Federal Courts
Established by the U.S. Constitution

State Courts
Established by the laws of each state

The State Courts

While our focus is on the federal judiciary, it is important to note that state courts handle the vast majority of court cases in the United States. Although states vary in how their judicial systems are structured and organized—including how judges are selected—the state court systems share a few common traits. State judicial systems handle both criminal and civil cases. Each state has a system of trial courts that does most of the work of the state's judiciary, handles cases arising under that state's laws, and possesses original jurisdiction. States also operate systems of specialized courts that typically handle issues like traffic violations, family disputes, and small claims. (See Figure 6.2.)

More than half of the states have an intermediate system of appellate courts that operate with appellate jurisdiction. Each state has at least one state supreme court, which acts as the highest court in that state's system and as the final level of appeal.[54]

A select group of cases may proceed to the federal judiciary from the highest state court of appeals. These types of cases generally involve a question arising under the Constitution, such as a claim that an individual's constitutional rights have been violated.

The Federal District Courts

federal district courts
the lowest level of the federal judiciary; these courts usually have original jurisdiction in cases that start at the federal level.

The federal court system is structured as a three-layered pyramid (Figure 6.2). At the bottom are the nation's **federal district courts**. Congress created the district courts in the Judiciary Act of 1789. In most federal cases, district courts act as the trial courts and possess original jurisdiction. As of 2017,[55] there were ninety-four district courts in the United States, and each state had at least one. (See Figure 6.3.) District court boundaries do not cut across state lines. The district courts handle most of the work of the federal courts, and a judge hears each case. The Constitution guarantees the right to a jury trial in all federal criminal cases (Sixth Amendment) and in some civil cases (Seventh Amendment).[56]

The Appellate Courts

federal courts of appeals
the middle level of the federal judiciary; these courts review and hear appeals from the federal district courts.

The **federal courts of appeals** occupy the middle level of the constitutional courts. There are thirteen courts of appeals; eleven have jurisdiction over regionally based "circuits," one has jurisdiction over the District of Columbia (which handles appeals involving federal agencies), and the thirteenth handles cases arising under international trade and patent law. (See Figure 6.3 in which the number of each regional circuit appears in a black circle.) The courts of appeals exercise appellate jurisdiction only, reviewing decisions made by the federal district courts and certain specialized federal courts.

The Supreme Court

The Constitution establishes the U.S. Supreme Court as the highest court in the nation. The Supreme Court resolves differences between the states, something that had not been

FIGURE 6.3

Map of the District and Appellate Courts

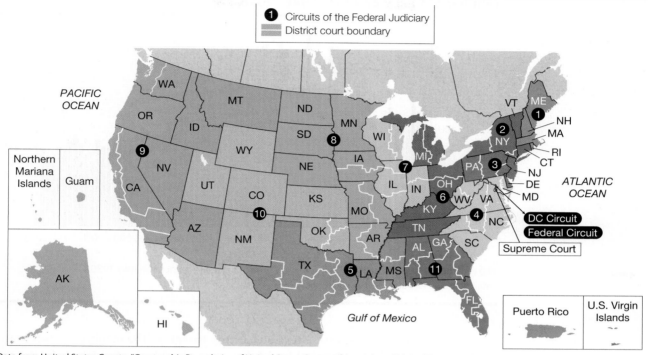

Data from United States Courts, "Geographic Boundaries of United States Courts of Appeals and United States District Courts"

provided for in the government created by the Articles of Confederation. The Court also resolves different interpretations of the law in the lower federal courts. Since 1869, the Court has consisted of nine justices, including a chief justice and eight associate justices. Each justice has a small number of clerks to assist in selecting, researching, and writing decisions. The Court meets in session roughly nine months out of the year, beginning on the first Monday in October. Those cases still on the docket (the schedule of cases to be heard) when a term ends continue to the next term's docket.

Cases in which the Supreme Court exercises original jurisdiction are few and are described in Article III of the Constitution: "In all Cases affecting Ambassadors, other public Ministers and Consuls, and those in which a State shall be a Party, the supreme Court shall have original jurisdiction."[57] In all other cases in which the federal judiciary has jurisdiction, the Court has appellate jurisdiction. The Court also has appellate jurisdiction over certain state cases, especially those involving a federal issue.

The Decision to Take Cases on Appeal

In exercising its appellate jurisdiction, the Supreme Court is confronted with two questions. First, the Court decides whether or not to hear the case. Second, if it does decide to hear the case, it issues its decision based on the merits of the case and applicable law. Almost all of the cases heard on appeal in the Court originate when a litigant who has lost in a lower court files a petition to have his or her appeal heard. The Supreme Court receives, on average, between eight thousand and nine thousand petitions a year but hears

FIGURE 6.4

Supreme Court Caseload on the Decline
Number of Cases by Term, 1946–2016

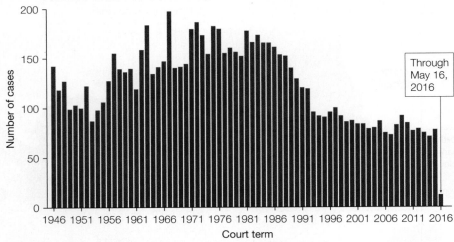

Through May 16, 2016

The number of cases heard by the Supreme Court has declined since the mid-1980s.
Data from Supreme Court Database, Scotusblog

less than 1 percent of these cases, or about seventy to eighty. The number of cases heard by the Supreme Court has dropped by 50 percent in recent years. See Figure 6.4 for the declining case load. See Figure 6.5, point 3, for how cases move from the courts of appeals.

The Constitution offers little guidance about which cases the Court should take, so justices have adopted the rule of four, which simply means that it will generally hear a case if four or more justices vote to do so. See Figure 6.5, point 4. If it decides to hear a case, the Court issues a writ of certiorari (from the Latin "to be more informed") to the lower court for the records of the case, a process that is commonly referred to as "granting cert." "Review on a writ of certiorari is not a matter of right, but of judicial discretion. A petition of a writ of certiorari will be granted only for compelling reasons."[58] See Figure 6.5, point 5.

The most important factor in the decision to grant cert is if there are different interpretations of a law or previous ruling among lower-level federal courts or state supreme courts. Cases presenting a question involving the Constitution, a federal law, or a treaty are also more likely to be heard.

precedent
a judicial decision that guides future courts in handling similar cases.

stare decisis
the practice of letting a previous legal decision stand.

Supreme Court decisions set a **precedent**, a judicial decision that acts as a basis for deciding similar cases in the future. An individual justice may be more or less likely to grant cert if there is a perceived likelihood that the outcome might be a precedent that the justice desires or wishes to avoid. Under the principle of **stare decisis**, the Supreme Court may avoid creating a new precedent by allowing a previous decision to stand.

Considering and Deciding on Cases

If the Supreme Court decides to grant cert in a case, it requests briefs from both sides laying out their full arguments. Interested non-parties may file amicus curiae (friend of the court) briefs to try to influence the precedential effect of the Court's ruling. Court clerks will assist the justices in reviewing these briefs. The case is then scheduled for oral argument

FIGURE 6.5

How Cases Move through the Court System

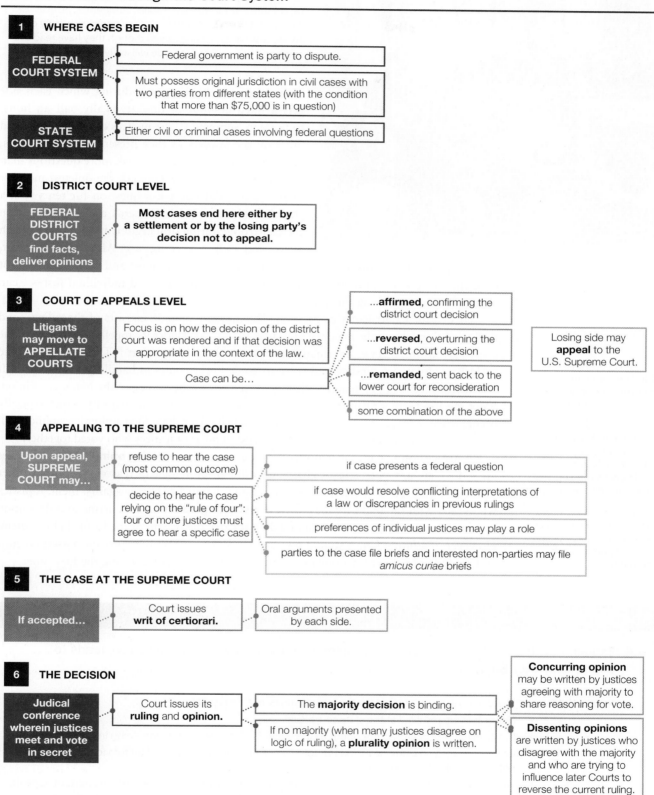

1 WHERE CASES BEGIN

FEDERAL COURT SYSTEM
- Federal government is party to dispute.
- Must possess original jurisdiction in civil cases with two parties from different states (with the condition that more than $75,000 is in question)

STATE COURT SYSTEM
- Either civil or criminal cases involving federal questions

2 DISTRICT COURT LEVEL

FEDERAL DISTRICT COURTS find facts, deliver opinions
- **Most cases end here either by a settlement or by the losing party's decision not to appeal.**

3 COURT OF APPEALS LEVEL

Litigants may move to APPELLATE COURTS
- Focus is on how the decision of the district court was rendered and if that decision was appropriate in the context of the law.
- Case can be…
  - …**affirmed**, confirming the district court decision
  - …**reversed**, overturning the district court decision
  - …**remanded**, sent back to the lower court for reconsideration
  - some combination of the above

Losing side may **appeal** to the U.S. Supreme Court.

4 APPEALING TO THE SUPREME COURT

Upon appeal, SUPREME COURT may…
- refuse to hear the case (most common outcome)
- decide to hear the case relying on the "rule of four": four or more justices must agree to hear a specific case
  - if case presents a federal question
  - if case would resolve conflicting interpretations of a law or discrepancies in previous rulings
  - preferences of individual justices may play a role
  - parties to the case file briefs and interested non-parties may file *amicus curiae* briefs

5 THE CASE AT THE SUPREME COURT

If accepted…
- Court issues **writ of certiorari.**
- Oral arguments presented by each side.

6 THE DECISION

Judical conference wherein justices meet and vote in secret
- Court issues its **ruling** and **opinion.**
  - The **majority decision** is binding.
  - If no majority (when many justices disagree on logic of ruling), a **plurality opinion** is written.

Concurring opinion may be written by justices agreeing with majority to share reasoning for vote.

Dissenting opinions are written by justices who disagree with the majority and who are trying to influence later Courts to reverse the current ruling.

In this sketch, Deputy Solicitor General Paul Clement is shown presenting his oral argument on behalf of the government before the Supreme Court on April 28, 2004, in the case of Yaser Esam Hamdi and Jose Padilla. Sometimes, justices ask the hardest questions of the side they agree with. Why do justices ask hard questions, even though they have read the briefs and know what each side will likely argue?
DANA VERKOUTEREN/AP Images

before the assembled justices, during which each side gets a fixed amount of time (typically half an hour) to present. Supreme Court justices often interrupt and question the lawyers as they present their arguments, although some justices tend to ask more questions than others. Justice Clarence Thomas, the quietest member of the Court, did not ask a question for ten years, a stretch broken in 2016. Cameras are not allowed in the courtroom during oral arguments, although sketch artists and audio recordings are. After oral argument, the case proceeds to judicial conference, in which the justices meet and vote in secret. Not even their clerks are present. The process can take months, and individual justices can change their votes during this phase.

Finally, the Court issues its decision. The majority opinion consists of the ruling—and the logic behind it—of the majority of justices in the case. Under its appellate jurisdiction, the court may affirm, reverse, or remand the case back to a lower court.[59] The decision and the **majority opinion** are binding and serve to guide lower courts in handling similar cases. If the chief justice is in the majority, then he or she selects the author of the majority opinion. If not, the most senior member of the majority does so. If there is no majority, which typically occurs when many justices disagree on the logic behind a ruling, then a plurality opinion will be written that expresses the views of the largest number of justices who voted together.

A justice voting with the majority may also write a **concurring opinion**. Concurrences are more common when a justice has some differences in logic or reasoning with the other members of the majority but not enough to cause that justice to side against them. A justice who voted with the minority may write a **dissenting opinion**. Concurring and dissenting opinions do not serve as precedent and do not carry the weight of the Court behind them. However, if a future Court should revisit precedent, a dissent may provide a useful record and analysis of why at least one justice thought the Court got it wrong the first time.

majority opinion
binding Supreme Court opinions, which serve as precedent for future cases.

concurring opinion
an opinion that agrees with the majority decision, offering different or additional reasoning, that does not serve as precedent.

dissenting opinion
an opinion that disagrees with the majority opinion and does not serve as precedent.

Section Review

6.4 Explain how the life tenure of justices, coupled with the power of judicial review, leads to controversy over Supreme Court nominations.

REMEMBER
- There are two levels of courts in the United States, federal and state.
- Most cases are resolved at the state court level.
- In a criminal case, a prosecutor brings a case against a defendant for wrong doing in the community.
- Civil cases involved a private action brought by a plaintiff against a defendant for violating a person's rights or breaking an agreement.
- The federal judiciary is organized into three levels: federal district courts, the federal courts of appeals, and the Supreme Court.

- *criminal law*: a category of law covering actions determined to harm the community. (p. 199)
- *civil law*: a category of law covering cases involving private rights and relationships between individuals and groups. (p. 199)
- *federal district courts*: the lowest level of the federal judiciary; these courts usually have original jurisdiction in cases that start at the federal level. (p. 200)
- *federal courts of appeals*: the middle level of the federal judiciary; these courts review and hear appeals from the federal district courts. (p. 200)
- *precedent*: a judicial decision that guides future courts in handling similar cases. (p. 202)
- *stare decisis*: letting a previous decision stand. (p. 202)
- *majority opinion*: binding Supreme Court opinions, which serve as precedent for future cases. (p. 204)
- *concurring opinion*: an opinion that agrees with the majority decision, offering different or additional reasoning, that does not serve as precedent. (p. 204)
- *dissenting opinion*: an opinion that disagrees with the majority opinion and does not serve as precedent. (p. 204)

THINK

- Why does having separate state and federal courts lead to conflicts under our system of federalism?
- Should the Supreme Court hear a great number of appeals? Why or why not?

6.4 Review Question: Free Response

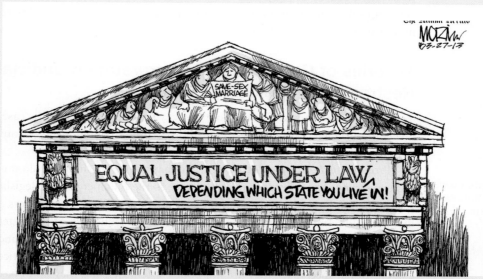

The Miami Herald, Jim Morin, March 27, 2013

The cartoon is about the Supreme Court's decision to take a case involving same-sex marriage. Use the cartoon and your knowledge of U.S. Government and Politics to respond to parts A, B, and C.

A. Describe the viewpoint shown in the cartoon.

B. Explain why the Supreme Court had jurisdiction over state laws involving same-sex marriage.

C. Describe two reasons why the Supreme Court might decide to take a case.

■ 6.5 Judicial Review, Constitutional Interpretation, and Judicial Decision Making

Supreme Court justices are not elected by the people but are appointed for life, removable only through impeachment. In striking down state or federal laws, a small group of unelected justices can overturn acts passed by representatives who *were* elected. The worry is that in striking down legislation, the Court "exercises control, not in behalf of the prevailing majority, but against it."[60] This is precisely what President Jefferson warned about when he feared the judiciary becoming a "despotic branch."[61]

In upholding the constitutionality of laws, the Supreme Court also exercises power over the legislative process by adding legitimacy in the minds of the American public to the laws passed by Congress.[62] However, in upholding the will of the majority, the Court risks trampling on the rights of minorities, thereby giving its stamp of approval to tyranny of the majority.

It is challenging to interpret and apply the Constitution. People have different ideas about the intent of the Founders and what the language of the Constitution means. As James Bradley Thayer cautioned in an 1893 article, "Much which will seem unconstitutional to one man, or body of men, may reasonably not seem so to another; [and] that the constitution often admits of different interpretations."[63] Justices use different philosophies in interpreting the Constitution.

Theories of Constitutional Interpretation: Judicial Restraint and Judicial Activism

Trying to figure out why justices vote the way they do on any specific case is very difficult given all of the factors that likely contribute to an individual justice's vote. There are two main theories about how justices should interpret the Constitution.

judicial restraint
a philosophy of constitutional interpretation that justices should be cautious in overturning laws.

Proponents of **judicial restraint** argue that the Court should seldom use the power of judicial review and whenever possible defer to the judgment of the legislative and executive branches. First, proponents of judicial restraint point to the dangers of going against majority rule and the potential undemocratic consequences of unelected justices overturning the actions of elected representatives. Further, declaring a law unconstitutional is more authoritative if the Supreme Court uses it sparingly. Finally, justices are legal and constitutional specialists; they are not policy specialists, and they don't have to implement their decisions. The public policies that may be affected by the use of judicial review may involve complex technical questions, the details of which justices may not fully understand.

judicial activism
a philosophy of constitutional interpretation that justices should wield the power of judicial review, sometimes creating bold new policies.

Proponents of **judicial activism**, on the other hand, argue that justices should be willing to overturn laws when necessary, sometimes creating bold new policy. The other two branches may make mistakes, or worse, trample on individual rights and liberties. The very power that fuels concerns that the Court can strike down the will of the majority also gives it the power to protect the rights of minorities, especially unpopular groups that may not have support in the other branches of government. Sometimes, elected officials act in ways that damage rights and liberties. Sometimes, the elected branches do not act at all. Free from concern about the popularity of their actions, Supreme Court justices can decide issues that Congress and the president are unwilling to tackle.

Judicial activism and restraint are not linked to political liberalism or conservatism. During the 1960s, an activist and liberal Court used the power of judicial review to strike

Interpreting an Author's Assumptions: Alexander Bickel on the Powers of Judicial Review

In his 1962 book, *The Least Dangerous Branch*, legal scholar Alexander Bickel explored the history of and controversies surrounding judicial review in American politics. Bickel pointed out the often overlooked fact that there are *three* possible outcomes when the Supreme Court ascertains the degree to which a federal law, state law, state constitutional provision, or governmental action is or is not in conflict with the Constitution.

In the first possible outcome, the Court overturns a law or provision. In doing so, it risks undermining democratic principles, acting, in Bickel's words, as "a countermajoritarian force in our system."[66] The "countermajoritarian difficulty" arises from the fact that a group of unelected justices will be overturning the will of a majority of citizens that is being exercised through their elected representatives, presidents, and governors.

The second possible outcome is that the Court upholds a law, giving the law its approval. In this case, the Court again inserts itself into the democratic process. In both of these cases, Bickel

notes, "the Court must act rigorously on principle, else it undermines the justification for its power."[67]

The third possible outcome occurs when the Court does not act at all and refuses to weigh in on the constitutionality of a law or action. To Bickel and other scholars, the act of *not acting* is an important tool in preserving judicial legitimacy. In the words of Justice Louis Brandeis, "The most important thing we do is not doing."[68] The tricky thing about refusing to hear a major constitutional case is that the Court is not required to say why it decided to avoid an issue.

1. Describe the three possible outcomes when the Supreme Court reviews a law.

2. Explain how the power of judicial review risks undermining democratic principles.

3. Explain how an independent judiciary with the power of judicial review protects democratic principles.

down state laws restricting the civil rights of Americans in the areas of education and voting. Conservative courts have used activism to protect the rights of states and private businesses. Sometimes people cannot agree on whether or not a decision represents judicial activism or restraint. For example, in *National Federation of Independent Business v. Sebelius*,[64] the Supreme Court upheld the provision of the Patient Protection and Affordable Care Act (ACA) requiring individuals to purchase health insurance or pay a fine.[65] This decision might be viewed as judicial activism because the Supreme Court broadened the definition of Congress's power to tax to include the power to impose fines under the ACA. The decision might also be characterized as an example of judicial restraint because the Supreme Court deferred to Congress in upholding the ACA.

AP® TIP

Make sure you understand the difference between judicial activism and judicial restraint. For the fifteen required Supreme Court cases, be able to make an argument about whether the decision represents judicial activism or restraint.

The Supreme Court and Policymaking

The Supreme Court has the unique power to use precedent to shape policymaking. Yet it does so in the face of multiple constraints on its independent use of authority.

Limitations on the Power of the Supreme Court

The legislative and executive branches have several powers that serve as a check on the power of the federal judiciary. The president nominates justices, and the Senate confirms them. Further, Congress sets the size of the Supreme Court and establishes other federal courts. Congress and the states may collectively amend the Constitution.

In addition, Congress may write legislation modifying the impact of a Supreme Court decision. For example, President Obama signed the Lilly Ledbetter Fair Pay Act on

January 29, 2009,[69] restoring the protection against pay discrimination. The Lilly Ledbetter Fair Pay Act was a response to the Supreme Court's decision in *Ledbetter v. Goodyear Tire & Rubber Co*, in which the Supreme Court disallowed a claim for wage discrimination.[70]

One of the biggest constraints on the power of the court is that it lacks the tools for implementing public policy and often must turn to the other two branches to enforce to its rulings. When a Court goes against the will of the president or Congress, the other branches may not implement the decision or even might ignore or defy the Court entirely.

In 1832, near the end of his long term as chief justice, John Marshall once again went toe to toe with a president—this time with Andrew Jackson in *Worcester v. Georgia*.[71] The case focused on federalism, specifically which level of government, state or federal, had authority over the treaties and laws covering Native American territories in the United States. Samuel Worcester, a missionary, had been arrested under a Georgia law for "residing within the limits of the Cherokee Nation without a license" and was convicted and sentenced to "hard labour in the penitentiary for four years."[72] The Supreme Court ruled that the federal government, not the states, had authority over Native American territories and declared the Georgia law to be unconstitutional. In doing so, Marshall sought to protect the rights of Native Americans secured by the treaties governing their autonomy. President Jackson, who, according to one historian, "had almost as little regard for the Supreme Court" as he had for Native Americans, is reported to have exclaimed, "Well, John Marshall has made his decision; now let him enforce it!"[73] Georgia continued to enforce its laws, and Jackson pursued his destructive policies toward the Cherokee Nation. This historical example is one of the relatively rare instances when a president defiantly refused to enforce a decision by the Supreme Court.

Even when the other two branches do not openly defy the Supreme Court, their lack of support of its rulings can limit the Court's power in setting national policy. The Supreme Court's landmark ruling in *Brown v. Board of Education* (1954)[74] declaring separate educational facilities unconstitutional was not implemented for more than a decade. As political scientist Gerald Rosenberg concluded, "For ten years the Court spoke forcefully while Congress and the executive did little."[75] It was only after the executive and the legislative branches began to use their own powers in shaping American public policy that desegregation gained momentum. The civil rights movement will be discussed in detail in Chapter 9.

Finally, although justices are appointed for life and do not have to worry about being reelected, they operate within the American political system, in which public opinion plays an important role. Political scientists continue to debate the degree to which Supreme Court justices pay attention to public opinion in crafting specific decisions. Scholars tend to agree that the influence of public opinion cannot be completely discounted.[76]

Justices have had to keep in mind that their power in exercising judicial review is tied to Americans' views of the legitimacy of their branch of government. It is no accident that, of all the branches, the federal judiciary, and the Supreme Court in particular, retains its traditions and independence. The prestige of the Court adds to its legitimacy in the view of the American people, and all justices—whatever their own political beliefs—know that they play a key role in preserving the important role of the judiciary as a check on the powers of Congress, the president, the states, and the will of the majority.

The Supreme Court and Controversial Issues

Supreme Court justices are able to bring some stability to controversial national questions. The Supreme Court rulings legalizing same-sex marriage is an example of this power. A member of Congress or a president may be afraid to weigh in on an important and controversial issue out of fear of public backlash, but a Court decision may resolve the issue. Providing political cover for elected representatives who wish to act on an issue may be one of the most important powers of the unelected branch of government.

The justices of the Supreme Court and the federal judiciary are not political in the ways that presidents, representatives, and senators are because they do not have to worry about reelection. They must consider the facts of the case and the letter of the law when ruling on cases. Justices are, however, political people, and their personal views on issues may affect their decisions. They must keep in mind the role their institution plays in the system of separation of powers and in Americans' views of the legitimacy of the institution.

In *Federalist* No. 78, Alexander Hamilton—a proponent of a strong national government—tried to reassure skeptics during the ratification debates that the Court was neither too political nor too powerful. Compared to the legislative and executive branches, the power of the federal judiciary in national policymaking is much less obvious. It cannot write laws, and it has no army. It has only the power of its decisions and the willingness of the people and the members of the other two branches to respect its decisions.

Section Review

6.5 Describe the Supreme Court's role in policymaking and how Congress and the president may limit the powers of the Supreme Court.

REMEMBER
- Proponents of judicial restraint argue that the Court should use the power of judicial review rarely and whenever possible defer to the judgment of the legislative and executive branches on decisions that those branches have made.
- Proponents of judicial activism argue that justices should be willing to overturn laws when they see a need to do so, sometimes making bold new policy.
- The Supreme Court may act as a national policymaker and agenda setter, but there are checks on its power.
- The Supreme Court relies on other branches of government to implement its decisions.
- While the Supreme Court is insulated from public opinion, the Court seeks to maintain legitimacy in the eyes of the public.

KNOW
- *judicial restraint*: a philosophy of constitutional interpretation that justices should be cautious in overturning laws. (p. 206)
- *judicial activism*: a philosophy of constitutional interpretation that justices should wield the power of judicial review, sometimes creating bold new policies. (p. 206)

THINK
- When should the Court use judicial activism to make bold new policy?
- When should the Court use judicial restraint, deferring to the judgment of elected officials?

6.5 Review Question: Free Response

The worst case [of judicial activism] was the Voting Rights Act case. That passed Congress overwhelmingly and I think it was unanimous in the Senate . . . if anyone knows about Voting Rights, how it affects the system, I think the elected representatives, have an appreciation of that, that the unelected judges don't have. Yet despite the overwhelming majority in Congress that passed the Voting Rights Act, the court said, that won't do.[77]

—Justice Ruth Bader Ginsberg

Use the quote and your knowledge of U.S. Government and Politics to respond to parts A, B, and C.

A. Define judicial activism.

B. Describe the viewpoint expressed in the quote.

C. Explain two ways in which judicial activism could be used to protect civil liberties.

Chapter 6 Review

AP® KEY CONCEPTS

- *federal judiciary (p. 186)*
- *Supreme Court (p. 186)*
- *original jurisdiction (p. 190)*
- *appellate jurisdiction (p. 190)*
- *Federalist No. 78 (p. 192)*
- *Marbury v. Madison (1803) (p. 197)*

- *judicial review (p. 197)*
- *criminal law (p. 199)*
- *civil law (p. 199)*
- *federal district courts (p. 200)*
- *federal courts of appeals (p. 200)*
- *precedent (p. 202)*

- *stare decisis (p. 202)*
- *majority opinion (p. 204)*
- *concurring opinion (p. 204)*
- *dissenting opinion (p. 204)*
- *judicial restraint (p. 206)*
- *judicial activism (p. 206)*

AP® EXAM PRACTICE and Critical Thinking Project

MULTIPLE-CHOICE QUESTIONS

1. Which of the following is an example of judicial review by the Supreme Court?
   A. deciding a case of original jurisdiction between New Mexico and Nevada over the issue of water rights
   B. hearing a case of appellate jurisdiction involving different interpretations of a federal law by the Ninth and Tenth Circuit Courts
   C. overturning a president's executive order about immigration because the order violates the Constitution
   D. hearing a case of appellate jurisdiction involving a contract dispute between a corporation and a labor union

2. Why is *Marbury v. Madison* significant?
   A. It established the power of judicial review, affirming that the Supreme Court is coequal with other branches.
   B. It established the power of the Supreme Court to overturn decisions by state supreme courts.
   C. It gives the Supreme Court more power than Congress because Congress has no way of overturning decisions by the court.
   D. It gives the Supreme Court the power to make decisions that serve as precedent for similar cases in the future.

The perfect Republican Supreme Court

ED FiSCHER

Fischer, Ed/Cartoon Stock

CartoonStock.com

3. Which of the following statements best describes the viewpoint in the cartoon?
   A. Republicans are more partisan than Democrats in nominating and confirming Supreme Court justices.
   B. Political parties attempt to nominate justices who share their political ideology.
   C. Supreme Court justices serve for life, and their appointment impacts decisions for a long time.
   D. Once justices are appointed to the Supreme Court, they pressure each other to adopt similar viewpoints.

   _____

4. The Constitution is "not a living document," [Justice Scalia] told the Southern Methodist University crowd in 2014. "It's dead, dead, dead. . . . The judge who always likes the results he reaches is a bad judge."[78] The quote supports which philosophy?
   A. judicial restraint
   B. judicial activism
   C. judicial independence
   D. judicial review

   There never can be danger that the judges, by a series of deliberate usurpations on the authority of the legislature, would hazard the united resentment of the body intrusted with it, while this body was possessed of the means of punishing their presumption, by degrading them from their stations.[79]

   —Alexander Hamilton, *Federalist* No. 81

5. Which of the following statements summarizes the argument made in *Federalist* No. 81?
   A. The Supreme Court might deliberately take power away from Congress.
   B. Congress must trust the court system to uphold the Constitution.
   C. Congress may check the Supreme Court by publicly degrading its decisions.
   D. Congress may check the Supreme Court through impeachment.

   _____

6. A Supreme Court Justice who writes the following words, "Generations from now, lawyers and judges will look back at today's ruling with utter contempt," is probably writing a
   A. concurring opinion
   B. majority opinion
   C. dissenting opinion
   D. per curiam opinion

Questions 7 and 8 refer to the following quote.

In *Federalist* No. 78, Alexander Hamilton wrote:

> Whoever attentively considers the different departments of power must perceive, that, in a government in which they are separated from each other, the judiciary, from the nature of its functions, will always be the least dangerous to the political rights of the Constitution; because it will be least in a capacity to annoy or injure them. The Executive not only dispenses the honors, but holds the sword of the community. The legislature not only commands the purse, but prescribes the rules by which the duties and rights of every citizen are to be regulated. The judiciary, on the contrary, has no influence over either the sword or the purse; no direction either of the strength or of the wealth of the society; and can take no active resolution whatever. It may truly be said to have neither FORCE nor WILL, but merely judgment; and must ultimately depend upon the aid of the executive arm even for the efficacy of its judgments.[80]

7. Which of the following statements best describes Hamilton's point of view?

   A. The executive is more powerful than the legislature or the judiciary because the president is commander in chief.

   B. The judiciary's power depends on an ability to convince the other branches of the strength of its reasoning.

   C. Judicial review should not be used against Congress because it determines the duties and rights of Americans.

   D. Judges should examine cases involving only legal rights, and not cases addressing political rights such as voting and gerrymandering.

8. Which of the following examples best reflects the statement Hamilton made in the final sentence of the quote?

   A. In 1957, President Dwight Eisenhower sent the National Guard to Little Rock, Arkansas to integrate the schools as ordered in *Brown v. Board of Education* (1954).

   B. In his 2010 State of the Union address, President Barack Obama sharply criticized the Supreme Court's decision in *Citizens United v. Federal Election Commission* (2010).

   C. In 2017, President Donald Trump nominated Neil Gorsuch to the Supreme Court, announcing he was "the very best judge in the country."[81]

   D. In 1983, President Ronald Reagan called for an amendment to overturn the Supreme Court's decision in *Roe v. Wade* (1973).

Questions 9 and 10 refer to the following table.

Supreme Court of the United States: Method of Disposition, 1970–2010

October Term	Petitions for certiorari granted	Cases argued	Cases disposed of by full opinion
1970	161	151	126
1980	162	144	144
1990	141	121	121
2000	99	86	83
2010	90	86	83

9. What is the most logical inference from the table, using data from the five years shown?

   A. The Supreme Court has been accepting fewer cases for review.

   B. The number of petitions for writ of certiorari has decreased.

   C. The Supreme Court has been issuing more opinions.

   D. The Supreme Court has heard more cases.

10. Which of the following best describes an inference that can be drawn from the table?

   A. Supreme Court Justices are more focused on writing books and in giving speeches than they are in making new law.

   B. As the Court resolves cases over time, fewer cases are being filed that address constitutional issues.

   C. The Justices have decided over time that they should devote more of their limited resources to resolving a smaller number of increasingly hard cases.

   D. Computerization has enabled the Justices to become more efficient over time.

FREE-RESPONSE QUESTIONS

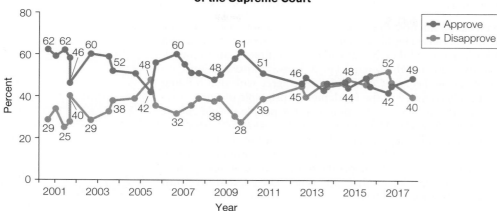

**Public Approval Ratings
of the Supreme Court**

Data from Gallup.

1. Use the graph and your understanding of U.S. Government and Politics to answer parts A, B, and C.

   A. Explain one reason why the data shown in the graph varies over time.

   B. Explain one reason why the Supreme Court is more insulated from public opinion than Congress or the president.

   C. Describe two ways in which public opinion may impact the Supreme Court.

———————————

2. In *United States v. Nixon* (1974),[82] the Supreme Court analyzed the scope of the president's claim of executive privilege. The president was broadly claiming that his executive privilege extended to every conversation he had, even those related to criminal conduct. For that reason, the president argued, the courts could not examine any transcript or hear any tape of his conversations. In addressing that argument, the Court noted:

   > [I]n Baker v. Carr . . . the Court stated: "Deciding whether a matter has in any measure been committed by the Constitution to another branch of government, or whether the action of that branch exceeds whatever authority has been committed, is itself a delicate exercise in constitutional interpretation, and is a responsibility of this Court as ultimate interpreter of the Constitution." Notwithstanding the deference each branch must accord the others, the "judicial Power of the United States" vested in the federal courts by Art. III, § 1, of the Constitution can no more be shared with the Executive Branch than the Chief Executive, for example, can share with the Judiciary the veto power, or the Congress share with the Judiciary the power to override a Presidential veto. Any other conclusion would be contrary to the basic concept of separation of powers and the checks and balances that flow from the scheme of a tripartite government . . . We therefore reaffirm that it is the province and duty of this Court "to say what the law is" with respect to the claim of privilege presented in this case.[83]

   Use the quote and your understanding of U.S. Government and Politics to respond to parts A, B, and C.

   A. Describe one similarity between the Supreme Court's ruling in *United States v. Nixon* (1974) and the Supreme Court's ruling in *Marbury v. Madison* (1803).

   B. Describe one difference between the Supreme Court's ruling in *United States v. Nixon* (1974) and the Supreme Court's ruling in *Marbury v. Madison* (1803).

   C. Explain one way in which your answers in parts A and B relate to the "basic concept of separation of powers and the checks and balances that flow from the scheme of a tripartite government," as stated in the quote.

ARGUMENTATION QUESTION

In *U.S. Term Limits v. Thornton*, the U.S. Supreme Court considered a law passed by the Arkansas State Legislature imposing term limits on those running for the federal Congress. The majority opinion, written by Justice John Paul Stevens, stated,

> Today's cases present a challenge to an amendment to the Arkansas State Constitution that prohibits the name of an otherwise-eligible candidate for Congress from appearing on the general election ballot if that candidate has already served three terms in the House of Representatives or two terms in the Senate. The Arkansas Supreme Court held that the amendment violates the Federal Constitution. We agree with that holding. Such a state-imposed restriction is contrary to the fundamental principle of our representative democracy, embodied in the Constitution, that the people should choose whom they please to govern them. *Powell* v. *McCormack*, 395 U.S. 486, 547 (1969) (internal quotation marks omitted). Allowing individual States to adopt their own qualifications for congressional service would be inconsistent with the Framers' vision of a uniform National Legislature representing the people of the United States. If the qualifications set forth in the text of the Constitution are to be changed, that text must be amended. *U.S. Term Limits v. Thornton (1995)*[84]

Take a position on whether the Supreme Court's ruling in *U.S. Term Limits v. Thornton* represents judicial activism or judicial restraint.

In your essay:

- Articulate a claim or thesis that responds to the prompt, and use a line of reasoning to defend it.
- Use at least TWO pieces of relevant and accurate evidence to support your claim.
- At least ONE piece of evidence must be from one of the listed foundational documents:
  - Constitution of the United States
  - *Federalist* No. 78
  - Brutus No. 1
- Use a second piece of evidence from another foundational document from the list or from your study of the judiciary.
- Use reasoning to explain why the evidence you provided supports your claim or thesis.
- Use refutation, concession, or rebuttal to respond to an opposing or alternative perspective.

CRITICAL THINKING PROJECT

How Should the Court Decide?

1. Visit the Supreme Court blog at http://www.scotusblog.com/case-files/petitions-were-watching/.
2. Look through the cases pending before the Supreme Court, and pick one that interests you.
3. Read the briefs filed by each side of the case.
4. Write an opinion paper explaining which side should win. Your paper should contain the following:
   a. An introductory paragraph explaining the facts of the case, the issue the Court was asked to resolve, and your analytical thesis statement about which side should win and why.
   b. A paragraph summarizing the best arguments on your side of the case.
   c. A paragraph summarizing the best arguments on the opposing side of the case.
   d. A paragraph explaining why you believe one side of the case should win.

7 The Federal Bureaucracy
Putting the Nation's Laws into Effect

To many Americans, the word *bureaucracy* refers to an unnecessary and confusing set of rules created by faceless government employees. Formally, the term *bureaucracy* does not carry any positive or negative meanings. A bureaucracy is simply an organization designed to carry out specific tasks according to a prescribed set of rules and procedures.

In this chapter, you will learn about the **federal bureaucracy**—the departments and agencies within the executive branch that carry out the laws of the nation. You will also be asked to wrestle with the complicated question of what Americans want from the bureaucracy, which often impacts their

Houston residents hitch a ride on a construction vehicle being used in the rescue of their neighborhood after Hurricane Harvey flooded it with rain water in August 2017.
Joe Raedle/Getty Images

federal bureaucracy
the departments and agencies within the executive branch that carry out the laws of the nation.

lives in a more personal way than the actions of the president, Congress, or the judiciary. Formally, the federal bureaucracy is part of the executive branch of the national government, charged with executing, or putting into action, the laws passed by Congress. The federal bureaucracy is a powerful player in the American political scene, but it seldom makes the news unless something goes wrong.

Americans often have contradictory views of the bureaucracy. At times, Americans complain that bureaucracy is too powerful, capable of making their lives more difficult or expensive. At other times, they complain that it is powerless to help them, incompetent, wasteful, and inefficient. A tried-and-true campaign strategy is to promise to reform a bloated and inefficient bureaucracy.

In this chapter, we examine the federal bureaucracy through the lenses of recent natural disasters—three hurricanes that rampaged through the Caribbean, the Gulf of Mexico region, and the United States mainland in 2017 along with one extraordinarily destructive hurricane whose impacts along the Gulf Coast are still being felt twelve years later. In considering the responses of the federal bureaucracy to these natural disasters, you will gain a deeper understanding of its complexity, change over time, and efforts to make it more efficient and successful given the myriad tasks Americans place upon it.

LEARNING TARGETS

After reading this chapter, you will be able to

7.1 Explain how the federal bureaucracy carries out the responsibilities of government.

7.2 Explain how the federal bureaucracy uses its authority to create and implement regulations.

7.3 Explain the role of the bureaucracy in the policymaking process.

7.4 Explain how Congress, the president, and the courts can hold the bureaucracy accountable.

The Summer of Disastrous Hurricanes

The first of the 2017 Atlantic monsters was Hurricane Harvey. It would become the costliest tropical cyclone in U.S. history. Harvey made landfall at Rockport, Texas, after it had swiftly intensified into a Category 4 storm (5 being the most dangerous).

The worst of Harvey was not the wind so much as the rain, torrents of rain. In much of South Texas, it dropped astonishing amounts of rain, as much as 60 inches in the areas worst hit. The flooding in Houston was so severe that, according to a scientist in NASA's Jet Propulsion Laboratory (another federal bureaucracy), the weight of the water pushed down the earth and bedrock in West Houston and nearby areas by two centimeters, leaving scientists unsure when it would bounce back.[1]

Yet to some experts and observers, it could have been far worse. Warnings went out to residents ahead of time, low-lying roads were barricaded, and—as the devastation became clear for all to observe—"thousands of ordinary folks walked out into the rain, some with just a scant idea of how they might be of assistance."[2] Officials and staff of the Federal Emergency Management Agency (FEMA) had pre-positioned supplies in Texas. In addition to members of other agencies and the National Guard, more than 31,000 people delivered millions of meals and millions of liters of water.[3]

As always, the aftermath of the storm raised questions about what the government could have done better. Some pointed to the placement of two reservoirs built by the Army Corps of Engineers in the 1940s to protect Houston residents. By 2017, however, Houstonians had moved far beyond the reservoirs and the land they were designed to protect so that 5,000 of 14,000 homes outside the two reservoirs flooded.

While the recovery efforts continued from Harvey, Irma landed, and with force. With Harvey, it was the rain and flooding. With Irma, it was the wind and the "storm surge," the ocean water pushed landward by the power of the storm and the differences in air pressure between the cyclone and the surrounding ocean water.

At the peak of its power, Irma was a Category 5 hurricane. It devastated the Virgin Islands, the Caribbean, and then Key West, Florida. From Key West to South Carolina, Irma and its storm surge wreaked havoc. In the United States, at least ninety people lost their lives.

On the U.S. mainland, five million Floridians lost power. Federal and state officials struggled to reach them. "Basically, every house in the Keys was impacted some way," according to a FEMA administrator. FEMA deployed thousands of people, and transferred even more meals and liters of water than it had done when Harvey ravaged Texas.[4]

And then Maria thundered across the Caribbean. Maria was kinder to the U.S. mainland. Instead, Puerto Rico, a United States territory, bore the brunt of Maria's extraordinary power. Maria was even more devastating, destroying the entire infrastructure of Puerto Rico.

As of February 2018, six months after the hurricane, 40 percent of people living in Puerto Rico remained without power, the largest and longest blackout in U.S. history. Many questioned the federal bureaucracy's handling of relief efforts to repair the damage Maria brought. President Trump cited the difficulties of reaching the island territory: "It's very tough because it's an island," Trump said. "In Texas, we can ship the trucks right out there, you know, we've got A-pluses on Texas and Florida and we will also on Puerto Rico, but the difference is this is an island sitting in the middle of an ocean, and it's a big ocean."[5]

The severity of the 2017 Atlantic hurricane season brought to mind one more notable storm, Hurricane Katrina of August 2005. Not only did Katrina produce devastation that still shapes New Orleans, the Gulf Coast, and many lives twelve years after it hit, Hurricane Katrina resulted in strong and persistent questioning of the actions of federal bureaucracies as they prepare for and respond to natural disasters.

Before exploring the controversy about the federal government's disaster relief efforts, we will consider what the federal bureaucracy is, how it developed, and what Americans expect it to do.

Irma Maldanado stands with Sussury, her parrot, and her dog in what Hurricane Maria left of her home in Corozal, Puerto Rico, on September 27, 2017.
Joe Raedle/Getty Images

In this December 21, 2017, photo, Jose Luis Gonzalez illuminates his path with a lantern on a street of the Barrio Patrón, in Morovis, Puerto Rico. In mid-December, experts estimated that only half of customers had electrical power, roughly twelve weeks after Maria hit the island on September 20.

Carlos Giusti/AP Images

◼ 7.1 How the Bureaucracy Is Organized

Unlike their relationship to the Congress, the president, or the Supreme Court, Americans have contact with the bureaucracy in their personal or professional lives, often without giving it much thought. The federal bureaucracy affects the lives of average Americans before they get out of bed. Alarm clocks comply with time zones and Daylight Savings Time set by federal agencies.[6]

bureaucrat
an official employed within a government bureaucracy.

If a person's mattress, pillows, sheets, and blankets were made in the United States, **bureaucrats**, officials employed with government agencies, were involved in making sure that the factory was safe for its employees, that it did not discriminate in hiring, that it dealt with labor issues and complaints fairly, and that it did not degrade the environment. If the bedding was not manufactured in the United States, the bureaucracy created regulations that the country of origin had to follow, including rules to make products safe for consumers. Driving much of this bureaucratic involvement in daily life are the demands of Americans themselves—for safe products, fair labor practices, and environmentally conscious factories. The federal bureaucracy regulates much of the nation's economy and private life.[7]

Development of the American Federal Bureaucracy

From its beginnings as a small set of departments employing few people, the bureaucracy has grown enormously and as of 2016 had nearly three million civilian employees working across the country.

This growth has not been steady and gradual, but—like the power of the national government itself—has experienced periods of relatively little growth and periods of intense expansion. The increase in the nation's population and boundaries, the complexity of tasks performed by the federal government, and greater demands for services by citizens have all contributed to this process. Also, responses to crises—economic, social, and military—have produced some of the most dramatic expansions in the size, scope, and complexity of the federal bureaucracy.

The Constitution and the Early Years of the Republic

Much of the constitutional basis for the bureaucracy lies in Article II, which lays out the functions and processes of the executive branch of government.[8] In it, the president is authorized to "require the Opinion, in writing, of the principal Officer in each of the executive Departments, upon any Subject relating to the Duties of their respective Offices."[9] This section forms the basis for the executive branch departments, which are special organizations created by acts of Congress to assist the president in executing the laws of the nation. The heads of these departments are referred to as secretaries. Those secretaries form the president's cabinet, along with the vice president and the heads of other offices given cabinet-level status. Under the Constitution, the president nominates cabinet secretaries, and the Senate must approve them. (Turn back to Figure 5.1, The Organization of the Cabinet, on page 158, for a list of cabinet-level departments.) Presidents may also remove officials in the executive branch, which is related to their role of ensuring that laws are faithfully executed.[10]

Geno DeSanto and Bob Schofield, inspectors from the Agricultural Marketing Service of the U.S. Department of Agriculture, examine bananas at the Philadelphia Food Distribution Center in Pennsylvania.
USDA

The First Administration and the First Cabinet Departments

President George Washington's cabinet included just four men and three official departments. Secretary of State Thomas Jefferson oversaw the Department of State, handling the young nation's dealings with foreign nations as well as publishing laws and overseeing the hiring of civil officials. The Department of War (later consolidated into the Department of Defense) oversaw the nation's small military with fewer than one hundred civilian employees. Alexander Hamilton used his position as secretary of the Treasury to advance his goal of expanding the role of the federal government in the nation's economic affairs. Finally, Washington's attorney general (later made the head of the Department of Justice) acted as a legal advisor to the president and members of his cabinet. In the centuries since, Congress has created new departments and reorganized others (see Figure 7.1).

FIGURE 7.1

Executive Branch Departments: Year of Establishment and Their Main Tasks

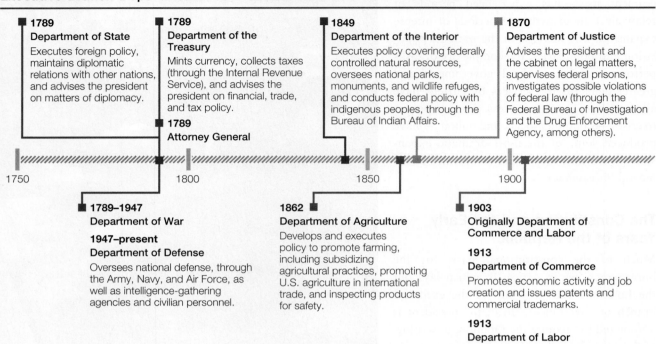

1789
Department of State
Executes foreign policy, maintains diplomatic relations with other nations, and advises the president on matters of diplomacy.

1789
Department of the Treasury
Mints currency, collects taxes (through the Internal Revenue Service), and advises the president on financial, trade, and tax policy.

1789
Attorney General

1849
Department of the Interior
Executes policy covering federally controlled natural resources, oversees national parks, monuments, and wildlife refuges, and conducts federal policy with indigenous peoples, through the Bureau of Indian Affairs.

1870
Department of Justice
Advises the president and the cabinet on legal matters, supervises federal prisons, investigates possible violations of federal law (through the Federal Bureau of Investigation and the Drug Enforcement Agency, among others).

1750   1800   1850   1900

1789–1947
Department of War

1947–present
Department of Defense
Oversees national defense, through the Army, Navy, and Air Force, as well as intelligence-gathering agencies and civilian personnel.

1862
Department of Agriculture
Develops and executes policy to promote farming, including subsidizing agricultural practices, promoting U.S. agriculture in international trade, and inspecting products for safety.

1903
Originally Department of Commerce and Labor

1913
Department of Commerce
Promotes economic activity and job creation and issues patents and commercial trademarks.

1913
Department of Labor
Oversees relationships between firms and their employees, the federal minimum wage, and workplace safety.

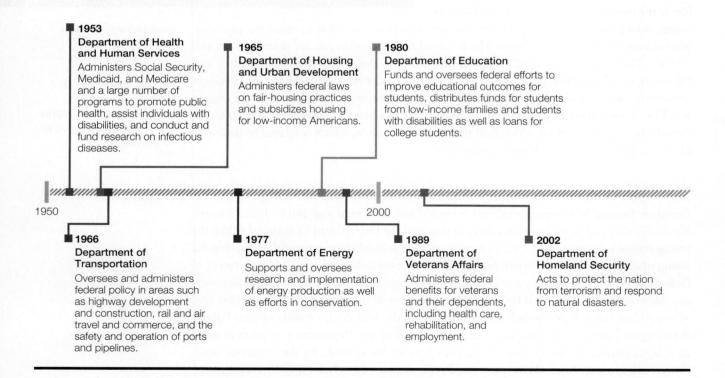

1953
Department of Health and Human Services
Administers Social Security, Medicaid, and Medicare and a large number of programs to promote public health, assist individuals with disabilities, and conduct and fund research on infectious diseases.

1965
Department of Housing and Urban Development
Administers federal laws on fair-housing practices and subsidizes housing for low-income Americans.

1980
Department of Education
Funds and oversees federal efforts to improve educational outcomes for students, distributes funds for students from low-income families and students with disabilities as well as loans for college students.

1950   2000

1966
Department of Transportation
Oversees and administers federal policy in areas such as highway development and construction, rail and air travel and commerce, and the safety and operation of ports and pipelines.

1977
Department of Energy
Supports and oversees research and implementation of energy production as well as efforts in conservation.

1989
Department of Veterans Affairs
Administers federal benefits for veterans and their dependents, including health care, rehabilitation, and employment.

2002
Department of Homeland Security
Acts to protect the nation from terrorism and respond to natural disasters.

The Jacksonian Era and the Rise of Political Patronage

President Andrew Jackson filled positions in the bureaucracy using **political patronage**—giving out administrative positions as a reward for support, rather than merit. Ironically, one of the consequences of patronage was to make the federal bureaucracy more impartial, neutral, and driven by standard operating procedures and technical expertise. If, after elections, a nation is constantly shuffling people in and out of important administrative positions—people who often have little expertise in the operations of those agencies and departments—it becomes necessary to standardize procedures. Otherwise, little would get done, and very little would be done well. Jackson and his supporters laid the foundations for the modern federal bureaucracy. As James Wilson put it, "Far from being enemies of the bureaucracy, the Jacksonians were among its principal architects."[11]

> **political patronage**
> filling of administrative positions as a reward for support, rather than solely on merit.

A Merit-Based Civil Service

With growing demands on the federal government and increasing concerns about the corruption that came with the spoils system, Congress passed the **Pendleton Act** of 1883 creating the first United States Civil Service Commission. Its task was to draw up and enforce rules on hiring, promotion, and tenure of office within the civil service.

Under these new rules, members of the **federal civil service** were hired and promoted using a **merit system**, in which competitive testing results, educational attainment, and other qualifications formed the basis for hiring and promotion rather than politics and personal connections. Even the test questions were prohibited from calling "for the expression or disclosure of any political or religious opinion or affiliation."[12] Also, civil service workers' participation in political campaigns was restricted—in particular, they could not be forced or coerced by superiors into donating to or participating in a political campaign.[13] In the early years after the act's passage, only a small percentage of federal bureaucrats were covered by the Pendleton Act; by 2016, more than 90 percent were. A merit-based civil service emphasizes the importance of professionalism and expertise in a particular policy area. Members of the civil service are supposed to behave neutrally, ensuring that regulations are enforced uniformly throughout the nation.

> **Pendleton Act**
> an act of Congress that created the first United States Civil Service Commission to draw up and enforce rules on hiring, promotion, and tenure of office within the civil service (also known as Civil Service Reform Act of 1883).
>
> **federal civil service**
> the merit-based bureaucracy, excluding the armed forces and political appointments.
>
> **merit system**
> a system of hiring and promotion based on competitive testing results, education, and other qualifications rather than politics and personal connections.

Section Review

This chapter's main ideas are reflected in the Learning Targets. By reviewing after each section, you should be able to

—**Remember** the key points,

—**Know** terms that are central to the topic, and

—**Think** critically about these questions.

7.1 Explain how the federal bureaucracy carries out the responsibilities of government.

REMEMBER
- Most of the federal bureaucracy lies within the executive branch. The bureaucracy make rules that impact people's daily lives.
- Bureaucrats are people who work within bureaucracies.
- The patronage system filled administrative positions as a reward for political support.
- The Pendleton Civil Service Act began the merit-based civil service, where jobs in the bureaucracy are awarded based on competitive testing and other qualifications.

KNOW
- *federal bureaucracy*: the departments and agencies within the executive branch that carry out the laws of the nation. (p. 216)
- *bureaucrat*: an official employed within a government bureaucracy. (p. 218)
- *political patronage*: filling of administrative positions as a reward for support, rather than solely on merit. (p. 221)
- *Pendleton Act*: an act of Congress that created the first United States Civil Service Commission to draw up and enforce rules on hiring, promotion, and tenure of office within the civil service (also known as Civil Service Reform Act of 1883). (p. 221)
- *federal civil service*: the merit-based bureaucracy, excluding the armed forces and political appointments. (p. 221)
- *merit system*: a system of hiring and promotion based on competitive testing results, education, and other qualifications rather than politics and personal connections. (p. 221)

THINK How does having a merit-based civil service advance the goals of democratic government?

7.1 Review Question: Free Response

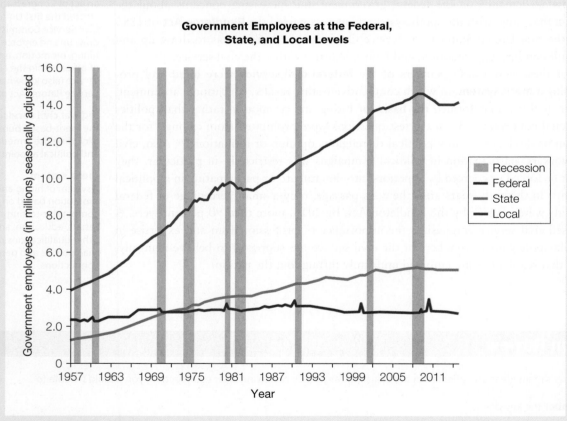

Government Employees at the Federal, State, and Local Levels

Data from U.S. Department of Labor

Use the graph and your knowledge of U.S. Government and Politics to answer parts A, B, and C.

A. Describe one trend shown in the graph.

B. Explain one reason why a civil service system may limit the growth of the federal bureaucracy more than a patronage system would.

C. Describe two advantages of a civil service system in policymaking.

7.2 The Structure of the Modern Federal Bureaucracy

The American federal bureaucracy is a complex web of organizations. As the head of the executive branch, the president's task is to ensure that the executive branch bureaucracy faithfully executes the laws of the nation. The president appoints (with Senate confirmation) people to the top levels of the bureaucracy and directs and advises the departments, bureaus, and agencies on how they should go about putting the laws into effect. When the American people feel that the federal bureaucracy has failed, the president becomes a lightning rod for their outrage.

The main administrative units in the federal bureaucracy are the fifteen cabinet departments. (See Figure 7.2.) Congress has the authority to establish and fund the departments, each of which is responsible for a major area of public policy. They are typically divided into subunits based on the policy in which they specialize.

Cabinet departments are headed by cabinet secretaries (or by the attorney general in the case of the Justice Department), who are nominated by the president and confirmed by a majority vote in the Senate. Cabinet secretaries formally work under the president. However, they also depend on Congress for appropriation of funds and for legislation that sets out specific goals and objectives for their departments. Further, cabinet secretaries often contend with pressure from those affected by the actions of their departments, such

FIGURE 7.2

Differences in Size and Expenditures between Cabinet Departments

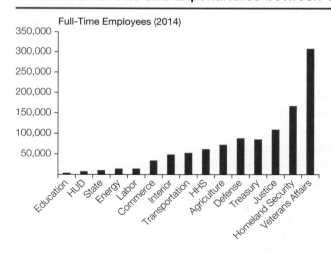
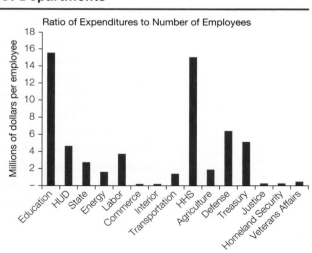

Note: HUD = Housing and Urban Development; HHS = Health and Human Services.

Employment data are from United States Office of Personnel Management, and data on expenditures are from Office of Management and Budget

as citizens or organized interest groups. It is a complicated job. Cabinet secretaries "are expected to perform an array of what might otherwise be viewed as distinctive tasks—building electoral support, making policy, and managing people and programs—while withstanding intense public scrutiny."[14] Secretaries have deputy secretaries, undersecretaries, and administrative staff to help with their efforts.[15]

The newest cabinet department, now considered one of the most influential, is the Department of Homeland Security (DHS), formed in 2002 in response to the terrorist attacks the previous September.[16] The DHS pulled together twenty-two agencies from eight cabinet departments to better coordinate preemption of and national responses to terrorist acts as well as oversee general preparedness for other national emergencies.

Federal Bureaucrats

The organization of the federal bureaucracy and the tasks that agencies undertake are important. Both can affect how well a bureaucracy functions and how easy it can be to reform an agency that has gone astray. Formally, authority across the federal bureaucracy is structured like a pyramid.[17] At the top are the executive political appointees, such as cabinet secretaries and deputy secretaries, who serve at the pleasure of the president and are subject to presidential removal. Of the roughly 6,500 political appointees in the executive branch, about 1,500 require Senate confirmation. Compared to the vast majority of federal bureaucrats, these individuals are short-timers. They do not expect to transition from one administration to the next. Presidents must juggle several considerations in selecting who will lead their departments and agencies. Experience and competence are certainly important, but so are political calculations and a desire to signal to important constituencies a willingness to work with them. The American people also expect a commitment to representing the wide diversity of interests, experiences, and backgrounds. (See Figure 7.3.)

Below this top level are the members of the Senior Executive Service (SES). These individuals—most of whom are drawn from the lower ranks of the federal bureaucracy—enjoy slightly more job security than high-level appointees and are paid and treated more like vice presidents of businesses than political figures. They are expected to use their authority to achieve concrete results.

The vast majority of employees occupy the bottom of the pyramid. They are the career civil servants, whose job ranks are clearly defined according to the General Service (GS) levels. Entrance into and advancement within the federal civil service is governed by the merit system, which relies on competitive examinations, educational qualifications, and performance reviews. Career civil servants enjoy considerable protections from termination, especially for political reasons. This job security is by design, although it presents presidents with a significant challenge. The federal bureaucracy is not a power station in which a president flips a switch and makes things happen automatically. Instead, it is a complex hierarchy of people, most of whom will still have their jobs long after the president and political appointees have moved on.

FIGURE 7.3

Diversity in Cabinet Appointments
How Diverse Have Different Cabinets Been?

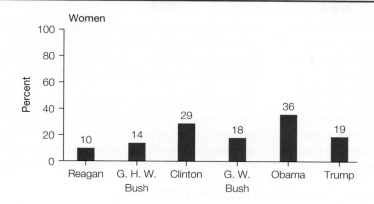

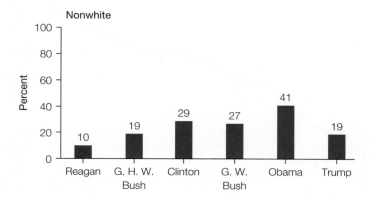

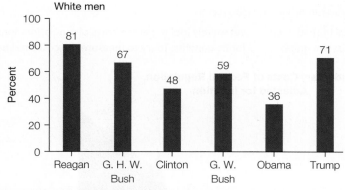

These bar charts compare the initial cabinet picks of the last five presidents alongside the picks President Trump has made for his cabinet as of February 2017. Trump's cabinet is shaping up to be about as woman-inclusive as those of the last few presidents (none of whose cabinets have approached the actual gender balance of the country), but far less racially diverse. White men make up nearly three-quarters of his picks thus far.

Data from National Public Radio

— Census Bureau classifications were used for race. Hispanics are counted as nonwhite.

Analyzing Data: The Growth of the Federal Bureaucracy

One of the common concerns about the federal bureaucracy has been its dramatic increase in size, number of regulations, and spending, especially over the last hundred years. This growth has sparked charges that the federal government is becoming too powerful and too involved in Americans' lives. Critics often imply that more power—and more money—should be found at the state and local level, or simply that government rules are just not needed for as many things as are currently regulated. Yet, the need for uniform rules for the economy has created the need for a greater role of the federal government. Many businesses want nationwide rules in order to avoid having to comply with fifty different sets of state-level rules. And often the states and local governments lack the expertise to deal with complex problems. One thing is for sure, bureaucracy is an inherent feature of modern life.

There are a number of ways to measure the growth of the federal bureaucracy, among them the total number of federal employees, the number of pages in the *Code of Federal Regulations* that publishes all the current rules made by agencies, and the cost of making these rules. Examine the graphs that follow.

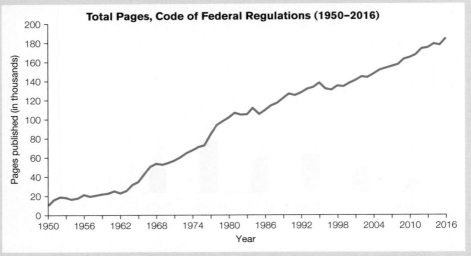

Total Pages, Code of Federal Regulations (1950–2016)

Data from George Washington University Regulatory Studies Center

Another way to measure the effects of the federal bureaucracy is the budgetary costs of making federal rules. See the graph.

Yet merely looking at the costs of regulation does not account for its benefits. To try to measure the costs and benefits of

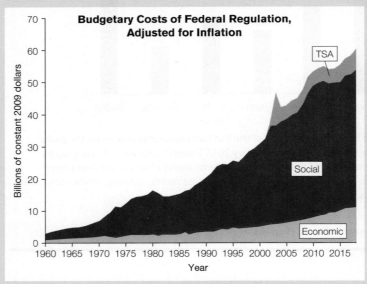

Budgetary Costs of Federal Regulation, Adjusted for Inflation

Data from George Washington University Regulatory Studies Center and the Weidenbaum Center on the Economy, Government, and Public Policy at Washington University in St. Louis

regulation, Congress requires the White House Office of Management and Budget to provide an annual report on the costs, including the cost of compliance with regulations, as well as the benefits of regulation. In its 2016 report, OMB estimated the annual benefits and costs of regulations made between 2005 and 2015, for agencies that monetized benefits and costs, and concluded that the aggregate annual benefits of regulation were between $269 billion and $872 billion, while estimated costs were between $74 billion and $110 billion (2014 dollars).

Government regulation cannot be evaluated by simply comparing economic costs to measurable benefits. Pollution control saves lives. In 1990, the Environmental Protection Agency, for example, estimated that Clean Air Act regulations alone were responsible for preventing 205,000 deaths that year. And in 2011 the EPA estimated air pollution regulation of particulate matter, as a result of the 1990 Clean Air Act, prevented 160,000 deaths in 2010, and by 2020 the number of deaths prevented would reach 230,000 per year.

1. Describe two different ways of measuring the growth of the federal bureaucracy.

2. Describe two factors that might lead to the growth of the federal bureaucracy.

3. Describe one limitation in measuring the effectiveness of the federal bureaucracy by its rate of growth.

4. Explain one way in which the effectiveness of the federal bureaucracy could be accurately assessed.

The bureaucracy is often criticized for making forms too complicated. This political cartoon compares federal tax forms to Egyptian hieroglyphics.
Dave Granlund

Iron Triangles and Issue Networks

iron triangle
coordinated and mutually beneficial activities of the bureaucracy, Congress, and interest groups to achieve shared policy goals.

As the term suggests, an **iron triangle** (see Figure 7.4) consists of three parts—the bureaucracy, Congress, and interest groups—each of which works with the other two to achieve their shared policy goals, even if achieving those goals runs counter to the general interests of society. In doing so, the members of the triangle act as factions, each helping the other two members and receiving benefits from the relationship.

Interest groups provide electoral support to members of Congress, who use their influence, especially on committees and subcommittees, to advance legislation favorable to the interest groups and reduce oversight of interest group activities. These same interest groups lobby on behalf of the relevant bureaucratic agencies to secure the agencies' desired funding and policy goals. In return, the agencies create regulations favorable to interest group objectives. Finally, members of Congress determine funding levels and pass legislation desired by the bureaucratic agencies, which, in turn, implement the laws as desired by those members of Congress.

issue network
webs of influence between interest groups, policymakers, and policy advocates.

Due to the growth in the number of interest groups and an increasingly fluid and complex policy landscape in recent decades, political scientists have employed the concept of the **issue network** to describe the webs of influence between interest groups, policymakers, and policy advocates. In contrast to iron triangles, issue networks are often temporary, arising to address a specific policy problem. Any one issue may give rise to competing issue networks, each of which advocates a different side of the issue. Issue networks also involve more interests than iron triangles. For example, beginning in the 1960s the iron triangle that included the tobacco industry was disrupted by the addition of public health groups opposed to smoking.

FIGURE 7.4

The Iron Triangle

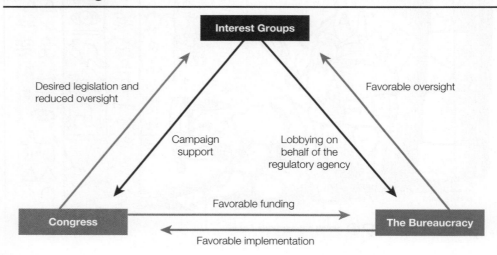

The iron triangle illustrates the linkage of benefits that each of the three members provides to the other two. While all members help each other, it is their common interest in the overall policy goal that drives individual decisions.

7.2 Explain how the federal bureaucracy uses its authority to create and implement regulations.

REMEMBER
- The federal bureaucracy has grown exponentially over time, as has the complexity of the tasks it must perform and the demands for services placed upon it by the American people.
- The Constitution calls for executive branch departments to assist the president in executing the laws of the nation. To control the power of the executive, Congress was given the power to approve nominees and impeach executive officers.
- There was not initially a set number of cabinet departments, nor were their responsibilities set in stone; they have changed over time according to the needs of the nation.
- Executive political appointees serve at the top of the federal bureaucracy, while career civil servants provide stability from administration to administration.
- Iron triangles are mutually beneficial relationships among the bureaucracy, members of Congress, and interest groups.

KNOW
- *iron triangle*: coordinated and mutually beneficial activities of the bureaucracy, Congress, and interest groups to achieve shared policy goals. (p. 228)
- *issue network*: webs of influence between interest groups, policymakers, and policy advocates. (p. 228)

THINK
- What are the advantages and disadvantages of policies that protect civil servants from termination?
- In what ways do iron triangles and issue networks benefit and harm representative democracy?

7.2 Review Question: Free Response

"We realized it is an unnecessary department, but the acronym was just too cool to shut it down."

Dave Carpenter/Cartoonstock.com

Use the cartoon and your knowledge of U.S. Government and Politics to respond to parts A, B, and C.

A. Describe the viewpoint shown in the cartoon.

B. Explain two reasons why the bureaucracy is organized into departments.

C. Explain one political reason why it is difficult to fire a federal bureaucrat.

■▬ 7.3 The Bureaucracy and Policymaking

The bureaucracy carries out executive actions and laws passed by Congress, and it is the key institution responsible for implementing policy. Making public policy involves a series of steps. The entire process is fluid, constantly changing, and, above all else, political. The American political system is designed to have multiple points of access and debate throughout the process.[18]

Defining the Problem and Getting Congress to Act

What may seem like the most simple—and nonpolitical—part of policymaking may be the most significant and the most consequential: defining the problem. (See Figure 7.5.) There are different ways of looking at an issue. Having one's definition of the problem accepted is an effective exercise of power in the policy process.

Getting on the policy agenda—the set of issues on which policymakers focus their attention—is a crucial goal of anyone who wants to influence the policymaking process. Getting on the agenda, or keeping an idea off it, is also an effective exercise of political power. The science of getting on the agenda remains somewhat *un*scientific because the ability to get one's concerns considered depends not only on the merits of the issue but also on the political and economic contexts in which the ideas are offered and on the ways in which the public views the issue at the time.

Getting a policy proposal on the agenda is only the beginning. The policies have to be debated and passed by the Congress and signed into law by the president. Financing an

---

FIGURE 7.5

The Policymaking Process

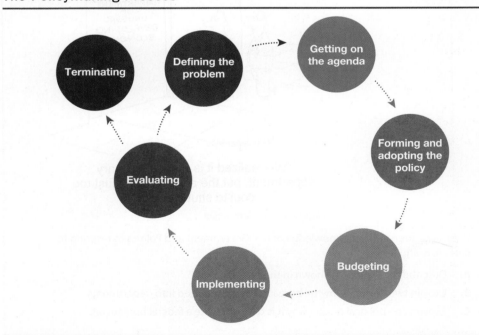

adopted policy is yet another political process. Congress must provide funds for an agency to carry out the policy. Although an agency may have the authority to act on a policy, Congress must provide the financial means to implement the policy.

Implementation, Rulemaking, Advising, and Representation

The main function of the federal bureaucracy is **implementation**, or putting into action, the laws that Congress has passed. Implementation is seldom a straightforward process.[19] New policies are not enacted in isolation. They are introduced into a body of existing policies, sometimes with competing demands.

The technical knowledge required of many federal bureaucrats to successfully implement public policies also acts as a brake on the ability of a president or his political appointees to shape bureaucrats' actions. High-level executive branch officials may lack the technical expertise necessary to evaluate or challenge the actions of their subordinates. As Herbert Kaufman cautioned, "Against this formidable array . . . of knowledge, outsiders and generalists and politicians whose principal skills are in the realm of partisan battle find they must defer to the technicians."[20]

Further, many front-line bureaucrats interact directly with citizens in an environment that makes it difficult to observe and control their behavior effectively. Law enforcement officers, teachers, and social workers all are examples of street-level bureaucrats.[21] Because of their close contact with citizens, street-level bureaucrats may conclude that they have to "bend the rules" to do their jobs.

When Congress passes laws, it often sets only general goals and targets, leaving many of the details, definitions, and specific procedures up to the bureaucratic agencies themselves. There is a sound logic behind this decision. The complexity involved in implementing policies, the technical and specialized knowledge often required to do so, and the flexibility to handle unforeseen circumstances mean bureaucrats must have the authority to flesh out parts of the laws in action. By doing so, however, Congress opens up a space for **bureaucratic discretion**, in which the bureaucrats have some power to decide how a law is implemented and, at times, what Congress meant when it passed a given law.

The process through which the federal bureaucracy fills in critical details of a law is called **regulation**. Agencies must first announce a proposed set of rules and allow interested parties to weigh in; this process is called *notice and comment*. Agencies may have to notify the president or Congress about the anticipated impact of a proposed rule or set of rules. Finally, the adopted rules, known as regulations, must be published in the *Federal Register*, which is published each year and typically runs more than 70,000 pages. These regulations matter because "they carry the same weight as congressional legislation, presidential executive orders, and judicial decisions."[22]

There are over one hundred agencies of the national government with regulatory powers. The overwhelming majority of these agencies is within the executive branch, such as the Environmental Protection Agency. Top officials in these agencies serve at the pleasure of the president and directly carry out the administration's agenda. At the same time, there are approximately twenty independent regulatory agencies, typically known as commissions, such as the Federal Communications Commission, where commissioners serve for set terms of office. See Figure 7.6 for some examples. Although they are political appointees, their set terms are supposed to insulate them from direct political influence. The first of these commissions was the Interstate Commerce Commission in 1887, which was empowered to regulate the railroads.

implementation
the bureaucracy's role in putting into action the laws that Congress has passed.

bureaucratic discretion
the power to decide how a law is implemented and to decide what Congress meant when it passed a law.

regulation
the process through which the federal bureaucracy makes rules that have the force of law, to carry out the laws passed by Congress.

FIGURE 7.6

Examples of Federal Independent Regulatory Agencies

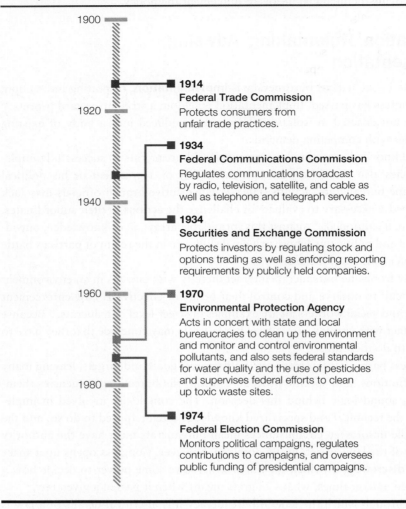

1900

1914
Federal Trade Commission
Protects consumers from
unfair trade practices.

1920

1934
Federal Communications Commission
Regulates communications broadcast
by radio, television, satellite, and cable as
well as telephone and telegraph services.

1940

1934
Securities and Exchange Commission
Protects investors by regulating stock and
options trading as well as enforcing reporting
requirements by publicly held companies.

1960

1970
Environmental Protection Agency
Acts in concert with state and local
bureaucracies to clean up the environment
and monitor and control environmental
pollutants, and also sets federal standards
for water quality and the use of pesticides
and supervises federal efforts to clean
up toxic waste sites.

1980

1974
Federal Election Commission
Monitors political campaigns, regulates
contributions to campaigns, and oversees
public funding of presidential campaigns.

At times the bureaucracy also acts somewhat like a court. It may settle disputes between parties that arise over the implementation of federal laws and presidential executive orders or determine which individuals or groups are covered under a regulation or program—a role called **bureaucratic adjudication**. Agencies may issue fines or other penalties against those who violate federal regulations.

Finally, and perhaps surprisingly, bureaucrats can act as representatives of the American public, especially if they have the ability to act on behalf of citizens, as street-level bureaucrats often do.[23] While cabinet secretaries are increasingly representative of the diversity of the American people, they still do not present a complete portrait of the nation. Members of the civil service, in contrast, do represent the nation's diversity in many ways, except for educational attainment (as it factors into the hiring and promotion process). In this view, having a "representative bureaucracy"—a civil service that truly reflects the diversity of the American people—may also act to legitimize its actions.[24]

bureaucratic adjudication
when the federal bureaucracy settles disputes between parties that arise over the implementation of federal laws or determines which individuals or groups are covered under a regulation or program.

Federal employees are restricted from engaging in political campaigns. The Hatch Act restricts the actions of federal workers in the political realm, with exceptions for the highest-level political appointees.[25] Federal workers were prohibited from participating in political campaigns, coercing other employees to participate, raising funds for a campaign, or holding all but a few elective offices. The Federal Employees Political Activities Act of 1993 relaxed some of the restrictions of the Hatch Act, allowing most federal employees to run in nonpartisan elections and contribute to and to participate in fund-raising for political campaigns, as long as they do not use their official authority to do so.[26]

Evaluation and (Maybe) Termination

What may seem like the least political part of the policymaking process is often far from it. Evaluation—determining if a policy is achieving its stated objectives—is just as consequential as the other stages of the policymaking process and, therefore, just as contested. Congress, state legislatures, academic institutions, federal and state courts, and policy entrepreneurs all weigh in on evaluations of different policies.

The last step in the policymaking process is one that does not always happen—at least formally—even when there is widespread agreement that a policy is not working. Congress has the authority to formally terminate a policy. There are, however, other ways in which a policy may be terminated. Courts, especially the Supreme Court, may terminate a policy using the power of judicial review.

AP® TIP

The bureaucracy has rulemaking authority. Some important departments and agencies to know are

Department of Homeland Security

Department of Transportation

Department of Veterans Affairs

Department of Education

Environmental Protection Agency

Federal Elections Commission

Securities and Exchange Commission

Section Review

7.3 Explain the role of the federal bureaucracy in the policymaking process.

REMEMBER
- The policymaking process involves the public agenda, lawmaking by Congress, rulemaking and implementation by the bureaucracy, feedback, and revision or termination.
- Implementing the laws passed by Congress is one of the bureaucracy's core tasks.
- Bureaucrats typically have some discretion over how the laws are implemented.
- Agencies also have critical rulemaking responsibilities and they may fill in the details of legislation, sometimes using bureaucratic adjudication to settle disputes that arise during implementation.
- The bureaucracy also can serve to represent the citizens.

KNOW
- *implementation*: the bureaucracy's role in putting into action the laws that Congress has passed. (p. 231)
- *bureaucratic discretion*: the power to decide how a law is implemented and, what Congress meant when it passed the law. (p. 231)
- *regulation*: the process through which the federal bureaucracy makes rules that have the force of law, to carry out the laws passed by Congress. (p. 231)
- *bureaucratic adjudication*: when the federal bureaucracy settles disputes between parties that arise over the implementation of federal laws or determines which individuals or groups are covered under a regulation or program. (p. 232)

THINK
What are the dangers in allowing an unelected bureaucracy to make rules and adjudicate whether or not those rules have been broken?

7.3 Review Question: Free Response

U.S. Food and Drug Administration, CPG Sec. 515.700
Chocolate & Chocolate Liquor—
Adulteration with Insect and Rodent Filth

Under the rules of the U.S. Food and Drug Administration, the agency may seize chocolate under the following conditions:

1. Insect Filth

a.   The chocolate in six (6) 100 gram subsamples contains an average of sixty or more insect fragments per 100 grams.

   or

b.   Any one subsample contains ninety or more insect fragments, even if the overall average of all the subsamples is less than sixty.

2. Rodent Filth

a.   The chocolate in six (6) 100 gram subsamples contains an average of more than one rodent hair per 100 grams, regardless of the size of the hairs or hair fragments.

   or

b.   Any one subsample contains more than three rodent hairs even if the overall average is less than one rodent hair.

After reading the regulation, and using your knowledge of U.S. Government and Politics, respond to parts A, B, and C.

A.   Describe the purpose of the regulation.

B.   Explain how the regulation represents the rulemaking function of the bureaucracy.

C.   Describe one criticism of allowing an agency to impose penalties for violations of the regulations it creates.

▰ 7.4 Checks on the Bureaucracy

Control, Oversight, and Reform

As mentioned earlier in the chapter, bureaucratic agencies participate in iron triangles, or issue networks, forming relationships with interest groups and congressional subcommittees. One concern, especially for bureaucrats in regulatory agencies, is that individuals may undermine effective regulation if their own interests are more closely aligned with the targets of regulation than the mission of the agency, a problem known as agency capture. If a regulator has close ties to the industry being regulated—either through previous employment or, perhaps, expected future employment—there may be temptations to "look the other way," instruct their subordinates to do so, or conduct their jobs in such a way as to benefit a few preferred clients.[27]

Controlling the Bureaucracy

The system of separation of powers that the framers designed poses a special challenge to controlling the bureaucracy. Because authority over the federal bureaucracy is divided among different branches, federal agencies and bureaus often have to answer to more than one overseer. According to political scientist Joel Aberbach, "Since usually no one set of institutional actors has clear control and signals often conflict, it is difficult to hold the bureaucracy, or any other institution, reasonably to account."[28]

The President

As head of the executive branch, the president formally controls most of the federal bureaucracy.[29] He or she has the authority to appoint and remove individuals at the top layers of the bureaucracy. Presidents appoint agency heads, subject to Senate confirmation, based on their ideology and willingness to carry out the administration's goals. Presidents can also shape bureaucratic priorities in the annual budgets that they present to Congress and, with congressional approval, by reorganizing agencies. As discussed in Chapter 5, executive orders carry the force of law and typically instruct departments, agencies, and bureaus on how they are to go about implementing policy.

Presidents, however, often confront restrictions in their control over the day-to-day functions of the bureaucracy. Bureaucratic discretion and the bureaucracy's size and complexity all conspire against achieving quick results. There are millions of federal bureaucrats, and it would be impossible for the president or Congress to oversee all of them. Bureaucrats have discretion in how to implement legislation, and they often behave independently. Bureaucrats, or their agencies, may disagree with the policies passed by Congress or the president, stalling or avoiding its implementation.

In one of the smaller battles of his presidency, Jimmy Carter (1977–1981) discovered one of the obstacles to his power when he confronted a problem that had apparently existed in the White House since the administration of Dwight David Eisenhower

AP® Political Science PRACTICES

Interpreting Political Cartoons

This political cartoon depicts octopus-shaped red tape from Washington, D.C., gripping the states with its tentacles.

Cagle Cartoons, Inc.

1. Describe the viewpoint expressed in the cartoon.

2. Explain how this cartoon relates to the federal bureaucracy rather than state bureaucracies.

3. Explain why the cartoonist chose a red octopus to represent the bureaucracy.

4. Explain one reason why most cartoons about the bureaucracy are negative.

(1953–1961): mice. With maintenance personnel unable to control the mouse population, Carter called on the bureaucracy. Unfortunately, the Department of the Interior said that the mice were a problem for the General Services Administration (GSA) because Interior was only responsible for the grounds of the White House and not the building itself. GSA countered that the problem was Interior's "since the mice were obviously migrating from outside." Only after Carter "ordered an immediate meeting in his office of all concerned officials of the GSA, Department of Interior, White House administrators, and others" was progress made.[30]

Congress

Congress plays a key role in controlling and guiding the bureaucracy. The Senate has power over confirmation for the higher levels of the federal service. Congress as a whole can pass legislation creating or terminating agencies and programs and, through the process of appropriation, has control over the resources that departments, bureaus, and agencies receive to carry out their tasks. Congressional committees, especially the House and Senate appropriations committees, are key players in these processes.

Legislation can shape bureaucratic behavior by setting goals, priorities, and an organizational structure. Congress also uses an oversight process to influence what happens when agencies are up and running. Members of the bureaucracy may be required to testify before Congress, justifying their actions. Further, Congress has established its own bureaucracies to keep tabs on executive branch implementation. The Government Accountability Office (GAO) is an example of this type of agency. Through its oversight functions, Congress checks on how executive agencies are exercising their authority and whether they are spending the funds appropriated to them wisely.

In a series of reports based on its investigations on preparedness and response regarding Hurricane Katrina, the GAO detailed a list of evaluations and suggestions for the future. The GAO's reports praised some parts of the bureaucracy, such as the Coast Guard. Much of what the office found, however, was unflattering, and it called out failed leadership, communication, and coordination within the executive branch. One report stated, "No one was designated in advance to lead the overall federal response in anticipation of the event despite clear warnings from the National Hurricane Center."[31]

Congressional oversight of the bureaucracy includes conducting hearings or requiring information from the agencies. While the GAO conducted its investigations into Katrina, Congress conducted its own hearings into the federal government's performance, at times grilling top officials on their actions or lack of action. Much of the sharpest questioning was directed at President Bush's top political appointees. Testifying before the Senate in February 2006, Secretary of Homeland Security Michael Chertoff "endured two and a half hours of intense political criticism" and offered an apology to Congress and the American people.[32] "The worst element of this catastrophe personally is not criticism I've received," he said, "but the derision of people who did have their suffering unnecessarily prolonged because this department did not perform."[33]

A report by a bipartisan investigative committee in the House of Representatives was also scathing. It documented, in page after page, "a litany of mistakes, misjudgments, lapses, and absurdities all cascading together."[34] The "American people," the report concluded, "don't care about acronyms or organizational charts. They want to know who was supposed to do what, when, and whether the job got done. And if it didn't get done, they want to know how we are going to make sure it does next time."[35]

Impact of the Judiciary and the Media

Decisions by the federal judiciary can significantly impact bureaucratic behavior. Judicial decisions may restrict and constrain the scope of accepted bureaucratic action. In *Michigan v. EPA* (2015),[36] the Supreme Court overturned the EPA's limits on mercury, arsenic, and acidic gases emitted by coal-fired power plants, known as mercury and air toxics standards (MATS).[37] Opponents, including the National Federation of Independent Business, challenged the regulation because compliance was expensive. The EPA estimated its rule would cost businesses $9.6 billion, although it might prevent up to 11,000 premature deaths and 130,000 asthma cases each year. The majority ruling, written by Justice Antonin Scalia, determined that the EPA "unreasonably" interpreted the Clean Air Act when it decided not to consider the costs of compliance and whether regulating the pollutants is "appropriate and necessary."[38]

In the days after Hurricane Harvey flooded Houston, Andrew White helps a neighbor down the street after he rescued her from her home in the River Oaks area of the city.
Scott Olson/Getty Images

In general, the media seldom cover the workings of the federal bureaucracy. For this reason, most Americans are not well informed of the day-to-day workings of the vast bureaucracy, and numerous agencies exist that many Americans just aren't aware of. As Walter Lippmann, scholar and commenter on American politics, noted in 1927, "The public will arrive in the middle of the third act and will leave before the last curtain, having stayed just long enough perhaps to decide who is the hero and who is the villain of the piece."[39] Therefore, public opinion rarely constrains bureaucratic behavior. When, however, the bureaucracy is involved in a major crisis or catastrophe—and especially when it appears that it has failed—it may find itself center stage in Lippmann's play, with a full and angry audience in attendance.

Such was the case after Katrina. A year after its landfall on the Gulf Cost, thousands of residents were still waiting for federal help, and public opinion had turned against President Bush on his handling of the disaster. A national poll found that only 31 percent of Americans approved of his management of the storm, and 56 percent did not "believe that the country [was] ready for another disaster."[40]

Reform and the Reliance on Private Organizations

Following Katrina, investigators and members of Congress began to question both the government's reliance on private contractors in relief efforts and governmental interference with private-sector efforts. Concerns included a lack of competition in awarding contracts for cleanup and recovery efforts, a failure to adequately employ local businesses and contractors, and a failure on the part of FEMA to have enough "sufficiently trained procurement professionals" to effectively manage and oversee the contracting process.[41] According to a local official in Louisiana, FEMA had blocked private relief efforts as well: "We had Wal-mart deliver three trailer trucks of water. FEMA turned them back. They said we didn't need them."[42]

As it became clear that the effects from Katrina would be felt for years, many private organizations and individuals stepped up to help. Habitat for Humanity dispatched thousands of volunteers to the Gulf Coast to rebuild housing for low-income residents. Mary Gray founded Minnesota Helpers, a "Mississippi-to-Minnesota arts pipeline," to provide opportunities for Gulf Coast artists to display and sell their work because few venues remained open in their own devastated communities.[43]

Trucks from Walmart with relief supplies for residents of the Gulf Coast. FEMA was widely criticized for hampering private efforts at assistance.

NICHOLAS KAMM/Getty Images

Not all private responses were viewed so positively. Some were accused of running scams to take advantage of the federal dollars that flowed into devastated areas, prompting the government to establish the Hurricane Katrina Fraud Task Force to "thwart and prosecute hurricane-related fraud."[44] Some initiatives, although not illegal, seemed to take advantage of the disaster. In January 2006, a local tour bus company planned to operate a "Hurricane Katrina Tour—America's Worst Catastrophe!" to offer tourists the chance to see the aftermath of the storm from air-conditioned buses, although the company promised that a portion of the $35 ticket price would benefit recovery efforts.[45]

Americans want the implementation of national policy to be effective and strong. When they believe that it is not—such as was the case with Hurricane Katrina—they demand change. However, Americans do not want the federal bureaucracy to be *too* strong. When they feel that it has become too powerful, they worry. Both the separation of powers and the realities of American federalism shape the behaviors of the federal departments, agencies, and bureaus. Such is the complex nature of the American federal bureaucracy.

Section Review

7.4 **Explain how Congress, the president, and the courts can hold the bureaucracy accountable.**

REMEMBER
- The president formally controls most of the federal bureaucracy, and he can influence the bureaucracy through the appointment of federal officials, by submitting a budget, and through executive orders.
- Congress can control the bureaucracy by passing laws that set priorities, through funding, and by holding oversight hearings.
- Judicial decisions may restrict bureaucratic action.
- Efforts to reform the bureaucracy to—limit its power, reduce its size, and fix inefficiencies—include devolving responsibilities to the states, deregulation, and privatizing government responsibilities to increase competitiveness.

THINK
Why is it difficult for the president and Congress to control the bureaucracy despite the tools they have for doing so?

7.4 **Review Question: Free Response**

Academic institutions and individual investigators often receive research funding from multiple federal agencies, but approaches to similar requirements—such as grant proposals, disclosure of financial conflict of interest, and animal care—are not harmonized across agencies. Regulations, reporting requirements, and congressional mandates frequently overlap, resulting in duplication of effort, multiple reporting of the same information in different formats, and multiple submissions of information on different schedules. Conflicting guidance on compliance requirements has created uncertainty and confusion.

—Inconsistent, Duplicative Regulations Undercut Productivity of U.S. Research Enterprise; Actions Needed to Streamline and Harmonize Regulations, Reinvigorate Government-University Partnership[46]

After reading the passage, use your knowledge of U.S. Government and Politics to respond to parts A, B, and C.

A. Describe the problem addressed in the passage.

B. Describe an oversight power Congress could use to address the complaints mentioned in the passage.

C. Describe a legislative action Congress could take to address the complaints mentioned in the passage.

Chapter 7 Review

AP® KEY CONCEPTS

- *federal bureaucracy* (p. 216)
- *bureaucrat* (p. 218)
- *political patronage* (p. 221)
- *Pendleton Act* (p. 221)
- *federal civil service* (p. 221)

- *merit system* (p. 221)
- *iron triangle* (p. 228)
- *issue network* (p. 228)
- *implementation* (p. 231)
- *bureaucratic discretion* (p. 231)

- *regulation* (p. 231)
- *bureaucratic adjudication* (p. 232)

AP® EXAM PRACTICE and Critical Thinking Project

MULTIPLE-CHOICE QUESTIONS

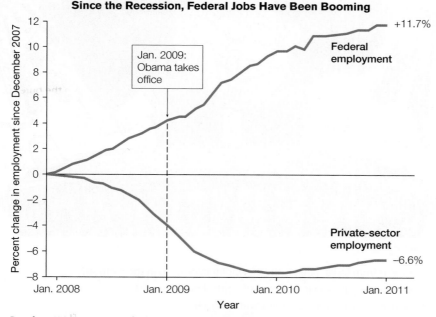

Since the Recession, Federal Jobs Have Been Booming

Data from U.S. Department of Labor, Bureau of Labor Statistics

1. The graph supports which of the following conclusions?

A. From January 2008 to January 2011, the percentage of federal workers has grown at twice the rate as the percentage of private sector employment.

B. As of January 2011, there was more than an 18 percent gap between the growth of federal and private-sector employment.

C. From January of 2008 to January 2011, private-sector employment steadily declined.

D. President Obama's policies favored federal employment over private-sector employment.

2. The following statement appears on the Food and Drug Administration Web site:

> The objective of FDA regulatory programs is to assure compliance with the Federal Food, Drug, and Cosmetic Act (the Act). Specific enforcement activities include actions to correct and prevent violations, remove violative products or goods from the market, and punish offenders. The type of enforcement activity FDA uses will depend on the nature of the violation. The range of enforcement activities include issuing a letter notifying the individual or firm of a violation and requesting correction, to criminal prosecution of the individual or firm.
>
> —U.S. Food and Drug Administration:
> FDA Enforcement Actions[47]

The quote refers to which of the following tasks of the bureaucracy?

A. regulation

B. oversight

C. compliance

D. discretion

_____

3. Iron triangles have been criticized because they benefit their members but limit the ability of outside groups to influence the policymaking process. This criticism represents which theory of democracy?

A. participatory

B. pluralist

C. representative

D. elitist

New Indian Express

4. The cartoon is from India. What is the viewpoint expressed in the cartoon?

A. The bureaucracy is similar to an out-of-control mad scientist.

B. The bureaucracy is overly complex and inefficient.

C. A storm is coming that will overwhelm the bureaucracy.

D. A merit-based civil service will make the bureaucracy more efficient.

_____

5. During the last week of July 2017, members of the Federal Communications Commission testified before Congress about net neutrality rules. In the same week, the House Homeland Security Committee heard testimony about the role of technology in policing the border.[48] These hearings are an example of

   A. The power of Congress to revise legislation pertaining to the bureaucracy

   B. Congressional oversight of executive agencies

   C. Iron triangles and issue networks

   D. The rulemaking and enforcement authority of the bureaucracy

6. Select the pair of answers that matches a branch of government with the correct check on the bureaucracy.

Branch of government	Check on the bureaucracy
A. Executive	Appropriates funds
B. Congress	Appoints agency heads
C. Supreme Court	Issues decisions overturning regulations
D. House of Representatives	Confirms Cabinet appointments

7. Which of the following makes it difficult for the executive branch to control the bureaucracy?

   A. Cabinet heads are appointed based on their expertise, and presidents defer to them.

   B. The bureaucracy is large and deals with complex issues.

   C. The Pendleton Civil Service Act protects bureaucrats from being fired.

   D. The Hatch Act protects the political independence of bureaucrats.

_____

Gatis Sluka/Cagle Cartoons, Inc.

8. The cartoon expresses which of the following criticisms of the bureaucracy?

   A. The bureaucracy is inefficient.

   B. There is too much congressional oversight of the bureaucracy.

   C. The average American does not benefit from the bureaucracy.

   D. Bureaucrats are underpaid for the hard work they do.

_____

9. Which of the following is a criticism of a patronage system in a democratic government?
   A. It rewards those who are loyal to past administrations.
   B. It is unrepresentative because there is no check on the appointment of cabinet heads.
   C. Appointees are frequently not qualified to serve the public interest.
   D. It prevents Congress and the judiciary from checking bureaucratic actions.

10. According to ABC News, the average chocolate bar contains **eight insect** parts. Anything less than **sixty insect** pieces per 100 grams of chocolate (two chocolate bars' worth) is deemed safe for consumption by the Food and Drug Administration.[49] This is an example of bureaucratic:
    A. discretion
    B. inefficiency
    C. red tape
    D. regulation

FREE-RESPONSE QUESTIONS

1. The following quote in *The Economist*, a U.K.-based periodical, is about the Dodd-Frank Banking Law, which was passed to increase the regulation of banks following the recession of 2007.

   But Dodd-Frank is far too complex, and becoming more so. At 848 pages, it is 23 times longer than Glass-Steagall, the reform that followed the Wall Street crash of 1929. Worse, every other page demands that regulators fill in further detail. Some of these clarifications are hundreds of pages long. Just one bit, the "Volcker rule," which aims to curb risky proprietary trading by banks, includes 383 questions that break down into 1,420 subquestions.[50]

   Use the excerpt and your knowledge of U.S. Government and Politics to respond to parts A, B, and C.
   A. Describe an action Congress could take to address the complaint expressed above.
   B. Describe an action the president could take to address the complaint expressed above.
   C. Explain two reasons why it is difficult for the president and Congress to control the bureaucracy.

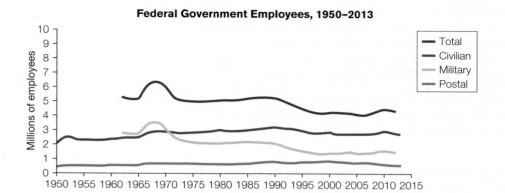

Federal Government Employees, 1950–2013

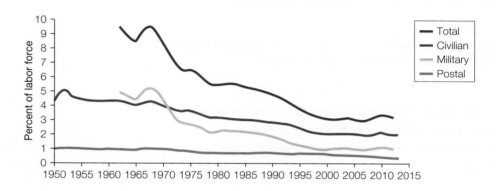

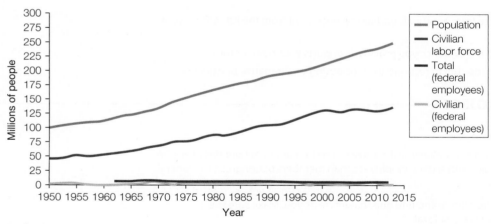

Data from Bureau of Labor Statistics

2. Use the graphs and your knowledge of U.S. Government and Politics to answer parts A, B, and C.

   A. Describe what each graph measures.

   B. Describe the graph that would be most useful in measuring the growth or decline of the federal bureaucracy in relation to the civilian workforce and explain why the graph is the most accurate.

   C. Identify one graph that does not accurately measure the growth of the federal bureaucracy in relation to the civilian workforce and explain why the graph is inaccurate.

ARGUMENTATION QUESTION

The 2008 financial crisis destabilized the economy and left millions of Americans economically devastated. Congress studied the causes of the recession to craft solutions; it determined that the financial services industry had pushed consumers into unsustainable forms of debt and that federal regulators had failed to prevent mounting risks to the economy, in part because those regulators were overly responsive to the industry they purported to police. Congress saw a need for an agency to help restore public confidence in markets: a regulator attentive to individuals and families. So it established the Consumer Financial Protection Bureau.[51]

Congress gave the CFPB a single director protected against removal by the president without cause. In *PHH Corporation v. Consumer Fraud Protection Bureau*, the director's protection against removal by the executive was challenged as an unconstitutional impediment to the president's power.[52]

Did Congress's creation of an agency head who cannot be removed by the president for five years except for cause violate the constitutional principle of checks and balances?

In your essay:

- Articulate a claim or thesis that responds to the prompt, and use a line of reasoning to defend it.
- Use at least TWO pieces of relevant and accurate evidence to support your claim.
- At least ONE piece of evidence must be from one of the listed foundational documents:
  - Constitution of the United States
  - *Federalist* No. 51
  - *Federalist* No. 70
- Use a second piece of evidence from another foundational document from the list or from your study of the bureaucracy.
- Use reasoning to explain why the evidence you provided supports your claim or thesis.
- Use refutation, concession, or rebuttal to respond to an opposing or alternative perspective.

CRITICAL THINKING PROJECT

Interviewing a Federal Employee

The bureaucracy consists of millions of employees who carry out tasks that impact our daily lives. We are more likely to personally interact with federal employees than members of Congress, the federal courts, or, of course, the president.

1. Research a federal agency in your area, and find one that interests you. Make sure the organization is federal and not state or local.

2. Call the agency or send an email and ask for the opportunity to speak with one of their employees. You might even ask them to meet with you or come to your school.

3. Conduct an interview, including these questions:
   a. What is your experience and educational background?
   b. Why did you want to work for the federal government?
   c. What do you do in an average day?
   d. What do you enjoy most about your work?
   e. What are the drawbacks of working in the federal bureaucracy?
   f. What is the biggest misconception about working for the federal government?

4. Present your findings to the class, using presentation software or any other method that will convey the information in an interesting way.

AP® EXAM PRACTICE and Critical Thinking Project

MULTIPLE-CHOICE QUESTIONS

Questions 1, 2, and 3 refer to these passages.

> The President of the United States would be liable to be impeached, tried, and, upon conviction of treason, bribery, or other high crimes or misdemeanors, removed from office; and would afterwards be liable to prosecution and punishment in the ordinary course of law. The person of the king of Great Britain is sacred and inviolable; there is no constitutional tribunal to which he is amenable; no punishment to which he can be subjected without involving the crisis of a national revolution . . .
>
> The President of the United States is to have power to return a bill, which shall have passed the two branches of the legislature, for reconsideration; and the bill so returned is to become a law, if, upon that reconsideration, it be approved by two thirds of both houses. The king of Great Britain, on his part, has an absolute negative upon the acts of the two houses of Parliament. . . . The qualified negative of the President differs widely from this absolute negative of the British sovereign; and tallies exactly with the revisionary authority of the council of revision of this State, of which the governor is a constituent part.
>
> —Alexander Hamilton, *Federalist* No. 69

1. Which of the following best describes the argument made by Alexander Hamilton?
   A. The president will have enough power to lead the nation, without having absolute power.
   B. Congress will have the power to check presidential actions, in contrast to the king of England, whose power is absolute.
   C. It is important to have an energetic single executive who can serve as the face of the nation and make decisions quickly.
   D. It will be easy for Congress to override a presidential veto, if Congress believes a law is in the best interests of the nation.

2. Which of the following constitutional provisions limits the power of the executive, according to Hamilton's argument?
   A. judicial review in Article III
   B. the necessary and proper clause in Article I
   C. expressed powers of Congress in Article I
   D. the supremacy clause in Article IV

3. Based on the text, which of the following statements would Hamilton most likely support?
   A. Congress should be the most powerful branch of government because it is closest to the people.
   B. Checks and balances are necessary to prevent a faction from taking too much power.
   C. Presidents are less able to abuse their power than unelected monarchs.
   D. Presidents are more qualified to lead a country than monarchs because presidents are elected.

4. Select the response that matches a constitutional power of the executive branch with a congressional check on that power:

Executive power	Congressional check
A. Approves treaties	Ratification in House of Representatives
B. Issues executive orders	Veto power
C. Commander in chief	Provides funding for military actions
D. Appoints judges	Holds oversight hearings

Questions 5 and 6 refer to the cartoon.

edsteinink.com

5. The cartoon reflects which of the following viewpoints?

   A. Most incumbents are reelected.

   B. Members of Congress are not likely to be reelected when the approval ratings for Congress are low.

   C. Members of Congress are not likely to be reelected when unemployment rates are high.

   D. Congress has few tools for controlling the unemployment rate.

6. Which of the following might lead to the result shown in the cartoon?

   A. an election for an open seat in Congress

   B. a political "tidal wave" sweeping across the nation

   C. a midterm congressional election

   D. increased campaign spending by incumbents

Questions 7 and 8 refer to the cartoon.

7. Which of the following viewpoints is expressed in the cartoon?

   A. Districts in Illinois were gerrymandered to benefit the Democratic Party.

   B. Both political parties use gerrymandering to increase their representatives in the U.S. House of Representatives.

   C. Both parties use gerrymandering to increase their representation in the U.S. Senate.

   D. Republicans and Democrats must compromise in the redistricting process.

8. Which of the following proposals would respond to the problem addressed in the political cartoon?

   A. Give state governors the power to redraw congressional district boundaries.

   B. Give politically independent commissions the power to redraw congressional district boundaries.

   C. Allow citizens to choose the congressional district in which they reside.

   D. Allow citizens to bring lawsuits challenging racial and ethnic gerrymandering.

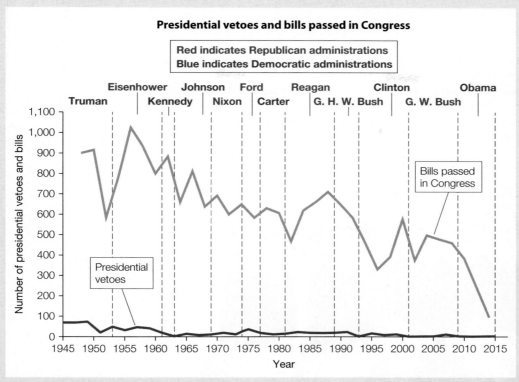

Presidential vetoes and bills passed in Congress

Red indicates Republican administrations
Blue indicates Democratic administrations

Truman · Eisenhower · Johnson · Ford · Reagan · Clinton · Obama
Kennedy · Nixon · Carter · G. H. W. Bush · G. W. Bush

Number of presidential vetoes and bills

Bills passed in Congress

Presidential vetoes

Year

Data from U.S. Senate

9. Which of the following statements is supported by the graph?

   A. Presidents are usually able to get more of their programs passed in Congress at the beginning of their first term than near the end of their first term.

   B. Congress has been less productive over time.

   C. The president is more likely to use his veto power during periods of divided government.

   D. Democratic presidents are more likely to veto legislation than Republican presidents.

   _____

10. In *Shelby v. Holder* (2013),[1] the Supreme Court overturned a provision of the Voting Rights Act of 1965 that requires some states to get approval from the federal government before changing their voting laws. The Court ruled that the provision violated the Tenth Amendment of the Constitution. Which of the following cases could be used as precedent in the Shelby ruling?

    A. *McCulloch v. Maryland* (1819)

    B. *Baker v. Carr* (1962)

    C. *United States v. Lopez* (1995)

    D. *Marbury v. Madison* (1803)

    _____

11. Which of the following best represents judicial restraint?
  A. The Supreme Court upholds key provisions of the Affordable Care Act under Congress's power to tax.
  B. A federal court overturns President Trump's executive order banning immigrants from seven predominantly Muslim countries.
  C. The Supreme Court overturns the Gun-Free School Zones Act on the grounds that Congress exceeded its authority under the Commerce Clause.
  D. The Supreme Court denies a petition from a death row inmate claiming a violation of his Eighth Amendment rights.

———————————

Ed Fischer/Cartoon Stock

12. Which of the following statements best represents the viewpoint expressed in the cartoon?
  A. Judicial appointments are a way for presidents to influence government after they leave office.
  B. Supreme Court justices influence each other to adopt a consistent political ideology.
  C. Supreme Court justices rarely stray from their ideology once they have been appointed.
  D. The Supreme Court should be balanced between liberals and conservatives.

> [O]rdinary Americans support electing judges. A whopping 65% of Americans favor the election of judges, and only 22% feel that judges should be appointed. Also, 69% of Americans feel judges should adhere to term limits as well.[2]
>
> —Bruce Walker

13. Which of the following arguments would support the viewpoint in the passage?

   A. Elected judges would be more qualified to interpret the Constitution than appointed judges.

   B. Elected judges would represent more diverse demographic groups and viewpoints than appointed justices.

   C. Presidents should not appoint judges based on political ideology.

   D. Lifetime appointments protect judicial independence.

14. Which of the following arguments would an opponent of the viewpoint in the passage make?

   A. Lifetime appointments allow judges to uphold the Constitution and protect the rights of unpopular groups.

   B. The judicial appointment process insulates judges from political ideology, so there is no reason to elect them.

   C. The president and Congress have the power to overturn judicial decisions, so there is no reason for the public to elect judges.

   D. Elected judges could change their minds about the issues after they are elected.

---

15. Which of the following statements best describes the constitutional basis for the decision in *Marbury v. Madison* (1803)?

   A. It was based on the Court's expressed powers in Article III.

   B. It was based on the argument made by Alexander Hamilton in *Federalist* No. 78.

   C. It was based on the full faith and credit clause of Article IV.

   D. It was based on the supremacy clause.

16. In *Obergefell v. Hodges* (2015),[3] the Supreme Court ruled that same-sex marriage is a fundamental right protected under the equal protection clause. What power could Congress use to overcome this ruling?

   A. Pass a law outlawing same-sex marriage.

   B. Approve a constitutional amendment that marriage is between one man and one woman and send the amendment to the states for ratification.

   C. Pass a law declaring that marriage is a state issue and cut funding for states that recognize same-sex marriage.

   D. Impeach the judges who voted to uphold same-sex marriage.

17. The Environmental Protection Agency has the power to enact regulations regarding air, water, and soil quality and to impose fines or other penalties when those regulations are violated. These rulemaking and compliance powers have been criticized because

   A. It violates the principle of checks and balances when agencies make rules, hold trials, and impose punishment.

   B. The bureaucracy is the least diverse branch of government, and it does not apply the law fairly to all groups.

   C. There are few checks on the power of the EPA, and the agency is unaccountable to the executive and Congress.

   D. EPA employees are political appointees who do not have the scientific knowledge and experience to write environmental regulations.

18. Which of the following is an advantage of a merit-based civil service?

   A. Civil servants are difficult to fire, so they are more efficient in carrying out policy.

   B. Agency budgets are insulated from the political ideology of the president and Congress.

   C. Appointed agency heads have little impact on the way policy is carried out.

   D. There is continuity of bureaucratic expertise regardless of presidential and congressional elections.

Pat Bagley, *Salt Lake Tribune*

19. The cartoon expresses which of the following viewpoints?
    A. The bureaucracy is underappreciated, even when it provides assistance.
    B. Religious Americans are more likely to rely on their churches for aid than on the federal government.
    C. The federal government's hurricane relief efforts in Texas were ineffective and underfunded.
    D. People who live in areas prone to natural disasters should not expect the federal government to provide disaster relief assistance.

    _____

20. Which of the following is an argument in favor of iron triangles?
    A. Iron triangles benefit the public interest because diverse groups of citizens are included in the policymaking process.
    B. The members of iron triangles are subject to election, which makes them accountable to the public.
    C. Interest groups are policy specialists, and they can provide needed expertise and information to members of Congress and bureaucratic agencies.
    D. Lobbyists are often former members of Congress, and this "revolving door" adds transparency to the policymaking process.

FREE-RESPONSE QUESTIONS

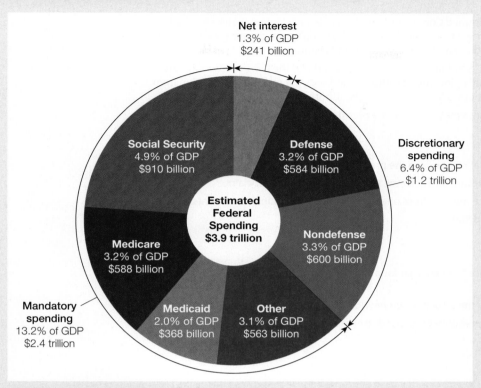

Net interest
1.3% of GDP
$241 billion

Social Security
4.9% of GDP
$910 billion

Defense
3.2% of GDP
$584 billion

Discretionary
spending
6.4% of GDP
$1.2 trillion

Estimated
Federal
Spending
$3.9 trillion

Medicare
3.2% of GDP
$588 billion

Nondefense
3.3% of GDP
$600 billion

Mandatory
spending
13.2% of GDP
$2.4 trillion

Medicaid
2.0% of GDP
$368 billion

Other
3.1% of GDP
$563 billion

Data from Congressional Budget Office, CBO Projections Unit

1. Use the pie chart and your knowledge of U.S. Government and Politics to answer parts A, B, and C.
   A. Identify the program that accounts for the largest portion of federal spending.
   B. Explain two reasons why it is difficult to reduce spending for the program you identified.
   C. Explain one reason, other than the program you identified in part (B), why it is difficult to reduce federal spending.

[The] U.S. Public Interest Research Group revealed that some [fidget] . . . spinners . . . contain dangerously high levels of lead.

The Fidget Wild Premium Spinner Brass tested at 33,000 parts per million for lead— some 300 times the 100 parts per million allowable for children's toys. The lead level in another model, the Fidget Wild Premium Spinner in Metal, tested at 1,300 parts per million.[4]   —Kathy Kristof, "Target Selling Fidget Spinners with High Levels of Lead"

2. Use the passage and your knowledge of U.S. Government and Politics to answer parts A, B, and C.
   A. Describe two oversight powers or legislative actions Congress could take to address the problem mentioned in the article.
   B. Describe an action a federal agency could take to address the problem.
   C. Describe one way in which an iron triangle relationship might impact policymaking regarding product safety.

ARGUMENTATION QUESTION

In April 2017, President Trump informed Congress of his plans to launch 59 Tomahawk cruise missiles, targeting the air base from which Syrian President Bashar Assad launched a chemical weapons attack against his own people, killing more than 80 men, women, and children.

According to a CBS News Report, "Sen. Mike Lee, R-Utah, insisted that if the U.S. increased the use of military force in Syria, 'we should follow the Constitution and seek the proper authorization from Congress.' Kentucky lawmakers Thomas Massie and Rand Paul, both Republicans, agreed."[5]

Develop an argument that explains whether or not the president has the power to order an airstrike without congressional approval.

In your essay:

- Articulate a claim or thesis that responds to the prompt, and use a line of reasoning to defend it.
- Use at least TWO pieces of relevant and accurate evidence to support your claim.
- At least ONE piece of evidence must be from one of the listed foundational documents:
  - Constitution of the United States
  - *Federalist* No. 70
  - *Federalist* No. 51
- Use a second piece of evidence from another foundational document from the list or from your study of Congress.
- Use reasoning to explain why the evidence you provided supports your claim or thesis.
- Use refutation, concession, or rebuttal to respond to an opposing or alternative perspective.

CRITICAL THINKING PROJECT

Creating a Board Game

The three branches of government, along with the bureaucracy, work together in the policymaking process. Rarely does the process work smoothly.

Create a board game where four players seek to advance through the institutions of government to create a policy at the end. Your playing pieces might represent different kinds of policies. For example, a tree might represent environmental policy, while a car might represent transportation policy. Be creative.

Your game board should have at least forty spaces. Your project should be entertaining and colorful, and make sure your content is accurate. Your game should include information about Congress, the presidency, the federal courts, and the bureaucracy.

Players may roll dice or spin to move ahead spaces. Spaces may be positive, like having a law passed by Congress, or negative, such as an unfavorable court decision. Make sure your board is structured so that a player cannot get permanently stuck between spaces. Some spaces should instruct players to draw from a set of quiz cards. Make at least thirty quiz cards, with AP®-level questions. Players can move on with correct answers. Players answering incorrectly lose a turn. The first player to reach the end is the winner.

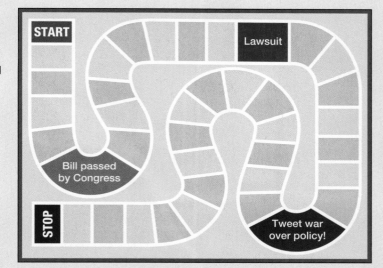

Building a board game will help you review the important powers of and checks on government institutions. Have fun!

Your game board can be informal and colorful. A pack of index cards may make a good set of quiz cards.

Unit 3

Civil Rights and Civil Liberties

Fearless Girl was installed near Wall Street in Lower Manhattan in March 2017. She caused controversy over her placement and her relation to the famous Charging Bull. Originally, Fearless Girl was intended as a temporary exhibit, but she proved immensely popular. Nira Desai organized an online petition to the New York authorities to keep the statue. In just two weeks, almost 25,000 people signed it.

Wang Ying/Xinhua/Alamy Live News

The Constitution and Bill of Rights protect individual freedoms. The government must balance the liberties of citizens with the need for public safety and order.

The due process and equal protection clauses of the Fourteenth Amendment protect individual liberties and civil rights from infringement by the government. The due process clause prohibits states from taking away life, liberty, or property without the protections of a fair trial. The equal protection clause protects groups from discrimination by the government.

The Supreme Court plays an important role in interpreting the equal protection and due process clauses. Through the process of selective incorporation, the Court has used the power of judicial review to prevent states

Chapter 8
Civil Liberties

Chapter 9
Civil Rights

Nira Desai @NiraDesai
Request is in @NYCMayor @NYCMayorsOffice to discuss #FearlessGirl's future on Wall Street. Hope we see you soon!
4:18 PM • Mar 15, 2017

Wang Ying/Xinhua/Alamy Live News

from infringing on fundamental rights. The Supreme Court has set important precedents in cases involving freedom of expression and religion, the right to bear arms, privacy, and the rights of criminal defendants.

African Americans, Latinos, women, LGBT citizens, the disabled, and others have used social movements to assert their rights and expand equality. Congress must decide how to weigh the rights of various groups with the claims of the majority. ∎

Mary Beth Tinker was thirteen years old when she protested against the Vietnam War at her junior high school in Iowa. She and her brother John are the named plaintiffs in *Tinker v. Des Moines Independent Community School District*, which protected free speech for students. She continues to tour the country as an advocate of free-speech rights.

Maria Bryk/Tinker Tour

8 Civil Liberties
Protecting Fundamental Freedoms

The American Republic was founded upon the idea that individuals are born with certain fundamental rights and freedoms. When the country began, these rights were given only to certain categories of people, but the rights of citizens have been expanded over time. Individual freedoms must be balanced with the need for order, and this balance leads to controversy over how much the government may restrict liberty.

Edward Snowden, currently living in Russia to avoid prosecution for leaking sensitive documents in protest over the government's monitoring of Americans' communications and activities, has become a hero to some but a traitor to others.
Baikal / Alamy

Civil liberties are the fundamental rights and freedoms of individuals that are protected from unreasonable governmental restriction. In contrast, the term **civil rights** refers to the government's protection of individuals from discrimination as members of particular groups.

Civil liberties are *protections citizens have against government action* that takes away fundamental freedoms. In contrast, civil rights are *protections provided by the government* to prevent discrimination. We will explore civil rights in the next chapter.

In this chapter, we will read stories about struggles to define and protect fundamental liberties.

civil liberties
fundamental rights and freedoms protected from infringement by the government.

civil rights
protections from discrimination as a member of a particular group.

After reading this chapter, you will be able to

8.1 Examine how the Constitution and Bill of Rights protect individual liberties.

8.2 Explain the doctrine of selective incorporation.

8.3 Explain the impact of the free exercise and establishment clauses on the relationship between government and religion.

8.4 Explain how the Supreme Court's decisions regarding the First and Second Amendments balance individual rights and freedoms with the need for public safety and order.

8.5 Examine the protections placed within the Bill of Rights for those accused of, tried for, and convicted of crimes.

8.6 Discuss the Supreme Court's affirmation of the right to privacy.

LEARNING TARGETS

■ Traitor or Hero?

Edward Snowden has been called "the most wanted man in the world."[1] To officials of the U.S. government, Snowden is a traitor, who compromised national security. To others, he is a hero, who publicized the government's collection of citizens' private conversations and electronic communications. Edward Snowden claims the American government used technology to spy on its own citizens without authority granted to it by a court. According to the Department of Justice, Snowden leaked valuable and sensitive national security secrets in violation of the Espionage Act of 1917, placing Americans involved in intelligence gathering at grave risk. The documents leaked by Snowden could reveal the identities of Americans operating undercover in other nations. Revealing their identities might result in the imprisonment or execution of men and women who have devoted their careers to protecting Americans.

In May 2013, Snowden, a contractor for the National Security Agency (NSA) and a former employee of the Central Intelligence Agency (CIA), flew to Hong Kong from Hawaii, where he had been working at an NSA facility. He brought more than a million classified files that he had downloaded from government databases. Snowden had

The *Guardian's* Web site hosts a section called "NSA Files: Decoded," which helps clarify the relevance of Snowden's leaks to the public. Here, *Guardian* writers explain the scope of the surveillance the National Security Agency undertook using rules that allowed them to gather enormous amounts of metadata on U.S. citizens. As the *Guardian* reported, the NSA argued that it "collected only a tiny proportion of the world's internet traffic, roughly equivalent to a 'dime on a basketball court.'" But as Congresswoman Zoe Lofgren put it, "Here's the deal. If you couldn't learn anything from that data, they wouldn't be collecting it."

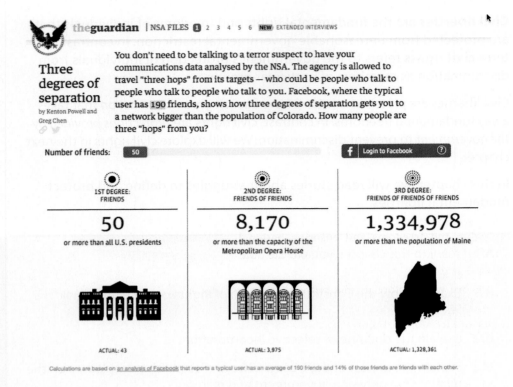

Three degrees of separation
by Kenton Powell and Greg Chen

You don't need to be talking to a terror suspect to have your communications data analysed by the NSA. The agency is allowed to travel "three hops" from its targets — who could be people who talk to people who talk to people who talk to you. Facebook, where the typical user has 190 friends, shows how three degrees of separation gets you to a network bigger than the population of Colorado. How many people are three "hops" from you?

Number of friends: 50   Login to Facebook

1ST DEGREE: FRIENDS	2ND DEGREE: FRIENDS OF FRIENDS	3RD DEGREE: FRIENDS OF FRIENDS OF FRIENDS
50	**8,170**	**1,334,978**
or more than all U.S. presidents	or more than the capacity of the Metropolitan Opera House	or more than the population of Maine
ACTUAL: 43	ACTUAL: 3,975	ACTUAL: 1,328,361

Calculations are based on an analysis of Facebook that reports a typical user has an average of 190 friends and 14% of those friends are friends with each other.

previously leaked thousands of pages of those classified documents, first to the British newspaper the *Guardian,* and then to other outlets, including the *Washington Post* and the *New York Times*.

In an interview with the *Guardian* released on June 9, 2013, Snowden defended what he had done. "The NSA has built an infrastructure that allows it to intercept almost everything," Snowden said. "With this capability, the vast majority of human communications are automatically ingested without targeting. If I wanted to see your emails or your wife's phone, all I have to do is use intercepts. I can get your emails, passwords, phone records, credit cards."[2]

If captured by American officials, Snowden would face prosecution under the Espionage Act of 1917, which was passed two months after the United States declared war on Germany and entered World War I. The Espionage Act makes it a felony to possess or distribute "any document, writing, code book, signal book, sketch, photographic negative, blue print, plan, map, model, instrument, appliance, or note relating to the national defense" that the possessor or distributor knows might pose a threat to the nation. In time of war, according to the act, certain violations could be "punished by death or by imprisonment for not more than thirty years."[3] If Snowden ever returns to the United States or gets on a plane over which the American government or its allies or partners has authority, he will most certainly be arrested and tried and could potentially be executed.

In an interview in May 2016, former U.S. attorney general Eric H. Holder Jr., who served in President Barack Obama's administration, reaffirmed the administration's position that Snowden's actions were "inappropriate and illegal" but added, "We can certainly argue about the way in which Snowden did what he did, but I think that he actually performed a public service by raising the debate that we engaged in."[4]

Snowden claimed that he was acting out of a duty to protect Americans' privacy and their fundamental rights and freedoms—to expose the power of the NSA in hopes it could

In October 2014, Edward Snowden appeared on screen at The New Yorker Festival. He is being interviewed by Jane Mayer, a prominent *New Yorker* writer and author.
Bryan Bedder/Getty Images

be reined in. His opponents, however, assert that his actions recklessly endangered the nation. One of the toughest issues in American constitutional law is the tension between protecting fundamental rights and freedoms and ensuring national security. Edward Snowden walked into the middle of that dilemma.

As we will explore in this chapter, controversy continues over the proper lines between the rights and freedoms of individuals and the power of the U.S. government to ensure order and security.

8.1 The Constitution and the Bill of Rights

The idea that a constitution should include a list of protections for the rights of individuals was not invented in 1787. Following American independence, most state governments included some protections for individual rights in their own constitutions.[5] However, the protections varied considerably and often lacked fundamental rights, such as freedom of the press or religion. Persecution of religious minorities by state legislatures and religious qualifications for holding office were not uncommon.

Well aware of the need to protect individual rights, the delegates placed certain protections in the U.S. Constitution, such as a strict limit on the definition of treason.[6] By defining treason in the specific manner outlined in Article III, the Constitution in effect protected the right to criticize the government—the equivalent of First Amendment speech protections. Many other protections of civil liberties appear in the original Constitution, as outlined in Hamilton's *Federalist* 84, including habeas corpus rights protected in Article I, jury trial rights protected in Article III, and religious freedom protected in Article VI. The delegates did not, however, include a **bill of rights**—a list of fundamental individual rights that a government cannot restrict without reason.

The delegates did debate the idea of a bill of rights, however. In the final days of the Constitutional Convention, two of the delegates moved to include one in the document, saying it "would give great quiet to the people," and to form a committee to draft one. The motion was defeated unanimously.[7] Two days later, another motion was offered "to insert a declaration 'that the liberty of the Press should be inviolably observed.'"[8] The failure to include a comprehensive list of restrictions on the power of the federal government in relation to individual rights resonated with the American people and served as a powerful argument for the Antifederalists against ratification.

bill of rights
a list of fundamental rights and freedoms that individuals possess. The first ten amendments to the U.S. Constitution are referred to as the Bill of Rights.

Federalists Versus Antifederalists, Ratification, and the Bill of Rights

The Antifederalists seized on the lack of a bill of rights during the ratification campaign following the Constitutional Convention. Some most likely used the lack of a bill of rights as a tactical weapon, hoping to defeat the Constitution entirely or push for a second convention during which they might secure a more favorable outcome. Some were opposed to the federal powers of taxation and regulation of commerce and wanted to see more protections for the rights of states, few of which were listed in the document.[9] Others argued that a list of fundamental rights was a necessary protection against what they feared would be the inexorable growth of centralized power in what was sure to become a large republic.

In response to the Antifederalists' charges, the Federalists offered several counterarguments. In *Federalist* No. 84, Hamilton made two fundamental arguments against the inclusion of a list of rights in the proposed Constitution. The first was that one was unnecessary. Hamilton argued that the government was designed to secure individual rights.[10]

Second, Hamilton argued that including a bill of rights would be dangerous to individual liberty, not supportive of it. Hamilton cautioned against the main danger of providing a list of individual rights in the constitution: that the list would necessarily be incomplete. Those in power might impose tyranny and deny additional rights not listed in the document.[11] Some rights are not specifically enumerated in the Constitution. These unenumerated rights are an important topic in the study of American civil liberties today.

The Antifederalists' strategy was effective in raising public concern. Historian Catherine Drinker Bowen wrote that "when the Constitution was published in the newspapers after the Convention rose, and the Antifederalists gathered their strength for opposition, nothing created such an uproar as the lack of a bill of rights."[12] As the ratification campaign progressed, the Federalists shifted their tactics. In Massachusetts, several of them proposed a series of nine amendments, not as a prerequisite to ratification but as modifications to be presented to Congress once ratification had been completed and the new government assembled. Similar promises were made in other state ratification debates.

As promised, on Monday, June 8, 1789, during the first session of Congress, James Madison "rose, and reminded the House that this was the day that he had heretofore named for bringing forward amendments to the constitution."[13] After reworking and revising the proposed list, Congress formally proposed twelve amendments to the Constitution and sent them to the states for ratification. Of these, ten were formally ratified on December 15, 1791.[14] The Bill of Rights had become part of the Constitution.

Ten Amendments, Proposed and Ratified

The First Amendment prevents the legislative branch from passing laws restricting a variety of individual rights, including religion, speech, the press, assembly, and the right to petition the government. The next two amendments deal with powers generally under the authority of the executive branch involving firearms, state militias, and the quartering of soldiers in people's homes and on their property. Of course, given the theory of separation of powers underlying the Constitution, these two amendments, like the others, also involved all of the

Federalist Alexander Hamilton, who opposed the inclusion of a bill of rights during the ratification debates. In *Federalist* No. 84, he argued that the U.S. Constitution was complete in itself: "It has been several times truly remarked, that bills of rights . . . have no application to constitutions professedly founded upon the power of the people, and executed by their immediate representatives and servants."
The Granger Collection

branches. For example, Congress might pass a law restricting the sales of firearms, the judicial branch would try those accused of violating such a law, and the Supreme Court would hear a case challenging the constitutionality of the law.

Amendments four through eight guarantee rights of Americans involved with the judicial system: including those accused of, tried for, and convicted of crimes, and those involved in noncriminal cases. The Ninth Amendment specifies that citizens have rights in addition to those listed in the Bill of Rights. This addressed the concerns raised by Alexander Hamilton in *Federalist* No. 84 that a Bill of Rights would limit the rights of citizens to those specifically listed and would be dangerous as a limitation on liberty. Finally, the Tenth Amendment declares that those powers not specifically delegated to the federal government are "reserved to the States respectively, or to the people." As we studied in Chapter 3, the Tenth Amendment is the basis of federalism. We will explore specific amendments in detail throughout this chapter. Table 8.1 summarizes the main provisions of the Bill of Rights.

TABLE 8.1 An Overview of Protections Contained within the Bill of Rights

Amendment	Protection
First Amendment	Restricts the lawmaking powers of Congress in the areas of religion, speech, the press, assembly, and petitioning the government
Second Amendment	The right to keep and bear arms
Third Amendment	No forced quartering of troops in homes
Fourth Amendment	Protects against unreasonable search and seizure and establishes the right to have warrants issued before an arrest or search
Fifth Amendment	Right to a grand jury indictment in criminal cases, protection against double jeopardy and self-incrimination, the right to due process of law, and the right to just compensation when private property is taken for public use
Sixth Amendment	Protections during criminal prosecutions for a speedy and public trial by an impartial jury, the right to confront witnesses, the right to compel favorable witnesses to testify in one's defense, and the right to the assistance of defense counsel
Seventh Amendment	Right to a trial by jury in certain civil suits
Eighth Amendment	Protections against excessive bail, excessive fines, and cruel and unusual punishment
Ninth Amendment	Protection of rights not listed in the Constitution
Tenth Amendment	Powers not delegated to the federal government, nor prohibited by it to the states, are reserved to the states or to the people

Section Review

This chapter's main ideas are reflected in the Learning Targets. By reviewing after each section, you should be able to

—**Remember** the key points,

—**Know** terms that are central to the topic, and

—**Think** critically about civil liberties and how they restrict each branch of government.

8.1 **Examine how the Constitution and Bill of Rights protect individual liberties.**

REMEMBER
- The Antifederalists were worried that the absence of a Bill of Rights would allow the federal government to infringe upon the rights of individuals.
- Protecting civil liberties involves placing restrictions upon the ability of the government to limit individual freedoms.
- The Bill of Rights enumerates a list of fundamental freedoms that the federal government cannot infringe upon.

KNOW
- *civil liberties*: fundamental rights and freedoms of citizens protected from infringement by the government. (p. 257)
- *civil rights*: protections from discrimination as a member of a particular group. (p. 257)
- *bill of rights*: a list of fundamental rights and freedoms that individuals possess. The first ten amendments to the Constitution are referred to as the Bill of Rights. (p. 259)

THINK
How does the case of Edward Snowden demonstrate the conflict between personal expression and the protection of national security?

8.1 **Review Question: Free Response**

The powers, rights and authority, granted to the general government by this Constitution, are as complete, with respect to every object to which they extend, as that of any State government—it reaches to every thing which concerns human happiness—life, liberty, and property are under its control. There is the same reason, therefore, that the exercise of power, in this case, should be restrained within proper limits, as in that of the State governments.

—Brutus No. 2

Use the quote and your knowledge of U.S. Government and Politics to answer parts A, B, and C.

A. Describe the argument made in the quote.

B. Describe two arguments made by proponents of the Constitution in response to the concerns raised in the quote.

C. Describe one way in which the concerns raised in the quote were resolved during the ratification process.

■ 8.2 Selective Incorporation

Like Edward Snowden, other dissidents have caused controversy in defense of the Bill of Rights. In 1919 Benjamin Gitlow was speaking about, writing on, and protesting against American involvement in World War I and its aftermath. Gitlow criticized the economic system as fundamentally unjust—so much so that it had driven the nation into global war. Gitlow oversaw the printing of a weekly newspaper, *The Revolutionary Age,* which included the slogan on its masthead, *Devoted to the International Communist Struggle,* and he also submitted articles to it. In an issue published in July 1919, Gitlow and his colleagues included "The Left Wing Manifesto," which decried American involvement in World War I, capitalism, and American imperialism. The manifesto proclaimed,

> The world is in crisis. Capitalism, the prevailing system of society, is in process of disintegration and collapse. . . . The predatory "war for democracy" dominated the world. But now it is the revolutionary proletariat in action that dominates, conquering power in some nations,

mobilizing to conquer power in others, and calling upon the proletariat of all nations to prepare for the final struggle against Capitalism. . . . The old machinery of the state cannot be used by the revolutionary proletariat. It must be destroyed.[15]

In November 1919, Gitlow and an associate were arrested during a series of police raids on radicals and charged under the New York State Criminal Anarchy Act, which made it a felony to advocate for "the doctrine that organized government should be overthrown by force or violence."[16]

Gitlow was convicted and sentenced to between five and ten years of hard labor at New York's Sing Sing prison, the maximum sentence allowable. He was assigned to shovel coal.[17]

Appealing his conviction, Gitlow argued that the New York law had violated his rights of due process under the Fourteenth Amendment. Gitlow lost. In his majority opinion, Justice Edward Terry Sanford affirmed that there are restrictions on speech and of the press that are legitimate if such expression sufficiently threatens the public welfare or safety, which, the Supreme Court found, Gitlow's revolutionary exhortations did. The New York law, as applied in this case, was not unconstitutional. The opinion stated, "It is a fundamental principle, long established, that the freedom of speech and of the press which is secured by the Constitution does not confer an absolute right to speak or publish, without responsibility, whatever one may choose, or an unrestricted and unbridled license that gives immunity for every possible use of language and prevents the punishment of those who abuse this freedom."[18]

Though separated in time by nearly a century, the stories of Benjamin Gitlow and Edward Snowden share some things in common. Both individuals knowingly broke a law based upon their convictions and their right to speak against war or national security policy. Each knew the likely consequences of his actions. Even though Gitlow lost his appeal, his case changed American constitutional law.

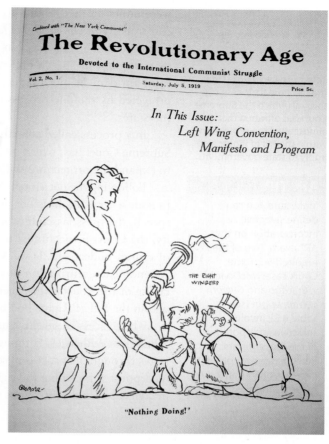

The cover of the July 1919 publication of *The Revolutionary Age*, which featured "The Left Wing Manifesto." Benjamin Gitlow was business manager of the newspaper, which was charged with illegally advocating violent overthrow of the government.

Marxists Internet Archive

Applying the Bill of Rights to State Laws and Actions

The language in the Bill of Rights does not restrict the actions of state governments and their officials. So, for much of the nation's history, the explicit protections contained within the Bill of Rights did not apply to state laws and actions, and the Supreme Court upheld this strict reading of the Constitution. The Fourteenth Amendment (1868) laid the foundation for extending the protections of the Bill of Rights to state laws and actions.[19] The Fourteenth Amendment's guarantee against the deprivation by any state of "life, liberty, or property without due process of law"—called the **due process clause**—laid the constitutional foundations for the extensions of the protections within the Bill of Rights to the actions and laws of the states. In its decision in *Gitlow v. New York* (1925), the Supreme Court formally incorporated the First Amendment and applied it to the states through the Fourteenth Amendment.[20] In doing so, it signaled to the states that there

due process clause
the clause in the Fourteenth Amendment that restricts state governments from denying citizens their life, liberty, or property without legal safeguards.

selective incorporation
the piecemeal process through which the Supreme Court has affirmed that almost all of the protections within the Bill of Rights also apply to state governments.

AP® TIP

Make sure you can define selective incorporation on the AP® exam. Two of the required Supreme Court cases, *McDonald v. Chicago* and *Gideon v. Wainwright* (see Table 8.2), involve selective incorporation of the Bill of Rights. See the table for other cases involving selective incorporation.

were limits on their ability to restrict expression. The freedoms of speech and the press constituted *fundamental freedoms* that states may not restrict unless there is a compelling reason to do so. The decision stated that "for present purposes, we may and do assume that freedom of speech and of the press which are protected by the First Amendment from abridgment by Congress are among the fundamental personal rights and 'liberties' protected by the due process clause of the Fourteenth Amendment from impairment by the States."[21]

In a process called **selective incorporation** because of its piecemeal development, the Supreme Court has, over time, used the due process clause of the Fourteenth Amendment to expand the protections within the Bill of Rights to also cover state laws and actions.

Following the decision in *Gitlow*, over the next two decades the Supreme Court began to issue a series of decisions incorporating most of the First Amendment's protections for speech, the press, assembly, and religion. Several decades later, in another burst of activity, the Court incorporated the protections for those accused of, tried for, and convicted of crimes under state laws. Most recently, in 2010 the Court incorporated the Second Amendment's affirmation of the right "to keep and bear arms" through the due process clause of the Fourteenth Amendment.[22] As of 2016, most, but not all, of the protections within the Bill of Rights had been incorporated (see Table 8.2).

The process of selective incorporation clarifies that states must protect their citizens' fundamental liberties. Although almost all of the rights in the Bill of Rights apply to the states through the process of selective incorporation, a few remaining rights have not been incorporated including the right to an indictment by a grand jury, the right to a jury trial in civil cases, and protections against excessive fines.

After World War I, the authorities engaged in a crackdown on dissenters and radicals that Benjamin Gitlow was caught up in. This office of a labor union, the Industrial Workers of the World, was ransacked during a raid by police.
University of Washington Libraries. Labor Archives Digital Collections.

TABLE 8.2 Selective Incorporation of the Bill of Rights

Amendment	Right Incorporated	Supreme Court Decision
First	Freedom from establishment of religion	*Everson v. Board of Education,* 330 U.S. 1 (1947)
	Freedom of religious expression	*Cantwell v. Connecticut,* 310 U.S. 296 (1940)
	Freedom of speech	*Gitlow v. New York,* 268 U.S. 652 (1925)
	Freedom of the press	*Near v. Minnesota ex rel. Olson,* 283 U.S. 697 (1931)
	Right to peaceably assemble	*De Jonge v. Oregon,* 299 U.S. 353 (1937)
Second	Right to keep and bear arms	*McDonald v. Chicago,* 561 U.S. 742 (2010)
Third	Right not to have soldiers quartered in homes	Not incorporated
Fourth	Protection against unreasonable searches and seizures	*Wolf v. Colorado,* 338 U.S. 25 (1949) (Illegally obtained evidence is still permissible in trial, however.)
	Warrant needed for search and seizure	*Mapp v. Ohio,* 367 U.S. 643 (1961) (Illegally obtained evidence cannot be used in trial.)
Fifth	Right to indictment by grand jury in cases involving a serious crime	Not incorporated
	Protection against double jeopardy	*Benton v. Maryland,* 395 U.S. 784 (1969)
	Protection against self-incrimination	*Malloy v. Hogan,* 378 U.S. 1 (1964)
	Right of just compensation for private property taken	*Chicago, Burlington, and Quincy Railroad v. City of Chicago,* 166 U.S. 226 (1897)
Sixth	Right to a speedy and public trial	*In re Oliver,* 333 U.S. 257 (1948); *Klopfer v. North Carolina,* 386 U.S. 213 (1967)
	Right to trial by an impartial jury	*Parker v. Gladden,* 385 U.S. 363 (1966)
	Right to confront witnesses	*Pointer v. Texas,* 380 U.S. 400 (1965)
	Right to compel witnesses to testify in the defendant's favor	*Washington v. Texas,* 388 U.S. 14 (1967)
	Right to counsel in cases involving capital punishment	*Powell v. Alabama,* 287 U.S. 45 (1932)
	Right to counsel in felony cases	*Gideon v. Wainwright,* 372 U.S. 335 (1963)
Seventh	Right to trial by jury in civil cases	Not incorporated
Eighth	Protection against excessive bail or fines	Not incorporated*
	Protection against cruel and unusual punishment	*Robinson v. California,* 370 U.S. 660 (1962)

*Note: Some constitutional scholars disagree on whether this right has been formally incorporated. See *Schilb v. Kuebel,* 404 U.S. 357 (1971).

8.2 Explain the doctrine of selective incorporation.

REMEMBER
- The protections set out in the Bill of Rights as written applied to the actions of the federal government and not of the state governments.
- In *Gitlow v. New York* (1925), the Supreme Court began the process of selective incorporation. On a case-by-case basis, most (but not all) of the rights in the Bill of Rights apply to actions by the states.

KNOW
- *due process clause*: the clause in the Fourteenth Amendment that restricts state governments from denying citizens life, liberty, or property without legal safeguards. (p. 263)
- *selective incorporation*: the piecemeal process through which the Supreme Court affirmed that almost all of the protections in the Bill of Rights also apply to state governments. (p. 264)

THINK
- How has selective incorporation expanded liberties over time?
- Do you believe the process of selective incorporation is complete? Why or why not?

8.2 Review Question: Free Response

In *West Virginia State Board of Education v. Barnette* (1943), a group of Jehovah's Witnesses, whose children attended public school, filed a lawsuit challenging this resolution passed by the West Virginia School Board: "All teachers and pupils shall be required to participate in the salute honoring the Nation represented by the Flag; provided, however, that refusal to salute the Flag be regarded as an act of insubordination, and shall be dealt with accordingly."[23]

Use the quote and your knowledge of U.S. Government and Politics to answer parts A, B, and C.

A. Define selective incorporation.

B. Explain how the doctrine of selective incorporation might apply in *West Virginia State Board of Education v. Barnette*.

C. Explain one reason why the Supreme Court might not apply the doctrine of selective incorporation in this case.

◼️ **8.3** The Right of Religious Freedom

The First Amendment restricts the power of Congress, which most delegates to the Constitutional Convention thought would be the most powerful, and potentially the most dangerous, branch.

Religion: Establishment and Free Exercise

The First Amendment begins, "Congress shall make no law respecting an establishment of religion, or prohibiting the free exercise thereof." These statements form the constitutional bases for protections of religious freedom and expression. The first statement is called the **establishment clause** because it protects individuals from the government requiring citizens to join or support a religion. The second statement is referred to as the **free exercise clause** because it protects the rights of individuals to exercise and express their religious beliefs.

Recall our discussion of Bridget Mergens in Chapter 1. Her request to form a Christian Bible study club at her public school involved questions about the boundaries of establishment protections and those of free exercise. Sometimes, the application of these clauses is clear-cut. For example, any attempt by a state to declare an official religion would be a

establishment clause
First Amendment protection against the government requiring citizens to join or support a religion.

free exercise clause
First Amendment protection of the rights of individuals to exercise and express their religious beliefs.

clear violation of the establishment clause. Similarly, any attempt to prohibit Americans' expressions of their religious faiths in their own homes, provided they did not violate others' fundamental rights and freedoms, would also be unconstitutional.

However, as with so many other areas of civil liberties, these clauses sometimes seem to conflict with one another. Consider a student who wants to say a prayer in her valedictory address at her public high school's graduation ceremonies. For the school to appear to condone her prayer implies a violation of the establishment clause. For it to restrict her right to say a prayer, however, implies a violation of the free exercise clause. It is in difficult cases like this one that the Supreme Court has had to decide what is and what is not constitutionally permissible.

Wariness about governmental power over religious practice is deep-rooted in the American experience. The desire to avoid religious persecution led to the establishment of several of the original colonial settlements. This history, however, did not mean that the colonies—or the later independent states—universally respected religious freedoms or separated the process of governing from the expression of faith. Members of certain denominations found themselves subject to state-imposed restrictions, including religious tests for the holding of office.

In a letter addressing the establishment clause, Thomas Jefferson stated, "I contemplate with sovereign reverence that act of the whole American people which declared that their legislature should make no law respecting an establishment of religion, or prohibiting the free exercise thereof, thus building 'a wall of separation between church and state.'"[24] The metaphor of a "wall of separation" is quite powerful, but how workable is it in the messy world of American politics? It is unrealistic to expect the government to be completely separate from religion. Supreme Court justices have had to wrestle with the balance between the establishment and free exercise clauses, just as school officials did in Bridget Mergens's case.

The Establishment Clause and the Supreme Court

Selective incorporation of these fundamental rights occurred over several decades in the twentieth century. We will begin our exploration of this with the Supreme Court's evolving treatment of the establishment clause and then move on to free exercise.

Taxpayer Funds and Private Religious Schools

In *Board of Education v. Allen* (1968), the Supreme Court affirmed the principle that there could be some permissible forms of taxpayer support for private religious schools. Divided 6–3, the Court ruled in favor of a New York law that provided free textbooks to middle and high school students, including those in private religiously affiliated schools. In his dissenting opinion, Justice Hugo Black critiqued the majority's reasoning and warned that it set a dangerous precedent: "It is true, of course, that the New York law does not, as yet, formally adopt or establish a state religion. But it takes a great stride in that direction. . . . And it nearly always is by insidious approaches that the citadels of liberty are most successfully attacked."[25]

Prayer in Public Schools

Perhaps no issue related to the establishment clause has been more vexing to the Supreme Court than prayer in public schools. In 1962, in *Engel v. Vitale*, the Court ruled that a school-sponsored prayer violated the establishment clause.[26]

It's important to read Supreme Court cases carefully so that you can explain their specific impact without overgeneralizing. The issue in *Engel v. Vitale* (1962)[27] was whether or not a school-sponsored prayer at a public high school violated the establishment clause of the First Amendment.

The following excerpt comes from the first part of the majority opinion: The prayer read, "Almighty God, we acknowledge our dependence upon Thee, and we beg Thy blessings upon us, our parents, our teachers and our Country."[28] Supporters of the prayer argued that it was nondenominational and students were permitted to remain silent or be excused from the classroom during the reading. The Supreme Court disagreed that the prayer was neutral, stating,

> When the power, prestige and financial support of government is placed behind a particular religious belief, the indirect coercive pressure upon religious minorities to conform to the prevailing officially approved religion is plain. But the purposes underlying the Establishment Clause go much further than that. Its first and most immediate purpose rested on the belief that a union of government and religion tends to destroy government and to degrade religion. The history of governmentally established religion, both in England and in this country, showed that whenever government had allied itself with one particular form of religion, the inevitable result had been that it had incurred the hatred, disrespect and even contempt of those who held contrary beliefs.[29]

Some people have wrongly concluded that the ruling in *Engel v. Vitale* outlaws prayer in schools, but the Court's opinion focuses on the fact that the school sponsored the prayer. A better explanation of the ruling is that it prevents government-sponsored prayer in public schools.

In his dissent, Justice Stewart mentioned the Pledge of Allegiance and the phrase "In God We Trust" on the national currency. Justice Stewart took the position that the prayer did not violate the spirit of the establishment clause:

> I do not believe that this Court, or the Congress, or the President has, by the actions and practices I have mentioned, established an "official religion" in violation of the Constitution. And I do not believe the State of New York has done so in this case. What each has done has been to recognize and to follow the deeply entrenched and highly cherished spiritual traditions of our Nation—traditions which come down to us from those who almost two hundred years ago avowed their "firm Reliance on the Protection of divine Providence" when they proclaimed the freedom and independence of this brave new world.[30]

When you read a dissent, focus on the points of disagreement with the majority opinion. In this case, Justice Stewart reads the establishment clause literally. He argues that because the prayer did not create an official religion in the school, it did not violate the Constitution.

1. Describe the rationale for the majority opinion.

2. Describe one point of agreement between the majority and dissenting opinions.

3. Explain whether or not the ruling in *Engel v. Vitale* should apply to public colleges and universities.

The next year, in *Abington School District v. Schempp*,[31] the Court struck down a program that involved the reading of ten verses from the Bible and a recitation of the Lord's Prayer at the beginning of each day in Pennsylvania's public schools.

Current Status of Prayer in Public Schools

Supreme Court justices are not the only ones who have had to try to balance the separation of government and religion against the need to protect the rights of individuals to express their own faiths. Administrators and teachers in the nation's public schools and universities also have to navigate this complicated constitutional tension.

According to guidelines produced for public schools and districts by the United States Department of Education, students may not pray during instructional time but may do so, at their own discretion, during noninstructional time, such as before school or during lunch. They may also, again on their own, pray during "moments of silence" in schools,

In this chapter, you will meet several required Supreme Court cases. The Political Science Practices feature on page 268 shows you how to read them. Of the many cases mentioned in this chapter, the following cases are required for the AP® U.S. Government and Politics course.

Case	Amendment
Engel v. Vitale	First Amendment, establishment clause
Wisconsin v. Yoder	First Amendment, free exercise clause
Schenck v. United States	First Amendment, political speech, "clear and present danger" test
New York Times Co. v. United States	First Amendment, freedom of the press, prior restraint
Tinker v. Des Moines Independent Community School District	First Amendment, symbolic speech
McDonald v. Chicago	Second Amendment, right to bear arms
Gideon v. Wainwright	Sixth Amendment, right to legal counsel
Roe v. Wade	Constitutional right to privacy

provided that the school makes it clear that such moments are not set aside to encourage prayer. Students may be excused from instruction "to remove a significant burden on their religious exercise . . . where doing so would not impose material burdens on other students," and they may participate in organized religious student groups and clubs under the same rules as the school sets for nonreligious groups. Students may express their religious beliefs in their homework and other assignments, but their work must be evaluated solely on its academic merits.

Teachers and administrators in public schools may not encourage or discourage prayer in their official capacity but may participate in religious activities when not in their official capacity, such as a Bible study group that meets outside of instructional time. While schools may not offer organized prayers during assemblies and extracurricular events, individual students may—on their own, and assuming they have been chosen as speakers based on nonreligious criteria—express their own faith. Schools, however, are free to "make appropriate, neutral disclaimers to clarify that such speech is the speaker's and not the school's."[32] If all of this sounds complicated, that's because it is, for students, parents, school officials, and Supreme Court justices.

Governmental Involvement with Religion

The Supreme Court created the Lemon test to set guidelines for what is permissible under the establishment clause. The test is named after the decision in

Students at Royal High School in Simi Valley, California—a public school—in prayer. As long as such meetings occur outside of instructional time and are both initiated and led by students, they are constitutionally permissible.
Anne Cusack/Getty Images

Lemon v. Kurtzman (1971).[33] The case dealt with Rhode Island and Pennsylvania programs that supplemented the salaries of teachers and provided educational materials in religiously based private schools for the purpose of teaching nonreligious subjects. The Court struck down both programs as violating the establishment clause. In doing so, it set out a three-pronged test for permissible government involvement in religious institutions. First, the underlying statute must have a "secular legislative purpose." Second, its effect "must be one that neither advances nor inhibits religion." Third, it must not foster "excessive entanglement between government and religion."

Free Exercise and the Supreme Court

Under the free exercise clause, Americans can hold any religious beliefs. However, they are not always free to act on them. As is the case with the establishment clause, the Supreme Court has wrestled with the boundaries of free exercise.

In *Wisconsin v. Yoder*,[34] Jonas Yoder and Wallace Miller, who were members of the Old Order Amish, and Adin Yutzy, who was a member of the Conservative Amish Mennonite Church, challenged Wisconsin's compulsory school attendance law that required their children to attend public or private school until the age of sixteen. They argued that the compulsory attendance law violated their rights under the free exercise clause because they believed that making their children attend high school, public or private, went against the Amish religion and way of life. The parents believed that, by sending their children to high school, they would expose themselves to the danger of the censure of their church community as well as endanger their own salvation and that of their children. The state of Wisconsin agreed that they sincerely held these religious beliefs.[35]

In the majority opinion, Chief Justice Burger emphasized the negative impact of the law on the Amish way of life:

> The conclusion is inescapable that secondary schooling, by exposing Amish children to worldly influences in terms of attitudes, goals, and values contrary to beliefs, and by substantially interfering with the religious development of the Amish child and his integration into the way of life of the Amish faith community at the crucial adolescent stage of development, contravenes the basic religious tenets and practice of the Amish faith, both as to the parent and the child.[36] However, the evidence adduced by the Amish in this case is persuasively to the effect that an additional one or two years of formal high school for Amish children in place of their long-established program of informal vocational education would do little to serve those interests. Respondents' experts testified at trial, without challenge, that the value of all education must be assessed in terms of its capacity to prepare the child for life. It is one thing to say that compulsory education for a year or two beyond the eighth grade may be necessary when its goal is the preparation of the child for life in modern society as the majority live, but it is quite another if the goal of education be viewed as the preparation of the child for life in the separated agrarian community that is the keystone of the Amish faith.[37]

In his dissent, Justice William Douglas expressed a concern that that Court was only listening to the Amish parents, without considering the desires of the children: "On this important and vital matter of education, I think the children should be entitled to be heard. While the parents, absent dissent, normally speak for the entire family, the education of the child is a matter on which the child will often have decided views. He may want to be a pianist or an astronaut or an oceanographer. To do so he will have to break from the Amish tradition."[38]

More recently, in *Employment Division v. Smith* (1990),[39] the Court adopted a neutrality test in deciding on conflicts between religious expression and legitimate state action.

Paul Skyhorse Durant and Buzz Berry were accused of possessing about 10,000 peyote buttons that were seized by the Ventura County sheriff's department in California. The two men argued that the use of peyote, a hallucinogen, was a constitutionally protected part of their First Amendment rights of free exercise of religion in spite of its classification as an illegal substance.
Steve Osman/Getty Images

In that case, two men had been fired from their jobs as rehabilitation counselors for using the sacramental religious drug peyote in violation of Oregon state law. They were also denied unemployment benefits as a result of their termination. The two men argued that the use of peyote was within their First Amendment rights of free expression as members of the Native American Church.[40] In its opinion, the Court ruled that the state law banning the use and possession of peyote was not targeted toward any religious group and that it represented a valid, compelling state interest and was religiously neutral, even if it restricted the religious expression of individuals.

Section Review

8.3 Explain the impact of the free exercise and establishment clauses on the relationship between government and religion.

REMEMBER The first two clauses in the First Amendment to the Constitution both involve religion; they prevent the federal government from establishing or favoring a religion and protect Americans' rights to exercise their religious freedoms.

KNOW
- *establishment clause*: First Amendment protection against the government requiring citizens to join or support a religion. (p. 266)
- *free exercise clause*: First Amendment protection of the rights of individuals to exercise and express their religious beliefs. (p. 266)

THINK Why do the free exercise and establishment clauses often conflict with one another?

8.3 Review Question: Free Response

Deborah Weisman graduated from Nathan Bishop Middle School, a public school in Providence, at a formal ceremony in June 1989. For several years the school board and superintendent followed a policy permitting principals to invite members of the clergy to give invocations and benedictions at middle school and high school graduations. Some of the principals decided to include prayers as part of the graduation ceremonies.

A rabbi was invited by Principal Robert Lee to deliver the prayer at Weisman's graduation ceremony, and he was given guidelines recommending that public prayers at nonsectarian civic ceremonies be composed with "inclusiveness and sensitivity" (*Lee v. Weisman*).[41] Deborah Weisman's parents sued Principal Lee to prevent the rabbi from speaking at the graduation ceremony. In this case the Supreme Court ruled that schools could not sponsor even non-denominational prayers.

Use the scenario and your knowledge of U.S. Government and Politics to answer parts A, B, and C.

A. Identify the constitutional provision that was challenged in both *Engel v. Vitale* (1962) and *Lee v. Weisman* (1992).

B. Describe one way in which the facts in *Engel v. Vitale* differ from the facts in *Lee v. Weisman*.

C. Explain how the ruling in *Engel v. Vitale* can be applied as precedent in *Lee v. Weisman*.

■ 8.4 The Right of Expression

freedom of expression
a fundamental right affirmed in the First Amendment to speak, publish, and protest.

Although they come after the two clauses about religion, those parts of the First Amendment that deal with **freedom of expression** are often considered the most fundamental affirmations of Americans' rights and liberties. They involve the expression of political beliefs and opinions.

Speech, Press, Assembly, and Petition

The right to criticize those in power is one of the cornerstones of American civil liberties. Thomas Jefferson's draft of the Declaration of Independence, the *Federalist Papers*, Antifederalist writings, Benjamin Gitlow's publication of essays on overthrowing the United States government, and Edward Snowden's release of classified documents all involve attempts to balance society's need for order with the rights of individuals to speak, to publish, and to assemble peaceably without fear of retribution or imprisonment.

National Security and Political Expression

One of the most difficult issues faced by the courts is how to balance the needs of national security with the fundamental right of political expression. The balance between the right of free speech and the protection of national security is especially important during wartime. The Espionage Act of 1917 was passed during World War I. Among other things, the act makes it a crime to interfere with military recruiting. Benjamin Gitlow—the radical socialist whose conviction by the New York State judicial system was upheld by the Supreme Court—was not the first American to criticize the nation's involvement in World War I. He was also not the first to lose his claim.

In 1917, Charles Schenck and Elizabeth Baer oversaw the printing and distribution of antiwar leaflets encouraging young men not to comply with the military draft. They were convicted under the Espionage Act of 1917. In *Schenck v. United States* (1919),[42] a unanimous Court ruled against the defendants, arguing that the restrictions on expression under the Espionage Act were permissible.

"The most stringent protection of free speech," Justice Oliver Wendell Holmes wrote in the unanimous decision, "would not protect a man falsely shouting fire in a theatre and causing a panic. . . . The question

REGISTER FOR THE WAR

All male persons who shall have attained their **TWENTY-FIRST** birthday and who shall not have attained their **THIRTY-FIRST** birthday, will present themselves at their respective voting places and register on

Tuesday, Fifth Day June, 1917

Between the hours of

7 o'clock a. m. and 9 o'clock p. m.

BOARD OF REGISTRATION OF GRANVILLE CO.

By S. C. HOBGOOD, Sheriff

Registrar Will Post.

When the United States entered World War I, local governments required young men to register for possible induction into the armed forces. Charles Schenck and Elizabeth Baer distributed leaflets urging men eligible for the draft not to comply with the war effort. Schenck and Baer were convicted under the Espionage Act of 1917. This same controversial act is the source of the charges against Edward Snowden a hundred years later.
WWI, Military Collection, State Archives of North Carolina

in every case is whether the words used are used in such circumstances and are of such a nature as to create a clear and present danger that they will bring about the substantive evils that Congress has a right to prevent."[43] In its decision, the Court established the **clear and present danger test** to evaluate whether restrictions on political speech are legitimate. As Holmes noted, the context of that expression must be taken into account: "When a nation is at war, many things that might be said in time of peace are such a hindrance to its effort that their utterance will not be endured so long as men fight, and that no Court could regard them as protected by any constitutional right."[44]

The risk with the clear and present danger test is its subjectivity. If a government can restrict statements suggesting that men should not comply with a draft, it might be able to restrict large amounts of political speech.

The modern standard for restrictions on political speech was set in 1969 in *Brandenburg v. Ohio*.[45] In that case, a leader of the American white supremacist group the Ku Klux Klan was convicted under an Ohio law for advocating "crime, sabotage, violence, or unlawful methods of terrorism as a means of accomplishing industrial or political reform." At issue was a speech at a filmed rally in which a cross was burned and Brandenburg threatened, "if our President, our Congress, our Supreme Court, continues to suppress the white, Caucasian race, it's possible that there might have to be some vengeance taken."[46] The Supreme Court overturned Brandenburg's conviction and established a two-pronged test of acceptable restrictions on such political speech: It must be "directed to inciting or producing imminent lawless action and [must be] likely to incite or produce such action."[47] The test that the Court developed placed a much higher standard on permissible restrictions of political speech.

Clarence Brandenburg, left, a Ku Klux Klan leader, with Richard Hanna, an admitted member of the American Nazi Party, in Cincinnati, Ohio, in August 1964. Brandenburg's case established a high standard of permissible speech, up to advocating for the legitimacy of violent action, as long as the speech does not advocate for imminent lawless action.
Anonymous/AP Images

clear and present danger test
legal standard that speech posing an immediate and serious threat to national security is not protected by the First Amendment.

prior restraint
the suppression of material prior to publication on the grounds that it might endanger national security.

The Press and National Security

The tension between national security and limits on free expression does not only apply to individuals and organizations. It also applies to the press. **Prior restraint** occurs when the government censors or suppresses material before it is published. The question of the permissibility of prior restraint was raised when the Nixon administration tried to prevent the *New York Times* and the *Washington Post* from publishing classified materials describing—often unflatteringly—high-level decision making on the part of U.S. officials in conducting the Vietnam conflict. In *New York Times v. United States* (1971), which was also known as the "Pentagon Papers case," there was no majority opinion, although six justices issued concurring opinions agreeing that the government did not demonstrate a sufficient interest to justify prior restraint.[48]

Justice Black included a history lesson in his concurrence, stating, "In the First Amendment, the Founding Fathers gave the free press the protection it must have to fulfill its essential role in our democracy. The press was to serve the governed, not the governors. The Government's power to censor the press was abolished so that the press would remain forever free to censure the Government."[49] Justice Douglas's concurrence asserted, "It should be noted at the outset that the First Amendment provides that 'Congress shall make no law . . . abridging the freedom of speech, or of the press.' That leaves, in my view, no room for governmental restraint on the press." [50] This set a very high bar for the ability of government to prevent publication.

The dissenters in *New York Times. v. United States* were just as divided as the majority, issuing three opinions. Chief Justice Burger emphasized that the documents published by the *New York Times* were stolen, and that the newspaper had a duty to report theft.[51] Justice Harlan argued that the case was rushed because the newspaper wanted to publish the document too quickly, and that the Justices needed more time to decide, given the serious national security issues raised in the case.[52]

Symbolic Speech

symbolic speech
protected expression in the form of images, signs, and other symbols.

The Supreme Court has protected the political expression of spoken and printed words and has also extended these protections to **symbolic speech**, such as images, signs, and symbols used as forms of political expression. These protections—like those for other forms of political expression—are not absolute.

In 1969, in *Tinker v. Des Moines Independent Community School District*, John and Mary Beth Tinker and Christopher Eckhardt wore black armbands to their public school in Des Moines, Iowa, in protest of the Vietnam War. Administrators became aware of the plan to wear armbands. They adopted a policy that any student wearing an armband to school would be asked to remove it and if he or she refused, the student would be suspended until returning to school without the armband. Petitioners were aware of the regulation that the school authorities adopted.

Mary Beth and Christopher wore black armbands to their schools on December 16. John Tinker wore his armband the following day. They were suspended from school and told to come back without their armbands. They did not return to school until after New Year's Day.[53]

The majority opinion argued that such restrictions were not necessary to preserve the school's ability to carry out its academic mission: "In order for the State in the person of school officials to justify prohibition of a particular expression of opinion, it must be able to show that its action was caused by something more than a mere desire to avoid the discomfort and unpleasantness that always accompany an unpopular viewpoint. Certainly where there is no finding and no showing that engaging in the forbidden conduct would 'materially and substantially interfere with the requirements of appropriate discipline in the operation of the school,' the prohibition cannot be sustained." [54]

In a dissenting opinion, Justice Black argued that the majority opinion would allow students to disobey reasonable requests by school administrators, harming education. He stated, "I think the record overwhelmingly shows that the armbands did exactly what the elected school officials and principals foresaw they would, that is, took the students' minds off their classwork and diverted them to thoughts about the highly emotional subject of the Vietnam war. And I repeat that, if the time has come when pupils of state-supported schools, kindergartens, grammar schools, or high schools, can defy and flout orders of school officials to keep their minds on their own schoolwork, it is the beginning of a new revolutionary era of permissiveness in this country fostered by the judiciary." [55]

As with other forms of political expression, though, the rights of students to express their political beliefs—through speech, writing, or symbols—are not absolute. Joseph Frederick and a group of students in Alaska held up a banner during a school-supervised off campus event, when the Olympic torch was carried through Juneau. The banner read, "BONG HITS 4 JESUS," which school officials concluded promoted drug use, a violation of school rules and conduct. Joseph Frederick was suspended from school for eight days. In yet another closely divided opinion, the Court ruled in *Morse v. Frederick* (2007)[56] that school officials can restrict students' rights of expression if that conduct occurs on school grounds or under school supervision and if it violates or disrupts the mission of the school.

Restrictions on Free Speech

None of the rights listed in the Bill of Rights is absolute. Society's need for order and safety must be balanced with the right of free expression. In attempting to achieve this balance, the government may place certain restrictions on expression.

Defamation: Libel and Slander

Expression that defames a person's reputation—whether in writing (**libel**) or in spoken form (**slander**)—is not protected in the same way as political expression.[57] To win a case based on libel or slander in the United States, an aggrieved party must show that the statements were made with the knowledge that they were untrue, which is rather difficult to prove. For public figures, the standard is even higher, although the line dividing those who qualify as public figures from those who do not often is unclear.

In 1964, in *New York Times v. Sullivan*,[58] the Supreme Court placed significant hurdles on the ability of public officials to successfully sue for libel. In a lower court, a Montgomery, Alabama, official won a $500,000 lawsuit against the *New York Times* for a full-page advertisement that the newspaper had published accusing Alabama officials of using excessive force during student protests. Even though some of the content of the advertisement was false, the Supreme Court, in a unanimous ruling, held that factual inaccuracies were not themselves sufficient to win a libel suit against a public official unless it could be demonstrated that they were published with "actual malice," meaning that the publishers knew the statements were untrue, or that they were published with "reckless disregard of the truth."[59]

libel
an untrue written statement that injures a person's reputation.

slander
an untrue spoken expression that injures a person's reputation.

Hate Speech in the Community and on College Campuses

Hate speech is speech that has no other purpose but to express hatred, particularly toward members of a group identified by racial or ethnic identity, gender, or sexual orientation. One of the most disturbing forms of hate speech is the burning of crosses—sometimes even in people's yards—by white supremacist groups such as the Ku Klux Klan. In response to these acts, many communities have passed ordinances prohibiting such expression.

In 1990 a group of teenagers was arrested in St. Paul, Minnesota, for burning a cross in the yard of an African American family. The teens were charged under a city ordinance that made it a misdemeanor to place "on public or private property" a symbol or object "including but not limited to, a burning cross or Nazi swastika," knowing that such an action might arouse "anger, alarm, or resentment in others on the basis of race, color, creed, religion or gender."[60]

While the Supreme Court agreed that the members of the group could have been legitimately arrested and prosecuted for committing other crimes—such as arson or making terroristic threats—it unanimously overturned their conviction under the hate speech ordinance and ruled the ordinance itself unconstitutional, stating, "The point of the First Amendment is that majority preferences must be expressed in some fashion other than silencing speech on the basis of its content."[61] Today, many college campuses have instituted hate speech codes for student conduct. While some of these policies have been challenged in federal court, the Supreme Court has yet to issue a decision on their constitutionality.

The Difficulty in Defining Obscenity and Pornography

obscenity and pornography
words, images, or videos that depict sexual activity in an offensive manner and that lack any artistic merit.

Finally, the Supreme Court has upheld restrictions on **obscenity and pornography**, although, as with other forms of expression, it has not always been clear just what constitutes an obscene statement or publication. In *Roth v. United States* (1957), the Court defined the standard for judging obscenity—and, therefore, constitutionally permissible restrictions on its expression—as "whether, to the average person, applying contemporary community standards, the dominant theme of the material, taken as a whole, appeals to prurient interest."[62]

In *Miller v. California* (1973),[63] the Supreme Court attempted to clarify the definition of obscenity. The Miller test sets out three criteria that all must be met for material to be considered obscene and, therefore, legitimately subject to restriction. First, the material must be "patently offensive." It must also be "utterly without redeeming social value." Finally, in determining the applicability of the first two parts of the test, "contemporary community standards" must be applied, meaning that different places may have different standards.[64]

Public Policy: Regulating the Internet

The Internet makes regulation of pornography challenging. It is difficult to define "community standards" for online material. In 1997, the Court struck down provisions of the 1996 Communications Decency Act, which was designed to protect minors from viewing obscene or pornographic material on the Internet. The Court held that the restrictions in the act were too vague and restrictive and that they carried the danger of having a "chilling effect on free speech."[65] Child pornography, however, is not protected by the First Amendment and is subject to full restriction and criminalization.

Regulating Time, Place, and Manner

The First Amendment grants special protection to free speech in public, such as sidewalks and public thoroughfares. There is a heavy burden placed on any government attempt to restrict speech in the public forum. But even in public, the government may impose reasonable restrictions on the time, place, or manner of protected speech. For example, cities may require protestors to file for a permit before conducting a march. The government must be able to justify time, place, and manner restrictions in the interest of public order or safety, and they cannot be based on the content of the regulated speech. Such regulations must be narrowly tailored and must address a significant governmental interest. Regulations must allow for other ways for people to communicate their goals.[66]

Freedom of Assembly

In comparison, the final two rights within the First Amendment—the right to peaceably assemble and to petition the government—have received less attention from the Supreme Court. Court decisions involving these rights usually regard them as cornerstones of civil liberties and rights that should be broadly protected.

The right to peacefully assemble was selectively incorporated in 1937 in *De Jonge v. Oregon*.[67] In that case, the Court overturned an Oregon law under which a member of the Communist Party had been convicted and sentenced to seven years in prison for holding a

LonelyDinosaur

In 2008 Sam Smith, a T-shirt designer, introduced his image of "Philosoraptor," a dinosaur appearing to be engaged in deep contemplation. The image quickly became the subject of countless Internet memes, some of which alluded to debates over the Second Amendment.

1. Describe the viewpoint of the meme on the left.

2. Describe the viewpoint of the meme on the right.

3. Identify two other issues have you encountered where memes were used to shape political opinion.

4. Explain whether or not humor is effective in generating debate and reflection on political issues.

5. Explain whether or not using humor to convey a viewpoint undercuts the seriousness of the underlying topic.

public meeting. In his opinion, quoting an earlier case, Chief Justice Charles Evans Hughes noted, "The very idea of a government, republican in form, implies a right on the part of citizens to meet peaceably for consultation in respect to public affairs and to petition for a redress of grievances."[68]

There has been a great deal of struggle, controversy, and Supreme Court action with regard to the First Amendment freedoms.[69]

The Second Amendment

Firearms ownership by Americans has become a highly charged topic. The Supreme Court did not rule directly on laws prohibiting personal possession of firearms until 2008. In a 5–4 decision in *District of Columbia v. Heller*, the Court overturned a District of Columbia ban on handgun ownership for the purpose of self-defense within an individual's home.[70]

As the *Heller* case involved Washington, D.C., and not a state, it was decided based on the Second Amendment directly. Incorporation of the Second Amendment right to bear arms happened two years later, in *McDonald v. Chicago*, when the Court—again splitting 5–4—overturned a Chicago ban on handgun ownership.[71] The majority opinion states that the right to bear arms is not less important than the other amendments in the Bill of Rights and that it was widely considered to be a fundamental right at the time it was ratified: "Antifederalists and Federalists alike agreed that the right to bear arms was fundamental to the newly formed system of government."[72] The majority opinion states, "The Second Amendment protects a personal right to keep and bear arms for lawful purposes, most notably for self-defense within the home."[73]

Justice Stevens dissented, arguing that the incorporation doctrine does not require the Supreme Court to treat all rights equally. He argued that judges in a federal system should not overturn carefully considered laws passed by the states: "Another key constraint on substantive due process analysis is respect for the democratic process. If a particular liberty interest is already being given careful consideration in, and subjected to ongoing calibration by, the States, judicial enforcement may not be appropriate."[74] Justice Breyer's dissent focused on the words "well regulated militia," concluding that the Second Amendment does not protect the individual ownership of firearms.[75]

While states still have the authority to place reasonable restrictions on firearms, under the Supreme Court's decision in *McDonald v. Chicago*, they may not prohibit individuals from owning firearms, which is an individual right protected by the Second Amendment.

Section Review

8.4 Explain how the Supreme Court's decisions regarding the First and Second Amendments balance individual rights and freedoms with the need for public safety and order.

REMEMBER
- Political speech and expression are considered particularly important fundamental freedoms.
- Expression may be limited if it presents a clear and present danger to national security, or is defamatory or obscene.
- In *McDonald v. Chicago* (2010), the Supreme Court incorporated the Second Amendment, ruling that individuals have the right to possess a firearm.
- The government balances freedoms under the First and Second Amendments with ensuring a secure and orderly society.

KNOW
- *freedom of expression*: a fundamental right affirmed in the First Amendment to speak, publish, and protest. (p. 272)
- *clear and present danger test*: legal standard that speech posing an immediate and serious threat to national security is not protected by the First Amendment. (p. 273)
- *prior restraint*: the suppression of material prior to publication on the grounds that it might endanger national security. (p. 273)
- *symbolic speech*: protected expression in form of images, signs, and other symbols. (p. 274)
- *libel*: an untrue written statement that injures a person's reputation. (p. 275)
- *slander*: an untrue spoken expression that injures a person's reputation. (p. 275)
- *obscenity and pornography*: words, images, or videos that depict sexual activity in an offensive manner and that lack any artistic merit. (p. 276)

THINK
Should hate speech be protected by the First Amendment, or should the Supreme Court create an exception that allows the regulation of hate speech on the basis of its content?

Review Question: Free Response

For more than twenty-five years, the congregation of the Westboro Baptist Church has picketed military funerals. Church members believe that God hates the United States, specifically its military, for its tolerance of homosexuality. The picketing has also condemned the Catholic Church for scandals involving its clergy. At the funeral of Marine Corporal Matthew Snyder, picketers held up signs that said, "Thank God for Dead Soldiers," "Fags Doom Nations," "America Is Doomed," "Priests Rape Boys," and "You're Going to Hell." The protest was peaceful and lasted for about thirty minutes before the funeral began. In *Snyder v. Phelps*,[76] the Supreme Court ruled that the protest was protected by the Constitution.

Use the scenario and your knowledge of U.S. Government and Politics to answer parts A, B, and C.

A. Identify a provision of the Constitution that is common to *Snyder v. Phelps* (2011) and *Schenck v. United States* (1919).

B. Explain why the facts of *Schenck v. United States* led to a different holding in *Snyder v. Phelps*.

C. Describe an action that city or state government officials who disagree with the holding in *Snyder v. Phelps* could take to limit its impact.

▄▄ 8.5 The Rights of Defendants

Before the addition of the Bill of Rights, the Constitution provided some protection to those accused and convicted of crimes. Article I prohibits Congress from passing **ex post facto laws** that criminalize conduct that was legal at the time it occurred. It also prohibits **bills of attainder**, laws passed by Congress punishing individuals without a trial.[77]

Article I also establishes the right to demand a **writ of habeas corpus** that sets out the reasons for an arrest or detention. Such a writ, if granted by a court, demands that authorities in charge of the person's detention establish the reasons for that detention. As discussed in Chapter 5, Yassar Hamdi claimed that his detention by the Obama administration violated his habeas corpus rights.

Despite these protections, fear remained that the federal government would violate citizens' rights. The Bill of Rights sets boundaries for the federal government in dealing with criminal defendants. Central to the protections for those accused, tried, or convicted of a crime is the idea of **procedural due process**, in which the standard of fairness is applied to all individuals equally.[78] Most of these standards have since been applied to the actions of the states through selective incorporation.

The Fourth Amendment: Search, Seizure, Warrants, and Evidence

Under British rule, the American colonists gained a vivid understanding of the dangers of allowing a government to search citizens or their homes without a warrant. Although the Bill of Rights protects against unreasonable searches, it is not easy to determine when a search is legitimate. With the development of modern technology, the issue is even more complicated.

Under the Fourth Amendment, the government must obtain a warrant before searching people or places. A **warrant** is a document issued by a judge authorizing some activity, such as tapping a phone line or searching an apartment. Warrants must be based on **probable cause**, or reasonable suspicion that a crime has been committed or that there is evidence relevant to a criminal investigation. There are several exceptions to the requirement that police obtain a warrant, such as when they are in "hot pursuit" of a suspect.[79]

ex post facto laws
laws criminalizing conduct that was legal at the time it occurred.

bill of attainder
a law passed by Congress punishing an individual without a trial.

writ of habeas corpus
a document setting out reasons for an arrest or detention.

procedural due process
a judicial standard requiring that fairness be applied to all individuals equally.

warrant
a document issued by a judge authorizing a search.

probable cause
reasonable belief that a crime has been committed or that there is evidence of criminal activity.

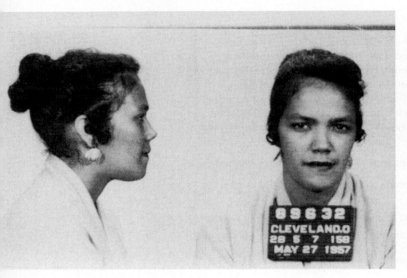

Under the **exclusionary rule**, established in *Mapp v. Ohio* (1961),[80] evidence obtained without a warrant is not admissible in court. While investigating a bombing, police searched Dollree Mapp's home without a warrant and found "lewd and lascivious books, pictures, and photographs," in violation of an Ohio anti-obscenity law.[81] The Court threw out her conviction and declared, "All evidence obtained by searches and seizures in violation of the Federal Constitution is inadmissible in a criminal trial in a state court."

As it has wrestled with the trickier issues in interpreting the exclusionary rule, the Court has ruled that the Fourth Amendment's protections are not absolute. In 1989, the Court upheld the conviction of a suspected drug dealer whose luggage had been searched without a warrant based on his behavior—

Dollree Mapp at the time of her arrest in 1957. The case of *Mapp v. Ohio* extended Fourth Amendment protections to the states by establishing that evidence gathered through an illegal search and seizure is inadmissible in criminal trials in a state court.
Anonymous/AP Images

exclusionary rule
a rule that evidence obtained without a warrant is inadmissible in court.

he had paid cash for his ticket, checked no bags, and appeared nervous, among other "tells." The Court found that the DEA agents conducting the search had "reasonable suspicion" of criminal activity "based on the totality of circumstances."[82]

The Court has also upheld the use of evidence connected with a crime (such as a weapon) that was not named in the warrant but that was discovered in plain sight while lawfully searching for a different type of evidence (the stolen property).[83] In 1996, the Court upheld the introduction of illegal drugs as evidence, though the drugs had been obtained as a result of a traffic stop in which the officers were found to have had a "reasonable cause" to believe that a traffic violation had occurred.[84]

The Court has placed some restrictions on the use of evidence when modern surveillance or communications technologies are involved. In 2001, a closely divided Court invalidated the use of a thermal imaging scan to obtain evidence of the cultivation of marijuana on the suspect's private property.[85] In 2014, the Court declared inadmissible evidence obtained from a suspect's cell phone without a warrant, although it allowed for some exceptions in emergencies.[86]

Drug testing is a controversial aspect of the law regarding searches. Private businesses may conduct drug testing of employees, but public hospitals may not conduct drug tests on patients without their consent.[87] Students in public schools have fewer protections against drug testing, because drug use goes against the schools' mission and endangers student safety. In 1995, the Court upheld random drug testing of student athletes[88] and in 2002 the Court upheld drug testing of students involved in extracurricular activities.[89]

The Fifth Amendment: The Grand Jury, Double Jeopardy, and Self-Incrimination

grand jury
a group of citizens who, based on the evidence presented to them, decide whether or not a person should be indicted on criminal charges and subsequently tried in court.

double jeopardy
protects an individual acquitted of a crime from being charged with the same crime again in the same jurisdiction.

The Fifth Amendment guarantees procedural due process for criminal defendants in federal cases. Those suspected of having committed serious crimes must have an indictment handed down by a **grand jury**—a group of citizens who, based on the evidence presented to them as a jury, decide whether or not there is enough evidence to take the defendant to trial. A grand jury is different from a jury, which decides whether a defendant is innocent or guilty. The Fifth Amendment also prohibits **double jeopardy**, which is the prosecution of an individual more than once for the same crime. An individual cannot be acquitted of a crime and then convicted for the same crime in the same jurisdiction. However, individuals can be acquitted for an offence in a state court and then tried and convicted for the same incident in a federal court under federal charges.

The Fifth Amendment also protects against self-incrimination. This means individuals cannot be compelled to give testimony that might lead to criminal charges against them.

One of the most important cases in delineating the rights of criminal defendants is *Miranda v. Arizona* (1966).[90] Ernesto Miranda was convicted of kidnapping and rape, based partly on evidence obtained while police officers questioned him without an attorney present. During this questioning, he signed a confession. The Supreme Court overturned Miranda's conviction, declaring, "Prior to any questioning, the person must be warned that he has a right to remain silent, that any statement he does make may be used as evidence against him, and that he has a right to the presence of an attorney, either retained or appointed. The defendant may waive effectuation of these rights, provided the waiver is made voluntarily, knowingly and intelligently."[91] Police officers now routinely inform suspected criminals that they have the right to remain silent and to have an attorney present during questioning. These rights are commonly referred to as **Miranda rights**.

The Sixth Amendment: Trials, Juries, and Attorneys

The Bill of Rights also guarantees defendants the right to a speedy trial, a right that was extended to the states in 1963.[92] It also ensures the right to be tried in front of an impartial jury, which has become more difficult because of the instantaneous spread of news and opinion with modern technology. The Sixth Amendment guarantees the right to have an attorney present at trial. For most of the nation's history, that meant the right to hire an attorney only if you could afford one.

In 1932, the Court extended this right to include the provision of attorneys in federal murder cases in which the death penalty might be imposed.[93] In 1938, the Court extended these protections to all federal criminal cases.[94] In 1963, the Court extended the right to an attorney for those unable to afford one in state criminal cases with its decision in *Gideon v. Wainwright,*[95] which involved the robbery conviction of Clarence Earl Gideon. A Florida trial court denied Gideon's request for an attorney, and he defended himself. He was convicted, and he appealed to the Supreme Court, arguing that the trial court violated his Sixth Amendment right to counsel in denying his request to have an attorney appointed for him. The majority opinion, written by Justice Black, states,

> The right of one charged with crime to counsel may not be deemed fundamental and essential to fair trials in some countries, but it is in ours. From the very beginning, our state and national constitutions and laws have laid great emphasis on procedural and substantive safeguards designed to assure fair trials before impartial tribunals in which every defendant stands equal before the law. This noble ideal cannot be realized if the poor man charged with crime has to face his accusers without a lawyer to assist him.[96]

More recently, the Court has strengthened these protections to try to ensure that criminal defendants receive "effective" legal representation and not just legal representation.[97]

The Eighth Amendment: Bail and Punishment

The Eighth Amendment prohibits excessive **bail**, an amount of money posted as a security to allow the defendant to be freed while awaiting trial, and cruel and unusual punishment. Legal challenges to the death penalty are often

Miranda rights
the right to remain silent and to have an attorney present during questioning; these rights must be given by police to individuals suspected of criminal activity.

bail
an amount of money posted as a security to allow the charged individual to be freed while awaiting trial.

In Clarence Gideon's case, *Gideon v. Wainwright*, the Court extended the right to an attorney for those unable to afford one in state criminal cases.
Bettmann/Getty Images

based on the Eighth Amendment. The death penalty remains contentious. Capital punishment was allowed at the time of ratification of the Constitution and the Bill of Rights, and the Fifth Amendment to the Constitution refers to circumstances in which individuals are "deprived of life." Proponents of the death penalty argue it can be an effective deterrent against the most heinous crimes, and that it is a just retribution for killing someone. Opponents point to the potential for errors in conviction, discriminatory sentencing, and the movement away from its use in other democracies, as well as the lack of actual evidence that the death penalty deters crimes.[98]

The Court's decision in *Furman v. Georgia* (1972) invalidated the use of the death penalty according to the state laws at the time, finding them arbitrary and discriminatory.[99] Rewritten death penalty statutes were held constitutional in *Gregg v. Georgia* (1976).[100] While the Supreme Court has held that the death penalty does not violate the Eighth Amendment's prohibition against cruel and unusual punishment, the Court has imposed restrictions on its imposition. For example, the Court has prohibited its use on defendants with significant cognitive disabilities[101] and on juveniles.[102]

The use of the death penalty is declining.[103] There are several reasons for this. Executions cost about $500,000 more than non-death penalty cases. The injection drugs used to execute prisoners are in short supply, hard to administer, and may result in painful, prolonged death. Others are concerned about wrongful convictions and racial disparities in imposing the death penalty.[104]

Section Review

8.5 Examine the protections placed within the Bill of Rights for those accused of, tried for, and convicted of crimes.

REMEMBER

- The Bill of Rights guarantees a set of protections for those accused of, tried for, and convicted of crimes.
- The exclusionary rule prohibits the use of evidence obtained without a warrant in court, although there are exceptions to this rule.
- Police are required to read Miranda rights to those accused of crimes.
- In *Gideon v. Wainwright* (1963), the Supreme Court incorporated the Sixth Amendment, ruling that defendants have a right to an attorney provided by the state if they cannot afford one.

KNOW

- *ex post facto laws*: laws criminalizing conduct that was legal at the time it occurred. (p. 279)
- *bill of attainder*: a law passed by Congress punishing an individual without a trial. (p. 279)
- *writ of habeas corpus*: a document setting out reasons for an arrest or detention. (p. 279)
- *procedural due process*: a judicial standard requiring that fairness be applied to all individuals equally. (p. 279)
- *warrant*: a document issued by a judge authorizing a search. (p. 279)
- *probable cause*: reasonable belief that a crime has been committed or that there is evidence of criminal activity. (p. 279)
- *exclusionary rule*: a rule that evidence obtained without a warrant is inadmissible in court. (p. 280)
- *grand jury*: a group of citizens who, based on the evidence presented to them, decide whether or not a person should be indicted for criminal charges and subsequently tried in court. (p. 280)
- *double jeopardy*: protects an individual acquitted of a crime from being charged with the same crime in the same jurisdiction. (p. 280)
- *Miranda rights*: the right to remain silent and to have an attorney present during questioning; these rights must be given by police to individuals suspected of criminal activity. (p. 281)
- *bail*: an amount of money posted as a security to allow the defendant to be freed while awaiting trial. (p. 281)

THINK

- Does the criminal justice system provide too many protections for defendants?
- Should the criminal justice system provide more protections for defendants?

stus.com

Use the cartoon and your knowledge of U.S. Government and Politics to answer parts A, B, and C.

A. Identify the Supreme Court case referred to in the cartoon.

B. Describe the ruling in the case you identified in part A.

C. Describe one action that could be taken by an interest group to advocate for the rights of criminal defendants.

■■ 8.6 Privacy and Other Rights

The Bill of Rights does not explicitly contain the word *privacy*. However, the Supreme Court has affirmed the right to privacy and applied it to several areas of Americans' lives.

Privacy in the Bedroom

In general, consenting adults have the right to keep their personal lives private from government interference. The Supreme Court has extended the right of privacy to issues such as birth control, abortion, and sexuality.

The Use of Contraceptives

In *Griswold v. Connecticut* (1965), the Supreme Court stated for the first time that the Constitution protects the right of privacy.[105] The Court overturned a Connecticut law passed in 1873, which prohibited the provision of contraceptives and medical advice about contraceptive techniques. In striking down the law, Justice Douglas cited affirmations of privacy in several amendments to the Constitution, including the First, which "has a penumbra where privacy is protected from governmental intrusion."[106] *Penumbra* is the Latin word for shadow. By reading the First, Third, Fourth, and Ninth Amendments together, the

Tyron Garner, left, and John Lawrence greet supporters at Houston City Hall where people had gathered to celebrate the landmark Supreme Court decision in the *Lawrence v. Texas* case on June 26, 2003. The court struck down a Texas sodomy law, a decision applauded by gay rights advocates as a historic ruling that overturned sodomy laws in thirteen states.
Reuters/Richard Carson

Court ruled that the Bill of Rights implicitly protects privacy. The Supreme Court ruled that married couples' right to privacy extended to the use of contraceptives.[107] Seven years later, in *Eisenstadt v. Baird*,[108] the Court extended this right to unmarried individuals.

Sexual Conduct between Consenting Adults

More recently, the Supreme Court extended the right to privacy beyond contraception. In 2003, in *Lawrence v. Texas*, the Court struck down a Texas sodomy law making same-sex sexual conduct illegal.[109] In his decision, Justice Kennedy stated, "Liberty presumes an autonomy of self that includes freedom of thought, belief, expression, and certain intimate conduct."[110] The Court used the "penumbra" of privacy in the Constitution to protect the right of consenting adults to express their sexuality in private without government interference.

Abortion as a Privacy Right

Abortion is one of the most controversial topics in American politics. Opponents of abortion believe the practice violates their deeply held religious conviction that terminating a pregnancy is murder of the unborn. Others assert that a woman should have the right to choose whether or not to terminate a pregnancy. In *Roe v. Wade* (1973),[111] the Court struck down a Texas law that made abortion illegal.

Jane Roe is a pseudonym used to protect the identity of Norma McCorvey, a single woman who lived in Dallas County, Texas. She filed a lawsuit in March 1970 against the district attorney of the county. She sought a judgment that the Texas criminal abortion statutes were unconstitutional and an injunction restraining Texas from enforcing the statutes. Roe was unmarried and pregnant. The lawsuit asserted that she wanted an abortion "performed by a competent, licensed physician, under safe, clinical conditions";[112] that she was unable to get a "legal" abortion in Texas because her life did not appear to be threatened by the continuation of her pregnancy; and that she could not afford to travel to another jurisdiction in order to secure a legal abortion under safe conditions.[113]

In ruling that the Constitution protects the right of a woman to obtain an abortion during the first three months of pregnancy, Justice Harry Blackmun drew on the Court's previous ruling in *Griswold*, stating, "This right of privacy, whether it be founded in the Fourteenth Amendment's concept of personal liberty and restrictions upon state action, as we feel it is, or . . . in the Ninth Amendment's reservation of rights to the people, is broad enough to encompass a woman's decision whether or not to terminate her pregnancy."[114] The Supreme Court also cited amicus curiae briefs submitted by the American Public Health Association and the American Medical Association.[115]

The right to terminate a pregnancy is not absolute and is subject to some limitation. At the end of the first trimester, the state has a compelling interest in regulating abortion. After the second trimester, once the fetus is viable, states may prohibit abortion.[116] In a dissenting opinion, Justice Rehnquist argued that the majority went beyond the scope of the Fourteenth Amendment stating, "To reach its result, the Court necessarily has had to find within the scope of the Fourteenth Amendment a right that was apparently completely unknown to the drafters of the Amendment."[117]

In subsequent decisions, the Court has continued to uphold the right of a woman to terminate a pregnancy, but it has also allowed state legislatures to place certain limits upon abortion. The Court has upheld state laws requiring minors to obtain parental consent and certain restrictions on late-term abortions.[118] Despite the Court's rulings, abortion remains very contentious. Since *Roe v. Wade*, a nominee's stance on abortion has become a key factor in the Senate's confirmation of justices to the Supreme Court and judges to the lower levels of the federal judiciary.

Pro-life demonstrators hold signs at the anti-abortion March for Life on January 27, 2017 in Washington, D.C. The demonstration is held each year during the week of the anniversary of the announcement of the decision in *Roe v. Wade*.
TASOS KATOPODIS/Getty Images

The Ninth Amendment: Rights Not Specified

The first eight amendments in the Bill of Rights limit the power of the federal government. The final two do not. The Ninth Amendment addresses one of the main worries about a bill of rights expressed during the ratification debates: that those fundamental rights and freedoms not listed might not be protected. The Ninth Amendment states that individuals have rights in addition to those expressly mentioned. It was ratified to make sure that governments in the future would not be able to take advantage of the incomplete listing of fundamental rights and freedoms.

As we studied in Chapter 3, the Tenth Amendment is the basis for federalism, reserving some power to the states.

The Evolving Nature of Civil Liberties

The stories regarding civil liberties in the United States are about tensions between fundamental rights and freedoms and the need for order and security. Civil liberties evolve, as generations of activists, Supreme Court justices, and politicians assert their ideas about the proper boundaries of American rights and freedoms.

Defining and defending the essential civil liberties in American democracy, and balancing them against the need for public order and safety, remains controversial and challenging.

8.6 Discuss the Supreme Court's affirmation of the right to privacy.

REMEMBER
- The Supreme Court, drawing upon several amendments, ruled that the Constitution establishes a right of privacy in areas such as reproductive rights and sexuality.
- The Supreme Court's decision in *Roe v. Wade* legalized abortion, although states may impose some restrictions on abortions.
- The Ninth Amendment provides that individuals have rights in addition to those expressly listed in the Bill of Rights.

THINK Did the Supreme Court exceed its power when it determined that the Constitution creates a penumbra of privacy? Why or why not?

8.6 Review Question: Free Response

The case . . . involve[s] two adults who, with full and mutual consent from each other, engaged in sexual practices common to a homosexual lifestyle. The petitioners are entitled to respect for their private lives. The State cannot demean their existence or control their destiny by making their private sexual conduct a crime. Their right to liberty under the Due Process Clause gives them the full right to engage in their conduct without intervention of the government.

—*Lawrence v. Texas*, 539 U.S. 558 (2003)

Use the quote and your knowledge of U.S. Government and Politics to answer parts A, B, and C.

A. Identify one constitutional clause that is common to both *Lawrence v. Texas* (2003) and *Roe v. Wade* (1973).

B. Based on the constitutional clause identified in part A, explain why the facts of *Roe v. Wade* led to a similar holding in *Lawrence v. Texas*.

C. Describe one way in which the facts in *Lawrence v. Texas* could have led to a different result than the one the Court reached in *Roe v. Wade*.

Chapter 8 Review

AP® KEY CONCEPTS

- *civil liberties* (p. 257)
- *civil rights* (p. 257)
- *Bill of Rights* (p. 259)
- *due process clause* (p. 263)
- *selective incorporation* (p. 264)
- *establishment clause* (p. 266)
- *free exercise clause* (p. 266)
- *freedom of expression* (p. 272)
- *clear and present danger test* (p. 273)

- *prior restraint* (p. 273)
- *symbolic speech* (p. 274)
- *libel* (p. 275)
- *slander* (p. 275)
- *obscenity and pornography* (p. 276)
- *ex post facto laws* (p. 279)
- *bill of attainder* (p. 279)
- *writ of habeas corpus* (p. 279)
- *procedural due process* (p. 279)

- *warrant* (p. 279)
- *probable cause* (p. 279)
- *exclusionary rule* (p. 280)
- *grand jury* (p. 280)
- *double jeopardy* (p. 280)
- *Miranda rights* (p. 281)
- *bail* (p. 281)

AP® EXAM PRACTICE and Critical Thinking Project

MULTIPLE-CHOICE QUESTIONS

1. Which of the following rulings is an example of selective incorporation?
   A. The right of privacy is extended to include the right to an abortion.
   B. The death penalty does not violate the Eighth Amendment.
   C. The federal government must provide habeas corpus rights to citizens in detention.
   D. A city may not ban law-abiding individuals from owning firearms.

2. Select the pair that correctly matches the name of the case with the constitutional amendment at issue in the case.

Supreme Court case	Amendment
A. Gideon v. Wainwright	Sixth
B. Engel v. Vitale	Fourth
C. McDonald v. Chicago	First
D. New York Times Co. v. United States	Fifth

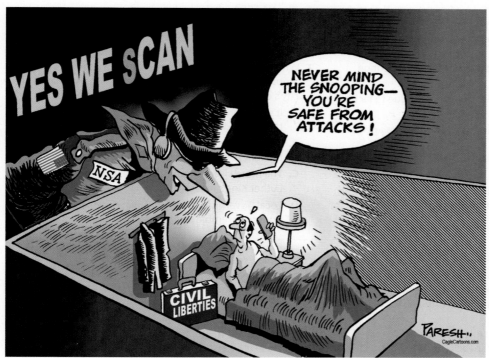

Paresh Nath/Cagle Cartoons

3. Which of the following best describes the viewpoint expressed in the cartoon?
   A. Data collection by the NSA infringes on civil liberties.
   B. The NSA should be free to collect data to keep Americans safe from terrorist attacks.
   C. The NSA only collects data from suspected terrorists.
   D. The government should not be able to collect data on its critics.

4. In *Minnesota v. Dickerson* (1993), the Supreme Court ruled that if an officer lawfully pats down a suspect's outer clothing and feels an object that indicates the presence of an illegal substance, like drugs, there has been no invasion of the suspect's privacy.[119] This Court ruling creates an exception to the

  A. exclusionary rule

  B. right against self-incrimination

  C. right to counsel

  D. right to a writ of habeas corpus

5. Some public colleges have adopted hate speech codes prohibiting speech that disparages people on the basis of race, color, national origin, religion, sex, sexual orientation, age, disability, or veteran's status. Which of the following is the best argument on behalf of a proponent of these codes?

  A. Hate speech presents a clear and present danger to public safety.

  B. Hate speech is often pornographic.

  C. Hate speech defames certain groups of people.

  D. The codes do not regulate content and are reasonable time, place, and manner restrictions.

Questions 6 and 7 refer to the scenario.

A few days before a Martin Luther King Day parade, the city of Arlington denied a parade permit because the city said it lacked sufficient funding to support the parade. The NAACP had planned to protest the parade, because it was opposed to the policies of Governor Greg Abbott, who was supposed to be the parade's honorary grand marshal.[120]

6. Which of the following best describes the argument on behalf of the city of Arlington, Texas?

  A. Denying the parade permit is reasonable, due to lack of money.

  B. The city has the legal right to prevent protests against controversial policies.

  C. The parade presented a clear and present danger to public safety.

  D. By issuing a parade permit, the city would be viewed as endorsing the message of the protest.

7. Which of the following best describes a constitutional argument that parade organizers might make to appeal the city's decision?

  A. It's up to the city to pay for the march because it would take place on the public roadways.

  B. The city may not deny a parade permit in an attempt to prevent controversial political speech.

  C. The march is important because it celebrates Martin Luther King's legacy.

  D. Local governments may not place restrictions on the right to assemble and protest.

8. *Bethel School District v. Fraser* is a Supreme Court case involving a public high school student who gave a speech at a voluntary assembly nominating his friend for student council. The assembly was held during the school day, and about 600 students attended. During the speech, the student referred to his candidate using an explicit sexual metaphor.[121]

Which of the following best explains why the Supreme Court ruled that the First Amendment did not protect the student's speech?

  A. The speech presented a clear and present danger to other students.

  B. The ruling in *Tinker v. Des Moines Independent Community School District* permits schools to limit speech that disrupts the educational process.

  C. School authorities have the right to censor speeches that contain controversial messages.

  D. Students leave their First Amendment rights behind when they enter the school building.

9. In situations where there is an imminent danger to the public, like suspected terrorist attacks where police are trying to ascertain the whereabouts of a bomb or knowledge of a future attack that's going to take place soon, officers are given some leeway to continue interrogation. Even if the person has invoked their . . . rights, their responses may still be admissible in court.[122]

From "3 Exceptions to the Miranda Rule," by Christopher Coble, *FindLaw Blotter*, December 27, 2017, http://blogs .findlaw.com/blotter/2017/12/3-exceptions-to-the-miranda-rule.html.

The excerpt describes an example of

A. the balance between state police powers and federal laws protecting national security.

B. the government's need to balance liberty with public safety.

C. limitations on the privacy rights of suspected terrorists.

D. limitations on speech that presents a clear and present danger to the public.

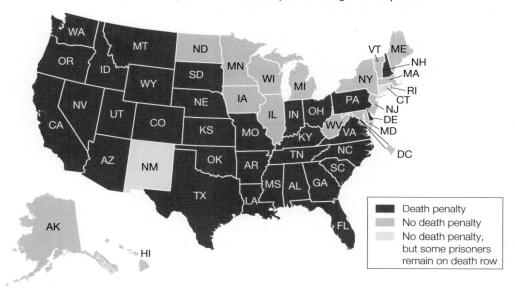

Data from Department of Justice, Death Penalty Information Center

10. Which two constitutional principles are relevant to the data shown in the map?

A. checks and balances and due process

B. judicial review and natural rights

C. separation of powers and civil rights

D. federalism and civil liberties

FREE-RESPONSE QUESTIONS

Ronald W. Rosenberger, a University of Virginia student, asked the University for $5,800 from a student activities fund to help pay for the cost of *Wide Awake: A Christian Perspective at the University of Virginia*. The University refused to provide funding for the publication solely because it promoted religious beliefs. Rosenberger sued the University of Virginia.[123] The Supreme Court ruled in favor of Rosenberger.

1. Use your knowledge of U.S. Government and Politics to answer parts A, B, and C.

A. Identify the constitutional clause that is common to both *Rosenberger v. University of Virginia* (1995) and *Engel v. Vitale* (1962).

B. Based on the constitutional clause identified in part A, explain why the facts of *Engel v. Vitale* led to a different holding than the holding in *Rosenberger v. University of Virginia*.

C. Describe an action that members of the public who disagree with the holding in *Rosenberger v. University of Virginia* could take to limit its impact.

2. In *Brandenburg v. Ohio* (1969),[124] a member of the Ku Klux Klan (KKK) was convicted of an Ohio state law prohibiting "criminal syndicalism," defined as membership in any organization advocating terrorism. At trial, the State of Ohio introduced into evidence a film of a KKK rally that the defendant attended, showing, as the Court noted, "12 hooded figures, some of whom carried firearms. They were gathered around a large wooden cross, which they burned." The defendant was filmed attending the rally, where he made a speech that included this statement: "We're not a revengent organization, but if our President, our Congress, our Supreme Court, continues to suppress the white, Caucasian race, it's possible that there might have to be some revengeance taken. We are marching on Congress July the Fourth. . . ."

The defendant appealed his conviction to the U.S. Supreme Court, claiming that the "criminal syndicalism" statute is unconstitutional as a violation of his First Amendment rights. The Supreme Court agreed, and overturned Brandenburg's conviction.[125]

Based on this scenario, and using your knowledge of U.S. Government and Politics, answer parts A, B, and C.

A. Identify the constitutional clause that is common to both *Brandenburg v. Ohio* (1969) and *Schenck v. United States* (1919).

B. Based on the constitutional clause identified in part A, explain why the facts of *Schenck v. United States* led to a different holding than the holding in *Brandenburg v. Ohio*.

C. Describe an action that state or local governments that disagreed with the ruling in *Brandenburg v. Ohio* could take to limit its impact.

ARGUMENTATION QUESTION

The following is an excerpt from an article in *the Denver Post*:

Denver Mayor Michael Hancock's administration banned the organizer of this year's 4/20 rally from hosting the event for three years citing a series of violations at the marijuana celebration.

In a letter released Saturday, the administration identified "substantial violations of city requirements" after conducting a review of the 2017 event and imposed $11,965 in fines and $190 in damages in addition to the temporary ban. "We will continue to ensure that events in our parks are safe, compliant and of high quality," said Happy Haynes, the executive director of Denver Parks and Recreation in a statement.

An attorney for the Denver 4/20 rally organization called the three-year ban "extreme overkill" on the part of Hancock's administration and suggested the real explanation is the mayor's opposition to marijuana. He pledged to get the decision overturned on appeal.[126]

From "Denver 4/20 rally organizers receive 3-year ban after event left Civic Center Park trashed," by John Frank and Alicia Wallace, *The Denver Post*, May 20, 2017.

Develop an argument about whether or not the City of Denver violated the civil liberties of the 4/20 rally organization in imposing the three-year ban.

In your essay:

- Articulate a claim or thesis that responds to the prompt, and use a line of reasoning to defend it.
- Use at least TWO pieces of relevant and accurate evidence to support your claim.
- At least ONE piece of evidence must be from one of the listed foundational documents:
  - United States Constitution
  - Declaration of Independence
- Use a second piece of evidence from another foundational document from the list or from your study of civil liberties.
- Use reasoning to explain why the evidence you provided supports your claim or thesis.
- Use refutation, concession, or rebuttal to respond to an opposing or alternative perspective.

CRITICAL THINKING PROJECT

Civil Liberties in the News

Stories involving civil liberties often make the news. Americans face difficult questions about how to ensure civil liberties and freedoms while protecting public order and safety.

Find a news story from the past year about a controversy surrounding civil liberties. Remember that civil liberties involve action by the government. For example, while the "take a knee" protest by NFL players received much media attention, it did not involve civil liberties because the government did not take any action against protesting players.

Prepare a script for a newscast that helps explain what happened. Your script should include

1. A description of the controversy
2. A reference to the constitutional provision(s) that might apply
3. An explanation of how the story relates to the balance between civil liberties and freedoms and the protection of public order and safety

As a trusted reporter, be sure to cite your sources.

9 Civil Rights
What Is Equality?

The preamble to the Declaration of Independence states that the purpose of representative government is to guard and protect the fundamental rights and freedoms of its citizens. The Constitution and later amendments secure these rights, but the American government does not run on autopilot. Rights evolve as Americans continue to advocate for protection from discrimination.

Judith Heumann, U.S. State Department special advisor for international disability rights, left, meets with German officials in Berlin in 2011 to discuss a set of measures to improve inclusion of people with disabilities. A disabled American herself, Heumann has spent a lifetime advocating for the rights of people with disabilities in America and across the globe.

Rainer Jensen/AP Images

Civil rights protect individuals from discrimination based on race, national origin, religion, sex, and other characteristics. They include the fundamental right of individuals to be treated equally under the laws and policies of governments.

Recall the discussion of civil liberties from Chapter 8. As a rule, the protection of civil liberties requires that a government does not infringe on the freedom of individuals. Unlike civil liberties, however, civil rights require positive action by the government to protect individuals from discrimination.

The challenge with civil rights comes from deciding how vigorously a government should act to protect them. How much action does a government need to take? How strongly does government have to act? How equal is equal? There is no single answer to these questions. Americans have always disagreed on how strongly government should act to protect civil rights. In this chapter, we will examine the efforts of individuals such as Thurgood Marshall and members of the National Association for the Advancement of Colored People (NAACP), as well as others hoping to achieve a broader vision of Americans' civil rights.

civil rights
protections for individuals from discrimination based on race, national origin, religion, sex, and other characteristics, ensuring equal treatment under the law.

> **AP® TIP**
>
> The Fourteenth Amendment protects both civil rights and civil liberties. Civil liberties stem from the due process clause, and they are protections individuals have from government action. Civil rights stem from the equal protection clause and protect people from discrimination because of their characteristics.

After reading this chapter, you will be able to

9.1 Describe the struggle to secure civil rights for people with disabilities.

9.2 Examine the fight against segregation, including the Supreme Court's decision in *Brown v. Board of Education*.

9.3 Describe the civil rights movement's fight for racial equality.

9.4 Examine the struggle by the women's rights movement for gender equality.

LEARNING TARGETS

▬▬ **9.1** Securing Rights for Those with Disabilities

In January 2016, writing in celebration of the American holiday devoted to Dr. Martin Luther King Jr., Judith Heumann, then a special advisor for international disability rights with the U.S. Department of State, posted an article to the State Department's official blog. In it, she looked both to the past and to the present:

> A stable, prosperous democracy succeeds when individuals can fully participate in political and public life. As we celebrate MLK Day and reflect on past struggles fought by Americans determined to uphold their individual rights, Dr. King's message of inclusion lives on. Dr. King encouraged everyone to participate when he said, "It is not possible to be in favor of justice for some people and not be in favor of justice for all people."

While change takes time, we must take action to: establish disabled people's organizations; adopt and enforce strong laws; create and enforce standards that advance inclusion of disabled people; and remove barriers—physical and attitudinal in all areas of life.[1]

Refusing to Be Called a "Fire Hazard"

Heumann has spent a lifetime advocating for, protesting, and changing American laws affecting those with disabilities. As a very young child in 1949, Heumann contracted polio, which requires her to use a wheelchair. In the 1950s, administrators refused to let her attend public elementary school in Brooklyn, New York. They cited her inability to gain access to the building because it had no ramps, which was pretty much universal at the time. They refused to let her attend even when her mother offered to carry her up and down the school's steps. "I was considered to be a fire hazard," Heumann recalled.[2]

In spite of these obstacles, Heumann earned two degrees, including a master of arts from the University of California at Berkeley in 1975. After graduation, she applied to become a teacher with the New York City schools but was rejected based on her disability. Instead of backing down, however, "she filed suit against them and won."[3]

In 1977, she helped to organize a series of rallies and sit-ins across the nation to protest the slowness of the federal government's implementation of an important law regarding disability rights, Section 504 of the Rehabilitation Act of 1973. This was the first federal law to prohibit discrimination against Americans with disabilities, but it was not being enforced. Officials in the executive branch had not signed key regulations implementing the act, likely because of how much it would cost.

People across the nation protested. In San Francisco, supporters of the act took over a federal office building. The protests were called the "504 sit-ins" after the section of the law that the protesters demanded be immediately and effectively implemented. According to one news account, "By the late 1970s, Americans were used to seeing civil rights marches. But this one was something new: people in wheelchairs, people on portable respirators, deaf people . . . And most were fighting mad."[4]

The protesters won. Four weeks into the San Francisco sit-in, the secretary of the Department of Health, Education, and Welfare endorsed the regulations. Heumann recalled what was at stake for the activists: "People weren't going to work, people were willing to risk arrest, people were risking their own health. Everybody was risking something. . . . Through the sit-in, we turned ourselves from being oppressed individuals into being empowered people. We demonstrated to the entire nation that disabled people could take control over our own lives and take leadership in the struggle for equality."[5]

Heumann also worked tirelessly for the passage of the Americans with Disabilities Act (ADA),[6] signed into law in 1990 by President George H. W. Bush. The ADA guarantees that people with disabilities are not discriminated against in employment, in buying goods and services, and in participating in government programs. The ADA protects those with a physical or mental impairment that substantially limits one or more major life activities, a person who has a history or record of such an impairment, or a person who is perceived by others as having such an impairment.[7] Among its provisions, the ADA offered protections for Americans with disabilities against discrimination in the workplace and improved their access to public transportation, public services, and other areas of public and commercial life.[8] The ADA required states to modify public buildings so disabled citizens can access them. Congress did not appropriate funds to help states pay for these modifications. This is an example of an unfunded mandate, as mentioned in Chapter 3.

Demonstrators converge on the offices of the Department of Health, Education, and Welfare in San Francisco in April 1977. They were part of a "504 sit-in" urging that civil rights law for disabled Americans be fully implemented. In the center, a woman briefs the group in American Sign Language.
JP/AP Images

Many advocates for the rights of Americans with disabilities drew connections between their struggles and those of African Americans decades before. A 1999 position paper for the American Civil Liberties Union—which noted that "people with disabilities are the poorest, least employed, and least educated minority in America"—pointed to a long history of discrimination against Americans with disabilities.[9] "Finally" the report noted, "thanks in part to the inspiration provided by the civil rights struggles of the 1960s, disability rights advocates began to press for full legal equality and access to mainstream society. Through lobbying and litigation, laws were passed and rights established; public education and advocacy were used to promote reason and inclusiveness rather than fear and pity."[10] Heumann helped lead that charge.

Section Review

This chapter's main ideas are reflected in the Learning Targets. By reviewing after each section, you should be able to

—**Remember** the key points,

—**Know** terms that are central to the topic, and

—**Think** critically about civil rights and how they offer protection from discrimination.

9.1 Describe the struggle to secure civil rights for people with disabilities.

REMEMBER
- Securing civil rights requires action, both on the part of individuals to advocate for their rights and on the part of government to secure and protect those rights.
- The ADA offered protections for Americans with disabilities against discrimination in the workplace and improved their access to public transportation, public services, and other areas of public and commercial life.

KNOW
civil rights: protections for individuals from discrimination based on race, national origin, religion, sex, and other characteristics, ensuring equal treatment under the law. (p. 293)

THINK
How does the Americans with Disabilities Act illustrate tensions between civil rights and federalism?

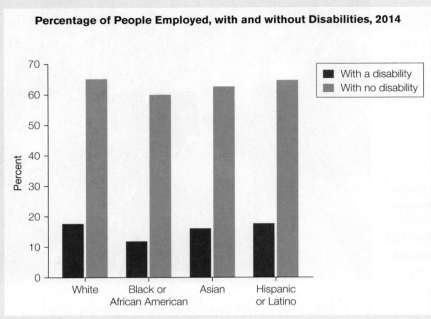

Percentage of People Employed, with and without Disabilities, 2014

Data from U.S. Bureau of Labor Statistics

Use the bar chart and your knowledge of U.S. Government and Politics to answer parts A, B, and C.

A. Define civil rights.

B. Describe one difference between the employment population ratios of disabled and nondisabled individuals.

C. Describe two tactics an individual or group might use to advocate for improved rights for the disabled.

■ 9.2 The Fight against Segregation

Before the Civil War, the rights of African Americans were severely restricted. In 1857, in *Dred Scott v. Sandford*,[11] the Supreme Court ruled that Scott, former slaves, and the descendants of slaves were not citizens of the United States, even if they were residents of free states or territories. The natural rights proclaimed in the Declaration of Independence and protected in the Constitution, Justice Roger Taney wrote in his opinion, did not extend to individuals "whose ancestors were negroes of the African race," who, at the time of the founding, were considered an "inferior class of beings who had been subjugated by the dominant race, and, whether emancipated or not, yet remained subject to their authority, and had no rights or privileges but such as those who held the power and the Government might choose to grant them."[12] The Court's decision further polarized public opinion on the question of slavery and galvanized both pro-slavery and antislavery forces in the United States.

In December 1860, South Carolina made the long-simmering threat of secession a reality. When the American Civil War finally ended in 1865, more than six hundred thousand soldiers had died. It was total war, and it did not end until the Union armies destroyed the ability of the Confederacy to support and conduct war. During the war, President Lincoln signed the Emancipation Proclamation, which took effect January 1, 1863, and declared

that all slaves in the states involved in the rebellion were "henceforward and forever free." However, Union troops and slaves themselves had to make that proclamation a reality.

Civil Rights Amendments and Backlash

At the conclusion of the war, southern states began to pass laws to preserve the status quo between whites and African Americans. Known as the black codes, these pieces of legislation attempted to restrict the economic and political rights of freedmen, to "make Negroes slaves in everything but name."[13]

Within five years of the conclusion of the Civil War, three amendments were added to the Constitution, in an effort to protect the civil rights of African Americans. In 1865, the **Thirteenth Amendment** prohibited slavery.[14] In 1868, the **Fourteenth Amendment** affirmed the citizenship of all persons "born or naturalized in the United States" and, for the first time in the history of the Constitution, placed explicit restrictions on the laws of states: "No State shall make or enforce any law which shall abridge the privileges and immunities of citizens of the United States; nor shall any State deprive any person of life, liberty, or property, without due process of law; nor deny to any person within its jurisdiction the equal protection of the laws."[15] The **equal protection clause** of the Fourteenth Amendment has been used to protect the civil rights of Americans from discrimination based on race, national origin, religion, gender, and other characteristics. The Fourteenth Amendment also overturned the Three-Fifths Compromise in the original Constitution.

The **Fifteenth Amendment**, ratified in 1870, granted voting rights to African Americans: "The right of citizens of the United States to vote shall not be denied or abridged by the United States or by any State on account of race, color, or previous condition of servitude."[16]

Thirteenth Amendment an amendment to the Constitution passed in 1865 prohibiting slavery within the United States.

Fourteenth Amendment an amendment to the Constitution passed in 1868 granting citizenship to all persons born or naturalized in the United States and placing restrictions on state laws that sought to abridge the privileges and immunities of citizens of the United States.

equal protection clause clause of the Fourteenth Amendment that has been used to protect the civil rights of Americans from discrimination based on race, national origin, religion, gender, and other characteristics.

Fifteenth Amendment an amendment to the Constitution passed in 1870 granting voting rights to African American men.

These amendments did not go unopposed. Southern states passed laws to preserve segregation and prevent African American men from exercising their Fifteenth Amendment right to vote. Known as Jim Crow laws, these efforts enforced segregation across all aspects of daily life, including transportation, entertainment, business, and education. Poll taxes, which required voters to pay a tax to vote, and literacy tests, which were used by registrars to determine whether voters were "qualified" to vote, combined to prevent African American men from voting.

Violence and the persistent threat of violence were used against African Americans who tried to exercise their rights and against whites who tried to help them. Schools were burned, and their white teachers were beaten and ostracized. Across the South, the Ku Klux Klan terrorized and murdered African American politicians and civic leaders.

A young African American man drinks from a segregated water fountain in Oklahoma City, Oklahoma, in 1939. Jim Crow laws persisted across the United States long after the civil rights acts of the late nineteenth century were passed.

The Granger Collection, New York

Plessy v. Ferguson: "Separate but Equal"

In the decades following the Civil War, the Supreme Court upheld the constitutionality of legalized racial segregation.[17] *Plessy v. Ferguson* (1896) was a test case organized by the African American community in New Orleans to challenge Louisiana's Jim Crow laws.[18] Homer Plessy, "a light-skinned man who described himself as 'seven-eighths Caucasian,'"[19] was arrested and fined for violating a state law requiring separate railroad cars for whites and African Americans. Under the Louisiana law, Plessy was considered African American. After losing in the state courts, he appealed his case to the Supreme Court.

In the majority decision in *Plessy*, Justice Henry Billings Brown ruled that Louisiana's law did not violate the Fourteenth Amendment to the Constitution. Arguing that "social prejudices cannot be overcome by legislation," Brown upheld Plessy's conviction and declared that "**separate but equal**" facilities did not violate the Constitution. Justice John Marshall Harlan, the lone dissenter on the Court, disagreed, stating, "Our Constitution is color-blind, and neither knows nor tolerates classes among citizens. In respect of civil rights, all citizens are equal before the law." Legal segregation, under the doctrine of "separate but equal," remained constitutional for almost sixty years.

separate but equal
the doctrine that racial segregation was constitutional so long as the facilities for blacks and whites were equal.

Thurgood Marshall and the NAACP

The attack on legal segregation was launched by Thurgood Marshall and the Legal Defense Fund of the National Association for the Advancement of Colored People (NAACP). *Plessy*, along with some later related cases, was precedent. Precedent is not always binding, yet the Court does not overturn precedent lightly, in part to preserve its legitimacy in the eyes of the American people. For the Court to declare that segregated education was *inherently* in violation of the Fourteenth Amendment, it would have to break from its own precedent. The members of the NAACP's legal team were also well aware of the fact that *Plessy* was a test case that had failed. Rather than overturning the Louisiana segregation laws, the case set the precedent for legal segregation well into the future. As they had no guarantee of success, the NAACP was risking the same fate for the segregated schools of twentieth-century America. Marshall and his team pushed ahead anyway.

By the morning of December 9, 1952, hundreds of Americans had already lined up outside the Supreme Court of the United States. The better prepared had brought food, knowing someone would take their place if they left. African Americans and whites stood together for a chance to witness history. Though the line was integrated, the public schools of the District of Columbia where they were gathered were not. By law, African American and white children in the nation's capital and elsewhere, predominantly in the South, attended separate schools. On this day, those laws would be challenged.

In the audience was the president of Howard University, a historically African American university whose law school had trained a generation of civil rights lawyers, including Thurgood Marshall. Marshall and his team of lawyers were arguing five cases in front of the Court.[20] The cases dealt with the same question—whether or not **legal segregation**, or the separation by law of African American and white children in the public schools based only on their race, was unconstitutional.

It had been a long journey through the courts for Marshall and the NAACP. They had been waging a legal attack on segregation for decades. The individuals who had filed the lawsuits, those who helped organize them, and the lawyers who had argued the cases had often done so in the face of personal danger. Some were threatened and assaulted. Many lost their jobs. Some had been shot at. In some cases, their homes and churches had been burned.

Marshall arrived in Washington ten days before the argument began to coordinate his team and make sure they were well prepared. Their main concern was that the Supreme Court might agree that the African American children in the five cases had been treated unfairly but only because their schools were not equal to the schools of the white children. It was not enough to have the Court declare that the educations of the African American children in the cases were unequal. Such a ruling would have forced the NAACP to fight on a case-by-case basis, to force thousands of school districts to equalize their educational facilities, with districts, counties, and states digging in their heels and trying to slow things down. According to a member of Marshall's legal team, if they won, "there would be momentous changes in the lives of black people, indeed of all Americans," and if they lost, "we would have spent our best chance and would face a long, dismal future of quibbling over the equality of school buildings, books, libraries, gyms, playgrounds."[21]

Marshall's legal team sought to have the Court overturn the *Plessy* decision and declare that segregation itself was unequal. Marshall had to prove that there was no possibility for equality in segregated education. The Court had to declare that segregation based on racial identity was *inherently* unequal and that it violated the Constitution of the United States.

legal segregation
the separation by law of individuals based on their race.

Thurgood Marshall, center, was special counsel for the NAACP in *Brown v. Board of Education*. Here, Marshall poses with two other members of his legal team, George E. C. Hayes (left) and James M. Nabrit Jr. (right), in front of the Supreme Court following their landmark victory in 1954.
Bettmann/Getty Images

Charles Hamilton Houston, Harvard-trained lawyer, was dean of the Howard University School of Law from 1929 to 1935 and Thurgood Marshall's mentor. As first special counsel to the NAACP, Houston was an early leader in the NAACP's efforts to overturn legal segregation in the United States. Houston was quoted as observing, "Nobody needs to explain to a Negro the difference between the law in books and the law in action."

The Granger Collection, New York

The NAACP's choice to base much of its strategy on winning in the Supreme Court was a risky move. In *Federalist* No. 78, Alexander Hamilton wrote that the "judiciary is beyond comparison the weakest of the three departments of power; that it can never attack with success either of the other two; and that all possible care is requisite to enable it to defend itself against their attacks."[22] In part, Hamilton was trying to reassure the American public in the face of Antifederalist charges that the federal courts would trample on people's rights. Furthermore, the founders had not given the judiciary powers to enforce its decisions. Justice Tom Clark, commenting on the decision in *Brown v. Board of Education*, cautioned that "we don't have money at the Court for an army and we can't take ads in the newspapers, and we don't want to go out on a picket line in our robes. We have to convince the nation by the force of our opinions."[23]

Brown v. Board of Education

Oliver Brown of Topeka, Kansas, was a railroad welder, a part-time minister, and a reluctant symbol for desegregation.[26] He tried to enroll one of his three daughters, Linda, in

AP® Political Science PRACTICES

Interpreting Images

Although admitted to the University of Oklahoma graduate school, George McLaurin "was made to sit at a desk by himself outside of the regular classroom. In the library, he was assigned a segregated desk behind half a carload of newspapers."[24] McLaurin challenged his separate treatment at the University of Oklahoma and won his case.[25]

1. Explain how Thurgood Marshall could have used the photo to support a sociological argument about the intangible effects of segregation.

2. Based on the photo, describe an argument the University of Oklahoma might have made that the segregation did not violate the equal protection clause.

3. Identify at least one other type of discrimination that is evident in the photo.

Bettmann/Getty Images

an all-white elementary school that was closer to their house than the all-black school and that did not require Linda to walk through the busy and dangerous Rock Island railroad yards. Brown's request was denied, so, with the help of the local NAACP, he and seven other parents sued. After losing in the state courts, they appealed to the Supreme Court. The Kansas case was joined with four others, and they collectively bore the name *Brown v. Board of Education.*

All evidence, including evidence that had been accepted by the Court in earlier cases, demonstrated that black and white children were equal in their educational potential. Educational segregation, therefore, had no legitimate basis. Marshall introduced social science research findings by psychologists Kenneth Clark and Mamie Clark. In those studies, the Clarks presented young African American and white children with a set of brown and white dolls. A majority of children stated that they preferred the white dolls over the brown dolls, and many had negative comments about the brown dolls.

The "doll study" research of Dr. Kenneth B. Clark and Dr. Mamie Clark, his wife, demonstrated the psychological harm of segregation and was used as evidence in *Brown v. Board of Education.* This photo comes from a series taken by the prominent Afircan American photographer Gordon Parks.
Photograph by Gordon Parks, Copyright The Gordon Parks Foundation

On May 17, 1954, the last day of the Supreme Court's term, Chief Justice Earl Warren read the Court's decision in *Brown*: "Does segregation in public schools solely on the basis of race, even though the physical facilities and other 'tangible' factors may be equal, deprive the children of the minority groups of equal educational opportunities? We believe that it does."[27] Arguing that the premise of *Plessy*—that separation based on race caused no harm—was flawed, Warren overturned the 1896 decision, saying, "We conclude that in the field of public education the doctrine of 'separate but equal' has no place. Separate educational facilities are inherently unequal. . . . We have now announced that such segregation is a denial of the equal protection of the laws." The Court was unanimous, a point that Warren inserted into his reading of the official decision.[28] It had to be; a deeply divided Court would not have had the legitimacy that was necessary to take on segregation.

The reaction of the nation was strong and immediate, but not uniform. Many cheered the moral stance the court had taken. "What the Justices have done," declared a Cincinnati newspaper, "is simply to act as the conscience of the American nation."[29] But there was also anger. Mobs blocked schools and universities. South Carolina governor James F. Byrnes proclaimed, "Ending segregation [will] mark the beginning of the end of civilization in the South as we have known it."[30]

Southern Resistance

The Court's decision in *Brown* had intentionally avoided setting a strict time line on achieving desegregation. The Court issued a follow-up decision the next year, in 1955. In what is now known as *Brown v. Board of Education of Topeka II,*[31] the Warren Court urged compliance with *Brown I* "with all deliberate speed," a contradictory word choice. The Court

AP® TIP

The Supreme Court's decision in *Brown v. Board of Education* did not end legal challenges to segregation. You may be asked to apply required Supreme Court cases to other scenarios. Make sure you can explain how the ruling in *Brown v. Board of Education* might apply in other cases.

de jure segregation
the separation of individuals based on their characteristics, such as race, intentionally and by law.

de facto segregation
a separation of individuals based on characteristics that arises not by law but because of other factors, such as residential housing patterns.

AP® TIP

The Supreme Court's decision in *Brown v. Board of Education* did not immediately end school segregation. Be ready to explain how the actions of other branches of government may impact the implementation of Supreme Court decisions.

affirmative action
a policy designed to address the consequences of previous discrimination by providing special consideration to individuals based upon their characteristics, such as race or gender.

placed federal district court judges in charge of desegregation efforts. Some southern district court judges were not sympathetic to the Court's ruling and tried to slow down compliance with it. In general, in spite of the second *Brown* decision, compliance across the South was slow. In 1964, ten years after the Court's ruling in *Brown v. Board of Education*, 98 percent of African American children in the South still attended completely segregated schools.[32]

Balancing Equal Protection with Other Rights

The segregation in the South that Thurgood Marshall and the NAACP had challenged in the courts was written into law—sometimes even into state constitutions. In many cases, these laws did not just allow segregation, they required it. This type of segregation is called **de jure segregation**, meaning that it is written into law. The efforts of activists and citizens had largely eliminated racially based de jure segregation by the end of the 1960s. Attention now focused on **de facto segregation**, segregation based not on law but on private choices, or the lingering social consequences of legal segregation even after those laws were no longer on the books. Addressing de facto segregation has proven to be even more complicated than addressing de jure segregation.

In 1971, the Court ruled in *Swann v. Charlotte-Mecklenburg Board of Education* that busing—the use of transportation to desegregate public schools, even if it meant sending students to schools farther away from their homes—was constitutionally permissible.[33] Often unpopular with parents, busing efforts stirred up considerable political opposition in both the North and the South. Those in favor argued that busing was necessary, given the depth of the roots of segregation. Those opposed argued that the role of government in securing equal protection was only to strike down unjust laws, not to implement plans to produce racially integrated schools.

The Supreme Court has been more cautious in addressing de facto segregation than de jure segregation. In 1974, in *Milliken v. Bradley*, the Court considered a case of educational segregation that had been caused by law but by residential housing patterns in and around Detroit, Michigan.[34] In the middle of the twentieth century, millions of people moved to the suburbs. This was made possible by the automobile and the interstate highway; this move was often described by the term *white flight*. Large numbers of whites moved outside the central cities, leaving the urban cores with high percentages of African Americans. Segregation had gone from being maintained within school districts, as it had been in the South, to being between urban and suburban districts. This pattern repeated across the industrial North.

The question in *Milliken* was of responsibility. How much action should be taken, and who should be required to take it, when there was no law that encouraged the segregation? In *Milliken*, the Court ruled that the schools would not be ordered to desegregate because the district boundaries had not been drawn for the purpose of segregating students.[35] The suburban districts did not have to participate in a plan that would move students across boundaries of school districts.

Affirmative Action

Affirmative action is policy designed to address the consequences of previous discrimination by providing special consideration to individuals based on their characteristics, such as race or gender. Affirmative action benefits individuals who are members of groups that faced discrimination in the past or are underrepresented. For example, some colleges and universities have sought to boost the enrollment of African Americans and members of other racial and ethnic minorities.

Opponents argue that affirmative action constitutes "reverse discrimination" against majority groups and harms minorities by tainting the admissions process. Proponents argue that affirmative action programs are necessary to ensure equality for those who face discrimination and the adversity of their circumstances. In recent years, the Supreme Court has tried to navigate among these viewpoints.

A 1978 Supreme Court decision in *Regents of the University of California v. Bakke* concerned the use of quotas, or the setting aside of a number of places at a school, contracts with the government, or job opportunities, for groups who have suffered past discrimination.[36] Allan Bakke, who is white, sued the regents of the University of California at Davis after he was denied admission to its medical school. Bakke argued that his academic record was superior to the group of sixteen minority applicants for whom seats had been set aside. He brought his suit under the equal protection clause of the Fourteenth Amendment. The Court agreed that the quota system violated Bakke's rights and those of other white applicants and instructed the school to admit him. However, the Court also affirmed the worthiness of the goal of increasing minority student enrollment, leaving open the possibility for affirmative action plans that did not involve strict quotas.[37]

In the years after *Bakke*, the Court issued several rulings that attempted to define the limits of permissible affirmative action. In 2003, the Court issued two rulings on the same day that tried to clarify its position. In *Gratz v. Bollinger*, the Court considered the use of a points system in undergraduate admissions decisions.[38] Like Alan Bakke, Jennifer Gratz had been denied admission to a university, in this case as an undergraduate of the University of Michigan at Ann Arbor. Rather than using a strict quota system, the university ranked applicants on a points system, much of which focused on academics. Some points, however, were awarded for having parents who attended the University of Michigan, being a Michigan resident, having shown a commitment to public service, or having strong athletic ability. Forty of the 150 points were awarded on the basis of "other factors." One of these factors was membership in a traditionally underrepresented racial or ethnic group. The university argued that having a diverse student body had an educational benefit on the entire learning community. In *Gratz*, the Court ruled that the points system was unconstitutional, but it did not strike down the use of race or ethnicity as factors in admissions decisions.

In *Grutter v. Bollinger*, also decided in 2003, the Court affirmed the possibility of using race and ethnicity in admissions decisions.[39] Barbara Grutter had also sued the University of Michigan, although this case involved the law school. Unlike the admissions system at the undergraduate level, the law school did not use a points system, but it did include race as a factor considered in admissions decisions. By a 5–4 vote, the Court ruled that the university could use race as a factor as long as it could show that it had a "compelling interest" to do so. The Court concluded that ensuring a diverse student body demonstrates such an interest.[40]

In June 2016, the Court, in a 4–3 ruling in *Fisher v. University of Texas at Austin*,[41] upheld the consideration of race in college admissions. President Obama said of the decision, "We are not a country that guarantees equal outcomes, but we do strive to provide an equal shot to everybody."[42]

AP® REQUIRED CASE

Case	Scope
Brown v. Board of Education (1954)	*Brown* is one of the required Supreme Court cases in AP® U.S. Government and Politics. Make sure you read it carefully and understand why the Supreme Court ruled that de jure racial segregation violates the equal protection clause of the Fourteenth Amendment.

9.2 Examine the fight against segregation, including the Supreme Court's decision in *Brown v. Board of Education*.

REMEMBER   In *Brown v. Board of Education*, the Supreme Court overturned the "separate but equal" doctrine of *Plessy v. Ferguson* and ruled that de jure segregation in schools violates the equal protection clause of the Fourteenth Amendment.

KNOW
- *Thirteenth Amendment*: an amendment to the Constitution passed in 1865 prohibiting slavery within the United States. (p. 297)
- *Fourteenth Amendment*: an amendment to the Constitution passed in 1868 granting citizenship to all persons born or naturalized in the United States and placing restrictions on state laws that sought to abridge the privileges and immunities of citizens of the United States. (p. 297)
- *equal protection clause*: clause of the Fourteenth Amendment that has been used to protect the civil rights of Americans from discrimination based on race, national origin, religion, gender, and other characteristics. (p. 297)
- *Fifteenth Amendment*: an amendment to the Constitution passed in 1870 granting voting rights to African Americans. (p. 297)
- *separate but equal*: the doctrine that racial segregation was constitutional so long as the facilities for blacks and whites were equal. (p. 298)
- *legal segregation*: the separation by law of individuals based on their race. (p. 299)
- *de jure segregation*: the separation of individuals based on their characteristics, such as race, intentionally and by law. (p. 302)
- *de facto segregation*: a separation of individuals based on their characteristics that arises not by law but because of other factors, such as residential housing patterns. (p. 302)
- *affirmative action*: a policy designed to address the consequences of previous discrimination by providing special consideration to individuals based upon their characteristics, such as race or gender. (p. 302)

THINK
- To what extent was *Brown v. Board of Education* successful in ending racial segregation in schools?
- Do affirmative action programs further racial equality, or do these programs result in reverse discrimination?

9.2 Review Question: Free Response

Following the ruling in *Brown v. Board of Education*, the Scotland Neck City School Board, located in North Carolina, devised a plan to desegregate its schools. The plan created one district with 695 students. Of them, 57 percent were white, and 43 percent were African American. Then, 360 students would be placed in a second district, which planned to use the facilities of the formerly all-white Scotland Neck High School. Of those students, 350 were white, and ten were African American. Teachers, African American children, and parents challenged the plan. In *United States v. Scotland Neck City School Board* (1972), the Supreme Court invalidated the plan on grounds that it did not meet the goal of desegregating the schools.[43]

Use the scenario and your knowledge of U.S. Government and Politics to answer parts A, B, and C.

A.   Identify the provision of the Constitution that is common to both *Brown v. Board of Education* and *United States v. Scotland Neck City School Board* (1972).

B.   Based on the constitutional clause identified in part A, explain why the facts of *Brown v. Board of Education* led to a similar holding in *United States v. Scotland Neck City School Board*.

C.   Describe one way in which the facts in *United States v. Scotland Neck City School Board* differ from the facts in *Brown v. Board of Education*.

9.3 The Civil Rights Movement

The decisions of the Supreme Court did not end segregation in the South. According to law professor Gerald Rosenberg, "For ten years the Court spoke forcefully while Congress and the executive did little."[44]

There were a few exceptions, however. In 1957, President Eisenhower sent federal troops to Little Rock, Arkansas, to enforce a Supreme Court order to segregate the schools against the will of the state's governor. The troops escorted nine African American students through an angry white mob. Also that year, Lyndon Johnson, senator and future president, sponsored the Civil Rights Act of 1957, the first piece of civil rights legislation to pass since Reconstruction. Its main purpose was to put pressure on the states by supporting the lawsuits of African Americans who had been denied the right to vote.

AP® Political Science PRACTICES

Interpreting Data

In *Federalist* No. 78, Alexander Hamilton argued that the Supreme Court had little power acting on its own "and must ultimately depend upon the aid of the executive arm even for the efficacy of its judgments." One scholar has collected data on the pace of integration in the South following *Brown v. Board* to make a similar argument: The Supreme Court cannot, acting on its own, produce social change on the ground. His data are displayed in the following chart.

1. Describe the trend shown in the graph.

2. Explain how the graph supports Alexander Hamilton's argument in *Federalist* No. 78.

3. Explain two reasons why, although the Supreme Court cannot enforce its decisions, it is still an important branch of government in bringing about social change.

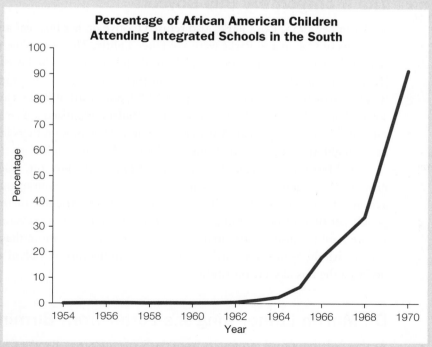

Data are from Table 2.1 in Gerald N. Rosenberg, *The Hollow Hope* (Chicago: University of Chicago Press, 2008)

By refusing to give up her seat on the bus, Rosa Parks, a secretary for the local chapter of the NAACP, became a civil rights icon. Her act of civil disobedience has had a strong impact on political culture.
Underwood Archives/Getty Images

social movement
large groups of citizens organizing for political change.

civil disobedience
the intentional refusal to obey a law to call attention to its injustice.

Citizens took increasingly strong action to end segregation in schools, workplaces, and the community, resulting in a large **social movement**. African American community leaders organized boycotts, in which people refused to buy services or products from businesses engaging in discrimination. Notable among these was the bus boycott in Montgomery, Alabama, which put economic pressure on the city to end racial segregation on buses. In 1955, Claudette Colvin, an African American high school student, refused to move to the "Negro section" of a Montgomery bus. She was not sitting in the "white section," but in "no man's land," a vaguely defined buffer between the two sections that, according to segregationists, was created "to give the driver some discretion to keep the races out of each other's way."[45] Colvin was handcuffed and placed under arrest.

Other African American women in Montgomery were arrested for similar acts of **civil disobedience**, which is intentionally breaking a law to protest its injustice.

The Montgomery Bus Boycott

In December 1955, Rosa Parks also refused to give up her bus seat and was arrested. The decisions of Colvin and Parks were not taken lightly. They faced the prospect of criticism within their own communities and physical violence at the hands of whites. "When she [Rosa] was allowed to call home," one historian has noted, "her mother's first response was to groan and ask, 'Did they beat you?'"[46] Upon word of Parks's arrest, English professor Jo Ann Robinson and other community leaders organized a boycott, getting the word out with the help of African American churches. They printed fliers in secret in the middle of the night at Alabama State College, where Robinson taught.

Dr. Martin Luther King Jr. was selected to lead the boycott. Addressing the community in a Montgomery church, King captured the simple, courageous reason behind the actions of the women of the city: "And you know, my friends, there comes a time when people get tired of being trampled over by the iron feet of oppression. . . . We are here— we are here because we are tired now."[47] After lasting for more than a year, the boycott ended with the Supreme Court's 1956 decision in the case of Colvin and three others that declared the bus law unconstitutional.[48]

Dr. Martin Luther King Jr.'s Letter from Birmingham Jail

As they led about forty protesters from the Sixteenth Street Baptist Church in Birmingham, Alabama, Rev. Martin Luther King Jr. and his close friend, Rev. Ralph David Abernathy, were dressed for jail. Wearing work shirts and jeans, carrying coats to ward off the cold and damp of Birmingham City Jail, King and Abernathy walked past hundreds of spectators, witnesses, and supporters. Some "sang freedom songs, some knelt in silence." A few cried.

Despite the seriousness of the situation, the two leaders tried to show calmness and strength. Before leaving for Birmingham, King lightened the mood of all present one evening when, looking at Abernathy and knowing well his friend's habits, he said, "Let me be sure to get arrested with people who don't snore." On the night before the march, King told the planners and supporters gathered at the Gaston Motel in Birmingham, "I don't know what will happen. I don't know where the money will come from. But I have to make a faith act."

Born in Atlanta in 1929, King received a doctorate in theology from Boston University and, like his father, joined the Christian clergy. After university, King moved back to the South, even though "there had been offers of jobs in safe northern universities." Later he became one of the founders and president of the Southern Christian Leadership Conference (SCLC), an organization devoted to challenging racial segregation and advocating for civil rights. In its founding statement, the conference's leaders pointed to the violence against those struggling for racial justice and announced that "We have no moral choice, before God, but to delve deeper into the struggle—and to do so with greater reliance on non-violence and with greater unity, coordination, sharing and Christian understanding."[49]

King, Abernathy, and other civil rights leaders faced a constant threat of violence. King's home in Montgomery, Alabama, was bombed in 1956. Both King and his wife escaped harm. King had also been threatened in an anonymous phone call—a clear attempt to intimidate him. It didn't work. King, as well as other leaders, members, and supporters of the SCLC, pressed ahead.

In 1963, King marched in Birmingham because the city was a bastion of segregation and protestors there were threatened with violence. King, Abernathy, and about fifty others were arrested for violating a ban on protesting and taken to Birmingham City Jail. King was thrown into solitary confinement—"the hole," as it was called—with only a cot with metal slats to sleep on. "You will never know the meaning of utter darkness," he recalled, "until you have lain in such a dungeon."

The White Clergy Urges Moderation

The morning after King's arrest, a copy of an article from the *Birmingham News* was slipped into his cell entitled "White Clergymen Urge Local Negroes to Withdraw from Demonstrations." The letter, written by eight white members of the Protestant, Catholic, and Jewish clergies, admonished King and the other leaders of the SCLC to slow down, to stop protesting, and to end the strategy of civil disobedience in Birmingham.

Calling the demonstrations "unwise and untimely" and "directed and led in part by outsiders," the

Southern Christian Leadership Conference leaders in Birmingham, Alabama, in May 1963. In the foreground, left to right, Rev. Fred L. Shuttlesworth, Rev. Ralph Abernathy, and Dr. Martin Luther King, are shown as they walked to a press conference.
Bettmann/Getty Images

eight clergy members argued that "honest convictions in racial matters could properly be pursued in the courts." They "commend[ed] the [Birmingham] community as a whole and the local news media and law enforcement officials in particular, on the calm manner in which these demonstrations have been handled." In closing, the clergy members urged Birmingham's "Negro community to withdraw support from these demonstrations."

King's Response Affirming Natural Rights

Beginning with notes written in the margins of the newspaper, Martin Luther King Jr. penned a response from jail. Paper was smuggled into the jail, and his notes were smuggled out, typed up, and eventually published by a group of Quakers as the "Letter from Birmingham Jail." Though it did not have the benefit of King's powerful speaking voice to increase its impact, it is one of the most important documents of the American civil rights movement.

King begins by offering his reply as a sincere response to the white clergymen's concerns, calling them "men of genuine goodwill." Then he defends his presence in Birmingham professionally, as president of the Southern Christian Leadership Conference. However, he also lays out a much more fundamental basis for his involvement. He declares, "I am in Birmingham because injustice is here." King defends his movement's tactics on the basis of natural rights, drawing a distinction between just and unjust laws: "A just law is a man-made code that squares with the moral law or the law of God. An unjust law is a code that is out of harmony with the natural law." Racial oppression, he asserts, in all of its legal manifestations, is unjust. Individuals, therefore, have the right to break these unjust laws, but "One who breaks an unjust law must do so openly, lovingly."

In a single sentence, more than three hundred words long, King lists the grievances, the injustices, and the evidence that led to his actions. Politically, one of the most important passages in the letter pointed to the white moderate as a severe obstacle to justice: "I have almost reached the regrettable conclusion that the Negro's great stumbling block in the stride toward freedom is not the White citizens' 'Councilor' or the Ku Klux Klanner, but the white moderate who is more devoted to 'order' than justice; who prefers a negative peace which

This photograph of a student activist being attacked by a police dog in Birmingham, Alabama, appeared on the front page of the *New York Times* in 1963. President John F. Kennedy is reported to have viewed it and said it sickened him. He also believed it would make the United States look bad across the world, as Birmingham was "a dangerous situation for our image abroad." Shortly afterward, Kennedy delivered his own famous civil rights speech, vindicating Martin Luther King Jr.'s statements in "Letter from Birmingham Jail."
AP Photo/Bill Hudson

is the absence of tension to a positive peace which is the presence of justice." By creating a crisis and a confrontation, King sought to force white moderates to decide if racial segregation and the oppression of African Americans were consistent with American values or not.

Civil Rights Act of 1964 and Voting Rights Act of 1965

There were many other acts of civil disobedience. In 1960, four African American college students sat down at a lunch counter reserved for whites at a Woolworth's in Greensboro, North Carolina, and requested service. They were denied. They returned the next day, and their numbers began to grow. College students, both African American and white, continued the sit-ins. The Student Nonviolent Coordinating Committee (SNCC) organized similar protests occurred across the South. Some protesters met with arrest, others with violence and intimidation.

In 1961, a group of African Americans and whites undertook another series of protests, aimed at pressuring the Kennedy administration to enforce Supreme Court decisions banning segregation in public facilities involved with interstate travel. These Freedom Riders faced arrest and violence. In one case, a bus was smoke-bombed, and protesters were beaten with baseball bats and iron pipes.[50]

The harsh treatment of these activists by local law enforcement, which was broadcast to Americans on their televisions, began to change public opinion toward the civil rights struggle. By voting in larger numbers, African Americans also began to make their presence felt in Washington, D.C. Close elections highlighted to politicians the importance of securing the African American vote, which might tip an election in their favor.

Congress, under intense pressure from President Johnson, passed two major pieces of civil rights legislation. A version of the **Civil Rights Act of 1964**[51] was part of President Kennedy's civil rights efforts before his assassination in 1963. The Civil Rights Act of 1964 authorized the federal government to withhold grants from districts that did not integrate their schools. The act outlawed racial segregation in schools and public places and authorized the attorney general to sue individual school districts that failed to desegregate. Further, the act outlawed employment discrimination based on race or ethnicity, religion, national origin, or gender.

The **Voting Rights Act of 1965**[52] outlaws literacy tests and authorizes the Justice Department to send federal officers to register voters in uncooperative cities, counties, and states. The effects on African American voter registration were immediate and significant.

In 2013, the Supreme Court overturned a provision of the Voting Rights Act of 1965 that required certain Southern states to obtain federal "pre-clearance" before they changed their voting laws or practices.[53] The Supreme Court acknowledged the effectiveness of the Voting Rights Act in achieving its goal of increasing registration among African Americans and protecting their right to vote. However, the Court ruled that the forty-year-old pre-clearance requirement was no longer relevant and violated the Tenth Amendment's principle of federalism.[54]

A black student protests outside a Woolworth's in Greensboro, North Carolina, in 1960. A white counterdemonstrator follows him. The efforts of those involved in the lunch counter protests helped call attention to the injustices of segregation in the American South.

The Granger Collection, New York

Civil Rights Act of 1964 legislation outlawing racial segregation in schools and public places and authorizing the attorney general to sue individual school districts that failed to desegregate.

Voting Rights Act of 1965 legislation outlawing literacy tests and authorizing the Justice Department to send federal officers to register voters in uncooperative cities, counties, and states.

9.3 Describe the civil rights movement's fight for racial equality.

REMEMBER
- In "Letter from Birmingham Jail," Dr. Martin Luther King Jr. justified the civil rights movement by referring to natural rights.
- The Civil Rights Act of 1964 outlaws racial segregation in schools and public places and authorizes the attorney general to sue individual school districts that failed to desegregate. In addition, the act outlaws employment discrimination based on race or ethnicity, religion, national origin, or gender.
- The Voting Rights Act of 1965 outlaws literacy tests and authorizes the Justice Department to send federal officers to register voters in uncooperative cities, counties, and states.

KNOW
- *social movement*: large groups of citizens organizing for political change. (p. 306)
- *civil disobedience*: the intentional refusal to obey a law to call attention to its injustice. (p. 306)
- *Civil Rights Act of 1964*: legislation outlawing racial segregation in schools and public places and authorizing the attorney general to sue individual school districts that failed to desegregate. (p. 309)
- *Voting Rights Act of 1965*: legislation outlawing literacy tests and authorizing the Justice Department to send federal officers to register voters in uncooperative cities, counties, and states. (p. 309)

THINK
- Why was Dr. Martin Luther King Jr. successful in changing the public's perception of race discrimination?
- Why did the civil rights movement focus on getting legislation passed in Congress?

9.3 Review Question: Free Response

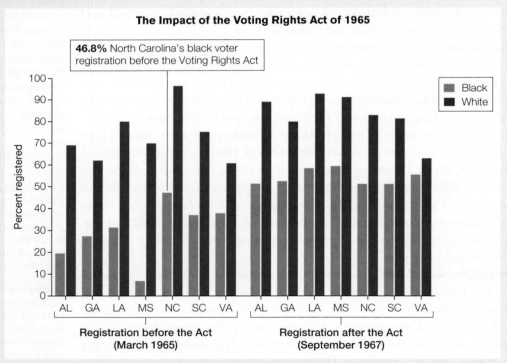

The Impact of the Voting Rights Act of 1965

46.8% North Carolina's black voter registration before the Voting Rights Act

Registration before the Act (March 1965)

Registration after the Act (September 1967)

Use the bar chart and your knowledge of U.S. Government and Politics to answer parts A, B, and C.

A. Describe one change in voter registration that occurred between March 1965 and September 1967.

B. Describe the Voting Rights Act of 1965 and explain how it had an impact on voter turnout among African Americans.

C. Describe one limitation of the data shown in the bar charts.

9.4 The Fight for Women's Rights

Although they constitute a slight majority of the American population, women have also fought to secure their civil rights throughout the nation's history. The women's rights movement took place in two waves. The first wave, in the nineteenth century, focused on the right to vote. The second wave, which began in the middle of the twentieth century, focused on equality in the classroom and the workplace.

The Nineteenth Amendment: Enfranchising Women

Unlike the efforts to secure the civil rights of African Americans through the judicial system, women's rights activists, especially in the first wave, used a legislative strategy. The Wyoming Territory granted the women the right to vote in 1869. By 1918, fifteen states had passed laws allowing women's suffrage.

The **Nineteenth Amendment**, ratified in 1920, gave women the right to vote nationwide. The amendment states, "The right of citizens of the United States to vote shall not be denied or abridged by the United States or by any State on account of sex. Congress shall have power to enforce this article by appropriate legislation."

Although the constitutional right to vote came later for women than it did for African Americans, women did not face the same kind of tactics to prevent them from voting. Yet even though women were allowed to vote, they continued to face significant discrimination.

Nineteenth Amendment
a 1920 constitutional amendment granting women the right to vote.

Beyond the Vote: The Second Wave

The second wave of the women's rights movement began in the 1960s. Like the first wave, much of the strategy involved changing laws. The second wave addressed inequalities at work and in the home, as well as protection from violence and sexual harassment.

Betty Friedan was one of the early leaders of this second wave. Her 1963 book, *The Feminine Mystique*, highlighted the ways in which American society assumed that women were best suited for roles as wives and mothers. Friedan challenged these assumptions and wanted a "dramatic reshaping of the cultural image of femininity that will permit women to reach maturity, identity, completeness of self, without conflict. . . ."[55] Friedan was the first president of the National Organization for Women (NOW), a women's rights advocacy group that pushed for change in both the legislature and the Supreme Court. NOW initially organized to pressure the federal government to enforce federal antidiscrimination laws. The organization's goals, however, became much more sweeping: "The purpose of NOW is to take action to bring women into full participation in the mainstream of American society now, exercising all the privileges and responsibilities thereof in truly equal partnership with men."[56]

The Civil Rights Act of 1964 was crucial to these legislative and legal efforts. Title VII of the act prohibits discrimination in employment based on race, color, religion, national origin, or sex.[57] In the 1960s and 1970s, women's rights activists secured several other important pieces of legislation. They also lobbied to ensure that these laws were vigorously enforced—to make sure that women were treated equally in the workplaces and schools. Women secured protections against discrimination based on gender, pregnancy, or childbirth. Many of these laws contain language making it illegal to retaliate against employees who file discrimination claims. Protections against gender discrimination apply not just to workplaces but also to schools, states, and local governments.

Betty Friedan in a 1970 protest march commemorating the fiftieth anniversary of the ratification of the Nineteenth Amendment. Friedan was a writer, an activist in efforts to secure equal rights for American women, and the first president of the National Organization for Women.
Fred W. McDarrah/Getty Images

Women's Rights and Public Policy: Title IX

One of the most notable provisions protecting women's equality in education is contained in a set of amendments to the Higher Education Act passed in 1972. **Title IX** of these amendments states, "No person in the United States shall, on the basis of sex, be excluded from participation in, or denied the benefits of, or subjected to discrimination under any educational program or activity receiving federal aid."[58] While its provisions apply equally to curriculum, health care, and residential life, Title IX has had a major impact on female participation in sports. Fewer than 300,000 girls played high school sports in 1974. By 2012, more than 3.1 million girls played high school sports.[59]

Speaking at a premiere of a documentary about Title IX, Olympic track and field gold medalist Jackie Joyner-Kersee stated, "We have to educate a generation that's continuing to benefit from it. A lot of people don't even know what Title IX is. And we can't let that happen. It's important that this generation be a voice to not let Title IX die."[60]

The Equal Rights Amendment

The women's rights movement failed to secure ratification of the Equal Rights Amendment (ERA). The proposed amendment read, "Equality of rights under the law shall not be denied or abridged by the United States or by any state on account of sex." The proposed amendment easily cleared the two-thirds vote requirement of the House of Representatives in 1971 and the Senate in 1972. By 1977, thirty-five of the required thirty-eight states had ratified the ERA. No more states, however, would ratify. Even though Congress extended its ratification deadline, the clock ran out on the ERA in 1982, and the amendment died.

Scholars continue to debate why the ERA failed. Part of the reason is that the Framers made it difficult to amend the Constitution. The two-stage process for ratification is a very high hurdle. Proponents were not as successful at the state level as they were in Congress. Many states ratified early, allowing opponents to concentrate their resources on a small number of remaining states.[61] Additionally, the controversy surrounding the Supreme Court's decision on abortion in *Roe v. Wade* (see Chapter 8) may have mobilized opponents to the proposed amendment.[62] Although the Equal Rights Amendment was not ratified, the debate over its ratification increased awareness of women's rights issues. In the absence of the Equal Rights Amendment, the Fourteenth Amendment and Title VII of the Civil Rights Act of 1964 provide a basis for the Supreme Court decisions regarding women's rights.

Supreme Court Decisions on Gender Discrimination and Sexual Harassment

The Court uses three different standards to determine the constitutionality of laws that treat people differently based on their characteristics. In cases involving race discrimination, the Court applies a standard of strict scrutiny. Under the strict scrutiny standard, a

Title IX of the Higher Education Amendments of 1972
legislation prohibiting sex discrimination in schools receiving federal aid, which had the impact of increasing female participation in sports programs.

government has to show a "compelling interest" to justify the unequal treatment, a high standard that is difficult to meet.

At the other end of the spectrum is the rational-basis standard, in which differential treatment must be shown to be reasonable and not arbitrary.[63] This is a much lower bar legally. Under the application of the rational basis standard, for example, air traffic controllers must retire at age fifty-six.[64]

Cases involving gender discrimination fall somewhere in between these two standards, and the Court uses intermediate scrutiny. While the Court doesn't place gender on the same level as race, it reviews claims of gender discrimination using a higher standard than, for example, age or disability. In general, the Court has found most forms of differential treatment for men and women to be unconstitutional, except when such treatment can be justified as serving important governmental objectives. For example, the Court has upheld the law that requires males, but not females, to register for the military draft.[65]

Although Title VII of the Civil Rights Act of 1964 does not specifically mention sexual harassment, the Court has ruled in several recent cases that sexual or gender-based harassment violates the act's antidiscrimination provisions.[66] The Court has identified two types of harassment. *Quid pro quo* harassment occurs when employers request or demand sexual favors in return for advancement or employment. A *hostile working environment* involves actions, statements, or conditions that unreasonably interfere with the ability of employees to do their jobs. In cases of quid pro quo harassment, employers can be found liable for the behavior of their offending employees, even if the employer did not know about the behavior at the time it occurred. In cases involving hostile working environments, employers are generally held liable only if they knew about the offending behavior but did nothing to stop it.

Civil Rights and the American Experience

In this chapter, we have focused on efforts to secure civil rights for Americans with disabilities, African Americans, and women. The right of gays and lesbians to marry was discussed in Chapter 3. Throughout the nation's history, however, members of many other groups have acted to secure their own rights.

Native Americans have fought to preserve their traditions and identities since the first arrival of the European colonists. Drawing upon lessons from the American civil rights movement, a group of Native American activists occupied Alcatraz Island in 1969 in protest of American policies that took away Native American lands and tried to force Native Americans to assimilate. The last of the protestors was removed nineteen months after the protest began, but the occupation had helped call national attention to historical and current grievances against the federal government.

Similarly, Latinos fight for their rights through protest, organization, education, and mobilization to challenge discrimination against members of their communities, especially on issues such as immigration, education, and labor policy. As they are the fastest growing group of Americans, issues of concern to Latinos are quickly gaining the attention of politicians and the major political parties. Individuals and groups have also mobilized to secure the rights of gay, lesbian, transgender, and transsexual Americans. Groups of Americans continue to assert their civil rights, based upon the Fourteenth Amendment's guarantee of equal protection of the laws.

In the United States in the twenty-first century, the concept of racial identity is complicated. Traditional racial and ethnic identifications have been used as the basis for evaluating compliance with the Civil Rights Act of 1964, the Voting Rights Act, and educational desegregation policies. Multiracial Americans have increasingly been carving out a space for themselves in discourse and policies involving race and ethnicity. In 2000, the

AP® TIP

Be ready to explain how the Fourteenth Amendment's equal protection clause has served as the basis for the expansion of civil rights to new groups, including the disabled and members of the LGBT communities.

United States Census allowed individuals to select more than one racial category. Slightly more than 2 percent chose to do so. By 2010 the number of Americans self-identifying as multiracial increased by 32 percent, to about nine million Americans. Where the most common combination in 2000 was "white and some other race," by 2010, the most common combination was "black and white." Furthermore, over the same ten-year period, the population of multiracial children increased by 50 percent, "making it the fastest growing youth group in the country."[67]

The twenty-first century is a time of major change in American civil rights policies, laws, and perceptions. The struggle to achieve equality has never been simple or clear, and it has only grown more complex. Whatever future attempts to secure civil rights in the United States bring, however, this much is certain: Those attempts will require learning from the past and approaching the future with courage and conviction.

Section Review

9.4 Examine the struggle by the women's rights movement for gender equality.

REMEMBER
- The first wave of the women's right movement focused on the right to vote.
- The second wave of the movement focused on equality in education and the workplace.
- Gender equality includes legal protections against sexual harassment.

KNOW
- *Nineteenth Amendment*: a 1920 constitutional amendment granting women the right to vote. (p. 311)
- *Title IX of the Higher Education Amendments of 1972*: legislation prohibiting sex discrimination in schools receiving federal aid, which had the impact of increasing female participation in sports programs. (p. 312)

THINK
Although Title IX provides women with equal educational opportunities in academics, why does most of the discussion around Title IX focus on athletics?

9.4 Review Question: Free Response

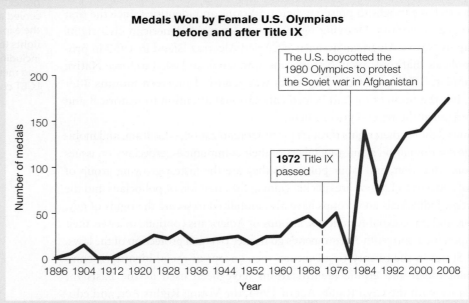

Medals Won by Female U.S. Olympians before and after Title IX

The U.S. boycotted the 1980 Olympics to protest the Soviet war in Afghanistan

1972 Title IX passed

Number of medals

Year

Data from International Olympic Committee

Use the graph and your knowledge of U.S. Government and Politics to answer parts A, B, and C.

A. Identify one trend shown in the graph.

B. Explain one way in which the Title IX of the Higher Education Act of 1972 impacted the trend shown in the graph.

C. Explain one other way in which Title IX impacted women's rights.

Chapter 9 Review

AP® KEY CONCEPTS

- *civil rights* (p. 293)
- *Thirteenth Amendment* (p. 297)
- *Fourteenth Amendment* (p. 297)
- *equal protection clause* (p. 297)
- *Fifteenth Amendment* (p. 297)
- *separate but equal* (p. 298)

- *legal segregation* (p. 299)
- *de jure segregation* (p. 302)
- *de facto segregation* (p. 302)
- *affirmative action* (p. 302)
- *social movement* (p. 306)
- *civil disobedience* (p. 306)

- *Civil Rights Act of 1964* (p. 309)
- *Voting Rights Act of 1965* (p. 309)
- *Nineteenth Amendment* (p. 311)
- *Title IX of the Higher Education Amendments of 1972* (p. 312)

AP® EXAM PRACTICE and Critical Thinking Project

MULTIPLE-CHOICE QUESTIONS

Today, education is perhaps the most important function of state and local governments. Compulsory school attendance laws and the great expenditures for education both demonstrate our recognition of the importance of education to our democratic society. It is required in the performance of our most basic public responsibilities, even service in the armed forces. It is the very foundation of good citizenship. Today it is a principal instrument in awakening the child to cultural values, in preparing him for later professional training, and in helping him to adjust normally to his environment. In these days, it is doubtful that any child may reasonably be expected to succeed in life if he is denied the opportunity of an education. Such an opportunity, where the state has undertaken to provide it, is a right which must be made available to all on equal terms.

—*Brown v. Board of Education*, 347 U.S. 493 (1954)

1. Which of the following constitutional principles are addressed in the quote?
   A. due process and equal protection
   B. due process and federalism
   C. judicial review and due process
   D. federalism and equal protection

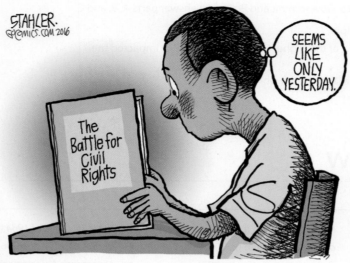

2. Which of the following best describes the viewpoint in the cartoon?

  A. The struggle for civil rights is ongoing.

  B. The civil rights movement is relatively new.

  C. Many schools are still segregated by race.

  D. Schools should teach students about the civil rights movement.

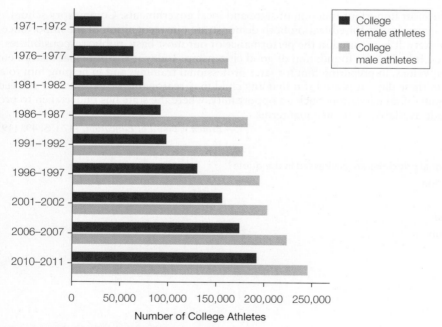

Data from National Collegiate Athletic Association

3. The bar chart best supports which of the following conclusions?

  A. The number of male college athletes increased every year from 1971 to 2011.

  B. Since the passage of Title IX of the Higher Education Act of 1972, the number of female athletes participating in college sports has increased each year.

  C. As of 2011, fewer men than women participated in college athletics.

  D. Title IX of the Higher Education Act of 1972 has been successful in increasing access for women to higher education.

4. Select the answer that matches the constitutional provision with the right it protects.

Constitutional provision	Protection
A. Equal protection clause	Prohibits discrimination based on race
B. Due process clause	Provides for affirmative action programs
C. Thirteenth Amendment	Provides African American men with the right to vote
D. Nineteenth Amendment	Provides equal rights for women

Use the table of data to answer question 5.

**Racial Composition of Schools Attended by
the Average Student of Each Race, December 2011**

Percent Race in Each School	Racial Composition of School Attended by Average:			
	White Student	Black Student	Asian Student	Latino Student
White	72.5%	27.6%	38.9%	25.1%
Black	8.3%	48.8%	10.7%	10.9%
Asian	3.9%	3.6%	24.5%	4.7%
Latino	11.8%	17.1%	22.1%	56.8%
Other	3.5%	2.9%	3.8%	2.5%

Note: Other represents students who identified as Native American or Multiracial.

Data from U.S. Department of Education, National Center for Education Statistics.

5. The table supports which of the following statements?
  A. *Brown v. Board of Education* successfully eliminated de jure segregation.
  B. *Brown v. Board of Education* successfully reduced de facto segregation.
  C. As of 2011, de facto segregation still existed in schools.
  D. Most public schools mirror the ethnic composition in their communities.

---

6. Which of the following best explains why many public schools in the South remained segregated in the immediate aftermath of the Supreme Court's decision in *Brown v. Board of Education*?
  A. The Supreme Court's decision was overturned by congressional legislation.
  B. The Supreme Court must rely on other branches of government to carry out its decisions.
  C. State governments had the authority to ignore the decision because education is a state issue.
  D. The civil rights movement began focusing on other issues, such as voting rights.

---

7. Select the pair that matches the correct legal standard with the type of discrimination.

Legal standard of review	Type of discrimination
A. Strict scrutiny	Disability
B. Mid-level review	Gender
C. Rational basis test	Race
D. Reverse discrimination test	Age

8. Which of the following best explains why the Equal Rights Amendment did not become part of the Constitution?

   A. At the time it was proposed, most Americans did not support equal rights for women.

   B. It failed to receive a two-thirds vote in Congress.

   C. It was not ratified by three-quarters of the states.

   D. It was unnecessary due to the passage of the Nineteenth Amendment.

Dear Director of Admissions, When you recently rejected my application, I'm not sure you were aware...

...THAT I IDENTIFY AS A Poor African-American Woman with a 4.0 average and a perfect S.A.T. score.

9. Which of the following best describes the viewpoint about affirmative action programs expressed in the cartoon?

   A. They help deserving students from underrepresented groups get into college.

   B. They benefit men and disadvantage women.

   C. They give minority students an unfair advantage over white students.

   D. They violate the equal protection clause of the Fourteenth Amendment.

Question 10 refers to this description.

Los Angeles last year pledged to spend $1.3 billion over three decades for massive infrastructure improvements—including fixing notoriously crumbling sidewalks . . . That too came out of a legal settlement, though this one was initiated by citizens and advocacy organizations. It appears to be the largest settlement of its kind in U.S. history, destined to not only transform the urban landscape, but also the way that priorities are set in City Hall.[68]

10. Which of the following laws did advocacy groups use in settling the case with Los Angeles described in the excerpt?

    A. The Americans with Disabilities Act

    B. The Civil Rights Act of 1964

    C. The Voting Rights Act of 1965

    D. Title IX of the Higher Education Act of 1972

FREE-RESPONSE QUESTIONS

1. In *Parents Involved in Community Schools v. Seattle School District No. 1*, the Supreme Court struck down a school district's plan to create more racially diverse schools by using race as a factor in determining whether a student could attend his or her school of choice, stating, "For schools that never segregated on the basis of race, . . . the way to achieve a system of determining admission to the public schools on a nonracial basis . . . is to stop assigning students on a racial basis. The way to stop discrimination on the basis of race is to stop discriminating on the basis of race."[69]

Use the scenario and your knowledge of U.S. Government and Politics to answer parts A, B, and C.

A. Identify the constitutional provision that is common to both *Parents Involved in Community Schools v. Seattle School District No. 1* (2007) and *Brown v. Board of Education* (1954).

B. Based on the constitutional provision identified in part A, explain how the facts of *Brown v. Board of Education* led to a different holding than in *Parents Involved in Community Schools v. Seattle School District No. 1*.

C. Other than the decision in *Brown v. Board of Education*, explain one way in which the civil rights movement has had an impact on public schools.

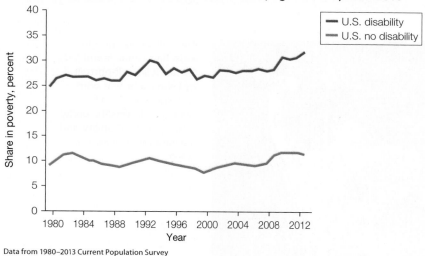

Share in Poverty, with or without Disabilities, Age 18 to 64, 1980–2018

Data from 1980–2013 Current Population Survey

2. Use the graph and your knowledge of U.S. Government and Politics to answer parts A, B and C.

A. Based on the graph, describe the relationship between having a disability and poverty.

B. Describe one provision of the Americans with Disabilities Act that was intended to address the problem shown in the graph.

C. Explain one strategy that activists could use to advocate for more civil rights for the disabled.

ARGUMENTATION QUESTION

In *United States v. Virginia* (1996),[70] the U.S. Supreme Court analyzed the question of whether Virginia's admissions policy to one of its state universities, the Virginia Military Institute (VMI), was unconstitutional because it restricted admissions to males. In describing the facts of that case, the Court noted the following:

> Founded in 1839, VMI is today the sole single-sex school among Virginia's 15 public institutions of higher learning. VMI's distinctive mission is to produce "citizen-soldiers," men prepared for leadership in civilian life and in military service. VMI pursues this mission through pervasive training of a kind not available anywhere else in Virginia. Assigning prime place to character development, VMI uses an "adversative method" modeled on English public schools and once characteristic of military instruction. VMI constantly endeavors to instill physical and mental discipline in its cadets and impart to them a strong moral code. The school's graduates leave VMI with heightened comprehension of their capacity to deal with duress and stress, and a large sense of accomplishment for completing the hazardous course.[71]

Develop an argument as to whether or not VMI's single-sex admissions policy is constitutional.

In your essay:

- Articulate a claim or thesis that responds to the prompt, and use a line of reasoning to defend it.
- Use at least TWO pieces of relevant and accurate evidence to support your claim.
- At least ONE piece of evidence must be from one of the listed foundational documents.
  - Brutus No. 1
  - United States Constitution
  - *Federalist* No. 78
- Use a second piece of evidence from another foundational document from the list or from your study of civil rights.
- Use reasoning to explain why the evidence you provided supports your claim or thesis.
- Use refutation, concession, or rebuttal to respond to an opposing or alternative perspective.

CRITICAL THINKING PROJECT

Civil Rights through Art

This collage by Chicago artist Riva Lehrer is entitled "At 54." It is a self-portrait by Lehrer, who was born with spina bifida. In her work, she depicts the body, adaptation to disability, and a strong will to overcome adversity.
Riva Lehrer

Art can be a powerful tool in getting your message across. Civil rights activists are often passionate about their causes, and artwork can convey powerful and emotional messages.

1. Choose a civil right group that interests you.
2. Research artwork that was created in connection with the group you chose.
3. Choose a piece of artwork that speaks to you. This can be a painting, poster, sculpture, collage, or any other artistic expression that represents civil rights.
4. Write a paragraph explaining how the work conveys the artist's message. Consider the mood, color, and composition of the work.

Alternate assignment: If you cannot find a work that sparks your interest, or if you'd like to be creative, make your own piece of art conveying a message about civil rights.

AP® EXAM PRACTICE and Critical Thinking Project

MULTIPLE-CHOICE QUESTIONS

1. Which of the following best describes the Supreme Court's ruling in a case of selective incorporation?
   - **A.** Government-sponsored prayers at a public high school graduation violate the establishment clause.
   - **B.** Cities may not prohibit the individual ownership of firearms.
   - **C.** De facto school segregation violates the equal protection clause.
   - **D.** Racial admissions quotas in public colleges violate the equal protection clause of the Fourteenth Amendment.

The description of the case applies to questions 2 and 3.

The city of Pawtucket, Rhode Island, along with several local businesses, sponsored a holiday display, which included a manger scene portraying the birth of Jesus, along with Santa Claus, reindeer, a clown, an elephant, a teddy bear, and holiday lights. A group of citizens brought a lawsuit claiming the display violated the Constitution. In *Lynch v. Donnelly* (1984), the Supreme Court ruled that Pawtucket's display did not violate the Constitution in a 5–4 decision.[1]

2. Which of the following provisions in the First Amendment was the basis for the lawsuit described?
   - **A.** Free exercise clause
   - **B.** Freedom of speech
   - **C.** Establishment clause
   - **D.** Right to petition

3. Which of the following best explains why the court ruled differently in *Lynch v. Donnelly* than it did in *Engel v. Vitale* (1962)?
   - **A.** The *Engel* case involved a Christian prayer.
   - **B.** The holiday display in Pawtucket was not state-sponsored.
   - **C.** Students have fewer rights in schools than citizens have in the community.
   - **D.** Taken as a whole, the holiday display did not advance or endorse a particular religion.

David Fitzsimmons/Cagle Cartoons, Inc.

4. The cartoon expresses which of the following viewpoints?
   - **A.** Hate speech should be subject to reasonable time, place, and manner restrictions.
   - **B.** Talk-radio hosts who engage in hate speech are a threat to the Constitution.
   - **C.** The government should be able to censor speech based on its content.
   - **D.** The First Amendment protects offensive speech.

5. In 2017, several players in the National Football League kneeled during the national anthem to draw the public's attention to racial inequality. President Trump responded to the protest with a statement that NFL owners should fire players who engage in such protests. Which of the following best describes how this issue relates to constitutional rights?

    A. This is not a free speech issue under the First Amendment because the NFL is a private organization.
    B. President Trump's statement violated the First Amendment because the government threatened to take action against a political protest.
    C. Congress has the authority to limit the players' political speech under the Commerce Clause.
    D. The First Amendment right to petition for a redress of grievances protects the players' political protest.

6. Which of the following best describes the exclusionary rule?

    A. Confessions are not admissible in court unless a suspect has an attorney present during questioning.
    B. Defendants found not guilty may not be tried again for the same offense in the same jurisdiction.
    C. Evidence obtained by authorities without a valid warrant is inadmissible in court.
    D. Defendants have the right to remain silent, which excludes their testimony from court proceedings.

7. The First Amendment does not protect which of the following types of speech?

    A. Protests that criticize government officials and call for their trial and impeachment
    B. Speech that disturbs the peace, in violation of reasonable local regulations
    C. Rallies led by white supremacist groups, advocating racial segregation
    D. Symbolic speech, such as burning a flag

8. The right to remain silent and to have a lawyer present during questioning are examples of:

    A. Equal protection under the law
    B. The right to petition for a writ of habeas corpus
    C. Protections for defendants provided by the Eighth Amendment
    D. Procedural due process

9. In the 1990s, several state legislatures passed "three-strikes" laws mandating that defendants convicted of a third serious offense be sentenced to twenty years or more in prison. Which of the following is the best constitutional argument against three-strikes laws?

    A. They violate the free speech clause of the First Amendment because defendants are not allowed to argue for shorter sentences.
    B. They violate the double jeopardy clause of the Fifth Amendment because defendants are being punished more than once for the same crime.
    C. They violate the equal protection clause of the Fourteenth Amendment because defendants with three convictions are not treated the same as defendants with fewer convictions.
    D. They violate the right to counsel under the Sixth Amendment because attorneys are not allowed to argue for shorter sentences for their clients.

10. The cartoon refers to civil liberties provided in the
    A. First Amendment
    B. Sixth Amendment
    C. Fourth Amendment
    D. Fifth Amendment

_____

11. A female college professor at a public university believes she was not granted tenure because of her gender. Which of the following is the best legal basis for her claim against the university?
    A. The Fourteenth Amendment's equal protection clause
    B. The Civil Rights Act of 1964
    C. Title IX of the Higher Education Act of 1972
    D. The Fourteenth Amendment's due process clause

12. Which of the following is a reason why civil rights activists might advocate for legislation, instead of filing lawsuits through the judicial system?
    A. Congress is more likely to protect the rights of minorities than the court system.
    B. The judiciary lacks the power to implement its decisions.
    C. Members of Congress are accountable to the majority, while the judiciary is not accountable to the majority.
    D. Legislation is more permanent than Supreme Court precedent.

Questions 13 and 14 refer to this scenario.

In *Milliken v. Bradley*,[2] the Supreme Court overturned a busing plan aimed at achieving racial diversity between the Detroit school system, where a high percentage of African Americans lived, and suburban school districts, where a high percentage of white children lived. The majority opinion stated, "Because of this inherent limitation upon federal judicial authority, federal court decrees exceed appropriate limits if they are aimed at eliminating a condition that does not violate the Constitution or does not flow from such a violation."[3]

13. Those who supported the busing plan relied on which of the following as part of their legal argument?
    A. The Voting Rights Act of 1965
    B. *Brown v. Board of Education* (1954)
    C. Title IX of the Higher Education Act of 1972
    D. *Plessy v. Ferguson* (1896)

14. According to the quotation, which of the following best explains the Supreme Court's decision to overturn the busing plan?

A. Suburban school districts did not engage in race discrimination.

B. Detroit city schools and suburban schools offered equal educational opportunities.

C. The busing plan resulted in reverse discrimination against students and parents who disagreed with the plan.

D. There is no significant government interest in increasing racial diversity in public schools.

_____

15. Select the answer where both columns correctly identify a civil right and a civil liberty.

Civil rights	Civil liberties
A. Right to a fair trial	Laws prohibiting discrimination against the disabled
B. Laws against sexual harassment	Laws preventing age discrimination
C. Equality for women in education	Right to privacy
D. Equal Rights Amendment	Voting Rights Act of 1965

_____

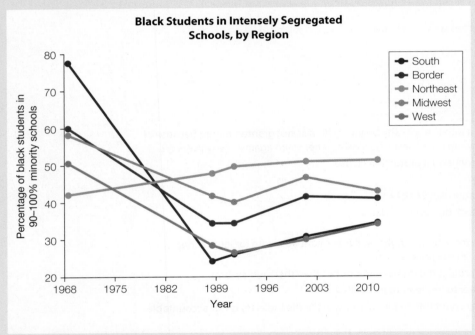

Black Students in Intensely Segregated Schools, by Region

Data from U.S. Department of Education, National Center for Education Statistics; before 1991, from the Office of Civil Rights

16. The graph supports which of the following statements?

A. The Court's decision in *Brown v. Board of Education* had no impact on segregation in the South.

B. In 2010, the percentage of African American students in intensely segregated schools was highest in the South.

C. The Court's decision in *Brown v. Board of Education* was unsuccessful in ending de facto segregation.

D. Court-ordered busing programs have successfully ended racial segregation in schools throughout the country.

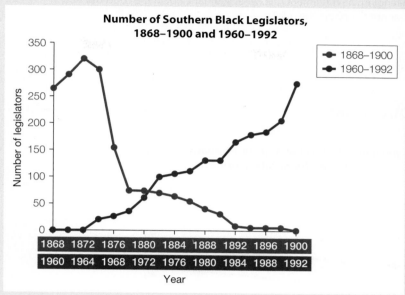

Number of Southern Black Legislators, 1868–1900 and 1960–1992

Data from U.S. Department of Justice, Civil Rights Division

17. Which of the following best describes a trend shown in the graph?

A. From 1964 to 1992, voter turnout among African Americans increased steadily.

B. From 1868 to 1900, voter turnout among African Americans decreased steadily.

C. Voter turnout among African Americans was not impacted by passage of the Fifteenth Amendment in 1870.

D. From 1964, the number of African Americans in the South elected to the legislature steadily increased.

18. The trend shown in the graph from 1960 until 1992 is best explained by the passage of which law?

A. Civil Rights Act of 1964

B. Voting Rights Act of 1965

C. Title IX of the Higher Education Amendments of 1972

D. Fourteenth Amendment equal protection clause

Question 19 refers to the quotation.

One who breaks an unjust law must do so openly, lovingly, and with a willingness to accept the penalty. I submit that an individual who breaks a law that conscience tells him is unjust, and who willingly accepts the penalty of imprisonment in order to arouse the conscience of the community over its injustice, is in reality expressing the highest respect for law.
—Dr. Martin Luther King Jr., "Letter from Birmingham Jail"

19. The quote from King advocates for which of the following tactics?

A. Civil disobedience

B. Public protest

C. The right to petition for a redress of grievances

D. Obeying the rule of law

20. The mandatory retirement age for most officers in the military is sixty-two.[4] If a military officer brought a lawsuit challenging the retirement rule, what standard would the court use in determining whether or not to uphold the rule?

A. rational basis test

B. mid-level scrutiny

C. compelling interest test

D. strict scrutiny

FREE-RESPONSE QUESTIONS

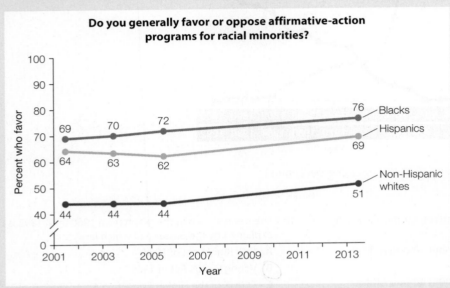

Data from Gallup

1. Use the graph and your knowledge of U.S. Government and Politics to answer parts A, B, and C.

A. Define affirmative action and describe one trend shown in the graph.

B. Explain how the equal protection clause of the Fourteenth Amendment might be used in an argument in favor of affirmative-action programs.

C. Explain how the equal protection clause of the Fourteenth Amendment might be used in an argument in opposition to affirmative-action programs.

2. The following is an excerpt from a speech given at a student assembly by Matthew Fraser in support of his friend Jeff Kuhlman's bid for student council "I know a man who is firm—he's firm in his pants, he's firm in his shirt, his character is firm—but most . . . of all, his belief in you, the students of Bethel, is firm. Jeff Kuhlman is a man who takes his point and pounds it in. If necessary, he'll take an issue and nail it to the wall. He doesn't attack things in spurts—he drives hard, pushing and pushing until finally—he succeeds. Jeff is a man who will go to the very end—even the climax, for each and every one of you." In *Bethel v. Fraser*, the United States Supreme Court ruled that the school did not violate Fraser's rights in suspending him.[5]

Use the scenario and your knowledge of U.S. Government and Politics to answer parts A, B, and C.

A. Identify the constitutional provision that was at issue in both *Tinker v. Des Moines Independent Community School District* (1969) and *Bethel v. Fraser* (1986).

B. Describe the ruling in *Tinker v. Des Moines Independent Community School District* (1969).[6]

C. Describe one way in which the facts in *Bethel v. Fraser* differ from the facts in *Tinker v. Des Moines Independent Community School District*, and explain how the difference you described impacted the ruling in *Bethel v. Fraser*.

ARGUMENTATION QUESTION

In the landmark decision in *Brown v. Board of Education* (1954), the Supreme Court ruled that de jure segregation in public schools violated the equal protection clause of the Fourteenth Amendment. Articulate a thesis about whether or not the Court's decision in *Brown v. Board of Education* was successful in reducing racial discrimination.

In your essay:

- Articulate a claim or thesis that responds to the prompt, and use a line of reasoning to defend it.
- Use at least TWO pieces of relevant and accurate evidence to support your claim.
- At least ONE piece of evidence must be from one of the listed foundational documents:
  - The Declaration of Independence
  - *Brown v. Board of Education* (1954)
  - United States Constitution
  - Martin Luther King Jr.'s "Letter from Birmingham Jail"
- Use a second piece of evidence from another foundational document from the list or from your study of civil rights.
- Use reasoning to explain why the evidence you provided supports your claim or thesis.
- Use refutation, concession, or rebuttal to respond to an opposing or alternative perspective.

CRITICAL THINKING PROJECT

Rights and Liberties around the World

Several organizations measure civil rights and liberties around the world. Freedom House rates countries according to their levels of civil rights and civil liberties and reports their status as not free, partially free, or free.

1. Pick a country that interests you. If you are planning to take AP® Comparative Government and Politics, you are encouraged to select one of the countries studied in that course: the United Kingdom, Mexico, Russia, China, Iran, or Nigeria.
2. Go to the Freedom House Web site at www.freedomhouse.org. Research the scores and status for the United States and your selected country.
3. In the Freedom House Web site, click on "regional trends," and read about the threats to civil rights and liberties throughout the world.
4. Create a table, graph, or chart using some of the data you collected.
5. Below the visual you created, write a paragraph about the biggest threat to civil rights and liberties worldwide. Does this threat apply to the United States and to the country you selected? Why or why not?

Unit 4

American Political Ideologies and Beliefs

Students and other members of the Oklahoma University community participate in the Indigenous Peoples' Day Parade. Parades affirm community, gauge public opinion, and often include politicians on floats looking for votes. For many young people, attending a Fourth of July parade is an early experience of political culture, and marching in a parade is a form of political participation.

Sarah Hussain/Red Dirt Report

Chapter 10
American Political Culture

Chapter 11
Public Opinion

Chapter 12
Political Ideology

Sarah Hussain/Red Dirt Report

American political culture consists of beliefs about government, politics, policies, and the individual's role in our democratic political system. Core American values include support for individualism, the rule of law, limited government, the free market, and equality of opportunity.

Citizens develop attitudes about government through political socialization, which occurs through contact with their families, schools, peers, and their social environment. Political attitudes are affected by someone's stage in life, called the lifecycle effect. Political events and national tragedies have an impact on generations that live through them. This is called the generational effect.

American political culture influences public policy. People have different ideals about how to balance individualism and freedom with order and security. These ideals influence their beliefs about economic and social policy. Some people favor active government involvement in promoting social equality and economic opportunity, while others believe excessive government regulation interferes with the free market and individual freedom.

The government influences the economy through fiscal and monetary policies. The Republican and Democratic parties have different views about how to use those policies to benefit the economy. The parties also disagree over social policies, such as health-care reform, and the role of government in providing social services to citizens. ■

At the age of five, George Takei was forced to go to a relocation camp in Arkansas during World War II. The reason? Because he is Japanese American. Now in his eighties, Takei has used his position as a cultural icon, the original Lieutenant Hikaru Sulu of *Star Trek,* to launch himself into the public sphere as an activist shaping public opinion against discrimination. His lively Facebook page has some 9 million followers.

Frazer Harrison/Getty Images

10 American Political Culture

What Americans Believe

Cowboys embody the American core values of individualism and self-determination. Western art and images are popular because they bring the past and present together in a lifestyle that still exists. Here, a cowboy rides across a field near the village of Lodge Pole, Montana.

Todd Klassy Photography

After reading this chapter, you will be able to

10.1 Describe Americans' core political values.

10.2 Describe how political socialization, cultural factors, and life experiences shape an individual's attitudes and beliefs about government.

10.3 Explain how American political culture has influenced other countries and been influenced by globalization.

Making a Difference Before She Could Vote

Hannah Sievers was a high school junior with strong political beliefs. Like her parents, Hannah supported the American core values of individualism, equality of opportunity, free enterprise, rule of law, and limited government. She was more conservative than most of her peers, and she proudly stood up for her values. At school, Hannah wore a necklace with a little gold elephant to represent her Republican beliefs.

Hannah was too young to vote, but she knew there were other ways to participate in politics in Colorado, where she lives. When her AP® U.S. Government and Politics teacher offered extra credit to volunteer in the 2016 campaign, Hannah decided to join in. The local Democratic Party offered several opportunities to volunteer. A recent graduate of Hannah's high school, representing the Democratic Party, visited the school asking for people to help with voter registration. None of these opportunities fit Hannah's core political beliefs. Then her teacher forwarded an email from Steve House, chairman of the Colorado Republican Party, asking for volunteers. Hannah became an intern for the Arapahoe County Republican Party, finding a place where she could help translate her beliefs into policy.

The Republican field office supported Donald Trump for the presidency, but its main focus was on getting Mike Coffman re-elected to the House of Representatives and on getting Darryl Glenn elected to the U.S. Senate. Coffman and Glenn supported traditional conservative positions. Glenn's Web site called the Patient Protection and Affordable Care Act a disaster.[1] Glenn argued that the Affordable Care Act should be repealed because it represents unnecessary government interference in individual choices. As we will see below, American individualism is one of America's core political values.

Coffman agreed with Glenn on health care and many other issues, including support for the Second Amendment right to own a firearm. Coffman believed that small businesses under the Obama administration were being "strangled by red tape."[2] He believed that under our current welfare system, "government often crosses the line to help those who can help themselves but have forgotten how."[3] Coffman's positions are consistent with another core American value, that of limited government. Breaking with many members of the Republican Party, Coffman supported the Deferred Action for Childhood Arrivals program, which allows individuals who were brought to the country as children to obtain legal status.

Darryl Glenn, running as the Republican candidate for U.S. Senate in 2016, talks to Norma Whitney during a visit to the Jefferson County Republican Party headquarters.
Michael Reaves/Getty Images

At age sixteen, Hannah Sievers joined the staff of the Arapahoe County Republican Party. She is shown here with her "war room" access pass. "Getting involved is an easy way to get your ideas out there," she says. "It will also make adults change the way they look at you and the generation you represent."[6]
Missy Sievers

Most of Hannah's political values aligned with Coffman and Glenn, and soon she was immersed in their campaigns. She recalled, "I was very nervous going into my first day, but I was also super excited. My first day, I asked a lot of questions. I was a high school student. I didn't know very much about the state parties or government. Most of the phone calls and emails I responded to were asking questions and I did not know the answers. My office manager was super helpful and very friendly, which made the job a lot easier."[4] She started at the front desk answering phone calls and emails. Hannah quickly learned about the policy positions of the candidates and about how to interact with callers.

Hannah then was asked to do projects for various employees in the office. These projects included researching laws, contacting government agencies, and creating spreadsheets. Hannah started writing letters and emails to constituents about how to get involved in the community, what events were coming up, and with reminders to vote.

Standing up for your core values isn't always easy, especially when you don't completely agree with the actions of your party's nominee. During the campaign, a news story broke featuring an old recording of President Trump making inappropriate comments about women.[5] Following the comments, Hannah had to do a lot of damage control. Many voters called her claiming they would stop supporting the Republican Party as long as the party supported Donald Trump. Although Hannah was uncomfortable with some of Donald Trump's behavior, she held firm to the core values that led her to the Republican Party, and she fully supported the candidacies of Mike Coffman and Daryl Glenn.

Hannah spent election day in the office calling citizens to remind them to go out and vote. While she was making phone calls, a friendly man came into the room and shook her hand. She looked up and saw Representative Mike Coffman. She was starstruck at first. Representative Coffman asked Hannah to set him up so that he could make calls, too.

Hannah had a long day. After the office closed, her boss asked her to go to the hotel to help set up the viewing party scheduled for later that night. She stamped passes and sold tickets. Once the doors closed, Hannah went to the viewing party the AP® U.S. Government and Politics teachers were throwing. She was bombarded by students, most of them liberal. Hannah left the party and grabbed some dinner. She hadn't eaten all day.

At home, with her parents by her side, Hannah watched the results. Mike Coffman won, but Darryl Glenn, the candidate Hannah did the most work for, lost.

Normally, Hannah is quiet and reserved, and she was taken out of her comfort zone, making her stronger and more committed to seeing the policies she favors become law. Hannah remains committed to her conservative beliefs, and she is not afraid to speak her mind, advocating for individualism, the free market, and limited government.

Hannah Sievers made a difference before she was old enough to vote, and you can, too. In Hannah's words, "Before the age of eighteen, it may seem pointless to volunteer with some aspect of the government, but it is a way to voice your opinions and concerns. Being viewed as a 'child' can be challenging, especially when you care about your community."[7] Hannah's story goes beyond the topic of individual political participation. Sievers chose to work for candidates she believed best represented America's core values.

◼ 10.1 Core Political Values

American **political culture** is the dominant set of beliefs, customs, traditions, and values that define the relationship between citizens and the government. American core political values include individualism, equality of opportunity, the free enterprise system, rule of law, and limited government. Americans have interpreted these values differently throughout American history, which influences how citizens perceive the actions and role of the federal government. Differences over core values affect the ways citizens interact with each other.

Individualism

One of the core political values of American political culture is **individualism**—the belief that individuals should be responsible for themselves and for the decisions they make. Alexis de Tocqueville wrote about American individualism after traveling through the nation in 1831–32.[8] *Democracy in America*[9] became one of the earliest and most influential essays on American political life and culture. *Democracy in America* is best known for its discussion of Americans as a "nation of joiners,"[10] a topic that will be discussed in more detail in Chapter 15, which is about interest groups.

Tocqueville also understood that democratic equality fosters individualism:

> As social conditions become more equal, the number of persons increases who, although they are neither rich enough nor powerful enough to exercise any great influence over their fellow-creatures, have nevertheless acquired or retained sufficient education and fortune to satisfy their own wants. They owe nothing to any man, they expect nothing from any man; they acquire the habit of always considering themselves as standing alone, and they are apt to imagine that their whole destiny is in their own hands.[11]

AP® REQUIRED DOCUMENTS

In this chapter, you will review three required documents. Read them carefully. The following documents are required for the AP® U.S. Government and Politics course:

Document	Importance
Declaration of Independence	• Philosophical statement of natural rights • Argument that governments are put in place to protect natural rights • Argument that citizens have the right to rebel when government infringes on citizens' rights
Federalist No. 51	• Explanation of checks and balances • Argument that checks and balances limit the power of the government and prevent it from taking away citizens' rights
Federalist No. 78	• Discussion of the independent judiciary • Argument that an independent judiciary prevents other branches of government from becoming too powerful and protects citizens' rights and the rule of law

Tocqueville warned about the perils of individualism, which could result in a tyranny of the majority, impinging on the rights of the minority.[12] He also believed that as a nation of joiners Americans could overcome the isolating selfishness that could result from individualism.[13]

The core value of individualism was a driving force during settlement. Immigrants who founded the United States brought with them the belief that they could create a better life for themselves. Settlers moving west encountered Native Americans who wanted to protect their ways of life and heritage, but in the minds of white settlers, land was bountiful.

According to historian Frederick Jackson Turner, the frontier encouraged individualism.[14] However, the frontier was not settled solely through the efforts of individuals. The federal government actively pursued policies that fostered the settlement of the frontier. The frontier was conquered by the U.S. Army, surveyed by the government, and land was distributed and property rights enforced by government. The railroad, the telegraph, and the mail all were subsidized by government or directly run by the government. Historian James Willard Hurst demonstrated that citizens benefited from federal laws and regulations, which were actively used to promote "the release of creative energy" in the economy.[15]

The "millennial" generation continues this spirit of individualism. According to a Pew Research Center survey, millennials are less likely to identify as members of the Republican or Democratic parties, less likely to marry, and less religious than previous generations, as well as less likely to describe themselves as patriotic.[16] By a large margin, millennials, the generation born after 1980 who became adults at the turn of the century,[17] are less likely to trust others.[18] See Figure 10.1 for differences in levels of trust, from a study published in 2014. The American core value of individualism continues to evolve, and it seems even stronger among young people born after 1995.

FIGURE 10.1

Social Trust by Age Group

Percentage saying that most people can be trusted

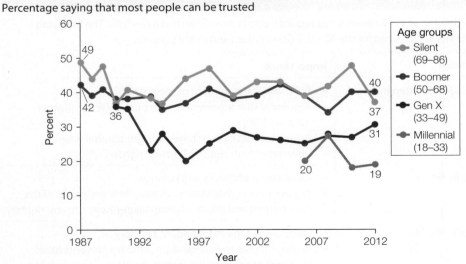

Data from the General Social Survey and Pew Media Center

Equality of Opportunity

The preamble to the Declaration of Independence includes the following statement about natural rights: "We hold these truths to be self-evident, that all men are created equal. . . ." It is a core American value that everyone should have a chance to succeed. The United States was founded on the idea that social status is based on effort, rather than inherited position. Americans also value political equality, which means that everyone should be able to influence government decision making.

While Americans value equality of opportunity, they do not support equality of result. The United States has not produced economic equality, in which everyone makes roughly the same amount of money or has the same amount of wealth. Rather, Americans value the opportunity to be rewarded for innovation, hard work, education, and determination. Affirmative action programs, discussed in Chapter 9, are one attempt to level the playing

AP® Political Science PRACTICES

Analyzing Implications of Visual Displays

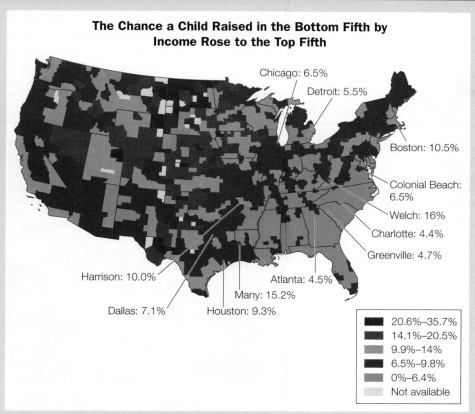

The Chance a Child Raised in the Bottom Fifth by Income Rose to the Top Fifth

Chicago: 6.5%
Detroit: 5.5%
Boston: 10.5%
Colonial Beach: 6.5%
Welch: 16%
Charlotte: 4.4%
Greenville: 4.7%
Harrison: 10.0%
Atlanta: 4.5%
Many: 15.2%
Dallas: 7.1%
Houston: 9.3%

Legend:
- 20.6%–35.7%
- 14.1%–20.5%
- 9.9%–14%
- 6.5%–9.8%
- 0%–6.4%
- Not available

Map based on data from the Equality of Opportunity Project

1. Identify one trend shown on the map.

2. Explain how the data in the map relate to the concept of equality of opportunity.

3. Based on the information in the map, explain whether or not the United States provides equality of opportunity to its citizens.

4. Describe a factor other than income that might be used to measure equality of opportunity.

field. Affirmative action is premised on the idea that American society and American government created an uneven playing field. Opponents of affirmative action programs argue that they hinder equality of opportunity by favoring some groups over others.

 Free Enterprise

laissez-faire or **free enterprise**
an economic system in which government intrudes as little as possible in the economic transactions among citizens and businesses.

Countries use different approaches in determining the proper level of government intervention in the economy. In a **laissez-faire**, or **free enterprise**, system, government plays as small a role as possible in the economic transactions among citizens and businesses. In a command-and-control economy, the government dictates much of the nation's economic activity: setting wages, prices, and production. America's economy is neither laissez-faire nor command-and-control. Rather, America has a mixed economy, in which many economic decisions are left to individuals and businesses, but the federal and state governments shape those decisions through taxation, spending, and regulation.

A culture of individualism is reflected in Americans' views on the economy. Americans tend to favor a free-market economy, with limited government intervention.[19]

Figure 10.2 shows how core values were used to promote patriotism.

The U.S. government is smaller and the social services it provides are more limited compared to the governments of most advanced industrialized democracies.[20] See Figure 10.3. A smaller percentage of the federal budget goes toward social services, and Americans pay lower taxes than their counterparts in European advanced democracies.[21]

FIGURE 10.2

A World War II Poster and Its Appeal to the U.S. System of Values

This poster was designed and published during World War II as part of the war effort on the home front. The poster advocates free enterprise and equality of opportunity as core American values.
Office for Emergency Management. Office of War Information. Domestic Operations Branch. Bureau of Special Services. 3/9/1943-9/15/1945

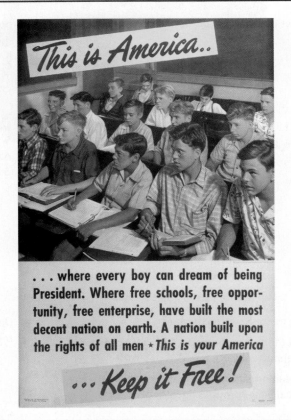

FIGURE 10.3

Welfare Benefits in High-Income Countries

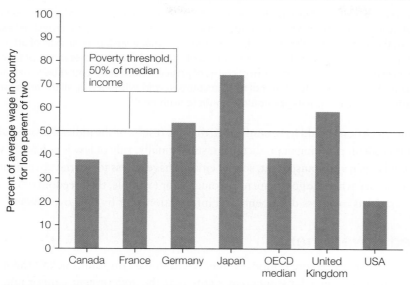

This bar chart compares need-based assistance, or welfare, benefits in the United States to those of five other countries, showing how close the combined benefits bring a recipient to the average wage. The OECD median bar represents the average of the thirty-five high-income countries of the Organisation for Economic Co-operation and Development.

Data from Organisation for Economic Co-operation and Development

Yet the federal government must balance the American core value of free enterprise with citizens' demands that the government ensure equality, stability, and protection from unforeseen life events, such as natural disasters.

The tension between being concerned with equality and individualism has long characterized American political culture. Since the 1960s political scientists have shown that most Americans are both suspicious of government and at the same time turn to government for help in meeting challenges, expanding opportunities, and providing for economic security. Most Americans believe that some inequality in wealth and income is appropriate, but are bothered by current levels of inequality.[22]

The vast majority of democracies provide national health care, run by the government. Although the Patient Protection and Affordable Care Act[23] (Obamacare) required Americans to purchase health care, it is not nationalized medicine because the doctors and hospitals are still private organizations. Many Americans opposed the Affordable Care Act because they believed that it brought more government regulation into the health-care system.

Rule of Law

In *Federalist* No. 51, James Madison stated, "If men were angels, no government would be necessary. In framing a government which is to be administered by men over men, the great difficulty lies in this: you must first enable the government to control the governed; and in the next place oblige it to control itself."[24] This quote refers to the principle of **rule of law**, which means no one, including public officials, is above the law. The constitutional system of checks and balances was designed to keep one branch from becoming so powerful that it is above the law.

The principle of rule of law goes beyond checks and balances within the structure of government. Citizens must respect the law and abide by it. This is part of the social contract,

rule of law
the principle that no one, including public officials, is above the law.

discussed on page 9 in Chapter 1. Judicial independence, discussed in Chapter 6, ensures that everyone has a fair trial and that court decisions are impartial. In *Federalist* No. 78, Alexander Hamilton emphasizes the role of the judiciary in protecting the rule of law:

> The complete independence of the courts of justice is peculiarly essential in a limited Constitution. By a limited Constitution, I understand one which contains certain specified exceptions to the legislative authority; such, for instance, as that it shall pass no bills of attainder, no ex-post-facto laws, and the like. Limitations of this kind can be preserved in practice no other way than through the medium of courts of justice, whose duty it must be to declare all acts contrary to the manifest tenor of the Constitution void. Without this, all the reservations of particular rights or privileges would amount to nothing.[25]

Further, a citizen should have confidence that the results of the judicial process should be based on precedent, resulting in predictable results. Finally, rule of law is enhanced when the government is open and transparent, so that citizens have access to official government documents and can see what the government is doing.[26] For example, the Freedom of Information Act allows citizens to access documents and information kept by the government.[27]

Limited Government

Limited government is a core political value. Based in part on John Locke's theory of natural rights, human beings have inherent rights that the government cannot take away.[28] As we studied in Chapter 1, the Declaration of Independence rests on the theory that the government's authority comes from the consent of the governed and that citizens are "endowed . . . with certain unalienable rights" such as "life, liberty, and the pursuit of happiness."[29] Government must be limited to prevent it from taking away rights and liberties, and the government's legitimacy is based on public support. In the Declaration of Independence, Jefferson argued that citizens have the right to rebel when the government goes beyond its limits and infringes on the rights of citizens:

> [W]henever any Form of Government becomes destructive of these ends, it is the Right of the People to alter or to abolish it, and to institute new Government, laying its foundation on such principles and organizing its powers in such form, as to them shall seem most likely to effect their Safety and Happiness.[30]

Several features of the American system limit government. Congress is limited by the enumerated powers set forth in Article I, Section 8. The federal courts have limited jurisdiction as prescribed in Article III. And as Madison wrote in *Federalist* No. 51, checks and balances and federalism are designed to create a double security limiting the power of government. In addition, free and fair elections, at regular intervals, give the public an opportunity to remove officials if they abuse their power. As discussed in Chapter 4, the Bill of Rights contains protections to protect citizens from government actions that infringe on civil liberties. An independent judiciary is designed to prevent the government from taking citizens' life, liberty, or property without due process of law.

American Core Values and Public Policy: Need-Based Assistance

While Americans share the core political values of individualism, equality of opportunity, free enterprise, rule of law, and limited government, they often disagree about how to balance those values. One of the biggest areas of disagreement is need-based assistance welfare programs. Unlike entitlement programs such as Social Security and Medicare, which are funded through payroll taxes (paid by the employer and employee on a percentage of salaries) and do not require a demonstration of need, need-based assistance programs involve a means test that is usually based on income. In assessing who qualifies for need-based assistance, the federal government uses the poverty line, which defines an income below which a family is considered poor. In 2015, the federally defined poverty threshold for a family of four was an annual family income of $24,600.[31] Need-based social welfare policies are funded through federal and/or state tax revenues rather than payroll taxes.

In addition to covering health services for low-income Americans, the federal government also provides other forms of need-based assistance. Aid to Families with Dependent Children (AFDC) was created in the 1930s to help families support their children in the event that a parent was deceased, disabled, unable to work, or out of work. In the decades following, AFDC was expanded to aid parents as well, increasing the number of covered individuals as well as the cost of the program. AFDC was sometimes accused of cultivating dependency among the families receiving it and creating generations of families that received welfare benefits without working. This dependency contradicts the core American values of individualism and free enterprise, but it furthers a different American value of providing a safety net for those in need. When AFDC was ended, the claims about lifetime dependency were on weak ground. Congressional reports showed that only 30 percent of recipients received benefits for eight years or more. For the overwhelming majority welfare was a short-time bridge between jobs.[32]

In 1996, Bill Clinton signed the Personal Responsibility and Work Opportunity Reconciliation Act of 1996 (PRWORA). PRWORA gave states more authority over the administration of social welfare programs. The law placed time limits on receipt of welfare assistance and added work requirements for beneficiaries. PRWORA demonstrates a compromise between the core political value of encouraging individualism with the belief that the government must provide a safety net for vulnerable citizens.

Section Review

This chapter's main ideas are reflected in the Learning Targets. By reviewing after each section, you should be able to

—**Remember** the key points,

—**Know** terms that are central to the topic, and

—**Think** critically about U.S. political culture and how core values influence the behavior of each branch of government.

10.1 Describe Americans' core political values.

REMEMBER	• Core American political values include individualism, equality of opportunity, free enterprise, rule of law, and limited government.
	• Americans differ in their interpretation of core political values.
KNOW	• *political culture*: the dominant set of beliefs, customs, traditions, and values that define the relationship between citizens and government. (p. 333)
	• *individualism*: the belief that individuals should be responsible for themselves and for the decisions they make. (p. 333)
	• *laissez-faire* or *free enterprise*: an economic system in which government intrudes as little as possible in the economic transactions among citizens and businesses. (p. 336)
	• *rule of law*: the principle that no one, including public officials, is above the law. (p. 337)
THINK	How do the Constitution and Bill of Rights reflect American core values?

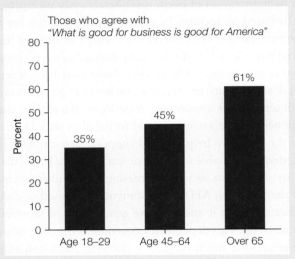

Those who agree with
"What is good for business is good for America"

Data from Aspen Institute American Values Survey

Use the bar chart and your knowledge of U.S. Government and Politics to answer parts A, B, and C.

A. Identify the trend shown in the bar chart.

B. Describe one core political value measured in the bar chart.

C. Explain how the U.S. government balances the core political value measured in the bar chart with another core political value.

political socialization
the experiences and factors that shape an individual's political values, attitudes, and behaviors.

political ideology
an individual's coherent set of beliefs about government and politics.

■ 10.2 Political Socialization

The formation and modification of opinions toward politics, public policy, and political figures is a lifelong process. Political scientists study how political attitudes are formed and change over time. **Political socialization** refers to the experiences and factors that shape an individual's **political ideology**, a coherent set of beliefs about government and politics.

Families, Schools, and Peers

> **AP® TIP**
>
> Make sure that you can distinguish political culture, political ideology, and political socialization. All three concepts are important, and students often get them confused.

The first and most important contributor to the process of political socialization is the family, especially when it comes to shaping children's views about political figures and political authority.[33] Party identification—the degree to which an individual identifies with and supports a particular political party—is strongly correlated with the family's political beliefs. Families are the first source of political information for children.[34] This process occurs through the parents' choice of news programs, comments made over the dinner table, and conversations about shared morals and values.

Schools play a role in political socialization. Several states require high school students to take an American government or civics class. These classes are meant to introduce students to how the government works and to the role of politics in our system.[35] Civic education can also transmit norms, such as the importance of civic participation.[36] As spaces of learning and community, schools are also important for their ability to create a respectful political climate. Schools introduce students to opportunities for political participation, and some schools require students to volunteer in their communities. Schools introduce political learners to students with different life experiences and viewpoints.[37] Discussing political issues with classmates may challenge a student's point of view, providing different perspectives. An individual's civic education does not occur on a blank canvas but one that has already been at least partially painted by his or her social class, race, religion, and education.

Civic and Religious Organizations

Churches and other religious organizations influence the political socialization of their members. In the past, Roman Catholics and Jews struggled for equality and were more liberal than Protestants. Today, Jews remain one of the most liberal groups in the country.[38] However, Catholics have become more conservative, mostly due to the Church's opposition to abortion. In the 2016 presidential election, the majority of white Catholics supported Donald Trump, while most Hispanic Catholics voted for Hillary Clinton.[39] Evangelical/born-again white Christians are one of the most conservative demographic groups.[40] Muslims strongly favor the Democratic Party, and three-quarters of them said they voted for Hillary Clinton in the 2016 presidential election.[41] Churches influence political socialization through their doctrinal positions on issues, sermons presented during their services, and through social interactions among members of the congregation.

Holy Ghost Catholic Church in Denver, Colorado, is the second oldest Catholic parish in the city. The church serves year round as a place where Catholics can express their faith as well as participate in volunteer work and social events. The Archdiocese of Denver runs a school system that socializes children by emphasizing Catholic values.
SuperStock/AGE Fotostock

Civic organizations also engage in political socialization. Volunteering for Habitat for Humanity or other local groups brings people together in their communities, where they learn to work for a common goal, compromise, and are exposed to different viewpoints. Habitat for Humanity organizes projects where volunteers and low-income families work together to build housing. The Better Block program brings volunteers together for painting, landscaping, rebuilding, and trash removal. In Chicago, Habitat for Humanity sponsors several additional programs that encourage community engagement.[42] In 2017, the Weatherization Collaboration brought 600 Chicagoans together to distribute and pick up kits to help people weatherize their homes. The West Pullman Tree Lighting ceremony, in partnership with several churches and community organizations, brings dozens of West Pullman community members together to light a tree and celebrate the holiday season.[43]

Civic engagement helps group members develop skills and experience in organizing, public speaking, fund-raising, and interacting with government officials. Group members learn about the norms of the organization.[44] These social interactions can influence an individual's political belief system.

Generational and Life-Cycle Effects

The political opinions that individuals hold tend to change for various reasons over the course of time. While families, schools, and peers play important early roles in political socialization, so do life experiences. The events that occur during a lifetime may also shape opinions on both individual and national levels, especially in times of crisis. People from the same generation have lived through the same events throughout the decades. This is known as the **generational effect**.

Views about political issues are also influenced by a person's stage in life. This is called the **life-cycle effect**. People who just graduated from college have different ideas about politics and the role of government from older Americans retiring from the workforce.

generational effect
the impact of historical events experienced by a generation upon their political views.

life-cycle effect
the impact of a person's age and stage in life on his or her political views.

For example, individuals who just graduated from high school may be more interested in college tuition assistance and the upcoming job market than workers who just retired and are concerned about Social Security and Medicare.

According to a Pew Research study, young people are far less likely than older adults to vote or to become involved in politics.[45] Young people may not be well informed about political issues, or they may not think they have much at stake in policy debates. As people age, they vote at higher rates and their levels of political interest and involvement rise. This does not mean that young people will never be interested in politics. According to the study, "Millennials are less engaged in politics today than are older generations, but the same was true of Baby Boomers in their youth. Today, Boomers are among the most likely to vote and participate in politics."[46]

Gertrude Gottschalk was one hundred years old in 2016, and she lived through the Great Depression and World War II. She has a long career of political participation, especially in the Democratic Party. Even as she passes the age of one hundred, though, Gottshalk remains politically active and doesn't understand people who don't vote.
Brad Coman/Nevada Appeal

One example of the generational effect is the impact of the Vietnam War and the Watergate affair on views of government. These events coincided with a sharp drop in public trust and confidence in government. Note the decline from 75 percent in 1965 to 45 percent in 1976, as shown in the graph. While trust in government has gone up and down since the 1970s, it has never returned to previous levels.[47]

Another example of a generational effect is the shift in public views on terrorism and national security following the terrorist attacks of September 11, 2001. After a brief period of patriotism and unity immediately following the attacks, a contentious debate emerged over how to balance security with personal liberty and privacy interests.[48]

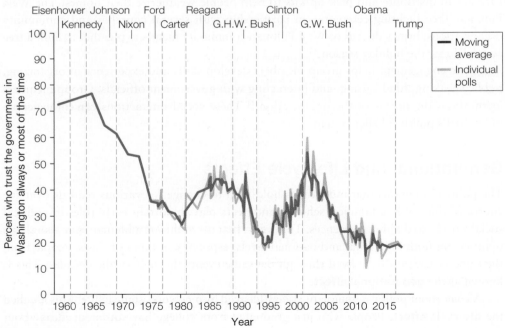

Public Trust in Government, 1958–2017

Data from Pew Research Center

Primary sources are statistics and data, eyewitness accounts, interviews, and original documents, such as the Constitution.[49] Secondary sources are interpretations, which are based on primary sources.[50]

As the 2016 presidential nomination process was under way, researchers, reporters, and political pundits weighed in on the potential impact of this generation's individual and collective decisions about whether or not to vote and who to vote for. One of the clearest themes that emerged was the effect of the economy on voting decisions. This factor had a profound impact on a generation maturing after the financial crisis of 2008 and saddled with levels of student debt unimaginable to earlier generations.

In a 2016 interview with *International Business Times*,[51] Tori Hall, a student at the Ohio State University and a board member of her school's Students for Bernie [Sanders] Club, countered criticisms that young adult Americans lacked interest in the elections, saying that she and her peers were constantly discussing the election. To Hall, her main reason for this interest was economic inequality in twenty-first-century America.

One of Hall's personal political interests is income inequality. She finds evidence for that in her own upbringing: Hall is paying for college herself. Her parents live paycheck-to-paycheck even though both of them have master's degrees.

"We went a winter without heat because we couldn't afford the gas bill. In the U.S., one of the wealthiest countries in the world, there shouldn't be anybody going through that. When I was 6, that's when 9/11 occurred. Then we entered two wars before I was even 8 years old. By 2008, we were in a financial crisis. . . . We're [looking for] the best candidate . . who's not part of the establishment."[52]

Young voters are united in their anger and disillusionment, having come of age during the Great Recession. President Trump tapped into that subset of those voters in the same way as Sanders, despite their radically different policy proposals, said Morley Winograd, a senior fellow at the University of Southern California who has authored books on millennials. Young voters think: "'The system is rigged, I need somebody to totally overthrow the system' and that's what Trump says he's going to do," he said. "You can understand where there might be those commonalities."[53]

Jeremy Wiggins, a junior at the University of Missouri and a delegate to the Republican National Convention, who supported Trump, echoed the same concern: "for somebody my age you're going to be in the job market very soon, starting your first job, getting health insurance and . . . we want the jobs to be there."[54]

On election day, roughly 37 percent of the millennial vote went to Trump, a larger segment of that population than expected, but virtually the same percentage that had voted for the 2012 Republican presidential candidate, Mitt Romney. Another way of looking at the voting percentages is that on election day, 63 percent of millennials voted for someone other than Trump, a greater percentage than was true for the overall population.

1. Identify one primary source and one secondary source within the excerpt. Describe the difference between a primary and a secondary source.

2. Explain why different members of the millennial generation, who shared the same experience of living through a recession, voted for opposing candidates on election day.

3. Describe one factor, other than generational effects, that shapes political socialization.

Historic events can have an outsized effect on members of one generation. During adolescence and young adulthood, people may become more aware of national and global affairs.[55] That's why members of the "Silent Generation," who lived through the Great Depression as teenagers, are often frugal and concerned about their economic security, even when they are doing well financially. Like their grandparents and great-grandparents, millennials experienced a major financial crisis in adolescence and early adulthood that has encouraged them to save money and spend conservatively.[56] On social issues, however, millennials are much more liberal than previous generations. For example, millennials are

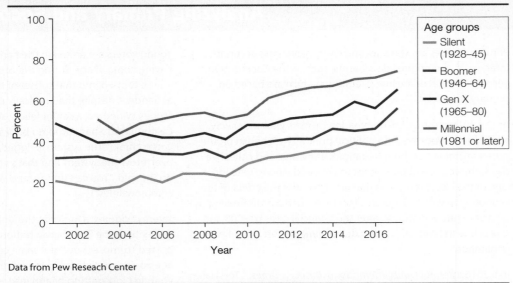

FIGURE 10.4

U.S. Adults Who Favor Same-Sex Marriage, by Generation (2001–2017)

Age groups
— Silent (1928–45)
— Boomer (1946–64)
— Gen X (1965–80)
— Millennial (1981 or later)

Data from Pew Reseach Center

almost twice as likely to support same-sex marriage as their grandparents.[57] See Figure 10.4 for a comparison across generations.

While parents, schools, and peers have an early influence on political beliefs and values, we continue to grow and change as we age and as we experience the events that impact our lives and the lives of those around us.

Section Review

10.2 Describe how political socialization, cultural factors, and life experiences have an impact on an individual's attitudes and beliefs about government.

REMEMBER
- The formation and modification of opinions toward politics, public policy, and political figures is a lifelong process.
- Family, peers, the media, and civic and religious organizations influence political beliefs and values.
- An individual's stage in life, as well as the events experienced by his or her generation, influence political beliefs and values.

KNOW
- *political socialization*: the experiences and factors that shape an individual's political values, attitudes, and behaviors. (p. 340)
- *political ideology*: an individual's coherent set of beliefs about government and politics. (p. 340)
- *generational effect*: the impact of historical events experienced by a generation upon their political views. (p. 341)
- *life-cycle effect*: the impact of a person's age and stage in life on his or her political views. (p. 341)

THINK In what ways are the political values of the Silent Generation similar to those of the millennial generation?

10.2 Review Question: Free Response

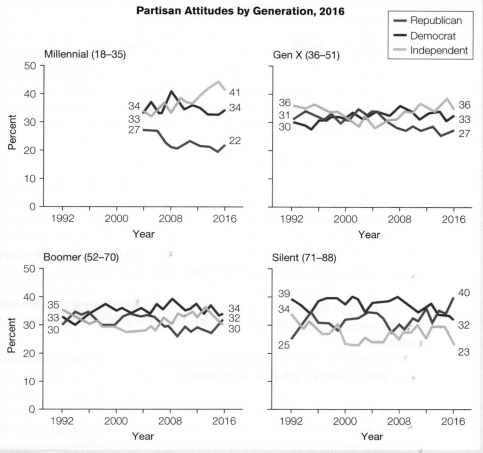

Partisan Attitudes by Generation, 2016

— Republican
— Democrat
— Independent

Millennial (18–35)

Gen X (36–51)

Boomer (52–70)

Silent (71–88)

Data from Pew Research Center

Use the graphs and your knowledge of U.S. Government and Politics to answer parts A, B, and C.

A. Describe what the graphs measure.

B. Describe one difference in partisanship between generations.

C. Explain how life-cycle and generational effects have an impact on the difference you identified in part B.

10.3 Globalization and American Core Values

Globalization refers to the increasing interconnectedness of people, businesses, and countries throughout the world. Globalization is not a new trend, and humans have connected with each other through trade and migration for centuries. In the twenty-first century, globalization has increased at a more rapid pace, due to complex worldwide networks involving communication, education, travel, and business. Globalization blurs the lines between international and domestic politics, and it presents policymakers with challenges.[58] They must consider the actions and potential actions of other governments and nongovernmental actors and institutions, the threat of military conflict, and the inescapable reality that their decisions will affect not just Americans but people across the globe.

globalization
the increasing interconnectedness of people, businesses, and countries throughout the world.

America's dominance as the only remaining superpower is being challenged. China has emerged as a global economic power and has undertaken a significant military buildup to protect its national interests. By 2015, Russia began to aggressively assert its own interests, especially over countries it considers to be within its sphere of influence. Russian troops invaded the Crimea region of the Ukraine. Russia has also defended the brutal authoritarian regime of Bashar al-Assad in Syria. As of 2017, the relationship between United States and Russia was strained, and some worried that a new Cold War was beginning.[59]

As the United States seeks to protect its core values and spread them throughout the world, it faces an increasingly complex network of global forces.

Actors on the World Stage

Countries are important because they set policies that affect their citizens and the rest of the world. A country is a set of government institutions that exert control over defined territory. In the past, countries were the most important international actors. Although countries are still relevant because their policies have influence across borders, other types of organizations are growing in importance. Multinational corporations (MNCs) are companies that make, transport, and market goods and services in two or more countries. Some large MNCs, like Nike, McDonalds, and Amazon produce an annual profit larger than the gross domestic product of most countries.[60] While the United States may regulate what these countries do within its borders, it is more difficult to control their activities overseas.

Nongovernmental organizations (NGOs) are independent groups outside of the government that work toward a public cause. Doctors Without Borders, for example, provides medical care to citizens who lack access to basic health care, improving the lives of citizens. NGOs can be a lifeline for the world's most vulnerable people. However, host countries sometimes oppose the actions of NGOs because they point out the government's ineffectiveness in delivering crucial services to citizens, thus decreasing the government's legitimacy.[61] NGOs that deliver free food may inadvertently put local producers out of business.[62] Furthermore, NGOs may have a corporate, religious, or foreign policy agenda that is inconsistent with the government's policy objectives.[63] As of 2017, there were more than 1.5 million NGOs operating within the United States, working on issues including women's rights, education, healthcare, child abuse, animal rights and a host of other issues.[64]

The greatest challenge to sovereignty, a country's ability to government itself without interference, may come from intergovernmental organizations (IGOs) consisting of member states. Countries join IGOs because they believe that the benefits of membership outweigh the loss of sovereignty over decision making.

Doctors Without Borders provides free medical care to the world's most vulnerable citizens. Here, children in Juba, South Sudan, receive basic medical care from a worker for Doctors Without Borders. In some respects, it operates as an alternate health-care system in countries with weak systems of public health, which can cause tensions in the host country.
CHARLES LOMODONG/AFP/Getty Images

One example of an IGO is the European Union (EU), which developed in the aftermath of World War II. To join the EU, countries must meet certain criteria for democratic government. EU member countries must agree to follow EU guidelines in three areas: economy and trade, justice and home affairs, and foreign and security policy. EU member countries give up sovereignty in exchange for the benefits of being part of the organization. For example, countries of the European Union that have adopted the euro as their currency gave up the authority to regulate their own currencies in favor of an international currency regulated by the European Central Bank.[65]

The World Trade Organization (WTO) is an IGO that focuses on free markets. As of 2016, the WTO had 164 member countries, including the United States.[66] It sets rules to encourage the free flow of capital, goods, and services between countries. For example, when China joined the WTO, it was required to reduce trade barriers and open its markets to foreign competition.[67] As an advocate for free trade policies, the WTO's goals include settling disputes between countries, stimulating economic growth, helping countries develop, cutting the costs for international businesses, and contributing to peace and stability.[68] Although the WTO has an ambitious agenda to improve conditions in developing countries, it has been criticized for supporting policies that widen the gap between the rich and the poor.[69]

The Globalized Economy

In the late twentieth century, American efforts to coordinate international economic policy focused on fostering free trade, which imposes few restrictions on the flow of goods and services across national borders. While overall global economic prosperity may benefit from free trade, those domestic producers who suffer from these policies—and the interest groups that represent them—will voice their concerns in Washington. When the free flow of goods and services involves authoritarian nations, which restrict civil rights and liberties, these trade relationships may come at a political cost for an administration that supports them.

Trade agreements may be bilateral, which means they are struck between the United States and only one other nation. Increasingly, however, the focus has been on regional trade agreements, which bring a group of nations into an overall agreement. In 1993, the United States entered into the North American Free Trade Agreement (NAFTA) with Canada and Mexico, increasing trade between the nations. NAFTA created some American jobs, such as positions in design and business services,[70] but it also cost Americans jobs in manufacturing, an outcome criticized by President Trump.[71] In fall 2016, President Obama pushed for congressional support for the Trans-Pacific Partnership (TPP), a regional trade agreement struck between twelve nations along the Pacific Rim, including Mexico, Australia, and East Asian and South American nations. President Trump abandoned the TPP shortly after assuming office.[72]

As a result of globalization, service jobs have increased, and some foreign manufacturers have placed plants in the United States. In 2015, a Chinese textile firm built a plant in South Carolina, and an Indian textile manufacturer announced plans to build a plant in Georgia.[73] Moreover, consumers have benefited due to lower prices, which has led to their ability to purchase more goods.

The effects of trade agreements are complicated, and politicians often simplify the discussion of globalization to advance their political agendas. In an article about the impact of NAFTA, market correspondent Sabri Ben-Anchour states, "Donald Trump and Bernie Sanders, who both used NAFTA as a favorite target during their presidential campaigns, will tell you it was a 'disaster' for the U.S. economy, that it cost the United States hundreds of thousands of jobs. The reality is not nearly as dramatic or tidy a story."[74]

Globalization and Democracy

Globalization can encourage democratization. Countries that join international organizations, such as the European Union, agree to abide by their rules. States must reach a certain level of democracy to be accepted as an EU member, and they must agree to make their actions transparent to their own citizens and to the outside world.[75] Countries may democratize their systems of government because they want to join the EU for trade benefits.

Globalization may make it more difficult for authoritarian states to operate without consequences. NGOs such as Reporters Without Borders, which compiles data about freedom of the press, Transparency International, which keeps track of government corruption, and Amnesty International and Human Rights Watch, which publicize human rights abuses and demand compliance with international laws, all engage in fact-finding, reporting, legal advocacy, and media campaigns to educate the public about human rights abuses. Human Rights Watch publishes more than one hundred reports annually about conditions in approximately ninety countries.[76] These powerful watchdog organizations may encourage countries to improve the treatment of their citizens.

Increased access to technology can impact government actions. It's easier than ever for citizens to organize protests and rallies through social media and to report on government wrongdoing. For example, when a collision between trains in China caused cars of both trains to derail and the deaths of forty people, government officials tried to literally bury the train. Outraged Chinese citizens took photos on their cell phones and demanded action. The Chinese government responded by acknowledging the mishandling of the accident and firing the railways minister.[77]

The Dark Side of Globalization

While globalization can spread new ideas, increase innovation, and encourage democracy, it also has negative consequences. If an MNC doesn't want to abide by labor regulations or environmental standards of a country, it can move its production elsewhere. **Outsourcing** occurs when a company moves its business to a place where labor costs are cheaper or production is more efficient because workers work longer hours. Outsourcing by U.S. companies resulted in job loss for employees in several industries, but especially in information-based businesses, like call centers, and in manufacturing. From 2000 to 2016, the United States has lost five million manufacturing jobs.[78] It is difficult for the workers left behind to find jobs that pay as well and offer as many benefits as their former positions.

Countries enticing international businesses to relocate may compete to lower their environmental and labor standards. While this strategy can increase employment, it may decrease quality of life in a phenomenon known as the "race to the bottom."[79]

Globalization can weaken traditional cultures. Fast-food restaurants make it difficult for local restaurants, serving traditional fare, to compete for customers. Mass-produced products are cheaper than hand-made traditional goods, like Navajo rugs, earthenware dishes, hand-loomed cloth, carved wooden bowls, and reed baskets.[80] Some worry that globalization will result in a homogenized culture that no longer reflects the historical values and connections formed within communities. Globalization can make people feel as if their way of life and values are under attack, which results in isolation and anxiety.

outsourcing
when a company moves its business to a place where labor costs are cheaper or production is more efficient because workers work longer hours.

A wellhead leaking oil has flared into a blaze in the Rivers State in Nigeria. The well had been used by a multinational corporation and abandoned. Why would the Nigerian government allow oil companies to drill in the Niger River Delta despite a long history of oil spills and protests by local communities?
Ed Kashi Photography

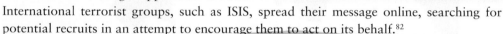

One of the most frightening consequences of globalization is its potential to connect people who want to incite violence and spread their message online. For example, white supremacist groups used online chats to plan violence at a march in Charlottesville, Virginia, sharing advice on weaponry and tactics, including a discussion about whether to drive vehicles through opposition crowds.[81] International terrorist groups, such as ISIS, spread their message online, searching for potential recruits in an attempt to encourage them to act on its behalf.[82]

Globalization also increases the ability of international crime syndicates to operate through the Dark Web. In July 2017, the Federal Bureau of Investigation, Drug Enforcement Agency, and Dutch National Police shut down underground criminal activity responsible for selling over 350,000 illegal drugs, weapons, and malware.[83] This illustrates both the ability of criminals to use technology to operate globally and the benefits of international cooperation in solving international crimes.

As a leading member of the global community, the United States asserts its interests and attempts to spread its core values. At the same time, the United States does not act alone and is influenced by global forces beyond its control.

Section Review

10.3 Explain how American political culture has influenced other countries and been influenced by globalization.

REMEMBER
- Individuals, businesses, and countries are becoming more interconnected.
- Actors on the world stage include countries, multinational corporations, international organizations, and nongovernmental organizations.
- The economy has become more globalized through free trade agreements.
- Globalization can spread democratic ideals, and technology can help citizens hold their governments more accountable.
- Negative consequences of globalization include poor working conditions, environmental degradation, loss of local culture, and the increased ease of planning terror attacks and other criminal activity.

KNOW
- *globalization*: the increasing interconnectedness of people, businesses, and countries throughout the world. (p. 345)
- *outsourcing*: when a company moves its business to a place where labor costs are cheaper or production is more efficient because workers work longer hours. (p. 348)

- Why do politicians overly simplify the impacts of globalization?
- Why is it difficult to measure the overall positive and negative impacts of globalization?

10.3 Review Question: Free Response

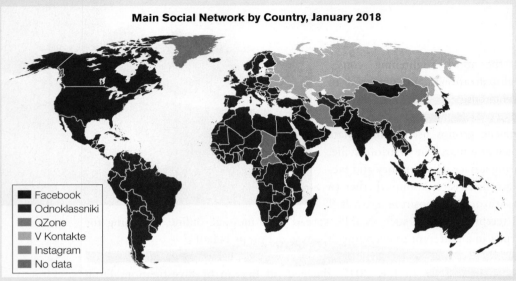

Main Social Network by Country, January 2018

- Facebook
- Odnoklassniki
- QZone
- V Kontakte
- Instagram
- No data

Data from Alexa, SimilarWeb, and Vincenzo Cosenza vincos.it

Use the map and your knowledge of U.S. Government and Politics to answer parts A, B, and C.

A. Describe the purpose of the map.

B. Use the map to explain one way in which technology impacts globalization.

C. Describe one policy enacted by the U.S. government in response to globalization.

Chapter 10 Review

AP® KEY CONCEPTS

- *political culture* (p. 333)
- *individualism* (p. 333)
- *laissez-faire* or *free enterprise* (p. 336)
- *rule of law* (p. 337)

- *political socialization* (p. 340)
- *political ideology* (p. 340)
- *generational effect* (p. 341)
- *life-cycle effect* (p. 341)

- *globalization* (p. 345)
- *outsourcing* (p. 348)

AP® EXAM PRACTICE and Critical Thinking Project

MULTIPLE-CHOICE QUESTIONS

1. Select the response that matches the American core political value with the appropriate example.

Core political value	Example
A. Individualism	Social welfare policies
B. Limited government	Restrictions on free speech
C. Free enterprise	Minimum wage regulations
D. Rule of law	Impeachment process

Questions 2 and 3 refer to the cartoon.

2. Which American core value is addressed in the cartoon?
   A. Equality of opportunity
   B. Limited government
   C. Free enterprise
   D. Individualism

3. A critic of the cartoon would make which of the following arguments?
   A. American is an individualistic country and is unlikely to join with other countries in creating economic policy.
   B. The American government is limited, and it relies on the principle of checks and balances to curb executive power.
   C. The cartoon overstates the possibility that the United States would become a socialist country, because the United States favors a free-market economy.
   D. When the United States cooperates with other countries in policy making, it runs the risk that other economies will negatively affect our economy.

4. Which of the following would have the greatest impact on an individual's political socialization?

A. The media report on a story about government corruption.

B. A pastor gives a sermon to explain the importance of charitable giving.

C. A father comments on political news while driving his daughter to school.

D. A grandmother washes and reuses plastic forks because of her experiences during the Great Depression.

I would not like to finish without saying a few words on a problem that affects you as you experience it in your current life: unemployment. . . . We cannot resign ourselves to losing a generation of young people who do not have the dignity of work!

—Pope Francis, Address to youth of the diocese of Abruzzo and Molise, Shrine of Our Lady of Sorrows, Castelpetroso, Italy, July 5, 2014[84]

5. Which of these political science concepts is reflected in the quote?

A. Political socialization

B. Life-cycle effects

C. Generational effects

D. Political ideology

Khalil Bendib/CorpWatch

6. The cartoon illustrates which of the following?

A. The race to the bottom

B. The impact of tariffs and other trade barriers

C. The decline of trade unions

D. The rapid pace of globalization

I have shown how it is that in ages of equality every man seeks for his opinions within himself: I am now about to show how it is that, in the same ages, all his feelings are turned towards himself alone.

—Alexis de Tocqueville, *Democracy in America*[85]

7. Which of the following statements best summarizes the excerpt?

A. Equality and individualism are contradictory core American values.

B. The core value of individualism leads Americans to turn away from their communities.

C. Individualism results in equality and opportunity.

D. As a "nation of joiners," Americans seek the opinions of their fellow citizens.

Question 8 refers to the quote.

That same system has helped lift more people out of poverty across the globe than any government program or competing economic system. The success of America's . . . system has been a bright beacon of freedom for the world. It has signaled to oppressed people to rise up against their oppressors, and given hope to the once hopeless.

—Mitt Romney, 2012 Campaign Speech[86]

8. Which of the following best describes the viewpoint expressed in the quote?

A. American core values inspire citizens throughout the world.

B. Democratic governments have a duty to try to spread their values to help citizens living in authoritarian states.

C. The American government has an obligation to reduce poverty among citizens.

D. America should fix its own problems before it tries to solve global issues.

9. The cartoon expresses which of the following viewpoints?

A. The millennial generation is pampered, and older people have earned their wealth.

B. Members of the millennial generation expect to get a trophy for doing everyday tasks.

C. Older generations benefited from a system that allowed them to get wealthy, while millennials are burdened with debt.

D. Members of the millennial generation are more likely to be depressed and are less engaged in their communities than older Americans.

Our security and prosperity are only found in wise, sustained, global engagement: In the cultivation of new markets for American goods. In the confrontation of security challenges before they fully materialize and arrive on our shores. In the fostering of global health and development as alternatives to suffering and resentment. In the attraction of talent, energy, and enterprise from all over the world. In serving as a shining hope for refugees and a voice for dissidents, human rights defenders, and the oppressed.

—George W. Bush, Speech at the National Forum on Liberty, October 19, 2017

10. Which of the following statements describes the viewpoint about globalization expressed in the quote?
   A. Free trade policies protect local artisans by allowing them to become more globally engaged.
   B. Globalization makes it difficult to confront increasing security challenges.
   C. Global health and development are slow to reach those who are suffering.
   D. Globalization provides the United States with an opportunity to spread its economic and political values.

FREE-RESPONSE QUESTION

Without liberty, law loses its nature and its name, and becomes oppression. Without law, liberty also loses its nature and its name, and becomes licentiousness.

—James Wilson[87]

1. Use the quote and your knowledge of U.S. Government and Politics to answer parts A, B, and C.
   A. Describe the viewpoint expressed in the quote.
   B. Describe a government policy that reflects the American core value of liberty.
   C. Explain how the policy you described in part B reflects the tension between liberty and order.

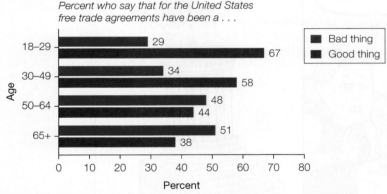

Age and Different Views of Free Trade Agreements

Percent who say that for the United States free trade agreements have been a . . .

Bad thing / Good thing

18–29: 29 (Bad), 67 (Good)
30–49: 34 (Bad), 58 (Good)
50–64: 48 (Bad), 44 (Good)
65+: 51 (Bad), 38 (Good)

Data from Pew Research Center

2. Use the bar chart and your knowledge of U.S. Government and Politics to answer parts A, B, and C.
   A. Describe one trend shown in the bar chart.
   B. Explain how the trend you described in part A reflects generational effects.
   C. Explain how a politician might use the information shown in the bar chart to target voters during a political campaign.

ARGUMENTATION QUESTION

American core values include individualism, equality of opportunity, free enterprise, rule of law, and limited government. Which one of these core values is the most important in ensuring democracy and a stable government?

In your essay:

- Articulate a claim or thesis that responds to the prompt, and use a line of reasoning to defend it.
- Use at least TWO pieces of relevant and accurate evidence to support your claim.
- At least ONE piece of evidence must be from one of the listed foundational documents:

  Declaration of Independence

  Constitution of the United States

  Federalist No. 78

- Use a second piece of evidence from another foundational document from the list or from your study of American political values.
- Use reasoning to explain why the evidence you provided supports your claim or thesis.
- Use refutation, concession, or rebuttal to respond to an opposing or alternative perspective.

CRITICAL THINKING PROJECT

The Generational Effect and You

People from different generations are influenced by the important events that occur during their lifetimes. The generational effect is already influencing you, sometimes in ways you don't always recognize. If you were born between 1980 and 2012, you are a member of the millennial generation, although some have called you the "iGeneration" because of the important role technology plays in your lives.[88]

Make a visual representing the generational effects on you.

1. On the left side, create a list of at least five news events that you remember well. These should be events shared by your generation, rather than things that happened in your personal life.
2. On the right side, make a list of five core beliefs you hold about government and politics.
3. Draw lines between the events your generation has experienced and their impact on your belief system. Some items may be connected in multiple ways, and other items may seem disconnected. The generational effect represents the connection between the events you have experienced as a member of your generation and your political beliefs.
4. Write a summary paragraph describing how events have impacted your political beliefs.

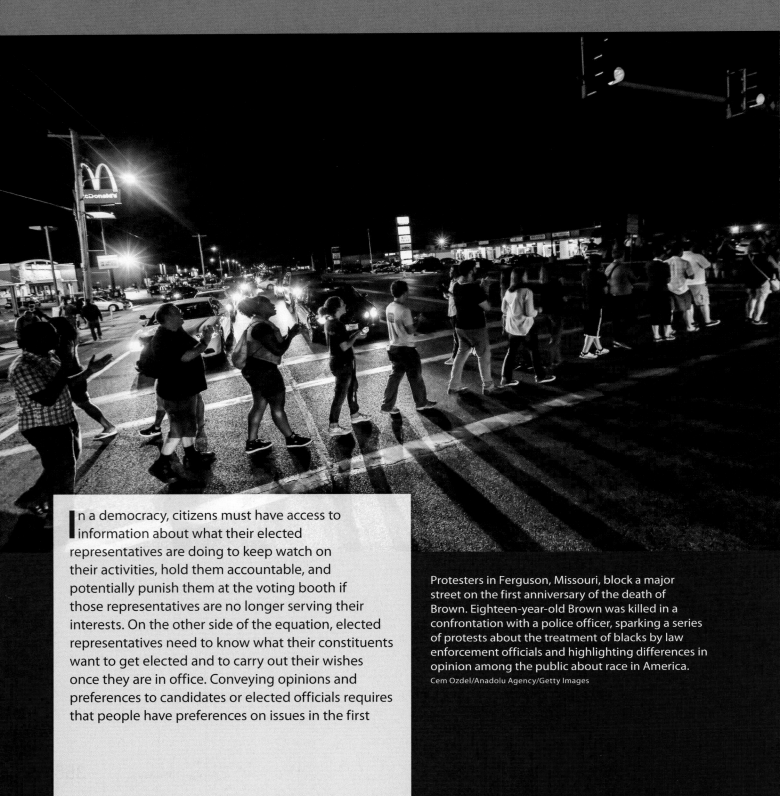

11 Public Opinion
Measuring Americans' Opinions

In a democracy, citizens must have access to information about what their elected representatives are doing to keep watch on their activities, hold them accountable, and potentially punish them at the voting booth if those representatives are no longer serving their interests. On the other side of the equation, elected representatives need to know what their constituents want to get elected and to carry out their wishes once they are in office. Conveying opinions and preferences to candidates or elected officials requires that people have preferences on issues in the first

Protesters in Ferguson, Missouri, block a major street on the first anniversary of the death of Brown. Eighteen-year-old Brown was killed in a confrontation with a police officer, sparking a series of protests about the treatment of blacks by law enforcement officials and highlighting differences in opinion among the public about race in America.
Cem Ozdel/Anadolu Agency/Getty Images

place and that these preferences are coherent and meaningful. These are the challenges of measuring **public opinion**, which is the sum of individual attitudes about government, policies, and issues. In this chapter, we will focus on American public opinion in one specific area: the treatment of young African Americans. Following several high-profile police shootings of unarmed African American men, protests erupted, including those by players in the National Football League. We will question whether or not these events have produced meaningful changes in American public opinion on issues involving both officer safety and civil liberties.

public opinion
the sum of individual attitudes about government, policies, and issues.

After reading this chapter, you will be able to

11.1 Define public opinion.

11.2 Describe the elements of a valid, scientific public opinion poll.

11.3 Explain how public opinion polling impacts elections and policymaking.

LEARNING TARGETS

 Differing Views of Race Discrimination in America

On August 9, 2014, law enforcement office Darren Wilson shot and killed Michael Brown following a confrontation in Ferguson, Missouri. In an interview with *ABC News* in fall 2014, Darren Wilson, who had announced his resignation from the Ferguson Police Department, argued that he acted in self-defense in killing Brown: "I had to. If I don't, he [Brown] will kill me if he gets to me."[1] Some eyewitnesses said that Brown had his hands raised in surrender when he was shot.[2]

The day after Brown's death protesters gathered peacefully in Ferguson. Tension, however, flared off and on through the evening. By nightfall, there was violence: "After a candlelight vigil, people smash[ed] car windows, carr[ied] away armloads of looted goods from stores and burn[ed] down a Quick Trip."[3] By the time the first wave of violence ended, "more than two dozen businesses in Ferguson and neighboring Dellwood were damaged or looted."[4] The protests, some peaceful and some violent, continued for weeks.

In the weeks following Brown's death, many of the protestors and other residents of Ferguson called for the arrest and prosecution of the officer who had shot Brown. Some chanted, "Black lives matter." The social movement to which the protesters were referring existed before Ferguson. It had begun with the Twitter hashtag #BlackLivesMatter, which sprang into use following the 2013 acquittal of George Zimmerman in the shooting death of Trayvon Martin in Florida. After Ferguson, however, Black Lives Matter became part of the national conversation in ways it had never been before. *Time* magazine included the protestors of Ferguson in its list of candidates for "Person of the Year."[5]

How Events at Ferguson Led to Change in Public Opinion

By 2015, the national conversation had changed. Maybe this was due to one specific tragic event or to several deaths of young African American men during police stops and arrests in 2014. Perhaps it was due to a complicated mixture of events, media coverage, and the use of social media that followed these deaths. Regardless of the exact reason, public opinion on the issue of police-citizen interactions, especially in predominantly African American communities, appeared to be shifting. To many Americans, especially whites, the protesters' anger over the events in Ferguson came as a surprise.

The Black Lives Matter movement began after the death of Trayvon Martin, an unarmed black Florida teenager who was shot to death by a white neighborhood watch volunteer in 2012. The group continued protesting in Ferguson after Michael Brown's death.
NICHOLAS KAMM/AFP/Getty Images

To individuals within African American communities across the country, the only surprising thing about the fallout from Ferguson was that the issue had not come to the public's attention sooner. According to former Representative John Conyers of Michigan, who was the dean of the Congressional Black Caucus at the time, "There are virtually no African American males—including congressmen, actors, athletes and office workers, who have not been stopped at one time or another for driving while black."[6]

Less than two weeks following Brown's death, the Pew Research Center published the results of a public opinion survey of Americans' responses to what Ferguson and racial identity meant in the larger national conversation. To conduct the survey, researchers had contacted a random sample of one thousand American adults, half via landlines and half via cell phones. The divisions between African Americans and whites on what Ferguson meant were clear. Eighty percent of blacks said that Brown's shooting raised "important issues about race." Only 37 percent of white respondents agreed. Forty-seven percent of whites said that "race [was] getting more attention than it deserves."

Police officers nationwide felt an impact from the events in Ferguson. According to a Pew Research Survey conducted in 2017, 86 percent of police officers reported that fatal incidents between law enforcement officers and African Americans have made their jobs harder, and 93 percent of police officers were more concerned about their safety.[7]

Take a Knee: Shaping Public Opinion in New Ways

Two years following the death of Michael Brown, race relations continued to occupy the public's attention. In August 2016, during the team's first preseason game of the National Football League against the Green Bay Packers, the San Francisco 49ers quarterback, Colin Kaepernick, refused to stand during the national anthem in protest of racism, especially in police-community relations. Kaepernick later told a reporter, "To me, this is bigger than football and it would be selfish to look the other way. There are bodies in the street and people [police officers] getting paid leave and getting away with murder."[9]

Assessing and Interpreting Changes in Public Opinion

In public opinion polls conducted by the Pew Research Center and the *Washington Post* in 2009, 2011, and March 2014, the percentage of Americans who agreed that the nation had "made the changes needed to give blacks equal rights with whites" did not change much. In each poll, a slight majority of Americans expressed the opinion that the nation had made these changes. Individual attitudes, however, diverged sharply by racial identity. A majority of white Americans felt that the nation had made the necessary changes, but the vast majority of African American survey respondents felt that it had not.

By the late summer of 2015, however, something appeared to have changed.[8] Between the polls conducted in March 2014,

six months before Brown's shooting, and July 2015, nearly a year after, there was what political scientists call a "break in trend," and a sharp one at that. In the 2015 survey, the percentages of Americans surveyed who thought that the nation had done enough to achieve equal rights had changed overall and for both groups of Americans.

1. Describe the break in trend that occurred in the survey results in July 2015.

2. Explain one reason why the break in trend occurred.

3. Describe one limitation in the data in evaluating public opinion about racial equality in America.

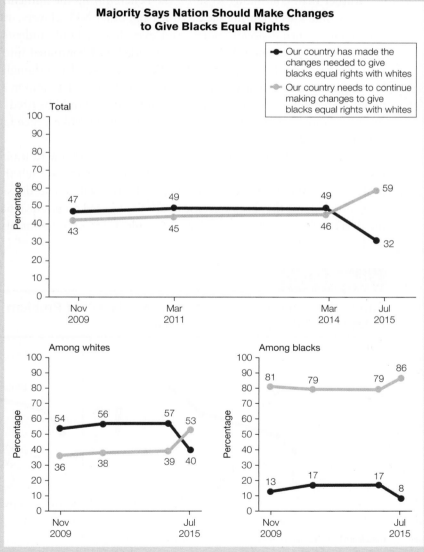

Majority Says Nation Should Make Changes to Give Blacks Equal Rights

Data from Pew Research Center

NFL quarterback Colin Kaepernick (center) kneels with fellow players Eric Reid (right) and Eli Harold (left) during the national anthem in a regular-season game against the Seattle Seahawks, 2016.

Michael Zagaris/San Francisco 49ers/Getty Images

Kaepernick added that he had not told his team ahead of time what he planned on doing, and he fully expected that there would be repercussions, although the NFL later issued a statement saying that players in the NFL are encouraged, but not required, to stand during the anthem. "If they take football away, my endorsements from me," Kaepernick, an American of mixed race and #BlackLivesMatter supporter, added, "I know that I stood up for what is right."[10]

Rather than continuing to sit on the bench during the anthem, Kaepernick decided that he would kneel. During the 2016 season, other NFL players, athletes in other men's and women's professional sports, and even high school students participated in the "take a knee" movement.[11] Protests expanded and continued into the 2017 NFL season. The level of tension grew, and so did the politics. Even though Kaepernick had not been signed to play on any NFL team, President Donald Trump in a series of tweets and public statements criticized Kaepernick and said he should be fired.[12] At a game between the 49ers and the Indianapolis Colts, Vice President Mike Pence left after several 49ers players kneeled during the anthem.

In August 2017, public opinion researchers with the Pew Research Center released the results of a survey asking Americans the degree to which they felt that racism was a "big problem" in American society. See Figure 11.1. While racial divisions continued, especially notable was the sharp increase in divisions based on political partisanship, reflecting the degree to which the NFL protests, President Trump's comments, and the role of the media impacted the racial divisions in America.

FIGURE 11.1

Gap in Perceptions of Whether Racism Is a "Big Problem" Relates to Political Party and Race

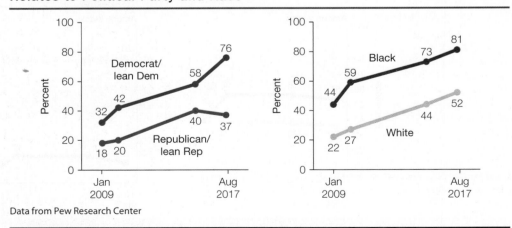

Data from Pew Research Center

■ 11.1 What Is Public Opinion?

One of the most interesting and important debates about American public opinion is whether or not something as broad as "public opinion" exists. Of course, many Americans *have* thoughts and ideas about politics and policies, but many others do not have well-formed views on these topics.

Public opinion, by definition, involves two components: an individual's own beliefs and attitudes, and the blending of these individual preferences into a larger concept that we call *public opinion*. Either of these two pieces—individual attitudes and the aggregation of individual attitudes—can make American public opinion difficult to understand. Individuals may not have meaningful preferences on any given issue, and even if they do, putting all of these individual preferences together may not yield meaningful and useful information.

A representative democracy cannot function without a reliable understanding of public opinion. If our elected representatives do not know what we want, they have a hard time trying to represent us in the policymaking process.

What Do We Mean When We Talk about "Public Opinion"?

Arguments about the meaning of public opinion in American political life fall into two general camps. One perspective is that the average citizen either doesn't have or is unable to express meaningful opinions on the vast array of issues facing the country. Another perspective holds that even though individuals sometimes lack the information they need to form opinions, they can find ways to overcome or work around these challenges by making inferences based on cues from their political ideology, peers, or political parties. Aggregating individual opinions—even if they are individually unclear or inconsistent—can send useful signals to elected representatives and government officials.

What Do Americans Know, or Not Know, about Politics, and Does It Matter?

There is a concern that the lack of coherent opinions among citizens poses a challenge to American representative democracy. In their 1996 book, *What Americans Know about*

An editorial cartoon by Tom Toles critiques the lack of influence of the American public following the financial crisis that began in 2008. Toles's cartoon refers to the Wall Street tycoons and financial analysts who were labeled "masters of the universe" in Tom Wolfe's *Bonfire of the Vanities*,[13] a popular book about ambition and greed that was made into a movie. Toles captures a general feeling of anger, but another question remains: What policies should the government enact in response to "angry" public opinion? Simply knowing that the public is angry doesn't tell us much about how to fix the problem. TOLES © 2009 The Washington Post. Reprinted with permission of Andrews McMeel Syndication

Politics and Why It Matters, two researchers examined decades of historical surveys of Americans' political knowledge. They also posed a series of political knowledge questions to a large sample of Americans.[14] The findings were troubling. Significant percentages of Americans were not able to answer basic questions about American government, such as being able to name one or more branches of the federal government or name constitutional protections in the Bill of Rights.

Younger Americans, lower-income Americans, and members of racial and ethnic minorities consistently fared worse in their answers to questions about factual knowledge of politics. These gaps have not narrowed over the past few decades. Researchers with the Pew Center periodically administer a "News IQ" quiz to a random sample of Americans. The test contains questions regarding political figures, knowledge of current issues in domestic and international politics, and geography (Figure 11.2). While the number of Americans who can correctly answer a question varies, significant numbers are unable to answer the questions correctly.

A More Optimistic View of American Public Opinion

Most scholars agree that Americans often lack opinions on many issues in politics and policy. However, researchers disagree about whether one person has to have an encyclopedic set of policy preferences to have an opinion. The aggregation of individuals' opinions, according to some scholars, can produce useful information.

Individuals' experiences and interactions with government, accumulated over a lifetime, can help them make sense of an issue or problem. This "gut rationality" may not help on a political knowledge quiz, but it can assist people in making meaningful political choices.[15] Also, individuals might rely on advice from friends and colleagues.[16]

Voters use their identification with a political party when evaluating candidates and forming opinions about specific issues.[17] If I identify as a Republican, I'm likely to be more

FIGURE 11.2

Public Awareness of Current Political Events

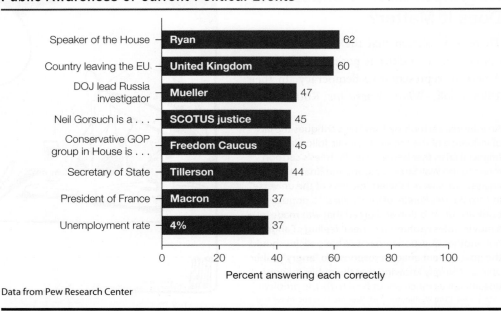

Data from Pew Research Center

favorable toward Republican candidates rather than Democratic candidates, even without knowing anything about them other than their party affiliations. Or if I identify as a Democrat, I am more likely to oppose a policy option that Republicans endorse than one Democrats endorse, even though I don't know much about the policy.

Finally, some political scientists have emphasized the possibility of the "wisdom of crowds,"[18] in which individuals who lack complete information can come up with a meaningful assessment of a problem or situation as a group. More recently, Benjamin Page and Robert Shapiro emphasized the possibility for a public to be collectively rational even in the presence of individually inconsistent and shapeable opinions.[19]

Section Review

This chapter's main ideas are reflected in the Learning Targets. By reviewing after each section, you should be able to

—**Remember** the key points,
—**Know** terms that are central to the topic, and
—**Think** critically about public opinion.

11.1 Define public opinion.

REMEMBER	• Public opinion is important in a representative democracy, because it helps policy makers understand citizens' preferences.
	• Even though individuals sometimes lack the information they need to form opinions, they can find ways to overcome or work around these challenges by making inferences based on cues from their political ideology, peers, or political parties.
	• Aggregating individual opinions can send useful signals to elected representatives and government officials.
KNOW	*public opinion*: the sum of individual attitudes about government, policies, and issues. (p. 357)
THINK	To what degree is it possible to accurately measure public opinion when most Americans lack understanding about complex policy issues?

11.1 Review Question: Free Response

Public Attention to Stem Cell Research

I'm going to read you a list of some stories covered by news organizations in the last month or so. As I read each one, tell me if you happened to follow this news story very closely, fairly closely, not too closely, or not at all closely. How closely did you follow this story?...

Government decision about the use of federal funding for stem cell research.

	Kaiser 9/00 (%)	Gallup[a] 7/10–7/11/01 (%)	Gallup[a] 8/3–8/5/01 (%)	Gallup[a] 8/10–8/12/01 (%)	Ipsos[b] 8/10–8/12/01 (%)	Kaiser[c] 9/28–10/1/01 (%)
Very closely	6	9	18	12	13	21
Fairly closely	14	29	37	45	38	30
Not too closely	19	28	22	23	27	20
Not at all closely	56	32	23	20	12	27
Don't know/refused	5	2	*	NA	10	2
Number of respondents	949	998	1,017	1,017	1,000	1,001

Note.—* = less than 0.5 percent; NA = not asked
Data from Public Opinion Quarterly

Use the table and your knowledge of U.S. Government and Politics to answer parts A, B, and C.

A. Define public opinion.

B. Use the information from the table to explain one reason why it is challenging to measure Americans' viewpoints on complex public policy issues.

C. Describe one factor that may influence an individual in forming an opinion about policy issues.

▄▄▄ 11.2 Trying to Measure Public Opinion Accurately

There are two basic requirements for effective representation in a democracy. First, voters must have opinions and preferences that can be communicated to their elected representatives. Second, elected officials must respond to these expressed preferences. This section will address how public opinion is measured.

Citizens may communicate directly with their elected officials, but people who take the time to write an email, call their representatives, or attend a town meeting are not typical voters. They are motivated people who have a strong view about an issue. While direct communication can tell an elected official about the strongly held views of a small group, it does not convey the overall preferences of the citizens as a whole.

An election is a better way to measure citizens' preferences. While we may not often think about an election as a tool for measuring public opinion, that is precisely what it is. However, elections have their own limitations. First, many eligible voters do not vote. The greater challenge with elections is that they tend to revolve around a small set of issues. For the majority of complex public policy issues, elections are too broad a tool to reveal useful information.

Rather than waiting for individuals to contact them or trying to decipher the results of an election, officials go directly to the citizens to find out what they want. One method is a **focus group**, a small group of individuals assembled for a conversation, usually led by a moderator, about specific issues. Focus groups can be useful in understanding what people think about a political topic. However, because they are small, focus groups cannot paint a picture of an entire constituency.

focus group
a small group of individuals assembled for a conversation about specific issues.

How Scientific Polling Works

scientific poll
a representative poll of randomly selected respondents with a statistically significant sample size, using neutral language.

In theory, scientific polling is simple. It would be unfeasible and expensive to get every constituent's opinion, so polling organizations select a smaller representative subset of that constituency and ask carefully written questions of the members of that group to find out what they think. This is a **scientific poll** (in a nutshell). The problem is deciding on whom to include in the **sample**. For some political polls, the population may be the entire voting-age population of the United States or of an individual state or congressional district. However, there are many other populations to sample, such as individuals with specific racial or ethnic identities or the student population of a college or university.

sample
a group of individuals from a larger population used to measure public opinion.

random selection
a method of choosing all poll respondents in a way that does not over- or underrepresent any group of the population.

Valid, scientific polling requires **random selection**, which means that everyone who is an appropriate subject of the poll has an equal chance of being selected for the particular survey. Pollsters cannot survey every person in a population, so researchers cannot know for certain what the true opinion of that population is. The goal is to minimize the uncertainty about the true opinion as much as possible while also conducting a poll that does not cost vast sums of money or take too long to conduct.

For the sample to be useful, it must represent the larger population as accurately as possible. This is why polls with voluntary responses, such as call-in polls, are always suspect. There is also a problem if a poll systematically oversamples or undersamples individuals based on characteristics that are relevant to what the poll is trying to measure. For instance, some polls have been limited to land lines, and it is widely believed that a poll taken using land lines will overrepresent older people. The goal, then, is a sample that reflects the characteristics of the population, which is called a **representative sample**.

Pollsters sometimes use the technique of **weighting** to adjust the results of a survey. Weighting adjusts the results based on differences between the percentages of specific groups participating in the survey and the demographics of the larger population.

When pollsters present their results, they include a measure of the **sampling error** (or margin of error) in their surveys. In larger national polls, known as a **mass survey**, which typically aim for about 1,500 respondents, the sampling error is often plus or minus three percentage points, meaning that pollsters can assert that about 95 percent of the time the true number lies within three points on either side of the measured number. If, for example, an opinion survey with a margin of error of three points shows that one party's candidate for president has the support of 49 percent of Americans and the other party's candidate the support of 47 percent, the race is too close for pollsters to make a confident prediction. Increasing the size of the sample decreases the error, but it also increases the cost.

Types of Surveys

In choosing how to administer a survey, a researcher has several options. The degree of confidence that you as a reader of poll results can place in the findings, however, depends critically on the ways in which the sample is selected. Surveys that allow anyone to participate are not random and are therefore not reliable. One example is a straw poll—an unofficial tally of opinion or support at a meeting or event, such as a political party meeting or caucus. While straw polls can be useful in exploring which individuals support a candidate and why, their target population is not randomly selected.

An **entrance survey** is a poll conducted of people who are coming into an event, such as attending a meeting of a political party or standing in line to vote. Entrance and exit polls are sometimes used to measure whether voters change their minds after attending an event, such as a party caucus.[20] An **exit poll** is a survey conducted following an event or at a polling place after individuals have voted. Individuals are asked who or what they just voted for and why. News outlets may use exit polling to get information out before their competitors, but there are risks in doing so. An exit poll may sample voters favoring a certain candidate. Also, announcing the results of exit polls while polling places are still open runs the risk of influencing an election. Learning that one candidate is supposedly winning may discourage another candidate's supporters from turning out to vote because they believe their votes would not matter. To avoid that problem, news networks have voluntarily agreed not to release exit poll results until all of a state's polling places have closed. Exit polls can be useful, though, in understanding patterns of voting—for example, who showed up at the polls, what issue was most on the minds of voters, who voted for a particular candidate and, more generally, which groups of voters supported each candidate.

Candidates use polling to decide how to address the issues and to determine their likelihood of winning. A **benchmark poll** is taken at the beginning of a political campaign in order to gauge support for a candidate and determine which issues are important to voters.

representative sample
a sample that reflects the demographics of the population.

weighting
a procedure in which the survey is adjusted according to the demographics of the larger population.

sampling error
the margin of error in a poll, which usually is calculated to plus or minus three percentage points.

mass survey
a survey designed to measure the opinions of the population, usually consisting of 1,500 responses.

entrance survey
a poll conducted of people coming to an event.

exit poll
a survey conducted outside a polling place in which individuals are asked who or what they just voted for and why.

benchmark poll
a survey taken at the beginning of a political campaign in order to gauge support for a candidate and determine which issues are important to voters.

tracking poll
a survey determining the level of support for a candidate or an issue throughout a campaign.

AP® TIP

Different types of polls are used for different purposes. Understand how different kinds of opinion polls, such as benchmark and tracking polls, and entrance and exit polls are used as part of the political process.

random digit dialing
the use of telephone numbers randomly generated by computer to select potential survey respondents.

question order
the sequencing of questions in public opinion polls.

question wording
the phrasing of a question in a public opinion poll.

Tracking polls determine the level of support for a candidate or an issue over the length of a campaign. The media have been criticized for using tracking polls to generate news about who is winning or losing a campaign at the moment, and focusing on the "horse race" between the candidates, instead of covering more important stories about the candidates' policies.

Because of the challenges posed by nonrandom selection, news organizations, media outlets, and research organizations rely mainly on the telephone in measuring public opinion. Even with **random digit dialing**, which uses telephone numbers randomly generated by a computer to select survey respondents, there are always risks that a sample is not truly representative of the overall population. Caller ID complicates the issue. Many people ignore calls from polling organizations, which makes it more challenging to obtain a random and representative sample.

Internet polls are not considered to be scientific. There are three criticisms of online polling.[21] Because people answer Internet polls voluntarily, the sample is not random. Furthermore, the respondents probably do not represent a cross section of all demographic groups. Internet polls do not have an established track record of reliability. As polling organizations establish new methods to evaluate Internet polling results, their track records of reliability may improve.[22]

On issues for which respondents have actual preferences, other factors may shape the results of a public opinion survey. First, the **question order** can affect the results. Consider a question about whether or not individuals should be permitted to burn an American flag in protest.[23] If the flag-burning question was preceded by a question about the importance of patriotism, it might produce more opinions against allowing flag burning.[24] Yet if the flag-burning question follows a question about the importance of free speech in American democracy, it might lead to a different pattern of responses.

Similarly, the **question wording** can, intentionally or not, guide respondents to a specific answer. For example, in a 2003 Pew Research Center survey about attitudes toward military action in Iraq, 68 percent of respondents said that they favored action when asked if they would "favor or oppose taking military action in Iraq to end Saddam Hussein's rule." However, when asked if they would "favor or oppose taking military action in Iraq to end Saddam Hussein's rule *even if it meant that U.S. forces might suffer thousands of casualties*," only 43 percent of respondents favored military action.[25]

Finally, the interviewers themselves may affect the results of a survey, especially one conducted in person. Political scientists have, for example, documented effects related to the race of an interviewer, in which the outcomes of surveys, even on questions only asking for political knowledge and information, may depend partly on the racial identities of respondents and survey takers.[26] Another problem with interpreting polls is that often they do not measure how strongly respondents feel about an issue. Expressing an opinion is not the same thing as caring about an issue.

One controversial tool that candidates or those supporting them may employ is a push poll, which is not really a poll but a negative campaign tactic. Disguised as surveys, push polls try to present voters with negative or damaging portrayals of opposing candidates, sometimes with false or exaggerated information.

The Challenges of Using Polling to Measure Public Opinion

The 2016 presidential campaign demonstrated the limits of polling data in predicting the outcome of an election. Most polls predicted that Hillary Clinton would win the election, and they forecasted that she would prevail in states such as Wisconsin and

Analyzing Limitations of Data: Question Wording and Its Effects

Public Perception of Police Misconduct

	Do you think number of cases of police officers using excessive force against civilians are going up, going down, or remaining about the same?			Do you think the police are too quick to use lethal force, or do they typically only use lethal force when necessary?	
	Going Up	**Going Down**	**Same**	**Too Quick**	**Only Necessary**
All	47%	7%	43%	45%	49%
Democrat	58%	4%	36%	61%	34%
Independent	52%	7%	38%	40%	50%
Republican	31%	10%	54%	24%	70%
Caucasian	38%	8%	49%	34%	59%
African American	73%	2%	25%	82%	16%
Hispanic	67%	2%	31%	72%	23%
<$45,000	53%	6%	38%	50%	44%
$45,000–$90,000	45%	5%	45%	48%	45%
$90,000+	32%	14%	51%	30%	63%
18–34	52%	6%	40%	55%	41%
35–54	49%	9%	39%	42%	53%
55+	40%	5%	49%	38%	52%
South	52%	6%	38%	43%	50%
West	49%	4%	44%	49%	43%
Northeast	45%	10%	41%	50%	45%
Midwest	38%	8%	52%	40%	55%
Rural	45%	7%	44%	35%	57%
Suburban	45%	7%	45%	42%	51%
Urban	50%	6%	39%	54%	40%
Favorable of Police	39%	8%	50%	35%	59%
Unfavorable of Police	71%	3%	24%	73%	22%

Data from Reason-Rupe Polls, October 2014

1. Identify wording within the survey questions that might impact the results of the survey.

2. Explain how the wording you identified in part 1 may affect the survey responses.

3. Describe one factor, other than the wording of the questions, that may impact the validity of a public opinion poll.

Pennsylvania that President Trump won.[27] The poll of polls immediately before the election showed Hillary Clinton up nationally by roughly 2 percent, which is a close estimate of the popular vote she received. On the morning of election day, statistician Nate Silver gave Donald Trump a 1 in 3 chance of winning, which is effectively the same chance as rolling a 1 or a 2 on a die.[28] In other words, the election result was within the margin of error of the polls.

Nevertheless, the polls underestimated the support for President Trump, even though more sophisticated surveying methods were used to poll voters in specific districts.[29]

Telephone polls were supplemented by use of aggregated polling data, which combined and averaged polling data from numerous sources. But some pollsters and analysts who used aggregated survey data got the results wrong, too.[30]

There are several explanations why it was difficult to predict the winner of the 2016 presidential election.[31] One is the type of people who are willing to answer polls. Some groups of voters, like less educated white voters, who supported Trump in large numbers,[32] are less likely to answer polls.[33] Some people may have been hesitant to admit they were voting for candidate Trump, given the large amount of criticism he received in many media outlets.[34] Pollsters also had difficulty identifying likely voters because some people who usually don't vote turned out to vote for Trump.[35]

One thing is certain—the election pointed out challenges pollsters will face in the future. Polling is important beyond the "horse race" of predicting who will win an election. Credible polls help representatives understand what their constituents want so that they can deliver policies the public favors.

Section Review

11.2 Describe the elements of a valid, scientific public opinion poll.

REMEMBER
- Valid, scientific public opinion polls use random and representative sampling, of at least 1,500 respondents.
- The way questions are worded, and the order in which they appear, may affect survey responses.
- Despite improved methods, many polls were not accurate in predicting the outcome of the 2016 presidential election.

KNOW
- *focus group*: a small group of individuals assembled for a conversation about specific issues. (p. 364)
- *scientific poll*: a representative poll of randomly selected respondents with a statistically significant sample size, using neutral language. (p. 364)
- *sample*: a subgroup of individuals from a larger population used to measure public opinion. (p. 364)
- *random selection*: a method of choosing all poll respondents in a way that does not over- or under-represent any group of the population. (p. 364)
- *representative sample*: a sample that reflects the demographics of the population. (p. 365)
- *weighting*: a procedure in which the survey is adjusted according to the demographics of the larger population. (p. 365)
- *sampling error*: the margin of error in a poll, which is usually calculated to around plus or minus three percentage points. (p. 365)
- *mass survey*: a survey designed to measure the opinions of the population, usually consisting of 1,500 responses. (p. 365)
- *entrance survey*: a poll conducted of people coming to an event. (p. 365)
- *exit poll*: a survey conducted outside a polling place in which individuals are asked who or what they just voted for and why. (p. 365)
- *benchmark poll*: a survey taken at the beginning of a political campaign in order to gauge support for a candidate and determine which issues are important to voters. (p. 365)
- *tracking poll*: a survey determining the level of support for a candidate or an issue throughout a campaign. (p. 366)
- *random digit dialing*: the use of telephone numbers randomly generated by computer to select potential survey respondents. (p. 366)
- *question order*: the sequencing of questions in public opinion polls. (p. 366)
- *question wording*: the phrasing of a question in a public opinion poll. (p. 366)

THINK   What tools and techniques might be developed in the future to make public opinion polling more reliable?

Poll	Right Direction	Wrong Track	Undecided	Spread
YouGov/Economist Jun 11 – Jun 13 1,500 Adults	33	**51**	16	Wrong Track +18
Rasmussen Jun 4 – Jun 8 2,500 Likely Voters	37	**57**	6	Wrong Track +20
Ipsos/Reuters Jun 2 – Jun 6 2,371 Adults	27	**58**	15	Wrong Track +31
Politico/Morning Consult Jun 1 – Jun 2 1,999 Registered Voters	42	**58**		Wrong Track +16
Rasmussen May 21 – May 25 2,500 Likely Voters	37	**56**	7	Wrong Track +19

Data from the polls listed and from Huffington Post

Use the table and your knowledge of U.S. Government and Politics to answer parts A, B, and C.

A. Describe what the polls in the table measure.

B. Describe two characteristics of a valid, scientific public opinion poll.

C. Identify one poll from the table that may not be reliable, and explain one reason why the results of the poll you identified may not be valid.

■ **11.3** The Effects of Public Opinion on Democratic Representation

Understanding Patterns within American Public Opinion

One of the single most effective predictors of public opinion is an individual's identification with a political party. Americans' response to Ferguson was no different. On the question of whether or not local law enforcement agencies could be trusted to administer the laws of the nation impartially and without regard to racial and ethnic identity, Americans were sharply divided according to party identification.

In a survey of one thousand adults in the week following the shooting, the Pew Research Center observed that while 61 percent of respondents who self-identified as Republicans thought that race was getting too much attention in the media coverage, 68 percent of Democrats thought that the shooting raised important issues about race in American society (Figure 11.3 on page 370).[36]

American public opinion is also often divided along gender lines. On many issues, such as comparative levels of spending on social welfare programs versus national defense, polls have consistently found differences between men and women. These differences in opinion are translated into differences in support for American political parties. Sometimes called the "gender gap," this pattern means that American women are more likely to vote for Democratic Party candidates than men, who are more likely to vote for Republican Party candidates (Figure 11.4 on the next page).

AP® TIP

Be careful in describing the gender gap, which is the tendency of women to vote for Democrats in higher percentages than men, and conversely, for men to vote for Republicans in higher percentages than women. Although women vote in slightly higher percentages than men, this is a difference in voter turnout, not the gender gap.

FIGURE 11.3

Partisan Divisions in Public Opinion about Ferguson

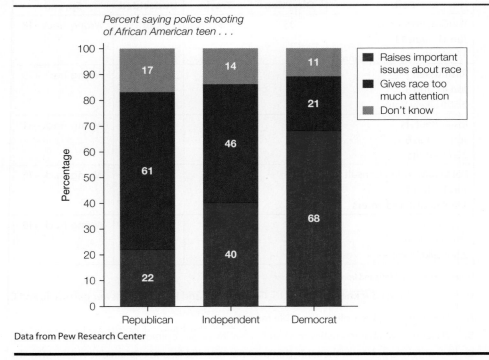

Percent saying police shooting of African American teen . . .

- Raises important issues about race
- Gives race too much attention
- Don't know

Data from Pew Research Center

FIGURE 11.4

The Gender Gap in American Politics

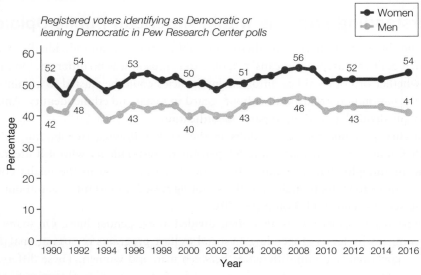

Registered voters identifying as Democratic or leaning Democratic in Pew Research Center polls

- Women
- Men

Data from Pew Research Center

FIGURE 11.5

Racial Divisions in Opinions of Authorities' Handling of the Ferguson Investigation

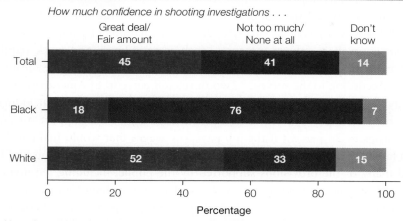

How much confidence in shooting investigations . . .

	Great deal/ Fair amount	Not too much/ None at all	Don't know
Total	45	41	14
Black	18	76	7
White	52	33	15

Percentage

Note: Survey conducted August 14–17, 2014. Whites and blacks include only those who are not Hispanic. Figures may not add to 100% because of rounding.

Data from Pew Research Center

American public opinion is also often divided on the basis of racial and ethnic identity. Members of American racial and ethnic minorities emphasize the importance of social justice and equality of opportunity more than white Americans do,[37] patterns that are correlated with the fact that racial and ethnic minorities are more likely to experience economic challenges and poverty.[38] In the days following the shooting in Ferguson, public opinion surveys revealed sharp racial divisions about how the events there were perceived. African Americans overwhelmingly felt that Brown's shooting raised important racial issues and that the police response to the shooting was inappropriate or insufficient. They also expressed a lack of confidence in the subsequent investigations into the shooting (Figure 11.5).[39]

How Polls Are Used

Public opinion polling is used by researchers, candidates, elected officials, interest groups, the media, and others who are interested in public policy to measure Americans' viewpoints about government and politics. But the relationship between public opinion and democratic government is complicated. Elected officials use polling to figure out what the public wants. They can also use polling data to shape the way they spin their policy decisions to the public.

Critics of the use of polling to make policy decisions argue that public officials are elected to lead, not to follow the whims of popular thought. A British pollster bluntly stated, "The public can be wrong. There are many areas where public understanding of an issue is well out of line with the facts."[40] Critics point to potential flaws in polling, such as citizens' lack of knowledge and the wording of poll questions.[41] In an article published by the Brookings Institute, E. J. Dionne and Thomas E. Mann state, "When analysts, sometimes innocently, use poll numbers as a definitive guide to public opinion . . . they are writing fiction."[42]

Public Opinion and Policymaking

It's difficult to measure the degree to which public opinion shapes the legislation passed by Congress because multiple factors influence Congress in the policymaking process. The Personal Responsibility and Work Opportunity Act (PRWORA) of 1996[43] was bipartisan legislation that addressed the public's dissatisfaction with the nation's welfare system. Before PRWORA was passed, a survey of Americans nationwide found that "the public supports strong welfare reform measures, such as time limits and work requirements, but is reluctant to simply cut people off and leave them without some means of basic support."[44] According to the survey, "Two-thirds (68 percent) of Americans favor ending welfare payments after two years for all able-bodied welfare recipients, including women with preschool children, and requiring them to take a job. But support for cutting off payments drops to 26 percent if the job pays low wages that would make it difficult to support a family, and to only 16 percent if the person is unable to find a job."[45] PRWORA contained many of the provisions supported by the public, including requirements that welfare recipients find a job within two years, and a five-year limit for receiving benefits.[46]

Members of Congress may decide to ignore public opinion in passing legislation. The Tax Cuts and Jobs Act,[47] passed by Congress in the fall of 2017, is an example of legislation passed despite public opposition. Research conducted by Gallup a couple of weeks before the tax bill was passed showed that only three in ten Americans supported the legislation.[48] There are several reasons why Congress would pass a bill opposed by most of the public. Supporters of the bill, who believe it will benefit citizens and grow the economy in the long run, speculate that public opinion will become more favorable over time, once many Americans see reduced taxes.[49] The media might follow suit, reporting more favorably on the public's opinion of the law. The Republican Party, which supported the tax bill, might improve its electoral successes in the 2018 midterm elections, and the approval rating for Congress as a whole might increase.[50] Another key factor was pressure from interest groups and donors. Congressman Chris Collins (R-NY) admitted, "My donors are basically saying, 'Get it done or don't ever call me again.'"[51] Even if the law remains unpopular with the public as a whole, the Republican base might be energized by the successful effort to reform the tax system, a promise made by President Trump in his 2016 campaign.[52] However, as the tax bill illustrates, members of Congress sometimes act contrary to the polls. The degree to which polling influences the voting decisions of members of Congress depends on whether they view themselves as delegates, who carry out the wishes of their constituents, or trustees, who make decisions based on their information and judgment (the delegate and trustee roles were discussed in Chapter 4). However, Congress ignores public opinion at its peril. If the legislation continues to be unpopular, dissatisfied voters may take out their anger against incumbents in the next election.

Public Opinion and the Response to Ferguson

In 2015, on the one-year anniversary of Michael Brown's death, protests and violence once again erupted in the city of Ferguson. News reports noted, "A peaceful day of protest and remembrance dissolved into chaos late Sunday after shots were fired and one person was hit by gunfire."[53]

The police response *had* changed, however. As reported by the *New York Times*, "No police officers in riot gear emerged Friday night when protesters arrived, a tactic that has drawn criticism. Rather, a small handful of officers calmly walked out and spoke with demonstrators. Many of the Ferguson police on the scene wore white polo shirts rather than their regular uniforms."[54] Political leaders and candidates for the 2016 presidential election were paying attention to public opinion and the protests. They began to talk about Ferguson and what it meant for the nation going forward. During the first Democratic Party presidential candidate debate in October 2015, one of the invited members of the public asked, "My question for the candidates is, do black lives matter, or do all lives matter?" Senator Bernie Sanders (I-VT) immediately replied, "Black lives matter."[55]

As shown in the graph, a poll conducted in 2014 revealed that 80 percent of African Americans and about 63 percent of Hispanics believed that police sometimes treat minority groups unfairly.[56] Members of Congress paid attention. In January 2015, as reported by the *St. Louis Post-Dispatch*, "On the eve of the Martin Luther King holiday, leading black members of Congress squeezed into a packed Ferguson church to deliver a specific message: We've got your backs. . . . There, they vowed to push for criminal justice reform."[57] The article quoted Representative Andrew Carson (D-IN), who said, "We're not here to tell you what to do . . . just to let you know you've got some firepower in Washington, D.C."

It is hard to assert that Ferguson *caused* a change in public opinion, only that there is a potentially meaningful *correlation* between Ferguson and Americans' changing perceptions of race discrimination. That said, politicians ignore public opinion at their peril, and changes in public opinon should not be taken lightly.

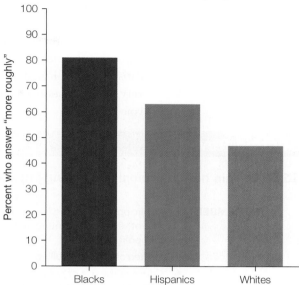

Race and Ethnicity as Factors in Perception of Police Treatment of Minorities, 2015

Data from Associated Press and National Opinion Research Center

Protestors prepared to march in downtown St. Louis on August 10, 2015, to mark the one-year anniversary of Michael Brown's death. The police response to the march was markedly different from previous protests and was much more measured and low key.
Rick Wilking/Reuters/Newscom

How to Understand Changing Public Opinion

In this chapter, we have examined what public opinion is, how it is measured, and how public opinion is used to impact policymaking. The events in Ferguson and the NFL protest highlight differences in the public's opinion about race relations. Public opinion evolves, impacting the media, interest groups, and politicians who must respond to it. Political scientist John W. Kingdon once asked, "But what makes an idea's time come?"[58] That is a very good question if people want to shape policies through public opinion and get their voices heard.

Section Review

11.3 Explain how public opinion polling impacts elections and policymaking.

REMEMBER
- Public opinion polling is used by researchers, candidates, elected officials, interest groups, the media, and others who are interested in public policy to measure Americans' viewpoints about government and politics.
- Elected officials use polling to figure out what the public wants and to shape the way the public views issues.
- Critics of the use of polling to make policy decisions argue that public officials are elected to lead, and not to follow the whims of the public.

THINK
When should elected officials rely on public opinion in making policy decisions, and under what circumstances should they ignore public opinion?

11.3 Review Question: Free Response

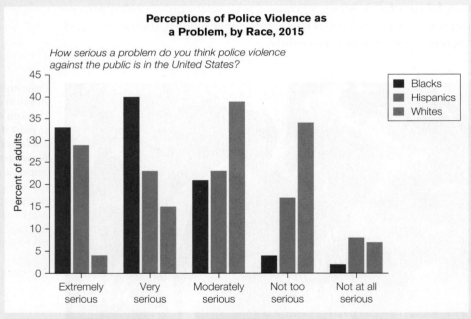

Perceptions of Police Violence as a Problem, by Race, 2015

How serious a problem do you think police violence against the public is in the United States?

Data from Associated Press and National Opinion Research Center

Use the bar charts and your knowledge of U.S. Government and Politics to answer parts A, B, and C.

A. Identify one trend shown in the bar charts.

B. Describe one limitation of the data shown in the bar charts in measuring public opinion.

C. Describe one way in which public opinion may shape the policymaking agenda.

Chapter 11 Review

AP® EXAM PRACTICE and Critical Thinking Project

MULTIPLE-CHOICE QUESTIONS

1. Which of the following poll questions is most likely to lead to a valid result, assuming the poll is taken using scientific methods?
   - **A.** Do you agree or disagree with the unjustified shooting of unarmed American citizens?
   - **B.** Do you agree that stem cell research has the potential to improve outcomes for patients suffering from cancer?
   - **C.** Do you agree or disagree with the way Donald Trump is doing his job as president?
   - **D.** Would you support a tax plan that benefits the rich at the expense of the poor?

2. In an effort to measure Americans' views on the death penalty, students in a high school government class take a poll of every fifth person entering the local coffee shop from 8:00 a.m. to 8:00 p.m. on a Saturday. Which of the following statements best describes the validity of the poll results?
   - **A.** The poll results are valid because respondents were selected at random.
   - **B.** The poll results are not valid because the respondents are not representative of the nation.
   - **C.** The poll results are scientific, as long as the sample size was large enough.
   - **D.** The poll results are not scientific, because the poll was not conducted by a reputable polling firm.

3. Which of the following best explains why it was more difficult for the polls to predict the outcome of the 2016 presidential election than it had been in the past?
   - **A.** Fewer polls were taken.
   - **B.** The media relied on exit polls, instead of public opinion polls.
   - **C.** The voters surveyed were not representative of those who voted.
   - **D.** The wording of the polls favored Hillary Clinton, overestimating her support.

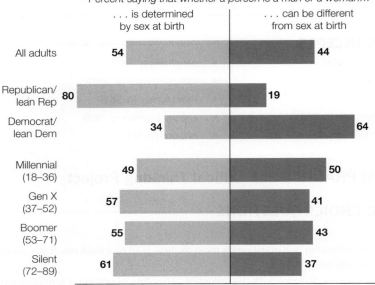

Views on Gender Identification Align with Party Affiliation

Percent saying that whether a person is a man or a woman...

	... is determined by sex at birth	... can be different from sex at birth
All adults	54	44
Republican/lean Rep	80	19
Democrat/lean Dem	34	64
Millennial (18–36)	49	50
Gen X (37–52)	57	41
Boomer (53–71)	55	43
Silent (72–89)	61	37

Data from Pew Research Center

4. The bar chart supports which of the following conclusions?

   A. Democrats are more likely to support the rights of transgendered persons than Republicans.

   B. Most members of Generation X believe that gender can be different from sex at birth.

   C. There is a significant difference in viewpoints about being transgendered between Baby Boomers and members of Generation X.

   D. Democrats and Republicans have starkly contrasting viewpoints on transgender issues.

Use the quote to answer question 5.

With public sentiment, nothing can fail; without it nothing can succeed. Consequently he who moulds public sentiment, goes deeper than he who enacts statutes or pronounces decisions. He makes statutes and decisions possible or impossible to be executed.

—Abraham Lincoln, Debate at Ottawa, Illinois, 1858[59]

5. Which of the following views about public opinion is conveyed in the quote?

   A. Public opinion plays a powerful role in shaping the policy agenda.

   B. It is important to use opinion polls to determine the public's view on an issue.

   C. Officials fail to lead when they rely too much on public opinion.

   D. Public opinion frequently shifts, making it hard for the government to create new policies.

"My pollster tells me it's 'position-switchero' time.'

Joseph Farris, www.cartoonstock.com

6. Which of the following best describes the viewpoint expressed in the cartoon?

  A. Americans are not very knowledgeable about candidates and campaigns.

  B. Exit polling is not an effective measure of how a voter will vote.

  C. Politicians change their stance on the issues based on polling results.

  D. Public opinion polls are more accurate when they are taken in person, rather than by phone.

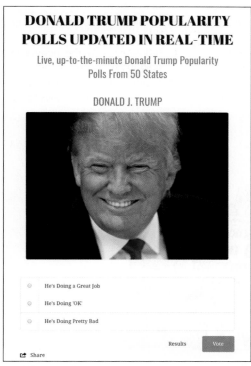

donaldtrumppolls.com

7. The screen capture is from an online polling organization. Which of the following best describes the validity of the results from this poll?

  A. The results of this online poll are more reliable than results from a telephone poll.

  B. The results are not reliable because there is no way to determine the sample size.

  C. The results are not reliable because the poll is conducted by an organization favorable to President Trump.

  D. The results are not reliable because the sample is not random.

Use this graph to answer questions 8 and 9.

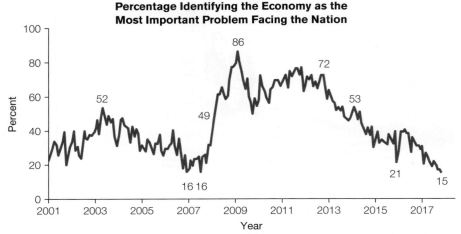

Percentage Identifying the Economy as the Most Important Problem Facing the Nation

Data from Gallup

8. Which of the following best describes a trend shown in the poll results?

   A. Since 2010, the economy has been the most important issue facing the nation.

   B. The percentage of people who mention the economy as the nation's most important problem has declined from 2014 to 2017.

   C. From 2001 to 2017, more than 50 percent of Americans identified the economy as the most important issue facing the nation.

   D. Presidential elections have a large impact on Americans' views about the importance of economic issues.

9. Which of the following is a criticism of the poll shown in the graph?

   A. It does not identify the aspects of the economy that concern respondents the most, such as unemployment or inflation.

   B. It does not accurately measure the economic growth rate.

   C. It does not take the income and wealth of the respondents into account.

   D. It defines the economy as a problem, and this wording results in negative views toward the economy.

Dave Granlund/Cagle Cartoons

10. Which of the following statements best describes the viewpoint expressed in the cartoon?

   A. Older Americans are more likely to trust polling data than younger Americans.

   B. Most Americans don't trust government officials.

   C. Polls purport to measure political attitudes, but most Americans don't trust the validity of polling data.

   D. Headlines often cover poll results, and people are more interested in poll results than news stories.

FREE-RESPONSE QUESTIONS

1. The polling data and commentary refer to the 2016 presidential election.

National Polling Average: Presidential Race, May–October 2016

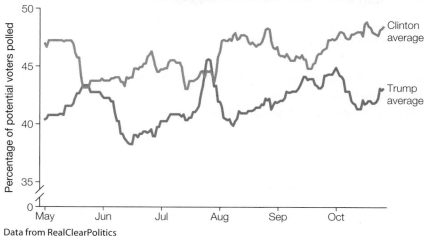

Data from RealClearPolitics

During the 2016 election, the *New York Times* Upshot column wanted to understand variation in poll results. The reporters gave the same raw data from a poll of Florida voters to four other pollsters to interpret. The result? As the *Washington Post* described it,

> Those four pollsters didn't all come back with the same result. The responses were a one-point Clinton lead, a three-point Clinton lead, a four-point Clinton lead, and a one-point lead for Donald Trump.[60]

Use the polling data, commentary, and your knowledge of U.S. Government and Politics to answer parts A, B, and C.

A. Identify one trend in the polling data shown in the graph.

B. Describe two elements of a valid, scientific public opinion poll.

C. Explain one reason why different pollsters using the same data might reach different conclusions.

2. By a faction, I understand a number of citizens, whether amounting to a majority or minority of the whole, who are united and actuated by some common impulse of passion, or of interest, adverse to the rights of other citizens, or to the permanent and aggregate interests of the community.

—James Madison, *Federalist* No. 10

Use the quote and your knowledge of U.S. Government and Politics to answer parts A, B, and C.

A. Describe the meaning of the term "faction," as defined in *Federalist* No. 10.

B. Using your description of faction in part A, describe one danger in using public opinion polling to establish public policy.

C. Describe one argument in favor of politicians using public opinion polling in making public policy.

ARGUMENTATION QUESTION

The Supreme Court's decision that state-sponsored prayer in public schools violates the establishment clause in *Engel v. Vitale*[61] has generated controversy. Should the Supreme Court overturn its decision in *Engel v. Vitale*? Some people believe that members of Congress should use public opinion polling in deciding which policies to support. Others believe that members of Congress should use their own judgment in making decisions about policies. Should members of Congress rely on public opinion as an important factor in making policies?

In your essay:

- Articulate a claim or thesis that responds to the prompt, and use a line of reasoning to defend it.
- Use at least TWO pieces of relevant and accurate evidence to support your claim.
- At least ONE piece of evidence must be from one of the listed foundational documents:
  - United States Constitution
  - *Federalist* No. 10
  - *Federalist* No. 51
- Use a second piece of evidence from another foundational document from the list or from your study of public opinion or Congress.
- Use reasoning to explain why the evidence you provided supports your claim or thesis.
- Use refutation, concession, or rebuttal to respond to an opposing or alternative perspective.

CRITICAL THINKING PROJECT

Analyzing and Manipulating Data

Pick an issue that interests you. You can find a list of important issues at PollingReport.com under "Issues Facing the Nation." Click on the issue, and find a poll about the issue that reports data as percentages.

Use the data to create a line graph, bar chart, or pie chart that accurately represents the poll results.

Now use the data to create a line graph, bar chart, or pie chart that *inaccurately* represents the poll results. One easy way to do this is to change the scale of the graph to make the percentages look closer or farther away from one another.

1. Write a sentence or two comparing the two graphs or charts you created.
2. Write a short paragraph explaining how the second graph or chart you created might be used for political purposes.
3. Describe two additional ways to present data in a misleading way, other than by changing the scale.

12 Political Ideology
How Beliefs Shape Our Choices

As we discussed in Chapter 10, political culture consists of Americans' shared values. While Americans share many of the same basic values, they often disagree sharply about the desired outcomes of the policymaking process. A **political ideology** is a set of beliefs about *what* should happen as the result of the process of governance. Individuals' political ideologies may differ on, for example, the degree to which government should regulate economic activity, how deeply government should be involved in individuals' decisions in their private lives, or how much government should act to ensure equality of opportunity.

The issue of health care policy often divides people along ideological lines. Here, members of the liberal group MoveOn.org protest in an effort to protect the Affordable Care Act and two other government-funded health-care programs, Medicare and Medicaid.
SAUL LOEB/AFP/Getty Images

political ideology
a set of beliefs about the desired goals and outcomes of a process of governance.

The high costs of health care and the provision of health insurance have been a source of continuing debate along ideological lines. Health care is paid for by a combination of private, out-of-pocket insurance and government funding. Many Americans receive insurance plans as a benefit offered by their employers, and some workers rely on plans administered by labor unions. Others buy health insurance for themselves and their families or simply pay for health care when they need it. Medicare is a federally run insurance program for those over age sixty-five, and Medicaid is a social program offering insurance for those with low income, jointly run by the states and the federal government. Debate continues about how to provide more access to health care and about whether insurance coverage should be universal.

right
something guaranteed, that the government cannot take away.

privilege
something a person may obtain or receive, but that the government can take away.

Health Care: A Right or a Privilege?

The debate over health-care policy reflects differences in political ideologies about the role of government. Some people believe health care is a **right**. Others view health care as a **privilege**, subject to political and market forces.

Ideological differences regarding health-care policy are demonstrated by the different approaches taken by President Obama and President Trump. As he prepared to take over the presidency in 2009, Barack Obama was about to face one of the most important decisions that any new president-elect has to confront: what to focus on in the early weeks and months of a new administration. At the beginning of their terms, presidents often have their greatest momentum and political opposition has not had a chance to crystallize.[1] In his speech before a joint session of Congress in February 2009, Obama called upon Congress to "address the crushing cost of health care."[2] Obama noted, "This is a cost that now causes bankruptcy in America every thirty seconds. By the end of the year, it could cause 1.5 million Americans to lose their homes."[3]

A printout of the nearly two-thousand-page Affordable Health Care for America Act sits on the podium following a news conference held by House Republicans. Only a single GOP member voted for the House version of the health-care bill.
Scott J. Farrell/Congressional Quarterly/Getty

By fall 2009, Democrats in the House of Representatives and the Senate had crafted their health-care reform proposals, which reflected their ideological belief that the government should require people to purchase health insurance, in an effort to make health care more universally available. In October, House Speaker Nancy Pelosi (D-CA) delivered a draft of a bill that ran 1,990 pages and weighed in at 20 pounds.[4] As she unveiled her bill, Pelosi said, "Leaders of all political parties, starting over a century ago, with President Theodore Roosevelt, have called and fought for health care and health insurance reform. . . ."[5] The quote reflects the fact that health care has been on the public agenda for a long time. However, parties have had ideological differences over the government's approach to health-care policy.

In 2009, Congress passed the Patient Protection and Affordable Care Act (ACA).[6] For Claire and Allen Secrist, the law provided coverage for their daughter that they would never have been able to pay for on their own. Their young daughter, Holly, developed eye cancer. With a combined income of $30,000, the Secrists could not afford the kind of health care she required except through the Affordable Care Act. With a variety of subsidies, including federal tax credits, the Secrists were able to obtain what would have been prohibitively expensive family medical care for less than $3,000 a year out of pocket. Her mother, Claire, later commented, "We would likely try to get some care—like vaccinations—at community health centers. But otherwise, I guess we would just be in a lot of trouble."[7]

Other Americans had a less positive experience under the ACA. Jennifer and Keith Gibbs live just 30 miles away from the Secrists in North Carolina, but the Gibbses saw the premiums for their self-purchased health insurance policy soar. Within a few years, their premiums spiked from $7,200 on their former insurance plan to $16,000 on their state's ACA exchange, partly because their new insurance plan covered a range of things, like mental health benefits and maternity coverage, that were not covered in their previous plan.[8] Insurers like Blue Cross Blue Shield of North Carolina—where the Gibbses had obtained their private plan—argued that the dramatic increases in premiums were necessary to pay for the ACA's promises.

During his campaign in the presidential election of 2016, Donald Trump promised to repeal and replace the ACA. President Trump's ideology regarding health care differed from President Obama's. President Trump does not believe it is the government's role to require individuals to purchase health insurance. Facing a highly charged political climate on Capitol Hill, as well as sharp ideological divisions within the Republican Party, President Trump was unable to completely repeal the ACA, although the tax penalty for not having insurance coverage was suspended, effective in 2019.[9] The ideological debate over the ACA and the question of the government's role in making health-care policy continues.

Before you continue into the chapter, examine Figure 12.1 about ideology. Place yourself ideologically on the graphics.

Claire, Holly, and Allen Secrist have needed the kind of financial assistance to buy comprehensive insurance coverage that the Affordable Care Act provides—and yet others argue that subsidies distort the market for health insurance.
Jonathan Cohn/The Huffington Post

After reading this chapter, you will be able to

12.1 Describe the different ideologies of the Republican and Democratic parties.

12.2 Describe liberal and conservative perspectives on economic policy making.

12.3 Describe monetary policy and how the Federal Reserve uses the money supply to regulate the economy.

12.4 Describe liberal and conservative perspectives on social policy.

LEARNING TARGETS

FIGURE 12.1

Thinking about Ideology and Shapers of American Ideology

This graphic is a way of thinking of ideology two-dimensionally. The left tends to favor shared economic action, and the right prefers individual economic initiative. Take a moment to place yourself and your ideas on the graphic.

Data from Wikimedia

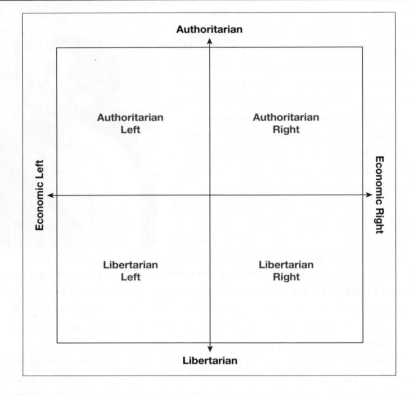

This graphic shows where the Political Compass ideology quiz places figures from recent U.S. presidential campaigns and several famous political figures from outside the United States. Do you agree with where the graphic places certain people?

Data from Political Compass blog

12.1 Party Ideology

The United States is a diverse society, and public policies reflect the attitudes and beliefs of citizens who participate in the political process. Because the United States is made up of so many different groups, policymakers must balance competing ideologies. Some people favor policies establishing order and stability over policies promoting individual liberties. Others favor the protection of liberty over policies to promote public order. Some people want the government to enforce strict codes of moral behavior, while others oppose government efforts to regulate moral behavior. The Republican and Democratic parties have different approaches in balancing these interests. As we have seen in previous chapters, debates over social and economic issues, such as welfare policies and immigration reform, reflect these party differences.

Party ideology refers to a party's philosophy about the proper role of government and its set of positions on major issues. **Party identification** is an individual's attachment to a political party.

The Republican Party is associated with **conservatism**, an ideology favoring more control of social behavior, fewer regulations on businesses, and less government intervention in the economy. The Democratic Party is associated with **liberalism**, an ideology supporting less government control over social behavior and more regulation of businesses and of the economy (Figure 12.2). **Libertarianism**, a third ideology, favors very little government regulation and intervention beyond protecting private property and individual liberty.

party ideology
a party's philosophy about the proper role of government and its set of positions on major issues.

party identification
an individual's attachment to a political party.

conservatism
an ideology favoring more control of social behavior, fewer regulations on businesses, and less government interference in the economy.

liberalism
an ideology favoring less government control over social behavior and more greater regulation of businesses and of the economy.

libertarianism
an ideology favoring very little government regulation and intervention beyond protecting private property and individual liberty.

FIGURE 12.2

Party Ideology: How Democrats and Republicans Differ on Public Policy

Democrat	Policy	Republican
Pro-choice	Abortion	Pro-life
Allow race-based preferences	Affirmative action	Prohibit race-based preferences
Focus on protecting the rights of the accused	Crime	Focus on strong punishment for offenders
Support regulation of businesses	Business	Ease regulation of businesses
Oppose	Death penalty	Support
Decrease or maintain	Defense spending	Increase
More regulation of firearms	Gun control	Less regulation of firearms
Support the Affordable Care Act	Health care	Repeal the Affordable Care Act
Allow a pathway to citizenship for undocumented immigrants, allow undocumented people to obtain drivers' licenses	Immigration	Oppose pathways to citizenship and drivers' licenses for undocumented immigrants
Increase	Minimum wage	Lower or eliminate
Support the current legality of same-sex marriages	Same-sex marriage	Support the idea that marriage should be defined as between one man and one woman
Less likely to support	School vouchers	More likely to support
Increase taxes, especially for wealthy	Taxes	Cut taxes, especially for businesses

Liberalism / *Conservatism*

The Republicans and Democrats have different ideologies about how to balance the competing values of liberty and order in addressing social and economic issues. Republicans favor the "liberty" to form a business relatively free of government regulation; this reflects a trust in the marketplace and a mistrust of government. In contrast, Democrats favor the "liberty" of sexual and marital privacy; this in turn reflects a mistrust of a tyranny of the majority, and a need for government to protect minority rights. Likewise, the Republicans seek "order" related to immigration, wanting to preserve traditional American values, while Democrats favor less strict immigration policies. In contrast, Democrats seek "order" regarding gun regulation, out of a mistrust of abuse from unrestricted gun use. Republicans are less supportive of gun regulations, favoring the individual liberty to own a firearm. Both parties seek "order" as well as "liberty." They just see the issues differently.

When balancing the competing values of order and liberty, Republicans favor a conservative ideology supporting stronger punishments for offenders, while Democrats are more concerned with liberal policies protecting the civil liberties of the accused. The Republican Party has adopted a pro-life platform, supporting the position that abortion should be banned. The Democratic Party is pro-choice, supporting the idea that the decision to have an abortion is part of the right of privacy. Conservative and liberal views about privacy differ depending on the type of government activity being used to restrict privacy. As shown in Figure 12.3, in 2014, during the Obama administration, conservatives were less likely to support NSA surveillance of phone and internet data than liberals.

The parties also differ on economic issues, with Democrats favoring tax increases for the wealthy, while Republicans favor tax cuts for businesses. Political ideology also impacts views of property rights and government regulations. Democrats tend to favor more regulation of businesses in the public interest, while Republicans prefer fewer regulations on business practices. Republicans tend to favor allowing individuals to use their property as they see fit, while Democrats favor rules that restrict uses of property that they believe might harm the community.

FIGURE 12.3

Party Ideology and Privacy: Americans' Opinions of NSA Surveillance

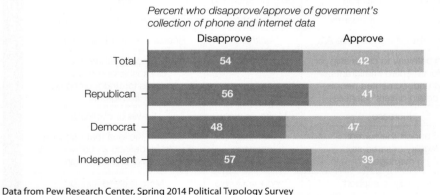

Percent who disapprove/approve of government's collection of phone and internet data

	Disapprove	Approve
Total	54	42
Republican	56	41
Democrat	48	47
Independent	57	39

Data from Pew Research Center, Spring 2014 Political Typology Survey

The issue of hydraulic fracturing, which is also called fracking, to extract natural gas illustrates these ideological tensions over regulations and property rights. Fracking involves using high-pressured injections of water and chemicals into rock to extract natural gas. Democratic-led governments in New York and Maryland banned fracking, despite the potential revenue from oil and natural gas.[10] Texas and Oklahoma, both conservative states controlled by Republicans, have gone in the opposite direction, passing laws to make sure that local towns and cities cannot outlaw the practice in their communities.[11] Opinions about fracking are divided along partisan lines. According to Hannah Wiseman, a Florida State University professor who researches environmental regulation, "[W]e have tended to see what would be expected, which is that the more liberal states tend to be more concerned about the environmental and social effects of fracking, whereas the more conservative states tend to welcome the money."[12]

It is important to remember that party ideology and party identification are not the same thing. Parties try to appeal to potential members by focusing on issues, policies, and solutions that might appeal to individuals with particular ideologies. As discussed in Chapter 10, however, an individual's political beliefs, including partisan identification, are formed through many influences, including family, education, and life experiences. Most people vote for candidates from the party whose ideology is most similar to their own.

Parties try to attract supporters by offering sharp ideological contrasts to each other. The Republican and Democratic national committees put out dozens of interviews, position papers, press releases, videos, tweets, and other social media presentations that seek to further a single larger point: Their position on the issues is right, and the other side's is wrong. Both parties display partisanship—they are less interested in fostering cooperation than they are in criticizing the ideological beliefs of their opponents. After the terrorist shootings in San Bernardino, California, in December 2015, Reince Priebus, who was the chair of the Republican National Committee, issued a statement saying that it proved Democrats "cannot be trusted to keep America safe from radical Islamic terrorists."[13] Meanwhile, Debbie Wasserman Schultz, who was the chair of the Democratic National Committee at the time, said her reelection to the House of Representatives was preferable to voters choosing "a bunch of radical Republicans who act like children."[14]

Section Review

This chapter's main ideas are reflected in the Learning Targets. By reviewing after each section, you should be able to

—**Remember** the key points,

—**Know** terms that are central to the topic, and

—**Think** critically about what ideology means in American life.

12.1 Describe the different ideologies of the Republican and Democratic parties.

REMEMBER
- The Republican Party is associated with conservatism, an ideology favoring more control of social behavior, fewer regulations of businesses, and less government interference in the economy.
- The Democratic Party is associated with liberalism, an ideology supporting less government control over social behavior and more regulation of businesses and the economy.

- *political ideology*: a set of beliefs about the desired goals and outcomes of a process of governance. (p. 382)
- *right*: something guaranteed, that the government cannot take away. (p. 382)
- *privilege*: something a person may obtain or receive, but that the government can take away. (p. 382)
- *party ideology*: a party's philosophy about the proper role of government and its set of positions on major issues. (p. 385)
- *party identification*: an individual's attachment to a political party. (p. 385)
- *conservatism*: an ideology favoring more control of social behavior, fewer regulations on businesses, and less government interference in the economy. (p. 385)
- *liberalism*: an ideology favoring less government control over social behavior and more regulation of businesses and of the economy. (p. 385)
- *libertarianism*: an ideology favoring very little government regulation and intervention beyond protecting private property and individual liberty. (p. 385)

THINK   How do the ideologies of the Democratic and Republican Parties reflect different views of the importance of individual liberty and social order?

12.1 Review Question: Free Response

Jim Morin, Miami Herald

Use your knowledge of AP® U.S. Government and Politics and the cartoon to answer parts A, B, and C.

A.   Describe the viewpoint expressed in the cartoon about party ideology.

B.   Pick one policy issue and describe one ideological difference between the Democratic and Republican parties regarding the issue you chose.

C.   Explain one way in which an ideological difference between the Democratic and Republican parties might impact the scope of government.

12.2 Ideology and Economic Policymaking

All societies wrestle with the question of the proper role of government in regulating economic activity. To what degree should individuals and businesses be left alone to pursue their own economic interests? To what degree should the government regulate working conditions, consumer safety, and the environment?

Government Intervention in the Economy

In 1776, Adam Smith wrote *An Inquiry into the Nature and Causes of the Wealth of Nations*, which is still used today to argue in support of a free market economy. Smith argued that national economic prosperity can best be obtained by allowing individuals to freely pursue their own economic interest and bargain with others in a competitive marketplace. In a **laissez-faire economy**, governments intervene as little as possible in the economic transactions between citizens and businesses. The term *laissez-faire* comes from a French expression, which means, "let us do it," or to leave alone. In reality, however, it has never been as simple as keeping the government out of the economy. Even in the nineteenth century, for example, the federal government acted in the economy to support broad policy goals, such as the building of the Transcontinental Railroad.

At the other end of the spectrum is a **command-and-control economy**, in which government dictates much of a nation's economic activity, including the amount of production and the price of goods. Before the Soviet Union collapsed in the early 1990s, it used command-and-control economic practices. China abandoned its command-and-control economy switching to a mixed market system in the 1980s. The result has been unprecedented economic growth.[15]

The United States has a **mixed economy**, in which many economic decisions are left to individuals and businesses, with the federal and state governments regulating economic activity. In Chapter 3, we discussed American federalism and the growth of national influence across a host of policy areas, including those involving the economy.

Monitoring the Health of the Economy

The federal government collects and distributes data about the health of the economy and uses this information to guide economic policy making. Federal policymakers rely on a few key data indicators.

Gross domestic product (GDP) measures the total value of goods and services produced by American economic activity. A decline or stagnation of the nation's GDP indicates that the country's economy is not firing on all cylinders and could be slipping into an **economic recession**, which is typically defined by two consecutive quarters of negative GDP growth. This is not good for American workers—or for their elected representatives should voters blame them for the recession.

Economists also focus on the **unemployment rate**, which is measured by the percentage of people actively looking for work who are unable to find jobs.[16] The unemployment rate underestimates the problem because it does not take into account people who would like to find a job but have become so discouraged that they have given up looking for work.

A third key indicator of the health of the American economy is the rate of **inflation**, or the rise in the prices of goods and services. A high rate of inflation, especially if not

laissez-faire economy
economic policy in which governments intrude as little as possible in the economic transactions between citizens and businesses.

command-and-control economy
economic policy in which government dictates much of a nation's economic activity, including the amount of production and price for goods.

mixed economy
economic policy in which many economic decisions are left to individuals and businesses, with the government regulating economic activity.

gross domestic product (GDP)
the total value of goods and services produced by an economy.

economic recession
a period of decline in economic activity, typically defined by two consecutive quarters of negative GDP growth.

unemployment rate
the percentage of people actively looking for work who cannot find jobs.

inflation
the rise in the prices of goods and services.

consumer price index (CPI)

the cost of a fixed basket of goods and services over time, used to measure the cost of living.

accompanied by an equal increase in wages, makes American workers poorer. One key measure of inflation is the **consumer price index (CPI)**, which measures the cost of a basket of fixed goods and services over time.[17] Every month, employees of the Bureau of Labor Statistics track the prices of about 80,000 items, including a variety of things like breakfast cereal, gasoline, pet food, college tuition, and funeral expenses.[18] Many programs that involve mandatory spending, such as Social Security payments, are tied to calculations of the nation's CPI. If the CPI goes up, for example, Social Security recipients may receive a cost-of-living raise in their benefits.

Oftentimes, there is a trade-off between inflation and unemployment. Republicans are usually willing to accept higher unemployment rates to achieve lower rates of inflation. Democrats are more willing to tolerate inflation to lower the unemployment rate.[19]

Business Cycles and Theories of Economic Policymaking

Policymakers have different ideas about how to define economic problems and how to solve them. Even when policymakers agree that an economic problem exists, they often differ in explaining why it happened and on how to fix it.

Economists use the term business cycle to describe this cyclical nature of economic activity. An economy experiencing a generally upward trend of positive GDP growth may still experience periods of contraction and expansion (Figure 12.4). Keynesianism, supply-side economics, and monetarism are three theories that explain how government activities affect the performance of the economy as a whole.

Keynesianism

One theory of business cycles comes from the work of John Maynard Keynes, whose highly influential work, *The General Theory of Employment, Interest, and Money*, was published in 1936 during the depths of the Great Depression.[20] For Keynes, the combined

FIGURE 12.4

The Business Cycle

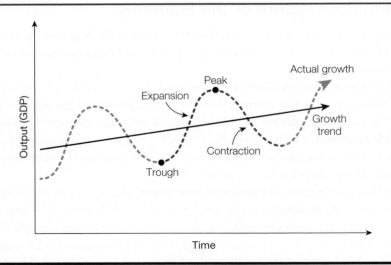

effect of individual decisions with regard to saving and spending drives business cycles. During periods of expansion, individuals become overconfident about future economic conditions and may make excessive, unwise investing decisions, thus exacerbating the economic boom. In periods of economic contraction, individuals become excessively gloomy and cut back on spending and investing, thereby exacerbating the contraction, possibly to the point of a national economic depression.

For Keynes, therefore, governmental economic policy should counterbalance a contraction by injecting more money into the economy. Democrats often support Keynesian policies, such as the creation of public works projects by the Roosevelt administration as part of the New Deal during the Great Depression. During the 2007–2009 recession, President Obama proposed a massive public works project with the goal of creating 2.5 million jobs.[21]

Supply-Side Theory

In stark contrast to Keynesian economic theory, which emphasizes the demand for goods and services, supply-side theory emphasizes the role of supply in fostering economic growth. Often called "Reaganomics" in reference to one of the theory's most influential proponents, President Ronald Reagan, supply-side theory proposes lower taxes on individuals and businesses as the most effective tool to combat economic downturns.

Critics of supply-side theory often use the term *trickle-down economics* to describe it, arguing that these policies benefit the wealthy and that it is unlikely these benefits will make their way to individuals not directly impacted by lower tax rates. Proponents of supply-side economics argue that excessive taxation is a drag on the economy, hindering the growth of businesses. In recent years, Republicans have tended to support supply-side economics. In December 2017, the Trump Administration successfully enacted legislation to cut individual and business taxes to boost economic growth.[22]

Managing the nation's economy is not an exact science. There are too many variables to predict all of the consequences of economic policy decisions. In spite of these uncertainties, federal authorities attempt to influence the economy through two important tools—monetary policy and fiscal policy. Through **fiscal policy** the government uses taxation and spending to attempt to lower unemployment, support economic growth, and stabilize the economy. As discussed in Chapters 4 and 5, fiscal policy is shaped mostly by Congress and the president.

fiscal policy
government use of taxes and spending to attempt to lower unemployment, support economic growth, and stabilize the economy.

Guiding the Nation's Economy through Decisions on Spending and Taxation

Republicans and Democrats have different ideologies about fiscal policy. Republicans often support budgets that increase military spending and decrease taxes. For example, the Bush tax cuts passed in 2001 and 2003 reduced income tax rates for wealthy Americans and for those earning below average income.[23] At the same time, military spending increased to fund the wars in Iraq and Afghanistan. The budget showed a record federal deficit of $374 billion in 2003.[24] President Obama's fiscal policy focused on tax increases for the wealthiest Americans[25] and government spending programs to stimulate the economy. In his final budget proposal, submitted in 2016, the president proposed boosting total spending by 4.9 percent, mostly as a result of increases in mandatory programs, such as Social Security.[26] The deficit at the end of 2016 was $548 billion.[27] President Trump's

TABLE 12.1 What Is the Best Way to Handle Economic Cycles?

According to ...	The government should ...
Monetary Theory	Match the growth of the money supply to the growth in economic productivity
Keynesianism	Stimulate the economy during times of economic recession by spending money to encourage economic growth
Supply-Side Theory	Stimulate the economy by cutting taxes to encourage businesses to grow and taxpayers to spend more money

federal budget for 2018 shows a budget deficit in excess of $1 trillion, largely due to a combination of tax cuts and increases in military and defense spending.[28] Although Democrats and Republicans differ about how to use taxing and spending to influence the economy, the budget is difficult to manage, and deficits will most likely occur well into the future.

Section Review

12.2 Describe liberal and conservative perspectives on economic policymaking.

REMEMBER
- The government uses fiscal policy to influence the economy through decisions about taxing and spending.
- The United States has a mixed economy in which many economic decisions are left to individuals and businesses, with federal and state regulation of economic activity.
- Gross domestic product, the unemployment rate, the inflation rate, and the consumer price index are economic indicators.
- Keynesian economics emphasizes government spending to stimulate the economy.
- Supply-side theory emphasizes tax cuts to stimulate the economy.

KNOW
- *laissez-faire economy*: economic policy in which governments intrude as little as possible in the economic transactions between citizens and businesses. (p. 389)
- *command-and-control economy*: economic policy in which government dictates much of a nation's economic activity, including the amount of production and prices for goods. (p. 389)
- *mixed economy*: economic policy in which many economic decisions are left to individuals and businesses, with the government regulating economic activity. (p. 389)
- *gross domestic product (GDP)*: the total value of goods and services produced by an economy. (p. 389)
- *economic recession*: a period of decline in economic activity, typically defined by two consecutive quarters of negative GDP growth. (p. 389)
- *unemployment rate*: the percentage of people actively looking for work who cannot find jobs. (p. 389)
- *inflation*: the rise in the prices of goods and services. (p. 389)
- *consumer price index (CPI)*: the cost of a fixed basket of goods and services over time, used to measure the cost of living. (p. 390)
- *fiscal policy*: government use of taxing and spending to attempt to lower unemployment, support economic growth, and stabilize the economy. (p. 391)

THINK
- What factors make it difficult for the federal government to influence the economy?
- What are the similarities of and differences between Keynesian and supply side economic theories?

There's an old saying: When you tax something, you get less of it. When you tax something less, you get more of it. Why is it so hard to believe that taxing investment and labor less will mean more of it? Trump has said from the start that this tax bill is about "making America more competitive" in a global economy.[29]

—Stephen Moore

Use the quote and your knowledge of AP® U.S. Government and Politics to answer parts A, B, and C.

A. Identify the economic theory supported by the quote.

B. Describe a strategy to improve the economy that would be used by policymakers who support the economic theory you identified in part A.

C. Describe a strategy to improve the economy that would be used by policymakers who support a different theory from the one you identified in part A.

12.3 Monetary Policy

According to monetary theory, the primary driver of business cycles is the supply of money in an economy, including the amount of credit available to people and businesses who want to borrow money. According to this theory, a policy that makes more money available will lead to inflation, with too much money chasing too few goods. Monetarists argue against government efforts to fine-tune the nation's economy through Keynesian policies that stimulate it, such as large public works projects, or supply-side policies that encourage economic growth, such as decreasing taxes. Instead, monetarists believe the government should try to match the access to money to the growth in economic productivity.

Monetary policy can unleash powerful and destructive forces. Countries facing bankruptcy sometimes resort to printing money with no financial backing. Controlling a nation's printing press can be a very dangerous responsibility. One of the worst instances of misusing monetary policy occurred in Germany, Austria, and Hungary in the 1920s, after the defeat of those nations in World War I. Those governments printed so much money that people used sacks to carry enough currency to buy food. Although there were many complicated reasons for the rise of the Nazi Party in Germany leading up to World War II, hyperinflation certainly contributed to the rise of fascism.[30] Societies in monetary chaos are vulnerable to anarchy, violence, and political extremism.

The Federal Reserve System

One way the federal government attempts to influence the economy is through the **Federal Reserve System**, often referred to as "the Fed." The system consists of a seven-member panel of governors, twelve regional Federal Reserve banks, and six thousand member banks. The members of the board of governors are appointed by the president and confirmed by the Senate. They serve fourteen-year, nonrenewable terms, except for the chair, who serves for a four-year term. The governors cannot be removed, except for cause, giving them some independence in making economic decisions.

The Fed sets **monetary policy**, regulating the amount of money in the economy. The Fed has three main tools to influence the economy. The Fed buys and sells Treasury

Federal Reserve System
a board of governors, Federal Reserve Banks, and member banks responsible for monetary policy.

monetary policy
a set of economic policy tools designed to regulate the amount of money in the economy.

Janet Yellen, chair of the U.S. Federal Reserve (at left), chairs a meeting of the board members. Yellen tried to chart a course for the economy to steer it back to health following the 2008 financial crisis. In 2018, Jerome Powell, who is seated second from her left, replaced Yellen.
Cliff Owen/Associated Press

securities. Buying a Treasury bill is investing in the U.S. government. The purchaser loans money to the government, and the government pays the money back when the Treasury bill is cashed, plus a set amount of interest. The Fed also sets reserve rates that require banks to have a certain amount of deposits kept in reserve. The higher the reserve rate, the less money banks have available to loan to their customers. The Fed also influences the interest rates banks pay to borrow money from the federal government. Lowering the federal funds rate stimulates the economy by encouraging businesses to borrow money because interest rates are lower. This influences other interest rates in the economy because banks and credit card companies usually adjust the rates that they charge their own customers in response to the actions of the Fed.

The goal in employing these tools is to encourage healthy economic growth without causing damaging levels of inflation, in which prices rise in response to a growth in the supply of money (too much money chasing too few goods). The Fed's policies may also be used to prevent the country from falling into an economic depression. The Fed lowered interest rates in response to the economic crisis of 2008 in an attempt to avoid the kind of crushing downturn characterized by the Great Depression in the 1930s.

The Challenges and Risks of Conducting Monetary Policy

The Federal Reserve System has critics. Some question whether or not it is truly independent of politics, especially when Congress or the president pressures it to take action. Others disagree with the Fed's stated goal of maintaining a "moderate inflation" of about 2 percent. While a 2 percent rise in the price of goods and services might not seem so drastic in one year, over time persistent moderate inflation undercuts the spending power of Americans if their wages don't go up.

International governments, financial firms, businesses, and individuals in America and abroad continues to have confidence in the nation's currency. The American dollar remains strong against other nations' currencies.

Interpreting Text-Based Sources: "Helicopter Ben" and Extreme Monetary Policy Options

In a speech in November 2002, Ben Bernanke, former chair of the Federal Reserve, discussed the powers of monetary policy in the face of the kind of crushing downturn that gripped the United States during the Great Depression.[31] Bernanke suggested the possibility that in extreme economic crisis, the Federal Reserve, operating in coordination with the federal government, could print enough money to finance a massive tax cut and economic stimulus. Bernanke was drawing from a 1969 essay published by economist Milton Friedman, in which Friedman suggested that if a helicopter flew over a community and dropped $1,000 in bills from the sky, and individuals were sure that it would be a one-time event, the unconventional policy might result in fiscal stimulus.[32]

Bernanke's reference in the 2002 speech, drew many sharp rebuttals in images, speeches, and text. In some media circles, he was called "Helicopter Ben." Consider this political cartoon, published in 2005. Bernanke was the chair of the Federal Reserve, missed signs that the mortgage industry was in trouble, and was blindsided when a financial crisis hit the nation in 2008.[33]

The political cartoon depicts a helicopter drop of money to struggling homeowners drowning in their mortgages.
Daryl Cagle/Cagle Cartoons

1. Describe the viewpoint conveyed in the cartoon.

2. Describe one way in which the federal government attempts to influence the economy.

3. Explain one way in which the federal government might use monetary policy to influence the economy during a recession.

Section Review

12.3 Describe monetary policy and how the Federal Reserve uses the money supply to regulate the economy.

REMEMBER
- Monetary policy is using the amount of money in circulation to influence the economy.
- The Federal Reserve System influences the economy by selling treasury bills, setting the interest rate for banks to borrow money from the federal government, and requiring that banks keep a certain amount of deposits on hand.

KNOW
- *Federal Reserve System*: a board of governors, Federal Reserve Banks, and member banks responsible for monetary policy. (p. 393)
- *monetary policy*: a set of economic policy tools designed to regulate the amount of money in the economy. (p. 393)

THINK
What are the dangers of using the money supply in an attempt to influence economic growth?

Risks to the forecast now seem more balanced than they have been for some time. In particular, the global picture has brightened as growth and inflation have broadly moved up for the first time in several years. Here at home, risks seem both moderate and balanced, including the downside risk of lower inflation and the upside risk of labor market overheating. The Committee has been patient in raising rates, and that patience has paid dividends. . . . If the economy performs about as expected, I would view it as appropriate to continue to gradually raise rates.[34]

—Jerome Powell, speech to the Economic Club of New York, June 2017

Jerome Powell became chair of the Federal Reserve in 2018. Use the quote from Powell's speech and your knowledge of AP® U.S. Government and Politics to answer parts A, B, and C.

A. Describe the viewpoint expressed in the quote.

B. Describe one way in which the members of the Federal Reserve board of governors are insulated from politics.

C. Explain one reason why the use of monetary policy to influence the economy has been criticized.

12.4 Ideology and Social Policy

Now we will shift our focus from economic to social policy. As with the economy, Democrats and Republicans have different ideas about social policy, and how to balance the values of individualism, freedom, and equality of opportunity.

The Federal Government and Health Care

Medicare
a federal program that provides health insurance to seniors and the disabled.

In the 1960s, President Lyndon Johnson's Great Society program created a social insurance program, amending the Social Security Act to establish Medicare, which provides health insurance to senior citizens (age sixty-five or older). In 1972, President Nixon signed a law extending Medicare benefits to the disabled. **Medicare** covers hospitalization and physicians' services. In 2003, President George W. Bush signed a law adding a prescription drug benefit to Medicare.[35] Collectively, Social Security and Medicare are massive programs, constituting by far the largest part of federal social welfare spending and much of the federal budget. This is expected to increase in the next decade and then level off in 2030 (Figure 12.5). Political forces have led to an expansion of the government's role in health care.

Medicaid
a federal program that provides health care for the poor.

In 1965, during the administration of President Johnson, Congress also enacted the **Medicaid** program, which covers health services for low-income Americans. While Medicare (along with Social Security) is run by the federal government and supported by federal taxes, Medicaid is jointly funded and administered by the states and the federal government. For fiscal year 2016, total spending on Medicaid was roughly $553.5 billion.[36]

In the late twentieth and early twenty-first centuries, both parties agreed that the nation's health-care system needed reform. In 2012, the United States had the highest medical care costs in the world, spending $8,233 per person, more than two-and-a-half times the average spent in other highly developed nations.[37]

The Patient Protection and Affordable Care Act

Most Americans obtain health insurance through their employers. However, in 2010, approximately 48 million Americans were uninsured, and millions of others were struggling to pay the costs of care and treatment.[38]

FIGURE 12.5

Projected Growth in Social Security and Medicare Payments

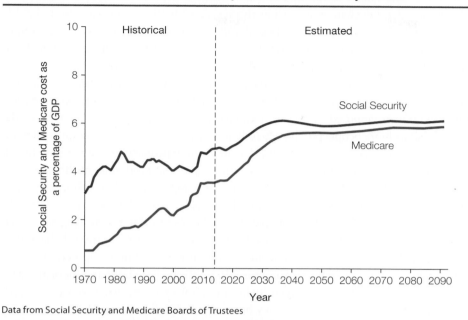

Data from Social Security and Medicare Boards of Trustees

On March 23, 2010, Obama signed the Patient Protection and Affordable Care Act into law. Not one Republican attended the signing. The Affordable Care Act (ACA), which is also called Obamacare, resulted in a major overhaul of the American health-care system. Among its key provisions were the following:

- A requirement that employers with more than fifty full-time employees provide health-care insurance for their employees or pay a penalty for not doing so
- A requirement for individuals to obtain health-care insurance (with some exceptions for religious beliefs or financial hardship) or pay a penalty for not doing so
- An expansion of Medicaid benefits for low-income Americans
- The creation of health-care exchanges in the states, with federal subsidies, to help individuals and small businesses obtain health-care insurance
- A requirement for health insurers to cover young adults up to the age of twenty-six on their parents' or guardians' plans
- A prohibition against excluding individuals with pre-existing medical conditions in most plans

As the ACA was implemented, there were bumps in the road. Many individuals initially found it hard to navigate the Web site to enroll. More significantly, by 2015 and 2016, many insurers were raising their premiums on the exchange policies or dropping out of the program entirely. On the positive side, however, in 2015 reports showed that more than 16 million Americans had obtained health-care coverage since the law's passage.[39]

The Republican Congress during Obama's second term was unsuccessful in attempting to overturn the ACA. Opponents of

President Barack Obama hunkers down with volunteer phone bank workers in October 2012 at an Organizing for America field office in Williamsburg, Virginia, to make phone calls to thank supporters who helped back his health-care efforts.
Nikki Kahn/The Washington Post via Getty Images

the ACA turned to the Supreme Court. In 2012, in *National Federation of Independent Businesses v. Sebelius*, the Court upheld the constitutionality of the individual mandate provision in the law.[40] In 2015, in *King v. Burwell*, the constitutionality of the tax credits in the ACA for federal exchanges as well as those created by the states was also upheld.[41]

The ACA is an interesting study in liberal and conservative ideologies on the complicated issue of health care. The ACA is not the same as nationalized health care owned and managed by the government, which is typical in most developed nations.

The requirement that individuals purchase health insurance or pay a fine is called the individual mandate. The original idea of the individual mandate came from conservative economists, who were opposed to President Clinton's health-care plan.[42] Supporters of the ACA argued that as more people purchase health insurance because the law requires them to, the overall costs of health care should decline. Healthy young people who did not have health insurance before the ACA would subsidize costs for people who need more health care.

Liberals argue that health care should be made widely available to all members of the public, and they supported the ACA for this reason. Republicans oppose the individual mandate, because they believe people should be responsible for making their own decisions about whether or not to purchase health insurance. Conservatives believe that health care should be subject to economic and market forces, and they opposed the ACA, especially the individual mandate. Furthermore, Republicans argued that Americans who buy insurance on the market are charged higher premiums to subsidize lower-cost health exchanges. Republicans opposed this policy because it redistributes wealth.[43]

President Donald Trump's successful tax overhaul legislation eliminated the mandate that individuals purchase health insurance or pay a fine. Republicans believe the individual mandate was an unnecessary government intrusion on individual freedom. The

AP® Political Science PRACTICES

Analyzing the Role of Ideology in Supreme Court Decisions: Chief Justice John Roberts and the Republicans

Dave Granlund/Cagle Cartoons

Many Republicans were surprised and upset by the Supreme Court's decision to uphold the constitutionality of the Affordable Care Act, especially considering the fact that Chief Justice John Roberts—who had been appointed by Republican president George W. Bush—sided with the majority. The Court ruled that Congress had the power to pass the ACA, using its expressed power of taxation provided in Article I, Section 8 of the Constitution. Consider the political cartoon, published in 2012 after the Court's decision in *National Federation of Independent Businesses v. Sebelius*. The elephant wearing a button with the abbreviation GOP (for Grand Old Party) is the traditional symbol of the Republican Party.

1. Describe the viewpoint expressed in the cartoon.

2. Describe one way in which political ideology impacts the appointment of Supreme Court justices.

3. Explain one reason why a Supreme Court justice might make a decision that goes against the ideological views of the president who appointed the justice.

Republican Party wants to repeal most of the rest of the ACA because they believe it interferes with the free market.

School Choice, Competition, and the Markets

Like health care, Republicans and Democrats differ ideologically on how to reform public education. School-choice reforms allow parents and guardians to choose their students' schools, which may encourage competition between the schools to attract students. School-choice advocates support vouchers, which use taxpayer money to pay for tuition in private and religious schools. Voucher programs blur the line between public and private schools, raising a host of issues.

Fannie M. Lewis, shortly before her death in 2008, in the Hough neighborhood of Cleveland.
John Kuntz/Cleveland Plain Dealer

Proponents argue that by offering alternatives to traditional public schools, vouchers create an environment in which all schools compete for students. The pressure put on the traditional public schools to retain their students and their funding by improving their standards would also benefit those unable to participate in the voucher programs. Opponents of vouchers fear the consequences of draining much-needed monies from traditional public schools and the creation of a lucky few schools that would gain at the expense of the many left behind. Opponents also argue that using tax dollars to support religious schools violates the First Amendment's establishment clause.[44]

Not all proponents of school vouchers are conservative. One key advocate of vouchers was Fannie M. Lewis, a Democratic councilwoman from one of Cleveland's poorest wards. One journalist called Lewis "the closest thing Cleveland has to a flesh-and-blood folk hero."[45] A devout Christian, Lewis advocated tirelessly for the voucher program, giving voice to the desperation she and many other Cleveland parents, grandparents, and guardians felt about their students' futures.

Most of Lewis's constituents, however, disagreed with the idea of providing taxpayer money to send kids to private schools. All twelve African American members of the Ohio House of Representatives eventually voted against it.[46] Many feared that the diversion of taxpayer money to private schools would put even more pressure on an already burdened system, leaving most public school students behind and denying them equality of opportunity. The controversial issue of school choice demonstrates ideological tensions between the core values of equality of opportunity and support for individualism and the free market.

Section Review

12.4 Describe liberal and conservative perspectives on social policy.

REMEMBER
- The Republican and Democratic parties have different ideas about social policies and about how to balance individual freedom, equality of opportunity, and societal order.
- Democrats supported the Patient Protection and Affordable Care Act (Obamacare), which included a requirement that most individuals purchase health insurance or pay a fine.
- Republicans opposed the Affordable Care Act because they believe it redistributes wealth and interferes with the free market.
- School-choice programs, like vouchers, provide market incentives to encourage competition between schools to improve.
- Republicans generally favor voucher programs, while Democrats usually oppose them.

- *Medicare*: a federal program that provides health insurance to seniors and the disabled. (p. 396)
- *Medicaid*: a federal program that provides health care for the poor. (p. 396)

THINK

- Should the American government be responsible for providing health care to citizens, or should the decision to purchase health care be an individual choice?
- Do school-choice programs, like vouchers, make schools better through competition, or do they drain necessary funds from the schools that need them the most?

12.4 Review Question: Free Response

In *Zelman v. Simmons-Harris*,[47] the Supreme Court considered a school voucher pilot program in Ohio providing tuition aid for certain students in the Cleveland City School District to attend participating public or private schools of their parent's choosing and tutorial aid for students who chose to remain enrolled in public school. Both religious and nonreligious schools in the district participated in the program.

The Supreme Court ruled that because the program was enacted for the valid secular purpose of providing educational assistance to poor children in a demonstrably failing public school system, the program was neutral with respect to religion and provided assistance directly to a broad class of citizens who, in turn, directed government aid to religious schools wholly as a result of their own genuine and independent private choice.

A. Identify the constitutional provision that is common to both *Zelman v. Simmons-Harris* (2002) and *Engel v. Vitale* (1962).

B. Based on the provision identified in part A, explain how the facts of *Engel v. Vitale* led to a different ruling than in *Zelman v. Simmons-Harris*.

C. Explain how members of the public who disagree with the ruling in *Zelman v. Simmons-Harris* could act to limit its impact.

Chapter 12 Review

AP® KEY CONCEPTS

- *political ideology* (p. 382)
- *right* (p. 382)
- *privilege* (p. 382)
- *party ideology* (p. 385)
- *party identification* (p. 385)
- *conservatism* (p. 385)
- *liberalism* (p. 385)
- *libertarianism* (p. 385)

- *laissez-faire economy* (p. 389)
- *command-and-control economy* (p. 389)
- *mixed economy* (p. 389)
- *gross domestic product (GDP)* (p. 389)
- *economic recession* (p. 389)
- *unemployment rate* (p. 389)
- *inflation* (p. 389)

- *consumer price index (CPI)* (p. 390)
- *fiscal policy* (p. 391)
- *Federal Reserve System* (p. 393)
- *monetary policy* (p. 393)
- *Medicare* (p. 396)
- *Medicaid* (p. 396)

AP® EXAM PRACTICE and Critical Thinking Project

MULTIPLE-CHOICE QUESTIONS

1. Select the pair that best represents the ideological positions of the two major parties.

Democratic Party	Republican Party
A. Increase the minimum wage	Increase environmental regulations
B. Oppose the death penalty	Increase taxes for the middle class
C. Protect the rights of the accused	Ban abortion
D. Expand school-choice programs	Oppose affirmative action

2. Which of the following best represents a conflict between liberty and order?
  A. Providing due process to criminal defendants and protecting the rights of crime victims
  B. Increasing the minimum wage and providing tax cuts for businesses
  C. Increasing taxes for the wealthy and providing social welfare for the poor
  D. Increasing the interest rate on loans and reducing the rate of inflation on consumer goods

Read the quote to answer questions 3 and 4.

> Our true choice is not between tax reduction, on the one hand, and the avoidance of large Federal deficits on the other. It is increasingly clear that no matter what party is in power, so long as our national security needs keep rising, an economy hampered by restrictive tax rates will never produce enough revenues to balance our budget just as it will never produce enough jobs or enough profits . . . it is a paradoxical truth that tax rates are too high today and tax revenues are too low and the soundest way to raise the revenues in the long run is to cut the rates now.[48]
>
> —John F. Kennedy

3. The quote is most consistent with which policy?
  A. Command-and-control policy
  B. Keynesian economics
  C. Monetarism
  D. Supply-side economics

4. Which of the following is a criticism of the viewpoint expressed in the quote?
  A. Cutting taxes decreases government revenue in the short run, and there is no guarantee that tax cuts will generate government revenues in the long run.
  B. It is better to cut spending on social programs than to cut taxes because tax cuts only benefit the wealthy.
  C. Tax cuts for the wealthy should be balanced with increased spending on social programs so that both the wealthy and the poor will benefit.
  D. Tax cuts result in job loss because businesses no longer need to increase productivity in order to keep up with their tax payments.

Library of Congress

5. The Civilian Conservation Corps, shown in the poster, was a New Deal program employing young men to work on projects to conserve and manage natural resources. This program is an example of which economic theory?

A. Monetarism

B. Keynesianism

C. Supply-side economics

D. Fiscal theory

The Two Largest Owners of U.S. Government Debt: Federal Reserve and China

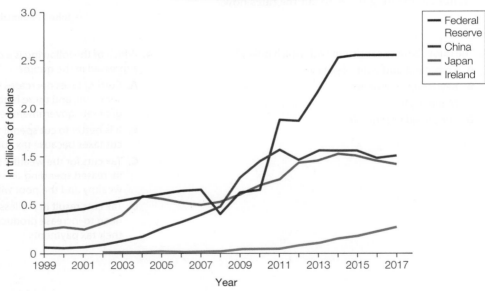

Data from the U.S. Treasury and the Federal Reserve

6. The graph supports which of the following statements?

A. The U.S. government is in more debt than China, Japan, or Ireland.

B. China and Japan are the largest international owners of U.S. government debt.

C. Interest on treasury bills constitutes an uncontrollable expenditure in the federal budget.

D. American citizens own most of the debt incurred through treasury securities.

7. The cartoon represents which of the following viewpoints?

   A. Government spending has gotten too big, at the taxpayers' expense.

   B. The federal government spends too much on the military and not enough on social programs.

   C. The Democratic Party is more likely to support big government.

   D. Government programs offer assistance to struggling citizens.

Mandatory Spending More Than Doubled as a Share of the Economy

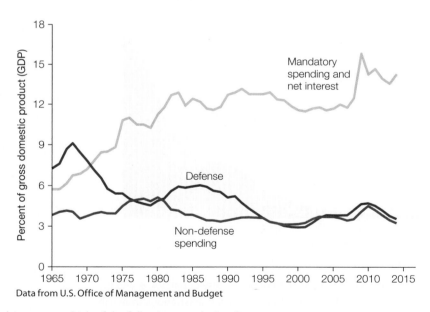

Data from U.S. Office of Management and Budget

8. The graph supports which of the following conclusions?

   A. From 1965 to 1995, there was a strong positive correlation between defense and nondefense spending.

   B. From 1965 to 2015, defense spending was consistently the largest discretionary item in the federal budget.

   C. Mandatory spending increased from 1965 to 2010.

   D. Mandatory spending increases the amount of discretionary spending in the federal budget.

9. Which of the following is a constitutional criticism of tuition vouchers?

   A. They violate the First Amendment because they limit freedom of expression and choice.

   B. They violate the equal protection clause of the Fourteenth Amendment because schools receive unequal funding.

   C. They violate the establishment clause of the First Amendment because tax dollars go to support religious schools.

   D. They violate the Fourth Amendment right of privacy because they allow schools access to financial information.

10. Which of the following describes how the Federal Reserve System influences the economy?

    A. The Fed raises interest rates in an attempt to increase the amount of credit available to consumers.

    B. The Fed increases the amount of money in circulation in an attempt to lower inflation rates.

    C. The Fed increases the reserve rate in an attempt to raise the amount of money banks keep in deposits.

    D. The Fed provides Congress and the president with advice about taxing and spending levels in the budget.

FREE-RESPONSE QUESTIONS

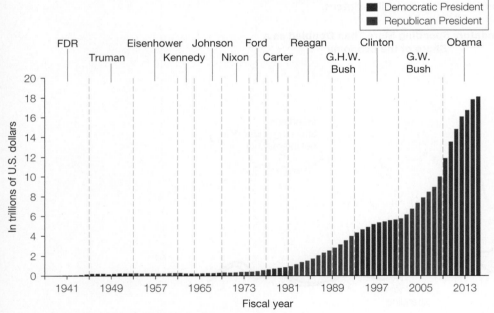

U.S. Federal Debt by President and Political Party

Data from U.S. Office of Management and Budget

1. Use the graph and your knowledge of U.S. Government and Politics to answer parts A, B, and C.

   A. Describe one similarity in the trends of Republican and Democratic administrations shown in the chart.

   B. Describe one proposal supported by either the Democratic Party or the Republican Party to decrease the national debt.

   C. Explain one reason why it is difficult for the federal government to reduce the national debt.

Excerpts from the 2016 Platform of Party A

Our agenda is high on job creation, expanding opportunity and providing a better chance at life for everyone willing to work for it. Our modern approach to environmentalism is directed to that end, and it starts with dramatic change in official Washington. We propose to shift responsibility for environmental regulation from the federal bureaucracy to the states and to transform the EPA into an independent bipartisan commission . . . with structural safeguards against politicized science. We will strictly limit congressional delegation of rule-making authority, and require that citizens be compensated for regulatory takings. . . . We firmly believe environmental problems are best solved by giving incentives for human ingenuity and the development of new technologies, not through top-down, command-and-control regulations that stifle economic growth and cost thousands of jobs.

Excerpts from the 2016 Platform of Party B

Climate change is an urgent threat and a defining challenge of our time. Fifteen of the 16 hottest years on record have occurred this century. . . . The best science tells us that without ambitious, immediate action across our economy to cut carbon pollution and other greenhouse gases, all of these impacts will be far worse in the future. We cannot leave our children a planet that has been profoundly damaged. . . . We will work to expand access to cost-saving renewable energy by low-income households, create good-paying jobs in communities that have struggled with energy poverty, and oppose efforts by utilities to limit consumer choice or slow clean energy deployment. . . . We will phase down extraction of fossil fuels from our public lands, starting with the most polluting sources, while making our public lands and waters engines of the clean energy economy and creating jobs across the country.[49]

2. Use the quotes and your knowledge of U.S. Government and Politics to answer parts A, B, and C.

   A. Describe the viewpoint about environmental regulation expressed in each platform.

   B. Pick one of the platforms and describe whether it is more consistent with liberal or conservative ideology.

   C. Describe one other policy area where liberals and conservatives propose different approaches.

ARGUMENTATION QUESTION

Tuition vouchers give families a monetary credit that can be used at public or private schools, including religious schools, in an effort to give families more choice in their children's education. Vouchers remain controversial. Discuss whether or not voucher programs that allow students to use public money for religious schools are consistent with the founders' intent for American democracy.

- Articulate a claim or thesis that responds to the prompt, and use a line of reasoning to defend it.

- Use at least TWO pieces of relevant and accurate evidence to support your claim.

- At least ONE piece of evidence must be from one of the listed foundational documents:
  - U.S. Constitution
  - *Federalist* No. 10
  - *Federalist* No. 51

- Use a second piece of evidence from another foundational document from the list or from your study of political ideology.

- Use reasoning to explain why the evidence you provided supports your claim or thesis.

- Use refutation, concession, or rebuttal to respond to an opposing or alternative perspective.

CRITICAL THINKING PROJECT

Writing a Blog Entry

Where should the U.S. government draw the line between what is a right and what is a privilege? Some people think that access to quality health care and education are basic human rights. Others believe that individuals, rather than the government, should be in charge of decisions about health care and education.

What do you believe?

Use your personal experience to write a blog entry about whether either health care or education is a right that should be provided by the government or a privilege subject to individual choices. Your blog entry should contain the following:

1. A catchy title that conveys your viewpoint
2. A picture of you that relates to the topic
3. A personal story that demonstrates how the topic has had an impact on you
4. Supporting evidence from at least two credible outside sources
5. Your proposal for improving the health-care or educational system

AP® EXAM PRACTICE and Critical Thinking Project

MULTIPLE-CHOICE QUESTIONS

Questions 1 and 2 refer to the quote.

> In addition to the rights of the students to learn, and the teachers to teach, there is the right of society to insist the educational system it supports will further the goals and the aspirations and the moral principles and precepts of that society. There is no question that the publicly supported colleges and universities contributed to the emerging greatness not only of California but also of our nation, and that is good; but we have a right to insure that they do not, in some far-out interpretation of "freedom," weaken the social structure essential to the nation's strength and to the perpetuation of these very educational institutions. —**Ronald Reagan, speech given at Chico State College, 1967**[1]

1. Which of the following statements best describes the viewpoint about American political culture expressed in the quote?

   A. The educational system should support core American values.

   B. The right to a college education is an important American value.

   C. The public should provide more financial support to colleges and universities.

   D. Colleges and universities should make more effort to hire conservative professors.

2. A critic of the viewpoint expressed in the quote might make which of the following arguments in rebuttal?

   A. The government may not place limits on the right to an education.

   B. The freedom to disagree over core values strengthens the social structure of the nation.

   C. Most college professors are politically neutral in expressing their beliefs.

   D. The government has the authority to regulate speech in public colleges because they receive federal funding.

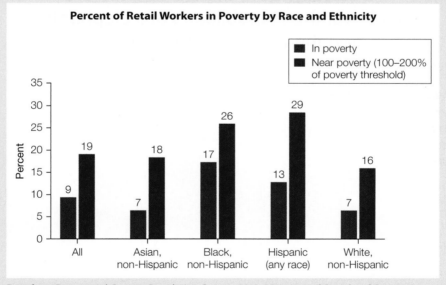

Percent of Retail Workers in Poverty by Race and Ethnicity

Data from Demos and Current Population Survey, 2012–2014 Annual Social and Economic Supplements

3. Which of the following conclusions regarding American core values is supported by the bar chart?

   A. People who decide to work in retail are more likely to live in poverty than those who choose to work in other occupations.

   B. Different wages for people from different racial and ethnic groups are the result of market forces.

   C. Hispanic and black retail workers are more likely to live in poverty than Asian and white retail workers.

   D. The government should regulate businesses so that all workers receive equal pay.

4. Which of the following strengthens transparency and the rule of law?
   A. The Freedom of Information Act allows citizens to request information kept by the government.
   B. Judges may impose different sentences for criminal defendants, depending on the circumstances.
   C. Under the system of federalism, states have independent powers that the federal government may not take away.
   D. The government may use prior restraint to prevent the publication of news stories that are critical of its actions.

"Basically, Son, the Democrats are donkeys, the Republicans are elephants, and the rest of us are roadkill."

Baloo-Rex May/Cartoon Stock

5. The cartoon best illustrates which of the following terms?
   A. Political culture
   B. Political ideology
   C. Political indoctrination
   D. Political socialization

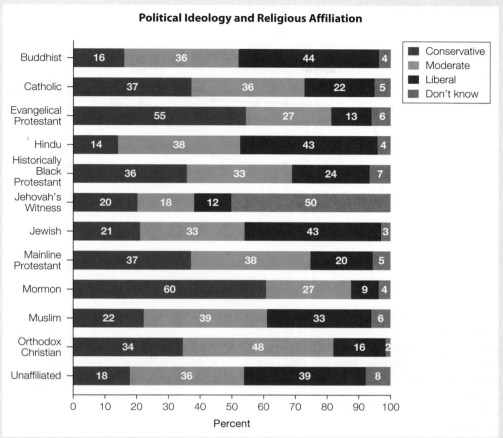

Political Ideology and Religious Affiliation

Legend:
- Conservative
- Moderate
- Liberal
- Don't know

Affiliation	Conservative	Moderate	Liberal	Don't know
Buddhist	16	36	44	4
Catholic	37	36	22	5
Evangelical Protestant	55	27	13	6
Hindu	14	38	43	4
Historically Black Protestant	36	33	24	7
Jehovah's Witness	20	18	12	50
Jewish	21	33	43	3
Mainline Protestant	37	38	20	5
Mormon	60	27	9	4
Muslim	22	39	33	6
Orthodox Christian	34	48	16	2
Unaffiliated	18	36	39	8

Percent

Data from Pew Research Center

6. Which of the following statements about the data in the bar chart is true?

   A. Most Catholics are liberal.

   B. Most Historically Black Protestants are liberal.

   C. Jews remain one of the most liberal religious groups.

   D. Muslims are one of the most conservative religious groups.

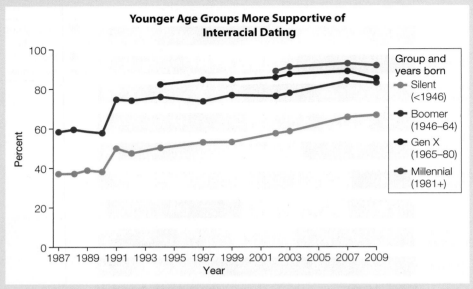

Younger Age Groups More Supportive of Interracial Dating

Data from Pew Research Center

7. The graph supports which of the following statements?

A. In 2009, most people born between 1946 and 1964 opposed interracial dating.

B. There is no difference in support for interracial dating between members of Generation X and Millennials.

C. In 2009, more than 80 percent of people born after 1946 supported interracial dating.

D. Baby boomers showed the greatest increase in support for interracial dating between 1987 and 2009.

8. The graph most closely measures

A. life-cycle effects.

B. generational effects.

C. political socialization.

D. changes in demographics.

9. Which of the following is a consequence of globalization for the U.S. economy?

A. Consumer goods are more expensive because most goods are made overseas and transportation costs are high.

B. The United States is losing some manufacturing jobs in certain industries to other countries.

C. Globalization spreads democratic values, encouraging free and fair elections and civil rights and liberties.

D. Stricter environmental regulations worldwide have improved air and water quality in the United States.

Who Will Win The Presidency?

Hillary Clinton **69.2%** **30.7%** Donald Trump
Chance of winning

Data from polling during summer 2016. Data used in map are from digitaltrends.com and FiveThirtyEight.com

10. Which of the following best describes the information shown on the map?
    A. Of voters polled, 69.2 percent supported Hillary Clinton.
    B. Although most voters supported Hillary Clinton, the electors in the most populous states favored Donald Trump.
    C. Most Hillary Clinton supporters live in the West.
    D. According to polling data, there was about a 69 percent chance Hillary Clinton would win the presidency.

11. Which of the following most likely explains why poll results shown in the map were inaccurate in predicting the winner of the 2016 presidential election?
    A. The polls favored voters on the East and West Coasts.
    B. The polls did not accurately reflect the opinions of citizens who went to the polls.
    C. The language in the polls was more favorable toward Hillary Clinton.
    D. The polls did not reach a sample of voters large enough to accurately predict the results.

12. Which of the following poll questions would lead to the most accurate result?
    A. Do you favor policies that improve access to healthy nutrition for American's poorest children?
    B. Do you agree that parents who pay taxes should be able to choose the best place for their child's education?
    C. Do you agree that hydraulic fracturing is an untested and dangerous threat to our quality of life and the environment?
    D. Do you agree or disagree with the way Donald Trump is doing his job as president?

In modern politics, polls often serve as the canary in the mine—an early warning signal of danger or trends. But polls can also be used to wag the dog—diverting attention from something significant.

—Donna Brazile[2]

13. Which of the following statements best describes an effective use of polling reflected in the quote?

A. Polling can help politicians decide how to present an issue to the public.

B. Candidates can use polling data to determine campaign strategy.

C. Polling can help the government understand long-term trends.

D. Polling can serve as an indicator of coming changes.

14. Which of the following statements best describes a negative impact of polling reflected in the quote?

A. Polling causes voters to focus too much on who is winning, rather than on the issues.

B. Polling about one issue can cause the government to ignore other, more important issues.

C. Politicians who rely too much on the polls are following, rather than leading.

D. Polls are often inaccurate and reflect the views of a vocal minority.

ImediaEthics

15. The cartoon reflects which of the following viewpoints?

A. Poll results are influenced by the organization conducting the poll.

B. There is no such thing as a valid, scientific, public opinion poll.

C. Polls done by conservative media organizations are more accurate than polls done by liberal media organizations.

D. The media uses polls in an attempt to measure public opinion.

16. Which of the following best describes an ideology supported by a political party?

    A. The Republican Party favors policies that reduce regulations on businesses and encourage the free market.

    B. The Democratic Party favors school voucher policies to encourage equality of opportunity.

    C. The Democratic Party favors supply-side economics to encourage economic growth.

    D. The Republican Party seeks to lower the unemployment rate, even if it means higher rates of inflation.

17. Which of the following is an example of a Keynesian economic policy?

    A. Increasing the number of tax deductions available to families

    B. Lowering taxes for corporations

    C. Government spending programs to build roads and bridges

    D. Raising interest rates to encourage savings

18. Which of the following types of spending make it difficult for the federal government to control the budget?

    A. Social Security and Medicare

    B. Payments under the Patient Protection and Affordable Care Act

    C. Defense

    D. Need-based assistance programs

Daryl Cagle/Cagle Cartoons

19. The cartoon expresses which of the following viewpoints?

    A. The Republican and Democratic parties cannot agree on the basic nature of the budget deficit.

    B. The deficit is caused by pork-barrel spending projects.

    C. The Republican and Democratic parties both agree that the deficit is a serious problem.

    D. The deficit is caused by disagreements between the Democratic and Republican parties.

20. Which of the following statements best describes the political party's stance on a social issue?

    A. Democrats support privatizing Social Security.

    B. Republicans support individual freedom, including the right to abortion.

    C. Democrats support an individual mandate, requiring most people to purchase health insurance.

    D. Republicans support expanding the due process rights of criminal defendants.

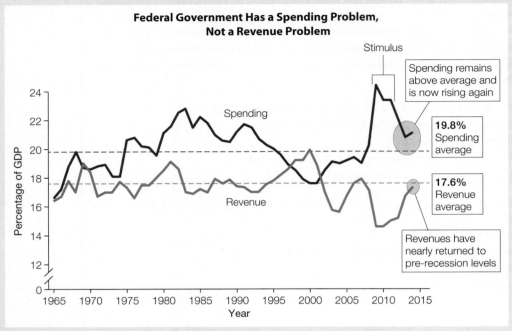

Data from the Office of Management and Budget

1. Use the graph and your knowledge of U.S. Government and Politics to answer parts A, B, and C.
   A. Identify one trend shown in the graph.
   B. Describe two policies favored by conservatives to address budget deficits.
   C. Describe two policies favored by liberals to address budget deficits.

Rick McKee/Cagle Cartoons

2. Use the cartoon and your knowledge of U.S. Government and Politics to answer parts A, B, and C.
   A. Describe the viewpoint expressed in the cartoon.
   B. Describe one policy favored by liberals or one policy favored by conservatives to influence the economy.
   C. Explain two reasons why it is difficult for the government to influence the economy.

ARGUMENTATION QUESTION

Political polling is used to measure the public's opinions about policy issues. Some people believe that elected officials should use polling data in policymaking. Others believe that elected officials should make policy based on their own opinions, rather than on the opinions of the public. Take a position on whether or not elected officials should rely on public opinion polling in making public policy.

In your essay:

- Articulate a claim or thesis that responds to the prompt, and use a line of reasoning to defend it.

- Use at least TWO pieces of relevant and accurate evidence to support your claim.

- At least ONE piece of evidence must be from one of the listed foundational documents:

  - Declaration of Independence

  - Constitution of the United States

  - *Federalist* No. 10

- Use a second piece of evidence from another foundational document from the list or from your study of public opinion polling, Congress, and the president.

- Use reasoning to explain why the evidence you provided supports your claim or thesis.

- Use refutation, concession, or rebuttal to respond to an opposing or alternative perspective.

CRITICAL THINKING PROJECT

Generational Research

People's beliefs are impacted by their stage in life and the events experienced by their generation. To fully understand these lifecycle and generational effects, it's important to talk to people from older generations and listen to their perspectives.

1. Set up an interview with someone from a different generation. Your interviewee might be an older relative, a teacher or coach, someone you work with, or a resident of an assisted living center. Make sure the person chosen understands the purpose of the interview and wants to share life experiences and political beliefs.

2. Generate a list of questions. Questions about how important historical events influence political beliefs will measure generational effects. Questions about how the person's political viewpoint has changed through different stages of his or her life will measure lifecycle effects. Write eight to ten questions.

3. Listen carefully during the interview. Be sure to get the interviewee's permission if you want to record the session. Otherwise, take good notes.

4. In a ten-minute presentation, share your reflections with the class. Include the following:

   a. A description of the person you interviewed and why you chose that person

   b. The impact of generational effects on political attitudes

   c. The impact of lifecycle effects on political attitudes

   d. How your generation's attitudes and experiences are similar to and different from those of the person you interviewed

Unit 5

Political Participation

College students organize and participate in a voter registration drive at their school. Voter-registration drives, canvassing, and other grassroots events are ways that Americans participate in their communities, learn about their neighbors' concerns, and gain knowledge of issues at a local and national level.

Ariel Skelley/Getty Images

Democracy depends on participation by citizens, who seek to influence the policymaking process. Elections, political parties, interest groups, and the media are channels that connect citizens with government.

Citizens choose policymakers through elections. The franchise has expanded over time. The Fifteenth, Nineteenth, and Twenty–Sixth Amendments extended the right to vote to African Americans, women, and eighteen-year-olds.

Political parties run candidates for office in an attempt to win seats in government and enact the policies they favor. The United States is a two-party system, with barriers to third-party candidates and candidates outside the mainstream of their parties.

Interest groups and social movements allow people to join together to influence the policy agenda. Interest groups represent people who care about a particular policy or issue. Social movements are less organized and more diffuse than interest groups. They

Chapter 13
Elections and Campaigns

Chapter 14
Political Parties

Chapter 15
Interest Groups and Social Movements

Chapter 16
The Media

Ariel Skelley/Getty Images

concentrate on broad policies like civil rights or wealth inequality.

The media report political information and influence the policy agenda by highlighting problems to get the attention of the public and government officials. Technology has changed the way news is delivered, and new technologies, like social media, pose both opportunities and challenges for democratic participation. ■

BallotReady is a mobile-ready online voter guide that helps voters assess candidates, create a sample ballot with all of the races in the voter's district, and print out a sample ballot to take to the polling station. Alex Niemczewski and Aviva Rosman started BallotReady because they found that people sometimes "guessed" when voting in less visible races like judges, school council members, and park districts. BallotReady appeals to voters of all ages, but especially to first-time voters, who often aren't aware of all the races to make decisions about.

Manuel Martinez/Reprinted with permission, Crain's Chicago Business, May 15, 2017. © Crain Communications, Inc.

13 Elections and Campaigns
Candidates and Voters in an Era of Demographic Change

Representative democracy cannot survive without action. Citizens must make their wishes known to representatives, who make laws and policies, as the Californians in the photograph are doing. They must find candidates they support and help those candidates win political office; they must also hold those representatives accountable after they are elected. Individuals rally others to their causes and speak as a member of a group that can wield political power and influence. Through political participation, people act to shape the laws and policies of the nation.

Activists gather in the California Assembly chambers in 2014 to show their support for a bill to place a nonbinding advisory question about *Citizens United* on the state ballot. Political participation often includes joining community groups, helping to draft legislation, and voting on ballot measures. Proposition 59 directing state officials to work to overturn *Citizens United* was on the ballot in California in 2016 and won.

Rich Pedroncelli/Associated Press photo

Political participation in a representative democracy can take many forms. One of them is voting in an election. Participating as a voter is critical to the health of a representative democracy and acts, as James Madison noted, as a counterweight to the dangers of faction.[1]

Yet many Americans do not vote. Level of educational attainment, racial and ethnic identity, economic background, gender, and age are all factors influencing whether someone will vote. Further, institutional barriers, such as voter registration, also affect voter turnout. Some states make it easier to register to vote and to cast a ballot on election day than other states. Young adult Americans are consistently underrepresented at the voting booth, for reasons that are both individual and institutional. While young people vote at lower rates than members of older generations, they participate in government through other means, such as volunteering, protesting, organizing, and the use of social media.

Citizens United: Money as Speech, Corporations as People

Candidates use campaigns to convince voters that they are the best choice to represent the people, to make the people's wishes known in Washington, and to enact legislation and policies favored by the public. Yet getting the word out about a candidate during a political campaign also costs a great deal of money. *Citizens United v. Federal Election Commission*, the 2010 decision that opened the floodgates to unlimited corporate campaign contributions, was opposed by eight out of ten Americans across the political spectrum.[2] The case is central to understanding the ways money is deployed in today's political campaigns.[3]

Since the Tillman Act of 1907, federal campaign finance laws have prohibited corporations from making direct campaign contributions to candidates for federal office.[4] In 1974, Congress amended the Federal Election Campaign Act of 1971,[5] in response to the Watergate scandal. Limits were placed on money given directly to candidates by political action committees and individuals.[6] **Political action committees** (PACs) are organizations that raise money to elect and defeat candidates.[7] Individuals, corporations, and unions can form PACs, which are registered with the Federal Election Commission. Under the 1974 law, PACs can donate money directly to a candidate's campaign, subject to monetary limits. No limits, though, were placed on donations that were made in support of a candidate but that were separate from the candidate's campaign. This was often called the soft money loophole. There could be no coordination between PACs and a campaign, and any advertisements separate from a campaign could not explicitly include such words as "vote" for or against a candidate. Such ads could, however, call into question the judgment, character, and positions of a candidate, which meant that, even though they were supposed to stick to issues, in reality, they served as veiled campaign ads.

In *Buckley v. Valeo*, the Supreme Court upheld limits on how much money an individual could donate directly to someone else's campaign, to prevent corrupting a government official or giving the appearance of corruption, but struck down limits on how much a candidate could spend on his or her own campaign.[8]

political participation
the different ways in which individuals take action to shape the laws and policies of a government.

political action committee
an organization that raises money to elect and defeat candidates and may donate money directly to a candidate's campaign, subject to limits.

In 2002, the Bipartisan Campaign Reform Act (BCRA), which is also called McCain-Feingold after its sponsors, tried to close the soft money loophole by prohibiting issue ads on television or radio (not the internet or books) that mentioned a candidate's name, were paid for by corporations or unions, and aired thirty days before a primary election and sixty days before a general election.[9] In 2003, the Supreme Court upheld these limitations on independent ads,[10] but six years later, the court's membership had changed and with it came a new interpretation of the law.

David Bossie, a Republican Party activist, brought the case. As a teenager in the 1980s, he became involved in Republican politics, volunteering for the Reagan campaign. He rose to national prominence in the 1990s as a congressional investigator targeting President Bill Clinton, but was forced to resign.[11] In 2001, he became head of Citizens United, a conservative political advocacy group.

Citizens United describes itself as a "tax-exempt non-profit [corporation] dedicated to informing the American people about public policy issues which relate to traditional American values: strong national defense, Constitutionally limited government, free market economics, belief in God and Judeo-Christian values, and the recognition of the family as the basic social unit of our society."[12] Part of its mission involved producing documentaries, including *Hillary: The Movie*, a film highly critical of Hillary Clinton as she geared up her 2008 campaign for the Democratic nomination for president. It was aired in theaters and available on DVD, but Bossie wanted it aired on cable television video-on-demand services, which ran afoul of the ban on corporate electioneering communications.

Bossie argued that video-on-demand services should not be covered by BCRA and that his movie did not constitute "electioneering communication" because it did not contain express advocacy. Bossie lost at the Federal Election Commission and in the lower courts.

Once the case made it to the Supreme Court, though, what had started as a small case hinging on technical interpretations of the law turned into a watershed decision about money and free speech. Representing Citizens United before the Court was Ted Olson, who in 2003 as an attorney for the George W. Bush administration had defended BCRA. In this appeal, Olson stressed that Congress had only intended to ban television and radio advertisements, not feature-length documentaries. He never questioned the constitutionality of the law's prohibition on corporate-funded electioneering.[13] The Supreme Court saw things differently and took the unusual step of calling for a second round of oral arguments on this issue. Court watchers immediately realized that this rare event was a signal.

In January 2010, the Court issued its landmark 5-4 decision that prohibitions on corporate (and union) independent campaign expenditures were unconstitutional.[14] Corporations and unions are entitled to the same First Amendment free speech protections as any individual. The Court reiterated its 1976 *Buckley v. Valeo* decision that equated the spending of money to speech, which is entitled to First Amendment free speech protections.[15]

The dissenters in *Citizens United* argued that no candidate would be unaware or uninfluenced by supporters who spent millions of dollars on "independent" expenditures, and massive corporate-financed independent ads placed right before an election could have a corrupting effect.[16] Moreover, corporations should not be entitled to First Amendment free speech protections concerning campaign spending because they are not people engaged in self-expression.[17] The dissenters also reminded the Court's majority that just the year before the Court had ruled in *Caperton v. Massey* that independent expenditures could have a corrupting effect on judicial elections.[18] (*Caperton* was described in more detail in Chapter 6.)

The decision immediately sparked controversy. In an unusual step, President Obama criticized it during his State of the Union Address in front of the Court's justices. It also rippled through the legal system. A few months later, a federal appeals court, in light of *Citizens United*, ruled that contributions to political action committees (PACs) that made independent expenditures also constituted free speech, opening up so-called Super PACs.[19] Unlike regular PACs, Super PACs can take unlimited donations, but they cannot contribute funds directly to candidates.

The financial results of these decisions are easy to see. Independent expenditures took off between 2008 and 2012, increasing from $338 million to $1 billion. In 2012, Sheldon Adelson led all donors, channeling $92 million to Republicans, while the top Democratic donor was Fred Eychaner who donated $14 million.[20]

In the 2016 elections, Tom Steyer topped Adelson by donating $86 million to the Democratic cause, while Sheldon Adelson donated $78 million to Republicans. By 2016, the number of large campaign contributions (more than $1 million) increased by more than 40 percent, compared to 2012, and outside spending surged from $1 billion to $1.5 billion.[21] In twenty-six truly competitive congressional races, outside groups outspent the combined total of both of the major party candidates.[22]

After reading this chapter, you will be able to

13.1 Describe different forms of political participation.

13.2 Explain how individual choice as well as state and federal laws influence voter turnout in elections.

13.3 Describe different models of voting behavior.

13.4 Describe the purpose and role of the Electoral College in our constitutional system.

13.5 Describe the rules governing political campaigns.

LEARNING TARGETS

13.1 Forms of Political Participation

While Americans often equate political participation with voting, casting a ballot is only one of the many forms of political participation. By voting, citizens choose representatives to carry out their wishes. Along with political parties, interest groups, and the media, elections are a **linkage institution**, connecting individuals with government. Other forms of participation also influence elected officials and citizens. According to political scientists Sidney Verba, Kay Lehman Schlozman, and Henry E. Brady, "Studies of political participation traditionally have begun with—and too often ended with—the vote. Although voting is an important mode of citizen involvement in political life, it is but one of many political acts."[23]

Citizens may call, email, or use social media to contact elected officials, making their preferences known or expressing their displeasure. People may also work on political campaigns, and some people donate money to candidates. Through all of these activities, people try to make their voices heard. See Figure 13.1.

Individuals might join together to work cooperatively for a shared set of political goals. In joining a **social movement** people come together to make social and political change with the goal of placing issues on the policy agenda. Members of social movements may participate in protests, attend political meetings, contact elected officials, or reach out to other citizens to educate them about the issues. While Americans vote at lower rates than citizens in other democracies, their rates of nonelectoral participation are equal to or higher than their counterparts in other nations.[24] See Figure 13.2 for an international comparison.

linkage institution
channels that connect individuals with government, including elections, political parties, interest groups, and the media.

social movement
the joining of individuals seeking social or political change with the goal of placing issues on the policy agenda.

FIGURE 13.1

Americans' Participation in Elections outside the Voting Booth

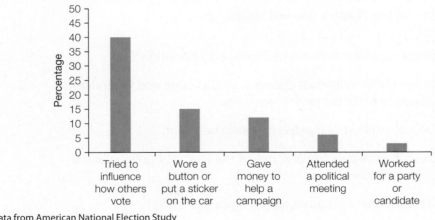

Data from American National Election Study

FIGURE 13.2

Participation in Campaigns

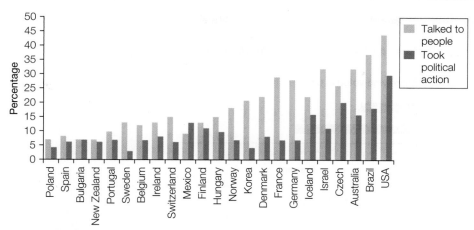

Data from Steven Weldon and Russell Dalton, "Democratic Structures and Democratic Participation: The Limits of Consensualism Theory," *Elections and Democracy*, ed. Jacques Thomassen, Oxford University Press, 2014: Table 7.1, "Levels of Political Participation."

Section Review

This chapter's main ideas are reflected in the Learning Targets. By reviewing after each section, you should be able to

—**Remember** the key points,

—**Know** terms that are central to the topic, and

—**Think** critically about these questions of how Americans participate in politics.

13.1 Describe different forms of political participation.

REMEMBER
- Political parties, interest groups, the media, and elections are linkage institutions, connecting individuals with government.
- Political participation includes voting, calling, emailing, or using social media to contact elected officials, making their preferences known or expressing their displeasure.
- People may also work on political campaigns and donate time and money to candidates.

KNOW
- *political participation*: the different ways in which individuals take action to shape the laws and policies of a government. (p. 419)
- *political action committee (PAC)*: an organization that raises money to elect and defeat candidates and may donate money directly to a candidate's campaign, subject to limits. (p. 419)
- *linkage institution*: channels that connect individuals with government , including elections, political parties, interest groups, and the media. (p. 422)
- *social movement*: the joining of individuals seeking social or political change with the goal of placing issues on the policy agenda. (p. 422)

13.1 Review Question: Free Response

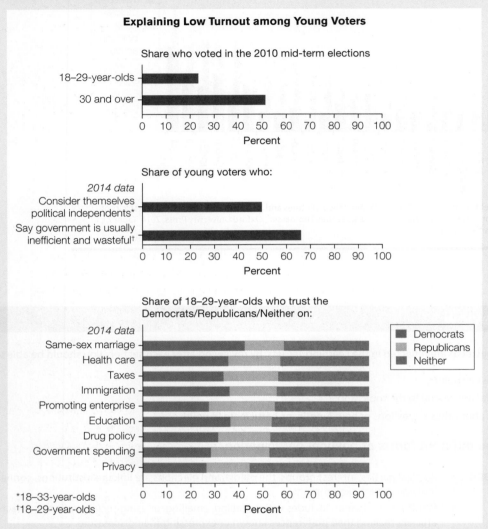

Explaining Low Turnout among Young Voters

Data from Pew Research Center, Reason-Rupe Public Opinion Survey

Use the graphs and your knowledge of U.S. Government and Politics to answer parts A, B, and C.

A. Describe the difference in voter turnout in the 2010 midterm elections between eighteen-to twenty-nine-year-olds and those over thirty.

B. Explain one reason why citizens under thirty have lower voter turnout rates than older generations.

C. Describe one form of political participation other than voting.

13.2 The Right to Vote and Exercising That Right

Voting is the most direct way for citizens to select policymakers. Democracies allow almost all citizens to vote, and the franchise has been expanded over time.

The Expansion of Voting Rights

Article I, Section 4, of the U.S. Constitution gives states the power to regulate their own voting laws. After the Constitution was ratified, most states set a property requirement for voting, and most voters were white male landholders. When George Washington was elected in 1789, only 6 percent of the population could vote.[25] States gradually opened the vote to white men who did not own property, and in 1856, North Carolina became the last state to end the property requirement for voting.[26]

Five of the seventeen amendments ratified since the Bill of Rights expand the **franchise** (or **suffrage**), or right to vote. The Fifteenth Amendment (1870) prohibits states from discriminating against prospective voters on the basis of race. Although the amendment technically gave African American men the right to vote, as discussed in Chapter 9, southern states adopted methods to block this right. The Voting Rights Act of 1965 was an effort to secure the voting rights of African Americans by protecting their rights to register and vote. Women were granted the right to vote with the ratification of the Nineteenth Amendment in 1920, although some states allowed women to vote earlier. The expansion of voting rights for women was also discussed in Chapter 9.

The **Twenty-Sixth Amendment**, ratified in 1971, lowered the voting age from twenty-one to eighteen. All of these amendments expanded the number of people who could vote.

Two other amendments expanded voters' rights. In the original Constitution, U.S. senators were selected by state legislatures. The Seventeenth Amendment (1913) provides for the direct election of senators. The **Twenty-Fourth Amendment**, ratified in 1964, prohibits the state and federal governments from charging a **poll tax**, a method used to depress voter turnout among the poor. The Fifteenth, Seventeenth, Nineteenth, Twenty-Fourth, and Twenty-Sixth Amendments expanded the opportunity for political participation.

Obtaining the right to vote is an important first step in democratic participation. The second step is deciding to exercise that right.

Factors That Shape Electoral Participation

Voting is an essential component of a representative democracy. Voting holds elected representatives accountable for their promises and actions. Voting is the foundation of what James Madison called the "Democratic Remedy" to the dangers of faction and the tyranny of the minority that we examined in Chapter 2.

Large percentages of Americans, however, do not vote. In the 2016 presidential election, only about 58 percent of eligible voters showed up at the polls, placing the United States near the bottom of democratic nations based on **voter turnout**. Turnout in midterm elections is even lower. In 2014, roughly 36 percent of eligible voters cast ballots, continuing a trend of decline that has persisted over decades and marking the lowest level of voter turnout since 1942.[27]

franchise (or **suffrage**) the right to vote.

Twenty-Sixth Amendment allows those eighteen years old and older to vote.

Twenty-Fourth Amendment prohibits Congress and the states from imposing poll taxes as a condition for voting in federal elections.

poll tax a payment required by a state or federal government before a citizen is allowed to vote.

voter turnout the number of eligible voters who participate in an election as a percentage of the total number of eligible voters.

What Causes a Person to Vote—or Not to Vote?

Many factors shape a person's decision of whether or not to vote. Some contributors to voter turnout are institutional, shaped by the laws and procedures surrounding the electoral process. Others depend upon whether it takes place during a presidential election year or the issues on the ballot. Voter turnout in the United States also varies with **demographic characteristics**, including economic status, education, age, race or ethnicity, and gender. In many other countries, these demographic characteristics do not have the same effect.

Socioeconomic Status and Educational Attainment

Voting is costly. It takes time, commitment, and intellectual engagement. A key factor in American voter turnout is an individual's **socioeconomic status (SES)**, which is a measure of an individual's wealth, income, occupation, and educational attainment.

A clear and consistent pattern in electoral participation is that Americans with higher levels of SES participate more in elections.[28] Individuals with higher incomes have more money to donate to political campaigns. Educated professionals are more likely to associate with interest groups, which bring political issues to their members' attention. Labor unions serve the same function in calling attention to political issues, and voter turnout among members of labor unions is higher than turnout among nonunionized workers.[29]

The most important contributor to an individual's SES, and one of the most important determinants of voter turnout rates, is educational attainment. (Figure 13.3.) Higher levels of educational attainment are associated with higher incomes, making the registration process and the issues involved in an election easier to navigate.

demographic characteristics
measurable characteristics of a population, such as economic status, education, age, race or ethnicity, and gender.

socioeconomic status (SES)
a measure of an individual's wealth, income, occupation, and educational attainment.

FIGURE 13.3

Voting and Registration by Educational Attainment in the United States, 2016

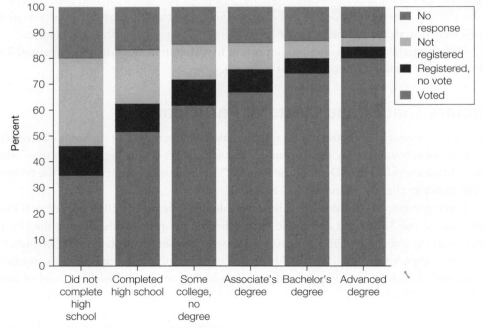

Data from Current Population Survey, Voting and Registration Supplement

Political Efficacy

Education also plays a role in shaping how individuals think about themselves as political actors and potential voters. The intellectual resources and skills that higher levels of education produce also increase an individual's sense of **political efficacy**, the confidence that he or she can make effective political change.

Changes in Participation as People Age

Another trend is also clear: Young adult voting-eligible Americans vote at lower rates than members of older generations (Figure 13.4).[30] Like income and education, age is connected to many other factors. Older Americans are more likely to have higher levels of income and wealth. Another factor may be the challenges registering to vote, especially for college students or people who have moved to a new state. While a 1979 Supreme Court ruling affirmed the right of college students to vote in their states of school attendance,[31] state voting laws and local practices "often make students travel a rocky road."[32]

Racial and Ethnic Identities

Voter turnout is also highly correlated with racial and ethnic identity (Figure 13.5 on page 428), which is often connected to SES. While turnout rates between whites and African Americans have narrowed in recent years, the turnout rate among Hispanic American citizens is lower than that of Americans with other racial and ethnic identities. As a group, Hispanic Americans are younger, and, as we have discussed, younger Americans vote in far fewer numbers than their older counterparts. As eligible Hispanic voters grow older, and grow in numbers, the political landscape may shift.

Gender and Voter Turnout

Since the presidential election of 1980, women have voted at a slightly higher rate than men, usually by a difference of a few percentage points.[33] Before 1980, voting-eligible men voted at higher rates than women. The differences between men's and women's modern

AP® TIP

The demographic factors that impact voter turnout, such as SES, income, and racial and ethnic identities are intertwined. Avoid simplistic assertions about the impact of race and ethnicity on voter turnout.

FIGURE 13.4

Historical Patterns of Voter Turnout Midterm and Presidential Elections, by Age

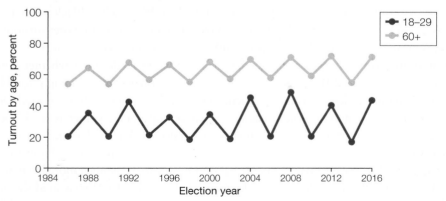

Data from U.S. Census Bureau

FIGURE 13.5

American Voter Turnout in Midterm Elections by Racial and Ethnic Identity

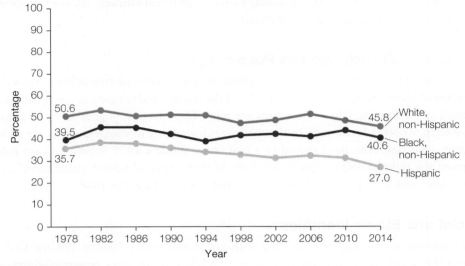

Data from U.S. Census Bureau

voting patterns hold true across racial and ethnic identities, with the largest percentage difference between African American men and women, which was more than 9 percent in the 2012 presidential election. The difference in voter turnout rates among African American men and women may be partly a result of felon disenfranchisement, which disproportionately affects African American men.[34] Differences in voter turnout between men and women are also connected with age. A higher percentage of women ages eighteen to forty-four voted than men in the same age cohort, while men seventy-five and up voted at higher rates than women within the same age group.

Candidate Characteristics and Voter Turnout

The demographic characteristics of the candidates may impact voter turnout. As shown in Figure 13.6, turnout among African American voters steadily increased from 1996 to 2012, when it reached a high point. The high level of voter turnout among African Americans in the 2008 and 2012 elections is sometimes called the "Obama effect." This trend in increasing voter turnout among African Americans stalled in 2016, when black voter turnout decreased.[35] The race of the candidates may have had some impact on voter turnout rates among African Americans, although this is difficult to measure with certainty.

Voters might also consider the gender of a candidate in deciding whether, and for whom, to vote. In the 2016 presidential race, women voted overwhelmingly for Hillary Clinton. White noncollege-educated women, however, overwhelmingly supported Donald Trump, with 62 percent of the vote.[36] The voter turnout rate among women was 63.7 percent in 2012 and 63.3 percent in 2016, which is not a significant change. Turnout among white women was 66.8 percent in 2016, up slightly from 65.6 percent in 2012.[37] From these figures, it appears that having a female on the ballot does not make women more likely to vote.

A Pew Research Center Survey conducted in 2016 (Table 13.1) measured the impact of other candidate traits. Voters view military service as a positive trait in presidential candidates.[38] Most respondents said it wouldn't matter to them if a candidate attended a

FIGURE 13.6

Voter Turnout by Racial and Ethnic Identity, 1988–2016

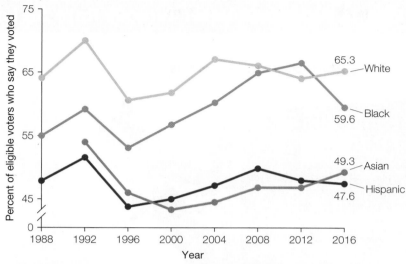

Note: Eligible voters are U.S. citizens ages 18 and older. The categories whites, blacks, and Asians include only non-Hispanics. Hispanics are of any race. Data for non-Hispanic Asians were not available in 1988.

Data from Pew Research Center

TABLE 13.1 Effect of Candidate Characteristics on Americans' Choice of President

Percent of U.S. adults who would be more/less likely to support a candidate who . . .

Traits	More likely	Less likely	Wouldn't matter	Don't know
Has served in the military	50	4	45	1
Attended prestigious university	20	6	74	*
Is Catholic	16	8	75	1
Is an evangelical Christian	22	20	55	3
Is Jewish	8	10	80	2
Has longtime Washington experience	22	31	46	1
Has used marijuana in the past	6	20	74	1
Is Mormon	5	23	69	3
Is gay or lesbian	4	26	69	1
Had personal financial troubles	8	41	49	2
Had extramarital affair in past	3	37	58	2
Is Muslim	3	42	53	2
Does not believe in God	6	51	41	1

Data from Pew Research Center survey conducted January 7–14, 2016.

Explaining Patterns and Trends in Data: Why Is America's Voter Turnout Rate So Low?

Percent of Registered Voters Who Voted in 2016

	47–54 (3)
	54–61 (15)
	61–68 (25)
	68–74 (8)

Data from U.S. Census Bureau

In May 2017, the Pew Research Center published a table depicting voter turnout in national elections in member nations of the Organisation for Economic Co-operation and Development (OECD) since 2012 (see page 431). Some countries, such as Australia, have laws compelling citizens to vote or pay a fine, and this influences their voter turnout rates.[39] However, voter turnout in the United States lagged behind that of almost all of its peer nations, including those twenty-one nations that do not have laws requiring people to vote.[40]

The percentage of the *voting-age* population that voted in recent national elections in the United States is far below that of most other members of the OECD. Notice the column that depicts voter turnout as a percentage of registered voters. By that measure, voter turnout in the United States does not appear to be very different from the other countries, and it leads most other nations.

Voting-age and *registered voters* are two very different terms. Large numbers of voting-age Americans are not eligible to vote. U.S. residents who aren't citizens as well as Americans convicted of felonies are not allowed to vote. The numbers of people who cannot vote because of a felony conviction have grown in recent decades.[41] A large percentage of disenfranchised felons were convicted for drug offenses. In 2016, 6 million Americans lost their right to vote because of felony convictions.[42]

prestigious university, is Catholic, Jewish, Muslim, Mormon, or evangelical Christian, had used marijuana in the past, had an extramarital affair, or is gay or lesbian.[43]

Besides demographic characteristics, voters may consider a candidate's appearance in deciding whether, and for whom, to vote. Candidates want to convey a positive image, and they often hire consultants to give them advice about what to wear, how to style their hair, what tone of voice to use, and how to use body language to project self-confidence.[44] A British research study concluded that attractive candidates have an advantage in winning elections.[45] However, another study looked at U.S. Senate elections between 1990

OECD Countries' Recent National Elections as a Percentage of Registered Voters and Voting Age Population

Country	% of voting-age population	% of registered voters	Country	% of voting-age population	% of registered voters
Belgium (2014)*	87.2%	89.4%	Canada (2015)	62.1%	68.3%
Sweden (2014)	82.6%	85.8%	Greece (2015)*	62.1%	56.2%
South Korea (2017)	77.9%	77.2%	Portugal (2015)	61.8%	55.8%
Denmark (2015)	80.3%	85.9%	Spain (2016)	61.2%	66.5%
Australia (2016)*	79.0%	91.0%	Czech Republic (2013)	60.0%	59.4%
Norway (2013)	78.0%	78.3%	Slovakia (2016)	59.4%	59.8%
Netherlands (2017)	77.3%	81.9%	Ireland (2016)	58.0%	65.1%
Iceland (2016)	76.8%	79.2%	Estonia (2015)	56.8%	64.2%
Israel (2015)	76.1%	72.3%	United States (2016)	55.7%	86.8%
New Zealand (2014)	73.2%	77.9%	Luxembourg (2013)*	55.1%	91.1%
Finland (2015)	73.1%	66.9%	Slovenia (2014)	54.1%	51.7%
Italy (2013)	70.6%	72.2%	Poland (2015)	53.8%	55.3%
France (2017)	67.9%	74.6%	Japan (2014)	52.0%	52.7%
Germany (2013)	66.1%	71.5%	Latvia (2014)	51.7%	58.8%
Mexico (2012)*	66.0%	63.1%	Chile (2013)	50.6%	49.4%
Austria (2013)	65.9%	74.9%	Switzerland (2015)*	38.6%	48.4%
United Kingdom (2016)	65.4%	72.2%	Turkey (2017)*	NA	85.4%
Hungary (2014)	63.3%	61.8%			

Note: Voting-age population (VAP) turnout is derived from estimates of each country's VAP by the International Institute for Democracy and Electoral Assistance. Registered-voter (RV) turnout derived from each country's reported registration data. Because of methodology differences, in some countries estimated VAP is lower than reported RV. Current voting-age population estimates for Turkey unavailable.
*National law makes voting compulsory. In addition, one Swiss canton has compulsory voting.
Data from Pew Research Center.

1. Describe the difference between an individual of voting age, a registered voter, and an eligible voter.

2. Describe the most accurate method for comparing voter turnout rates among countries.

3. Describe one institutional factor that might account for different voter turnout rates among countries.

and 2006 and did not find an instance where good looks helped a candidate win.[46] According to Ryan Enos, a political scientist at Harvard, "Politics and voting are greatly affected by factors such as partisanship, the economy, campaigning, and even policy—all of which leave little room for voters to cast votes based on politicians' looks."[47]

Voting decisions are complicated. It can be difficult to measure the degree to which demographic and other characteristics of candidates influence decisions about whether to vote.

Partisan Attachment

political mobilization
efforts by political parties to
encourage their members
to vote.

Individuals with a strong attachment to a political party are more likely to vote than those without one.[48] **Political mobilization**, such as efforts to "get out the vote" (GOTV), can be decisive in an election. These efforts may be direct, through recruiting, sponsoring meetings, or requesting contributions, or indirect, such as building social networks where potential voters can engage with their friends and associates.[49]

Legal and Institutional Factors That Influence Voter Turnout

Most Americans are eligible to vote, but institutional factors impact voter turnout. State laws vary in whether a felony conviction bars someone from voting. Compared to other countries, the U.S. has one of the most restrictive laws in the world.[50]

registration requirements
the set of rules that govern
who can vote and how,
when, and where they vote.

Voting involves two actions: registering to vote and casting a ballot. States have different **registration requirements** setting rules for who can vote, how ballots may be cast, and where a person may go to vote. As of April 2018, twelve states automatically register all citizens as voters.[51] In most states, however, would-be voters must register before the election, often as much as thirty days. Otherwise they will not be allowed to vote.[52]

To register to vote, Americans are required to show identification or proof of residency in their state or both. Others require another form documenting residency. As of March 2018, sixteen states allow same-day registration, which means that voters can register on election day. (See Figure 13.7.) Even in states that allow same-day

FIGURE 13.7

States Allowing Same-Day Voter Registration

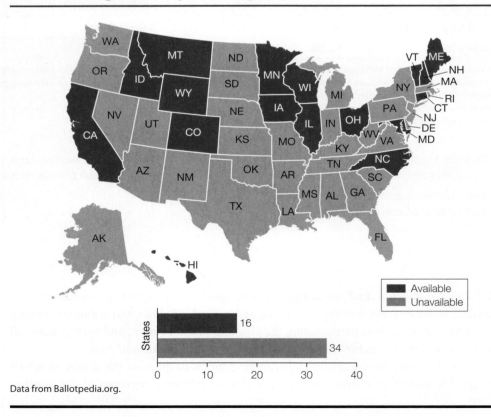

Legend:
- Available
- Unavailable

States: 16 / 34

Data from Ballotpedia.org.

registration, however, residency requirements may result in the disenfranchisement of certain Americans, such as the homeless, who may lack documentation like utility bills that can prove state residency.

As of March 2018, eighteen states require a photo identification to be shown when casting a vote. (See Figure 13.8 for states' required voting-day identification.)

College students may be disenfranchised by voter identification laws. Across the nation, state lawmakers are debating whether or not students should be able to use a college ID as proof of residency, especially if the college or university is a private institution. Refer again to Figure 13.8. When such policies were being debated in Texas, Natalie Butler, a graduate and former student government president of the University of Texas at Austin, spoke out against a state law that prohibited the use of school IDs as proof of residence. She noted the law's impact on participation in local elections, stating, "If we're going to make it even harder for students to impact city politics, that's a huge problem."[53]

Some advocates of electoral reform hope to make the registration process easier and less costly in terms of time and energy. In contrast to most modern representative democracies, in the United States the burden of registering to vote falls entirely on the potential voter, and there is no federal governmental action to register citizens automatically. The National Voter Registration Act of 1993,[54] commonly called the Motor Voter Law, allows Americans to register to vote when applying for or renewing their driver's licenses. The law also makes it easier for Americans with disabilities to register. As of March

FIGURE 13.8

State Requirements for Identification at the Polling Place

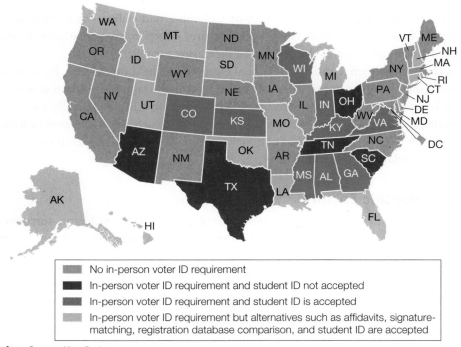

- No in-person voter ID requirement
- In-person voter ID requirement and student ID not accepted
- In-person voter ID requirement and student ID is accepted
- In-person voter ID requirement but alternatives such as affidavits, signature-matching, registration database comparison, and student ID are accepted

Data from Campus Vote Project

FIGURE 13.9

States Allowing Online Voter Registration

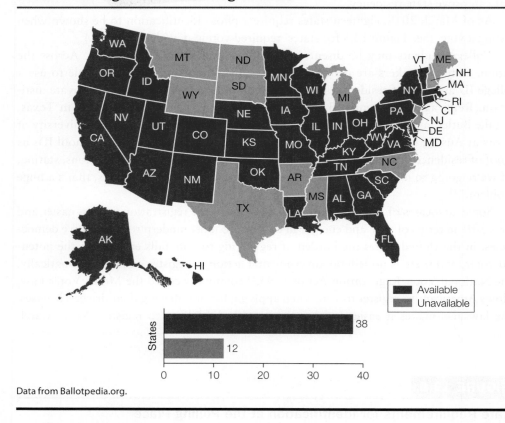

Available

Unavailable

States

38

12

0 10 20 30 40

Data from Ballotpedia.org.

absentee ballot

voting completed and submitted by a voter before the day of an election without going to the polls.

AP® TIP

Demographic factors, like SES, educational attainment, gender, age, and racial and ethnic identities can have a strong influence on voter turnout. Structural factors, like registration and ID requirements, also affect turnout. Read questions about voter turnout carefully to determine whether the question refers to demographic factors or structural factors.

2018, thirty-eight states and the District of Columbia had online voter registration.[55] (See Figure 13.9.) While online registration requires efforts to make the process secure and free from fraud, it offers the promise of increasing turnout.

National presidential and congressional elections are held on the first Tuesday after the first Monday of November. This scheduling may discourage voting because it is challenging for some Americans to get to their polling place on what is normally a workday. Although states are increasingly allowing voters to vote early or cast **absentee ballots**, some reformers have proposed that national elections be held on weekends or that election day be declared a national holiday.

Election-Specific Factors

Also contributing to the level of voter turnout in a given election are factors surrounding the election itself. If it is a presidential election year, then voters will turn out in higher numbers than if it is not (Figure 13.10).

FIGURE 13.10

Comparing Voter Turnout in Presidential and Midterm Election Years

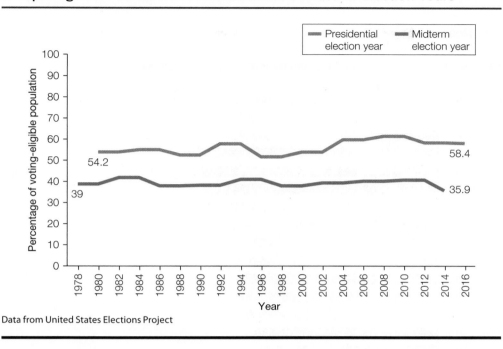

Data from United States Elections Project

Section Review

13.2 Explain how individual choice and state and federal laws influence voter turnout in elections.

REMEMBER
- Voting is the most direct way for citizens to select policymakers.
- The Fifteenth, Nineteenth, and Twenty-Sixth Amendments expanded the right to vote to include African Americans, women, and eighteen-year-olds.
- Demographic factors, such as age, income, and educational attainment, have an influence on an individual's decision about whether to vote.
- Structural factors, such as the timing of elections, registration, and identification laws, affect voter turnout.

KNOW
- *franchise* (or *suffrage*): the right to vote. (p. 425)
- *poll tax*: a payment required by a state or federal government before a citizen is allowed to vote. (p. 425)
- *Twenty-Fourth Amendment*: prohibits Congress and the states from imposing poll taxes as a condition for voting in federal elections. (p. 425)
- *Twenty-Sixth Amendment*: allows those eighteen years and older to vote. (p. 425)
- *voter turnout*: the number of eligible voters who participate in an election as a percentage of the total number of eligible voters. (p. 425)
- *demographic characteristics*: measurable characteristics of a population, such as economic status, education, age, race or ethnicity, and gender. (p. 426)
- *socioeconomic status (SES)*: a measure of an individual's wealth, income, occupation, and educational attainment. (p. 426)
- *political efficacy*: a person's belief that he or she can make effective political change. (p. 427)
- *political mobilization*: efforts by political parties to encourage their members to vote. (p. 432)
- *registration requirements*: the set of rules that govern who can vote and how, when, and where they vote. (p. 432)
- *absentee ballot*: voting completed and submitted by a voter before the day of an election without going to the polls. (p. 434)

THINK

- Why is voter turnout lower in the United States than in other democracies?
- What steps could the state and national governments take in an effort to increase voter turnout?

13.2 Review Question: Free Response

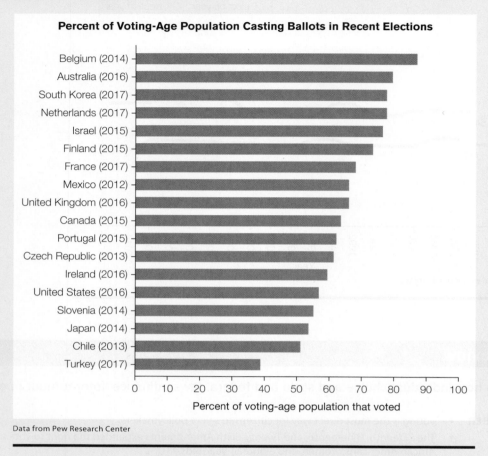

Percent of Voting-Age Population Casting Ballots in Recent Elections

Percent of voting-age population that voted

Data from Pew Research Center

Use the bar chart and your knowledge of U.S. Government and Politics to answer parts A, B, and C.

A. Describe how turnout among the voting age population in the United States compares to turnout among the voting-age population in most of the countries shown in the bar chart.

B. Describe one government policy that might make it more difficult for a citizen to vote.

C. Describe one policy a government might enact in an effort to increase voter turnout.

◼ 13.3 Democratic Representation and Theories of Voting Behavior

The framers of the Constitution did not want the system they created to be *too* democratic. They feared the potential mischief of faction and the dangers of tyranny of the majority. Therefore, they built in roadblocks to protect against the passions of the majority. Senators, for example, were originally chosen by state legislatures rather than directly by voters, and the president is selected indirectly through an Electoral College. The election of senators was discussed in Chapter 4, and the Electoral College was covered in Chapter 5.

Another safeguard against faction is the system of American federalism, which divides sovereignty between the nation and the states. One consequence of American federalism, as provided for in Article I, Section 4 of the Constitution, is that "The Times, Places and Manner of holding Elections for Senators and Representatives, shall be prescribed in each State by the Legislature thereof."[56] As discussed above, this means states set the rules for elections. Following the Civil War, southern states enacted laws, including grandfather clauses and literacy tests, in an effort to disenfranchise African Americans, as discussed in Chapter 8. Before ratification of the Nineteenth Amendment, women could vote in some states but not others. And today the language in Article I, Section 4, ensures that states can devise their own voting technologies, whether electronic or paper-based, as well as having different policies about whether convicted felons are allowed to vote.[57]

Compared to other democracies in the world, Americans get to exercise their right to vote often. Americans vote for more than half a million positions in local, state, and federal government. However, many American citizens do not vote, or they are shut out of the process. Barriers to voting include the registration process, voter identification laws, difficulty in making it to the polling place during a workday, and felony disenfranchisement.

American elections occur on fixed and predictable schedules. Unlike in parliamentary systems, in which the prime minister decides when to "call" an election, in the United States, voters elect the president every four years, regardless of what is happening in the nation or world.

How Citizens Make Voting Decisions and the Functions of Elections

Elections serve as a signal, a way of transmitting information to elected officials about voters' preferences and priorities. In a representative democracy, elections are the key way Americans can keep their elected officials in line. Citizens may vote an incumbent out of office and vote in a challenger if the incumbent's performance has not been in line with voters' policy preferences.

Voting based on what a citizen believes is in his or her own best interest is called **rational choice voting**. Anthony Downs, who concluded that voters behave "sensibly and efficiently," presented the rational choice model.[58] Under this model, voters are purposive, which means that they want to achieve their goals, acting as rationally as they can, given their knowledge and situation.[59] Voters want to see the policies they favor enacted. Members of Congress want to get reelected. Under rational choice theory, candidates in democratic systems seek to maximize their chance of winning elections, and parties adopt policies that are popular with most voters.

Reflecting back on an incumbent's past performance before making a choice in an election is called **retrospective voting**.[60] Several interest groups, including the National Rifle Association and the Human Rights Campaign, issue "congressional scorecards" to help their members keep up with the voting records of members of Congress. While retrospective voters take their cues from past behavior, prospective voters look to the future. **Prospective voting** means casting a ballot for a candidate who promises to enact policies favored by the voter. President Trump appealed to prospective voters with his promise to "Make America Great Again." In the speech when he announced his presidential bid, he promised, "I would build a great wall, and nobody builds walls better than me, believe me, and I'll build them very inexpensively."[61]

Some voters simply cast ballots for members of one political party for all of the offices on the ballot. This is called **party-line voting**. As we will examine in Chapter 14 about

rational choice voting
voting based on what a citizen believes is in his or her best interest.

retrospective voting
voting based on an assessment of an incumbent's past performance.

prospective voting
casting a ballot for a candidate who promises to enact policies favored by the voter in the future.

party-line voting
voting for candidates who belong only to one political party for all of the offices on the ballot.

political parties, party labels serve as a cue to voters. When people identify with a party they generally agree with most of the positions supported by that party. A voter might not know much about all of the candidates running for office at the local, state, or national level, but a party label is a cue for them to vote for candidates they most likely would support anyway, if they studied each candidate's positions individually. For these voters, party-line voting simplifies the election process. A recent work in political science, based on extensive survey research, described voters as mostly identifying "with ethnic, racial, occupational, religious, or other sorts of groups, and often—whether through group ties or hereditary loyalties—with a political party."[62]

Elections help define or change the national agenda. Elections can increase the government's legitimacy in enacting laws and policies, especially when elected officials win by margins large enough to give them a mandate to carry out their policies. Citizens use their power at the ballot box—to put people in office that will support the policies they favor and protect their constitutional rights and liberties. Elections can also be used as a weapon—to get rid of office holders who have disappointed or angered voters. Elections remind Americans that they live in a representative democracy.

Section Review

13.3 Describe different models of voting behavior.

REMEMBER
- Elections serve as a signal to elected officials about voters' preferences and priorities.
- Elections can increase the government's legitimacy in enacting laws and policies.
- Voters make choices based on what officials have done in the past and what they promise to do in the future.
- Some voters use party affiliation as the deciding factor in voting.

KNOW
- *rational choice voting*: voting based on what a citizen believes is in his or her best interest. (p. 437)
- *retrospective voting*: voting based on an assessment of an incumbent's past performance. (p. 437)
- *prospective voting*: casting a ballot for a candidate who promises to enact policies favored by the voter in the future. (p. 437)
- *party-line voting*: voting for candidates who belong only to one political party for all of the offices on the ballot. (p. 437)

THINK
What are the benefits and drawbacks for democratic government of rational-choice, retrospective, prospective, and party line voting?

13.3 Review Question: Free Response

Voters' lack of decisiveness changes everything. Voting is not a slight variation on shopping. Shoppers have incentives to be rational. Voters do not. The naive view of democracy, which paints it as a public forum for solving social problems, ignores more than a few frictions. It overlooks the big story inches beneath the surface. When voters talk about solving social problems, their primary aim is to boost their self-worth by casting off the workaday shackles of objectivity.[63]

—Bryan Caplan, Professor of Economics, George Mason University

Use the quote and your knowledge of U.S. Government and Politics to answer parts A, B, and C.

A. Identify the model of voter behavior discussed in the quote.

B. Describe the viewpoint conveyed in the quote.

C. Describe one function of elections in a representative democracy, besides the selection of office holders.

13.4 The Politics of Presidential Elections

The basics of presidential elections are laid out in Article II, Section 1 of the U.S. Constitution. Presidents must be at least thirty-five years old, be born in the United States, and have resided in the country for fourteen years. Presidential elections occur every four years.

Presidents are selected through the Electoral College. Under the Twelfth Amendment (1804), the Electoral College votes for the president and vice president separately. This means the president and vice president run for office together on their party's ticket. When a candidate wins the presidency, his or her running mate becomes the vice president.

The Stages of Presidential Campaigns

Presidential elections have two official campaign phases: the nomination campaign, in which candidates try to secure the nomination of their political party, and the general election campaign, in which successful nominees compete for the presidency. The general trend in modern campaigns has been one of increasing openness, taking some of the power away from party elites and placing it in the hands of party activists and average Americans. However, party leaders still have more power to shape the nomination than the average American voter.

Before the Official Campaign

Presidential hopefuls lay the foundations for their bids years before the official process begins. They begin raising money and contacting party officials, trying to win the favor of the party elite. An exploratory committee may attract media coverage, and it allows a potential candidate to test the waters by traveling around the country, conducting public opinion polls, and making outreach phone calls to attract potential voters. If a candidate decides to run, his or her campaign becomes official.

The Nomination Process

Declared candidates from the same party compete for that party's nomination. Federal and state laws set many of the rules governing the nomination process, but the parties control most of the details of how a candidate gets nominated. Key differences exist across states and between the parties themselves.

Most states hold presidential primary elections, in which a state's voters choose delegates who support a particular candidate. In some states, these elections may be open primaries where all eligible voters may vote, regardless of partisan affiliation. Some states require voters to affiliate with a party on the day of the primary to participate in an open primary. Other states may hold closed primaries, which are open only to voters who affiliated with a political party weeks or months before the date of the primary. Some states hold caucuses, in which party members gather to discuss candidates and issues and to select delegates to represent them in later stages of the nomination process. The national conventions, held by the parties late in the summer, conclude the nomination phase

George W. Bush and his wife, Laura, enjoy nachos on the campaign trail. Candidates encourage people to vote for them by eating local fare. As the saying goes: All politics is local. The road to the presidency is paved with food.

Paul J. Richards/Getty Images

Marco Rubio @marcorubio · 13 Apr 2015
I'm running for President of the United States.
Become a Day One Supporter at tinyurl.com/ofl2kk8
VISIT MARCORUBIO.COM
GIF
619
746

Senator Marco Rubio of Florida announces his bid for the U.S. presidency in a tweet in April 2015.
@marcorubio, Twitter

of the presidential campaign. The role of political parties in nominations and campaigns will be discussed in more detail in Chapter 14.

The General Election

After the national party conventions, the nominees are seasoned campaigners, having polished their talking points and interactions with the media. The problem is that now, instead of speaking mainly to their base of core supporters, nominees also have to appeal to independent and undecided voters, who are more moderate ideologically than voters in primaries and caucuses.

Candidates must maintain the energy of core party voters while also appealing to the undecided middle. The worry is not that voters who represent the wings of a nominee's party will vote for a candidate from the other party. The worry is that if core partisan voters think their nominee has moved too far to the center and abandoned core party goals, they will not make phone calls, knock on doors, and mobilize undecided voters during the campaign. If a candidate has survived the nomination campaign by appealing primarily to the extremes of the party, then he or she may be seen as too far left or too far right to appeal to independents and undecided voters.

The Electoral College

Electoral College
a constitutionally required process for selecting the president through slates of electors chosen in each state, who are pledged to vote for a nominee in the presidential election.

winner-take-all system
a system of elections in which the candidate who wins the plurality of votes within a state receives all of that state's votes in the Electoral College.

Voters do not cast ballots directly for the president. Instead, they are voting for a slate of electors pledged to vote for a nominee. The **Electoral College** is described in Article II, Section 1, which also places limits on who may serve as an elector. This Electoral College chooses the president.

The number of Electoral College votes to win the presidency is 270. Each state is allocated a number of electoral votes based on its representation in Congress, one for each of its two senators and one for each member of the House of Representatives, guaranteeing each state at least three electoral votes. Adding the three electoral votes allocated to the District of Columbia brings the total to 538. All states, except Maine and Nebraska, award electoral votes using a **winner-take-all system**. In Maine and Nebraska, whoever wins the state wins the two electoral votes allocated for the Senate and the rest are awarded for winning a plurality of votes within each of the state's congressional districts.

Electors are chosen from party leaders and loyal activists. Although they have pledged to vote for their party's candidate, there is a risk that they may change their minds in between the general election and the electors' vote, which takes place in December after the presidential election. Electors who do not vote for the candidate supported by the majority of the voters in their states are called *faithless electors*. Faithless electors are rare and have never changed the outcome of a presidential election.

If no nominee wins a majority of electoral votes, then the presidential election goes to Congress, with the House of Representatives choosing among the top three electoral vote winners. Each state gets one vote, and the candidate with a majority of votes wins. The Senate chooses the vice president. This process was used twice in the nation's history but not since the election of 1824.

A presidential candidate can win the presidency without winning more than half of the popular vote. This has happened several times in U.S. history.[64] In 1992, Bill Clinton

FIGURE 13.11

Electoral College Results, 2016

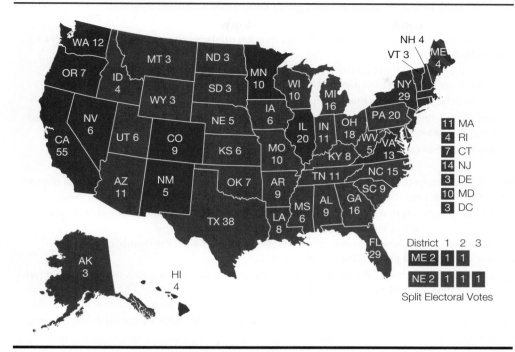

won the presidential election with 43 percent of the popular vote. Ross Perot, a third-party candidate, won nearly 19 percent of the popular vote, making it difficult for either of the major party candidates to win with a majority.[65] Sometimes the candidate who wins the popular vote loses the Electoral College vote and the presidency. This has happened five times, in U.S. history, twice recently,[66] in 2000, when George W. Bush defeated Al Gore, and again in 2016 when Donald Trump defeated Hillary Clinton. (See Figure 13.11.)

The Electoral College shapes candidate strategies. Given that all but two states award their electoral votes in a block, candidates tend to focus their campaigns on states with a large number of electoral votes and those whose electoral votes seem to be in play, largely ignoring other states. For example, Republicans can count on a majority of Texans to support their party, and Democrats can count on Californians, so there is little incentive for candidates to allocate scarce resources on those states, even though they have large populations. Instead, candidates focus on **battleground states**, where the polls show a close contest, and **swing states**, where levels of support for the parties are similar and elections swing back and forth between the Democrats and Republicans.

Critics of the Electoral College claim it is undemocratic because it does not reflect the will of the majority, causing the government to lose legitimacy. The Electoral College may lower voter turnout. For example, a Republican living in California may be discouraged from voting in the presidential election because most Californians vote for the Democratic nominee. When voters don't show up for presidential elections, they miss an opportunity to influence the outcome of state and local elections and ballot initiatives. Proponents of the Electoral College argue that it was established to provide a check on the passions of the majority. It protects the influence of the states under our system of federalism. Furthermore, if the president were selected through the popular vote, candidates would focus on large population centers, ignoring rural voters.

battleground state
a state where the polls show a close contest between the Republican and Democratic candidate in a presidential election.

swing state
a state where levels of support for the parties are similar and elections swing back and forth between Democrats and Republicans.

13.4 Describe the purpose and role of the Electoral College in our constitutional system.

REMEMBER
- Candidates are nominated by their political parties through primaries or caucuses and are announced at a national convention.
- Under Article II, Section 1, of the Constitution, presidents must be at least thirty-five years of age, natural born citizens, and have lived in the United States for fourteen years.
- Presidents are selected indirectly through the Electoral College.
- Most states use a winner-take-all system where the candidate who receives the most votes is awarded all of the state's votes in the Electoral College.
- Candidates focus their campaigns on large battleground and swing states.

KNOW
- *Electoral College*: a constitutionally required process for selecting the president through slates of electors chosen in each state, who are pledged to vote for a nominee in the presidential election. (p. 440)
- *winner-take-all system*: a system of elections in which the candidate who wins the plurality of votes within a state receives all of that state's votes in the Electoral College. (p. 440)
- *battleground state*: a state where the polls show a close contest between the Republican and Democratic candidate in a presidential election. (p. 441)
- *swing state*: a state where levels of support for the parties are similar and elections swing back and forth between Democrats and Republicans. (p. 441)

THINK
What are the advantages and disadvantages of selecting the president through an Electoral College, rather than a popular vote?

13.4 Review Question: Free Response

Jeff Parker/ Cagle Cartoons

Use the cartoon and your knowledge of U.S. Government and Politics to answer parts A, B, and C.

A. Describe the viewpoint expressed in the cartoon.

B. Explain how the Electoral College impacts the way presidential nominees allocate their resources during a campaign.

C. Explain one reason why the Electoral College system was created.

13.5 Money and Campaigns

In the 2016 presidential campaign, roughly $1.5 billion in total was raised in support of each of the campaigns of Democratic candidate Hillary Clinton and Republican candidate Donald Trump.[67] Clinton's campaign committee raised a staggering $563 million, while the Trump campaign raised $333 million, not including money raised from outside sources.[68] The 2016 presidential election proves that raising the most money doesn't guarantee victory, but candidates need staggering amounts of money to run their campaigns.

What Money Buys

Money is a strategic weapon. For all of the reasons we will discuss here, the cost of elections has only gone up (Figure 13.12). Money buys media time, on television and radio, in print, and in social media outlets. Some campaign advertisements focus on the candidate's qualities and creating a positive image. Others focus on policy differences between the candidate and his or her opponents. Finally, negative campaign advertisements attack an opponent in an effort to raise doubts about him or her. Negative campaigning has been part of presidential politics since the election of 1800. Polls show that most voters dislike negative ads, and most people think that campaigns would be improved by reducing them.[69] Political scientists disagree about the impact of negative advertising on the political process. John Geer has argued that negative campaign ads may actually "increase the quality of information available to voters as they make choices in elections."[70]

Candidates use money to hire professional consultants. Political consultants use political science to target the candidate's message to voters. Campaign consultants also

FIGURE 13.12

Comparing the Cost of Presidential Campaigns and the U.S. Gross Domestic Product

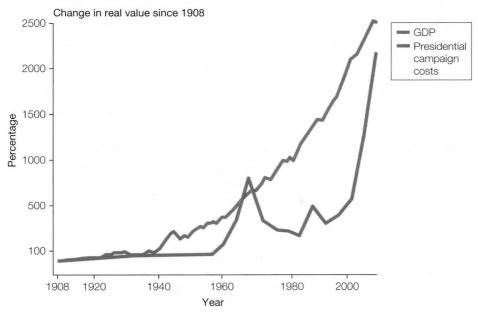

Data from Center for Responsive Politics and U.S. Bureau of Labor Statistics

figure out the districts, and even the neighborhoods, where voter turnout will be crucial. Campaigns need money to hire staff, help manage their message, coordinate media strategy, arrange public appearances, and conduct public opinion polls. Efforts to mobilize voters, called **get out the vote (GOTV)** efforts, also cost money. Finally, having a sizeable war chest, especially early in a campaign, might discourage potential challengers from entering a race in the first place.

One of many things that money buys in a campaign is the ability to reach voters, in this case by financing travel to give campaign speeches, rally supporters, and meet with members of the community.
Paul Marotta/Getty Images

Get out the vote (GOTV) efforts to mobilize supporters.

Campaign Finance Reform

Many people are concerned about the powerful role money plays in politics, and laws have been passed to limit its influence. In 1971, following the Watergate scandal, Congress passed the Federal Election Campaign Act, which created the Federal Election Commission (FEC), an independent agency that oversees campaign finance laws.[71] The act also set rules requiring disclosure of the source of campaign funds, placed limits on campaign contributions, and instituted a system for public financing of presidential elections. As discussed earlier in this chapter, in 1976, in *Buckley v. Valeo*, the Supreme Court upheld the constitutionality of restrictions on campaign contributions by individuals, although not on monies spent independently or money spent by candidates on their own campaigns.[72]

When it comes to money and elections, however, controlling the influence of money has often been like handling a balloon—squeeze it in one place and it expands somewhere else. In 2002, Congress passed the Bipartisan Campaign Reform Act (BCRA), which placed stricter limits on campaign contributions by individuals and PACs. Under BCRA, independent groups were not allowed to run ads thirty days before a primary or sixty days before the general election. As discussed in the beginning of this chapter, these limits were challenged as a violation of the First Amendment right to free speech. In *Citizens United v. Federal Election Commission* (2010), in a 5–4 decision, the Court struck down portions of the BCRA, ruling that corporations and labor unions are "persons" under the law protected by the First Amendment.[73]

Justice Anthony Kennedy delivered the majority opinion. The Court addressed the difficult standard laws must meet if they restrict speech: "Laws burdening such speech are subject to strict scrutiny, which requires the Government to prove that the restriction 'furthers a compelling interest and is narrowly tailored to achieve that interest.'"[74] According to the majority opinion, BCRA's prohibitions against independent ads thirty days prior to a primary and sixty days before a general election constitute a restriction of speech based on its content. This is precisely the kind of speech the First Amendment was meant to protect. The majority opinion states:

Premised on mistrust of governmental power, the First Amendment stands against attempts to disfavor certain subjects or viewpoints or to distinguish among different speakers, which may be a means to control content. The Government may also commit a constitutional wrong when by law it identifies certain preferred speakers. There is no basis for the proposition that, in the political speech context, the Government may impose restrictions on certain disfavored speakers. Both history and logic lead to this conclusion.[75]

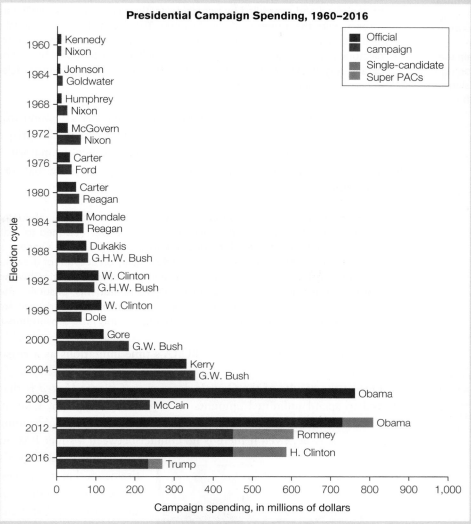

Presidential Campaign Spending, 1960–2016

Legend:
- Official campaign
- Single-candidate Super PACs

Y-axis: Election cycle
X-axis: Campaign spending, in millions of dollars

Data from Federal Election Commission

1. Describe one trend shown in the bar chart.

2. Use the bar chart to draw a conclusion about the role of money in campaigning.

3. Explain why it would be difficult to pass an amendment limiting campaign contributions.

The Court reasoned that "All speakers, including individuals and the media, use money amassed from the economic marketplace to fund their speech, and the First Amendment protects the resulting speech. . . . Differential treatment of media corporations and other corporations cannot be squared with the First Amendment."[76]

There were two concurring opinions in the *Citizens United* case, along with two opinions that concurred in part and dissented in part. These multiple opinions demonstrate a variety of viewpoints among the Supreme Court Justices. A dissenting opinion, authored by Justice Stevens (joined by Justices Ginsberg, Breyer, and Sotomayor), took issue with the majority's characterization of corporations as persons under the law:

> In the context of election to public office, the distinction between corporate and human speakers is significant. Although they make enormous contributions to our society, corporations are not actually members of it. They cannot vote or run for office. Because they may be managed and controlled by nonresidents, their interests may conflict in fundamental respects with the interests of eligible voters. The financial resources, legal structure, and instrumental orientation of corporations raise legitimate concerns about their role in the electoral process. Our lawmakers have a compelling constitutional basis, if not also a democratic duty, to take measures designed to guard against the potentially deleterious effects of corporate spending in local and national races.[77]

The dissent predicted that the outcome of the majority's decision would harm democracy in stating, "The Court's ruling threatens to undermine the integrity of elected institutions across the Nation."[78] Furthermore, the dissent rejected the majority's contention that BCRA imposed unconstitutional restrictions on speech, arguing that the first amendment is not absolute:

> The First Amendment provides that "Congress shall make no law . . . abridging the freedom of speech, or of the press." Apart perhaps from measures designed to protect the press, that text might seem to permit no distinctions of any kind. Yet in a variety of contexts, we have held that speech can be regulated differently on account of the speaker's identity, when identity is understood in categorical or institutional terms. The Government routinely places special restrictions on the speech rights of students, prisoners, members of the Armed Forces, foreigners, and its own employees. When such restrictions are justified by a legitimate governmental interest, they do not necessarily raise constitutional problems.[79]

super PAC
an organization that may spend an unlimited amount of money on a political campaign, as long as the spending is not coordinated with a campaign.

The dissent would have upheld BCRA's time limitations as a reasonable regulation on speech.

One of the results of the Court's decision in *Citizens United* is that **super PACs** are allowed to spend unlimited amounts on a political campaign. Like other PACs, super PACs must not be coordinated with a candidate's campaign. Spending by super PACs raises a tricky issue. Even if there is no contact between a super PAC and members of a campaign, if the super PAC runs advertisements that are successful in getting its point across, candidates will take notice. Information will still change hands, even if this transfer is uncoordinated and legal.

David Bossie, who brought *Citizens United* to the U.S. Supreme Court, summed up his feeling about the decision: "I'm responsible for *Citizens United*. I am not sorry," calling it "a sweeping

Protests were held on the fifth anniversary of the Supreme Court's decision in *Citizens United* that corporations and labor unions have free speech rights under the First Amendment. What are the dangers of limiting the First Amendment?

Drew Angerer/Getty Images

Donald Trump's 2016 electoral victory is announced against the backdrop of a Manhattan skyscraper. Before becoming president, Donald Trump was a real estate developer and reality TV star. How does the image reflect both his past and the future?
Brazil Photo Press/Getty Images

victory against government censorship of free speech. . . ."[80] Yet the 2010 decision that opened the floodgates to unlimited corporate campaign contributions was opposed by eight out of ten Americans across the political spectrum.[81] The case is central to understanding the ways that money is deployed in today's campaigns.

Representative democracy depends on the actions of citizens. People can make their voices heard through voting, volunteering for a campaign, donating money, joining interest groups, contacting elected officials, and protesting. Political campaigns seek to convince voters that a candidate will enact the policies they favor. Although all citizens have the right to run for office, it takes a lot of money to run a campaign. The high cost of campaigning raises questions about whether money plays too big a role in politics. This concern, along with worries about low voter turnout rates, raises questions about how to ensure the representative nature of our democracy.

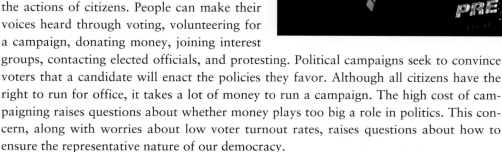

Section Review

13.5 Describe the rules governing political campaigns.

REMEMBER
- Campaigns are expensive, and candidates need money to hire professional consultants, pay for travel, and run media ads to reach potential voters.
- Several efforts have been made to reduce the influence of money in politics, including the Federal Election Campaign Act of 1971 and the Bipartisan Campaign Reform Act of 2002 (BCRA).
- In *Citizens United v. United States* (2010), the Supreme Court ruled that corporations and labor unions are persons under the law and that the provisions of BCRA banning independent ads before elections violated the First Amendment.

KNOW
- *Get out the vote (GOTV)*: efforts to mobilize supporters. (p. 444)
- *super PAC*: an organization that may spend an unlimited amount of money on a political campaign, as long as the spending is not coordinated with a campaign. (p. 446)

THINK
What is the proper balance between protecting the First Amendment right of free speech and limiting the influence of money in politics?

13.5 Review Question: Free Response

[T]he formalistic obsession with whether a corporation should have the legal status of a "person" with a "right" to free speech quite misses the substantive issues at stake, which concern how the principle of free expression should be applied to the political speech of certain types of social groups. In particular, is there something uniquely harmful and/or unworthy of protection about political messages that come from corporations and unions, as opposed to, say, rich individuals, persuasive writers, or charismatic demagogues? . . . The very idea that political speech in an open democracy can be "corrupting" rests on fundamentally illiberal assumptions about individuals' capacity for reasoned deliberation and self-government.[82]

—Anthony Dick, "Defending *Citizens United*"

Use the quote and your knowledge of U.S. Government and Politics to answer parts A, B, and C.

A. Describe the ruling in the Supreme Court case referenced in the quote.

B. Describe the viewpoint expressed in the quote about the Supreme Court case discussed in part A.

C. Explain one reason why the decision you discussed above has faced criticism.

Chapter 13 Review

AP® KEY CONCEPTS

- *political participation* (p. 419)
- *political action committee* (p. 419)
- *linkage institution* (p. 422)
- *social movement* (p. 422)
- *franchise* or *suffrage* (p. 425)
- *Twenty-Sixth Amendment* (p. 425)
- *Twenty-Fourth Amendment* (p. 425)
- *poll tax* (p. 425)
- *voter turnout* (p. 425)

- *demographic characteristics* (p. 426)
- *socioeconomic status (SES)* (p. 426)
- *political efficacy* (p. 427)
- *political mobilization* (p. 432)
- *registration requirements* (p. 432)
- *absentee ballot* (p. 434)
- *rational choice voting* (p. 437)
- *retrospective voting* (p. 437)
- *prospective voting* (p. 437)

- *party-line voting* (p. 437)
- *Electoral College* (p. 440)
- *winner-take-all system* (p. 440)
- *battleground state* (p. 441)
- *swing state* (p. 441)
- *Get out the vote (GOTV)* (p. 444)
- *super PAC* (p. 446)

AP® EXAM PRACTICE and Critical Thinking Project

MULTIPLE-CHOICE QUESTIONS

1. Which of the following describes the person most likely to vote, based on the demographic characteristics?

    A. A twenty-five-year-old white male, with a high school diploma

    B. A sixty-five-year-old Hispanic female, with a PhD

    C. A thirty-five-year-old African American male, with a bachelor's degree

    D. An eighteen-year-old white female, entering college

2. Which of the following is the most accurate measure of voter turnout?

   A. The percentage of those registered who vote

   B. The percentage of the total population that votes

   C. The percentage of the voting-age population that votes

   D. The percentage of those living in a country who vote

Questions 3 and 4 refer to the cartoon.

Jeff Parker/Cagle Cartoons

3. Which of the following best describes the viewpoint in the cartoon?

   A. It is unreasonable to ask voters to present identification.

   B. Voting is similar to renting a movie or going to a bar and should require an ID.

   C. Voter ID laws make it too difficult for people to exercise their right to vote.

   D. Voter ID laws are an attempt to prevent fraud at the polls.

4. A critic of the cartoon would make which of the following political arguments?

   A. Unlike renting a movie or going to a bar, voting is an important political right that should not be restricted through ID laws.

   B. Voter ID laws are an infringement on the basic right of privacy.

   C. If a form of identification is acceptable to travel or go to a bar, it should be acceptable for voting.

   D. Voter identification laws are a reasonable way to prevent fraud.

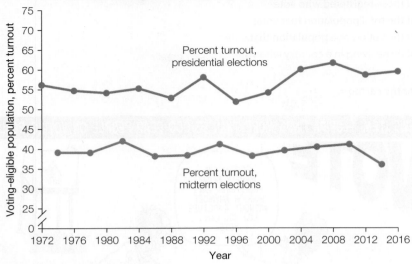

Voter Turnout among U.S. Voting-Eligible Population, 1972–2016

Data from United States Elections Project

5. Which of the following best describes a trend shown in the graph?
   A. Turnout in all federal elections is usually below 50 percent.
   B. Turnout is lower in midterm congressional elections than in presidential elections.
   C. Turnout in presidential elections decreased every year from 1992 to 2008.
   D. Turnout in midterm congressional elections is more unpredictable than turnout in presidential elections.

Questions 6 and 7 refer to the quote.

Allowing corporate influence to flow unfettered into federal campaigns will only undermine the confidence the American people have in their government, and serve only to stack the deck further in favor of special interests at the expense of hardworking Americans.

—Senator Michael Bennet (D.-Colorado)[81]

6. The quote refers to which of the following?
   A. The Bipartisan Campaign Reform Act of 2002
   B. *Buckley v. Valeo* (1976)
   C. *Citizens United v. Federal Election Commission* (2010)
   D. The Federal Election Campaign Act of 1971

7. A critic of the quote would make which of the following arguments?
   A. The First Amendment protects the right of individuals to participate in the political process.
   B. Corporations and labor unions should not be considered as persons protected under the Bill of Rights.
   C. Advertising is expensive, and candidates need large donations in order to conduct their campaigns.
   D. The First Amendment protects all political speech, including campaign spending by groups.

8. Which of the following is an argument that the Electoral College favors small states?

  A. Small states have at least three votes in the Electoral College, and this gives them influence disproportionate to their populations.

  B. Small states are often the deciding factor in presidential elections, and candidates focus on them more than on large states.

  C. Large states, like California and Texas, are easy to predict, so they have little impact on the outcome of presidential elections.

  D. Voter turnout is very high in small states, making them more important than large states.

9. Which of the following is an argument that the Electoral College favors large states?

  A. Candidates focus on the swing states and battleground states that have the most votes in the Electoral College.

  B. Candidates focus on all large states because they have the most votes in the Electoral College.

  C. It is easier to win a majority of votes in large states than in small states because most people in large states live in cities.

  D. Large states are overrepresented in comparison with their populations because large states have a lot of members in the House of Representatives.

Pat Bagley/Cagle Cartoons

10. Which of the following best describes the viewpoint in the cartoon?

  A. Spending by Super PACs has too much influence on Supreme Court decisions.

  B. Super PAC spending is a threat to representative democracy.

  C. Super PACs have become so big that they will collapse under their own weight.

  D. Citizens have as much power as Super PACs because they have the ability to choose policymakers.

TWO THIRDS OF ELIGIBLE TEXANS DON'T VOTE

1. Use the cartoon and your knowledge of U.S. Government and Politics to answer parts A, B, and C.
   A. Describe the viewpoint expressed in the cartoon.
   B. Explain one reason why voting is important in a democracy.
   C. Describe one proposal to increase voter turnout rates.

2. Head Count is a voter-registration drive aimed at young people. Following a march to end gun violence held in March, 2018, in Washington, D.C, members of Head Count raised their fists and chanted "demonstration without registration leads to frustration" before sending out volunteers with clipboards to sign up new voters.[82]

   Use the scenario and your knowledge of U.S. Government and Politics to answer parts A, B, and C.
   A. Describe the viewpoint expressed by members of Head Count in the scenario.
   B. Describe one policy a state might enact to address the issue described in the scenario.
   C. Explain one reason why a citizen might attend a demonstration but not register to vote.

ARGUMENTATION QUESTION

Although there have been several efforts to limit the role on money in politics, campaign spending continues to increase. Discuss whether increased campaign spending threatens representative democracy. In your essay:

- Articulate a claim or thesis that responds to the prompt, and use a line of reasoning to defend it.
- Use at least TWO pieces of relevant and accurate evidence to support your claim.
- At least ONE piece of evidence must be from one of the listed foundational documents:
  - Constitution of the United States
  - *Federalist* No. 10
  - *Federalist* No. 78
- Use a second piece of evidence from another foundational document from the list or from your study of elections and campaigns.
- Use reasoning to explain why the evidence you provided supports your claim or thesis.
- Use refutation, concession, or rebuttal to respond to an opposing or alternative perspective.

CRITICAL THINKING PROJECT

Working as a Campaign Consultant

The photo is from one of the most famous negative campaign ads. It was run in 1964 by Democrat Lyndon Johnson's campaign against Republican challenger Barry Goldwater. For nearly thirty seconds, a freckled, brown-eyed little girl plucks daisy petals in a lovely park. A countdown begins at ten, the camera zooms to a close-up of her eye, and at zero, a nuclear bomb detonates, producing a mushroom cloud. The ad implied that Goldwater would lead the country into a nuclear war.
Democratic National Committee

Negative advertisements have always been a part of American political campaigns. TV and social media allow campaign managers to combine words and images to paint negative, and sometimes frightening, pictures of their opponents.

Your party's imaginary nominee for president has hired you to create an ad campaign that will give him or her the best chance of winning.

1. Go to the Web site for the Museum for the Moving Image at http://www.livingroomcandidate .org/. View ads from twenty-first-century presidential campaigns to get some idea of how campaigns have been run in the recent past.
2. Compare at least five ads run by the winners with at least five ads run by the losers.
3. Based on your research, write a memo to your candidate, and explain whether the campaign should use mostly positive or mostly negative ads. Explain your reasoning for why you favor one model of advertising. In your memo, refer specifically to at least two ads from recent campaigns, and explain why those ads serve as models for what your campaign should, or should not, do.

14 Political Parties
The Outsiders versus the Establishment

Republican presidential candidate Donald Trump speaking at a rally in West Virginia in May 2016. Trump's campaign challenged his Republican Party by breaking many rules about how candidates should run their campaigns. Trump's win raised questions about whether traditional wisdom about political parties still applies.
Brendan Smialowski/AFP/Getty Images

Representative democracy involves uncertainty about which candidates might win an election and how citizens figure out which candidates to support. The variety of governmental policies makes it extremely challenging for even the most attentive voters to know all of the details about what a candidate stands for or hopes to accomplish.

Political parties organize and support candidates running for office. A candidate's affiliation with a political party serves as a shortcut, helping voters choose which candidate to support. Political parties (along with elections, interest groups, and the media) are linkage institutions connecting citizens with government.

Party leaders face a challenge. They must craft an appealing and consistent message that gets their candidates elected and maintains party cohesion. American political parties have often been successful in doing this, but not always. Once in a while, a party is challenged not by another party but by members within its own ranks who believe party leadership has ignored their opinions.

In 2016 both the Democrats and the Republicans confronted challenges from within. Two candidates, Senator Bernie Sanders of Vermont, and entrepreneur and television celebrity Donald Trump—far apart on the political spectrum— emerged as major forces in their parties. Sanders and Trump changed the national political debate. Both men were outside the mainstream positions within their parties, and many Americans responded to their campaigns.

The presidential election of 2016 turned conventional wisdom on its head. Experts in American politics were surprised by both campaigns, and the established leaders of America's dominant political parties scrambled to figure out what was going on and what to do about it.

The election of 2016 provides an opportunity to do much more than analyze one presidential election. It offers the chance to better understand the role that parties play in American representative democracy.

political party
an organized group of party leaders, officeholders, and voters who work together to elect candidates to political office.

After reading this chapter, you will be able to

14.1 Describe the functions and impacts of political parties on the government and its citizens.

14.2 Explain how political parties have developed and adapted to new circumstances.

14.3 Explain the role of political parties in nominating candidates.

14.4 Explain why it is difficult for third parties and independent candidates to win elections.

LEARNING TARGETS

▪ Two Presidential Candidates Shake Up the Field

American presidential elections often are filled with drama. Traditionally, though, most of the drama goes on between the parties. The election of 2016 was different. Two of the leading candidates, Republican multimillionaire Donald Trump and Vermont senator Bernie Sanders capitalized on voters' profound disgust with politics as usual. While Sanders failed to get the Democratic nomination, in winning the presidency Trump became the first to do so without previously holding public office or serving as a high ranking military officer.

Unlike many presidential contenders, neither candidate concentrated on courting the best-known activists and leaders in their parties, the so-called party establishment or party elites. In fact, their campaigns went out of their way to alienate those elites.

Other presidential candidates have run similar campaigns. What made Trump and Sanders more noteworthy was that their criticisms struck such a deep chord with so many voters. Each kept winning state nomination contests long after many political observers were certain they would fade.

Americans have become less attached to political parties in recent years. At the same time, the country has grown increasingly more polarized by political ideology. More conservatives hold strongly conservative views than in the past, and more liberals hold strongly liberal views. Both parties have fostered an environment in which the two sides seem locked in combat. Despite this ongoing battle, the parties haven't become any stronger. According to journalist Jonathan Rauch, "Here is the reigning political paradox of our era: Partisanship is strong, but parties are weak."[1]

To many within the Democratic and Republican parties, the Sanders and Trump campaigns represented the opposite of what parties should present to voters: a range of interests and policies, linked by a shared goal, forming a larger, unified system.

Sanders didn't even belong to the Democratic Party when he announced he was running for the nomination. Instead, he described himself as an "independent socialist," favoring the idea that government and society should meet the needs of the public, even if the result is that rich people can't earn as much. He criticized so-called corporate welfare, such as special provisions in the tax code that give businesses preferential treatment. As public resentment toward financial companies rose during the 2008–2010 recession, the Occupy Wall Street movement protested income inequality. Sanders endorsed the movement's widespread demonstrations. Sanders's message that the playing field was unacceptably tilted toward the top 1 percent of Americans resonated with many voters, especially young adults struggling with student loan debt.

Sanders's proposal to make public colleges and universities tuition free made him popular with young liberals. Sanders said his campaign involved creating a "political revolution" that could serve "millions of Americans, working people who have given up on the political process."[2] But Sanders's Democratic opponent, Hillary Clinton, and many others in the mainstream of the Democratic Party, said Sanders's proposals were unrealistic. They did not want the Democratic Party to be associated with tax increases and big government for fear they would lose the support of centrist voters. In the end, Sanders won 43 percent of the popular vote during the primaries and 46 percent of the pledged delegates.

Like Sanders, Trump was an outsider in his party. He had never held a public office. That disturbed some in the GOP ("Grand Old Party" or Republican Party) who believed that those seeking the nation's highest post should have prior political experience. Trump has switched political parties several times, which led many conservative Republicans to question whether Trump would remain faithful to the party.

Trump called for building a wall on the U.S.–Mexico border to keep out those coming into the country illegally. After the 2015 terrorist attacks in

An attendee holds up a sign in support of Democratic presidential candidate Bernie Sanders at a rally in Brooklyn, New York, in April 2016. Sanders's call for a "political revolution" was a rallying cry, especially among young voters.
Victor J. Blue/Bloomberg via Getty Images

San Bernardino, California, and overseas, Trump called for a ban on Muslims being allowed to enter the United States. Trump campaigned on a theme of "Make America Great Again." He blamed all politicians for their inability to solve the country's problems. That included the GOP's establishment, which he bluntly described as ineffective.

Trump tapped into many voters' deep frustration with politics and political parties. They agreed with Trump's call to upend the entire system and described him as refreshingly authentic and blunt. "He disrupts a broken political process and beats establishment candidates who've long ignored their interests," a lawyer in a poor, rural North Carolina town wrote in explaining Trump's widespread appeal there. "When you're earning $32,000 a year and haven't had a decent vacation in over a decade, it doesn't matter who Trump appoints to the [United Nations]."[3]

Donald Trump addresses contestants on the NBC reality show *The Apprentice*. Trump's unconventional candidacy, including his criticisms of many of his own party's leaders, resonated with many voters.
NBC/Photofest © NBC

Trump and Sanders had completely different styles and messages, but they shared some things in common. Both argued that politicians can be bought with large campaign contributions. Another trait they shared was a message of economic pessimism. Both drew strong support from voters who were anxious about where the economy was headed.[4] Both actively criticized their parties' mainstream beliefs on trade with other countries. They accused the parties of supporting trade deals that had led to the outsourcing of thousands of American jobs to foreign competitors.

In a normal presidential election campaign, Sanders and Trump might have made a splash, but neither would probably have had a real chance at securing the nomination. In 2016, the leaders of political parties faced challenges to the way they had operated in the past. Donald Trump not only secured his party's nomination. He became president.

In a well-known incident during the 2016 presidential primaries, a house finch landed on the lectern as Bernie Sanders was speaking at a rally in Portland, Oregon. Both Sanders and Trump drew large crowds at their rallies, presenting themselves as candidates who weren't beholden to the political establishment.
Steve Dykes/AP Images

14.1 Functions of Political Parties

Parties are linkage institutions, which connect citizens with government. A healthy party serves as a check on the opposition, promoting ideas and candidates that differ from the other party's positions, so voters can choose how they want to be represented.

The Roles That Parties Play

Political scientist V. O. Key Jr. identified three main roles that political parties play in American representative democracy:[5]

1. As organizations, political parties recruit, nominate, and support candidates for political office.
2. In the electorate, parties provide labels that voters can use as shortcuts in identifying candidates closer to their own political ideologies.
3. In government, a party enacts the policy positions of its members and acts as an opposition to the majority party when it is in the minority.

Parties as Organizations

A political party unites people with shared social, economic, and ideological goals. It finds and supports candidates to run for federal, state, and local offices. Parties educate and mobilize voters. They raise money and develop a media strategy to try to get their candidates elected. If those candidates win, parties try to keep them in office. The parties also come up with policy platforms that they want their candidates to follow.

Today, however, national party organizations are struggling. That's partly because of the ability of outside groups to raise and spend large amounts of money on behalf of political causes. As we studied in the last chapter, the Supreme Court's decision in *Citizens United v. Federal Election Commission* (2010)[6] allows for unlimited spending independent of a campaign or candidate. The campaign finance system restricts the ability of parties to raise and spend money and to coordinate campaigns so that candidates of the same party can pool their expenses.

party identification
the degree to which a voter is connected to and influenced by a particular political party.

The Party in the Electorate

Party identification is the degree to which voters are connected to a particular party. We have already explored the individual contributors to Americans' political beliefs (Chapter 10) and the factors that contribute to voters' choices—and whether or not they vote at all (Chapter 12).

Parties influence voter choices. Parties support policies consistent with a broad set of political beliefs. An "R" or a "D" next to a candidate's name serves as a cue to voters about what that candidate stands for. Voters use party labels as a shortcut in the voting booth. Some

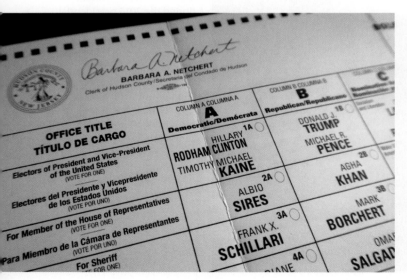

This ballot from the 2016 presidential election shows the candidates' party affiliation. How does party affiliation serve as a cue to voters?
Gary Hershorn/ZUMA Press/Newscom

states have ballots that enable voters to cast their votes for all of the candidates from one political party. Party-line voters, who pick candidates based on their party affiliation, use the process of **straight-ticket voting** to mark their ballots.

Since the 1980s, more people have identified themselves as Democrats than as Republicans. But one frustration for both parties is that larger numbers of people consistently have not identified with either party (Figure 14.1). In fact, a Gallup poll taken in 2015 showed that just 29 percent of those surveyed called themselves Democrats—the lowest figure in the past twenty-seven years and probably the lowest since the early 1950s. Meanwhile, 26 percent considered themselves Republican—just one percentage point above

straight-ticket voting
voting for all of the candidates on the ballot from one political party.

FIGURE 14.1

Americans' Party Identification over Time: Two Perspectives, with and without "Leaners"

U.S. Party Identification, Yearly Averages, 1988–2017

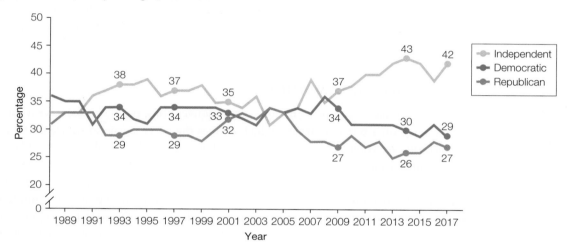

U.S. Party Identification Including Independent Leanings, Yearly Averages, 1991–2017

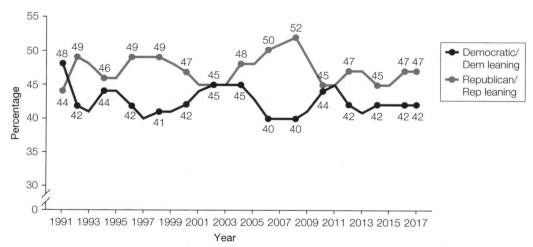

Note: Gallup began regularly measuring independent's party leanings in 1991. Data are through 2017.

Data from Gallup

the historically low figure of 25 percent recorded two years earlier.[7] In contrast, the percentage of independent voters has grown sharply. A big part of slipping party identification is Americans' deep frustration with the inability of the federal government to enact policies. A Gallup poll published in December 2017 asked Americans what they felt was the nation's top problem. Twenty-two percent of those polled reported that dissatisfaction with the government was the most important problem, several percentage points ahead of the economy.[8]

In recent elections voters have been less likely to support candidates of different parties in a single election, a practice known as **split-ticket voting**. From 1964 until 1988, as many as one-third of House elections featured a candidate of one party winning even though a presidential candidate of the other party got the most votes in that candidate's district. Once people identify a group to which they belong, "they are much more likely to vote for their party and less likely to split a ticket," according to political scientist Matthew Levendusky. "They are more likely to become devoted cheerleaders."[9]

In 2012, only 26 out of the House's 435 members won elections in districts where someone who was not from their party got the most presidential votes. The resulting split-ticket percentage of 5.7 was the lowest it had been since 1920.[10] In 2016, every state that went for Trump elected a Republican senator. On the other side of the aisle, every state that went in Clinton's favor elected a Democrat to the Senate.

The Party in Government

At the national level, during national party conventions, party members write, argue over, and agree on a **party platform**, which defines the party's general stance on issues. These platforms are voted on at the conventions. Because of the difficulty in getting large groups of people, even those with similar beliefs, to agree on something, the platforms can be the source of great controversy. In 2012, Democrats initially took out a sentence in their party's platform about helping individuals reach their "God-given potential." But that would have removed any references to God in the platform, and Democrats feared it would lead Republicans to depict them as out of touch with religious Americans. The sentence was reinstated.[11]

When its candidates win, a party's members take office and begin the process of governing. While it is usually much easier for a political party to get its policies passed when it controls both houses of Congress and the presidency, party platforms are not binding, and elected officials from the same party do not always agree on the issues.

Party Leadership

The president generally chooses the chair of his or her national party. The national party chair raises money and serves as a prominent spokesperson in the media. Yet the national party organization's power over the state and local parties is advisory. It can't tell them what to do. In fact, the state parties can put pressure on national parties. In 2014, as public opinion in the United States shifted toward greater acceptance of same-sex marriage, Nevada's Republican Party dropped language from its party platform opposing same-sex marriage.[12] The national committee later rejected proposed resolutions that were critical of same-sex marriage, reflecting its responsiveness to state party organizations.[13]

Recruiting and Supporting Candidates

Parties use **recruitment** to seek candidates who best reflect the party's philosophy and who will draw voters to them. The parties look for people who can contrast sharply with their opponents. Parties try to discourage prospective candidates who don't have a good chance of winning.

Parties provide expertise and support for their candidates. As discussed in Chapter 13, campaigning is expensive. Parties hire political consultants to help them raise money and to refine their message to specific targeted groups of voters. Parties hire campaign staff, arrange for public appearances, coordinate media strategy, and conduct public opinion polls to help their candidates win.

Parties maintain voter databases to collect information about potential voters and how to target them. In the 2016 campaign, the Democratic Party developed a complex algorithm, named Ada (after a female nineteenth-century mathematician), which ran 400,000 simulations a day to determine which battleground states were the most important.[14] The algorithm played a role in almost every decision made by the Clinton campaign, including where to run ads.[15] President Trump's Campaign hired Cambridge Analytica, a data management firm, to target voters. The firm is accused of harvesting personal information from fifty million Facebook users in an effort to sway their votes.[16]

Section Review

This chapter's main ideas are reflected in the Learning Targets. By reviewing after each section, you should be able to

— **Remember** the key points,

— **Know** terms that are central to the topic, and

—**Think** critically about U.S. political parties and their role in government.

14.1 Describe the functions and impacts of political parties on the government and its citizens.

REMEMBER	• Political parties recruit, nominate, and support candidates for office.
	• Parties provide labels that voters can use as shortcuts in identifying candidates close to their own political ideologies.
	• In government, elected officials work to enact their party's policies.

KNOW	• *political party*: an organized group of party leaders, officeholders, and voters that work together to elect candidates to political office. (p. 455)
	• *party identification*: the degree to which a voter is connected to and influenced by a particular political party. (p. 458)
	• *straight-ticket voting*: voting for all of the candidates on the ballot from one political party. (p. 459)
	• *split-ticket voting*: voting for candidates from different parties in the same election. (p. 460)
	• *party platform*: a set of positions and policy objectives that members of a political party agree to. (p. 460)
	• *recruitment*: the process through which political parties identify potential candidates. (p. 460)

THINK	How does the competition between political parties further representative democracy?

14.1 Review Question: Free Response

The excerpt is from an article about research on Get Out the Vote (GOTV) efforts.

First, they found that a good GOTV effort increased the likelihood that a voter would turn out by 7 percentage points. Second, they found that GOTV interventions were additive in their effectiveness. Which is to say that if you knocked on a voter's door a second time, the percentage chance that they would turn out for your candidate increased *again*, by another 7 percentage points.[17]

Use the excerpt and your knowledge of U.S. Government and Politics to answer parts A, B, and C.

A. Describe the results of the research referenced in the quote.

B. Explain one way in which a political party could use the information from the passage to help its candidates win.

C. Explain one way in which political parties use technology in an attempt to increase their electoral success.

■ 14.2 The Development of American Political Parties

party coalition
groups of voters who support a political party over time.

For about the last 150 years, most politicians have belonged to either the Democratic or Republican Party. Parties seek to build a **party coalition** consisting of groups of voters who will continue to support the party's policies and, most important, vote for the party's candidates. However, coalitions that support a political party shift over time, with some groups leaving to join the other political party. For example, the New Deal coalition was made up of northern liberals, African Americans, and white southerners. That coalition was bound to fracture over the issue of civil rights, which it did in 1964. The concept of shifting coalitions explains how Nixon was able to turn the South Republican and how in 2016 Trump succeeded in winning over blue-collar whites in the Rust Belt. It also explains why each major party seeks to appeal to the weakest link in the opposing party's coalition.

realignment
when the groups of people who support a political party shift their allegiance to a different political party.

Control of government has shifted back and forth between the parties in periods of **realignment**, which is a major shift in allegiance to the political parties that is often driven by changes in the issues that unite or divide voters. Periods of realignment may be ushered in by **critical elections**, a major national election that shifts the balance of power between the two parties.[18] Periods when one party wins most national elections are called **party eras**.[19] Political scientists debate the boundaries of major eras in party control and how decisive a particular election was in signaling a change in those boundaries.

critical election
a major national election that signals a change in the balance of power between the two parties.

From 1969 until 2016, government has often been divided, with one party controlling one or both houses of Congress with a president from the opposing party. Some political scientists refer to this as the **era of divided government**.[20]

party era
time period when one party wins most national elections.

Modern American Party Politics

era of divided government
a trend since 1969, in which one party controls one or both houses of Congress and the president is from the opposing party.

In the mid-1960s, the Republican Party's base began shifting away from the Northeast and toward the rapidly growing South and West, enabling Nixon to win the presidency in 1968 and even more decisively in the 1972 election. Much of this change had been driven by a realignment in which large numbers of southern white voters shifted from the Democratic Party to the Republican Party. Nixon strategist Kevin Phillips had urged the president to pursue a "southern strategy" and play on some whites' negative reaction to the Civil Rights Act of 1964. Nixon also capitalized on the backlash against hippies and protestors against the Vietnam War, calling on "the great silent majority of my fellow Americans" to support Republican policies.[21]

The Republican Party's fortunes declined temporarily as a result of the Watergate scandal, which led to Nixon's resignation in 1974. In 1976, Democratic presidential candidate Jimmy Carter swept the entire South—and failed to win a single state west of

Texas—by emphasizing his deeply religious beliefs and his born-again status, reclaiming to the Democratic Party the southern whites who had supported Nixon.

But Ronald Reagan reinvigorated the party with his landslide election win in 1980 against Jimmy Carter. Reagan's message of lower taxes, smaller government, and a strong defense remains highly influential in the GOP today. "Reagan Democrats" were white working-class voters who had supported the Democratic Party in the past but switched their allegiance to the Republican Party and voted for Reagan.[22]

In 1992, Bill Clinton became the first Democrat since Carter to occupy the White House, partly by prodding his party toward the ideological center and partly by arguing that then-President George H. W. Bush caused an economic recession in 1991–1992.[23] But two years later, the Republican Party broke the Democrats' forty-year hold on the House and also regained control of the Senate. Yet the continued conflict between the parties helped propel Clinton to reelection in 1996.

With Republicans in search of someone who could unite the party, Texas governor George W. Bush campaigned in 2000 as a "compassionate conservative" and eked out a narrow electoral college victory while barely losing the popular vote. He carried every southern state while drawing 83 percent of the Evangelical Christian vote.[24] Throughout this period, other changes in the South led to a dwindling number of conservative Democrats serving in Congress and a corresponding increase in the election of conservative Republicans. At the state level, the Republican Party began using the congressional redistricting process to redraw districts to move greater numbers of Democrats into cities, making the Republican Party more competitive in suburban areas.

Since the mid-1990s, party control has swung wildly back and forth (see Figure 14.2). Democrats won back control of the House and Senate in 2006. In 2008 Republicans nominated Arizona senator John McCain, hoping that McCain's experience in Congress, national security credentials, and heroic story of survival as a prisoner of war in Vietnam would appeal to voters. The Democrats nominated Barack Obama, who had been a community organizer and senator prior to the nomination. Obama took 53 percent of the popular vote, the best Democratic percentage since 1964.[25] Democrats also kept control of the House and

FIGURE 14.2

Changes in Party Control, 2000–2016

Election	Presidency	House	Senate
2000	Republican George W. Bush	Republican	Democrat
2002		Republican	Republican
2004	Republican George W. Bush	Republican	Republican
2006		Democrat	Democrat
2008	Democrat Barack Obama	Democrat	Democrat
2010		Republican	Democrat
2012	Democrat Barack Obama	Republican	Democrat
2014		Republican	Republican
2016	Republican Donald Trump	Republican	Republican

The 2016 election showed the decline of the influence of the Tea Party. Instead, a movement aligned with President Trump emerged, as in the photo from a rally in Phoenix in August 2017.
AP Photo/Alex Brandon

Senate and eventually had a majority of sixty votes in the Senate to give them even more clout.

Nevertheless, the party's dominance was extremely short-lived. President Obama pushed several measures in response to the economic downturn of 2008–2010, including hundreds of billions of dollars in federal spending and extensions of bailouts to the banking, investment, and automobile industries.[26] These actions led to a political backlash called the Tea Party movement. Members of the Tea Party were not hostile to all government programs, however. A Harvard University study found that their opposition to Obama's health care overhaul came even as members liked programs such as Social Security and Medicare.[27] The Tea Party was credited with helping Republicans regain control of the House in the 2010 elections.

The weakened economy, with an unemployment rate stuck at around 8 percent, led Republicans to confidently predict they could recapture the White House in 2012. The Republican Party, and its candidate Mitt Romney, sought to make the elections a referendum on the president's handling of the economy, but Democrats portrayed Romney as a wealthy corporate executive with an inability to understand average Americans. Obama won, and Democrats kept their majority in the Senate.

After the election, the Republican Party decided to take a hard look at how it could do better. The RNC formed a panel of experienced activists who made a series of recommendations, including putting out a positive message and creating a diverse, nationwide operation of local activists.

Despite the lowest overall percentage turnout rate among voters since 1942, Republicans turned out in much greater numbers than Democrats in the 2014 midterms, swinging control of the Senate back to their party.[28] That led the DNC to do its own post-election assessment of how to improve. It called for a better long-term strategy for winning state elections that could help the party redraw future congressional districts. But most of its report said the party should continue its existing goals of ensuring voting rights and recruiting a diverse set of candidates.[29]

How Political Parties Change and Adapt

The Democratic and Republican parties are trying to stay relevant in an age of intense polarization. That polarization has grown and has led some voters to participate in politics not just because they support their party but out of an intense dislike of the other side.

In the 2016 election, both party establishments witnessed major challenges to their parties' status quo. Sanders, though ultimately unsuccessful in his pursuit of the nomination, challenged the Democratic Party to focus more on issues of economic inequality and the power of Wall Street and the nation's financial institutions.

The Trump candidacy may have exposed a deep rupture between the party's corporate-backed wealthier donors and its less affluent blue-collar supporters. Many Trump voters shared his deep distrust of government and the party elites, electing an unconventional candidate to the presidency. At the same time, voters returned congressional Republicans who did not embrace Trump to the House and Senate. Party loyalist Paul

Ryan, who kept his job as Speaker of the House, offered to work with Trump, saying, "We are eager to work hand in hand with the new administration to advance an agenda to improve the lives of the American people."[30]

Today's Republican Party coalition may well be dominant. But, like all party coalitions, it is unstable. For example, fiscal conservatives who want a balanced budget might turn against Republicans who favor tax cuts that raise the deficit. Republicans who are social liberals, supporting same-sex marriage and the legalization of recreational marijuana, might clash with social conservatives, who oppose both policies. Some Republicans favor reducing international trade barriers, while others are more isolationist.

The Democratic Party has its own problems. Even though Obama easily won election in both 2008 and 2012, Democrats were unable to generate broader enthusiasm for the party. This made it difficult to recruit successful candidates for lower political offices. During Obama's two terms, the Democrats lost seats in the House, Senate, and state legislatures as well as more than half of state governorships. By 2016, Democrats controlled fewer elected offices nationwide than at any time since the 1920s.[31] Part of the reason was Republicans' ability in many states to redraw congressional districts after the 2010 census to make it easier for members of their party to win and remain in office. Democrats tend to cluster in cities, where they can win local elections, but they have less success in congressional or statewide offices. Another reason was the continued inability of Democrats to turn out their most loyal supporters in midterm elections, when a presidential candidate isn't on the ballot. The Democratic Party is also weakened by the split between those who supported Sanders, who seek dramatic change, and the centrist voters who supported Clinton.

The landscape is changing dramatically for both the Democratic and Republican parties. Both parties must adapt to new technologies and changing demographics if they want to remain relevant in American national politics.

Section Review

14.2 Explain how political parties have developed and adapted to new circumstances.

REMEMBER
- Control of government has shifted back and forth between the parties during periods of realignment, which occur when public support shifts substantially from one party to the other.
- During the 1960s, white voters in the South shifted away from the Democratic Party, and today the South favors the Republican Party.
- Democrats are more popular in cities, and rural voters tend to support Republicans.
- Parties are becoming more polarized, and some voters cast ballots because they support their party and intensely dislike the other party.
- Political parties try to predict and adapt to demographic changes.

KNOW
- *party coalition*: groups of voters who support a political party over time. (p. 462)
- *realignment*: when the groups of people who support a political party shift their allegiance to a different political party. (p. 462)
- *critical election*: a major national election that signals a change in the balance of power between the two parties. (p. 462)
- *party era*: a time period when one party wins most national elections. (p. 462)
- *era of divided government*: a trend since 1969, in which one party controls one or both houses of Congress and the president is from the opposing party. (p. 462)

THINK   What advice would you give both the Democratic and Republican parties to help them retain the party faithful while encouraging new groups of voters to support them?

Florida Politics by ZIP Code

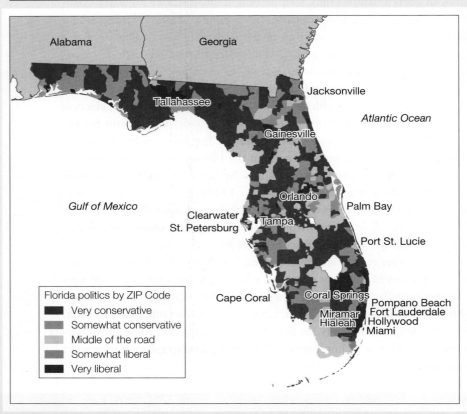

Map based on data from Esri

Use the map and your knowledge of U.S. Government and Politics to answer parts A, B, and C.

A. Describe one pattern shown on the map.

B. Describe one way in which the geographic support for the Democratic and Republican parties has shifted over time throughout the United States.

C. Explain one reason why support for both the Democratic and Republican parties has declined over time.

▬ **14.3** Parties and Political Campaigns

Parties play a key role in national, state, and local political campaigns. There are several phases to a campaign, each with its own dynamics. First, candidates decide to run, often with the help of party leaders and activists. Second, parties choose a nominee to represent their party during the election. Finally, parties support their nominees during the election campaign. We examined the decision to run for national office (Chapter 4) and the dynamics of political campaigns (Chapter 13) earlier in this book.

nomination
the formal process through which parties choose their candidates for political office.

The Nomination Process

At the beginning of congressional and presidential campaigns, declared candidates compete with others in their own party for that party's **nomination**. Beginning early in the election year, candidates seek the support of party **delegates**, whose votes they will need to secure the party's nomination. State and federal laws set many of the rules governing the nomination process, but most of the details about *how* things work are hammered out by the parties.

Most states hold **primary elections**, in which a state's voters choose delegates who support a particular presidential candidate (see Figure 14.3). In congressional primaries, the candidate with the most votes becomes the party's candidate. Some states hold

delegate
a person who acts as the voters' representative at a convention to select the party's nominee.

primary election
an election in which a state's voters choose delegates who support a presidential candidate for nomination or an election by a plurality vote to select a party's nominee for a seat in Congress.

FIGURE 14.3

Presidential Primary and Caucus Systems by State, as of 2017

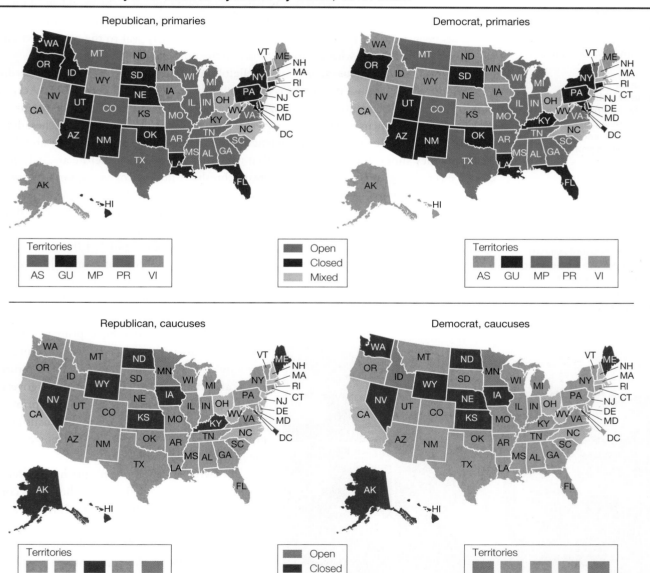

Data from http://www.uspresidentialelectionnews.com; updated to reflect changes in Colorado as of December 2016

open primaries, in which all eligible voters may vote in a party's primary election, regardless of that voter's partisan affiliation. Others hold **closed primaries**, in which only those voters who have registered with a political party can participate. While open primaries encourage undecided and independent voters to participate in choosing a party's nominee, they also allow the possibility that some voters will cast their votes to sabotage a candidate from the opposing party if they see the candidate as a threat to their own preferred candidate.

Critics of open primaries contend that only voters registered to a party should have a say in selecting the party's nominee. It is not fair to allow nonaffiliated voters to diminish the voices of the party faithful. Closed primaries produce candidates who are in line with what that party's voters want. Advocates of open primaries say they help make elections more competitive by taking power away from senior party officials, who serve as gatekeepers, favoring some candidates over others. "The problem [with politics] isn't the money. The problem is the parties themselves," said John Opdycke, the president of Open Primaries, a group seeking to implement the process nationwide.[32] Those favoring open primaries believe closed primaries incentivize candidates to appeal to the party's extremists, leading to nominees who are too far outside the political mainstream.

Some states hold **caucuses**, meetings of eligible voters to select delegates. Caucuses differ from primaries because the voting is done in public instead of by secret ballot. At their most basic level, the caucuses are organized by voting precincts within cities and towns. At a typical precinct caucus meeting, supporters from various campaigns give speeches about why they back their candidate. Then participants break into groups depending on which candidate they support, or they indicate that they are still undecided. Before any delegates can be elected, a group has to meet a certain threshold number of votes. Groups try to persuade people to join them to increase their size.[33]

Because caucuses have complex rules and are time-consuming, they tend to draw fewer participants than primaries, typically attracting those who are more committed to a candidate. In February 2016, more than 186,000 Republicans and 171,000 Democrats took part in the Iowa caucus, a turnout rate of just under 16 percent of eligible voters.[34] In the first twelve presidential primary election contests that followed that year, the combined average turnout rate was only 17.3 percent for Republicans and 11.7 percent for Democrats.[35]

Alan Nelson, a caucus chair for the Bernie Sanders campaign, counts caucus attendees at a Democratic caucus at Jackson Township Fire Station in Keokuk, Iowa, in February 2016.
Michael B. Thomas/AFP/Getty Images

Why do some states have primaries while other have caucuses? If a state holds a primary, the state government has to finance it. In return, political parties must abide by state laws governing the process, such as the date of the primary and who can participate. Holding a caucus gives political parties more flexibility and power over the nomination process.

The two major political parties have differed in how they award delegates. The rules continue to change. The Republican Party awards delegates either to the winning candidate statewide or, more commonly, by splitting delegates between winners in the state overall and winners in individual congressional districts. The Democratic Party has tended to award delegates through a proportional system in which delegates

FIGURE 14.4

Who Are the Democratic Party's Superdelegates?

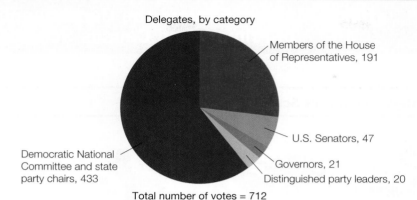

Delegates, by category

- Members of the House of Representatives, 191
- U.S. Senators, 47
- Governors, 21
- Distinguished party leaders, 20
- Democratic National Committee and state party chairs, 433

Total number of votes = 712

Data from Pew Research Center and Wikipedia

are divided based upon total vote share. However, the elite within the Democratic Party is given special representation. **Superdelegates** are members of the Democratic Party, usually elected officials or party activists, who can support any candidate they choose, regardless of the outcome of the primaries or caucuses in their state. They account for 15 percent of the total number of delegates.[36] The Republicans designate three delegates from each state based upon their positions within the state party. Unlike delegates selected in primaries and caucuses, they are not pledged to vote for a particular candidate. (See Figure 14.4.)

There are risks with either approach to awarding delegates. Awarding delegates through the proportional system used by the Democratic Party tends to push back the date when a candidate wins enough delegates to secure the nomination; awarding them based on the winner-take-all system used by the Republican Party tends to speed it up. A quicker conclusion to a nomination season benefits a party by allowing it to focus its efforts on the general election. On the other hand, a rapid conclusion to the process may end the nomination process before some potentially viable candidates have a chance to gain traction with voters.

The schedule of primary elections and caucuses affects the outcome of the nomination process. By tradition, Iowa holds the first caucus and then New Hampshire holds the first primary. While neither state has a large number of delegates, their early position gives them a disproportionate amount of attention. Neither state is representative of the demographics of the nation as a whole. Both states are more rural and less ethnically diverse than the rest of the country. Holding an early caucus or primary gives a state enormous influence over the nominating process, and it attracts candidate and media attention—and large amounts of money.

A win in an early state helps candidates establish momentum. Issues that are important to specific states may become policies later if a candidate becomes president, and state party leaders have a strong incentive to hold their primary election as early as possible. States **front-load** their primaries or caucuses, pushing them as early in the season as possible. National party leaders set a schedule for state primaries and caucuses and have punished states that jump the line. There's an inherent conflict in the nominating process. On the one hand, states have a desire to front-load to increase their importance in the nominating process, but the national party has a conflicting desire to create an orderly series of

superdelegate
usually a party leader or activist who is not pledged to a candidate based on the outcome of the state's primary or caucus.

front-loading
a decision by a state to push its primary or caucus to a date as early in the election season as possible to gain more influence in the presidential nomination process.

Analyzing and Interpreting Quantitative Data: Using Maps to Explore the Consequences of Primary and Caucus Schedules

FIGURE A

Front-Loading: Presidential Primary and Caucus Scheduling by State, 2016

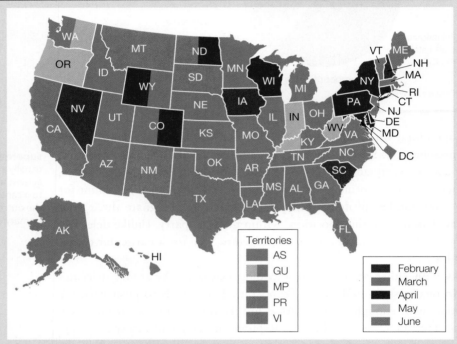

Territories	
	AS
	GU
	MP
	PR
	VI

	February
	March
	April
	May
	June

Note: In states where Democrats and Republicans hold primaries and caucuses in different months, the timing of the Democratic elections is shown on the left and the timing of the Republican elections is shown on the right.

Data from FrontloadingHQ, accessed June 15, 2016

Geographical representations of data can be useful tools in exploring important topics in political science. The schedule of state caucuses and primaries has important political consequences. One of the issues with this scheduling involves the degree to which voters in states that participate early in the cycle may have an advantage in selecting nominees. Figure A displays the month of a state's primary or caucus in the 2016 presidential elections.

Keeping Figure A in mind, consider Figure B, which displays counties in which racial or ethnic minorities constituted a majority of voters in 2014. Although the data are shown by county, focus on the patterns from state to state, connecting these population patterns to the data presented in Figure A.

primaries and caucuses. In 2012, Florida moved its primary ahead of schedule to January, and the RNC punished it by taking away half of its delegates at the national convention.[37]

The final phase of the nomination process is the **national convention**, held in the summer of the presidential election year. During the conventions, delegates vote to select the party's nominee, and committees of delegates write the party platform on the issues. For much of American history, national conventions were sources of high drama, with many rounds of delegate voting required to select a nominee.

national convention
a meeting where delegates officially select their party's nominee for the presidency.

Counties in Which Racial and Ethnic Minorities Constitute a Majority of the Population

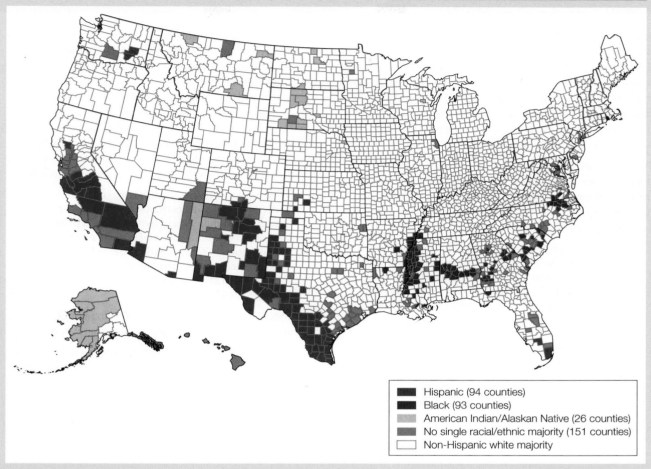

Hispanic (94 counties)
Black (93 counties)
American Indian/Alaskan Native (26 counties)
No single racial/ethnic majority (151 counties)
Non-Hispanic white majority

Data from Pew Research Center

Use the maps to answer the questions.

1. Describe the pattern of states that front-load their primaries and caucuses, as shown in Figure A.

2. Describe the distribution of counties where ethnic and racial minorities make up a majority of the population, as shown in Figure B.

3. Explain how front-loading impacts the representation of racial and minority groups in the nomination process, and support your conclusion with data from Figures A and B.

At the national convention, most, but not all, delegates are pledged to vote for the candidate that voters have chosen in their state. If no candidate gets the number of delegates required to win, more rounds of votes are held until someone does. This process includes much behind-the-scenes courting of delegates to switch their votes and is known as a "brokered" or "contested" convention. In recent decades, the nominee has been determined before the convention.

Comparing Political Processes: The Parties Rethink Their National Strategies

After Mitt Romney lost the 2012 presidential election, the Republican National Committee appointed a task force of long-time party activists called the Growth and Opportunity Project to make recommendations on how the party needed to change. In 2013, it issued its report, claiming, "It is time to smartly change course, modernize the party, and learn once again how to appeal to more people, including those who share some but not all of our conservative principles."[38]

The report talked about the enduring influence of former president Ronald Reagan but warned that the party seemed too dependent on invoking Reagan's legacy without trying to appeal to younger voters who did not remember Reagan's 1981–1989 tenure. It stated,

> Our party knows how to appeal to older voters, but we have lost our way with younger ones. We sound increasingly out of touch. The Republican Party needs to stop talking to itself. . . . Devastatingly we have lost the ability to be persuasive with, or welcoming to, those who do not agree with us on every issue. . . . we need a Party whose brand of conservatism invites and inspires new people to visit us. We need to remain America's conservative alternative to big-government, redistribution-to-extremes liberalism, while building a route into our party that a non-traditional Republican will want to travel.[39]

Overwhelming Republican gains in the 2014 midterm elections, in which Democrats lost majority control of the Senate, led Democratic Party officials to form their own task force in 2015 to examine how their party could improve. The task force specifically pointed to how poorly Democrats have done in contrast to the Republicans in recruiting talented young candidates who can rise through the ranks. Democratic Party task force members also said the party had not communicated its message effectively. Their report stated that the party would create a National Narrative Project to better articulate what the party stands for:

> One of the most striking findings of the Task Force's initial conversations was the difficulty faced by candidates, elected officials, activists and others in concisely, consistently answering the question, "What does it mean to be a Democrat?" The beauty of the Democratic Party lies in the very fact that we are not one-size-fits-all. We are enriched by our diversity.[40]

1. Describe one similarity between the findings of the Growth and Opportunity Project and the National Narrative Project.

2. Describe one difference in the approaches suggested by the Growth and Opportunity Project and the National Narrative Project.

3. Explain one reason why national party organizations are not as powerful as they were in the past.

Conventions have become more like pep rallies, designed to energize and mobilize voters. A key speaking spot at a national convention can be a stepping-stone to future prominence on the national stage. In 2004 Barack Obama, then an Illinois state senator and candidate for the U.S. Senate, gave the keynote address at the Democratic National Convention (DNC), which signaled his status as a rising star within the Democratic Party.

Party leaders used to play a big role in selecting the nominee, but party elites are losing some of this power. Some candidates are developing their own strategies and raising money independently because they do not believe party leadership is serving their goals. Political scientist John Aldrich says, "In such cases politicians turn elsewhere to seek the means to win."[41] As campaigns have become more **candidate-centered**, party elites are losing influence over the nomination process. Parties want to steer the nomination process toward the most "electable" candidates in the general election, but voters in primaries and caucuses may not select the nominee favored by the party elite. National party organizations are not as powerful as they used to be, and their role in selecting and supporting candidates for office continues to evolve.

candidate-centered campaign
a trend in which candidates develop their own strategies and raise money with less influence from the party elite.

Parties typically select their nominees for president at their national conventions amidst much fanfare but without much drama. In 2016, both the Republican National Convention in Cleveland, OH (left), and the Democratic National Convention in Philadelphia, PA (right), had more drama than usual. At the Republican Convention, some Republican Party leaders refused to endorse Trump. Some Sanders supporters disrupted the proceedings in Philadelphia at several points. Eventually, however, both Donald Trump and Hillary Clinton received their party's endorsement.

left: Jim Watson/AFP/Getty Images; right: Ricky Carioti/Washington Post via Getty Images

Section Review

14.3 Explain the role of political parties in nominating candidates.

REMEMBER

- Parties recruit candidates to run for offices at all levels, selecting people who reflect the ideas of the party and who would make strong challengers for office.
- Parties shape the candidate selection process by setting rules for how candidates are nominated.
- Candidates for the presidency must seek the support of delegates who will later vote for their nomination.
- In conjunction with federal and state laws, state parties establish the rules by which their candidates are nominated for the presidency, including what type of primary election process that state will have and when it will be held.
- At the national convention, most state delegates are bound to vote for the candidate voters have chosen in their state primaries or caucuses.
- The rise of candidate-centered campaigns reduces the role of party elites in choosing the party's nominee.

KNOW

- *nomination*: the formal process through which parties choose their candidates for political office. (p. 466)
- *delegate*: a person who acts as the voters' representative at a convention to select the party's presidential nominee. (p. 467)
- *primary election*: an election in which a state's voters choose delegates who support a candidate for nomination. (p. 467)
- *open primary*: a primary election in which all eligible voters may vote, regardless of their partisan affiliation. (p. 468)
- *closed primary*: a primary election in which only registered voters from a political party may vote. (p. 468)
- *caucus*: a process through which a state's eligible voters meet to select delegates to represent their preferences in the nomination process. (p. 468)
- *superdelegate*: usually a party leader or activist who is not pledged to a candidate based on the outcome of the state's primary or caucus. (p. 469)
- *front-loading*: a decision by a state to push its primary or caucus to a date as early in the season as possible to become more influential in the nomination process. (p. 469)
- *national convention*: a meeting where delegates officially select their party's nominee for the presidency. (p. 470)
- *candidate-centered campaign*: a trend in which candidates develop their own strategies and raise money with less influence from the party elite. (p. 472)

THINK

Should the leaders of political parties have more power than party members in selecting candidates? Why or why not?

Dave Granlund/Cagle Cartoons

Use the cartoon and your knowledge of U.S. Government and Politics to answer parts A, B, and C.

A. Describe the viewpoint expressed in the cartoon.

B. Describe one criticism of front-loading in the nomination process.

C. Explain one way in which a candidate might benefit from front-loading.

◼◼ **14.4** Third Parties

two-party system
a system in which two political parties dominate politics, winning almost all elections.

proportional representation system
an election system for a legislature in which citizens vote for parties, rather than individuals, and parties are represented in the legislature according to the percentage of the vote they receive.

single-member plurality system
an election system for choosing members of the legislature where the winner is the candidate who receives the most votes, even if the candidate does not receive a majority of the votes.

There is no law requiring a **two-party system** in the United States, but with a few exceptions, a two-party system has been dominant for most of the nation's history. Many other countries have a multiple-party system, and some have a single-party-dominant system. (See Figure 14.5 on page 475.) Some countries have **proportional representation systems**, in which citizens vote for parties, rather than individuals, and parties are represented in the legislature according to the percentage of the vote they receive. For example, in a proportional representation system, a party winning 10 percent of the nationwide vote would be awarded 10 percent of the seats in the legislature.

With a few exceptions, a two-party system has been dominant for most of America's political history. Why? Let's consider a few factors: The United States uses a **single-member plurality system**, in which voters have a single vote for one candidate, and the candidate who gets the most votes (a plurality) in a state or congressional district wins the election, even if her or she does not have the support of more than 50 percent of the voters. In presidential elections, the candidate who wins the popular vote in a state wins all of that state's electoral votes (except for Maine and Nebraska). This is known as a winner-take-all system.

The winner-take-all system means that the Democratic and Republican parties win almost every office because a candidate from one of the two major parties almost always receives the most votes in a district or state. Proponents of the system say this promotes stability, and voters can continue to elect members from the same party if they think they are doing a good job in office.

FIGURE 14.5

Differences across Countries in the Number of Major Political Parties

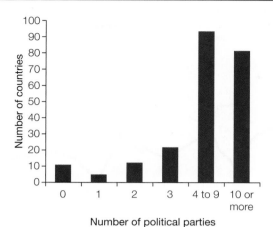

Data from CIA World Factbook, accessed June 15, 2016

But many people live in areas where one party dominates. Conservatives living in districts or states dominated by the Democratic Party don't have much of a voice in politics. The same is true of liberals living in Republican strongholds. This can discourage people from participating in politics.

Minor Parties in the Twenty-First Century

Although they almost never win office, **third parties** may influence elections. Third-party candidates often focus on a single issue that they think the major parties are not addressing. Sean Wilentz, a professor of history at Princeton University, explains, "There'll be an issue that's being neglected or that is being purposely excluded from national debate because neither party wants to face the political criticism that it would bring."[42] Sometimes the two major parties incorporate third-party agendas into their platforms, undercutting the third party's chances of winning.

The winner-take-all feature makes it difficult for third-party candidates to win votes in the Electoral College because they rarely win a plurality of the votes within a state. However, sometimes third-party candidates are able to win some votes in the Electoral College because they are popular in a region. In 1968, George Wallace ran for president as an independent candidate on a platform in favor of segregating blacks and whites. Wallace took nearly 14 percent of the vote, and because he was popular in the South, he won a plurality in four southern states and was awarded their votes in the Electoral College.[43] Twelve years later, John Anderson, an Illinois GOP congressman, ran under the banner of the National Unity Party as a moderate alternative to Democratic president Jimmy Carter and the more conservative Republican Ronald Reagan, and received 6.6 percent of the vote.[44] Because Anderson's popularity was dispersed, he did not win a plurality in any state and was not awarded any votes in the Electoral College.

Sometimes third parties are built around a popular candidate. In 1992, billionaire businessman H. Ross Perot ran as an independent with the Reform Party on a platform of cutting the federal budget deficit. He captured nearly 19 percent of the vote but did not win any electoral college votes.[45] And eight years later, consumer activist Ralph Nader ran for president under the liberal Green Party banner. He won 2.74 percent of the popular

third party
a minor political party in competition with the two major parties.

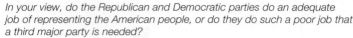

FIGURE 14.6

Americans' Opinions of the Need for Third Parties in the United States

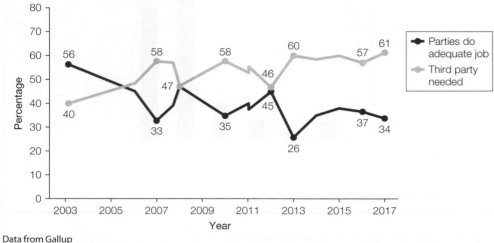

In your view, do the Republican and Democratic parties do an adequate job of representing the American people, or do they do such a poor job that a third major party is needed?

Data from Gallup

vote, pulling votes away from Democratic candidate Al Gore.[46] Sometimes there is a backlash against third party candidates like Nader because their campaigns probably pull votes away from the party most similar to them and help the opposing party win. This phenomenon discourages people from voting for third parties.

The Democratic and Republican parties hope to discourage third-party candidacies. One way is to prevent third-party candidates from participating in televised presidential debates. To qualify for national televised debates, candidates must be supported by at least 15 percent of the respondents in five national public opinion polls.[47] Local officials may set stringent requirements for candidates to collect a certain number of signatures before they can appear on a ballot, making it difficult for many third-party hopefuls.

During the 2016 presidential election, as the Clinton and Trump campaigns both struggled against heavily negative perceptions, third-party challengers emerged, drawing votes from both. Gary Johnson, candidate for the Libertarian Party, Jill Stein, the Green Party candidate, and Independent Party candidate Evan McMullin all vied to establish their respective parties as credible challengers to the Democratic and Republican parties. While Johnson won around 3.3 percent of the national vote, and Stein won roughly 1 percent, neither of them presented a serious challenge to Hillary Clinton or Donald Trump.[48] Figure 14.6 shows how Americans' opinions about the need for viable third parties have varied recently.

2016 and the Challenges to Mainstream Political Parties

As the 2016 presidential nomination season progressed, both Bernie Sanders and Donald Trump surprised political scientists, political pundits, and their own party leaders with their unconventional campaigns. Both candidates took positions that were outside the mainstream of their parties.

Bernie Sanders and Donald Trump presented challenges to their own parties' establishment. The larger story about the election of 2016 may not be only about divisions within political parties, but about how both political parties will adapt to the changing nature of political campaigns.

Section Review

14.4 Explain why it is difficult for third parties and independent candidates to win elections.

REMEMBER
- A two-party system has been dominant for most of America's history.
- The United States uses a single-member plurality system for electing members of Congress, which means the Democratic and Republican parties win almost every office.
- The winner-take-all feature of the Electoral College contributes to the dominance of two major parties.
- Third parties often form around a particular issue or the personality of a candidate.

KNOW
- *two-party system*: a system in which two political parties dominate politics, winning almost all elections. (p. 474)
- *proportional representation system*: an election system for a legislature in which citizens vote for parties, rather than individuals, and parties are represented in the legislature according to the percentage of the vote they receive. (p. 474)
- *single-member plurality system*: an election system for choosing members of the legislature where the winner is the candidate who receives the most votes, even if the candidate does not receive a majority of the votes. (p. 474)
- *third party*: a minor political party in competition with the two major parties. (p. 475)

THINK
- Will the Democratic and Republican parties continue to control politics well into the future?
- What are the circumstances under which a third party might successfully rise to replace one of the dominant parties?

14.4 Review Question: Free Response

In this rigged, two-party system, third parties almost never win a national election. It's obvious what our function is in this constricted oligarchy of two corporate-indentured parties—to push hitherto taboo issues onto the public stage, to build for a future, to get a young generation in, keep the progressive agenda alive, push the two parties a little bit on this issue and that.

—Ralph Nader[49]

Use the quote and your knowledge of U.S. Government and Politics to answer parts A, B, and C.

A. Describe the viewpoint expressed in the quote.

B. Explain one reason why third parties seldom win national elections.

C. Explain one reason why an individual might not vote for a third party, aside from the fact that third parties rarely win elections.

Chapter 14 Review

AP® KEY CONCEPTS

- *political party* (p. 455)
- *party identification* (p. 458)
- *straight-ticket voting* (p. 459)
- *split-ticket voting* (p. 460)
- *party platform* (p. 460)
- *recruitment* (p. 460)
- *party coalition* (p. 462)
- *realignment* (p. 462)
- *critical election* (p. 462)

- *party era* (p. 462)
- *era of divided government* (p. 462)
- *nomination* (p. 466)
- *delegate* (p. 467)
- *primary election* (p. 467)
- *open primary* (p. 468)
- *closed primary* (p. 468)
- *caucus* (p. 468)
- *superdelegate* (p. 469)

- *front-loading* (p. 469)
- *national convention* (p. 470)
- *candidate-centered campaign* (p. 472)
- *two-party system* (p. 474)
- *proportional representation system* (p. 474)
- *single-member plurality system* (p. 474)
- *third party* (p. 475)

AP® EXAM PRACTICE and Critical Thinking Project

MULTIPLE-CHOICE QUESTIONS

Questions 1 and 2 refer to the quote.

The last two legislative sessions have seen a small push to eliminate the straight-ticket option. . . . Especially in Texas—as independent-minded as we are, with the spirit of independence we have in Texas—we ought to be voting for individuals.[50]

—*Texas state senator Jeff Wentworth*

1. Which of the following is a potential outcome if the proposal referred to above becomes law?

A. More third-party candidates will be elected.

B. Divided government may occur more frequently.

C. The Republican Party in Texas will win more legislative seats.

D. Voter turnout will decrease.

2. Which of the following would be most likely to support the proposal discussed in the quote?

A. Party-line voters

B. Third party candidates

C. Leaders of the two major parties

D. Incumbent candidates

Use the excerpt to answer questions 3 and 4.

[A]lthough Sanders voters are quite liberal, *a lot of them aren't Democrats*, or at least don't like to identify themselves as Democrats. Clinton crushed Sanders among self-identified Democrats, winning them by 27 percentage points, based on exit polls. But Sanders won independents who voted in the Democratic primary by 31 percentage points.[51]

—*Nate Silver*

3. Which of the following would improve Hillary Clinton's chances of winning the nomination?

A. Closed primaries

B. Open primaries

C. Caucuses

D. Split-ticket voting

4. Which of the following explains why the percentage of delegates awarded to Hillary Clinton in the Democratic primaries exceeded the percentage of primary voters who supported her?

A. There was a backlash against superdelegates who supported Sanders.

B. Superdelegates usually support the candidate favored by the party elite.

C. Voter turnout was higher among self-identified Democrats than among independents.

D. Independent voters are more likely to vote in primaries than in the general election.

Mike Luckovich/Creators Syndicate, Inc.

5. The cartoon expresses which of the following viewpoints?

　A. Republican Party leaders were surprised by Donald Trump's unconventional campaign.

　B. Donald Trump had difficulty controlling Republican Party leadership during his campaign.

　C. Donald Trump ran an unconventional and unpredictable campaign.

　D. Voters were drawn to Donald Trump's message as a political newcomer.

---

6. Select the response that matches a political practice with its impact.

Practice	Impact
A. Proportional representation	Two-party system
B. Closed primary	Selection of moderate candidates
C. Front-loading	Early states are more influential
D. Fund-raising by candidates	Strengthens national parties

Question 7 refers to the pair of bar charts.

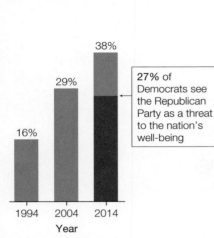

Democratic attitudes about
the Republican Party:
Very unfavorable

38%

29%

27% of
Democrats see
the Republican
Party as a threat
to the nation's
well-being

16%

1994   2004   2014
Year

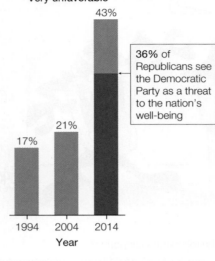

Republican attitudes about
the Democratic Party:
Very unfavorable

43%

36% of
Republicans see
the Democratic
Party as a threat
to the nation's
well-being

17%   21%

1994   2004   2014
Year

Data from Pew Research Center

7. The bar charts refer to which of the following trends?
   A. An increase in party-line voting
   B. An increase in party polarization
   C. A decrease in trust and confidence in government
   D. A decrease in bipartisanship

   _____

8. According to the Pew Research Center, more than 28.5 percent of all eligible voters cast ballots in the 2016 presidential primaries, compared to 30.4 percent turnout in the 2008 primaries.[52] Which of the following conclusions is supported by the data?
   A. Voters in primaries and caucuses are more radical than voters in the general election.
   B. Most eligible voters do not participate in presidential primaries.
   C. Voter turnout in primaries increased substantially from 2008 to 2016.
   D. Turnout in Democratic primaries was higher in 2008, while turnout in Republican primaries was higher in 2016.

Independent Florida, http://independentflorida.com/tag/vote-third-party/

9. The graphic addresses which of the following problems of voting for a third party?

   A. Third parties rarely win elections.

   B. Third-party candidates are not well known to the American public.

   C. Voting for a third party benefits the opposing party.

   D. Voting for a third party is perceived as throwing away a vote.

   _____

10. Suppose the Green Party of the United States won 5 percent of the votes throughout the country in congressional races. How many seats in Congress would the Green Party likely win?

    A. Five seats in the Senate, and no seats in the House of Representatives

    B. Five percent of the seats in both the House of Representatives and the Senate

    C. Twenty-two seats in the House of Representatives and none in the Senate

    D. No seats in either house of Congress

FREE-RESPONSE QUESTIONS

After a Decline, Primary Turnout Goes Up

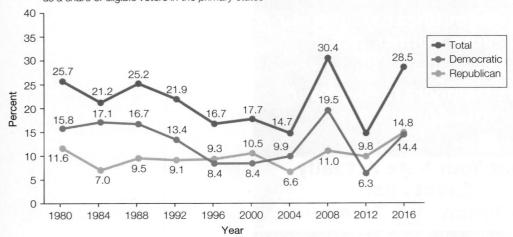

Votes cast in Democratic and Republican primaries as a share of eligible voters in the primary states

Data from Pew Research Center

1. Use the graph and your knowledge of U.S. Government and Politics to answer parts A, B, and C.

   A. Describe one difference in the trends in primary turnout for the Republican and Democratic parties.

   B. Explain one reason why turnout in primaries for both parties increased in 2016.

   C. Explain one reason why turnout in primaries and caucuses is lower than voter turnout in general elections.

2. On May 4, 2018, the *New York Times* reported the following, in an article entitled, "They Voted for Obama, Then Went for Trump. Can Democrats Win Them Back?"[53]

   > Sharla Baker . . . picked Barack Obama for president . . . Her great-grandmother, who grew up poor in Pennsylvania, always said that Democrats look out for the poor people.
   >
   > In 2016, though, she voted for Donald J. Trump . . . she liked how he talked about jobs and wages and people being left out of the economy . . .
   >
   > Of the more than 650 counties that chose Mr. Obama twice, about a third flipped to Mr. Trump. Many were in states critical to Mr. Trump's win, like Iowa, Michigan, Ohio and Wisconsin.

   Use the excerpt and your knowledge of U.S. Government and Politics to answer parts A, B, and C.

   A. Define party coalition.

   B. Describe one reason why a coalition of voters might switch from one political party to a different political party.

   C. Explain one reason why divided government has been more prevalent during the twenty-first century than single party control.

ARGUMENTATION QUESTION

The American two-party system often results in gridlock, because the Democratic and Republican parties have different ideas about the role of government. However, America's two-party system has remained for nearly 150 years. Does the two-party system foster representative democracy within our constitutional system of checks and balances?

In your essay:

- Articulate a claim or thesis that responds to the prompt, and use a line of reasoning to defend it.
- Use at least TWO pieces of relevant and accurate evidence to support your claim.
- At least ONE piece of evidence must be from one of the listed foundational documents:

  Constitution of the United States

  Federalist No. 10

  Federalist No. 51

- Use a second piece of evidence from another foundational document from the list or from your study of political parties.
- Use reasoning to explain why the evidence you provided supports your claim or thesis.
- Use refutation, concession, or rebuttal to respond to an opposing or alternative perspective.

CRITICAL THINKING PROJECT

Political cartoons use symbolism to convey a point of view. In the cartoon below, the elephant is a symbol, representing the Republican Party, and the donkey symbolizes the Democratic Party. The point of view is that the parties are polarized, blaming each other for a government shutdown.

Daryl Cagle/Cagle Cartoons

1. Read a news article from the past two weeks about political parties.
2. Draw a political cartoon based on the article. Be sure to include symbolism and a point of view. Decide whether you want to color your cartoon or use black and white. It's okay if you are not a good artist. Use images from the Internet as inspiration, but don't rely on another political cartoon. Be creative!
3. On the back of your cartoon, summarize the article you read, complete with a citation in MLA format.
4. Explain how you used symbolism to convey a point of view in your cartoon.

15 Interest Groups and Social Movements

Collective Action, Power, and Representation

Music needs net neutrality.

Without an open internet, music today just wouldn't sound the same. Net neutrality gives every artist a fair shot at getting heard.

#ListenBetter

SONO

We'r
tod
of

We need music.

If we let net neutrality get strip
powerful gatekeepers could sti
and hold back tomorrow's taler

#ListenBetter

In the American political system, elected officials formally represent the interests of citizens in government. If the people don't like the policies they put into place, they can vote them out of office. Elected officials, however, are not the only people who try to represent citizens' interests. **Interest groups** are voluntary associations of people who come together with the goal of getting the policies they favor enacted. **Social movements** are loosely organized groups that educate the public and put pressure on policymakers in an effort to bring about

The Sonos music store in the SoHo neighborhood in New York has closed for a day in January 2018 to protest the vote by the Federal Communications Commission that overturned rules mandating net neutrality.

Mark Lennihan/AP Images

societal change. Interest groups, along with political parties, elections, and the media, are linkage institutions that connect people with government.

The distinction between an interest group and a social movement is fuzzy. Interest groups tend to focus on specific issues. Social movements tend to be larger and more diffuse. For example, the National Association for the Advancement of Colored People (NAACP) is an interest group that focuses its efforts on filing lawsuits to end legal segregation. The NAACP is also part of a larger social movement in the struggle for civil rights.

interest groups
voluntary associations of people who come together with the goal of getting the policies that they favor enacted.

social movements
diffuse groups that educate the public and put pressure on policymakers in an effort to bring about societal change.

After reading this chapter, you will be able to

15.1 Describe the factors that impact whether or not interest groups will be effective in reaching their policy objectives.

15.2 Describe the tactics used by interest groups to achieve their goals and how they interact with bureaucratic agencies and members of Congress through iron triangles and issue networks.

15.3 Explain how social movements have an impact on policymaking.

LEARNING TARGETS

Net Neutrality: Who Owns the Pathways of Communication?

In 2015, under the administration of President Obama, "net neutrality" became the regulatory framework for the internet. Under FCC rules, internet service providers (ISPs) were prohibited from "speeding up, slowing down, or blocking" content.[1]

In 2017, the chairperson of the Federal Communications Commission under President Donald Trump issued an order designed to overturn net neutrality rules. The FCC would no longer require ISPs to provide equal access to the internet. Under the old rules, ISPs were not allowed to interfere with users' ability to reach websites, apps or services. The new rules allow ISPs to create "fast lanes" for users who pay for special treatment.[2]

Americans rely on the internet to access information, shop, and connect with friends. In particular, the growth of e-commerce has burgeoned as the internet has become more widespread and accessible. Here, an artisan is preparing an internet site that is a virtual shop window, showing off handmade leather goods.
Luca Sage/Getty Images

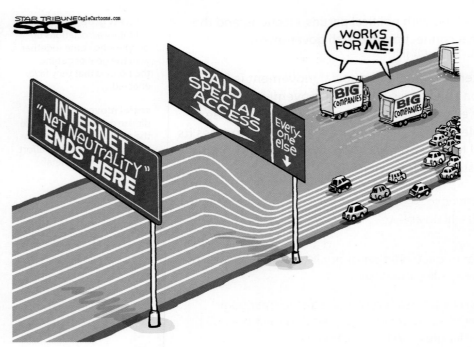

Like many public policy issues involving technology, regulating the internet is complicated, and interest groups weigh in on all sides. This cartoon advocates the view of those who oppose ending net neutrality. They think that the internet would become a "divided highway" with extra charges imposed on users by ISPs.

Steve Sack/Cagle Cartoons

Certain interest groups lobbied against the changes: "Supporters of net neutrality fear its demise will lead to broadband companies favoring their own content over that of rivals, blocking material more frequently, and running online 'fast lanes' that let some businesses pay a premium to get their traffic delivered more swiftly than others—a move that would favor wealthy existing companies over startups."[3] Members of the Electronic Frontier Foundation, a nonprofit interest group dedicated to protecting civil liberties for those who use digital technology, tried to persuade Congress to overturn the FCC's decision.[4]

Some business interest groups, particularly those in the communications industry, supported the end of net neutrality rules. A spokesperson from AT&T wrote: "We do not block websites, nor censor online content, nor throttle or degrade traffic based on the content, nor unfairly discriminate in our treatment of internet traffic. . . . In short, the internet will continue to work tomorrow just as it always has."[5] These groups argued that excessive regulations from the Obama administration made it hard for them to provide internet service to their customers.

Government officials and interest groups will debate net neutrality in the years ahead, and the issue may find its way to the Supreme Court. The debate over net neutrality demonstrates how interest groups participate in the political process in an attempt to get the policies they favor enacted.

■ 15.1 Acting Collectively

Americans' rights to organize and petition the government for change are protected in the Constitution, specifically in the First Amendment, which states: "Congress shall make no law . . . abridging the freedom of speech . . . or the right of the people peaceably to assemble, and to petition the Government for a redress of grievances."

Interest Groups in American Representative Democracy

In exercising these fundamental rights, people create what James Madison described in *Federalist* No. 10 (see Chapter 2) as a faction, which he defined as "a number of citizens, whether amounting to a majority or a minority of the whole, who are united and actuated by some common impulse of passion, or of interest, adverse to the rights of other citizens, or to the permanent and aggregate interests of the community."[6] Madison believed factions were potentially dangerous. Their actions risk trampling upon the rights of others or damaging the community. Yet the freedoms protected under the Constitution almost guarantee that factions will form. We can eliminate faction at its source, Madison argued, but only by preventing individuals from coming together and asking the government to address their concerns. Such restrictions upon liberty would go against the very principles of a representative democracy. If you have freedom, Madison concluded, you will have factions. The challenge is not how to eliminate factions but how to make sure that no one faction can do too much damage.

In the absence of an acceptable way to eliminate factions, Madison made an insightful observation about how to lessen the dangers of faction. He believed many factions would compete with each other in the large American Republic, making any one faction less of a danger to the nation as a whole. As Madison stated,

> Extend the sphere, and you take in a greater variety of parties and interests; you make it less probable that a majority of the whole will have a common motive to invade the rights of other citizens; or if such a common motive exists, it will be more difficult for all who feel it to discover their own strength, and to act in unison with each other.[7]

In other words, factions will form, but if there are many competing factions all vying to achieve their goals in a system that allows each a voice, then their most dangerous consequences can be contained.

Theories of Interest Group Formation

Although people might form factions around a number of issues, inequality of wealth posed the greatest danger, according to James Madison. He wrote, "But the most common and durable source of factions has been the various and unequal distribution of property. Those who hold, and those who are without property, have ever formed distinct interests in society."[8]

As discussed in Chapter 1, three main theories explain the impact of groups on the political process. Under the **theory of participatory democracy**, citizens impact policymaking through their involvement in **civil society**, which is made up of groups outside the government that advocate for policies. While one person may not be able to make a difference, joining a group allows people with a common interest to have their voices heard.

Under **pluralist theory**, the distribution of political power among many competing groups serves to keep any one of them in check. Groups that lack one resource, like money, may have other resources, like a large number of members, enabling them to compete in the political process.

theory of participatory democracy
the belief that citizens impact policymaking through their involvement in civil society.

civil society
groups outside the government that advocate for policy.

pluralist theory
a theory that political power is distributed among many competing groups, which means that no single group can grow too powerful.

AP® REQUIRED DOCUMENTS

Federalist No. 10 is one of the nine foundational documents required in AP® U.S. Government and Politics. Make sure you read it carefully and understand Madison's arguments about how the Constitution controls the negative consequences of faction.

Document	Scope
Federalist No. 10	Madison argues that the Constitution reduces the negative consequences of faction by creating a large, representative republic.

FIGURE 15.1

Where Do Americans Participate?

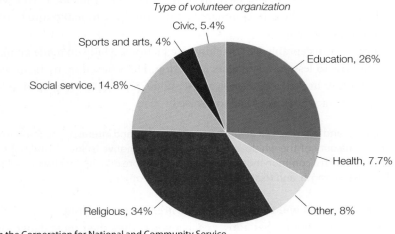

Type of volunteer organization

Civic, 5.4%
Sports and arts, 4%
Education, 26%
Social service, 14.8%
Health, 7.7%
Religious, 34%
Other, 8%

Data from the Corporation for National and Community Service

elitist theory
a theory that the wealthy elite class has a disproportionate amount of economic and political power.

policy agenda
the set of issues to which government officials, voters, and the public are paying attention.

In contrast to pluralism, under **elitist theory**, the wealthy elite class has a disproportionate amount of power, holding the top positions in government and industry. Those who support elite theory claim that the elites control the **policy agenda**, which is the set of issues policymakers are paying attention to.[9] It is based upon the claim that the wealthy class has more access to policymakers than average citizens. Members of Congress and their staff have limited time, and they are more likely to spend time with lobbyists and wealthy donors. While some scholars point to the dominance of corporate interest groups in giving campaign contributions (as we will see below), others point out that wealthy and powerful interest groups often compete against each other. Figure 15.1 shows the diversity of U.S. civil society and points to competing policy agendas.

Ironically, when Madison became one of the authors of the *Federalist Papers*, he was acting as part of an interest group. As you will recall from Chapter 2, the *Federalist Papers* were written to convince state ratifying conventions to approve the Constitution. According to political scientist David B. Truman, "The entire effort of which *The Federalist* was a part was one of the most skillful and important examples of pressure group activity in American history."[10] The *Federalist Papers* are now viewed as one of the most important expositions on the theory of the Constitution, but the essays were also political propaganda, designed to push for the ratification of the Constitution. The Antifederalists, a competing interest group, opposed the Constitution because it created a strong central government.

Challenges Facing Interest Groups

collective action
political action that occurs when individuals contribute their energy, time, or money to a larger group goal.

collective good
also called a public good; a public benefit that individuals can enjoy or profit from even if they do not help achieve it.

Differences in size, wealth, and political power shape the strategies available to interest groups as they try to overcome the challenges of **collective action**, when individuals come together to contribute their energy, time, or money to a larger group goal. Some interest groups work for a **collective good** (also called a public good), which is a public benefit, such as strong national defense, clean air, or a really nice fireworks display.[11] The problem with collective goods is that people can enjoy the benefits achieved by an interest group without contributing to it, so there is no incentive to join the group.

This political cartoon illustrates the concept of free riding. In "right-to-work" states, employees who don't join the union obtain the same negotiated benefits as those who join the union and pay dues.
Barry Deutsch

People who benefit from the actions of an interest group without joining are called **free riders**, and they pose a serious challenge to interest groups working for the collective good. The free rider problem occurs in states with "right-to-work" laws, where employees of unionized companies have the right not to join the union. If the union negotiates for higher salaries and better benefits, all employees will benefit, including those who did not join the union and pay dues (see the cartoon and its dialogue). Using cost-benefit logic, individuals should "free ride" and devote their energies elsewhere, knowing that others will make up for their inaction.

Interest groups have ways of overcoming the free rider problem. One tactic is to offer **selective benefits**, available only to those who join or contribute to the group, including discounts on goods and services, access to group publications and information, special offers, travel opportunities, or other benefits available only to members. AARP (formerly known as the American Association of Retired Persons) is widely known for the travel benefits and discounts it provides for its members. Professional associations may provide their members with the credentials needed to operate in their profession. Trade unions work to help their members earn higher wages and better benefits.

free riders
individuals who enjoy collective goods and benefit from the actions of an interest group without joining.

selective benefits
benefits available only to those who join the group.

Section Review

This chapter's main ideas are reflected in the Learning Targets. By reviewing after each section, you should be able to

—**Remember** the key points,

—**Know** terms that are central to the topic, and

—**Think** critically about how interest groups and social movements influence the behavior of government.

15.1 Describe the factors that impact whether or not interest groups will be effective in reaching their policy objectives.

REMEMBER	• In *Federalist* No. 10, James Madison described factions as self-interested groups, either of a majority or a minority, that have the potential to cause harm to the community.
	• According to the participatory model of democracy, citizens impact policymaking through their activities as members of interest groups.
	• Pluralist theory contends that political influence is distributed among groups, which compete for the policies they favor with groups that check each other's power.
	• Elitist theorists believe that wealthy interest groups have a disproportionate influence over policymaking.
	• The free rider problem arises when an interest group works for a collective good that people will benefit from even if they don't contribute to the interest group.

KNOW	• *interest groups*: voluntary associations of people who come together with the goal of getting the policies that they favor enacted. (p. 485)
	• *social movements*: diffuse groups that educate the public and put pressure on policymakers in an effort to bring about societal change. (p. 485)
	• *theory of participatory democracy*: the belief that citizens impact policymaking through their involvement in civil society. (p. 487)
	• *civil society*: groups outside the government that advocate for policy. (p. 487)
	• *pluralist theory*: a theory that political power is distributed among many competing groups, which means that no single group can grow too powerful. (p. 487)
	• *elitist theory*: a theory that the wealthy elite class has a disproportionate amount of economic and political power. (p. 488)
	• *policy agenda*: the set of issues to which government officials, voters, and the public are paying attention. (p. 488)
	• *collective action*: political action that occurs when individuals contribute their energy, time, or money to a larger group goal. (p. 488)
	• *collective good*: also called a public good; a public benefit that individuals can enjoy or profit from, even if they do not help achieve it. (p. 488)
	• *free riders*: individuals who enjoy collective goods and benefit from the actions of an interest group without joining. (p. 489)
	• *selective benefits*: benefits available only to those who join the group. (p. 489)

THINK	• Was James Madison correct in his assumption that the Constitution would reduce the dangers of faction?
	• What are the advantages of joining an interest group instead of just being a free rider?

15.1 Review Question: Free Response

What Madison failed to grasp is that in the very extended republic he was advocating, permanent majority faction gives way to temporary, transient factions of both the majority and minority varieties. Faction allies with faction to form majorities that further their own parochial interests at the expense of everyone else. Within each transient majority there is likely to exist a permanent minority faction or group of permanent minority factions at the core (e.g., the military-industrial complex, the banking cartel, labor unions and so forth), which transcends each episodic faction.[12]

–Lawrence Hunter

Use the quote and your knowledge of U.S. Government and Politics to answer parts A, B, and C.

A. Describe the viewpoint expressed in the quote.

B. Describe James Madison's argument in *Federalist* No. 10 about the impact of a large republic on factions.

C. Explain how James Madison's argument in *Federalist* No. 10 supports pluralist theory.

15.2 Interest Group Tactics

There are several broad categories of interest groups. **Economic interest groups** advocate on behalf of the financial interests of their members. These groups by far form the largest category of interest groups and they are large donors to political campaigns. Business groups advocate for the policies that favor their firms or broader corporate interests, such as tax reform or reducing the rights of labor unions. Labor groups, such as trade unions, advocate on behalf of the workers that they represent and sometimes advocate for policies that will benefit the working class in general. Finally, farm groups have a long tradition in American politics. Farm groups support subsidies and trade policies that benefit American agriculture.

In contrast, **public interest groups** act on behalf of the collective interests of a broad group of individuals and not just their members. Groups advocating in the areas of civil rights, civil liberties, social welfare, education, or the environment are all examples of public interest groups. Associations that focus on one specific area of public policy are called **single-issue groups**. Single-issue groups often form around a moral issue about which their members are passionate and committed. For example, members of right-to-life organizations strongly believe that abortion is the murder of an unborn baby. On the other side of the issue, members of pro-choice organizations believe that women should have the right to make a decision to have an abortion, under the right of privacy. Single-issue groups are less likely to compromise because of their vehement belief that they are right and the other side is wrong.

Finally, **government interest groups** act on behalf of state, regional, local, or even foreign governments. Groups representing state and local governments are often concerned about laws and regulations that affect their particular regions. State government interest groups work to obtain grant money from the federal government, which is allocated through the appropriations process in Congress.

economic interest groups groups advocating on behalf of the financial interests of their members.

public interest groups groups that act on behalf of the collective interests of a broad group of individuals.

single-issue groups associations focusing on one specific area of public policy, often a moral issue about which they are unwilling to compromise.

government interest groups organizations acting on behalf of local, state, or foreign governments.

Lobbying by Interest Groups

The First Amendment guarantees the right of any citizen "to petition the Government for a redress of grievances." Interest groups use **lobbying**, or interacting with government officials, to advance a group's goals. Lobbying involves efforts to shape policy across all three branches; legislative lobbying seeks to influence how legislation is written in Congress, executive branch lobbying focuses on how laws are implemented by the bureaucracy, and judicial lobbying centers on how laws are interpreted by the courts.

In 2017, roughly 11,500 paid lobbyists spent a total of $3.37 billion lobbying Congress and federal agencies.[13] Because these figures are based only on registered lobbyist activities, however, they understate the actual numbers of total activity, both in the number of lobbyists and the amount of money they spent.

Lobbyists need solid, useful knowledge about the particular policy area and access to those in government. For this reason, former government officials are often in high demand by lobbying firms. Government agencies may recruit individuals from lobbying firms and the private sector for their experience and expertise.

The movement of individuals between positions in government and lobbying positions is called the **revolving door**. Those who believe that the revolving door is beneficial to the policymaking process argue that effective lobbying depends on the kind of knowledge and experience former government officials can bring to the table. Critics of the revolving door worry that paying large sums to hire well-connected lobbyists tilts public policy in favor of the wealthy and powerful. They point out that former members of Congress serving

lobbying interacting with government officials in order to advance a group's public policy goals.

revolving door the movement of individuals between positions in government and lobbying positions.

TABLE 15.1 After They Work for Government, How Do People Use the "Revolving Door"?

One of the databases maintained and published by the Center for Responsive Politics is "The Revolving Door," a door, the Web site's editors note, "that shuttles former federal employees into jobs as lobbyists, consultants and strategists just as the door pulls former hired guns into government careers." This table shows the top ten organizations hiring people who have come from government, excluding lobbying firms themselves.

Top Ten Organizations	Number of "Revolving Door" Employees
U.S. Chamber of Commerce	104
Pharmaceutical Research & Manufacturers of America	56
National Association of Manufacturers	52
General Electric	43
Lockheed Martin	42
Center for American Progress	42
Boeing Co.	40
Goldman Sachs	40
National Federation of Independent Business	38
Citigroup Management Corp.	37

Data from Center for Responsive Politics and OpenSecrets.org

as lobbyists have much greater access to policymakers than average citizens, which may influence government officials to give greater weight to the opinions of lobbyists than to the views of their constituents. Almost half the members of Congress who left in 2017 became lobbyists.[14] Table 15.1 highlights some of the top revolving-door organizations.

Lobbying Congress: Influencing Legislation

Congress is a natural target for lobbyists, and lobbyists use several strategies to influence legislation. Sometimes lobbyists contact members of Congress or their staff directly to advocate for their group's position. This is called inside, or direct, lobbying. In addition, lobbyists prepare research reports and briefs to bring more attention to their issues.[15] Interest groups draft bills, lobby members of Congress to introduce the legislation, and help them plan legislative strategy as the bills work their way through committees. Lobbyists also focus on the levels of funding Congress appropriates for agencies and programs.

Much of the power of inside lobbying is providing useful and timely information. Research by an interest group might save congressional staff valuable time. Studies sponsored by an interest group may persuade a member of Congress that constituents support an issue. Lobbyists might testify about an issue at committee or subcommittee hearings.

Lobbying Government Agencies

Interest groups take advantage of federal laws requiring executive branch agencies to notify the public and solicit input when establishing rules and procedures.[16] Proposed regulations

This political cartoon depicts the perception that the revolving door benefits certain economic interest groups. The cartoonist drew both Washington and Wall Street on the door. How might term limits cause the revolving door to turn faster? Is this a persuasive argument against term limits, or would the benefits of term limits outweigh the drawbacks?

R.J. Matson/Cagle Cartoons

are often complicated. Interest groups generate data and hire experts with knowledge of regulations and politics.[17] Interest groups encourage agencies to provide benefits, such as subsidies, to the members they represent and to issue favorable regulations.

Influencing the Judiciary

Interest groups try to shape how the nation's laws are interpreted by the judiciary. Interest groups may file lawsuits, but litigation is expensive and time-consuming, even when it goes well. As we explored in Chapter 9, in *Brown v. Board of Education* (1954),[18] the Legal Defense Fund of the NAACP undertook a lengthy, expensive, and risky strategy in using the federal judiciary to end legal segregation in the United States. Interest groups may weigh in on a case filed by other parties by filing a brief as a "friend of the court," also known as an **amicus curiae brief**, which describes the group's position on the issues in an attempt to persuade the Court to agree with its arguments. As we learned in Chapter 6, Supreme Court decisions serve as precedent for future cases. By filing amicus curiae briefs, interest groups attempt to influence how the laws in their policy area will be interpreted well into the future.

Interest groups also try to influence judicial appointments, either through the presidential nomination or Senate confirmation process. Given the importance of the federal judiciary and its influence over a host of issues, interest groups often have a very strong desire to shape the appointment process. In 2016, as Judge Merrick Garland, President Obama's nominee to fill the Supreme Court seat left vacant by the death of Justice Antonin Scalia, awaited Senate action, interest groups such as the National Federation of Business, the National Rifle Association, Planned Parenthood, and many others weighed in on his confirmation. However, the Republican majority in the Senate blocked Garland's nomination from coming up for a vote, and the seat remained vacant until President Trump nominated Neil Gorsuch, who became a member of the Court in April 2017. As with the

amicus curiae brief
a brief filed by someone who is not a party to a case in an attempt to persuade the Court to agree with the arguments set forth in the brief.

Garland nomination, interest groups weighed in on the Gorsuch nomination, hoping to influence the direction of the Supreme Court.

Iron Triangles and Issue Networks

iron triangle
the coordinated and mutually beneficial activities of the bureaucracy, Congress, and interest groups to achieve shared policy goals.

issue network
the webs of influence between interest groups, policymakers, and policy advocates.

As discussed in Chapter 7, the **iron triangle** is a classic depiction of the connections between interest groups and government (refer back to Figure 7.4 on page 228). It consists of three parts—interest groups, Congress, and the bureaucracy. Some political scientists believe the iron triangle model is simplistic. They use the term **issue network** to describe the webs of influence between interest groups, policymakers, and policy advocates. Complicated issues may give rise to competing issue networks, each of which advocates on a different side of the issue.

Issue networks may temporarily unite groups that are normally on different sides of most issues. The effort to legalize recreational marijuana has united some states' rights advocates, who tend to be conservative, with legalization advocates, who tend to be liberal. The immigration reform effort unites some business groups (seeking skilled and unskilled labor) that tend to be conservative and immigrant rights groups that tend to be liberal. While the iron triangle model emphasizes the power of special interests to work with government officials to achieve their goals, the issue network model represents pluralism, with multiple groups participating in the political process.

> **AP® TIP**
>
> Different interest groups use different tactics depending on their resources. A group weak in one resource, like money, may be strong in another resource, like numbers of members. Be prepared to explain why an interest group would choose one tactic over another in pursuing its goals.

Money and Campaigns

Interest groups often are heavily involved in the electoral process. Money is a powerful strategic tool that can pay for media coverage, a solid ground campaign, and research. Money can also act as a weapon to discourage underfunded candidates from running for election.

Political action committees (PACs) have limits on how much money they can contribute directly to a campaign or candidate. As discussed in Chapter 13, since the Supreme Court's decision in *Citizens United v. Federal Election Commission*, American politics has seen the proliferation of independent expenditure organizations and super PACs, which may raise and spend unlimited amounts of money as long as they do not coordinate with a campaign.[19] An interest group might form a PAC to give money directly to a candidate. It would form a super PAC to run its own ads independent from a candidate or campaign.

> **AP® TIP**
>
> *Citizens United v. Federal Election Commission* is one of the required Supreme Court cases. Be prepared to apply the ruling to a new court case or scenario.

In addition to financial contributions and spending, interest groups try to influence elections by mobilizing voters through efforts to encourage their members to go to the polls and vote for the candidates endorsed by the interest group. Many interest groups keep scorecards on the voting records of members of Congress and publicize the results to their members and the public in an effort to influence their vote. For example, the National Rifle Association's Political Victory Fund website has an interactive map where members can click on their state to see how the organization has rated a candidate's support for gun rights, on a scale from A to F.[20]

Acting from Outside: Mobilizing Members through Grassroots Lobbying and Political Protest

grassroots lobbying
mobilizing interest group members to pressure their representatives by contacting them directly through phone calls, email, and social media.

Interest groups may use **grassroots lobbying** to mobilize their members to pressure elected representatives directly through phone calls, emails, and social media. Interest groups that are not well funded may use this tactic because it is relatively inexpensive, and it can effectively get the attention of a member of Congress. As we will see in the discussion of social

Analyzing Data:
Campaign Contributions by Economic Sector

Reportable Campaign Contributions by Economic Sector, 2016 Elections

Rank	Sector	Amount	To Candidates/ Parties	Democrats	Republicans	To Democrats / To Republicans
1	Finance/insurance/ real estate	$1,133,203,884	$606,013,276	45.9%	53.8%	
2	Other	$751,124,095	$640,337,306	59.2%	40.3%	
3	Ideology/ single-issue	$570,270,261	$374,832,691	62.7%	37.1%	
4	Miscellaneous business	$487,750,719	$345,355,620	45.6%	54.0%	
5	Communications/ electronics	$323,458,087	$208,742,250	70.6%	29.0%	
6	Health	$280,632,601	$204,295,038	51.8%	47.9%	
7	Lawyers and lobbyists	$258,022,492	$242,874,489	70.7%	29.0%	
8	Labor	$216,789,052	$67,341,173	87.9%	12.0%	
9	Energy/natural resources	$172,005,013	$114,590,761	22.9%	77.0%	
10	Construction	$129,998,419	$87,348,986	31.1%	68.6%	
11	Agribusiness	$116,011,016	$85,088,267	26.4%	73.1%	
12	Transportation	$92,771,145	$75,053,758	30.4%	69.4%	
13	Defense	$29,712,784	$28,130,572	39.4%	60.3%	

Note: Percentages may not add up to 100% as money can be given to third-party candidates and party committees.

METHODOLOGY: The numbers on this page are based on contributions from PACs and individuals giving $200 or more to candidates and party committees, and from donors (including corporate and union treasuries) giving to super PACs and other outside groups, as reported to the Federal Election Commission.

All donations took place during the 2015–2016 election cycle and were released by the Federal Election Commission on November 27, 2017.

Data from Center for Responsive Politics and OpenSecrets.org, accessed May 11, 2018

The OpenSecrets.org project by the independent nonprofit Center for Responsive Politics collects, analyzes, and shares data on money, lobbying, politics, and elections. The center focuses a considerable amount of its efforts on tracking reportable campaign contributions. The table presents the total amounts of campaign contributions in the 2016 election cycle reported to the Federal Election Commission, broken down by sector of the economy. It includes contributions from individuals (of $200 or more) and PACs, as well as contributions given to super PACs and other groups.

1. Identify a sector that gives most of its donations to the Republican Party, and explain one reason why it prefers to donate money to the Republican Party.

2. Identify a sector that gives most of its donations to the Democratic Party, and explain one reason why it prefers to donate money to the Democratic Party.

3. Explain why an interest group might donate money to both political parties.

movements, protest can be another relatively inexpensive way for an interest group to call attention to an issue. Protests may gain the attention of the media, informing the public about the group's issues and goals. Coverage of protests on social media may spread a group's message quickly and cheaply to thousands, and sometimes millions, of viewers.

15.2 Describe the tactics used by interest groups to achieve their goals and how they interact with bureaucratic agencies and members of Congress through iron triangles and issue networks.

REMEMBER
- Interest groups may advocate for a variety of goals, including those focused on business and the economy, public issues, and the interests of state and local governments.
- Single-issue groups are narrowly focused, often around a moral issue, and they are usually unwilling to compromise.
- When lobbying the federal government, interest groups act to influence the actions of the legislative, executive, and judicial branches.
- Interest groups participate in iron triangles and issue networks that form around a particular policy area.
- Interest groups also act to influence campaigns and elections.

KNOW
- *economic interest groups*: groups advocating on behalf of the financial interests of their members. (p. 491)
- *public interest groups*: groups that act on behalf of the collective interests of a broad group of individuals. (p. 491)
- *single-issue groups*: associations focusing on one specific area of public policy, often a moral issue about which they are unwilling to compromise. (p. 491)
- *government interest groups*: organizations acting on behalf of local, state, or foreign governments. (p. 491)
- *lobbying*: interacting with government officials in order to advance a group's public policy goals. (p. 491)
- *revolving door*: the movement of individuals between positions in government and lobbying positions. (p. 491)
- *amicus curiae brief*: a brief filed by someone who is not a party to a case in an attempt to persuade the Court to agree with the arguments set forth in the brief. (p. 493)
- *iron triangle*: the coordinated and mutually beneficial activities of the bureaucracy, Congress, and interest groups to achieve shared policy goals. (p. 494)
- *issue network*: the webs of influence between interest groups, policymakers, and policy advocates. (p. 494)
- *grassroots lobbying*: mobilizing interest group members to pressure their representatives by contacting them directly through phone calls, email, and social media. (p. 494)

THINK
- How do the tactics used by wealthy interest groups differ from the tactics used by groups with fewer monetary resources?
- What are the advantages and disadvantages of the revolving door in the policymaking process?

15.2 Review Question: Free Response

The following is an excerpt from an article that appeared before Congress adopted a tax plan that was signed by President Trump in December 2017.

Alliance to Save Energy wants reinstatement of green energy subsidies for residential and commercial builders. Realtors want to pump the brakes on tax reform unless Congress scraps a proposal to double the standard deduction. . . . Not to be outdone, BUILD Coalition wants to maintain the full deduction for business interest expenses.[21]

Use the excerpt and your knowledge of U.S. Government and Politics to answer parts A, B, and C.

A. Describe the type of interest group addressed in the excerpt.

B. Describe one tactic used by interest groups to influence the political process.

C. Explain one reason why the tactic you described in part B has faced criticism.

15.3 Social Movements

As discussed in Chapter 9, the civil rights movement and the struggle for the rights of women, disabled Americans, and LGBT Americans are social movements that achieved major policy change. Although their specific goals differed, they often employed similar tactics.

Choice of Effective Tactics

Social movements often use **protest**, a public demonstration designed to call attention to the need for change. Members of social movements may use **civil disobedience**, intentionally breaking of a law to call attention to injustice. Protest and civil disobedience can be powerful and effective tactics, especially in altering the political agenda. They attract media attention to an issue, forcing the public and policymakers to confront it. Protest and civil disobedience can be risky, however, not only for the individuals involved, but also for the movement itself. Individuals who protest or engage in civil disobedience may endanger their freedom, jobs, physical safety, or even their lives. There is a chance that these activities may alienate rather than mobilize the public. There is also the risk that the protesters will be ignored.

protest
a public demonstration designed to call attention to the need for change.

civil disobedience
intentionally breaking a law to call attention to an injustice.

AP® TIP

Social movements have broader and more diffuse goals than interest groups. Be sure you know the difference between interest groups and social movements, and be ready to explain why they choose various strategies in an effort to achieve their goals.

Successes and Failures of Social Movements

According to Piven and Cloward, social movements arise under particular circumstances and are short-lived. Protestors need to feel that the system has lost some legitimacy, and individuals who are normally pessimistic about change start to believe they can assert their rights and have the capacity to make a difference. The success of social movements depends upon the impact that protest has on the electoral system, and on whether elected officials accommodate the demands of protestors, or decide to ignore them.[22]

The Occupy Wall Street (OWS) Movement was an example of a social movement with an ambitious agenda. After the collapse of the mortgage industry in 2007 and the bank bailout that followed, the movement's members believed that the government adopted policies to favor wealthy financial interests. Critics of the bailout believed that big financial firms had been rescued from suffering the consequences of their risky behavior, thanks to the federal government. On the other hand, many unfortunate homeowners lost their homes. The protesters saw this as not only an inequality of wealth but also an inequality of justice.

As they struggled to convey their message to American citizens, OWS members also struggled to clearly define their message. As Rachel Pletz, a participant in the Zuccotti Park protests who helped to organize similar efforts in Philadelphia, put it, "This is about solidarity. This is about

An Occupy Wall Street activist takes part in a protest at Zuccotti Park in New York City on July 11, 2012, asserting the right to form a social movement.
REUTERS/Eduardo Munoz/Newscom

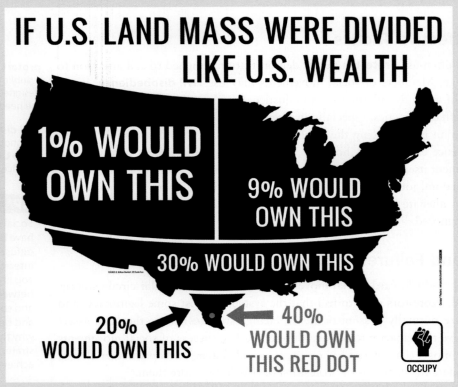

IF U.S. LAND MASS WERE DIVIDED LIKE U.S. WEALTH

1% WOULD OWN THIS

9% WOULD OWN THIS

30% WOULD OWN THIS

20% WOULD OWN THIS

40% WOULD OWN THIS RED DOT

OCCUPY

Using data on wealth and income concentrations in the United States compiled by academic researchers, individuals associated with Occupy Wall Street created this image, which found its way into major media outlets and onto T-shirts and posters.

How effective do you think this image is in conveying the inequality of wealth in the United States? Although the figure is based on actual data, the creator acknowledges, "I drew the lines in a somewhat impressionistic manner."[23]

1. Describe the message about income inequality conveyed by the mapmaker.

2. Describe two limitations of using a map, instead of a graph or chart, in conveying information about income inequality.

3. Explain one reason why someone would use a map to convey information, rather than a chart or graph.

getting people together and figuring it out. We just know something's wrong."[24] It is a particular challenge to successfully mobilize Americans to respond to political and economic inequalities when economic regulations are so complex. "What do you say about a financial crisis where the villains are obscure and the solutions are obscure," wondered a noted British music critic. And one college student who attended a musical performance on behalf of OWS commented, "I have not heard a single song that sums up what we are trying to do here."[25]

By spring 2012, tents set up by OWS protestors had mostly disappeared from New York, Boston, Los Angeles, and other cities. Protests continued, but without the same level of media coverage. Some debated what had been accomplished.[26] OWS did not appear to have built the necessary infrastructure to sustain it over the long haul. According to one reporter, "Many pundits suggest that it's time for the activists to hire political consultants and assemble a list of demands—in short, to become much more involved in electoral politics."[27] Some people argued it was time for OWS to stop trying to form a broad social movement and become a more focused interest group. However, forming an interest group might not be an effective way for OWS to meet its goals.

Piven and Cloward have argued that social movements lose leverage when they become interest groups because they have to compete alongside other groups with more financial resources and well-connected lobbyists.[28] However, in our exploration of political parties in Chapter 14, we studied the candidacy of Senator Bernie Sanders, who highlighted American economic inequality in his campaign. The efforts of Sanders and others to call attention to this issue illustrate that OWS may have influenced the political agenda. As OWS faded from the nation's attention, another social movement arose.

In the fall of 2017, the #MeToo social movement gained national attention. The #MeToo movement started with the revelation that Ashley Judd, a country music singer and actress, had faced inappropriate advances from Harvey Weinstein, a successful Hollywood producer. According to a *Time* magazine article, "In 1997, just before Ashley Judd's career took off, she was invited to a meeting with Harvey Weinstein, head of the star-making studio Miramax, at a Beverly Hills hotel. Astounded and offended by Weinstein's attempt to coerce her into bed, Judd managed to escape. But instead of keeping quiet about the kind of encounter that could easily shame a woman into silence, she began spreading the word."[29] Judd claimed that Weinstein ruined her career in retribution for her allegations. The #MeToo movement went viral on social media, with women of all walks of life who had been subjected to sexual harassment posting the hashtag #MeToo.

The #MeToo movement had measurable success in holding some very successful men accountable for sexual harassment. It caused the resignation of several members of Congress, state legislators, and business executives, including Harvey Weinstein, who was charged with rape. Roy Moore, a candidate for an Alabama Senate seat, lost the election following allegations that he had preyed on young women and girls earlier in his career. States and corporations revised policies on how to respond to complaints of sexual harassment. And while Congress hasn't yet taken any action, future legislation may further the goals of the #MeToo movement.

While social movements often fail, successful social movements have expanded equality in the United States.

Section Review

15.3 Explain how social movements have an impact on policymaking.

REMEMBER
- Social movements are broad-based efforts to achieve major policy change.
- Social movements tend to be more diffuse than interest groups.
- Social movements often use protest and civil disobedience as a way to call attention to their issues.
- Some social movements lack leadership, resources, infrastructure, and clear policy objectives, which hinders their success.
- Some social movements, such as the #MeToo movement, gather momentum and result in policy change.

KNOW
- *protest*: a public demonstration designed to call attention to the need for change. (p. 497)
- *civil disobedience*: intentionally breaking a law to call attention to an injustice. (p. 497)

THINK

- What are the advantages and disadvantages of forming a social movement, rather than an interest group?
- Why are some social movements successful in achieving their policy objectives while other social movements fail?

15.3 Review Question: Free Response

Rob Rogers, Pittsburgh Post-Gazette. Reprinted with permission of Andrews McMeel Syndication. All Rights Reserved.

Use the cartoon and your knowledge of U.S. Government and Politics to answer Parts A, B, and C.

A. Describe the viewpoint conveyed in the cartoon.

B. Describe one difference between the tactics used by an interest group and the tactics used by a social movement, such as the tactic depicted in the cartoon.

C. Explain one reason why social movements may be less likely to achieve their goals than interest groups.

Chapter 15 Review

AP® KEY CONCEPTS

- *interest groups* (p. 485)
- *social movements* (p. 485)
- *theory of participatory democracy* (p. 487)
- *civil society* (p. 487)
- *pluralist theory* (p. 487)
- *elitist theory* (p. 488)
- *policy agenda* (p. 488)
- *collective action* (p. 488)

- *collective good* (p. 488)
- *free riders* (p. 489)
- *selective benefits* (p. 489)
- *economic interest groups* (p. 491)
- *public interest groups* (p. 491)
- *single-issue groups* (p. 491)
- *government interest groups* (p. 491)
- *lobbying* (p. 491)

- *revolving door* (p. 491)
- *amicus curiae brief* (p. 493)
- *iron triangle* (p. 494)
- *issue network* (p. 494)
- *grassroots lobbying* (p. 494)
- *protest* (p. 497)
- *civil disobedience* (p. 497)

AP® EXAM PRACTICE and Critical Thinking Project

MULTIPLE-CHOICE QUESTIONS

After tallying publicly available information on constituent calls, the *Washington Post* reported 59,337 calls made to members of Congress to urge them to oppose the repeal of the [Patient Protection and Affordable Care Act] with just 1,130 messages in support. As Representative Gerry Connolly of Virginia noted, "You organized across the country. . . . You called your Representatives and asked them to vote no. Members of Congress reported receiving thousands of calls from constituents almost uniformly against repeal."[30]

1. The passage describes which tactic used by interest groups?

A. protest

B. lobbying

C. grassroots lobbying

D. electoral support

"Our industry is committed to the environment.
All of our lobbyists are 100% recycled congressmen."

Chris Wildt/Cartoon Stock

2. The cartoon refers to which of the following?

A. environmental interest groups

B. the iron triangle

C. the revolving door

D. issue networks

Questions 3 and 4 refer to the quote.

It should be clear from my remarks that Congress has always had, and always will have, lobbyists and lobbying. We could not adequately consider our work load without them. We listen to representatives from the broadest number of groups: large and small; single-issue and multi-purposed; citizens groups; corporate and labor representatives; the public spirited and the privately inspired.

—**Senator Robert C. Byrd, Address to the Senate, September 1987**[31]

3. Which of the following concepts is best represented in the quote?

A. Interest group pluralism
B. Grassroots lobbying
C. The dangers of faction
D. Polarization and gridlock

4. According to the quote, the role of a lobbyist in the political process is to

A. provide expertise to members of Congress.
B. help members of Congress win campaigns.
C. represent a diverse group of interests.
D. advocate for policies to benefit the public as a whole.

---

5. Select the pair that matches the branch of government with a tactic used by interest groups to influence government officials.

Branch of government	**Interest group tactic**
A. President	Civil disobedience
B. Congress	Grassroots lobbying
C. Courts	Monetary donations
D. Bureaucracy	Support for election campaigns

Questions 6 and 7 refer to the bar chart.

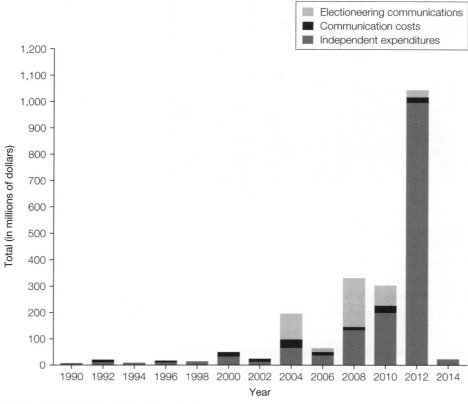

Spending by Interest Groups, 1990–2014 Elections

Data from the *Washington Post* and Open Secrets

6. Which of the following describes a trend in spending by interest groups as shown in the bar chart?

   A. Spending in midterm congressional elections increased steadily from 1990 until 2014.

   B. Less money is spent in midterm congressional election years than in the presidential election two years later.

   C. Communication costs have increased every year from 2004 to 2014.

   D. The amount of money donated directly to candidates is greater than the amount spent independently.

7. Which of the following best explains a reason for the upward trend in interest group spending shown in the bar chart?

   A. The Supreme Court's decision in *Citizens United v. Federal Election Commission*

   B. The increased cost of campaigning through social media

   C. The increased ability of candidates to spend their own personal wealth on campaigns

   D. The increased ability of candidates to raise and spend money independent of political parties

A SHORT INTERVIEW WITH AN OCCUPY WALL ST. PROTESTER:

PEOPLE SAY WE'VE BEEN VAGUE, INCOHERENT AND UNFOCUSED, BUT WE REJECT THAT DESCRIPTION...

KIND OF.

8. Which of the following best describes the viewpoint expressed about the Occupy Wall Street movement in the cartoon?

A. It was not effective in appealing to average Americans.

B. It did not have a single leader.

C. It was not effective in conveying a clear message about its goals.

D. It was made up of people who wanted to receive benefits without paying for them.

_____

9. The Tobacco Division of the Department of Agriculture, interest groups representing cigarette manufacturers, interest groups representing farmers, and the subcommittees in the House of Representatives and Senate work to create tobacco policy. This is an example of

A. An iron triangle

B. Interest group pluralism

C. Grassroots lobbying

D. The policy agenda

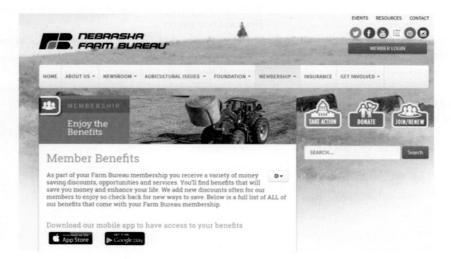

10. The program advertised at the Web site is an example of

A. Interest group pluralism

B. Free riders who benefit without joining a group

C. A tactic to reduce the free rider problem

D. Grassroots lobbying by interest group members

FREE-RESPONSE QUESTIONS

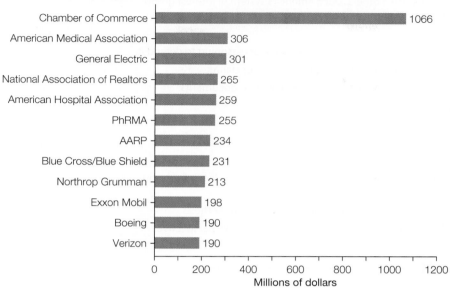

Groups Spending the Most on Federal Lobbying, 1998–2014

Group	Millions of dollars
Chamber of Commerce	1066
American Medical Association	306
General Electric	301
National Association of Realtors	265
American Hospital Association	259
PhRMA	255
AARP	234
Blue Cross/Blue Shield	231
Northrop Grumman	213
Exxon Mobil	198
Boeing	190
Verizon	190

Data from Vox.com and Center for Responsive Politics

1. Use the bar chart and your knowledge of U.S. Government and Politics to answer parts A, B, and C.

   A. Define lobbying.

   B. Explain one reason why the Chamber of Commerce spent more than twice as much on lobbying as any other interest group shown in the graph.

   C. Other than lobbying, identify one other tactic used by interest groups to influence members of Congress, and explain why an interest group might use the tactic you identified.

2. Amicus curiae briefs abound in the U.S. Supreme Court . . . According to Justice [Ruth Bader] Ginsburg these briefs along with other secondary sources can aid the Court in its decision-making: "There is useful knowledge out there in friend of the court briefs . . . in . . . grappling with the same difficult questions."[32]

   —Dr. Adam Feldman

   After reading the excerpt, use your knowledge of U.S. Government and Politics to answer parts A, B, and C.

   A. Define the term *amicus curiae brief*.

   B. Explain one reason why an amicus curiae brief filed by an interest group might help the Supreme Court in making a decision.

   C. Describe two other tactics an interest group might use in an effort to influence the policymaking process, other than filing an amicus curiae brief.

ARGUMENTATION QUESTION

Interest groups are linkage institutions that connect citizens with government. However, some interest groups have more wealth and power than others. Does America's system of interest group participation best represent the pluralist model or the elitist model of democracy?

In your essay:

- Articulate a claim or thesis that responds to the prompt, and use a line of reasoning to defend it.
- Use at least TWO pieces of relevant and accurate evidence to support your claim.
- At least ONE piece of evidence must be from one of the listed foundational documents:

    Constitution of the United States

    Federalist No. 10

    Federalist No. 51

    Brutus No. 1

- Use a second piece of evidence from another foundational document from the list or from your study of elections and campaigns.
- Use reasoning to explain why the evidence you provided supports your claim or thesis.
- Use refutation, concession, or rebuttal to respond to an opposing or alternative perspective.

CRITICAL THINKING PROJECT

By forming or joining an interest group, you can have some impact on the political process before you are old enough to vote.

1. By yourself or with a group of classmates, brainstorm a list of problems in your school or community that you would like to see addressed. Create a group that shares your interest and pick one problem to focus on. Perhaps your class will vote on which issue to support, or maybe you will be a part of a smaller group that shares your concerns. If you are homeschooled, you might want to join with others who are homeschooled or contact other groups to which you belong.
2. Research your issue. Be prepared to explain why the issue you selected poses a problem in your school or community. If possible, support your claim with credible data. For example, if there is a dangerous intersection in your neighborhood, you might compile data from the police department about the number and seriousness of accidents in that location.
3. Decide who can solve your problem. This might be your school principal, the school board, the city council, or county or state officials. If you plan to present your issue to the school board, notify your principal first.
4. Select the tactics most likely to help your group achieve its goal. You might conduct a publicity campaign in the school newspaper, select someone from your group to lobby on your behalf, or even protest.
5. Take action! After carefully planning your tactics, follow through. You may or may not be successful, but you will learn more about how to advocate for your group's interests.

16 The Media
New Technologies, Enduring Issues

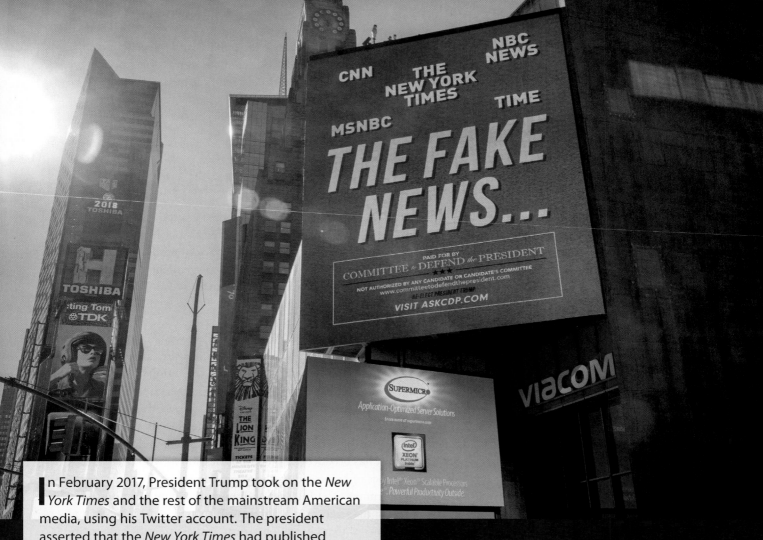

In February 2017, President Trump took on the *New York Times* and the rest of the mainstream American media, using his Twitter account. The president asserted that the *New York Times* had published an inaccurate and poorly sourced story about his ties to the Russian government. During the spring and summer, the president accused CNN, MSNBC, the *New York Times*, and other mainstream media outlets of broadcasting "fake news," with the goal of undermining his presidency.

On February 5, 2017, the Committee to Defend the President ran advertising on an electronic billboard in Times Square in New York. Times Square was once the home of the *New York Times,* and as the photo shows, Times Square still buzzes with messages from various media. It is the ideal place for a battle over what is news.
Richard Levine/Alamy Stock Photo

Donald J. Trump ✔
@realDonaldTrump

(Follow) ⌄

After being forced to apologize for its bad and inaccurate coverage of me after winning the election, the FAKE NEWS @nytimes is still lost!

5:39 AM - 4 Feb 2017

The Trump tweet about the *New York Times* that launched another skirmish over what is "fake" news.
@realDonaldTrump, Tweet, February 4, 2017

The term *fake news* is often thrown about, but what does it mean? To some, it means the intentional use of the media to support a political party. To others, it means the intentional presentation of material that the news agency knows to be untrue or, at least, unverified. To others, it means the intentional use of the mass media to deceive the public, with the goal of changing political outcomes. To still others, it is used to discredit media stories that, while accurate, are critical. And, for some, the term is used to discredit the media in general. The challenge for readers and viewers of American media is to discern fact from fiction. This is not an easy task, especially in a new politically charged media environment that moves at warp speed.

What Do We Mean by "Media"?

news media
a broad term that includes newspapers, magazines, radio, television, internet sources, blogs, and social-media postings that cover important events.

social media
forms of electronic communication that enable users to create and share content or to participate in social networking.

The media are an important source of information about political issues. The **news media** is a broad term that includes newspapers, magazines, radio, television, internet sources, blogs, and social media postings that cover important events. **Social media** are forms of electronic communication that enable users to create and share content or to connect through social networking. Much of the news transmitted through social media is generated in traditional ways, through previously produced stories, videos, and commentaries linked or posted on Facebook, YouTube, Snapchat, or Twitter.

Keep in mind that the word *media* is a plural that refers collectively to many sources of communication. The way media are funded, who their audiences are, and what technologies they use shape the presentation, influence, and even the definition of the news.

Today, the pace of change in the media seems mind-boggling. Americans are simultaneously witnessing a major decline in daily newspaper readership, the rise of social media, and increasingly divisive language in political talk shows. The lines between the roles of reporter, entertainer, and celebrity are blurred in an effort to capture the public's attention.

The idea of who is a journalist has broadened, and nonprofessionals who cover events by filming them on their cell phones or by providing their own commentaries and analysis generate news stories and commentary. The Internet and modern communications technologies provide the ability to capture, report on, and transmit news more quickly and cheaply than ever. Some scholars argue that citizen journalism makes America more democratic. Others worry that while large news organizations have the resources to carefully fact-check their stories and do in-depth investigations, social media journalists do not.

The Power of the News Media

agenda setting
the media's ability to highlight certain issues and bring them to the attention of the public.

The media exercise a great deal of power by selecting which stories are covered. In their **agenda setting** role, the media highlight which issues are worthy of coverage and, as a consequence, worthy of the public's attention. Agenda setting is a key function of the media in a representative democracy. According to political scientist Harold Lasswell, the media perform three important and interconnected functions: to survey and report on political events and outcomes, to interpret those events and outcomes to the public, and to educate citizens.[1]

There is no doubt that the recent revolution in communications technologies has changed the delivery of political news and opinion. How do the news media shape Americans' political understanding? And how will Americans' understanding of government and politics be impacted by rapidly evolving technologies that change our perceptions of journalism?

After reading this chapter, you will be able to

16.1 Explain how increased media choices, consumer-driven media, and new technologies have impacted the level of citizens' political knowledge.

16.2 Explain how consolidation and ideologically driven news media have impacted the delivery of the news.

16.3 Explain the debate over the impact of bias in the news and how the media shape political understanding and behaviors.

LEARNING TARGETS

16.1 The Evolving News Media

From before the country's founding to today, the news media have played an important role in shaping American political culture and influencing Americans' attitudes toward government and politics. Along with political parties, interest groups, and elections, the media are a linkage institution connecting citizens with government, making it easier for the government to communicate with citizens. The connection between the nation's media and American politics has been shaped by technological change.

The Print Media and a New Nation

The delegates to the Constitutional Convention, as we explored in Chapter 2, had been careful to prevent information from being leaked to the newspapers. The publication of the proposed Constitution spurred a flood of editorials for and against the document, and newspapers took their place at the forefront of American political life in the late 1780s.

Freedom of the Press, the Constitution, and the Ratification Debates

The press played a pivotal role in the ratification debates, as proponents and opponents of the document made their cases through the nation's newspapers, often writing under pseudonyms. The *Federalist Papers*, the classic statement of the theory behind the Constitution, authored by Alexander Hamilton, James Madison, and John Jay, first appeared as a series of essays written under the pseudonym Publius in the New York newspapers. The Antifederalists produced essays warning that the proposed Constitution posed dangers to liberty.

While the Bill of Rights was not part of the original document, a promise that the new government would create one through a series of amendments during the session of Congress in 1789 proved crucial to securing ratification. The First Amendment states: "Congress shall make no law . . . abridging the freedom of speech, or of the press." This provided the foundation for press freedoms.

The Media Go "Mass": Penny Presses, Partisanship, and Scandal

In the late eighteenth and early nineteenth centuries, however, newspapers only reached a relatively small part of the population. They were expensive and often only available through an annual subscription, which required putting down a large sum of money all at once rather than for each issue.

The cost to produce a newspaper fell during the 1830s with the development of cheaper methods of printing, and readership grew rapidly. The penny press, so labeled because an individual newspaper cost one penny, could be bought on the street from newsboys hawking their products. Within just a few months of its introduction, the *New York Sun* was the city's top-selling paper. By 1834, the *Sun* was selling 15,000 copies a day. The penny press was an example of the **mass media**—sources of information and entertainment (including newspapers, television and radio broadcasts, and internet content) designed to reach large audiences.

Newspapers depended on sales and on providing an audience for their advertisers, and so they often focused on dramatic stories of crime, riots, and scandalous behavior.[2]

mass media
sources of information designed to reach a wide audience, including newspapers, radio, television, and internet outlets.

Journalists as Investigators and Activists

A faster and cheaper printing press was not the only technological development that shaped the newspaper in the nineteenth century. The telegraph allowed news to travel instantaneously over distances that might have taken days or weeks otherwise. The Associated Press created a **wire service**, an organization that gathers the news and offers it for sale to other media outlets.

The nineteenth century also witnessed a new approach to news coverage, **investigative journalism**, in which journalists act as detectives and dig into stories rather than simply conveying the speeches and opinions of political leaders. During the Progressive Era, an important group of investigative reporters became known as *muckrakers*; the name was a reference to a rake used to dig up mud. Theodore Roosevelt made the term popular, and at first it was seen as a criticism of journalists. Muckrakers used investigative journalism to expose wrongdoing and also to shape public opinion in support of regulating businesses and reducing corruption in government.[3]

wire service
an organization that gathers and reports on news and then sells the stories to other outlets.

investigative journalism
an approach to newsgathering in which reporters dig into stories, often looking for instances of wrongdoing.

Direct to Americans' Homes: Radio and Television

Technological advances during the twentieth century brought political figures directly into Americans' homes. Radio and television, which are examples of **broadcast media**, brought political news to citizens directly and immediately. Listening to the radio or watching

broadcast media
outlets for news and other content including radio and television that bring stories directly into people's homes.

television was often a shared experience, with only one radio or television set in the home or in the neighborhood. People could learn about the news while doing other things, such as driving, doing chores, working, or having dinner. Mass media was a shared experience because people nationwide were exposed to the same stories. By breaking down geographic barriers, the broadcast media were truly national in scope.

If the 1930s signaled the emergence of radio as a powerful new force in political news, the late 1950s did the same for television. In 1960, candidates John F. Kennedy and Richard Nixon participated in the first televised presidential debates in American history. While experts and radio listeners did not declare a clear winner, those who watched on television thought that Kennedy won the debate. Kennedy's image on television came across as robust and energetic, while Nixon, who had been fighting the flu, appeared pale and sweaty.[4] In 1961, having won the presidency, Kennedy gave the first live televised news conference.

As more Americans relied upon the major television networks for their news and coverage of political events, news anchors became trusted figures in describing and interpreting these events. As the Vietnam War progressed, American casualties mounted, and protests against American involvement spread, trusted television journalist Walter Cronkite questioned if the war had become unwinnable. It was widely reported that President Lyndon Johnson observed, "If I've lost Cronkite, I've lost Middle America."[5] The idea that a trusted news anchor could affect American public opinion so strongly in an area as vital as foreign policy speaks to the power of television news anchors during the heyday of network news.

Beginning in the 1980s, the mass media changed, appealing to narrower audiences. Radios crackled with political commentary and harsh criticism of those who shared different viewpoints. Some programs were clearly Republican, such as *The Rush Limbaugh Show*. Other radio shows appeal to a liberal audience. These talk radio broadcasts have been criticized for their efforts to provoke emotional responses, such as anger, fear, and moral indignation through the use of overgeneralization, sensationalism, misleading or patently inaccurate information, and ridicule of opponents.[6]

The 1980s and 1990s witnessed the rise of a new outlet for television and television news. First broadcasting in 1980, CNN, the Cable News Network, provided Americans with twenty-four-hour news coverage. The American political news media had broken the clock, going 24/7, and America tuned in. In 1996, Australian media entrepreneur Rupert Murdoch launched Fox News, which provided a conservative interpretation of the nation's news and political events. Americans who felt that network news coverage was too liberal switched to Fox News. Cable television news is subject to fewer government regulations, and it has become unapologetically partisan. Figure 16.1 on page 512 shows how sources of political news have changed in recent years.

The twenty-first century has also witnessed a marked decline in the number of people who read printed newspapers. Traditional papers have gone online, sometimes for free and with advertisements, sometimes behind firewalls that require registration and/or a subscription fee.

Some political scientists worry that ideologically driven news increases polarization and leads people to support more partisan policies. One study suggests that most Americans are moderate, but politically interested people who consume ideologically driven news may become more entrenched in their partisan beliefs.[7] People who consistently watch a single news source are less trusting of other sources of news and are more likely to have friends who share their own political views than viewers of multiple news sources.[8]

FIGURE 16.1

Changes in Americans' Main Sources of News

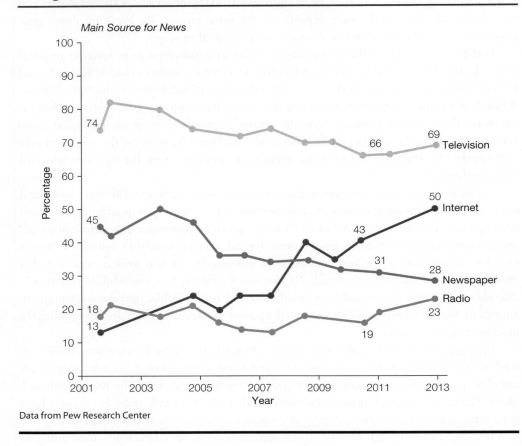

Data from Pew Research Center

New Media: New Freedom and New Problems

The twenty-first century gave rise to new forms of media. The term *new media* is used to refer to all of the various digital platforms through which individuals receive, share, and produce content. Broadband reception, the Internet, and other communications technologies enable Americans to receive and send text, sound, and video at increasingly fast speeds and in increasingly large volumes.

These new forms of media communication have revolutionized far more than the speed of delivery. In the era of 24/7 news coverage and the merging of entertainment and news media, individuals can be journalists, citizens can be editors and commentators, and members of the media can be celebrities. Throughout much of the nation's history, most Americans had a limited number of choices in their news media outlets—generally, one or two daily newspapers, several radio stations, and a few major television broadcast networks. The rise of cable television expanded the number of options, and the internet increased these options even further. Newspapers and TV news broadcasts are struggling to remain relevant in the face of rapidly changing technology. See Figure 16.2 to assess the rate of change.

New media can bring us together by shattering geographic boundaries, but they can polarize us politically by allowing people to select information and political news, shutting out other viewpoints.

FIGURE 16.2

Pace of Change in Adoption of Communications Media

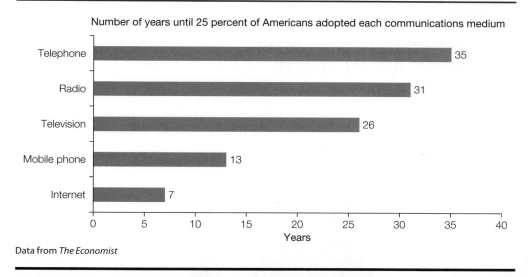

Number of years until 25 percent of Americans adopted each communications medium

Medium	Years
Telephone	35
Radio	31
Television	26
Mobile phone	13
Internet	7

Data from *The Economist*

Section Review

This chapter's main ideas are reflected in the Learning Targets. By reviewing after each section, you should be able to

—**Remember** the key points,

—**Know** terms that are central to the topic, and

—**Think** critically about the role of the media as it relates to government and politics.

16.1 Explain how increased media choices, consumer-driven media, and new technologies have impacted the level of citizens' political knowledge.

REMEMBER
- The media are a linkage institution, which allows the government to more easily communicate with the people.
- Pamphlets and, later, weekly and daily newspapers were among the first print media in the United States.
- Costs to produce newspapers decreased, making the news more affordable and able to reach a mass audience.
- The nineteenth and twentieth centuries saw the rise of other technologies, such as the telegraph (which brought us wire services) and radio and television (which brought us broadcast news).
- Cable news offers around-the-clock news coverage, often with a partisan slant.
- Newer technologies, such as the internet, broadband, and social media, have not only increased the pace and volume of news content but have also blurred the lines between information and entertainment, and between citizens and journalists.

KNOW
- *news media*: a broad term that includes newspapers, magazines, radio, television, Internet sources, blogs, and social media postings that cover important events. (p. 508)
- *social media*: forms of electronic communication that enable users to create and share content or to participate in social networking. (p. 508)
- *agenda setting*: the media's ability to highlight certain issues and bring them to the attention of the public. (p. 508)
- *mass media*: sources of information designed to reach a wide audience, including newspapers, radio, television, and internet outlets. (p. 510)
- *wire service*: an organization that gathers and reports on news and then sells the stories to other outlets. (p. 510)
- *investigative journalism*: an approach to newsgathering in which reporters dig into stories, often looking for instances of wrongdoing. (p. 510)
- *broadcast media*: outlets for news and other content including radio and television that bring stories directly into people's homes. (p. 510)

16.1 Review Question: Free Response

Bob Krohmer/Cartoon Stock

Use the cartoon and your knowledge of U.S. Government and Politics to answer parts A, B, and C.

A. Describe the viewpoint expressed in the cartoon.

B. Describe one impact of talk radio shows on government and politics.

C. Explain one way in which new forms of media have changed the way news is covered.

◼ 16.2 Public Policy Regulating Content and Ownership

While the media provide information that helps citizens hold elected officials and government employees accountable, the government also regulates the media. Government regulation has focused mainly on two things: content and ownership.

The Changing Nature of Regulation

When radio and television became popular in the twentieth century, both citizens and the federal government pushed for regulation of the broadcast media.[9] Some wanted to regulate the content beamed directly into Americans' homes to ensure it was suitable for children. Others wanted to regulate the political content of radio and television broadcasts to ensure that multiple political viewpoints were presented.

The Radio Act (1927) established the Federal Radio Commission and required broadcasters to obtain a license to broadcast on specific frequencies.[10] The Communications Act of 1934 expanded the federal government's role in regulating the nation's broadcast media, creating the Federal Communications Commission (FCC) to oversee the implementation of its provisions.[11]

AP® TIP

New York Times Co. v. United States is a required case. Make sure you understand the facts, issue, decision, and rationale and are able to apply the case to non-required cases involving the role of the media and the First Amendment.

Regulation of the media raises concerns about the appropriate balance between the constitutional right of freedom of the press and the government's need to protect liberty and order. As discussed in Chapter 8, the government attempted to block a story by the *Washington Post* during the Vietnam War. In *New York Times Co. v. United States* (1971),[12] the Supreme Court ruled that the government may not censor a story before it is published, unless publication would endanger national security.

In the latter half of the twentieth century, changes in the ways news stories were created and distributed forced the government to rethink the rules governing telecommunications. Deregulation led to increasing consolidation as news firms tried to maximize their profits in the face of declining sales and advertising revenue. Subscriptions to print magazines and newspapers are being canceled because people can read online magazines, blogs, and newspapers for free.

It would be difficult to regulate political content on social media to ensure equality and fairness of opposing viewpoints because the First Amendment protects freedom of expression. Political candidates who are also celebrities, for example, can obtain disproportionate attention based on their celebrity status. In the 2016 presidential campaign, Republican candidate Donald Trump used his large following on Twitter to get media coverage without having to purchase as much airtime as other candidates. As president, Donald Trump has made unprecedented use of Twitter to convey his viewpoints to the public.

President Barack Obama was a vocal advocate for net neutrality rules that prevent Internet and broadband companies from charging more for content providers who chew up more bandwidth. In June 2016, the D.C. Circuit Court of Appeals, in a 2–1 vote, upheld the FCC's net neutrality rules.[13] Net neutrality also came up in the 2016 presidential election. Following the Court's decision, Democratic candidate Bernie Sanders tweeted that the ruling "will help ensure we don't turn over our democracy to the highest bidder," while Republican senator Ted Cruz labeled net neutrality "Obamacare for the Internet," implying that the government was placing too many regulations on the Internet.[14] As discussed in Chapter 15, the Trump Administration reversed net neutrality rules on the grounds that they were excessive, unnecessary, and deter investment in new technologies.[15]

Public Policy and Media Consolidation

The Federal Communications Commission was created in 1934 and, until the early 1980s, the federal government enacted regulations to preserve media diversity and prevent consolidation. **Media consolidation** is the concentration of ownership of the media in fewer corporations. The FCC regulations prevented a corporation from holding too many TV stations or newspapers, reaching too big of an audience. In 1945, the Supreme Court blocked a merger among various media companies and the Associated Press. The majority opinion states, "The widest possible dissemination of information from diverse and antagonistic sources is essential to the welfare of the public." In this decision, the Court prevented media consolidation to strengthen the First Amendment.

media consolidation
the concentration of ownership of the media into fewer corporations.

FIGURE 16.3

Consolidation of Ownership of the Media as of 2011

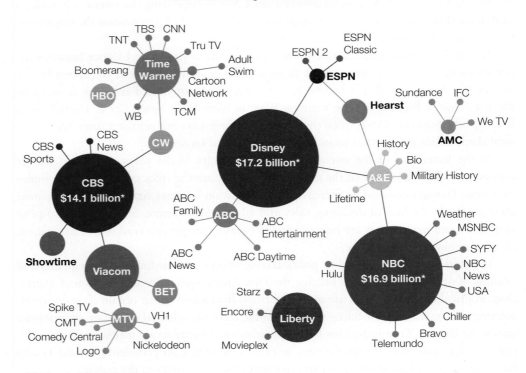

Who owns the big TV networks?

*2010 entertainment revenue

Data from Nielsen, Disney, Hollywood Reporter, Bloomberg, Wikipedia, Businesswire, and Value Investing Center, and based on entertainment revenue.

In the 1980s, FCC Chairman Mark Fowler, who was appointed by Ronald Reagan, began deregulating the media, paving the road to consolidation. The Telecommunications Act of 1996, signed by President Bill Clinton, significantly raised the percentage of a national audience a corporation was allowed to reach. It also raised the limits on the number of media outlets one corporation could hold.[16] President Trump's FCC chair has relaxed rules preventing media consolidation, making it possible for news sources to be held by fewer and fewer companies.[17] In 2018 a federal court decision paved the way for even further consolidation when it approved the $85 billion merger between AT&T and Time Warner.[18] Figure 16.3 is a graphic illustrating media consolidation, using 2011 data as a starting point, although several companies have changed hands since.

This means that national and even local news coverage is dictated from afar—and by business leaders, not by journalists on the ground.[19] Corporate executives make financial decisions that impact how the news is reported. The ability of the media to control the policy agenda means some issues will get more attention than others. News about human rights, climate change, and foreign affairs is often ignored or underreported.[20]

16.2 Explain how consolidation and ideologically driven news media have impacted the delivery of the news.

REMEMBER
- Some efforts to regulate the news media have focused on ownership; others have focused on content.
- The Radio Act of 1927 established the Federal Communications Commission (FCC) and required broadcasters to obtain licenses.
- The Telecommunications Act of 1996 modified regulations on media ownership and led to a period of consolidation.
- Social media challenges the ability to ensure fairness and equal coverage of opposing viewpoints.

KNOW *media consolidation*: the concentration of ownership of the media into fewer corporations. (p. 515)

THINK
- Should the government regulate the broadcast media to ensure fair and equal treatment of candidates?

16.2 Review Question: Free Response

Consolidation

1983

50

In 1983, 90% of American media was owned by 50 companies

2011

6

In 2011, that same 90% is controlled by 6 companies

These six companies are:

COMCAST
Notable properties:
- NBC
- Universal Pictures
- Focus Features

NEWS CORP
Notable properties:
- Fox
- *Wall Street Journal*
- *New York Post*

DISNEY
Notable properties:
- ABC
- ESPN
- Pixar
- Miramax
- Marvel Studios

VIACOM
Notable properties:
- MTV
- Nick Jr.
- BET
- CMT
- Paramount Pictures

TIME WARNER
Notable properties:
- CNN
- HBO
- *TIME*
- Warner Bros.

CBS
Notable properties:
- Showtime
- Smithsonian Channel
- NFL.com
- *Jeopardy*
- *60 Minutes*

Data from Business Insider

Use the chart and your knowledge of U.S. Government and Politics to answer parts A, B, and C.

A. Define media consolidation.

B. Describe one way in which media consolidation has an impact on the amount of political information available to citizens.

C. Explain one reason why media consolidation may increase political polarization.

16.3 How the Media Shape American Politics Today

Earlier in the chapter, we explored historical attempts to regulate the American news media and how those efforts were driven by changes in technology, which drove changes in how citizens access the news and the structure of news organizations themselves. Today is no different. The more power the media have, the more concern there is about who is providing political news and whether or not they are fair and unbiased.

The Political Perils of the New Media

One of the most important developments in the Internet age has been the rise of social media outlets, such as Facebook and Twitter. These interactive media environments allow individuals to create or share text, image, and video as well as comment on content and forward it to other members of their personal networks. We have already discussed the effects of new technologies in supporting citizen journalism and addressed concerns about the ability to verify reports for accuracy. Politicians can now easily and directly communicate to citizens through Facebook, Instagram, and Twitter. President Trump, for example, has millions of followers on his Twitter account.

For politicians, however, there is another worry. As they are often acting and speaking in a sea of cell-phone cameras, they must always be aware that any spontaneous, off-the-cuff remarks might be posted on YouTube or Facebook within minutes. The use of social media as the main source of political news has grown tremendously in recent years, and these trends show strong generational differences (as shown in Figure 16.4).

FIGURE 16.4

Generational Differences in Main Sources of Political News

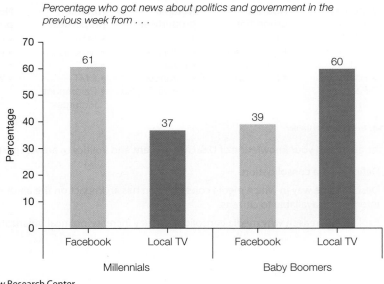

Percentage who got news about politics and government in the previous week from . . .

Data from Pew Research Center

The New Media and the Reshaping of What Is News

The pressure to attract an audience in a marketplace with so many easily accessible alternatives has led news outlets to focus on infotainment, the merging of information and entertainment in a way designed to attract viewers and gain market share. This dynamic includes pressures to provide soft news, stories that focus on celebrities, personalities, and entertaining events rather than on events of local, national, or international political or economic significance.

There are other concerns with the merging of news with entertainment. Scholars have found that viewership of political comedy shows, such as *The Daily Show*, may decrease individuals' support for the government, exposing them to political issues but increasing cynicism in the process.[21] There are also concerns that soft news may decrease the amount of knowledge about public affairs—knowledge that is necessary for effective democratic governance.[22]

Bias and Coverage of the News

Some claim the American news media has a **partisan bias**. Those who believe the media have a liberal bias point out that journalists are more likely to self-identify as liberal than members of the general population.[23] Others claim that even though most journalists are liberal, they are supposed to operate under norms and professional expectations that reward objectivity. Finally, the perception that the media are politically biased might be shaped by certain media outlets that run stories on the "biased media," thereby encouraging their readers, listeners, or viewers to believe a bias exists.[24] The percentage of Americans who think that there is a "great deal" of political bias in the news has risen recently, fueled by repeated claims made by politicians and political commentators.

Concerns about bias in the media have been accompanied by a lack of trust in the news sources. Confidence in television news, in particular, has fallen dramatically (Figure 16.5).

partisan bias
the slanting of political news coverage in support of a particular political party or ideology.

AP® TIP

Be prepared to explain how partisan news media, perceptions of bias, and the decline of trust in confidence in the news media impact government and politics.

FIGURE 16.5

Americans' Assessment of Bias in the News Media

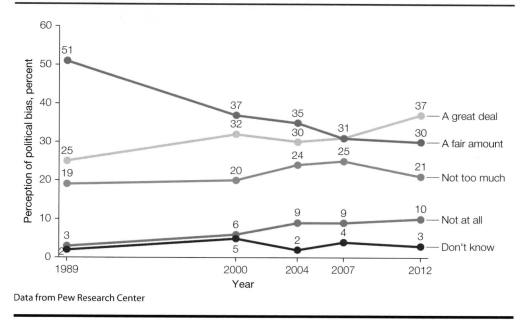

Data from Pew Research Center

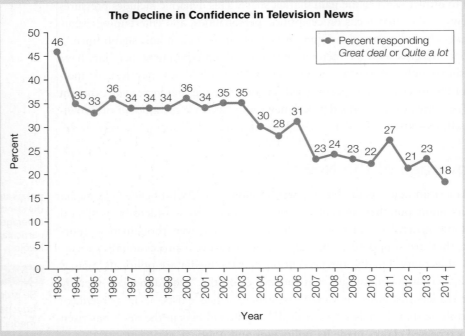

The Decline in Confidence in Television News

Percent responding *Great deal* or *Quite a lot*

Data from Gallup

It is important to read political science graphs and charts with a critical eye. The graph tracks the decline in confidence in political news on television, but it does not draw any conclusions about why trust in television news has declined.

1. The graph tracks data from respondents who said they trust the news "a great deal/or quite a lot." Explain whether or not these data are the best way to measure whether trust in the news has declined.

2. Describe one other piece of information that would be useful in determining whether trust in TV news has declined.

3. Explain how a political scientist might gather information about the reasons for the decline of trust in TV news.

4. Describe the most useful way to convey information about the reasons for the decline of trust in the television news, and explain whether you would use a graph, bar chart, or another type of visual representation.

When thinking about bias in news coverage, we should not ignore one of the most important potential sources of the problem: us. The news media—even outlets that are operated as nonprofit entities—need to attract an audience. They need us to listen to and watch what they are producing, and they shape their coverage accordingly. Some news outlets pursue inflammatory, sensational coverage to secure their corner of the marketplace.

Stories about government regulation or public policies are often seen as boring narratives that will not attract a large audience, unless a major disaster or event shines a spotlight on some underlying problem. In a competitive marketplace, news is based on providing interesting narratives—stories that we want to read, hear, watch, and re-tweet. It is easy to criticize the news media for failing to report on the "important stories." However, very few people would watch the "Federal Bureaucracy Channel."

The Media as Shapers of Political Campaigns and Elections

The drive to attract an audience shapes how media outlets cover political campaigns and elections, and it affects how candidates try to present themselves. When covering political campaigns, news outlets may focus on the latest polls. Emphasizing the drama of who is winning, rather than the policy differences between candidates, is called **horse-race journalism**. Scandals also sell, tempting media outlets to focus on wrongdoing and crowding out discussions of policy, a pattern that political scientist Larry Sabato has called a "feeding frenzy."[25]

Candidates and politicians are not bystanders in the coverage of politics; they actively try to shape the media's agenda. Politicians and their staff members try to get their message out and shape how viewers will react to it. The goal is to control the message, sometimes obsessively, by focusing on one message per news cycle, per day. Allowing or restricting access by journalists is also a strategic decision, made according to which choice seems most likely to "spin" a story in the desired way.

A Digital Divide?

At first glance, the proliferation of news sources in the twenty-first century might help Americans become more informed about government and politics. Americans who were previously disconnected from the political process might become interested in American politics by connecting with friends and family in their social networks. It may not be that simple. People do not use new media in the same way. According to political scientist Markus Prior, the new technologies and media avenues may be dividing Americans, making them more partisan.[26] Some people may follow the news more closely, but others may avoid news entirely because there are so many other forms of digital entertainment available to them.[27]

Perhaps more worrisome, Americans with the skills to navigate this "Brave New World"[28] of multiple media options may benefit from the increased access to information, but those who cannot, or choose not to, may be left behind. The Internet, according to Prior, "has widened gaps in news exposure, political knowledge, and turnout between those who like news and those who prefer entertainment."[29] Older, low-income, rural, Spanish-speaking, and disabled Americans are less likely to make use of the Internet, as are those with lower levels of educational attainment.[30] We call these gaps the digital divide.

horse-race journalism coverage of political campaigns that focuses more on the drama of the campaign than on policy issues.

Presidential candidate Donald Trump appears with Jimmy Fallon on the *Tonight Show*. Reaching audiences through popular TV shows is a way for candidates to gain exposure to viewers who might not otherwise be tuned into political news.
NBC

Do the media make us more knowledgeable about politics? In a study published in 2007, the Pew Research Center reported the findings of a study of Americans' political knowledge and media use.[31] Part of the study was a political knowledge quiz, in which the roughly 1,500 respondents were asked to identify individuals and answer questions about the U.S. government. According to the poll results, more Americans could identify Beyoncé Knowles and Peyton Manning than Barack Obama, who was running for president at the time.

Shown here is a more recent bar chart, based on 2017 data. How well-informed are Americans?

1. Describe a conclusion about Americans' level of political knowledge based on the data shown in the bar chart.

2. Explain how the media's role in setting the policy agenda is reflected in the data shown in the bar chart.

3. Explain one reason why many respondents could not identify important political figures, even though Americans have more access to news sources than at any time in history.

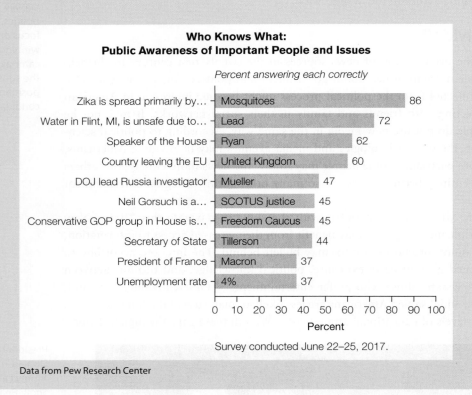

Who Knows What:
Public Awareness of Important People and Issues

Percent answering each correctly

Question	Answer	Percent
Zika is spread primarily by…	Mosquitoes	86
Water in Flint, MI, is unsafe due to…	Lead	72
Speaker of the House	Ryan	62
Country leaving the EU	United Kingdom	60
DOJ lead Russia investigator	Mueller	47
Neil Gorsuch is a…	SCOTUS justice	45
Conservative GOP group in House is…	Freedom Caucus	45
Secretary of State	Tillerson	44
President of France	Macron	37
Unemployment rate	4%	37

Survey conducted June 22–25, 2017.

Data from Pew Research Center

A Credibility Divide?

Traditional news media, citizen journalism, and comedy satire programs can provide useful information to viewers. Yet it can be difficult to sort credible sources from those that are poorly researched, inaccurate, biased, or satirical. More than ever, it's our job to view the news with a critical eye. It's our job as Americans to stay informed. In our representative democracy, the news media provide a critical link between citizens and government.

16.3 Explain the debate over the impact of bias in the news and how the media shape political understanding and behaviors.

REMEMBER
- With the proliferation of news sources, media outlets are under pressure to draw audiences, increase ratings, and raise revenue for the network and its owners.
- The media have a powerful role in setting the political agenda, which has an impact on which issues the public and government are paying attention to.
- The media often focus more on campaign strategy and on who is winning or losing, rather than the substance of policy.
- Multiple media options increase access to information, but a digital divide exists for low-income, rural, Spanish-speaking, and disabled Americans, making it harder for them to access political information.

KNOW
- *partisan bias*: the slanting of political news coverage in support of a particular political party or ideology. (p. 519)
- *horse-race journalism*: coverage of political campaigns that focuses more on the drama of the campaign rather than on policy issues. (p. 521)

THINK
How should we balance freedom of the press with the public's desire for access to credible, unbiased information?

16.3 Review Question: FREE RESPONSE

Consider the broadcast networks' desperate struggle to hold on to an ever-shrinking news audience. The problem is not that shallow, loud, or negative coverage of politics causes viewers to tune out in disgust. It's that for many people shallow, loud entertainment offers greater satisfaction, and it always has. Now, such entertainment is available around the clock and in unprecedented variety. Television viewers have not abandoned the evening news out of frustration—they just found something more enjoyable.
—**Markus Prior**[32]

Use the quote and your knowledge of U.S. Government and Politics to answer parts A, B, and C.

A. Describe the viewpoint expressed in the quote.

B. Explain one reason why the expansion of news sources has not increased Americans' knowledge of government and politics.

C. Explain one reason why the media's role in setting the policy agenda is important in a representative democracy.

Chapter 16 Review

AP® KEY CONCEPTS

- *news media* (p. 508)
- *social media* (p. 508)
- *agenda setting* (p. 508)
- *mass media* (p. 510)
- *wire service* (p. 510)
- *investigative journalism* (p. 510)
- *broadcast media* (p. 510)
- *media consolidation* (p. 515)
- *partisan bias* (p. 519)
- *horse-race journalism* (p. 521)

MULTIPLE-CHOICE QUESTIONS

Question 1 refers to this quote from a newspaper.

> A poll conducted by JMC Analytics finds that Roy Moore is ahead in the Alabama special election by five percentage points. According to the poll, Moore holds a 48–43 lead.[33]

1. The excerpt is an example of
   A. agenda setting.
   B. biased journalism.
   C. horse-race journalism.
   D. partisan reporting.

Questions 2 and 3 refer to the graph.

Thirty-Year Decline of Viewers of Television Evening News

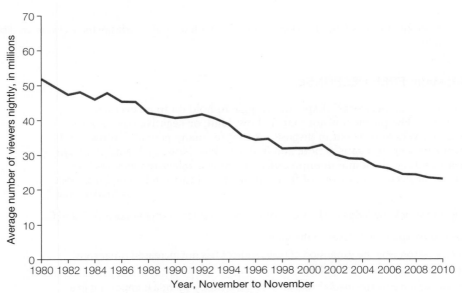

Data from Pew Research Center and Nielsen Media Research

2. The graph supports which of the following conclusions?
   A. Americans know less about government and politics than they did thirty years ago.
   B. While fewer people are watching nightly newscasts, there is an increase in the number of people watching cable newscasts.
   C. Americans are watching fewer news reports than they did thirty years ago.
   D. The number of people watching the evening news has declined over the past thirty years.

3. Which of the following best describes the impact of new media on the trend shown in the graph?
   A. Americans have more news sources available to them than they did thirty years ago, and fewer Americans watch the nightly news.
   B. Americans are less interested in politics than they were thirty years ago.
   C. Nightly news shows have always been biased, and Americans are turning to other sources for unbiased news.
   D. There are fewer nightly national newscasts and more local newscasts.

Not so long ago, we had a superb public school system, but now we trail most countries. In math, we're thirty-eighth in the world among developed countries in terms of how 15-year-olds perform. And it's getting worse, not better.

—F. H. Buckley, Fox News[34]

4. The excerpt is an example of the role of the media in

 A. partisan reporting.

 B. agenda setting.

 C. investigating corruption.

 D. electioneering.

Partisanship and Impartiality: How the Audience Rates the News

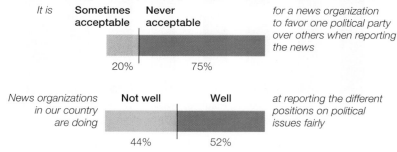

	Sometimes acceptable	Never acceptable	
It is	20%	75%	*for a news organization to favor one political party over others when reporting the news*

	Not well	Well	
News organizations in our country are doing	44%	52%	*at reporting the different positions on political issues fairly*

Note: Percentages are global medians based on 38 countries.
Data from Pew Research Center and the Spring 2017 Global Attitudes Survey

5. The bar chart supports which of the following conclusions?

 A. Most viewers prefer impartial reporting of political news.

 B. Most Americans believe the news media is biased.

 C. Most newscasts are biased toward a political party.

 D. There has been a loss of trust and confidence in the credibility of news sources.

Matt Wuerker Editorial Cartoon used with the permission of Matt Wuerker and the Cartoonist Group. All rights reserved.

6. The cartoon refers to which of the following?

 A. The growth of cable TV programming

 B. The increasing threat of partisan bias in the news

 C. Increasing concentration of media sources among fewer providers

 D. The fusion of news programming with entertainment

Questions 7 and 8 refer to the bar chart.

Adoption of Broadband by Demographic Group, 2013

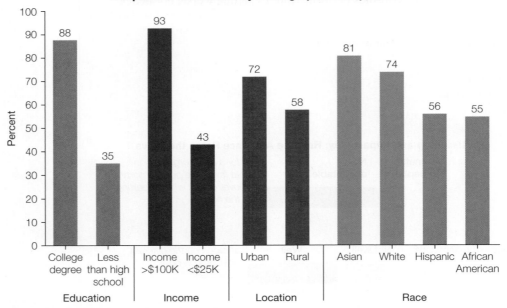

Data from White House Broadband Report, June 2013

7. The bar chart supports which of the following conclusions?

   A. White households have a higher percentage of broadband access than any other group.

   B. Rural Americans are half as likely to have broadband access as people living in urban areas.

   C. Those with college degrees are more than twice as likely to have broadband access as those who did not graduate from high school.

   D. Hispanic Americans have less access to broadband than any other group.

8. Which of the following statements best describes a direct consequence of the information shown on the bar chart?

   A. Those with higher incomes are more likely to vote than low-income individuals.

   B. Rural Americans are less interested in politics than people who live in cities.

   C. Asian Americans have the highest levels of education of all groups.

   D. Lack of access to technology makes it more difficult for some groups to access political information.

By permission of Chip Bok and Creators Syndicate, Inc.

9. The cartoon expresses which of the following viewpoints?

   A. Fox News has a partisan bias toward conservatives.

   B. MSNBC has a partisan bias against Republicans.

   C. The media have an important role in agenda setting.

   D. The media focus too much on horse-race journalism.

...a hereditary chief strictly limited, the right of war vested in the legislative body, a rigid economy of the public contributions, and absolute interdiction of all useless expences, will go far towards keeping the government honest and unoppressive. But the only security of all is in a free press. [T]he force of public opinion cannot be resisted, when permitted freely to be expressed. [T]he agitation it produces must be submitted to. [I]t is necessary to keep the waters pure. [W]e are all, for example in agitation even in our peaceful country. [F]or in peace as well as in war the mind must be kept in motion.

—**Thomas Jefferson to Marquis de Lafayette, November 4, 1823**[35]

10. The quote expresses which of the following viewpoints?

 A. A free press must be impartial and not favor one political party over another.

 B. The rights of a free press must be balanced with the need for public order and security.

 C. A free press is necessary to keep Americans secure from foreign influence.

 D. Freedom must outweigh stability in protecting the rights of the press.

FREE-RESPONSE QUESTIONS

Politics and Social Media, 2016: Fatigue Factor?
Social media users are stressed out by political content and opinions

Opinion of users about the amount of politics they find on social media, percent

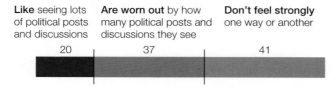

Like seeing lots of political posts and discussions — 20
Are worn out by how many political posts and discussions they see — 37
Don't feel strongly one way or another — 41

How socal-media users describe discussions of politics with people they disagree with, percent

Interesting and informative — 35
Stressful and frustrating — 59

How much they find in common with people they disagree with, percent

More in common politically — 29
Less in common politically — 64

Note: Survey conducted July 12–August 8, 2016.
Data from Pew Research Center

1. Use the bar charts and your knowledge of U.S. Government and Politics to answer parts A, B, and C.

 A. Describe one finding shown in the bar charts about the impact of social media on viewers of political news.

 B. Describe one way in which social media has changed the way news is delivered.

 C. Explain one reason why viewers of news on social media may have less trust and confidence in news sources than viewers of traditional nightly TV newscasts.

President Donald Trump has made unprecedented use of his personal Twitter account to make announcements about his administration and to express his political views and criticize his opponents. His followers have the opportunity to engage in political commentary through their responses. The president blocked certain followers based on their posts criticizing the president and his stance on the issues. The Knight First Amendment Institute at Columbia University brought a lawsuit challenging the president's actions in blocking certain Twitter followers.

In May 2018, in *Knight First Amendment Institute at Columbia University v. Donald Trump* the U.S. District Court for the Southern District of New York ruled that President Trump may not block Twitter followers.[36]

2. Use the scenario and your knowledge of U.S. Government and Politics to answer parts A, B, and C.

  A. Identify the constitutional clause that is common to both *Knight First Amendment Institute at Columbia University v. Donald Trump* (2018) and *New York Times Co. v. United States* (1971).

  B. Based on the constitutional clause identified in part A, explain why the facts of *Knight First Amendment Institute at Columbia University v. Donald Trump* led to a ruling similar to that in *New York Times Co. v. United States*.

  C. Describe one way in which the facts of the *Knight First Amendment* case differ from those in *New York Times Co. v. United States*, and explain how this difference might lead a court to overturn the *Knight First Amendment* case on appeal.

ARGUMENTATION QUESTION

The media have become increasingly diverse, and partisan news channels attract viewers who tend to agree with their viewpoints. Does partisan news reporting endanger American representative democracy?

In your essay:

- Articulate a claim or thesis that responds to the prompt, and use a line of reasoning to defend it.
- Use at least TWO pieces of relevant and accurate evidence to support your claim.
- At least ONE piece of evidence must be from one of the listed foundational documents:

  Constitution of the United States

  Federalist No. 10

- Use a second piece of evidence from another foundational document from the list or from your study of the Constitution, civil liberties, and the media.
- Use reasoning to explain why the evidence you provided supports your claim or thesis.
- Use refutation, concession, or rebuttal to respond to an opposing or alternative perspective.

CRITICAL THINKING PROJECT

Many people are worried that news reporting is too biased. Bias can have several negative effects on government and politics. It may reinforce viewers' political preferences, increasing polarization. It may cause some viewers to lose interest in politics. It may make it hard to know whether or not information is trustworthy.

1. Pick a news story that has happened in the past two weeks. Choose a topic involving U.S. government and politics that interests you.
2. Read a least four different news articles about the story from different perspectives. Fox News offers a conservative perspective, while MSNBC is liberal. Highlight examples of bias in each of the stories you read.
3. Write your own article about the topic. Be sure to include verifiable facts about what happened, as well as both liberal and conservative perspectives on the topic. Clearly separate fact from opinion.
4. Create a headline that will grab viewers' attention and give them a preview of the topic.
5. Include a picture, with a caption, that captures viewers' attention.

Your article should demonstrate that it is possible to write balanced, informative news stories, without boring your audience.

AP® EXAM PRACTICE and Critical Thinking Project

MULTIPLE-CHOICE QUESTIONS

Questions 1 and 2 refer to the quote.

> Several commentators . . . have called the current generation of voter ID laws "a solution in search of a problem." But that doesn't give enough respect to the argument that we should as a nation strive to be as accurate as possible with our voting.[1]
>
> —Andrew Cohen

1. Which of the following best summarizes the viewpoint expressed in the quote?

  A. Voter ID laws are unnecessary because there is not much evidence of fraud at the polls.

  B. Even though some people don't think they are necessary, voter ID laws may help officials make sure election results are fair.

  C. States should not pass voter ID laws because they are expensive.

  D. Voter ID laws are important to prevent those who are unregistered from attempting to vote.

2. Which of the following is a criticism of the viewpoint expressed in the quote?

  A. The federal government should determine the qualifications for voting, rather than the states.

  B. Voter ID laws are necessary because voting fraud undermines the government's legitimacy.

  C. Voter ID laws disproportionately impact minority and poor voters, making it difficult for them to exercise their right to vote.

  D. Voter ID laws disproportionately impact the elderly because many of them have driver's licenses.

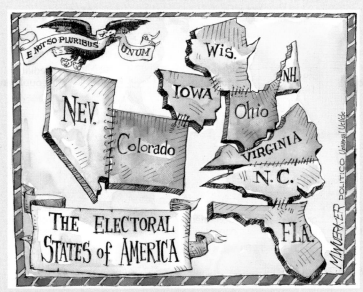

3. The cartoon expresses which of the following viewpoints?

  A. Small states are overrepresented in the Electoral College as a percentage of their population.

  B. Election outcomes are driven by a few key battleground and swing states.

  C. Campaigns focus too much on states in the East and South, ignoring Western states.

  D. The winner-take-all feature of the Electoral College unfairly disadvantages small states.

4. Select the pair of responses that explains why the election system results in a two-party system:

Presidential elections	Congressional elections
A. Electoral College	Proportional representation
B. Presidential primaries	Reapportionment
C. Winner-take-all feature	Single member plurality districts
D. Direct elections	Nonpartisan redistricting

Questions 5 and 6 refer to the graphs.

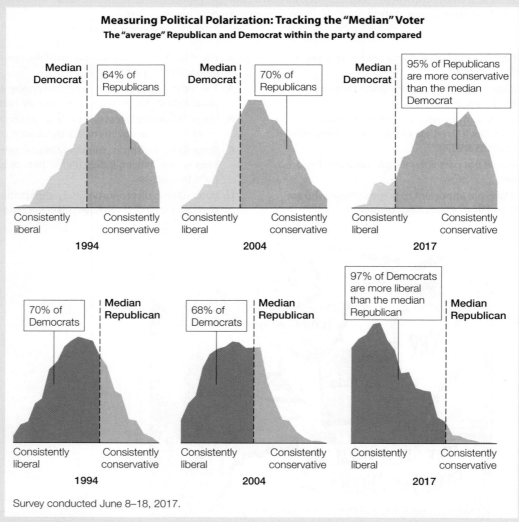

Measuring Political Polarization: Tracking the "Median" Voter
The "average" Republican and Democrat within the party and compared

Survey conducted June 8–18, 2017.

Data from Pew Research Center

5. The graphs support which of the following conclusions?
   A. From 1994 to 2017, both political parties adopted more centrist positions.
   B. In 2017, the average Democrat moved farther away from the center than the average Republican.
   C. Campaigns by Bernie Sanders and Donald Trump attracted voters outside the mainstream of their parties.
   D. Members of the Democratic and Republican Parties are becoming more polarized.

6. The trend shown in the graphs is likely to lead to what result?
   A. Gridlock, as a result of divided government
   B. Bipartisanship, as a result of split-ticket voting
   C. Party realignment, resulting in a critical election
   D. More reliance on superdelegates by both parties

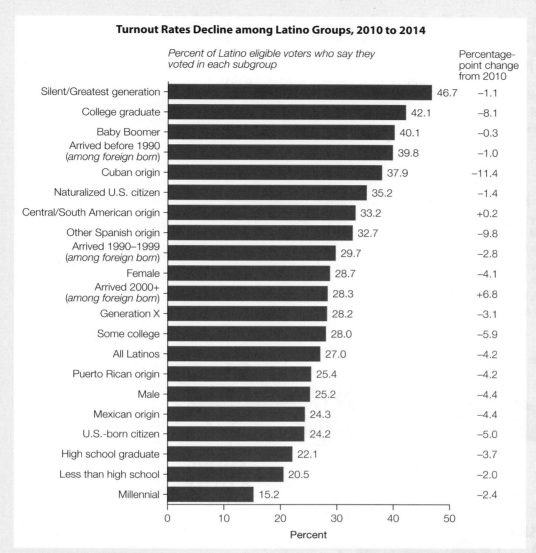

Turnout Rates Decline among Latino Groups, 2010 to 2014

Percent of Latino eligible voters who say they voted in each subgroup

	Percent	Percentage-point change from 2010
Silent/Greatest generation	46.7	−1.1
College graduate	42.1	−8.1
Baby Boomer	40.1	−0.3
Arrived before 1990 (*among foreign born*)	39.8	−1.0
Cuban origin	37.9	−11.4
Naturalized U.S. citizen	35.2	−1.4
Central/South American origin	33.2	+0.2
Other Spanish origin	32.7	−9.8
Arrived 1990–1999 (*among foreign born*)	29.7	−2.8
Female	28.7	−4.1
Arrived 2000+ (*among foreign born*)	28.3	+6.8
Generation X	28.2	−3.1
Some college	28.0	−5.9
All Latinos	27.0	−4.2
Puerto Rican origin	25.4	−4.2
Male	25.2	−4.4
Mexican origin	24.3	−4.4
U.S.-born citizen	24.2	−5.0
High school graduate	22.1	−3.7
Less than high school	20.5	−2.0
Millennial	15.2	−2.4

Data from Pew Research Center

7. The bar chart supports which of the following conclusions?

   A. Cuban Americans have the highest voter turnout rates among other groups of Latino ethnicity.

   B. Turnout is higher among Latinos born in the United States than it is among naturalized citizens.

   C. Latino turnout is lower than voter turnout for other ethnic groups.

   D. Latino voter turnout is higher among those who arrived after 2000 than among those who arrived before that time.

Almost all millennials think people like them can have an impact in the U.S. to make it a better place to live. Only 5 percent of respondents do not think people like them can have an impact at all. As with other trends, male millennials more than female millennials believe a person can have a big impact in the U.S.[2]   —Ryan Scott

8. The quote refers to which of the following?
   A. Partisan attachment
   B. Political socialization
   C. Political ideology
   D. Political efficacy

---

9. How do participants in primaries and caucuses differ from voters in a general election?
   A. They are more likely to support a centrist candidate so that their party has the best chance of winning the general election.
   B. They are more likely to identify as independent or nonaffiliated.
   C. They are more likely to favor candidates on the far right or the far left compared to voters in the general election.
   D. They are more likely to split their tickets in the general election by voting for candidates from different parties for different offices.

Dave Granlund/Cagle Cartoons

10. The cartoon expresses which of the following viewpoints?
   A. The New Hampshire primary has too much influence because New Hampshire is a rural state.
   B. Primaries are more important than caucuses because voters may choose from a wide variety of candidates.
   C. It is difficult for voters in New Hampshire to choose their party's nominee because the field of candidates has not been narrowed down.
   D. Primaries are important because they help candidates decide whether or not to stay in the race for their party's nomination.

Questions 11 and 12 refer to the quote.

People matter politically only as members of groups, and groups matter only when they act, but political life is complicated: nobody is a member of only one interest group, and no interest group stands apart from other groups and behaves in a single, consistent way. Alliances are constantly shifting. No realm of government is immune to interest-group pressures, including the judiciary.[3]
—Nicholas Lemann

11. Which of the follow theories of interest groups is expressed in the quote?

A. elitism

B. pluralism

C. republicanism

D. factionalism

12. According to the quote, how do interest groups interact with the government?

A. Interest groups try to influence all three branches of government.

B. Interest groups focus on the judiciary.

C. Interest groups that are weak in one resource may be strong in another resource.

D. Members of Congress are often aligned with several different interest groups.

Omaha World-Herald

13. The cartoon refers to which of the following?

A. Lobbying by interest groups

B. The decision in *Citizens United v. Federal Election Commission* (2010)

C. Interest groups that help candidates write their campaign speeches

D. Politicians who act as "free riders" in taking interest group donations

———————

For me, the overarching issue here is that we need regulatory agencies that are standing up for us [instead of hiring former employees of] Monsanto, and then suddenly Monsanto lobbyists are in charge of telling us whether GMOs are good for our food or not.
—Jill Stein[4]

14. The quote refers to

A. the revolving door.

B. grassroots lobbying by powerful interest groups.

C. campaign contributions by wealthy interest groups.

D. social movements on behalf of consumer safety.

The Catholic bishops of the United States have long and consistently supported the right of workers to organize for purposes of collective bargaining. Because this right is substantially weakened by so-called right-to-work laws, many bishops—in their dioceses, through their state conferences, and through their national conference—have opposed or cast doubt on such laws, and no U.S. bishop has expressed support for them.

—Statement of the Catholic Church filed in *Janus v. American Federation of State, County and Municipal Employees*[5]

15. The statement is an example of
- **A.** an direct lobbying tactic.
- **B.** a brief filed by a petitioner.
- **C.** an amicus curiae brief.
- **D.** an excerpt from a Supreme Court opinion.

Questions 16 and 17 refer to the data in the table.

Sources of Stories and Their Geographic Focus: A Study of Eight Newspapers

	National	Foreign affairs	Local
Washington, D.C.-based staff	12 %	12 %	4 %
Non-D.C. staff	28 %	6 %	9 %
Wire services	63 %	25 %	1 %
Other national media	56 %	31 %	1 %

Data from Pew Research Center

16. The table supports which of the following conclusions?
- **A.** Wire services are more likely to cover foreign affairs than all other media outlets.
- **B.** Most national news reporters are based in Washington, D.C.
- **C.** Local news is not as important to consumers as national news.
- **D.** Wire services cover more national news than other media outlets.

17. Which of the following is a concern regarding the media's reliance on wire services?
- **A.** Broadcast news stories have become less diverse.
- **B.** Local news channels are less likely to cover community events and news.
- **C.** Wire services are more biased than cable news channels.
- **D.** Wire services have little time to fact-check stories in their rush to convey breaking news.

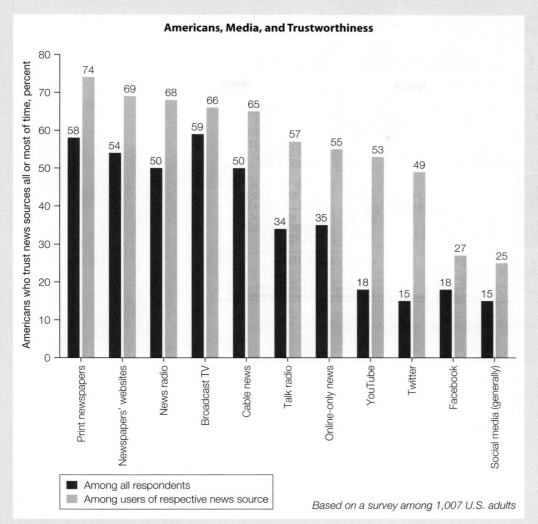

Americans, Media, and Trustworthiness

Americans who trust news sources all or most of time, percent

Source	Among all respondents	Among users of respective news source
Print newspapers	58	74
Newspapers' websites	54	69
News radio	50	68
Broadcast TV	59	66
Cable news	50	65
Talk radio	34	57
Online-only news	35	55
YouTube	18	53
Twitter	15	49
Facebook	18	27
Social media (generally)	15	25

■ Among all respondents
▨ Among users of respective news source

Based on a survey among 1,007 U.S. adults

Data from Ipsos survey

18. The bar chart supports which of the following conclusions?
   A. Among all respondents, more trust print newspapers than they trust broadcast TV newscasts.
   B. Those who use Facebook trust it more than they trust YouTube.
   C. News radio has a higher level of trust than talk radio.
   D. More than half of all Americans have lost trust in in traditional news sources.

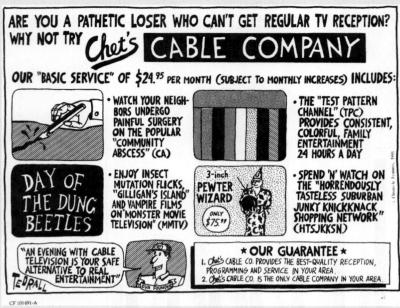

19. How does the topic addressed in the cartoon relate to government and politics?

   A. Because cable TV is not as regulated as broadcast TV, there are fewer news channels on cable.

   B. There are many viewing options on cable, and Americans can avoid the news entirely.

   C. Cable TV is ideologically biased, and viewers watch stations that confirm their viewpoints.

   D. Cable TV is expensive, which contributes to the digital divide between Americans living in rural and urban areas.

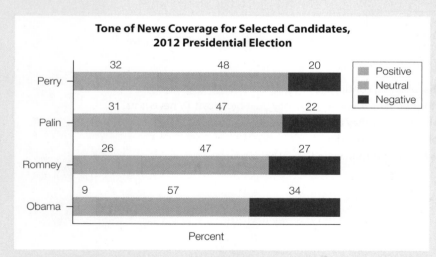

Date range: May 2 to October 9, 2011, for all candidates.

Data from Pew Research Center, Project for Excellence in Journalism

20. The bar chart supports which of the following conclusions?

   A. The tone of news coverage of President Obama was more negative than positive.

   B. More than half of news coverage of politicians is negative.

   C. Sarah Palin received more negative news coverage than the rest of the politicians.

   D. More than 60 percent of news coverage is neutral.

FREE-RESPONSE QUESTIONS

[A] lawsuit, which was filed last month, marks the first time AARP's legal team has sued a long-term care organization over alleged "patient dumping," in which providers evict residents in favor of more lucrative patients. Attorneys with the AARP Foundation called for a federal investigation into nursing home evictions in California last year; a citizens group also sued the state in 2015 over the practice.[6]

—Emily Mongon

1. Use the quote and your knowledge of U.S. Government and Politics to answer parts A, B, and C.

   A. Describe the tactic used by interest groups that is referred to in the excerpt.

   B. Explain one reason why an interest group might use the tactic you describe in part A.

   C. Identify another tactic used by interest groups to achieve their goals, and describe one reason why an interest group might use that tactic.

   ───────────

In 2012, Shaun McCutcheon donated to the Republican National Committee, state and local Republican committees, and individual candidates. The Bipartisan Campaign Reform Act limited the aggregate amount an individual could contribute during an election cycle. McCutcheon wanted to donate more than allowed under federal law. McCutcheon sued the Federal Election Commission arguing that the limits on the total amount of money an individual may donate during an election cycle violate the Constitution.

In *McCutcheon v. Federal Election Commission*,[7] the Supreme Court ruled in favor of McCutcheon on the ground that the aggregate spending limit forced donors to choose which candidates and issues they would be able to support during an election cycle.

2. Use the scenario and your knowledge of U.S. Government and Politics to answer parts A, B, and C.

   A. Identify the constitutional clause that is common to both *McCutcheon v. Federal Election Commission* (2014) and *Citizens United v. United States* (2010).

   B. Based on the constitutional clause identified in part A, explain why the Court reached a decision in *McCutcheon v. Federal Election Commission* that is similar to its decision in *Citizens United v. United States*.

   C. Describe one action an interest group might take in an effort to limit the impact of the Supreme Court's decisions in the *Citizens United* and *McCutcheon* cases.

ARGUMENTATION QUESTION

In a representative democracy, political parties are linkage institutions that connect citizens with government. Are modern political parties effective in connecting citizens with government and representing their interests in the policymaking process?

In your essay:

- Articulate a claim or thesis that responds to the prompt, and use a line of reasoning to defend it.

- Use at least TWO pieces of relevant and accurate evidence to support your claim.

- At least ONE piece of evidence must be from one of the listed foundational documents:

- Constitution of the United States

- *Federalist* No. 10

- *Federalist* No. 51

- Use a second piece of evidence from another foundational document from the list or from your study of political parties.

- Use reasoning to explain why the evidence you provided supports your claim or thesis.

- Use refutation, concession, or rebuttal to respond to an opposing or alternative perspective.

CRITICAL THINKING PROJECT

Throughout this class, you have learned about government and politics and about the importance of citizen participation in our representative democracy. At the beginning of a new year, people often make resolutions about what they hope to accomplish in the future. Now that you are at the end of this course, it's time to think about how you will participate in civic life in your future.

Successful resolutions include specific and measurable goals within a time frame. For example, "I will exercise more in the future" is not a very good resolution because it is vague. "I will run at least a mile twice a week for the next year" is a much better resolution because it is clear and measurable.

1. Think about what you have learned about U.S. government and politics and about how you plan to use this information to influence the system in the future.
2. Make a draft of three political resolutions that are specific and measurable over a period of time. For example, you might resolve to register to vote within three months of turning eighteen.
3. Review your resolutions and ask yourself if they are realistic.
4. Put your resolutions on paper. Add a border, pictures, words, sayings, and color to illustrate your thoughts.
5. Sign your resolutions and put them in a place where they can serve as a reminder that your actions can make a difference.

SECTION I: MULTIPLE-CHOICE QUESTIONS

Use the table of data to answer questions 1 and 2.

U.S. Population, by Age, Projected

Year	Population (thousands)				Percentage 65 or older
	All ages	Under 20	20–64	65 or older	
	Projected*				
2020	339,269	87,547	198,213	53,510	16
2040	376,856	92,268	207,416	77,172	20
2060	402,079	96,760	218,777	86,543	22
2080	428,214	101,159	230,137	96,918	23

Data from Social Security Administration, Board of Trustees, 2006

NOTE: For the purpose of this table, the U.S. population is the Social Security area population, comprising residents of the 50 states and the District of Columbia (adjusted for net census undercount); civilian residents of Puerto Rico, the Virgin Islands, Guam, American Samoa, and the Northern Mariana Islands; federal civilian employees and persons in the armed forces abroad and their dependents; crew members of merchant vessels; and all other U.S. citizens abroad.

* Projected using the intermediate assumptions in the 2006 annual report of the Board of Trustees of the Federal Old-Age and Survivors Insurance and Disability Insurance Trust Funds.

1. Which of the following is an accurate description of the projections provided in the table?
   A. By 2080, Americans over the age of 65 will be the largest age group in the U.S. population.
   B. The number of people under the age of 20 will decrease between 2020 and 2080.
   C. The total number of Americans will double between 2020 and 2080.
   D. There will be a steady increase in the number of Americans over the age of 65 between 2020 and 2080.

2. Which of the following describes the most likely effect of these projections on federal expenditures?
   A. Entitlement spending will decrease.
   B. Discretionary spending will decrease.
   C. Means-tested social welfare spending will increase.
   D. Defense spending will decrease.

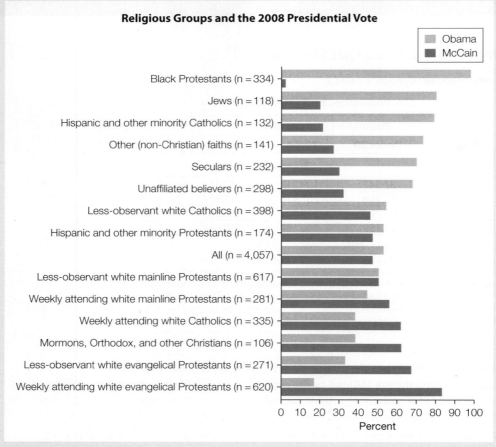

Data from Pew Research Center

3. The chart supports which of the following conclusions?

   A. Jewish voters were more likely to vote for Obama than black Protestants.

   B. Among those who attend church every week, white Catholics were more likely to vote for McCain than white evangelical Protestants.

   C. Unaffiliated believers were more likely to vote for Obama than McCain.

   D. Hispanic and other minority Catholics were more likely to vote for Obama than black Protestants.

4. Which of the following groups would the Republican Party most likely target in an effort to encourage them to switch the majority of their groups' votes to Republican candidates in the next election?

   A. Black Protestants

   B. Hispanic and other minority Protestants

   C. White evangelical Protestants

   D. Mormons, Orthodox, and other Christians

Use the bar chart to answer questions 5 and 6.

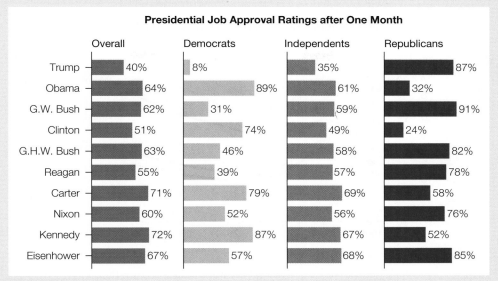

Presidential Job Approval Ratings after One Month

	Overall	Democrats	Independents	Republicans
Trump	40%	8%	35%	87%
Obama	64%	89%	61%	32%
G.W. Bush	62%	31%	59%	91%
Clinton	51%	74%	49%	24%
G.H.W. Bush	63%	46%	58%	82%
Reagan	55%	39%	57%	78%
Carter	71%	79%	69%	58%
Nixon	60%	52%	56%	76%
Kennedy	72%	87%	67%	52%
Eisenhower	67%	57%	68%	85%

Data from Gallup and NBC News

5. The bar chart best supports which of the following conclusions?

A. Most presidents enter office with an approval rating near 50 percent.

B. The approval ratings of presidents entering office have steadily dropped since the Eisenhower administration.

C. Presidents George H. W. Bush and Obama had similar approval ratings entering office.

D. Independents are more likely to show support for an incoming president than those affiliated with a political party.

6. Based on the information shown in the bar chart, which of the following best describes the impact of the public approval ratings on a president's ability to get the policies enacted that he favors?

A. A majority of both Democrats and Republicans approved of President Eisenhower, giving him a strong mandate to pass the policies he favored.

B. Divided government made it difficult for President Obama to get the policies he favored enacted.

C. It was easier for President Reagan to get policies passed at the beginning of his term than during the lame-duck period.

D. High public approval ratings among independent voters made it easier for President George H. W. Bush to get the policies he favored enacted.

Use the graph to answer questions 7 and 8.

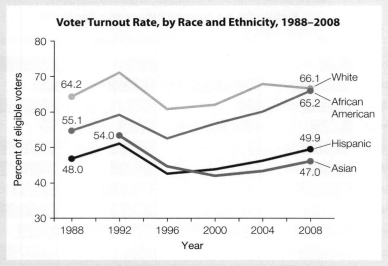

Voter Turnout Rate, by Race and Ethnicity, 1988–2008

Note: Whites include only non-Hispanic whites. Blacks include only non-Hispanic blacks. Asians include only non-Hispanic Asians. Native Americans and mixed-race groups not shown. Voter turnout rate for Asians not available prior to 1990. Data from Pew Research Center and Current Population Survey

7. The graph supports which of the following statements?

A. In 2008, the voter turnout among Hispanic Americans was lower than the voter turnout among Asian Americans.

B. The gap between voter turnout among white Americans and Hispanic Americans narrowed between1988 and 2008.

C. In the 2008 election, voter turnout among African Americans was greater than voter turnout among white Americans.

D. From 1998 to 2008, voter turnout among African Americans has been consistently higher than the voter turnout among Hispanic Americans.

8. Based on the chart, which of the following is likely to occur, assuming voting patterns among racial groups remain consistent?

A. America will have a minority-majority by 2040.

B. Electoral support for the Democratic Party will increase.

C. Electoral support for the Republican Party will increase.

D. There will be an increase in the percentage of independent voters.

Use the cartoon to answer questions 9 and 10.

Ann Telnaes Editorial Cartoon used with the permission of Ann Telnaes and the Cartoonist Group. All rights reserved.

9. Which of the following best describes the viewpoint in the cartoon?
   A. Those who donate large amounts of money to political campaigns have more influence than average citizens.
   B. Big corporations have more influence in policymaking than other interest groups.
   C. Members of Congress are unlikely to enact legislation favored by the majority of citizens.
   D. The First Amendment protects campaign donations by large corporations.

10. Which of the following Supreme Court cases is most relevant to the topic of the cartoon?
   A. *Shaw v. Reno* (1993)
   B. *New York Times Co. v. United States* (1971)
   C. *Baker v. Carr* (1962)
   D. *Citizens United v. Federal Election Commission* (2010)

Use the graph to answer questions 11 and 12.

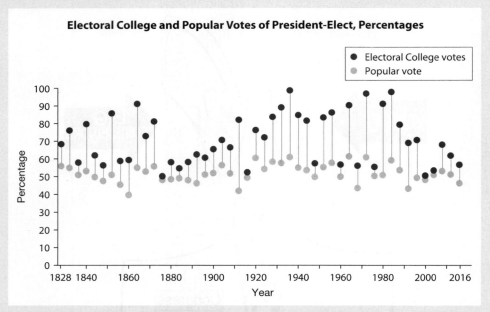

Electoral College and Popular Votes of President-Elect, Percentages

Data from Pew Research Center, National Archives, Dave Leip's Atlas of Presidential Elections, Dave Leip's *America Votes,* and *Washington Post*

11. The graph supports which of the following conclusions?

　A. In most presidential elections, the winning candidates receive a higher percentage of the popular vote than the percentage of votes they receive in the Electoral College.

　B. In most presidential elections, the percentage of the popular vote received by the winning candidate is similar to the percentage of votes they receive in the Electoral College.

　C. Most candidates who win the presidential election do so with slightly more than 50 percent of the votes in the Electoral College.

　D. Most candidates who win the presidential election receive a higher percentage of the Electoral College vote than the percentage they receive of the popular vote.

12. Which of the following best describes the impact of the Electoral College on campaign strategy?

　A. Candidates focus on building their base of voters in states that have traditionally supported their political party.

　B. States with the largest urban populations receive the most attention because it is more efficient for candidates to focus their attention on big cities.

　C. Candidates focus on battleground states.

　D. Candidates focus on states with the most votes in the Electoral College, regardless of how those states have voted in the past.

Steve Greenberg/Cartoonstock.com

13. Which of the following best describes the viewpoint in the cartoon?

    A. Nonpartisan committees should draw congressional district boundaries.

    B. Congressional districts are drawn into strange shapes to benefit political parties.

    C. The redistricting process is confusing for voters.

    D. It is a challenge to draw congressional district boundaries so that each district is roughly equal in population.

14. Which of the following Supreme Court cases is most relevant to the topic of the cartoon?

    A. *Baker v. Carr* (1962)

    B. *Citizens United v. Federal Election Commission* (2010)

    C. *McCulloch v. Maryland* (1819)

    D. *Schenck v. United States* (1919)

Use the map to answer questions 15 and 16.

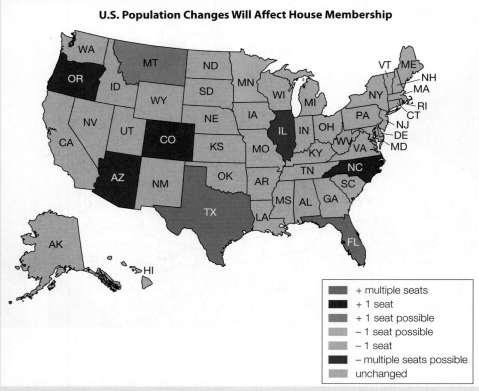

U.S. Population Changes Will Affect House Membership

Legend:
- + multiple seats
- + 1 seat
- + 1 seat possible
- − 1 seat possible
- − 1 seat
- − multiple seats possible
- unchanged

Data from U.S. Census Bureau, Election Data Services

15. According to the map, which region(s) will receive more seats in the House of Representatives following the 2020 census?

A. The South and Southwest

B. Midwestern states

C. Heavily populated areas on the East and West Coasts

D. States in the Great Lakes region

16. What is the likely effect of the changes shown on the map on political party representation?

A. The number of Democrats serving in the House of Representatives is likely to increase.

B. Rural areas will lose representation in the House of Representatives.

C. The number of Republicans serving in the House of Representatives is likely to increase.

D. Western states will become less influential in the House of Representatives.

A FIRM Union will be of the utmost moment to the peace and liberty of the States, as a barrier against domestic faction and insurrection. It is impossible to read the history of the petty republics of Greece and Italy without feeling sensations of horror and disgust at the distractions with which they were continually agitated, and at the rapid succession of revolutions by which they were kept in a state of perpetual vibration between the extremes of tyranny and anarchy. If they exhibit occasional calms, these only serve as short-lived contrast to the furious storms that are to succeed. If now and then intervals of felicity open to view, we behold them with a mixture of regret, arising from the reflection that the pleasing scenes before us are soon to be overwhelmed by the tempestuous waves of sedition and party rage. If momentary rays of glory break forth from the gloom, while they dazzle us with a transient and fleeting brilliancy, they at the same time admonish us to lament that the vices of government should pervert the direction and tarnish the lustre of those bright talents and exalted endowments for which the favored soils that produced them have been so justly celebrated.

—Alexander Hamilton, *Federalist* No. 9

17. Which of the following statements is most consistent with the author's argument in the passage?
    - **A.** A republican form of government is necessary to ensure tranquility.
    - **B.** State governments are likely to infringe on individual rights.
    - **C.** A strong national government is necessary to prevent turmoil.
    - **D.** Checks and balances will prevent tyranny.

18. Hamilton makes the argument that the constitution will
    - **A.** ensure peace and maintain order.
    - **B.** balance state and national power.
    - **C.** encourage pluralism.
    - **D.** foster participatory democracy.

19. Hamilton makes which of the following concessions?
    - **A.** At the time of the statement, the country was at peace and relatively free from turmoil.
    - **B.** The American republic is not as subject to corruption as Greece or Italy.
    - **C.** States are better able to represent the interests of their citizens than a large national government.
    - **D.** A bill of rights is necessary to protect individual liberties.

20. A critic of Hamilton's viewpoint in the passage would most likely support the ratification of which of the following amendments?
    - **A.** Second
    - **B.** Tenth
    - **C.** Seventh
    - **D.** Ninth

In this present crisis, government is not the solution to our problem; government is the problem. From time to time we've been tempted to believe that society has become too complex to be managed by self-rule, that government by an elite group is superior to government for, by, and of the people. Well, if no one among us is capable of governing himself, then who among us has the capacity to govern someone else? All of us together, in and out of government, must bear the burden. The solutions we seek must be equitable, with no one group singled out to pay a higher price.

We hear much of special interest groups. Well, our concern must be for a special interest group that has been too long neglected. It knows no sectional boundaries or ethnic and racial divisions, and it crosses political party lines. It is made up of men and women who raise our food, patrol our streets, man our mines and factories, teach our children, keep our homes, and heal us when we're sick—professionals, industrialists, shopkeepers, clerks, cabbies, and truck drivers. They are, in short, "We the people," this breed called Americans.　　　　　—Ronald Reagan, Inaugural Address, January 20, 1981

21. Which of the following statements is most consistent with the author's argument in the passage?

A. Participation by citizens is the foundation of American democracy.

B. Policymaking is complicated, and it is important to rely on the opinion of experts.

C. Special interest groups have too much influence in the policymaking process.

D. Democracy is superior to other forms of government.

22. Which of the following models of democracy is most consistent with the passage?

A. pluralist

B. elitist

C. participatory

D. factionalist

23. The passage refers directly to which constitutional principle?

A. states' rights in the Tenth Amendment

B. right to free speech in the First Amendment

C. popular sovereignty in the Preamble

D. supremacy clause in Article VI

24. Voter turnout in the United States is low when compared to other electoral democracies. On the other hand, interest groups have a significant impact in the policymaking process. Which of the following forms of democracy best describe this system?

   A. elite democracy

   B. republicanism

   C. participatory democracy

   D. pluralist democracy

25. In a letter to John Adams written in 1789, Thomas Jefferson stated that the Constitution should be a "living document." Jefferson supported the idea that the U.S. Constitution should expire every twenty years. This idea is most closely associated with which of the following constitutional provisions?

   A. supremacy clause in Article VI

   B. enumerated powers in Article I

   C. amendment process in Article V

   D. necessary and proper clause in Article I

26. The USA PATRIOT Act and subsequent legislation expanded the government's authority to monitor cell phone records. This increased surveillance ability most directly illustrates which of the concerns expressed during the debates over the ratification of the Constitution?

   A. The conflict between the power of the new central government to ensure order and protect the liberty of individuals.

   B. The balance between the power of the new central government and the powers left to state governments.

   C. The tension between having a strong president and creating too much power in the executive.

   D. The conflict between the right of privacy and the government's power to collect demographic information about citizens.

27. Which type of federal grants gives states the most flexibility in deciding how to spend federal money?

   A. block grants

   B. categorical grants

   C. formula grants

   D. project grants

28. Which of the following Supreme Court decisions increased the power of national government relative to the states?

   A. *United States v. Lopez* (1995)

   B. *McCulloch v. Maryland* (1819)

   C. *Schenck v. United States* (1919)

   D. *McDonald v. Chicago* (2010)

29. A member of Congress who wanted to be involved in the initial creation of tax legislation would request a position on which of the following committees?

   A. House Rules Committee

   B. Senate Appropriations Committee

   C. House Ways and Means Committee

   D. Senate Budget Committee

30. A majority vote is necessary to pass legislation in the Senate. However, unless sixty senators support a significant piece of legislation, it is unlikely to pass. This is a result of the process of

    A. placing a hold on a bill.
    B. presenting a motion for cloture.
    C. introducing a concurrent resolution.
    D. filing for a discharge petition.

31. Critics of the Civil Rights Act of 1964 argued that Congress did not have the constitutional authority to pass civil rights legislation. However, the Supreme Court decided that, based on Congress's authority to regulate interstate commerce, Congress may pass civil rights legislation.

    Which of the following constitutional provisions gives Congress the authority to extend its power under the commerce clause to pass civil rights legislation?

    A. due process clause in the Fourteenth Amendment
    B. supremacy clause in Article VI
    C. emoluments clause in Article I
    D. necessary and proper clause in Article I

32. The Supreme Court's decision in *Baker v. Carr*, which resulted in the "one person, one vote" doctrine, was the result of a challenge to

    A. voter registration laws.
    B. gerrymandering.
    C. voter identification laws.
    D. reapportionment.

33. Members of Congress who believe their main responsibility is to represent the wishes of their constituents are acting mainly as?

    A. delegates
    B. partisans
    C. politicos
    D. trustees

34. A president who wanted to carry out foreign policy without the advice and consent of the Senate would most likely use which of the following?

    A. treaties
    B. executive agreements
    C. executive orders
    D. signing statements

35. According to political scientists, over the last half-century, the power of most two-term presidents has declined during their second term in office. The decline in presidential power during a second term is most likely a result of the

    A. Fifteenth Amendment.
    B. Nineteenth Amendment.
    C. Twenty-Second Amendment.
    D. Twenty-Fifth Amendment.

36. Which of the following is a result of the decision in *Marbury v. Madison* (1803)?

    A. the Supreme Court's ability to act as a final court of appeal
    B. an expansion of the appellate jurisdiction of the federal courts
    C. an expansion of the Supreme Court's original jurisdiction
    D. the power of the Supreme Court to nullify an executive action or law passed by Congress

37. During the confirmation process, potential Supreme Court justices are often questioned about the degree to which they believe justices should adhere to stare decisis. Which of the following is the best description of the philosophy of strict adherence to stare decisis?

- **A.** Previous court decisions that result in unequal treatment under the law should be overturned.
- **B.** Justices should focus on the original intent of the Founding Fathers when interpreting the Constitution.
- **C.** Justices should be guided by the previous decisions made by the Supreme Court.
- **D.** The Constitution is a "living document" and justices should apply modern standards in interpreting it.

38. Which of the following is an accurate comparison of the demographic characteristics of a typical Democratic versus a typical Republican voter?

Democratic voter	Republican voter
A. over 65	under 30
B. African American	non-Cuban Hispanics
C. urban	rural
D. Evangelical Christian	Jewish

39. Which of the following is an accurate comparison of the nomination process used by the Democratic and Republican parties during the 2016 presidential nomination?

Democratic Party	Republican Party
A. open and closed primaries	closed primaries
B. primaries only	primaries and caucuses
C. candidates run on a ticket	candidates run independently
D. some superdelegates	delegates chosen by voters

40. Which of the following is an accurate comparison of political parties compared to interest groups?

Political parties	Interest groups
A. nominates candidates for public office	advocates for public policies
B. avoids taking stances on issues	educates the public on issues
C. forms super PACs	forms PACs
D. endorses candidates in campaigns	does not endorse candidates

41. Which of the following is an accurate comparison of the philosophies of judicial activism and judicial restraint?

Judicial activism	Judicial restraint
A. more likely to uphold precedent	less likely to uphold precedent
B. less likely to overturn legislative action	more likely to uphold legislative action
C. more likely to make bold new policy	less likely to create new policy
D. less likely to overturn executive action	more likely to overturn executive action

42. Which of the following accurately describes a demographic difference between those who are more likely to vote and those who less likely to vote?

Those more likely to vote	Those less likely to vote
A. college degree	high school diploma
B. low incomes	high incomes
C. male	female
D. hourly employees	union members

43. The policymaking process is often influenced by alliances of various interest groups and individuals who come together to promote a common policy agenda. Which of the following terms most accurately describes this type of broad alliance of interest groups and individuals who attempt to influence public policymaking?

   A. iron triangle
   B. issue network
   C. coalition
   D. social movement

44. The Supreme Court has consistently placed a high standard on any attempt by a government to restrict political speech or the press. In one of its most important decisions, the Court argued that the freedom of speech protection afforded in the First Amendment to the U.S. Constitution could only be restricted if the words spoken or printed represented a "clear and present danger." This "clear and present danger" doctrine was first established by which of the following Supreme Court decisions?

   A. *Engel v. Vitale* (1962)
   B. *Tinker v. Des Moines Independent Community School District* (1969)
   C. *New York Times Co. v. United States* (1971)
   D. *Schenck v. United States* (1919)

45. The Supreme Court originally ruled that the Bill of Rights only limited the actions of the federal government. Through a series of decisions over time, the Supreme Court has ruled that state governments may not infringe on individual liberties protected in the Bill of Rights.
   Which of the following correctly identifies the process that was used by the Supreme Court to gradually apply the Bill of Rights to the states?

   A. judicial review
   B. stare decisis
   C. selective incorporation
   D. judicial activism

46. The Supreme Court's decision in *Roe v. Wade,* which recognized a woman's right to an abortion while acknowledging the government interest in potential life, was based on which of the following implied rights?

   A. natural rights
   B. equal protection
   C. due process
   D. privacy

47. The Supreme Court's decision in *Brown v. Board of Education* (1954) was based mainly on which of the following?

   A. First Amendment, free exercise clause
   B. Fifth Amendment, due process clause
   C. Ninth Amendment, implied rights
   D. Fourteenth Amendment, equal protection clause

48. Which of the following has the greatest influence on the development of individuals' political attitudes and values?

   A. family
   B. education
   C. peer group
   D. media

49. Which of the following fiscal policies is consistent with Keynesian economic theory?

    A. reducing the number of federal government regulations on businesses

    B. increasing taxes for families at all income levels

    C. increasing government spending to spur economic activity

    D. lowering interest rates to encourage business investment

50. Which of the following would result in the most valid scientific public opinion poll about a policy issue?

    A. a voluntary poll of subscribers to an internet news source

    B. a poll conducted through random sampling techniques

    C. a representative sample of 1,000 Americans

    D. a poll that includes only registered voters

51. The framers of the Constitution designed the Senate to be less responsive to the will of the people than the House of Representatives. Over time, the Senate has become more responsive to public opinion. Which of the following amendments to the Constitution most directly increased the Senate's responsiveness to public opinion?

    A. Seventeenth Amendment

    B. Nineteenth Amendment

    C. Twenty-Fourth Amendment

    D. Twenty-Sixth Amendment

52. Many voters compare the issue positions of candidates and then vote based on their belief that when those candidates are elected they will work to pass the policies they advocated during the campaign. Which of the following best explains this type of voting behavior?

    A. party-line voting

    B. prospective voting

    C. rational-choice voting

    D. retrospective voting

53. Which of the following is a result of the single-member district system for electing members of the legislature, coupled with the winner-take-all feature in the Electoral College?

    A. The electoral system acts as a structural barrier to minor-party electoral success.

    B. The system makes it more likely that candidates from ethnic and racial minorities will be elected.

    C. It is difficult for third parties to run candidates for office.

    D. Third-party candidates are more likely to win seats in the House of Representatives than in the Senate.

54. Which of the following correctly describes the "free rider" problem faced by many interest groups?

    A. Interest groups have to form coalitions to get the policies they favor passed.

    B. People can join multiple interest groups, diluting the importance of individual interest groups.

    C. People can benefit from an interest group's public-policy work without becoming a member of that interest group.

    D. Interest groups endorse candidates, providing free advertising for campaigns.

55. Which of the following best describes the effect of the Supreme Court's decision in *Citizens United v. Federal Election Commission* (2010) on the financing of political campaigns?

    A. It is more difficult for corporations and labor unions to spend money because they must report their donations to the Federal Election Commission.

    B. It has allowed the federal government to increase its regulation of independent expenditures made by individuals or groups.

    C. It increased the amount of money PACs may donate directly to campaigns.

    D. It has led to increasing amounts of independent expenditures by Super PACs.

Directions: It is suggested that you take a few minutes to plan and outline each answer. It is also suggested that you spend approximately twenty minutes each on questions 1, 2, and 3 and forty minutes on question 4. Unless directions indicate otherwise, respond to all parts of all four questions. In your response, use substantive examples where appropriate.

> The Trump . . . presidency has brought a flurry of changes—both realized and anticipated—to U.S. environmental policy. Many of the actions roll back Obama-era policies that aimed to curb climate change and limit environmental pollution, while others threaten to limit federal funding for science and the environment.
> —Greshko, Parker, and Howard, *National Geographic*[1]

1. After reading the scenario, respond to parts A, B, and C.
   A. Describe a power Congress could use to address the comments outlined in the scenario.
   B. In the context of the scenario, explain how the use of the congressional power described in part A can be affected by its interaction with the presidency.
   C. In the context of the scenario, explain how the interaction between Congress and the presidency can be affected by linkage institutions.

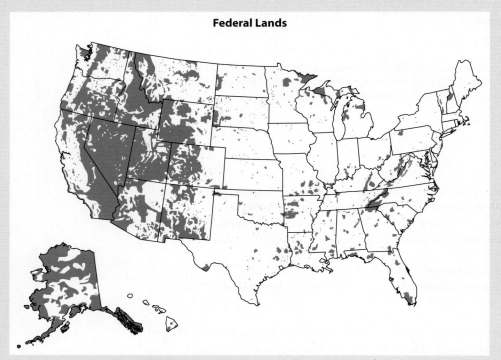

Federal Lands

Data from United States Geological Survey

2. Use the map to answer parts A, B, and C.
   A. Describe the data represented in the map.
   B. Based on your answer in part A, describe a similarity or difference in the amount of public lands by region, as illustrated in the map. Draw a conclusion about that similarity or difference.
   C. Explain how the distribution of public lands as shown on the map might impact the relationship between the states and the federal government.

3. Students at Hazelwood East High School in Missouri published a newspaper called the *Spectrum*. The *Spectrum* was written and edited by the Journalism II class and was published approximately every three weeks during the 1982–83 school year. More than 4,500 copies of the newspaper were distributed during that school year to students, school personnel, and members of the community. The board of education of the Hazelwood School District allocated funds from its annual budget for the printing of the *Spectrum*. Students who were members of the Journalism II class and the *Spectrum*'s staff wrote articles concerning student experiences with pregnancy and the impact of divorce on students at the school. The principal of Hazelwood East directed the teacher advisor of the *Spectrum* not to publish the articles on pregnancy and divorce. The students, whose articles were censored, claimed that this was a violation of their constitutional rights.

   In *Hazelwood School District v. Kuhlmeier* (1988), the Supreme Court of the United States in a 5–3 decision determined that school administrators could censor the publication of school-sponsored expression, such as curriculum-based student newspapers and assembly speeches, if the censorship is "reasonably related to legitimate pedagogical (educational) concerns." The majority decision reasoned that school-sponsored student newspapers were not presumed to be operating as public forums for student expression unless there is evidence indicating otherwise. The Supreme Court ruled that the school's censorship of the articles was not a violation of the students' constitutional rights.

   A. Identify the constitutional amendment clause that is common to both *Hazelwood School District v. Kuhlmeier* (1988) and *Tinker v. Des Moines Independent Community School District* (1969).

   B. Based on the constitutional clause identified in part A, explain why the facts in *Tinker v. Des Moines Independent Community School District* (1969) led to a different holding from the holding in *Hazelwood School District v. Kuhlmeier* (1988).

   C. Describe an action that public school students who disagree with the holding in *Hazelwood School District v. Kuhlmeier* could take to limit its impact.

4. Develop an argument that explains whether or not the Constitution should be amended to abolish the Electoral College and replace it with direct election as the method of selecting the president of the United States.

   In your essay, you must

   - Articulate a defensible claim or thesis that responds to the prompt and establishes a line of reasoning.

   - Support your claim with at least TWO pieces of accurate and relevant information.

   - At least one piece of evidence must be from one of the following foundational documents:

     The Declaration of Independence

     The Constitution of the United States

     Federalist No. 10

   - Use a second piece of evidence from another foundational document from the list or from your study of the electoral process.

   - Use reasoning to explain why your evidence supports your claim or thesis.

   - Respond to an opposing or alternative perspective using refutation, concession, or rebuttal.

Political Party Affiliations in Congress and the Presidency, 1789–2017

Year	Congress	House Majority party	House Principal minority party	Senate Majority party	Senate Principal minority party	President
1789–1791	1st	AD-38	Op-26	AD-17	Op-9	F (Washington)
1791–1793	2nd	F-37	DR-33	F-16	DR-13	F (Washington)
1793–1795	3rd	DR-57	F-48	F-17	DR-13	F (Washington)
1795–1797	4th	F-54	DR-52	F-19	DR-13	F (Washington)
1797–1799	5th	F-58	DR-48	F-20	DR-12	F (John Adams)
1799–1801	6th	F-64	DR-42	F-19	DR-13	F (John Adams)
1801–1803	7th	DR-69	F-36	DR-18	F-13	DR (Jefferson)
1803–1805	8th	DR-102	F-39	DR-25	F-9	DR (Jefferson)
1805–1807	9th	DR-116	F-25	DR-27	F-7	DR (Jefferson)
1807–1809	10th	DR-118	F-24	DR-28	F-6	DR (Jefferson)
1809–1811	11th	DR-94	F-48	DR-28	F-6	DR (Madison)
1811–1813	12th	DR-108	F-36	DR-30	F-6	DR (Madison)
1813–1815	13th	DR-112	F-68	DR-27	F-9	DR (Madison)
1815–1817	14th	DR-117	F-65	DR-25	F-11	DR (Madison)
1817–1819	15th	DR-141	F-42	DR-34	F-10	DR (Monroe)
1819–1821	16th	DR-156	F-27	DR-35	F-7	DR (Monroe)
1821–1823	17th	DR-158	F-25	DR-44	F-4	DR (Monroe)
1823–1825	18th	DR-187	F-26	DR-44	F-4	DR (Monroe)
1825–1827	19th	AD-105	J-97	AD-26	J-20	DR (John Q. Adams)
1827–1829	20th	J-119	AD-94	J-28	AD-20	DR (John Q. Adams)
1829–1831	21st	D-139	NR-74	D-26	NR-22	DR (Jackson)
1831–1833	22nd	D-141	NR-58	D-25	NR-21	D (Jackson)
1833–1835	23rd	D-147	AM-53	D-20	NR-20	D (Jackson)
1835–1837	24th	D-145	W-98	D-27	W-25	D (Jackson)
1837–1839	25th	D-108	W-107	D-30	W-18	D (Van Buren)
1839–1841	26th	D-124	W-118	D-28	W-22	D (Van Buren)
1841–1843	27th	W-133	D-102	W-28	D-22	W (W. Harrison)
						W (Tyler)
1843–1845	28th	D-142	W-79	W-28	D-25	W (Tyler)
1845–1847	29th	D-143	W-77	D-31	W-25	D (Polk)

Key to abbreviations:

AD—Administration

DR—Democratic-Republican

NR—National Republican

U—Unionist

AM—Anti-Masonic

F—Federalist

Op—Opposition

W—Whig

D—Democratic

J—Jacksonian

R—Republican

		House		Senate		
Year	Congress	Majority party	Principal minority party	Majority party	Principal minority party	President
1847–1849	30th	W-115	D-108	D-36	W-21	D (Polk)
1849–1851	31st	D-112	W-109	D-35	W-25	W (Taylor)
						W (Fillmore)
1851–1853	32nd	D-140	W-88	D-35	W-24	W (Fillmore)
1853–1855	33rd	D-159	W-71	D-38	W-22	D (Pierce)
1855–1857	34th	R-108	D-83	D-42	R-15	D (Pierce)
1857–1859	35th	D-131	R-92	D-35	R-20	D (Buchanan)
1859–1861	36th	R-113	D-101	D-38	R-26	D (Buchanan)
1861–1863	37th	R-106	D-42	R-31	D-11	R (Lincoln)
1863–1865	38th	R-103	D-80	R-39	D-12	R (Lincoln)
1865–1867	39th	U-145*	D-46	U-42	D-10	U (Lincoln)
						U (A. Johnson)
1867–1869	40th	R-143	D-49	R-42	D-11	R (A. Johnson)
1869–1871	41st	R-170	D-73	R-61	D-11	R (Grant)
1871–1873	42nd	R-139	D-104	R-57	D-17	R (Grant)
1873–1875	43rd	R-203	D-88	R-54	D-19	R (Grant)
1875–1877	44th	D-181	R-107	R-46	D-29	R (Grant)
1877–1879	45th	D-156	R-137	R-39	D-36	R (Hayes)
1879–1881	46th	D-150	R-128	D-43	R-33	R (Hayes)
1881–1883	47th	R-152	D-130	R-37	D-37	R (Garfield)
						R (Arthur)
1883–1885	48th	D-200	R-119	R-40	D-36	R (Arthur)
1885–1887	49th	D-182	R-140	R-41	D-34	D (Cleveland)
1887–1889	50th	D-170	R-151	R-39	D-37	D (Cleveland)
1889–1891	51st	R-173	D-159	R-37	D-37	R (B. Harrison)
1891–1893	52nd	D-231	R-88	R-47	D-39	R (B. Harrison)
1893–1895	53rd	D-220	R-126	D-44	R-38	D (Cleveland)
1895–1897	54th	R-246	D-104	R-43	D-39	D (Cleveland)
1897–1899	55th	R-206	D-134	R-46	D-34	R (McKinley)
1899–1901	56th	R-185	D-163	R-53	D-26	R (McKinley)
1901–1903	57th	R-198	D-153	R-56	D-29	R (McKinley)
						R (T. Roosevelt)
1903–1905	58th	R-207	D-178	R-58	D-32	R (T. Roosevelt)
1905–1907	59th	R-250	D-136	R-58	D-32	R (T. Roosevelt)
1907–1909	60th	R-222	D-164	R-61	D-29	R (T. Roosevelt)
1909–1911	61st	R-219	D-172	R-59	D-32	R (Taft)
1911–1913	62nd	D-228	R-162	R-49	D-42	R (Taft)
1913–1915	63rd	D-290	R-127	D-51	R-44	D (Wilson)
1915–1917	64th	D-231	R-193	D-56	R-39	D (Wilson)

Year	Congress	House Majority party	House Principal minority party	Senate Majority party	Senate Principal minority party	President
1917–1919	65th	D-216	R-210	D-53	R-42	D (Wilson)
1919–1921	66th	R-237	D-191	R-48	D-47	D (Wilson)
1921–1923	67th	R-300	D-132	R-59	D-37	R (Harding)
1923–1925	68th	R-225	D-207	R-51	D-43	R (Coolidge)
1925–1927	69th	R-247	D-183	R-54	D-40	R (Coolidge)
1927–1929	70th	R-237	D-195	R-48	D-47	R (Coolidge)
1929–1931	71st	R-267	D-163	R-56	D-39	R (Hoover)
1931–1933	72nd	R-218	D-216	R-48	D-47	R (Hoover)
1933–1935	73rd	D-313	R-117	D-59	R-36	D (F. Roosevelt)
1935–1937	74th	D-322	R-103	D-69	R-25	D (F. Roosevelt)
1937–1939	75th	D-333	R-89	D-75	R-17	D (F. Roosevelt)
1939–1941	76th	D-262	R-169	D-69	R-23	D (F. Roosevelt)
1941–1943	77th	D-267	R-162	D-66	R-28	D (F. Roosevelt)
1943–1945	78th	D-222	R-209	D-57	R-38	D (F. Roosevelt)
1945–1947	79th	D-243	R-190	D-56	R-38	D (F. Roosevelt) D (Truman)
1947–1949	80th	R-246	D-188	R-51	D-45	D (Truman)
1949–1951	81st	D-263	R-171	D-54	R-42	D (Truman)
1951–1953	82nd	D-234	R-199	D-48	R-47	D (Truman)
1953–1955	83rd	R-221	D-213	R-48	D-46	R (Eisenhower)
1955–1957	84th	D-234	R-201	D-48	R-47	R (Eisenhower)
1957–1959	85th	D-233	R-200	D-49	R-47	R (Eisenhower)
1959–1961	86th	D-283	R-153	D-64	R-34	R (Eisenhower)
1961–1963	87th	D-262	R-175	D-64	R-36	D (Kennedy)
1963–1965	88th	D-258	R-176	D-67	R-33	D (Kennedy) D (L. Johnson)
1965–1967	89th	D-295	R-140	D-68	R-32	D (L. Johnson)
1967–1969	90th	D-248	R-187	D-64	R-36	D (L. Johnson)
1969–1971	91st	D-243	R-192	D-58	R-42	R (Nixon)
1971–1973	92nd	D-255	R-180	D-54	R-44	R (Nixon)
1973–1975	93rd	D-242	R-192	D-56	R-42	R (Nixon) R (Ford)
1975–1977	94th	D-291	R-144	D-60	R-37	R (Ford)
1977–1979	95th	D-292	R-143	D-61	R-38	D (Carter)
1979–1981	96th	D-277	R-158	D-58	R-41	D (Carter)
1981–1983	97th	D-242	R-192	R-53	D-46	R (Reagan)
1983–1985	98th	D-269	R-166	R-54	D-46	R (Reagan)
1985–1987	99th	D-253	R-182	R-53	D-47	R (Reagan)
1987–1989	100th	D-258	R-177	D-55	R-45	R (Reagan)
1989–1991	101st	D-260	R-175	D-55	R-45	R (G. H. W. Bush)

Year	Congress	House Majority party	House Principal minority party	Senate Majority party	Senate Principal minority party	President
1991–1993	102nd	D-267	R-167	D-56	R-44	R (G. H. W. Bush)
1993–1995	103rd	D-258	R-176	D-57	R-43	D (Clinton)
1995–1997	104th	R-230	D-204	R-52	D-48	D (Clinton)
1997–1999	105th	R-226	D-207	R-55	D-45	D (Clinton)
1999–2001	106th	R-223	D-211	R-55	D-45	D (Clinton)
2001–2003	107th	R-221	D-212	D-50	R-50	R (G. W. Bush)
2003–2005	108th	R-229	D-204	R-51	D-48	R (G. W. Bush)
2005–2007	109th	R-232	D-202	R-55	D-44	R (G. W. Bush)
2007–2009	110th	D-233	R-202	D-49	R-49	R (G. W. Bush)
2009–2011	111th	D-254	R-175	D-57	R-40	D (Obama)
2011–2013	112th	R-242	D-193	D-51	R-47	D (Obama)
2013–2015	113th	R-232	D-200	D-53	R-45	D (Obama)
2015–2017	114th	R-246	D-188	R-54	D-44	D (Obama)
2017–	115th	R-241	D-194	R-52	D-46	R (Trump)

For data through the 33rd Congress, see U.S. Bureau of the Census, *Historical Statistics of the United States, Colonial Times to 1970* (Washington, D.C.: Government Printing Office, 1975), 1083–84; for data after the 33rd Congress, see U.S. Congress, Joint Committee on Printing, *Official Congressional Directory* (Washington, D.C.: Government Printing Office, 2008), 553–54; for 2008 election data, see *CQ Politics Election 2008*; for 2010 election data, see http://www.rollcall.com/politics/. For 2012 election data, see the Office of the Clerk of the U.S. House of Representatives, http://clerk.house.gov/member_info/cong.aspx.

Notes: Figures are for the beginning of the first session of each Congress.

*The Republican Party ran under the Union Party banner in 1864.

Summary of Presidential Elections, 1789–2016

Year	Number of states	Candidates		Electoral vote		Popular vote	
1789[a]	10	F George Washington		F 69		——[b]	
1792[a]	15	F George Washington		F 132		——[b]	
1796[a]	16	F John Adams	DR Thomas Jefferson	F 71	DR 68	——[b]	
1800[a]	16	DR Thomas Jefferson Aaron Burr	F John Adams Charles Cotesworth Pinckney	DR 73	F 65	——[b]	
1804	17	DR Thomas Jefferson George Clinton	F Charles Cotesworth Pinckney Rufus King	DR 162	F 14	——[b]	
1808	17	DR James Madison George Clinton	F Charles Cotesworth Pinckney Rufus King	DR 122	F 47	——[b]	
1812	18	DR James Madison Elbridge Gerry	F DeWitt Clinton Jared Ingersoll	DR 128	F 89	——[b]	
1816	19	DR James Monroe Daniel D. Tompkins	F Rufus King John Howard	DR 183	F 34	——[b]	
1820	24	DR James Monroe Daniel D. Tompkins	——[c]	DR 231	——[c]	——[b]	
1824[d]	24	DR Andrew Jackson John C. Calhoun	DR John Q. Adams Nathan Sanford	DR 99	DR 84	DR 151,271 41.3%	DR 113,122 30.9%
1828	24	DR Andrew Jackson John C. Calhoun	NR John Q. Adams Richard Rush	DR 178	NR 83	DR 642,553 56.0%	NR 500,897 43.6%
1832[e]	24	D Andrew Jackson Martin Van Buren	NR Henry Clay John Sergeant	D 219	NR 49	D 701,780 54.2%	NR 484,205 37.4%

Key to abbreviations:

AD—Administration	AM—Anti-Masonic	D—Democratic
DR—Democratic-Republican	F—Federalist	J—Jacksonian
NR—National Republican	Op—Opposition	R—Republican
U—Unionist	W—Whig	

Year	Number of states	Candidates		Electoral vote		Popular vote	
1836[f]	26	D	W	D	W	D	W
		Martin Van Buren	William H. Harrison	170	73	764,176	550,816
		Richard M. Johnson	Francis Granger			50.8%	36.6%
1840	26	W	D	W	D	W	D
		William H. Harrison	Martin Van Buren	234	60	1,275,390	1,128,854
		John Tyler	Richard M. Johnson			52.9%	46.8%
1844	26	D	W	D	W	D	W
		James Polk	Henry Clay	170	105	1,339,494	1,300,004
		George M. Dallas	Theodore Frelinghuysen			49.5%	48.1%
1848	30	W	D	W	D	W	D
		Zachary Taylor	Lewis Cass	163	127	1,361,393	1,233,460
		Millard Fillmore	William O. Butler			47.3%	42.5%
1852	31	D	W	D	W	D	W
		Franklin Pierce	Winfield Scott	254	42	1,607,510	1,386,942
		William R. King	William A. Graham			50.8%	43.9%
1856[g]	31	D	R	D	R	D	R
		James Buchanan	John C. Fremont	174	114	1,836,072	1,342,345
		John C. Breckinridge	William L. Dayton			45.3%	33.1%
1860[h]	33	R	D	R	D	R	D
		Abraham Lincoln	Stephen A. Douglas	180	12	1,865,908	1,380,202
		Hannibal Hamlin	Herschel V. Johnson			39.8%	29.5%
1864[i]	36	R	D	R	D	R	D
		Abraham Lincoln	George B. McClellan	212	21	2,218,388	1,812,807
		Andrew Johnson	George H. Pendleton			55.0%	45.0%
1868[j]	37	R	D	R	D	R	D
		Ulysses S. Grant	Horatio Seymour	214	80	3,013,650	2,708,744
		Schuyler Colfax	Francis P. Blair Jr.			52.7%	47.3%
1872[k]	37	R	D	R	D	R	D
		Ulysses S. Grant	Horace Greeley	286	0	3,598,235	2,834,761
		Henry Wilson	Benjamin Gratz Brown			55.6%	43.8%
1876	38	R	D	R	D	R	D
		Rutherford B. Hayes	Samuel J. Tilden	185	184	4,034,311	4,288,546
		William A. Wheeler	Thomas A. Hendricks			47.9%	51.0%
1880	38	R	D	R	D	R	D
		James A. Garfield	Winfield S. Hancock	214	155	4,446,158	4,444,260
		Chester A. Arthur	William H. English			48.3%	48.2%
1884	38	D	R	D	R	D	R
		Grover Cleveland	James G. Blaine	219	182	4,874,621	4,848,936
		Thomas A. Hendricks	John A. Logan			48.5%	48.2%
1888	38	R	D	R	D	R	D
		Benjamin Harrison	Grover Cleveland	233	168	5,443,892	5,534,488
		Levi P. Morton	Allen G. Thurman			47.8%	48.6%

Year	Number of states	Candidates		Electoral vote		Popular vote	
1892[l]	44	D	R	D	R	D	R
		Grover Cleveland	Benjamin Harrison	277	145	5,551,883	5,179,244
		Adlai E. Stevenson	Whitelaw Reid			46.1%	43.0%
1896	45	R	D	R	D	R	D
		William McKinley	William J. Bryan	271	176	7,108,480	6,511,495
		Garret A. Hobart	Arthur Sewall			51.0%	46.7%
1900	45	R	D	R	D	R	D
		William McKinley	William J. Bryan	292	155	7,218,039	6,358,345
		Theodore Roosevelt	Adlai E. Stevenson			51.7%	45.5%
1904	45	R	D	R	D	R	D
		Theodore Roosevelt	Alton B. Parker	336	140	7,626,593	5,028,898
		Charles W. Fairbanks	Henry G. Davis			56.4%	37.6%
1908	46	R	D	R	D	R	D
		William H. Taft	William J. Bryan	321	162	7,678,395	6,408,985
		James S. Sherman	John W. Kern			51.6%	43.0%
1912[m]	48	D	R	D	R	D	R
		Woodrow Wilson	William H. Taft	435	8	6,293,152	3,486,333
		Thomas R. Marshall	James S. Sherman			41.8%	23.2%
1916	48	D	R	D	R	D	R
		Woodrow Wilson	Charles E. Hughes	277	254	9,126,300	8,546,789
		Thomas R. Marshall	Charles W. Fairbanks			49.2%	46.1%
1920	48	R	D	R	D	R	D
		Warren G. Harding	James M. Cox	404	127	16,133,314	9,140,884
		Calvin Coolidge	Franklin D. Roosevelt			60.3%	34.2%
1924[n]	48	R	D	R	D	R	D
		Calvin Coolidge	John W. Davis	382	136	15,717,553	8,386,169
		Charles G. Dawes	Charles W. Bryant			54.1%	28.8%
1928	48	R	D	R	D	R	D
		Herbert C. Hoover	Alfred E. Smith	444	87	21,411,991	15,000,185
		Charles Curtis	Joseph T. Robinson			58.2%	40.8%
1932	48	D	R	D	R	D	R
		Franklin D. Roosevelt	Herbert C. Hoover	472	59	22,825,016	15,758,397
		John N. Garner	Charles Curtis			57.4%	39.6%
1936	48	D	R	D	R	D	R
		Franklin D. Roosevelt	Alfred M. Landon	523	8	27,747,636	16,679,543
		John N. Garner	Frank Knox			60.8%	36.5%
1940	48	D	R	D	R	D	R
		Franklin D. Roosevelt	Wendell L. Willkie	449	82	27,263,448	22,336,260
		Henry A. Wallace	Charles L. McNary			54.7%	44.8%
1944	48	D	R	D	R	D	R
		Franklin D. Roosevelt	Thomas E. Dewey	432	99	25,611,936	22,013,372
		Harry S. Truman	John W. Bricker			53.4%	45.9%

Year	Number of states	Candidates		Electoral vote		Popular vote	
1948[o]	48	D	R	D	R	D	R
		Harry S. Truman	Thomas E. Dewey	303	189	24,105,587	21,970,017
		Alben W. Barkley	Earl Warren			49.5%	45.1%
1952	48	R	D	R	D	R	D
		Dwight D. Eisenhower	Adlai E. Stevenson II	442	89	33,936,137	27,314,649
		Richard M. Nixon	John J. Sparkman			55.1%	44.4%
1956[p]	48	R	D	R	D	R	D
		Dwight D. Eisenhower	Adlai E. Stevenson II	457	73	35,585,245	26,030,172
		Richard M. Nixon	Estes Kefauver			57.4%	42.0%
1960[q]	50	D	R	D	R	D	R
		John F. Kennedy	Richard M. Nixon	303	219	34,221,344	34,106,671
		Lyndon B. Johnson	Henry Cabot Lodge			49.7%	49.5%
1964	50*	D	R	D	R	D	R
		Lyndon B. Johnson	Barry Goldwater	486	52	43,126,584	27,177,838
		Hubert H. Humphrey	William E. Miller			61.1%	38.5%
1968[r]	50*	R	D	R	D	R	D
		Richard M. Nixon	Hubert H. Humphrey	301	191	31,785,148	31,274,503
		Spiro T. Agnew	Edmund S. Muskie			43.4%	42.7%
1972[s]	50*	R	D	R	D	R	D
		Richard M. Nixon	George McGovern	520	17	47,170,179	29,171,791
		Spiro T. Agnew	Sargent Shriver			60.7%	37.5%
1976[t]	50*	D	R	D	R	D	R
		Jimmy Carter	Gerald R. Ford	297	240	40,830,763	39,147,793
		Walter F. Mondale	Robert Dole			50.1%	48.0%
1980	50*	R	D	R	D	R	D
		Ronald Reagan	Jimmy Carter	489	49	43,904,153	35,483,883
		George H. W. Bush	Walter F. Mondale			50.7%	41.0%
1984	50*	R	D	R	D	R	D
		Ronald Reagan	Walter F. Mondale	525	13	54,455,075	37,577,185
		George H. W. Bush	Geraldine Ferraro			58.8%	40.6%
1988[u]	50*	R	D	R	D	R	D
		George H. W. Bush	Michael S. Dukakis	426	111	48,886,097	41,809,074
		Dan Quayle	Lloyd Bentsen			53.4%	45.6%
1992	50*	D	R	D	R	D	R
		William J. Clinton	George H. W. Bush	370	168	44,909,326	39,103,882
		Albert Gore	Dan Quayle			43.0%	37.4%
1996	50*	D	R	D	R	D	R
		William J. Clinton	Robert J. Dole	379	159	47,401,185	39,197,469
		Albert Gore	Jack F. Kemp			49.2%	40.7%
2000	50*	R	D	R	D	R	D
		George W. Bush	Albert Gore	271	266	50,455,156	50,992,335
		Richard B. Cheney	Joseph I. Lieberman			47.9%	48.4%

Year	Number of states	Candidates		Electoral vote		Popular vote	
2004	50*	R	D	R	D	R	D
		George W. Bush	John Kerry	286	252	62,025,554	59,026,013
		Richard B. Cheney	John Edwards			50.7%	47.3%
2008	50*	D	R	D	R	D	R
		Barack Obama	John McCain	365	173	69,498,459	59,948,283
		Joe Biden	Sarah Palin			52.9%	45.6%
2012	50*	D	R	D	R	D	R
		Barack Obama	Mitt Romney	332	206	62,611,250	59,134,475
		Joe Biden	Paul Ryan			51.5%	48.5%
2016	50*	D	R	D	R	D	R
		Hillary Clinton	Donald Trump	232	306	65,853,514	62,984,828
		Tim Kaine	Mike Pence			48.2%	46.1%

Data from Harold W. Stanley and Richard G. Niemi, *Vital Statistics on American Politics, 2007–2008*; *CQ Press Guide to U.S. Elections*; for the 2008 election: for presidential race electoral vote data, see *CQ Politics Election 2008*. For presidential race popular vote data, see the *New York Times*'s Presidential Big Board. 2012 election data from Politico.

Notes:

a. Elections from 1789 through 1800 were held under rules that did not allow separate voting for president and vice president.

b. Popular vote returns are not shown before 1824 because consistent, reliable data are not available.

c. 1820: One electoral vote was cast for John Adams and Richard Stockton, who were not candidates.

d. 1824: All four candidates represented Democratic-Republican factions. William H. Crawford received 41 electoral votes and Henry Clay received 37 votes. Because no candidate received a majority, the election was decided (in Adams's favor) by the House of Representatives.

e. 1832: Two electoral votes were not cast.

f. 1836: Other Whig candidates receiving electoral votes were Hugh L. White, who received 26 votes, and Daniel Webster, who received 14 votes.

g. 1856: Millard Fillmore, Whig-American, received 8 electoral votes.

h. 1860: John C. Breckinridge, southern Democrat, received 72 electoral votes. John Bell, Constitutional Union, received 39 electoral votes.

i. 1864: Eighty-one electoral votes were not cast.

j. 1868: Twenty-three electoral votes were not cast.

k. 1872: Horace Greeley, Democrat, died after the election. In the Electoral College, Democratic electoral votes went to Thomas Hendricks, 42 votes; Benjamin Gratz Brown, 18 votes; Charles J. Jenkins, 2 votes; and David Davis, 1 vote. Seventeen electoral votes were not cast.

l. 1892: James B. Weaver, People's Party, received 22 electoral votes.

m. 1912: Theodore Roosevelt, Progressive Party, received 88 electoral votes.

n. 1924: Robert M. La Follette, Progressive Party, received 13 electoral votes.

o. 1948: J. Strom Thurmond, States' Rights Party, received 39 electoral votes.

p. 1956: Walter B. Jones, Democrat, received 1 electoral vote.

q. 1960: Harry Flood Byrd, Democrat, received 15 electoral votes.

r. 1968: George C. Wallace, American Independent Party, received 46 electoral votes.

s. 1972: John Hospers, Libertarian Party, received 1 electoral vote.

t. 1976: Ronald Reagan, Republican, received 1 electoral vote.

u. 1988: Lloyd Bentsen, the Democratic vice-presidential nominee, received 1 electoral vote for president.

* Fifty states plus the District of Columbia.

Glossary/Glosario

English	Español
A	
absentee ballots voting completed and submitted by a voter before the day of an election.	**votos en ausencia** voto completado y presentado por un votante antes del día oficial de la elección.
affirmative action a policy designed to address the consequences of previous discrimination by providing special consideration to individuals based upon their characteristics, such as race or gender.	**acción afirmativa** política diseñada a abordar las consecuencias discriminatorias de políticas previas, dando consideración especial a los individuos según sus características, como la raza o el sexo.
agency capture when agencies tasked with regulating businesses, industries, or other interest groups are populated by individuals with close ties to the very firms that they are supposed to regulate.	**captura de agencia** cuando las agencias, cuya tarea es regular a negocios, industrias u otros grupos de interés, incluyen a individuos con vínculos cercanos a las mismas firmas que se supone están regulando.
agenda setting the media's ability to highlight certain issues and bring them to the attention of the public.	**configuración de la agenda** capacidad de los medios para realizar ciertos tópicos y así llamar la atención del público.
aggregating a process through which internet and other news providers relay the news as reported by journalists and other sources.	**agregación** proceso mediante el cual proveedores de noticias de internet y otros medios retransmiten lo reportado por periodistas y otras fuentes.
amendment a constitutional provision for a process by which changes may be made to the Constitution.	**enmienda** recurso constitucional para un proceso por el cual pueden hacerse cambios a la constitución.
the American dream the idea that individuals should be able to achieve prosperity through hard work, sacrifice, and their own talents.	**el sueño americano** la idea de que los individuos deberían ser capaces de alcanzar la prosperidad mediante el esfuerzo laboral, el sacrificio y su propio talento.
American political culture the set of beliefs, customs, traditions, and values that Americans share.	**cultura política norteamericana** conjunto de creencias, costumbres, tradiciones y valores que comparten los estadounidenses.
amicus curiae brief a brief filed by someone who is not a party to a case in an attempt to persuade the court to agree with the arguments set forth in the brief.	**informe amicus curiae** escrito presentado por alguien que, sin ser parte del caso, trata de persuadir a la corte para que acepte los argumentos expuestos en dicho escrito.
Antifederalist a person opposed to the proposed Constitution who favored stronger state governments.	**antifederalista** persona opuesta a la constitución propuesta, que favorece la fortaleza de los gobiernos estatales.
appellate jurisdiction the authority of a court to hear and review decisions made by lower courts in that system.	**jurisdicción de apelación** la autoridad de un tribunal para escuchar y revisar las decisiones hechas por tribunales inferiores del mismo sistema.
apportionment the process of determining the number of representatives for each state using census data.	**distribución** proceso para determinar la cantidad de representantes por estado usando los datos del censo.
appropriation the process through which congressional committees allocate funds to executive branch agencies, bureaus, and departments.	**apropiación** proceso a través del cual comités del congreso asignan fondos a las distintas agencias ejecutivas, oficinas y departamentos.
Articles of Confederation and Perpetual Union a governing document that created a union of thirteen sovereign states in which the states, not the union, were supreme.	**Artículos de Confederación y Unión Perpetua** documento oficial que creó la unión de trece estados soberanos, donde se estipula que los estados, y no la unión, eran supremos.
B	
bail an amount of money posted as a security to allow the charged individual to be freed while awaiting trial.	**fianza** cantidad de dinero pedida como seguro que permite a un acusado salir en libertad mientras espera el juicio.
bargaining and persuasion an informal tool used by the president to persuade members of Congress to support his or her policy initiatives.	**negociación y persuasión** herramienta informal usada por el presidente para persuadir a los miembros del congreso de que apoyen sus iniciativas políticas.

battleground state a state where the polls show a close contest between the Republican and Democratic candidate in a presidential election.	**estado en disputa** estado donde los sondeos de opinión muestran un estrecho margen de victoria entre los candidatos demócrata y republicano en las elecciones presidenciales.
benchmark poll a survey taken at the beginning of a political campaign in order to gauge support for a candidate and determine which issues are important to voters.	**encuesta comparativa** encuesta hecha al comienzo de una campaña electoral para medir el apoyo a un candidato y determinar qué asuntos son de importancia para los votantes.
bicameral a two-house legislature.	**bicameral** asamblea legislativa que incluye dos cámaras.
bill of attainder when the legislature declares someone guilty without a trial.	**condena sin derechos civiles** cuando la asamblea legislativa declara culpable a alguien sin pasar por un juicio.
Bill of Rights a list of fundamental rights and freedoms that individuals possess. The first ten amendments to the U.S. Constitution are referred to as the Bill of Rights.	**Declaración de Derechos** lista de los derechos y libertades fundamentales que poseen los individuos. Las primeras diez enmiendas de la Constitución de Estados Unidos se conocen como la Declaración de Derechos.
bipartisanship agreement between the parties to work together in Congress to pass legislation.	**bipartidismo** acuerdo entre los partidos de trabajar juntos en el congreso para aprobar una ley.
block grant a type of grants-in-aid that gives state officials more authority in the disbursement of federal funds.	**subvención en bloque** tipo de subvención que da a los oficiales del estado más autoridad en el desembolso de fondos federales.
broadcast media outlets for news and other content that rely on mass communications technology to bring stories directly into people's homes.	**medios de difusión** canales de noticias y otros contenidos que dependen de la tecnología de comunicación de masas para hace llegar las noticias directamente a todos los hogares.
Brutus No. 1 an Antifederalist paper arguing that the country was too large to be governed as a republic and that the Constitution gave too much power to the national government.	**Brutus N.º 1** documento antifederalista que argumentaba que el país era demasiado grande para ser gobernado como república y que la Constitución daba demasiado poder al gobierno nacional.
budget deficit the difference when a government takes in less money than it spends.	**déficit presupuestario** cantidad de dinero faltante cuando un gobierno ingresa menos dinero del que gasta.
budget surplus the amount of money remaining when the government takes in more money than it spends.	**superávit presupuestario** cantidad de dinero sobrante cuando un gobierno ingresa más dinero del que gasta.
bully pulpit presidential appeals to the public to pressure other branches of government to support his or her policies.	**púlpito soberbio** cuando el presidente apela al público para presionar a otras ramas del gobierno a apoyar sus políticas.
bureaucrat an official employed within a government bureaucracy.	**burócrata** persona empleada dentro de la burocracia gubernamental.
bureaucratic adjudication when the federal bureaucracy settles disputes between parties that arise over the implementation of federal laws or determines which individuals or groups are covered under a regulation or program.	**sentencia burocrática** cuando la burocracia federal resuelve disputas que surgen entre partidos acerca de la implementación de las leyes federales, o determina cuáles individuos o grupos están amparados bajo una regulación o un programa.
bureaucratic discretion the power to decide how a law is implemented and, at times, what Congress actually meant when it passed a given law.	**discreción burocrática** el poder de decidir cómo las leyes son implementadas y, en ciertos casos, lo que el congreso haya querido decir cuando aprobó una ley.
business cycle the fluctuation of economic activity around a long-term trend, with periods of expansion and contraction.	**ciclo de los negocios** la fluctuación de la actividad económica en el curso de una tendencia a largo plazo, con períodos de expansión y contracción.

C

candidate-centered campaign a trend in which candidates develop their own strategies and raise money with less influence from the party elite.	**campaña centrada en el candidato** tendencia en la que el candidato desarrolla su propia estrategia y consigue fondos con menos influencias de la élite del partido.
capitalist system a way of structuring economic activity in which private firms are allowed to make most or all of the decisions involving the production and distribution of goods and services.	**sistema capitalista** manera de estructurar la actividad económica en la cual a las firmas privadas se les permite tomar la mayoría de las decisiones concernientes a la producción y distribución de bienes y servicios.
categorical grants grants-in-aid provided to states with specific provisions on their use.	**subvenciones categóricas** subvenciones de ayuda otorgadas a los estados con fines específicos para su uso.
caucus a process through which a state's eligible voters meet to select delegates to represent their preferences in the nomination process.	**cónclave** proceso en el que los votantes de un estado se reúnen para seleccionar a los delegados que representarán sus preferencias en el proceso de nominación.

certiorari the process through which most cases reach the Supreme Court; after four justices concur that the Court should hear the case, a writ of certiorari is issued to the lower court to request the relevant case records.	**cercioramiento** proceso a través del cual la mayoría de los casos llegan a la Corte Suprema. Después de que cuatro jueces concuerdan en que la Corte debería escuchar el caso, se emite un escrito de *certiorari* a la corte inferior para pedir los archivos relevantes del caso.
checks and balances a design of government in which each branch has powers that can prevent the other branches from making policy.	**control y equilibrio de poderes** diseño del gobierno en el que cada rama puede controlar y evitar el que otras ramas tomen decisiones políticas.
civil disobedience the intentional refusal to obey a law to call attention to its injustice.	**desobediencia civil** la negativa intencionada de obedecer la ley para llamar la atención sobre una injusticia.
civil law a category of law covering cases involving private rights and relationships between individuals and groups.	**derecho civil** conjunto de normas jurídicas que regulan los casos que involucran derechos privados y relaciones entre individuos y grupos.
civil liberties fundamental rights and freedoms protected from infringement by the government.	**libertades civiles** derechos y libertades fundamentales que el gobierno no puede infringir.
civil rights protections from discrimination as a member of a particular group.	**derechos civiles** derechos que protegen contra la discriminación por ser miembro de un determinado grupo.
Civil Rights Act of 1964 legislation outlawing racial segregation in schools and public places and authorizing the attorney general to sue individual school districts that failed to desegregate.	**Ley de Derechos Civiles de 1964** legislación que prohíbe la segregación en escuelas y espacios públicos, autorizando al fiscal general a demandar a los distritos escolares que incumplan esta ley.
civil society group an independent association outside the government's control.	**grupo de sociedad civil** asociación independiente que se halla fuera de las estructuras gubernamentales.
clear and present danger test legal standard that speech posing an immediate and serious threat to national security is not protected by the First Amendment.	**prueba de peligro claro e inminente** normativa legal según la cual un discurso que represente una amenaza inmediata y seria para la seguridad nacional no está protegido por la Primera Enmienda.
closed primary a primary election in which only those who have registered as a member of a political party may vote.	**primarias cerradas** elección primaria donde solamente quienes estén registrados en el partido político pueden votar.
cloture a procedure through which senators can end debate on a bill and proceed to action, provided three-fifths of senators agree to it.	**clausura** procedimiento por el cual los senadores pueden poner fin a las discusiones de una ley y proceder a la toma de decisiones, solo si tres quintas partes del Senado están de acuerdo con ello.
collective action political action that occurs when individuals contribute their energy, time, or money to a larger group goal.	**acción colectiva** acción política que ocurre cuando los individuos aúnan su esfuerzo, tiempo o dinero para alcanzar una meta colectiva.
collective good also called a public good; a public benefit that individuals can enjoy or profit from even if they do not help achieve it.	**bien colectivo** también llamado bien público, es un beneficio público del que pueden disfrutar y beneficiarse todos los individuos aunque no hayan ayudado a conseguirlo.
command-and-control economy economic policy in which government dictates much of a nation's economic activity, including the amount of production and prices for goods.	**economía de control y mando** política económica en la que el gobierno dicta la mayoría de la actividad económica de la nación, incluida la cantidad de producción y precios de los bienes.
commerce clause grants Congress the authority to regulate interstate business and commercial activity.	**cláusula de comercio** garantiza al Congreso la autoridad para regular los negocios interestatales y su actividad comercial.
committee chair leader of a congressional committee who has authority over the committee's agenda.	**presidente del comité** líder de un comité del Congreso que tiene autoridad para establecer las prioridades.
Committee of the Whole consists of all members of the House and meets in the House chamber but is governed by different rules, making it easier to consider complex and controversial legislation.	**Comité Plenario** está compuesto por todos los miembros de la Cámara y se reúne en la Cámara, pero se rige por reglas diferentes, para facilitar la discusión de leyes complejas y polémicas.
Compromise on Importation Congress could not restrict the slave trade until 1808.	**Acuerdo en Importación** el Congreso no pudo restringir la trata de esclavos hasta 1808.
concurrent powers powers granted to both states and the federal government in the Constitution.	**competencias concurrentes** poderes otorgados por la Constitución al gobierno federal como a los estados.
concurring opinion an opinion that agrees with the majority decision, offering different or additional reasoning that does not serve as precedent.	**opinión concurrente** opinión que está de acuerdo con la decisión mayoritaria. Ofrece un razonamiento diferente o agregado, que no sirve como precedente.
confederal system a system where the subnational governments have most of the power.	**sistema confederal** sistema donde los gobiernos subnacionales tienen la mayoría del poder.

Congressional Budget Office (CBO) the federal agency tasked with producing independent analyses of budgetary and economic issues to support the congressional budget process.	**Oficina de Presupuestos del Congreso** agencia federal encargada de producir análisis independientes de asuntos económicos y presupuestarios para respaldar el proceso de presupuesto del congreso.
conservatism an ideology favoring more regulation of social behavior and less government interference in the economy.	**conservadurismo** ideología que favorece más regulación del comportamiento social y menos interferencia gubernamental en la economía.
constituency a body of voters in a given area who elect a representative or senator.	**electorado** grupo de votantes de un área particular quienes eligen a un representante o a un senador.
constitution a document that sets out the fundamental principles of governance and establishes the institutions of a government.	**constitución** documento que expone los principios fundamentales de gobernabilidad y establece las instituciones de un gobierno.
Constitutional Convention a meeting attended by state delegates in 1787 to fix the Articles of Confederation.	**Convención Constitucional** reunión a la que asistieron los delegados de estado en 1787 para definir los Artículos de la Confederación.
constitutional republic a democratic system with elected representatives in which the constitution is the supreme law.	**república constitucional** sistema democrático con representantes elegidos en el cual la constitución es la ley suprema.
consumer price index (CPI) a basket of fixed goods and services over time, used to measure the cost of living.	**índice de precios de consumo (IPC)** índice económico de bienes y servicios determinados en un período de tiempo. Sirve para calcular el costo de vida.
cooperative federalism a form of American federalism in which the states and the national government work together to shape public policy.	**federalismo cooperativo** forma de federalismo estadounidense en la que el gobierno nacional y los estados trabajan unidos para dar forma a las políticas públicas.
criminal law a category of law covering actions determined to harm the community itself.	**derecho penal** categoría de leyes que establece penas sobre delitos contra la comunidad.
critical election a major national election that signals a change in the balance of power between the two parties.	**elección definitoria** elección a nivel nacional que señala un cambio en el equilibrio de poder entre dos partidos políticos importantes.

D

de facto segregation a separation of individuals based on characteristics that arises not by law but because of other factors, such as residential housing patterns.	**segregación _de facto_** separación de individuos basada en características no surgidas de la ley sino de otros factores, como los patrones residenciales.
defendant a person or group against whom a case is brought in court.	**acusado** persona o grupo en contra de quien o quienes es presentado un caso en la corte.
de jure segregation the separation of individuals based on their characteristics, such as race, intentionally and by law.	**segregación _de iure_** separación intencionada y legal de individuos según sus características, tales como la raza.
delegate a person who acts as the voters' representative at a convention to select the party's nominee.	**delegado** persona que actúa como representante de los votantes en una convención para seleccionar el candidato de un partido político.
delegate role the idea that the main duty of a member of Congress is to carry out constituent wishes.	**rol del delegado** la idea de que la responsabilidad principal de un miembro del Congreso es hacer valer los deseos de sus electores.
democracy a system of government where power is held by the people.	**democracia** sistema de gobierno donde el poder pertenece al pueblo.
demographic characteristics measurable characteristics of a population, such as economic status, education, age, race or ethnicity, gender, and partisan attachment.	**características demográficas** características medibles de una población, como el nivel económico, la educación, la edad, la raza o grupo étnico, sexo y afiliación política.
demographics the grouping of individuals based on shared characteristics, such as ancestry, race, ethnicity, and gender.	**demografías** la agrupación de individuos basada en características compartidas, como la ascendencia, la raza, el origen étnico y el sexo.
deregulation the reduction or elimination of government power in a particular industry, usually to create more competition within the industry.	**desregulación** reducción o eliminación del poder estatal en una industria en particular, usualmnte para incentivar la competencia dentro de la misma.
descriptive representation the degree to which a body of representatives in a legislature does or does not reflect the diversity of that nation's identities and lived experiences.	**representación descriptiva** el grado con el cual un cuerpo de representantes de una legislatura refleja o no la diversidad y experiencias de vida de las identidades de la nación.
devolution returning more authority to state or local governments.	**descentralización** otorgar más autoridad a los estados o gobiernos locales.
digital divide divisions in society that are driven by access to and knowledge about technologies; these gaps often fall along the lines of partisanship, class, race, and ethnicity.	**brecha digital** divisiones en la sociedad impulsadas por el acceso y conocimiento de tecnologías; estas diferencias están a menudo alineadas con la afiliación política, clase, raza y grupo étnico.

direct democracy a political system in which citizens vote directly on public policies.	**democracia directa** sistema político en el que los ciudadanos votan directamente sobre las políticas públicas.
discharge petition a motion filed by a member of Congress to move a bill out of committee and onto the floor of the House of Representatives for a vote.	**petición de votación** acción promovida por un miembro del Congreso para sacar una legislación del comité y llevarla a la Cámara de Representantes para que sea votada.
discretionary spending spending for programs and policies at the discretion of Congress and the president.	**gasto discrecional** gastos para programas y políticas a discreción del Congreso y el presidente.
dissenting opinion an opinion that disagrees with the majority opinion and does not serve as precedent.	**opinión discrepante** opinión que está en desacuerdo con lo que opina la mayoría y no se usa como precedente.
divided government a situation that occurs when control of the presidency and one or both chambers of Congress is split between the two major parties.	**gobierno dividido** situación que ocurre cuando el control de la presidencia y una o ambas Cámaras del Congreso se dividen entre los dos partidos más importantes.
double jeopardy protects an individual acquitted of a crime from being charged with the same crime again in the same jurisdiction.	**doble riesgo** protege a quien sea absuelto de un delito de que lo imputen por el mismo delito nuevamente en la misma jurisdicción.
dual federalism a form of American federalism in which the states and the nation operate independently in their own areas of public policy.	**federalismo dual** forma de federalismo estadounidense donde los estados y la nación operan independientemente en sus áreas particulares de política pública.
due process clause the clause in the Fourteenth Amendment that restricts state governments from denying their citizens their life, liberty, or property without legal safeguards.	**cláusula del proceso debido** cláusula de la Decimocuarta Enmienda que restringe a los gobiernos estatales negarle a sus ciudadanos la vida, sus libertades o propiedades sin salvaguarda legal.

E

earmark an addition to a piece of legislation that directs specific funds to projects within districts or states.	**asignación de fondos** adición a una legislación que destina fondos específicos para proyectos dentro de los estados o distritos.
economic interest group a group advocating on behalf of the financial interests of members.	**grupo de interés económico** grupo que aboga en beneficio del interés financiero de sus miembros.
economic policy the efforts of government to regulate and support the economy to protect and expand citizens' financial well-being and economic prospects and to support businesses in the global financial system.	**política económica** los esfuerzos del gobierno para regular y apoyar la economía, para proteger y expandir el bienestar financiero y la perspectiva económica de los ciudadanos, también para brindar apoyo a los negocios en el sistema financiero mundial.
economic recession a period of decline in economic activity, typically defined by two consecutive quarters of negative GDP growth.	**recesión económica** período de declive en la actividad económica, definido típicamente por dos cuartos consecutivos de crecimiento negativo del PIB.
economy the systems and organizations through which a society produces and distributes goods and services.	**economía** sistemas y organizaciones a través de los cuales una sociedad produce y distribuye sus bienes y servicios.
Electoral College a constitutionally required process for selecting the president through slates of electors chosen in each state, who are pledged to vote for a nominee in the presidential election.	**Colegio Electoral** proceso constitucional requerido para seleccionar al presidente a través de una lista de electores escogidos en cada estado, quienes han prometido votar por un nominado en la elección presidencial.
elite a small number of individuals (who tend to have well-informed and well-reasoned opinions).	**élite** grupo reducido de personas (quienes tienden a tener opiniones bien informadas y bien razonadas).
elitist theory theory of democracy that the elites have a disproportionate amount of influence in the policymaking process.	**teoría elitista** teoría de democracia según la cual las élites tienen una cantidad desproporcionada de influencia en el proceso de crear políticas.
entitlement program a program that provides benefits for those who qualify under the law, regardless of income.	**programa de ayuda social** programa que ofrece beneficios a aquellos que cumplen los requisitos según la ley, independientemente de sus ingresos.
entrance survey a poll conducted of people coming to an event.	**encuesta de entrada** encuesta hecha a personas que asisten a un evento.
enumerated powers powers explicitly granted to the national government through the Constitution; also called *express powers*.	**poderes enumerados** poderes explícitamente garantizados al gobierno nacional a través de la Constitución, también conocidos como poderes expresos.
equal protection clause a clause of the Fourteenth Amendment that requires the states to treat all citizens alike with regard to application of the laws.	**cláusula sobre protección igualitaria** cláusula de la Decimocuarta Enmienda que requiere que los estados traten a sus ciudadanos con igualdad en lo que respecta a la aplicación de la ley.

Equal Rights Amendment a proposed but not ratified amendment to the Constitution that sought to guarantee equality of rights based upon sex.	**Enmienda de Igualdad de Derechos** propuesta de enmienda a la Constitución, no ratificada, que busca garantizar la igualdad de derechos basada en el sexo.
era of divided government a trend since 1969, in which one party controls one or both houses of Congress and the president is from the opposing party.	**etapa de gobierno dividido** tendencia desde 1969, según la cual un partido controla una o ambas cámaras del Congreso y el presidente pertenece al partido opositor.
establishment clause First Amendment protection against the government requiring citizens to join or support a religion.	**cláusula de establecimiento** protección de la Primera Enmienda en contra de que el gobierno requiera a los ciudadanos unirse o apoyar una religión.
exclusionary rule a rule that evidence obtained without a warrant is inadmissible in court.	**regla excluyente** regla de que una prueba obtenida sin autorización es inadmisible en la corte.
exclusive powers powers only the national government may exercise.	**poderes exclusivos** poderes que solo el gobierno nacional puede ejercer.
executive agreement an agreement between a president and another nation that does not have the same durability in the American system as a treaty but does not require Senate ratification.	**acuerdo ejecutivo** acuerdo entre el presidente y otra nación que en el sistema estadounidense no tiene la misma duración que un tratado, mas no requiere ratificación del Senado.
executive branch the institution responsible for carrying out laws passed by the legislative branch.	**poder ejecutivo** institución encargada de hacer cumplir las leyes aprobadas por el poder legislativo.
Executive Office of the President a collection of offices within the White House organization designed mainly to provide information to the president.	**Oficina Ejecutiva del Presidente** grupo de oficinas dentro de la organización de la Casa Blanca diseñada principalmente para dar información al presidente.
executive order policy directives issued by presidents that do not require congressional approval.	**orden ejecutiva** directivas políticas emitidas por los presidentes que no requieren aprobación del Congreso.
executive privilege a right claimed by presidents to keep certain conversations, records, and transcripts confidential from outside scrutiny, especially that of Congress.	**privilegio ejecutivo** derecho que ejercen los presidentes de mantener ciertas conversaciones, registros y transcripciones en secreto y fuera del escrutinio externo, especialmente fuera del escrutinio del Congreso.
exit poll a survey conducted outside a polling place in which individuals are asked who or what they just voted for and why.	**sondeo a boca de urna** encuesta que se realiza a la salida de un centro de votación en la que se le pregunta a los individuos qué o a quién votaron y por qué.
ex post facto law a law punishing people for acts that were not crimes at the time they were committed.	**ley *ex post facto*** ley retroactiva que castiga a las personas por actos que no eran delito en el momento en el que se cometieron.
expressed or enumerated powers authority specifically granted to a branch of the government in the Constitution.	**poderes expresados o enumerados** autoridad específicamente garantizada en la Constitución para una rama del gobierno.
extradition the requirement that officials in one state return a defendant to another state where the crime was committed.	**extradición** el requisito de que los oficiales de un estado entreguen a un acusado a otro estado donde se cometió el crimen.

F

faction a group of self-interested people.	**facción** grupo de personas con intereses propios.
federal bureaucracy the departments and agencies within the executive branch that carry out the laws of the nation.	**burocracia federal** departamentos y agencias dentro del poder ejecutivo que hacen cumplir las leyes de la nación.
federal civil service the merit-based bureaucracy, excluding the armed forces and political appointments.	**servicio civil federal** burocracia basada en el mérito, excluídas las fuerzas armadas y los cargos políticos.
federal courts of appeals the middle level of the federal judiciary; these courts review and hear appeals from the federal district courts.	**cortes federales de apelación** nivel medio de la justicia federal; estas cortes revisan y escuchan apelaciones de las cortes de distrito federal.
federal district courts the lowest level of the federal judiciary; these courts usually have original jurisdiction in cases that start at the federal level.	**cortes de distrito federal** el nivel más bajo de la judicatura federal; estas cortes usualmente tienen jurisdicción de primera instancia en casos que empiezan a nivel federal.
federalism the sharing of power between the national government and the states.	**federalismo** el reparto de poder entre el gobierno nacional y los estados.
Federalist supporter of the proposed Constitution, who called for a strong national government.	**federalista** partidario de la Constitución propuesta, que abogaba por un gobierno nacional fuerte.

Federalist No. 10 an essay in which Madison argues that the dangers of faction can be mitigated by a large republic and republican government.	**Federalista N.º 10** ensayo en el que Madison argumenta que los peligros de las facciones pueden ser mitigados por una gran república y un gobierno republicano.
Federalist No. 51 an essay in which Madison argues that separation of powers and federalism will prevent tyranny.	**Federalista N.º 51** ensayo donde Madison argumenta que la separación de poderes y el federalismo evitarán la tiranía.
Federalist No. 78 argument by Alexander Hamilton that the federal judiciary would be unlikely to infringe upon rights and liberties but would serve as a check on the other two branches.	**Federalista N.º 78** argumento de Alexander Hamilton según el cual la judicatura federal no podrá violar los derechos y libertades, mas servirá como vigilante de los otros dos poderes.
Federalist Papers a series of eighty-five essays written by Alexander Hamilton, James Madison, and John Jay and published between 1787 and 1788 that lay out the theory behind the Constitution.	**Documentos Federalistas** serie de ochenta y cinco ensayos escritos por Alexander Hamilton, James Madison y John Jay, publicados entre 1787 y 1788, que exponen la teoría que sustenta la Constitución.
federal judiciary the branch of the federal government that interprets the laws of the nation.	**judicatura federal** la rama del gobierno federal que interpreta las leyes de la nación.
Federal Reserve System a board of governors, Federal Reserve Banks, and member banks responsible for monetary policy.	**Sistema de la Reserva Federal** la junta de gobernadores, bancos de la Reserva Federal y bancos miembros responsables de la política monetaria.
federal system a system where power is divided between the national and state governments.	**sistema federal** un sistema donde el poder se divide entre los gobiernos de la nación y de los estados.
Fifteenth Amendment constitutional amendment that gave African Americans the right to vote.	**Decimoquinta Enmienda** enmienda constitucional que dio a los afroamericanos el derecho al voto.
filibuster a tactic through which an individual senator may use the right of unlimited debate to delay a motion or postpone action on a piece of legislation.	**obstruccionismo** táctica a través de la cual un senador individual puede usar el derecho al debate sin límites para demorar una moción o posponer la acción sobre un proyecto de ley.
fiscal federalism the federal government's use of grants-in-aid to influence policies in the states.	**federalismo fiscal** uso que hace el gobierno federal de las subvenciones para influir en las políticas de los estados.
fiscal policy government use of taxes and spending to attempt to lower unemployment, support economic activity, and stabilize the economy.	**política fiscal** uso que hace el gobierno de los gastos e impuestos en un intento de reducir el desempleo, apoyar la actividad económica y estabilizar la economía.
focus group a small group of individuals assembled for a conversation about specific issues.	**grupo de enfoque** pequeño grupo de individuos formado para conversar acerca de temas específicos.
formal or enumerated powers powers of the president expressly granted in the Constitution.	**poderes formales o enumerados** poderes del presidente expresamente garantizados en la Constitución.
Fourteenth Amendment constitutional amendment asserting that persons born in the United States are citizens and prohibits states from denying persons due process or equal protection under the law.	**Decimocuarta Enmienda** enmienda constitucional que afirma que las personas nacidas en los Estados Unidos son ciudadanos de este país y prohíbe a los estados negar a las personas el proceso debido o la igualdad ante la ley.
franchise (or suffrage) the right to vote in political elections.	**sufragio (o voto)** el derecho a votar en elecciones políticas.
freedom of expression a fundamental right affirmed in the First Amendment to speak, publish, and protest.	**libertad de expresión** derecho fundamental de hablar, publicar y protestar respaldado por la Primera Enmienda.
free exercise clause First Amendment protection of the rights of individuals to exercise and express their religious beliefs.	**cláusula de libre ejercicio** protección de la Primera Enmienda a los derechos de individuos a ejercitar y expresar sus creencias religiosas.
free rider individual who enjoys collective goods and benefits from the actions of an interest group without joining.	**consumidor parásito** individuo que disfruta de los bienes colectivos y se beneficia de las acciones de grupos de interés sin unirse a ellos.
front-loading a decision by a state to push its primary or caucus to a date as early in the election season as possible to gain more influence in the presidential nomination process.	**anticipar** decisión de un estado de mover sus primarias o conclave a la fecha más temprana posible de la temporada electoral para ganar así más influencia en el proceso de nominación presidencial.
full faith and credit clause constitutional clause requiring states to recognize the public acts, records, and civil court proceedings from another state.	**cláusula de entera fe y crédito** cláusula constitucional que requiere a los estados reconocer los actos públicos, registros y procedimientos de las cortes civiles de otro estado.

G

gender gap a term that refers to the fact that American women are more likely to identify with and vote for Democratic Party candidates than men, who are more likely to vote for Republican Party candidates.	**brecha de género** término que hace referencia al hecho de que las mujeres en Estados Unidos son más proclives a identificarse y votar por los candidatos del Partido Demócrata que los hombres, quienes son más proclives a votar por el candidato del Partido Republicano.

generational effect the impact of historical events experienced by a generation upon their political views.	**efecto generacional** el impacto de los sucesos históricos experimentados por una generación sobre sus puntos de vista políticos.
gerrymandering the intentional use of redistricting to benefit a specific interest or group of voters.	**manipulación electoral (gerrymandering)** el uso intencionado de redistribuir distritos electorales para beneficiar a un interés específico o a un grupo de votantes.
get out the vote (GOTV) efforts to mobilize voters.	**sacar el voto (GOTV, en inglés)** esfuerzos para movilizar a los votantes.
globalization the increasing interconnectedness of people, businesses, and countries throughout the world.	**globalización** la creciente interconexión de personas, negocios y países de todo el mundo.
going public a tactic through which presidents reach out directly to the American people with the hope that the people will, in turn, put pressure upon their representatives and senators to press for a president's policy goals.	**hacer público** táctica a través de la cual los presidentes se comunican directamente con los estadounidenses con la esperanza de que estos, como respuesta, presionen a sus representantes y senadores para impulsar los objetivos políticos del presidente.
government the rules and institutions that make up that system of policymaking.	**gobierno** reglas e instituciones que conforman el sistema de hacer política.
government interest group organization acting on behalf of local, state, or foreign governments.	**grupo de interés gubernamental** organización que actúa en beneficio de gobiernos locales, estatales o extranjeros.
Grand Committee a committee at the Constitutional Convention that worked out the compromise on representation.	**Gran Comité** comité presente en la Convención Constitucional que elaboró el compromiso de representación.
grand jury a group of citizens who, based on the evidence presented to them, decide whether or not a person should be indicted and subsequently tried in a court of law.	**gran jurado** grupo de ciudadanos que, según las pruebas ante ellos presentadas, decide si una persona debe o no ser acusada y, consecuentemente, juzgada en una corte judicial.
grants-in-aid federal money provided to states to implement public policy objectives.	**subvención de ayuda** dinero federal otorgado a los estados para implementar los objetivos de la política pública.
grassroots lobbying mobilizing interest group members to pressure their representatives by contacting them directly through phone calls, email, and social media.	**cabildeo de base** movilizar a miembros de grupos de interés a presionar a sus representantes contactándoles directamente por teléfono, email y redes sociales.
Great Compromise an agreement for a plan of government that drew upon both the Virginia and New Jersey Plans; it settled issues of state representation by calling for a bicameral legislature with a House of Representatives apportioned proportionately and a Senate apportioned equally.	**Gran Compromiso** un acuerdo para un plan de gobierno que se basaba en los Planes de Virginia y New Jersey; resolvió cuestiones de representación de estado haciendo un llamado por una legislatura bicameral, con una Cámara de Representantes repartida proporcionalmente y un Senado también repartido equitativamente.
gridlock a slowdown or halt in Congress's ability to legislate and overcome divisions, especially those based on partisanship.	**estancamiento** desaceleración o un alto en la capacidad del Congreso para legislar y sobreponerse a las divisiones, especialmente las basadas en el partidismo.
gross domestic product (GDP) the total value of goods and services produced by an economy.	**producto interno bruto (PIB)** valor total de los bienes y servicios producidos por una economía.

H

hold a delay placed on legislation by a senator who objects to a bill.	**moción de protesta** reclamación hecha en la legislatura por un senador que se opone a un proyecto de ley.
horse-race journalism coverage of political campaigns that focuses more on the drama of the campaign than on policy issues.	**periodismo hípico** cobertura de campañas políticas que se enfoca más en el drama de la campaña que en los aspectos políticos.
House majority leader the person who is the second in command of the House of Representatives.	**líder mayoritario de la Cámara** la segunda persona al mando de la Cámara de Representantes.
House Rules Committee a powerful committee that determines when a bill will be subject to debate and vote on the House floor, how long the debate will last, and whether amendments will be allowed on the floor.	**Comité de Reglas de la Cámara** un poderoso comité que determina cuándo un proyecto de ley estará sujeto a debate y votado en la Cámara, cuánto durará el debate y si las enmiendas estarán permitidas.

I

implementation the bureaucracy's role in putting into action the laws that Congress has passed.	**implementación** el papel de la burocracia en la puesta en acción de las leyes que el Congreso ha aprobado.
implied powers authority of the federal government that goes beyond its expressed powers; powers not granted specifically to the national government but considered necessary to carry out the enumerated powers.	**poderes implícitos** autoridad del gobierno federal que va más allá de sus poderes expresos; poderes no garantizados específicamente al gobierno nacional pero considerados necesarios para llevar a cabo los poderes enumerados.

inalienable rights rights the government cannot take away.	**derechos inalienables** derechos que el gobierno no puede retirar.
incumbency advantage institutional advantages held by those already in office who are trying to fend off challengers in an election.	**ventajas de titularidad** ventaja institucional que tienen los que ya trabajan en el gobierno y que están tratando de eludir a los contendientes en una elección.
incumbent a political official who is currently in office.	**funcionario en ejercicio** funcionario político que está ejerciendo un cargo.
independent executive agency agency otherwise similar to cabinet departments but existing outside of the cabinet structure and usually having a narrower focus of mission.	**agencia ejecutiva independiente** agencia parecida a los departamentos del gabinete pero que existe fuera de la estructura del gabinete, usualmente con una misión declarada más específica.
independent regulatory agency organization that exists outside of the major cabinet departments and whose job is to monitor and regulate specific sectors of the economy.	**agencia regulatoria independiente** organización que existe fuera de los departamentos mayores del gabinete, cuyo trabajo es evaluar y regular sectores específicos de la economía.
individualism the belief that individuals should be responsible for themselves and for the decisions they make.	**individualismo** la creencia de que los individuos deben ser responsables de sí mismos y de las decisiones que toman.
inflation the rise in the prices of goods and services.	**inflación** el aumento de los precios de bienes y servicios.
informal powers powers not laid out in the Constitution but used to carry out presidential duties.	**poderes informales** poderes no asentados en la Constitución pero usados para llevar a cabo deberes presidenciales.
interest group voluntary association of people who come together with the goal of getting the policies that they favor enacted.	**grupo de interés** asociación voluntaria de personas que se juntan con la meta de hacer que se aprueben las políticas que ellos apoyan.
interest rates the rates paid to borrow money.	**tasas de interés** cuotas que se pagan al pedir dinero prestado.
investigative journalism an approach to newsgathering in which reporters dig into stories, often looking for instances of wrongdoing.	**periodismo de investigación** una manera de recopilar noticias en la que los reporteros investigan muy a fondo, usualmente delatando irregularidades.
iron triangle coordinated and mutually beneficial activities of the bureaucracy, Congress, and interest groups to achieve shared policy goals.	**triangulo de hierro** actividades coordinadas y mutuamente beneficiosas entre la burocracia, el Congreso y grupos privados para alcanzar metas políticas compartidas.
issue network webs of influence between interest groups, policymakers, and policy advocates.	**red temática** red de influencia que se forma entre grupos de interés, legisladores y activistas políticos.

J

judicial activism a philosophy of constitutional interpretation that justices should wield the power of judicial review, sometimes creating bold new policies.	**activismo judicial** filosofía de la interpretación constitucional en la que los jueces deben tener el poder de hacer revisiones judiciales, algunas veces creando políticas nuevas y audaces.
judicial branch the institution responsible for hearing and deciding cases through federal courts.	**poder judicial** la institución responsable de oír y decidir casos a través de las cortes federales.
judicial restraint a philosophy of constitutional interpretation that asserts justices should be cautious in overturning laws.	**contención judicial** filosofía de la interpretación judicial que afirma que los jueces deben ser cautelosos al anular leyes.
judicial review the authority of the Supreme Court to strike down a law or executive action if it conflicts with the Constitution.	**revisión judicial** la autoridad de la Corte Suprema para derogar una ley o acción ejecutiva si está en conflicto con la Constitución.

L

laissez-faire or free enterprise an economic system in which government intrudes as little as possible in the transactions among citizens and businesses.	**laissez-faire o liberalismo económico** sistema económico en el que el estado interfiere lo menos posible en las transacciones de los ciudadanos y los negocios.
lame duck period period at the end of a presidential term when Congress may block presidential initiatives and nominees.	**período de "pato rengo"** período final de un ciclo presidencial, en el que el Congreso bloquea las iniciativas del Presidente y a sus nominados.
legal segregation the separation by law of individuals based on their race.	**segregación legal** separación legal de los individuos según su raza.
legislative branch the institution responsible for making laws.	**poder legislativo** institución responsable de hacer las leyes.
libel an untrue written statement that injures a person's reputation.	**libelo** declaración escrita falsa que daña la reputación de una persona.
liberalism an ideology favoring less government control over social behavior and greater regulation of the economy.	**liberalismo progresista** ideología a favor de tener menos control del gobierno sobre el comportamiento social y mayor regulación de la economía.

libertarianism an ideology favoring very little government intervention beyond protecting private property and individual liberty.	**libertarianismo** ideología a favor de la no intervención del gobierno más allá de la protección de la propiedad privada y las libertades individuales.
liberty social, political, and economic freedoms.	**libertades** aperturas sociales, políticas y económicas.
life-cycle effect the impact of a person's age and stage in life on his or her political views.	**efecto de ciclo de vida** el impacto que tienen la edad y la etapa de la vida de una persona sobre sus puntos de vista políticos.
linkage institutions channels that connect individuals with government, including elections, political parties, interest groups, and the media.	**instituciones vinculantes** los canales que conectan a los individuos con el gobierno, incluidas las elecciones, los partidos políticos, los grupos de interés y los medios.
lobbying interacting with government officials in order to advance a group's public policy goals.	**cabildeo** interactuar con oficiales del gobierno para impulsar las metas de las políticas públicas de un grupo.
logrolling trading of votes on legislation by members of Congress to get their earmarks passed into legislation.	**amiguismo** intercambio de votos entre miembros del Congreso sobre una legislación para lograr que sus asignaciones se aprueben como ley.

M

majority-minority district a district in which voters of a minority ethnicity constitute an electoral majority within that electoral district.	**distrito mayoría-minoría** distrito en el cual los votantes de una etnia minoritaria constituyen una mayoría electoral dentro de ese distrito electoral.
majority opinion binding Supreme Court opinions, which serve as precedent for future cases.	**opinión mayoritaria** vincular opiniones en la Corte Suprema, que sirven como precedente para casos futuros.
majority party leader the head of the party with the most seats in Congress, chosen by the party's members.	**líder del partido mayoritario** el cabeza del partido con más escaños en el congreso, elegido por los mismos miembros del partido.
malapportionment the uneven distribution of the population between legislative districts.	**mal proporcionado** distribución desigual de la población entre los distritos legislativos.
mandatory spending spending required by existing laws that is "locked in" the budget.	**gasto obligatorio** gasto requerido por la ley vigente que es parte "fija" del presupuesto.
***Marbury v. Madison* (1803)** a Supreme Court decision that established judicial review over federal laws.	***Marbury v. Madison* (1803)** decisión de la Corte Suprema que creó la revisión judicial sobre las leyes federales.
markup a process during which a bill is revised prior to a final vote in Congress.	**redacción** proceso durante el cual un proyecto de ley es revisado antes de su voto final en el Congreso.
mass media sources of information that appeal to a wide audience, including newspapers, radio, television, and Internet outlets.	**medios de comunicación** fuentes de información que llegan a una vasta audiencia, incluida la prensa, la radio, la televisión e internet.
mass survey a survey designed to measure the opinions of the population, usually consisting of 1,500 responses.	**encuesta de masas** encuesta diseñada para medir las opiniones de la población, usualmente consiste de 1500 respuestas.
media consolidation the concentration of ownership of the media into fewer corporations.	**consolidación mediática** la concentración de propiedad de los medios en manos de unas pocas corporaciones.
media effects the power of the news media in shaping individuals' political knowledge, preferences, and political behavior.	**efecto de los medios** el poder de los medios noticiosos de dar forma al conocimiento, las preferencias y el comportamiento político de los individuos.
Medicaid a federal program that provides health care for the poor.	**Medicaid** programa federal que proporciona seguro médico para los pobres.
Medicare a federal program that provides health insurance to seniors and the disabled.	**Medicare** programa federal que proporciona seguro médico a personas mayores y a los discapacitados.
merit system a system of hiring and promotion based on competitive testing results, education, and other qualifications rather than politics and personal connections.	**meritocracia** sistema de contratación y promoción basado en los resultados competitivos de pruebas, la educación y otras calificaciones, en lugar de conexiones políticas y personales.
minority leader the head of the party with the second-highest number of seats in Congress, chosen by the party's members.	**líder minoritario** el cabeza del partido con la segunda más alta cantidad de escaños en el Congreso, elegido por los mismos miembros del partido.
Miranda rights the right to remain silent and to have an attorney present during questioning; these rights must be given by police to individuals suspected of criminal activity.	**derechos Miranda** el derecho a permanecer callado y de tener un abogado presente durante un interrogatorio; estos derechos deben dárselos los oficiales de policía a los individuos sospechosos de alguna actividad criminal.
mixed economy economic policy in which many economic decisions are left to individuals and businesses with the federal government regulating economic activity.	**economía mixta** política económica en la que muchas decisiones económicas se dejan a los individuos y negocios, al mismo tiempo que esta actividad económica es regulada por el gobierno federal.

monetary policy a set of economic policy tools designed to regulate the amount of money in the economy.	**política monetaria** serie de herramientas de política económica diseñadas para regular la cantidad de dinero que circula en la economía.
motor voter law a law allowing Americans to register to vote when applying for or renewing their driver's licenses and making it easier for Americans with disabilities to register to vote.	**ley *Motor Voter*** ley que permite a los estadounidenses registrarse para votar cuando están obteniendo o renovando la licencia de conducir; así se facilita también el acceso de los estadounidenses con discapacidad para que se registren para votar.

N

national convention a meeting where delegates officially select their party's nominee for the presidency.	**convención nacional** reunión donde los delegados eligen oficialmente al nominado a la presidencia del partido.
national debt the total amount of money owed by the federal government.	**deuda nacional** la cantidad total de dinero que debe el gobierno federal.
natural rights the right to life, liberty, and property, which government cannot take away.	**derechos naturales** el derecho a la vida, la libertad y la propiedad, los cuales el gobierno no puede eliminar.
necessary and proper or elastic clause language in Article I, Section 8, granting Congress the powers necessary to carry out its enumerated powers.	**necesaria y correcta o cláusula elástica** terminología del Artículo I, Sección 8, que garantiza al Congreso los poderes necesarios para ejecutar sus poderes enumerados.
need-based assistance social welfare programs whose benefits are allocated to individuals demonstrating specific needs.	**asistencia según la necesidad** programas de ayuda social cuyos beneficios son asignados a individuos que demuestran tener necesidades específicas.
net neutrality a Federal Communications Commission (FCC) rule that required internet service providers to treat all data and content providers equally and not discriminate based upon content or bandwidth demands.	**neutralidad de la red** regla de la Comisión Federal de Comunicaciones (FCC) que requiere del servicio de proveedores de internet tratar todos los datos y proveedores de contenidos con igualdad y no discriminar según los contenidos o los requisitos de banda ancha.
New Jersey Plan a plan of government that provided for a unicameral legislature with equal votes for each state.	**Plan New Jersey** un plan de gobierno que contempla una legislatura unicameral con la misma cantidad de votos para cada estado.
news media a broad term that includes newspapers, magazines, radio, television, radio, internet sources, blogs, and social media postings.	**medios de noticias** término amplio que incluye periódicos, revistas, radio, televisión, fuentes de internet, blogs y mensajes de las redes sociales.
Nineteenth Amendment a 1920 constitutional amendment granting women the right to vote.	**Decimonovena Enmienda** enmienda constitucional de 1920 que garantiza a las mujeres el derecho al voto.
nomination the formal process through which parties choose their candidates for political office.	**nominación** proceso formal a través del cual los partidos escogen a sus candidatos para los cargos políticos.

O

obscenity and pornography words, images, or videos that depict sexual activity in an offensive manner and that lack any artistic merit.	**obscenidad y pornografía** palabras, imágenes o videos que muestran actividad sexual en una manera ofensiva que carece de todo mérito artístico.
Office of Management and Budget (OMB) the executive branch office that assists the president in setting national spending priorities.	**Oficina de Gerencia y Presupuesto (OMB)** oficina del poder ejecutivo que asiste al presidente para establecer las prioridades del gasto nacional.
open primary a primary election in which all eligible voters may vote, regardless of their party affiliation.	**primarias abiertas** elecciones primarias donde todos los votantes pueden votar, sin importar su afiliación política.
oral argument presentation made by plaintiffs and attorneys before the Supreme Court.	**alegato oral** presentación oral hecha por los demandantes y abogados ante la Corte Suprema.
original jurisdiction the authority of a court to act as the first court to hear a case, which includes the finding of facts in the case.	**jurisdicción de primera instancia** autoridad de un tribunal a actuar como el primer tribunal donde se escuche un caso, lo que incluye hallar los hechos del mismo.
outsourcing when a company moves its business to a place where labor costs are cheaper or production is more efficient because workers work longer hours.	**subcontratación / tercerización** cuando una compañía muda sus negocios a un sitio donde los costos laborales son más baratos o la producción más eficiente porque las jornadas de trabajo son más largas.
oversight efforts by Congress to ensure that executive branch agencies, bureaus, and cabinet departments, as well as their officials, are acting legally and in accordance with congressional goals.	**supervisión** esfuerzos del Congreso para garantizar que las agencias del poder ejecutivo, oficinas y departamentos del gabinete, así como sus oficiales, actúan legalmente y de acuerdo con las metas del congreso.

P

participatory democracy the theory that widespread political participation is essential for democratic government.	**democracia participativa** teoría de que la participación política generalizada es esencial para el gobierno democrático.

partisan bias the slanting of political news coverage in support of a particular political party or ideology.	**parcialidad partidista** inclinación de la cobertura de noticieros políticos en apoyo de un partido político en particular o de una ideología.
partisan gerrymandering drawing of district boundaries into strange shapes to benefit a political party.	**manipulación partidista** el trazar los límites de los distritos electorales con formas extrañas para beneficiar a un partido político en particular.
party coalition interest groups and like-minded voters who support a political party over time.	**coalición partidista** grupos de interés y votantes con pensamientos afines, que apoyan a un partido político a través del tiempo.
party era time period when one party wins most national elections.	**era de un partido** período de tiempo en que un partido gana la mayoría en las elecciones nacionales.
party identification an individual's attachment to a political party.	**identificación partidista** apego de un individuo a un partido político.
party ideology a party's philosophy about the proper role of government and its consistent set of positions on major issues.	**ideología de un partido** filosofía de un partido acerca de la función adecuada de un gobierno y sus posiciones consecuentes en los problemas más importantes.
party-line voting voting for candidates who belong only to one political party for all of the offices on the ballot.	**votar según los lineamientos del partido** votar en todos los cargos de la papeleta electoral por candidatos que pertenecen a un solo partido político.
party platform a set of positions and policy objectives that members of a political party agree to.	**plataforma partidista** grupo de posiciones y objetivos políticos sobre los que todos los miembros del partido político están de acuerdo.
party system the number of stable parties that exist at a particular time.	**sistema partidista** número de partidos estables que existen en un período tiempo particular.
Pendleton Act an act of Congress that created the first United States Civil Service Commission to draw up and enforce rules on hiring, promotion, and tenure of office within the civil service. Also known as Civil Service Reform Act of 1883.	**Acto Pendleton** acto del Congreso que creó la primera Comisión de Servicios Civiles de Estados Unidos para trazar y hacer cumplir las reglas sobre contratación, promoción y tenencia de cargos dentro del servicio civil. También conocido como Acto de Reforma del Servicio Civil de 1883.
plaintiff a person or group who brings a case in court.	**demandante** persona o grupo que lleva un caso a la corte.
plea bargaining a legal process in which the defendant agrees to an outcome before the handing out of a verdict.	**negociación de clemencia** proceso legal en el cual el defendido llega a un acuerdo antes de que se dicte la sentencia.
Plessy v. Ferguson a Supreme Court case in 1896 that upheld legal racial segregation.	***Plessy v. Ferguson*** caso de la Corte Suprema en 1896 que mantuvo la segregación racial.
pluralism a theory of governmental influence that views the distribution of political power among many competing groups as serving to keep any one of them in check.	**pluralismo** teoría de influencia gubernamental que revisa la distribución de poder político entre varios grupos competidores y sirve para mantener a cualquiera de ellos a raya.
pluralist theory a theory of democracy that emphasizes the role of groups in the policymaking process.	**teoría pluralista** teoría de la democracia que enfatiza el papel de los grupos en el proceso de hacer políticas.
plurality when a candidate receives more votes than any other candidate.	**mayoría relativa** cuando un candidato recibe más votos que ningún otro candidato.
pocket veto an informal veto caused when the president chooses not to sign a bill within ten days, during a time when Congress has adjourned at the end of a session.	**veto indirecto** veto informal que ocurre cuando el presidente decide no firmar una legislación dentro de un período de diez días, mientras el Congreso ha cesado al final de una sesión.
polarization a sharp ideological distance between political parties.	**polarización** marcada distancia ideológica entre partidos políticos.
police powers a category of reserved powers that includes the protection of people's health, safety, and welfare.	**poderes policiales** categoría de poderes reservados que incluyen la protección de la salud de las personas, su seguridad y bienestar.
policy agenda the set of issues to which government officials, voters, and the public are paying attention.	**agenda política** grupo de temas tratados por los oficiales del gobierno, y que genera el interés de los votantes y el público en general.
political action committee (PAC) an organization that raises money for candidates and campaigns.	**comité de acción política (CAP)** organización que recauda fondos para candidatos y campañas.
political culture the shared set of beliefs, customs, traditions, and values that define the relationship between citizens and government.	**cultura política** conjunto de creencias, costumbres, tradiciones y valores compartidos que definen la relación entre los ciudadanos y el gobierno.
political efficacy a person's belief that he or she can make effective political change.	**eficacia política** creencia de una persona en que él o ella pueden hacer un cambio político efectivo.

political ideology an individual's coherent set of beliefs about government and politics.	**ideología política** grupo de creencias coherentes de un individuo acerca del gobierno y la política.
political institutions the structure of government, including the executive, legislature, and judiciary.	**instituciones políticas** la estructura del gobierno que incluye el ejecutivo, la legislatura y el poder judicial.
political mobilization efforts by political parties to encourage their members to vote.	**movilización política** esfuerzos de los partidos políticos para animar a sus miembros a que voten.
political participation the different ways in which individuals take action to shape the laws and policies of a government.	**participación política** las diferentes maneras en que los individuos toman medidas para dar forma a las leyes y políticas de un gobierno.
political party an organized group of party leaders, officeholders, and voters who work together to elect candidates to political office.	**partido político** grupo organizado de lideres políticos, funcionarios públicos y votantes quienes trabajan juntos para elegir candidatos a los puestos del gobierno.
political patronage filling administrative positions as a reward for support, rather than solely on merit.	**patrocinio político** ocupar posiciones administrativas, no solo a través del mérito personal, sino como recompensa por el apoyo dado.
political science the systematic study of the ways in which ideas, individuals, and institutions shape political outcomes.	**ciencia política** el estudio sistemático de las maneras en las que ideas, individuos e instituciones dan forma a los resultados políticos.
political socialization the experiences and factors that shape our political values, attitudes, and behaviors.	**socialización política** experiencias y factores que dan forma a nuestros comportamientos, actitudes y valores políticos.
politico role representation where members of Congress balance their choices with the interests of their constituents and parties in making decisions.	**rol como político** representación donde miembros del Congreso concilian sus preferencias con los intereses de sus electores y de los partidos al tomar decisiones.
politics the process of influencing the actions and policies of government.	**políticas** el proceso de influenciar las acciones y políticas de gobierno.
popular sovereignty the idea that the government's right to rule comes from the people.	**soberanía popular** la idea de que el derecho del gobierno a mandar radica en el pueblo.
pork barrel spending legislation that directs specific funds to projects within districts or states.	**gastos "barril con carne de cerdo"** legislación que dirige fondos específicos a proyectos dentro de los estados o distritos.
precedent a judicial decision that guides future courts in handling similar cases.	**precedente** decisión judicial que guía a las cortes en su manejo futuro de casos semejantes.
presidential pardon presidential authority to forgive an individual and set aside punishment for a crime.	**perdón presidencial** autoridad presidencial de perdonar a un individuo y dejar de lado el castigo dado por un crimen.
primary election an election in which a state's voters choose delegates who support a particular presidential candidate for nomination or an election by a plurality vote to select a party's nominee for a seat in Congress.	**elección primaria** elección en la cual los votantes de un estado escogen delegados que apoyan a un candidato presidencial en particular para ser nominado, o una elección por voto de mayoría relativa para seleccionar al nominado por el partido a un puesto en el Congreso.
prior restraint the suppression of material prior to publication on the grounds that it might endanger national security.	**restricción previa** La supresión de un material antes de que se publique dado que este puede ser peligroso para la seguridad nacional.
privacy a right not enumerated in the Constitution but affirmed by Supreme Court decisions that covers individuals' decisions in their private lives, including decisions regarding reproductive rights and sexuality.	**privacidad** derecho no enumerado en la Constitución pero asegurado por las decisiones de la Corte Suprema que protege las preferencias de los individuos en sus vidas privadas, incluidas sus decisiones sobre derechos de reproducción y sexualidad.
privilege something subject to political process.	**privilegio** algo sujeto a proceso político.
privileges and immunities clause prevents states from discriminating against people from out of state.	**cláusula de privilegios e inmunidades** evita que los estados discriminen a las personas que no sean de ese estado.
probable cause reasonable belief that a crime has been committed or that there is evidence indicating so.	**causa probable** creencia razonable de que un crimen se cometió o de que haya evidencia que así lo indique.
procedural due process a judicial standard requiring that fairness be applied to all individuals equally.	**garantías procesales** estándar judicial que requiere que la imparcialidad se aplique a todos por igual.
proportional representation system an election system for a legislature in which citizens vote for parties, rather than individuals, and parties are represented in the legislature according to the percentage of the vote they receive.	**sistema de representación proporcional** sistema de elección para una legislatura en la cual los ciudadanos votan a partidos en vez de a individuos, y los partidos son representados en la legislatura de acuerdo al porcentaje del voto que recibieron.

prospective voting casting a ballot for a candidate who promises to enact policies favored by the voter in the future.	**voto perspectivo** votar a un candidato que promete que en el futuro pondrá en vigor políticas apoyadas por el votante.
protest a public demonstration designed to call attention to the need for change.	**protesta** manifestación pública destinada a llamar la atención sobre la necesidad de un cambio.
public interest group group that acts on behalf of the collective interests of a broad group of individuals.	**grupo de interés público** grupo que actúa representando el interés colectivo de un gran número de individuos.
public opinion the sum of individual attitudes about government, policies, and issues.	**opinión pública** la suma de actitudes individuales acerca del gobierno, políticas y temas en general.
public policy the intentional use of governmental power to secure the health, welfare, opportunities, and national security of citizens.	**política pública** el uso intencionado del poder gubernamental para asegurar la salud, bienestar, oportunidades y seguridad nacional de los ciudadanos.

Q

question order the sequencing of questions in public opinion polls.	**orden de las preguntas** la secuencia de las preguntas en una encuesta de opinión pública.
question wording the phrasing of a question in a public opinion poll.	**redacción de la pregunta** la redacción de las preguntas en una encuesta de opinión pública.

R

random digit dialing the use of telephone numbers randomly generated by a computer to select potential survey respondents.	**marcar números aleatoriamente** uso de números de teléfono generados aleatoriamente por computadora para seleccionar participantes potenciales de una encuesta.
random selection a method of choosing all poll respondents in a way that does not over- or underrepresent any group of the population.	**selección aleatoria** método para seleccionar a todos los participantes de una encuesta de manera que no se sobrerepresente o subrepresente ningún grupo de la población.
rational choice voting voting based on what a citizen believes is in his or her best interest.	**voto de elección racional** voto basado en lo que un ciudadano cree que va a favorecer más sus intereses.
realignment when the groups of people who support a political party shift their allegiance to a different political party.	**realineamiento** cuando grupos de personas que apoyan a un partido cambian su apoyo a otro partido político.
recruitment the process through which political parties identify potential candidates.	**reclutamiento** proceso a través del cual los partidos políticos identifican candidatos potenciales.
redistricting states' redrawing of boundaries of electoral districts following each census.	**redistribuir distritos** cambiar el trazado de los límites de los distritos electorales después de cada censo.
registration requirements the set of rules that govern who can vote and how, when, and where they vote.	**requisitos de registro** grupo de reglas que rigen sobre quién puede votar y cómo, así como cuándo y dónde vota.
regulation the process through which the federal bureaucracy makes rules that have the force of law, to carry out the laws passed by Congress.	**regulación** proceso a través del cual la burocracia federal crea reglas que tienen fuerza de ley; así se implementan las leyes aprobadas por el Congreso.
representative democracy a political system in which voters select representatives who then vote on matters of public policy.	**democracia representativa** sistema político por el cual los votantes seleccionan a sus representantes, quienes luego votan en cuestiones de política pública.
representative sample a sample that reflects the demographics of the population.	**muestra representativa** muestra que refleja los datos demográficos de la población.
republic a government ruled by representatives of the people.	**república** gobierno regido por los representantes del pueblo.
republicanism a system in which the government's authority comes from the people.	**republicanismo** sistema en el cual la autoridad del gobierno viene del pueblo.
reserved powers powers not given to the national government, which are retained by the states and the people.	**poderes reservados** poderes no otorgados al gobierno nacional, los cuales son retenidos por los estados y el pueblo.
retrospective voting voting based on an assessment of an incumbent's past performance.	**voto retrospectivo** voto basado en la evaluación del desempeño pasado de un funcionario.
revenue sharing when the federal government apportions tax money to the states with no strings attached.	**repartición de ingresos** cuando el gobierno federal distribuye el dinero de los impuestos a los estados sin ataduras.

revolving door the movement of individuals between government and lobbying positions.	**puerta giratoria** el flujo de individuos entre posiciones de gobierno y de cabildeo.
right something fundamental to which all have access.	**derecho** algo fundamental a lo que todos tenemos acceso.
roll-call vote a recorded vote on a bill.	**voto nominal** voto registrado en proyecto de ley.
rulemaking the process through which the federal bureaucracy fills in critical details of a law.	**reglamentación** proceso a través del cual la burocracia federal complementa los detalles críticos de una ley.
rule of law the principle that no one, including public officials, is above the law.	**estado de derecho** el principio de que nadie, ni siquiera los funcionarios públicos, está por encima de la ley.

S

sample a group of individuals from a larger population used to measure public opinion.	**muestra** grupo de individuos tomado de una población extensa. Sirve para medir la opinión pública.
sampling error the margin of error in a poll, which usually is calculated to plus or minus three percentage points.	**error de muestreo** el margen de error de una encuesta el cual es usualmente calculado en más o menos tres puntos porcentuales.
scientific poll a representative poll of randomly selected respondents with a statistically significant sample size using neutral language.	**encuesta científica** encuesta representativa con participantes seleccionados aleatoriamente que usa una muestra de tamaño estadísticamente significativa y emplea un lenguaje neutral.
selective benefit benefit available only to those who join the group.	**beneficio selectivo** beneficio que solamente disfrutan aquellos que se unen a un grupo.
selective incorporation the process through which the Supreme Court applies fundamental rights in the Bill of Rights to the states on a case-by-case basis.	**incorporación selectiva** proceso a través del cual la Corte Suprema aplica a los estados los derechos fundamentales contemplados en la Carta de Derechos, basándose particularmente en cada caso.
Senate majority leader the person who has the most power in the Senate and is the head of the party with the most seats.	**líder de la mayoría del Senado** la persona con más poder en el Senado, que es el cabeza del partido con la mayoría de escaños.
separate but equal the doctrine that racial segregation was constitutional so long as the facilities for blacks and whites were equal.	**separados pero iguales** la doctrina en la que la segregación era constitucional mientras que las instalaciones para negros y blancos fueran iguales.
separation of powers a design of government that distributes powers across institutions in order to avoid making one branch too powerful on its own.	**separación de poderes** diseño del gobierno que distribuye los poderes entre las instituciones para evitar que una rama concentre mucho poder en si misma.
Shays's Rebellion a popular uprising against the government of Massachusetts.	**Rebelión de Shays** rebelión popular contra el gobierno de Massachusetts.
signing statement text issued by presidents while signing a bill into law that usually consists of political statements or reasons for signing the bill but that may also include a president's interpretation of the law itself.	**comunicado de firma** escrito entregado por los presidentes mientras firman un proyecto de ley que usualmente consiste en un a explicación de por qué se firma esa ley, pero que puede también incluir la interpretación del presidente de la ley misma.
single-issue group association focusing on one specific area of public policy, often a moral issue about which they are unwilling to compromise.	**grupo de tema único** asociación enfocada en un área especifica de la política pública, frecuentemente un hecho moral con el cual no están dispuestos a comprometerse.
single-member plurality system an election system for choosing members of the legislature where the winner is the candidate who receives the most votes, even if the candidate does not receive a majority of the votes.	**sistema de mayoría relativa de un solo miembro** sistema para elegir a miembros de la legislatura donde el ganador es el candidato que recibe más votos, incluso si ese candidato no recibe la mayoría de los votos.
slander an untrue spoken expression that injures a person's reputation.	**difamación** expresión hablada falsa que causa daño a la reputación de una persona.
social contract people allow their governments to rule over them to ensure an orderly and functioning society.	**contrato social** la gente permite a su gobierno que les rija para asegurar un funcionamiento ordenado de la sociedad.
social insurance programs programs such as Social Security that are financed by payroll taxes paid by individuals and that do not have income-based requirements to receive their benefits.	**programas de seguridad social** programas como el Seguridad Social que son financiados por la nómina de los impuestos pagados por los individuos y que no tienen requisitos basados en los ingresos para poder gozar de sus beneficios.
social media forms of electronic communication that enable users to create and share content or to participate in social networking.	**medios sociales** formas de comunicación electrónica que permiten a los usuarios crear y compartir contenidos y participar en redes sociales.

social movement large groups of citizens organizing for political change.	**movimiento social** grandes grupos de ciudadanos organizados para conseguir cambios políticos.
social welfare policies governmental efforts designed to improve or protect the health, safety, education, and opportunities for citizens and residents.	**políticas de asistencia social** esfuerzos gubernamentales diseñados para mejorar la salud, seguridad, educación y oportunidades de los ciudadanos y residentes.
socioeconomic status (SES) a measure of an individual's wealth, income, occupation, and educational attainment.	**estatus socio económico (SES)** nivel de riqueza, ingreso, ocupación y logros de educación de un individuo.
Speaker of the House the leader of the House of Representatives, chosen by an election of its members.	**Presidente de la Cámara de Representantes** líder de la cámara de diputados, escogido por elección entre sus miembros.
split-ticket voting voting for candidates from different parties in the same election.	**votación dividida** votar a candidatos de diferentes partidos en la misma elección.
standing the legal ability to bring a case in court.	**postulación procesal** capacidad legal para presentar un caso en la corte.
stare decisis the practice of letting a previous legal decision stand.	*stare decisis* **(mantener lo decidido)** la practica de dejar que una decisión legal previa prevalezca.
State of the Union Address the annual speech from the president to Congress updating that branch on the state of national affairs.	**Discurso del Estado de la Unión** discurso anual del presidente al Congreso para informar del estado de los asuntos de la nación.
statute a written law established by a legislative body.	**estatuto** ley escrita establecida por un cuerpo legislativo.
straight-ticket voting voting for all of the candidates on the ballot from one political party.	**votación de boleta directa** votar en la boleta por todos los candidatos de un mismo partido.
suffrage the right to vote in political elections.	**sufragio** el derecho a votar en una elección política.
superdelegate usually, a party leader or activist who is not pledged to a candidate based on the outcomes of the state's primary or caucus.	**superdelegado** usualmente un líder o activista de partido que no está comprometido con un candidato basado en el resultado de las primarias estatales o el conclave del partido.
super PAC an organization that may spend an unlimited amount of money on a political campaign, as long as the spending is not coordinated with the campaign.	**super PAC** organización que puede gastar una cantidad de dinero ilimitada en una campaña política, siempre que el gasto no esté coordinado con la campaña misma.
supremacy clause constitutional provision declaring that the Constitution and all national laws and treaties are the supreme law of the land.	**cláusula de supremacía** disposición constitucional que declara que la Constitución y todas las leyes y tratados nacionales son la ley suprema del país.
Supreme Court the highest level of the federal judiciary, which was established in Article III of the Constitution and serves as the highest court in the nation.	**Corte Suprema** el nivel más alto de la justicia federal, el cual fue establecido en el artículo III de la Constitución y funciona como el tribunal más alto en la nación.
swing state a state where levels of support for the parties are similar and elections swing back and forth between Democrats and Republicans.	**estado pendular** estado donde los niveles de apoyo a los partidos son similares y los resultados en las elecciones fluctúan entre Demócratas y Republicanos.
symbolic speech protected expression in the form of images, signs, and other symbols.	**expresión simbólica** expresión que se escuda en forma de imágenes, señales y otros símbolos.

T

Tenth Amendment reserves powers not delegated to the national government to the states and the people; the basis of federalism.	**Décima Enmienda** reserva poderes no delegados al gobierno nacional, para el estado y el pueblo; lo que es la base del federalismo.
terrorism the use of violence as a means to achieve political ends.	**terrorismo** el uso de la violencia como medio para conseguir metas políticas.
theory of participatory democracy the belief that citizens impact policymaking through their involvement in civil society.	**teoría de la democracia participativa** la creencia de que los ciudadanos tienen impacto en la creación de políticas a través de involucrarse en la sociedad civil.
third party a minor political party in competition with the two major parties.	**tercer partido** partido político minoritario que compite los dos partidos mayores.
Thirteenth Amendment constitutional amendment that outlaws slavery.	**Decimatercera Enmienda** enmienda constitucional que penaliza la esclavitud.

Three-Fifths Compromise an agreement reached by delegates at the Constitutional Convention that a slave would count as three-fifths of a person in calculating a state's representation.	**Compromiso de los Tres Quintos** acuerdo alcanzado por los delegados en la Convención Constitucional, de que un esclavo contaría como tres quintos de persona al calcularse la representación de un estado.
Title IX of the Higher Education Amendments of 1972 legislation prohibiting sex discrimination in schools receiving federal aid, which had the impact of increasing female participation in sports programs.	**Titulo IX de las Enmiendas de Educación Superior de 1972** legislación que prohíbe la discriminación sexual en escuelas que reciben ayuda federal, la cual tuvo el impacto de incrementar la participación femenina en los programas deportivos.
tracking poll a survey determining the level of support for a candidate or an issue throughout a campaign.	**encuesta de seguimiento** sondeo para determinar el nivel de apoyo a un candidato o a un tema particular a lo largo de una campaña.
treaty an agreement with a foreign government negotiated by the president and requiring a two-thirds vote in the Senate to ratify.	**tratado** acuerdo con un gobierno extranjero negociado por el presidente y que requiere dos tercios del voto del Senado para ser ratificado.
trustee role the idea that members of Congress should act as trustees, making decisions based on their knowledge and judgment.	**rol del fideicomisario** la idea que miembros del Congreso deben actuar como fideicomisarios, tomando decisiones basadas en sus conocimientos y buen juicio.
Twenty-Fourth Amendment prohibits Congress and the states from imposing poll taxes as a condition for voting in federal elections.	**Vigésimocuarta Enmienda** prohíbe al Congreso y a los estados imponer un impuesto electoral como condición para votar en elecciones federales.
Twenty-Sixth Amendment allows those eighteen years old and older to vote.	**Vigésimosexta Enmienda** permite votar a los que son mayores de 18 años de edad.
two-party system a system in which two political parties dominate politics, winning almost all elections.	**sistema bipartidista** sistema en el que dos partidos políticos dominan la vida política, ganando casi todas las elecciones.
tyranny of the majority when a large number of citizens use the power of their majority to trample on the rights of a smaller group.	**tiranía de la mayoría** cuando una mayoría de ciudadanos usa su poder para pisotear los derechos de un grupo minoritario.
tyranny of the minority when a small number of citizens trample on the rights of the larger population.	**tiranía de la minoría** cuando una minoría de ciudadanos pisotea los derechos de la mayoría.

U

unanimous consent agreement an agreement in the Senate that sets the terms for consideration of a bill.	**acuerdo de consentimiento unánime** acuerdo en el Senado que establece los términos para considerar una propuesta de ley.
unemployment rate the percentage of people actively looking for work who cannot find jobs.	**tasa de desempleo** el porcentaje de personas que están activamente buscando trabajo y no encuentran un empleo.
unfunded mandate federal requirement the states must follow without being provided with funding.	**mandato sin financiamiento** una imposición federal que los estados deben cumplir sin que le sean asignados fondos para ello.
unicameral a one-house legislature.	**unicameral** legislatura de una sola cámara.
unitary system a system where the central government has all of the power over subnational governments.	**sistema unitario** sistema donde el gobierno central tiene todo el poder sobre de los gobiernos subnacionales.

V

veto formal rejection by the president of a bill that has passed both houses of Congress.	**veto** rechazo formal del presidente a un proyecto de ley que ha sido aprobado por ambas cámaras del Congreso.
Virginia Plan a plan of government calling for a three-branch government with a bicameral legislature, where more populous states would have more representation in Congress.	**Plan Virginia** un plan de gobierno que propone un gobierno de tres ramas con una legislatura bicameral donde los estados más poblados tendrían más representación en el Congreso.
voter turnout the number of eligible voters who participate in an election as a percentage of the total number of eligible voters.	**participación electoral** número de votantes reales que participan en una elección con respecto al porcentaje total de votantes que podrían participar.
Voting Rights Act of 1965 legislation outlawing literacy tests and authorizing the Justice Department to send federal officers to register voters in uncooperative cities, counties, and states.	**Ley de Derecho al Voto de 1965** legislación que proscribe el tener que saber leer y escribir para registrarse como votante y que autoriza al Departamento de Justicia a enviar oficiales federales para registrar a esos votantes, en ciudades, condados y estados que no quieran cooperar.

War Powers Resolution a law passed over President Nixon's veto that restricts the power of the president to maintain troops in combat for more than sixty days without congressional authorization.	**Resolución sobre Poderes de Guerra** ley aprobada contra el veto del Presidente Nixon sobre la ley que restringía el poder del presidente de mantener tropas en combate por más de 60 días sin la aprobación del Congreso.
warrant a document issued by a judge authorizing a search.	**orden judicial** documento expedido por un juez que autoriza un registro.
weighting a procedure in which the survey is adjusted according to the demographics of the larger population.	**ponderación** procedimiento en el cual una encuesta es ajustada de acuerdo con las características demográficas de la población más extensa.
whip a member of Congress, chosen by his or her party members, whose job is to ensure party unity and discipline.	**jefe de la bancada** miembro del Congreso, escogido por los miembros de su partido cuyo trabajo es mantener la disciplina y unidad dentro del partido.
winner-take-all system a system of elections in which the candidate who wins the plurality of votes within a state receives all of that state's votes in the Electoral College.	**sistema en que el ganador se lleva todo** sistema de elecciones en el cual el candidato que gana la pluralidad de votos dentro de un estado recibe todos los votos de ese estado en el Colegio Electoral.
wire service an organization that gathers and reports on news and then sells the stories to other outlets.	**agencia de noticias** una organización que reúne y reporta acerca de noticias y luego las vende a otros medios de comunicación.
writ of habeas corpus the right of people detained by the government to know the charges against them.	**mandato de *habeas corpus*** el derecho de las personas detenidas por el gobierno a saber de qué cargos se les acusa.

Notes

Chapter 1

1. Equal Access Act of 1984, 20 U.S.C. § 4071.
2. Board of Education of Westside Community Schools v. Mergens, 496 U.S. 226 (1990).
3. Ruth Marcus, "Schools Brace for Fallout from Bible-Club Ruling: Some Officials Fear Disruptive Groups Will Enter through Door Opened by Court to Religion," *Washington Post*, June 11, 1990.
4. Boyd County High School Gay Straight Alliance v. Board of Education of Boyd County, KY, 258 F. Supp. 2d 667 (E.D. Ky. 2003).
5. Ibid. The ACLU had sent the letter in September, before the meeting in which the decision to deny was taken.
6. Ibid.
7. Ibid.
8. Ibid.
9. American Civil Liberties Union, "ACLU Wins Settlement for Kentucky School's Gay-Straight Alliance," February 3, 2014, https://www.aclu.org/news/aclu-wins-settlement-kentucky-schools-gay-straight-alliance.
10. National Legal Foundation, "Welcome," http://www.nlf.net.
11. Equal Access Act of 1984.
12. John Locke, *Second Treatise of Government* (1690).
13. Charles-Louis de Secondat, Baron de Montesquieu, *The Spirit of the Laws* (1748).
14. David Hume, *A Treatise of Human Nature* (1739).
15. Rodgers Smith, "Beyond Tocqueville, Myrdal, and Hartz: The Multiple Traditions in America," *American Political Science Review* 87, no. 3 (Sept. 1993): 549–66.
16. Ibid.
17. https://politicsofpoverty.oxfamamerica.org/2013/08/hard-work-hard-lives-the-new-american-dream/.
18. Robert Putnam, *The Collapse and Revival of American Democracy* (New York: Simon & Schuster, 2000).
19. Margaret Talbot, "Who Wants to Be a Legionnaire?," *New York Times* (June 25, 2000).
20. Alexis de Tocqueville, *Democracy in America* (1835), edited and translated by Harvey C. Mansfield and Debra Winthrop (Chicago: University of Chicago Press, 2000), quoted online at http://www.press.uchicago.edu/Misc/Chicago/805328.html.
21. Robert A. Dahl, *Who Governs? Democracy and Power in an American City* (New Haven, CT: Yale University Press, 1961).
22. Charles A. Beard, *An Economic Interpretation of the Constitution of the United States* (New York: Macmillan Company, 1913).
23. "Full transcript: Donald Trump's jobs plan speech," Politico, June 28, 2016, https://www.politico.com/story/2016/06/full-transcript-trump-job-plan-speech-224891.
24. Mark Levin, *Men in Black: How the Supreme Court Is Destroying America* (Washington, D.C.: Regnery, 2006), 63.
25. Declaration and Resolves of the First Continental Congress, October 14, 1774, The Avalon Project, Yale Law School, http://avalon.law.yale.edu/18th_century/resolves.asp.
26. Laura Stampler, "Chris Christie Defends Controversial Ebola Quarantine," *Time*, October 28, 2014.
27. Katie Zernike and Emma G. Fitzsimmons, "Threat of Lawsuit Could Test Maine's Quarantine Policy," *New York Times*, October 29, 2014.
28. Available at https://www.archives.gov/files/press/exhibits/dream-speech.pdf.

Chapter 2

1. Madison's two papers were titled "Notes of Ancient and Modern Confederacies," written in the spring of 1786, and "Vices of the Political System of the United States," written in the spring of 1787.
2. Articles of Confederation, art. III.
3. Ibid., art. V.
4. Ibid., art. II.
5. This idea of term limits is one that we continue to debate today. For a discussion of challenges of coordination under the Articles of Confederation, see Keith L. Dougherty, *Collective Action under the Articles of Confederation* (New York: Cambridge University Press, 2001).
6. Articles of Confederation, art. XIII.
7. Letter from James Madison to Thomas Jefferson, August 12, 1786, in Rutland and Rachal, *The Papers of James Madison*, Vol. 9: 1786-1787 with Supplement 1781-1784, 97 (Chicago: University of Chicago Press, 1975).
8. 1786 Chap. 0038 An Act To Prevent Routs, Riots, And Tumultuous Assemblies, and Evil Consequences Thereof.
9. Wilson Ring, "Did Shays' Rebellion Leader Hide Out in Vermont?," *Burlington Free Press*, August 3, 2014.
10. George Washington had been reluctant to be a delegate, in part, because the Society of the Cincinnati, an organization of former Revolutionary War officers of which he had been a president, was to meet in Philadelphia at the same time. The society was viewed with mistrust due to its potential to become a new aristocracy. See Catherine Drinker Bowen, *Miracle at Philadelphia: The Story of the Constitutional Convention, May to September 1787* (Boston: Little, Brown and Company, 1966).
11. Dougherty, *Collective Action under the Articles of Confederation*, 129.
12. Letter from Thomas Jefferson to James Madison, 30 January 1787, Founders Online, National Archives, https://founders.archives.gov/documents/Jefferson/01-11-02-0095.
13. Letter from George Washington to Henry Knox, 3 February 1787, Founders Online, National Archives, https://founders.archives.gov/GEWN-04-05-02-0006.
14. Letter to James Madison from George Washington, 5 November 1786, Founders Online, National Archives, last modified June 29, 2017, http://founders.archives.gov/documents/Madison/01-09-02-0070.
15. Max Farrand, ed., *The Records of the Federal Convention of 1787, Volume I* (New Haven, CT: Yale University Press, 1911), xi.
16. "Notes of James Madison, May 29, 1787," in Farrand, *The Records of the Federal Convention of 1787*, 15.
17. It is also known as the Connecticut Compromise, after Roger Sherman, a Connecticut delegate, member of the committee, and author of the proposal. One state delegation was split.
18. Native Americans not paying taxes would not count at all.
19. James Madison, *Federalist No. 54*, in George Carey and James McClellan, eds., *The Federalist Papers* (Mineola, NY: Dover Publications, 2014), 283.
20. "James Madison to Robert Evans, June 15, 1819." Library of Congress, https://www.loc.gov/item/mjm018592/, accessed August 5, 2016.
21. Richard E. Neustadt, *Presidential Power and the Modern Presidents: The Politics of Leadership from Roosevelt to Reagan* (New York: Free Press, 1990), 29.
22. Marbury v. Madison, 5 U.S. 137 (1803).
23. Bruce Ackerman, *We the People: Foundations* (Cambridge, MA: Harvard University Press, 1991).
24. William H. Riker, *The Strategy of Rhetoric: Campaigning for the American Constitution* (New Haven: Yale University Press, 1996), 81.
25. James Madison, *Federalist No. 10*, in Carey and McClellan, *The Federalist Papers*, 42.
26. Ibid., 44.
27. Ibid., 43.
28. Ibid.
29. Ibid.
30. Ibid., 46.
31. Brutus No. 1, Monticello Digital Classroom, https://classroom.monticello.org/media-item/brutus-no-1/.
32. "Brutus Essay I, October 18, 1787," in W. B. Allen and Gordon Lloyd, *The Essential Antifederalist* (Lanham, MD: University Press of America, 1985), 110.
33. "Brutus Essay V, December 13, 1787," in Allen and Lloyd, *The Essential Antifederalist*, 119.
34. "Brutus Essay I, October 18, 1787," in Allen and Lloyd, *The Essential Antifederalist*, 110.
35. Ibid.
36. Ibid.
37. Ibid.

38. Ibid.
39. Douglass Adair, "The Authorship of the Disputed *Federalist Papers*," in *Fame and the Founding Fathers: Essays by Douglass Adair*, ed. Trevor Colbourn (New York: W. W. Norton & Company, 1974), 28.
40. Madison, *Federalist* No. 51, in Carey and McClellan, *The Federalist Papers*.
41. Ibid.
42. Charles A. Beard, *An Economic Interpretation of the Constitution of the United States* (New Brunswick, NJ: Transaction Publishers, 1998).
43. Ibid.
44. Kenneth M. Dolbeare and Linda Medcalf, "The Dark Side of the Constitution," in *The Case against the Constitution from the Antifederalists to the Present*, ed. John F. Manley and Kenneth M. Dolbeare (Armonk, NY: M. E. Sharpe, 1987), 120–42.
45. James Madison's March 18, 1786, letter to Thomas Jefferson, accessible via https://founders.archives.gov/documents/Jefferson/01-09-02-0301.
46. Myers v. United States, 252 U.S. 52 (1926).
47. Justice Brandeis, dissenting, at 252 U.S. 293.
48. Charles Beard, "Framing the Constitution," in Peter Woll, ed., *American Government: Readings and Cases,* 11th ed. (New York: Harper Collins, 1993).
49. Letter from George Washington to John Jay, Deficiencies of the Constitution, *The Founders' Constitution*, Vol. 1, p. 162, accessed at http://press-pubs.uchicago.edu/founders/print_documents/v1ch5s11.html.

Chapter 3

1. Brian Anderson, "Women File Suit for Continued Access to Marijuana," *Contra Costa Times*, October 10, 2002; available from Lexis-Nexis Academic.
2. Dan Reed, "Medicinal Pot Users Renew Legal Challenge," *San Jose Mercury News*, October 10, 2002; available from Lexis-Nexis Academic.
3. Comprehensive Drug Abuse and Control Act of 1970, Pub. L. No. 91-513, 84 Stat. 1236 (Oct. 27, 1970).
4. Anderson, "Women File Suit for Continued Access to Marijuana."
5. Richard Willing, "Medical-Pot Fight Goes to Justices," *USA Today*, November 26, 2004; available from Lexis-Nexis Academic.
6. U.S. Const. art. I, § 8.
7. U.S. Const. art. I, § 8.
8. U.S. Const. art. VI.
9. U.S. Const. amend. X.
10. United States v. Darby, 310 U.S. 100 (1941).
11. Garcia v. San Antonio Metropolitan Transit Authority, 460 U.S. 528 (1985).
12. Ibid.
13. U.S. Const. art. I, §§ 2 and 4; U.S. Const. art. II, § 1.
14. U.S. Const. art. V.
15. Full Faith and Credit Clause, Legal Dictionary, https://legaldictionary.net/full-faith-and-credit-clause/.
16. Privileges and Immunities, Legal Dictionary, https://legaldictionary.net/privileges-and-immunities-clause/.
17. McCulloch v. Maryland, 17 U.S. (4 Wheat.) 316 (1819).

18. Ibid.
19. Ibid., 405.
20. Ibid.
21. Ibid., 415.
22. Ibid.
23. Ibid.
24. Ibid.
25. Gibbons v. Ogden, 22 U.S. (9 Wheat.) 11 (1824).
26. Ibid.
27. Plessy v. Ferguson, 163 U.S. 537 (1896).
28. Mark V. Tushnet, *The NAACP's Legal Strategy against Segregated Education, 1925–1950* (Chapel Hill: The University of North Carolina Press, 1987), 21.
29. James Bryce, *The American Commonwealth*, Vol. I (New York: Macmillan and Co., 1888), 432.
30. Tarble's Case, 80 U.S. (13 Wall.) 397 (1871).
31. The Northwest Ordinance of 1787, for example, stated, "Religion, morality, and knowledge, being necessary to good government and the happiness of mankind, schools and the means of education shall forever be encouraged." Henry Steele Commager, ed., *Documents of American History*, 8th ed. (New York: Appleton-Century-Crofts, 1968), 131.
32. Lochner v. New York, 198 U.S. 45 (1905).
33. Gitlow v. New York, 268 U.S. 652 (1925).
34. Daniel J. Elazar, *American Federalism: A View from the States* (New York: Thomas Y. Crowell Company, 1972), 190.
35. Jean Edward Smith, *FDR* (New York: Random House, 2007), 15.
36. History and Development of Social Security, Social Security Administration, https://www.ssa.gov/history/briefhistory3.html.
37. Works Progress Administration (WPA) (1935), The Living New Deal, https://livingnewdeal.org/glossary/works-progress-administration-wpa-1935/.
38. Ibid.
39. Ibid.
40. Ibid.
41. Joseph F. Zimmerman, *Contemporary American Federalism: The Growth of National Power* (New York: Praeger, 1992), 118.
42. National Minimum Drinking Age Act of 1984, 23 U.S. Code § 158.
43. Americans with Disabilities Act, Public Law 101-336, 1990.
44. Zimmerman, *Contemporary American Federalism*, 118–19.
45. Brown et al., *The Changing Politics of Federal Grants*, 7.
46. Ibid., 8.
47. "Acceptance Speeches: Reagan: 'Time to Recapture Our Destiny,'" in *CQ Almanac 1980*, 36th ed. (Washington, D.C.: Congressional Quarterly, 1981), http://library.cqpress.com/cqalmanac/cqal80-860-25879-1173673, accessed January 7, 2013.
48. Cheryl Cirelli, Examples of Block Grants, Lifestyle, http://charity.lovetoknow.com/Examples_of_Block_Grants.
49. Lindsey Gruson, "End of Federal Revenue Sharing Creating Financial Crises in Many Cities," *New York Times*, January 3, 1987.
50. Personal Responsibility and Work Opportunity Reconciliation Act of 1996, 110 Stat. 2105.

51. United States Elementary and Secondary Education Act of 1965, H. R. 2362, 89th Cong., 1st Sess., Pub. L. 89-10.
52. No Child Left Behind Act of 2001, Pub. L. 107-110, 20 U.S.C. § 6319 (2002).
53. Every Student Succeeds Act, Pub. L. 114-95, 129 Stat. 1802.
54. Ronald Reagan, Address Accepting the Presidential Nomination at the Republican National Convention in Detroit, July 17, 1980. Online by Gerhard Peters and John T. Woolley, The American Presidency Project. Access at http://www.presidency.ucsb.edu/ws/?pid=25970.
55. Gun-Free School Zones Act of 1990, Pub. L. 101-647, 104 Stat. 4789.
56. United States v. Lopez, 514 U.S. 549 (1995).
57. Ibid.
58. Ibid.
59. Ibid.
60. Ibid.
61. Printz v. United States, 521 U.S. 898 (1997).
62. Loving v. Virginia, 388 U.S. 1 (1967).
63. United States v. Windsor, 133 S. Ct. 2675, 570 U.S. ___ (2013).
64. Defense of Marriage Act, 1 U.S. Code § 7.
65. Ibid.
66. U.S. Const. art. IV, § 1.
67. United States v. Windsor, 570 U.S. ___ (2013).
68. Ibid.
69. Ibid.
70. ALS Association, "What Is ALS?," http://www.alsa.org/about-als/what-is-als.html, accessed March 12, 2016.
71. Chris Geidner, "Two Years after His Husband's Death, Jim Obergefell Is Still Fighting for the Right to Be Married," BuzzFeed.com, March 22, 2015, http://www.buzzfeed.com/chrisgeidner/his-husband-died-in-2013-but-jim-obergefell-is-still-fighting#.ldrnVM0Ag, accessed March 12, 2016.
72. Ibid.
73. Obergefell v. Hodges, 576 U.S. ___ (2015).
74. Richard Wolf, "Grieving Widower Takes Lead in Major Gay Marriage Case," *USA Today*, April 10, 2015, http://www.usatoday.com/story/news/nation/2015/04/10/supreme-court-gay-marriage-obergefell/25512405/, accessed March 12, 2016.
75. Gonzales v. Raich, 545 U.S. 1 (2005).
76. Reagan Ali and M. David, "Obama Effectively Tells Supreme Court to Legalize Marijuana," *Counter Current News*, January 17, 2016, http://countercurrentnews.com/2016/01/obama-tells-supreme-court-to-legalize/, accessed May 18, 2016.
77. Ariane de Vogue, "Obama Admin Weighs in on Legalized Marijuana at the Supreme Court," CNN.com, December 16, 2015, http://www.cnn.com/2015/12/16/politics/supreme-court-marijuana-colorado-obama/, accessed May 18, 2016.
78. Marijuana Resource Center: State Laws Related to Marijuana, Office of National Drug Control Policy, https://obamawhitehouse.archives.gov/ondcp/state-laws-related-to-marijuana.
79. "Number of Legal Medical Marijuana Patients (as of March 1, 2016)," ProCon.org, March 3, 2016, http://medicalmarijuana.procon.org

/view.resource.php?resourceID=005889, accessed March 5, 2016.

80. James M. Cole, "Memorandum for All United States Attorneys," U.S. Department of Justice, August 29, 2013, https://www.justice.gov/iso /opa/resources/3052013829132756857467.pdf, accessed March 5, 2016.

81. Jefferson B. Sessions III, Office of the Attorney General, letter to the Honorable Jay Inslee, Governor, the State of Washington, July 24, 2017, https://s3.amazonaws.com/big.assets .huffingtonpost.com/LtrfromSessions.pdf, accessed August 25, 2017.

82. Josh Gerstein and Cristiano Lima, "Sessions announces end to policy that allowed legal pot to flourish," Politico, January 4, 2018.

83. Brady Handgun Violence Prevention Act, Pub. L. 103–159, 107 Stat. 1536, enacted November 30, 1993.

84. Printz v. United States, 521 U.S. 898 (1997).

85. Alan Blinder and Tamar Lewin, "Clerk in Kentucky Chooses Jail over Deal on Same-Sex Marriage," New York Times, Sept. 3, 2015, accessed 28 February 2018 at https://www .nytimes.com/2015/09/04/us/kim-davis-same -sex-marriage.html

Unit 1 Review

1. 529 U.S. 598 (2000).
2. David Harsanyi, "Trump's Executive Moves Have Strengthened Checks and Balances," National Review, October 20, 2017.
3. Brady Handgun Violence Prevention Act, Pub. L. 103-159, 107 Stat. 1536.

Chapter 4

1. Hanna Fenichel Pitkin, The Concept of Representation (Berkeley: University of California Press, 1972).
2. U.S. District Court, Eastern District of Wisconsin, Case No. 11-CV-1011 JPS-DPW-RMD.
3. Matthew DeFour, "Democrats' Short-Lived 2012 Recall Victory Led to Key Evidence in Partisan Gerrymandering Case," Wisconsin State Journal, July 23, 2017.
4. Emily Bazelon, "The New Front in the Gerrymandering Wars: Democracy vs. Math," New York Times, August 29, 2017.
5. Docket No. 16-1161.
6. U.S. Const. art. I (compared with articles II and III).
7. James Madison, Federalist No. 62, in George W. Carey and James McClellan, eds., The Federalist (Indianapolis, IN: Liberty Fund, 2001), 321.
8. James Madison, Federalist No. 10, in Carey and McClellan, The Federalist, 321.
9. James Madison, Federalist No. 53, in Carey and McClellan, The Federalist, 279.
10. Although they are only required by the Constitution to live in the states that they represent, members of the House are, by custom, expected to maintain a residence in their electoral district.
11. James Madison, Federalist No. 52, in Carey and McClellan, The Federalist, 273.

12. James Madison, Federalist No. 63, in Carey and McClellan, The Federalist, 327.
13. See Stan Luger and Brian Waddell, What American Government Does Today (Baltimore: Johns Hopkins University Press, 2017), for policy histories of these areas and more.
14. Also referred to as the Congressional Budget Control and Impoundment Act of 1974, P.L. 93-344.
15. Martin Frost and Tom Davis, "How to Fix What Ails Congress: Bring Back Earmarks," Los Angeles Times, February 8, 2015, http:// www.latimes.com/nation/la-oe-frost-earmark -spending-20150209-story.html, accessed July 7, 2016.
16. If the president is being tried for impeachment, the chief justice of the Supreme Court presides (U.S. Const. art. I, § 3).
17. Apportionment Act of 1842, 5 Stat. 491.
18. Reapportionment Act of 1929, 46 Stat. 21, 2 U.S.C. § 2a.
19. "State-by-state redistricting procedures," Ballotpedia, https://ballotpedia.org /State-by-state_redistricting_procedures.
20. Sam Wang and Brian Remlinger, "Slaying the Partisan Gerrymander," The American Prospect, September 27, 2017.
21. Kim Soffen, "Independently Drawn Districts Have Proven to Be More Competitive," New York Times, July 1, 2015.
22. The Cook Political Report, "House Race Ratings," November 17, 2017.
23. Thomas Mann and Anthony Corrado, "Party Polarization and Campaign Finance," Center for Effective Public Management at Brookings, July, 2014, https://www.brookings.edu /wp-content/uploads/2016/06/Mann-and -Corrad_Party-Polarization-and-Campaign -Finance.pdf.
24. Gary C. Jacobson, The Politics of Congressional Elections, 7th ed. (New York: Pearson Longman, 2009), 13.
25. Carol M. Swain, Black Faces, Black Interests: The Representation of African Americans in Congress (Cambridge, MA: Harvard University Press, 1995), 5.
26. Baker v. Carr, 369 U.S. 186 (1962).
27. Gray v. Sanders, 372 U.S. 368 (1963).
28. Reynolds v. Sims, 377 U.S. 522 (1964).
29. Wesberry v. Sanders, 376 U.S. 1 (1964); Reynolds v. Sims, 377 U.S. 533 (1964).
30. Shaw v. Reno, 509 U.S. 630 (1993).
31. Center for Responsive Politics, Most Expensive Races, https://www.opensecrets.org/overview /topraces.php.
32. Alan I. Abramowitz, Brad Alexander, and Matthew Gunning, "Incumbency, Redistricting, and the Decline of Competition in U.S. House Elections," Journal of Politics 68, no. 1 (February 2006): 82.
33. David R. Mayhew, Congress: The Electoral Connection (New Haven, CT: Yale University Press), 5. See also David R. Mayhew, "Congressional Elections: The Case of the Vanishing Marginals," Polity 6, no. 3 (Spring 1974): 295–317.
34. Mayhew, Congress, 49–77.
35. Gary C. Jacobson and Samuel Kernell, Strategy and Choice in Congressional Elections (New Haven, CT: Yale University Press, 1981), 32.

36. U.S. Const. art. I, § 2.
37. "Leadership PACs," OpenSecrets.org, http:// www.opensecrets.org/industries/indus .php?ind=Q03, accessed May 24, 2013.
38. U.S. Const. art. I, § 3.
39. Woodrow Wilson, Congressional Government: A Study in American Politics (Boston: Houghton, Mifflin and Company, 1885), 79.
40. Thomas Mann and Norman Ornstein, The Broken Branch (New York: Oxford University Press, 2006), 170.
41. Richard F. Fenno Jr., Congressmen in Committees (Boston: Little Brown, 1973).
42. Ken Buck, Drain the Swamp (Washington, D.C.: Regnery Publishing, 2017), 38.
43. Schoolhouse Rock! "I'm Just a Bill," available on YouTube at https://www.youtube.com /watch?v=tyeJ55o3El0.
44. Scott Franklin Abernathy, No Child Left Behind and the Public Schools (Ann Arbor: University of Michigan Press, 2007), vii.
45. Barbara Sinclair, Unorthodox Lawmaking: New Legislative Processes in the U.S. Congress, 5th ed. (Washington, D.C.: CQ Press, 2017).
46. Elise Viebeck, "Seven Ways the Latest Republican Health-Care Effort Is Impulsive and Chaotic," Washington Post, September 25, 2017.
47. Lee Drutman and Steven Teles, "A New Agenda for Political Reform," Washington Monthly, March/April/May 2015.
48. Ibid., 15.
49. "Committee FAQs," Office of the Clerk, House of Representative, http://clerk.house.gov /committee_info/commfaq.aspx.
50. Sinclair, Unorthodox Lawmaking.
51. www.Senate.gov.
52. The term filibuster is generally also used to describe several other delaying tactics in the Senate.
53. Thomas Mann and Norman Ornstein, It's Even Worse Than It Looks (New York: Basic Books, 2013), 88.
54. Barbara Sinclair, Unorthodox Lawmaking: New Legislative Processes in the U.S. Congress, 2nd ed. (Washington, D.C.: CQ Press, 2000), 43.
55. Ashley Parker, "Rand Paul Leads Filibuster of Brennan Nomination," New York Times, March 6, 2013.
56. Shane Miller, @sash_miller, #StandWithRand, Twitter, March 6, 2013, https://twitter.com /sash_miller/status/309518378664611840.
57. Mark Memmott, "Nearly 13 Hours Later, Sen. Paul Ends His Filibuster; Here's the Video," NPR.org, the Two-Way, March 7, 2013, http://www.npr .org/blogs/thetwo-way/2013/03/07/173693133 /nearly-13-hours-later-sen-paul-ends-his-filibuster -heres-the-video, accessed May 30, 2013.
58. Tom LoBianco, "Five Politically Important Recent Filibusters," CNN, June 16, 2016.
59. Sinclair, Unorthodox Lawmaking, 58.
60. U.S. Const. art. I, § 7.
61. Mitch McConnell, "Democrats Want to Disregard Senate Rules," U.S. News & World Report, November 27, 2012. https://www .usnews.com/debate-club/should-the -filibuster-be-overhauled/mitch-mcconnell -democrats-want-to-disregard-senate-rules, accessed November 21, 2017.

62. Pub. L. 93–344, 88 Stat. 297, 2 U.S.C. §§ 601–688.

63. U.S. Const. amend. XVI (1913).

64. For a history of tax policy, see Stan Luger and Brian Waddell, *What American Government Does* (Baltimore: Johns Hopkins University Press, 2017).

65. https://www.treasurydirect.gov/NP/debt /current.

66. U.S. Department of Commerce, Bureau of Economic Analysis, "National Income and Product Accounts, Gross Domestic Product: Third Quarter 2017 (Advance Estimate)," https://www.bea.gov/newsreleases/national /gdp/gdpnewsrelease.htm, accessed November 3, 2017.

67. Pub. L. 74-271, 49 Stat. 620-648 (1935). The programs were collectively called Old Age Security and Disability Insurance (OASDI) and commonly referred to as Social Security.

68. Office of Social Security, "Frequently Asked Questions: What Is the Average Monthly Benefit for a Retired Worker?" https://faq.ssa .gov/link/portal/34011/34019/Article/3736 /What-is-the-average-monthly-benefit-for-a -retired-worker, accessed November 3, 2017.

69. Office of Social Security, "Social Security Basic Facts," April 2, 2014, http://www.ssa .gov/news/press/basicfact.html, accessed November 3, 2017.

70. Ibid.

71. Alicia Munnell, "Social Security's Financial Outlook: The 2017 Update in Perspective," Center for Retirement Research at Boston College, July 2017, Number 17-13, 2.

72. Richard F. Fenno, Jr., *Home Style: House Members in Their Districts* (HarperCollins Publishers, 1978).

73. John W. Kingdon, *Congressmen's Voting Decisions*, 3rd ed. (Ann Arbor: University of Michigan Press, 1989).

74. Fenno, *Home Style.*

75. Martin Gilens and Benjamin Page, "Testing Theories of American Politics: Elites, Interest Groups, and Average Citizens," *Perspectives on Politics* 12, no. 3 (September 2014): 564–81.

76. Jane Mansbridge calls the former *promissory representation* and the latter *anticipatory representation*. Jane Mansbridge, "Rethinking Representation," *American Political Science Review* 97, no. 4 (November 2003): 515–28.

77. Ibid.

78. Tracy Sulkin, *Issue Politics in Congress* (New York: Cambridge University Press, 2005).

79. Paige Winfield Cunningham, The Health 202: "Here's Why John McCain Voted 'No' on Health Care," *Washington Post*, August 4, 2017.

80. See Morris P. Fiorina, Samuel J. Abrams, and Jeremy C. Pope, *Culture War? The Myth of a Polarized America*, 3rd ed. (New York: Longman, 2011); and Alan I. Abramowitz, *The Disappearing Center: Engaged Citizens, Polarization, and American Democracy* (New Haven, CT: Yale University Press, 2010).

81. Jane Mansbridge, "Should Blacks Represent Blacks and Women Represent Women? A Contingent 'Yes,'" *Journal of Politics* 61, no. 3 (August 1999): 628.

82. Ibid., 632.

83. Pitkin, *The Concept of Representation*, 114.

84. Barbara Mikulski et al., *Nine and Counting: The Women of the Senate* (New York: Perennial, 2001), 197.

85. John Adams, "Letter to John Penn," as quoted in Pitkin, *The Concept of Representation*, 60.

86. Alexander Hamilton, John Jay, and James Madison. *The Federalist: A Commentary on the Constitution of the United States* (New York: Random House, 2010), 367.

87. David Lawder, "Two Conservative Republicans Booted from House Budget Panel," Reuters, December 4, 2012, https://www.reuters.com /article/us-usa-fiscal-conservatives/two -conservative-republicans-booted-from-house -budget-panel-idUSBRE8B30QV20121204.

88. H.R.184, 115th Congress (2017–2018).

89. https://www.cagw.org/reporting/pig-book.

90. Pub. L. No. 114-113, December 18, 2015.

Chapter 5

1. Executive Order No. 13223, "Ordering the Ready Reserve of the Armed Forces to Active Duty and Delegating Certain Authorities to the Secretary of Defense and the Secretary of Transportation," 66 Fed. Reg. 48201 (September 14, 2001); Executive Order No. 13224, "Blocking Property and Prohibiting Transactions with Persons Who Commit, Threaten to Commit, or Support Terrorism," 66 Fed. Reg. 49079 (September 23, 2001); Executive Order No. 13228, "Establishing the Office of Homeland Security and the Homeland Security Council," 66 Fed. Reg. 51812 (October 8, 2001). Congress later authorized the Department of Homeland Security as a cabinet-level department.

2. Hamdi v. Rumsfeld, 542 U.S. 507 (2002).

3. Ibid.

4. Ibid.

5. Dina Temple-Rastan, "Kill and Tell: Inside the President's Terrorist Hunt," *Washington Post*, June 17, 2012, B01, available from Lexis-Nexis Academic.

6. Mark Mazzetti, Charlie Savage, and Scott Shane, "A U.S. Citizen in America's Cross Hairs," *New York Times*, March 10, 2013, A1, available from Lexis-Nexis Academic.

7. "Details of Al-Awlaki's Death," *Yemen Times*, October 3, 2011, available from Lexis-Nexis Academic.

8. Mazzetti, Savage, and Shane, "A U.S. Citizen in America's Cross Hairs."

9. Ibid.

10. Scott Shane, "Judging a Long, Deadly Reach," *New York Times*, October 1, 2011, A1, available from Lexis-Nexis Academic.

11. Charlie Savage, "Top U.S. Security Official Says 'Rigorous Standards' Used for Drone Strikes," *New York Times*, May 1, 2012, A8, available from Lexis-Nexis Academic.

12. Karen DeYoung and Peter Finn, "4 Americans Killed in Drone Strikes since '09," *Washington Post*, May 23, 2013, A1, available from Lexis-Nexis Academic.

13. Mazzetti, Savage, and Shane, "A U.S. Citizen in America's Cross Hairs."

14. Pub. L. 170-40.

15. Scott Shane, "A Legal Debate as C.I.A. Stalks a U.S. Jihadist," *New York Times*, May 10, 2010, A1, available from Lexis-Nexis Academic.

16. John Nichols, "16 Years Ago Barbara Lee's Warning against the AUMF Was Ignored: Nevertheless, She Persisted," *The Nation*, June 30, 2017.

17. Azeem Ibrahim, "The Assassination of Al-Awlaki, American Citizen and al Qaeda Martyr," TheWorldPost/Huffington Post, https://www.huffingtonpost.com/azeem -ibrahim/anwar-al-awlaki-killed_b_996902 .html, accessed 20 November 2017.

18. Ulysses S. Grant unsuccessfully sought a third term in 1880.

19. In some states, widows with property were allowed to participate in public and political life.

20. Max Farrand, *The Framing of the Constitution of the United States* (New Haven, CT: Yale University Press, 1913), 163.

21. Noah Feldman, *The Three Lives of James Madison: Genius, Partisan, President* (New York: Random House, 2017), 264.

22. Many of these titles are in Clinton Rossiter, *The American Presidency*, 2nd ed. (Baltimore: Johns Hopkins University Press, 1987).

23. U.S. Const. art. II, § 1.

24. U.S. Const. art. II, § 1 and art. II, § 3.

25. Executive Order Enforcing Statutory Prohibitions on Federal Control of Education, issued April 26, 2017, https://www .whitehouse.gov/the-press-office/2017/04/26 /presidential-executive-order-enforcing -statutory-prohibitions-federal, accessed 20 November 2017. Quote is from https://www .whitehouse.gov/the-press-office/2017/04/26 /remarks-president-trump-signing-executive -order-federalism-education, accessed November 20, 2017. The quote also appears in Martin Levine, "Dept. of Ed. Executive Order: Combatting Bureaucracy or Retreating from Equity," *Nonprofit Quarterly*, May 2, 2017.

26. U.S. Const. art. II, § 2.

27. U.S. Const. art. II, §§ 2 and 3.

28. Rossiter, *The American Presidency*, 12.

29. U.S. Const. art. II, § 3.

30. Charles M. Cameron, *Veto Bargaining: Presidents and the Politics of Negative Power* (New York: Cambridge University Press, 2000).

31. U.S. Const. art. II, § 2.

32. Rossiter, *The American Presidency*, 9.

33. U.S. Const. art. II, § 2.

34. See, for example, Mark J. Rozell, "The Law: Executive Privilege: Definition and Standards of Application," *Presidential Studies Quarterly* 29, no. 4 (1999): 918–30.

35. U.S. Const. art. II, § 3.

36. Kenneth R. Mayer, *With the Stroke of a Pen: Executive Orders and Presidential Power* (Princeton, NJ: Princeton University Press, 2001).

37. William G. Howell, *Power without Persuasion: The Politics of Direct Presidential Action* (Princeton, NJ: Princeton University Press, 2003), 14.

38. Herbert J. Storing, ed., *Cato No. 4, Vol. 3 of The Complete Anti-Federalist* (Chicago: University of Chicago Press, 1981), 500.

39. U.S. Const. art. I and III.

40. U.S. Const. art. II, § 2.

41. War Powers Resolution, Pub. L. No. 93-148, 87 Stat. 555 (November 7, 1973). Codified in 50

U.S.C. 33, §§ 1541-48 (1973). It is also called the War Powers Act, which was the title of the version of the joint resolution passed in the Senate.

42. Louis Fisher and David Gray Adler, "The War Powers Resolution: Time to Say Goodbye," *Political Science Quarterly* 113, no. 1 (1998): 1.

43. War Powers Resolution, § 2(c).

44. War Powers Resolution, § 4(a). The president must notify both the Speaker of the House and the president of the Senate pro tempore.

45. War Powers Resolution, § 5(b).

46. See Fisher and Adler, "The War Powers Resolution."

47. U.S. Const. art. II, § 4.

48. The chief justice presides only when presidents are impeached. Otherwise, the presiding office of the Senate would chair the proceedings.

49. United States v. Nixon, 418 U.S. 683 (1974).

50. United States v. Texas, 579 U.S. __ (2016).

51. Trump v. Hawaii, No. 17-965, 585 U.S. __ (2018).

52. Glenn Thrush, "Trump's New Travel Ban Blocks Migrants from Six Nations, Sparing Iraq," *New York Times*, March 6, 2017.

53. "Syria Missile Strikes: US Launches First Direct Military Action against Assad," *The Guardian*, April 7, 2017, https://www.theguardian.com /world/2017/apr/06/trump-syria-missiles -assad-chemical-weapons, accessed 20 November 2017.

54. U.S. Const. art. I, § 3.

55. Arthur M. Schlesinger Jr., "Is the Vice Presidency Necessary?," *The Atlantic*, May 1, 1974, http://www.theatlantic.com/magazine /archive/1974/05/is-the-vice-presidency -necessary/305732/, accessed August 31, 2013.

56. Fred Greenstein, "Change and Continuity in the Modern Presidency," in Robert Hirschfield, ed., *The Power of the Presidency: Concepts and Controversy*, 3rd ed. (New York: Routledge, 2017), 451–81.

57. For a challenge to the argument that divided government necessarily leads to legislative gridlock, see David R. Mayhew, *Divided We Govern: Party Control, Lawmaking, and Investigations, 1946–1990* (New Haven, CT: Yale University Press, 1991).

58. Rossiter, *The American Presidency*, 54, 56.

59. Samuel Kernell, *Going Public: New Strategies of Presidential Leadership* (Washington, D.C.: CQ Press, 2007), 1–2.

60. James A. Stimson, "Public Support for American Presidents: A Cyclical Model," *Public Opinion Quarterly* 40, no. 1 (1976): 1–21.

61. Department of Homeland Security, "Consideration of Deferred Action for Childhood Arrivals (DACA)," https://www.uscis .gov/humanitarian/consideration-deferred -action-childhood-arrivals-daca, accessed August 3, 2017.

62. Bradley Jones, "Americans' Views of Immigration Marked by Widening Partisan, Generational Divides," Pew Research Center, April 15, 2016, http://www.pewresearch.org /fact-tank/2016/04/15/americans-views-of -immigrants-marked-by-widening-partisan -generational-divides/, accessed August 6, 2017.

63. Audrey Singer, Nicole Prchal Svajlenka, and Jill H. Wilson, "Local Insights from DACA for Implementing Future Programs for Unauthorized Immigrants," Brookings Metropolitan Policy Program, April, 2015, 2, https://www.brookings.edu/wp-content /uploads/2016/06/BMPP_Srvy _DACAImmigration_June3b.pdf, accessed August 6, 2017.

64. James Barragán, "Immigration Hard-Liners Try to Force Trump's Hand on DACA," *Dallas Morning News*, https://www.dallasnews.com /news/immigration/2017/07/03/immigration -hardliners-try-force-trumps-hand-daca, accessed August 4, 2017.

65. Tal Kopan, "States Try to Force Trump's Hand on DACA," *CNN*, July 1, 2017, http://www.cnn .com/2017/06/30/politics/trump-daca-bind /index.html, accessed August 4, 2017.

66. Pete Williams, "In a Blow to Trump, Supreme Court Won't Hear Appeal of DACA Ruling," NBC News, February 26, 2018.

67. Lester G. Seligman, "On Models of the Presidency," *Presidential Studies Quarterly* 10, no. 3 (1980): 356.

68. Hamdi v Rumsfeld, 542 U.S. 507, citing *Youngstown Sheet & Tube Co. v. Sawyer,* 343 U.S. at 587. Justice O'Connor's opinion was of the plurality, with three other justices concurring and two joining in part.

69. Attorney General Eric S. Holder Jr. to Patrick J. Leahy, Chairman on the Judiciary, United States Senate, May 22, 2013, https://www .justice.gov/slideshow/AG-letter-5-22-13.pdf.

70. Mark Mazzetti, "American Drone Strike in Yemen Was Aimed at Awlaki," *New York Times*, May 7, 2011, A11, available from Lexis-Nexis Academic.

71. Thomas E. Cronin and Michael A. Genovese, *The Paradoxes of the American Presidency*, 2nd ed. (New York: Oxford University Press, 2004).

72. "Address to the Nation on the September 11 Attacks," *Selected Speeches of President George W. Bush 2001–2008*, https:// georgewbush-whitehouse.archives.gov /infocus/bushrecord/documents/Selected _Speeches_George_W_Bush.pdf.

73. President Jackson's Veto Message Regarding the Bank of the United States, July 10, 1832. http://avalon.law.yale.edu/19th_century /ajveto01.asp.

74. Arthur Schlesinger Jr., "The Runaway Presidency," *The Atlantic*, November 1973, https://www.theatlantic.com/magazine /archive/1973/11/the-runaway-presidency /306211/.

Chapter 6

1. The subtitle refers to Alexander Hamilton's characterization in *Federalist* No. 78 of the federal judiciary as "least dangerous to the political rights of the Constitution." In *The Federalist Papers*, ed. George W. Carey and James McClellan (Indianapolis, IN: Liberty Fund, 2001), 402. Alexander M. Bickel also chose the phrase from the title of his critique of judicial power, *The Least Dangerous Branch: The Supreme Court at the Bar of Politics* (Indianapolis, IN: Bobbs-Merrill Educational Publishing, 1962).

2. Jed Handelsman Shugerman, *The People's Courts: Pursuing Judicial Independence in America* (Cambridge, MA: Harvard University Press, 2012), 6.

3. Adam Liptak, "U.S. Voting for Judges Perplexes Other Nations," *New York Times*, May 25, 2008.

4. Handelsman Shugerman, *The People's Courts*, 3.

5. Sandra Day O'Connor, Foreword, in James Sample, et al., "The New Politics of Judicial Elections 2000–2009: A Decade of Change," Brennan Center for Justice, August 16, 2010, https://www.brennancenter.org/publication /new-politics-judicial-elections-2000-2009 -decade-change.

6. John Kowal, "Judicial Selection for the 21st Century," Brennan Center for Justice, June 6, 2016, 1, https://www.brennancenter.org /publication/judicial-selection-21st-century.

7. "Spending by Outside Groups in Judicial Races Hits Record High, Secret Money Dominates," Brennan Center for Justice, November 16, 2016, https://www.brennancenter.org/press-release /spending-outside-groups-judicial-races-hits -record-high-secret-money-dominates.

8. Alicia Bannon, "Who Pays for Judicial Races?," Brennan Center for Justice, December 14, 2017, https://www.brennancenter.org /publication/politics-judicial-elections.

9. 556 U.S. 868 (2009).

10. Ibid.

11. Ibid., 884.

12. Ibid.

13. Ibid., 888.

14. Robert Barnes and Michael A. Fletcher, "Riskiest Choice on Obama's List Embodies His Criteria; President and Judge Cite Her Life Experience," *Washington Post*, May 27, 2009, available from Lexis-Nexis Academic.

15. Charlie Savage, "Conservatives Map Strategies on Court Fight," *New York Times*, May 17, 2009, available from Lexis-Nexis Academic.

16. Ibid.

17. Forrest McDonald, *Novus Ordo Seclorum: The Intellectual Origins of the Constitution* (Lawrence: University Press of Kansas, 1985), 253.

18. The delegates did debate the need to raise judges' salaries to keep up with changes in the cost of living, but they ultimately left the issue of pay raises out of the document.

19. U.S. Const. art. III, § 2.

20. U.S. Const. art. III, § 1.

21. U.S. Const. art. II, § 1.

22. U.S. Const. art. VI.

23. The term *jurisdiction* is also applied in other contexts, such as the authority of a specific law enforcement agency to investigate a case. However, we will focus only on the jurisdiction of courts in this chapter.

24. "Brutus," Essay XI, December 27, 1787, in *The Essential Antifederalist*, 2nd ed., ed. W. B. Allen and Gordon Lloyd (New York: Rowman & Littlefield Publishers, Inc., 2002), 188.

25. Hamilton, *Federalist* No. 78, in Carey and McClellan, *The Federalist Papers*, 402.

26. Ibid.

27. "The Judiciary Act of 1789," in *Documents of American History*, 6th ed., ed. Henry Steele Commager (New York: Appleton-Century-Crofts, Inc., 1958), 153.

28. Jeremy W. Peters, "In Landmark Vote, Senate Limits Use of Filibuster," *New York Times,* November 21, 2013.

29. Matt Flegenheimer, "Senate Republicans Deploy 'Nuclear Option' to Clear Path for Gorsuch," *New York Times,* April 6, 2017.

30. "Brutus," Essay I, December 27, 1787, in *The Essential Antifederalist,* 109.

31. Jefferson's party is often referred to as the Democratic-Republican Party, though it was more commonly called the Republican Party at the time. "Jeffersonian Republicans" is also a commonly used label today.

32. Jefferson's Republicans are viewed as having been better organized than the Federalists at the time.

33. The Twelfth Amendment to the Constitution (ratified in 1804) changed the presidential election rules by separating the votes for president and vice president. The House would continue to settle presidential elections if there was not a majority vote for one candidate by the electors, and the Senate would choose the vice president. While no presidential election has gone to Congress since 1824 (when John Quincy Adams, son of John Adams, was selected over the popular vote winner Andrew Jackson), this process remains in place today.

34. U.S. Const. amend. XII.

35. U.S. Const. art. III, § 1.

36. Kathryn Turner, "Federalist Policy and the Judiciary Act of 1801," *The William and Mary Quarterly* 22, no. 1 (January 1965): 32. Turner notes that as many of the provisions in the Judiciary Act of 1801 had been introduced prior to the election, there were other reasons for these provisions, particularly a desire to strengthen the power of the national government. The electoral results, however, "gave a driving urgency to the fight for its passage" (32).

37. The four plaintiffs were William Marbury, Dennis Ramsay, Robert Townsend Hope, and William Harper.

38. Oliver Ellsworth, the former chief justice, had retired shortly before.

39. Mark R. Killenbeck, *M'Culloch v. Maryland: Securing a Nation* (Lawrence, KS: University of Kansas Press, 2006), 81.

40. Marbury v. Madison, 5 U.S. (1 Cranch) 137 (1803).

41. Ibid., 164.

42. Ibid., 177.

43. Ibid.

44. Michael Stokes Paulsen, "The Irrepressible Myth of *Marbury,*" *Michigan Law Review* 101, no. 8 (August 2003): 2707.

45. Hamilton, *Federalist* No. 78, in Carey and McClellan, *The Federalist Papers,* 403–5.

46. 60 U.S. 393 (1856).

47. George Will, "A Law Arizona Can Live With," *Washington Post,* April 28, 2010.

48. Another category of law, called procedural law, refers to proceedings and rules through which laws are enforced, such as how law enforcement officials interact with those accused of crimes.

49. Many of the definitions of legal terms in this chapter are informed by Bryan A. Garner, ed.,

Black's Law Dictionary, 8th ed. (St. Paul, MN: Thompson/West, 2004).

50. The relevant federal law is the Controlled Substances Act, 21 U.S.C. 13 § 801 et seq. (1970). Under that act, marijuana, along with heroin, ecstasy, and other substances, is classified as having a high potential for abuse and no accepted medical use.

51. As discussed in Chapter 3, the process of incorporation has resulted in the application of most of the protections of the Bill of Rights to the states as well as the federal government.

52. U.S. Const. amend V.

53. As of September 2016, thirty states had the death penalty. (Death Penalty Information Center, "States with and without the Death Penalty," http://www.deathpenaltyinfo.org /states-and-without-death-penalty, accessed September 18, 2016.) The United States government also has the authority to impose the death penalty for conviction under certain federal laws. In addition, the military retains the death penalty for conviction of certain offenses under the Uniform Code of Military Justice, though it has not been carried out since 1961.

54. Two states, Texas and Oklahoma, have separate state supreme courts for criminal and civil cases.

55. http://www.uscourts.gov/about-federal -courts/court-role-and-structure, accessed November 7, 2017.

56. U.S. Const. amend. VI and VII.

57. U.S. Const. art. III, § 2.

58. United States Supreme Court, *Rules of the Supreme Court of the United States,* Rule 10.

59. Another option for the Court is to send it back to the lower court under the status of review being improvidently granted. In such a case, the Court has decided that, after review, it now chooses not to give a full hearing to the case. If so, the lower ruling stands, but the Court has not officially weighed in on that ruling.

60. Bickel, *The Least Dangerous Branch,* 17.

61. For historical perspectives on the counter -majoritarian difficulty, see Sylvia Snowiss, *Judicial Review and the Law of the Constitution* (New Haven, CT: Yale University Press, 1990), and Barry Friedman, "The History of the Countermajoritarian Difficulty, Part One: The Road to Judicial Supremacy," *New York University Law Review* 73, no. 2 (May 1998): 333–433.

62. Bickel, *The Least Dangerous Branch,* 29–33.

63. James B. Thayer, "The Origin and Scope of the American Doctrine of Constitutional Law," *Harvard Law Review* 7, no. 3 (October 25, 1893): 144.

64. 567 U.S. 519 (2012).

65. 42 U.S.C. § 18001 (2010).

66. Bickel, *The Least Dangerous Branch: The Supreme Court at the Bar of Politics* (Indianapolis, IN: Bobbs-Merrill, 1962), 16.

67. Ibid., 69.

68. Ibid., 71.

69. Pub. L. 111–2, S. 181.

70. 550 U.S. 618 (2007).

71. Worcester v. Georgia, 31 U.S. 515 (1832).

72. McDonald, *Novus Ordo Seclorum,* 254–55.

73. Loth, *Chief Justice: John Marshall and the Growth of the Republic* (New York: W. W. Norton & Company, 1949), 360, 367.

74. 347 U.S. 483 (1954).

75. Gerald N. Rosenberg, *The Hollow Hope: Can Courts Bring About Social Change?* (Chicago: University of Chicago Press, 1991), 49.

76. Kevin T. McGuire and James A. Stimson, "The Least Dangerous Branch Revisited: New Evidence on Supreme Court Responsiveness to Public Preferences," *Journal of Politics* 66, no. 4 (November 2004): 1018–35.

77. NCC Staff, "Justice Ruth Bader Ginsberg Talks about Judicial Activism," National Constitution Center, September 9, 2013.

78. Katie Glueck, "Scalia: The Constitution Is 'Dead,'" *Politico,* January 19, 2013.

79. *Federalist* No. 81 in *The Federalist and Other Contemporary Papers on the Constitution of the United States,* ed. Erastus Howard Scott (Chicago: Scott, Foresman and Co., 1894), 443.

80. Alexander Hamilton, *Federalist* No. 78, The Avalon Project, Yale University, http://avalon .law.yale.edu/18th_century/fed78.asp.

81. Robert Barnes, "Trump Picks Colo. Appeals Court Judge Gorsuch for Supreme Court," *Washington Post,* January 31, 2017.

82. 418 U.S. 683 (1974).

83. Ibid.

84. U.S. Term Limits, Inc. v. Thornton, 514 U.S. 779 (1995).

Chapter 7

1. "Crushing Weight of Harvey's Floodwaters Pushed Houston Down, GPS Data Reveals," ABC13.com, September 13, 2017, http://abc13 .com/science/crushing-weight-of-harvey -flood-pushed-houston-down/2413363/, accessed November 3, 2017.

2. Mike Tolson and Cindy George, "Harvey's Heartbreaking Losses: Collective Human Damage Tells a Story of Its Own," *Houston Chronicle,* September 15, 2017, http://www .houstonchronicle.com/news/houston-texas /houston/article/Harvey-s-heartbreaking -losses-12201961.php, accessed November 1, 2017.

3. Eric Levenson, "3 Storms, 3 Responses: Comparing Harvey, Irma, and Maria," *CNN,* September 27, 2017, http://www.cnn .com/2017/09/26/us/response-harvey-irma -maria/index.html, accessed November 5, 2017.

4. Ibid.

5. Ibid.

6. United States Department of Transportation. The Uniform Time Act of 1966 (15 U.S.C. §§ 260–64) established the system of uniform Daylight Saving Time. States are allowed to opt out of the national daylight savings program. If they do participate, they must change the time according to a federally set schedule.

7. See Stan Luger and Brian Waddell, *What American Government Does* (Baltimore: Johns Hopkins University Press, 2017), chap. 7, "The Regulatory State."

8. U.S. Const. art. II, § 2.

9. U.S. Const. art. II, § 2.

10. Myers v. United States, 272 U.S. 52 (1926).
11. James Q. Wilson, "The Rise of the Bureaucratic State," *Public Interest* 41 (fall 1975): 82. See also Michael Nelson, "A Short, Ironic History of the American National Bureaucracy," *Journal of Politics* 44, no. 3 (August 1982): 757–62.
12. David H. Rosenbloom, *The Federal Service and the Constitution: The Development of the Public Employment Relationship* (Ithaca, NY: Cornell University Press, 1971), 76, quoting from Civil Service Rule VIII (1884).
13. The U.S. Supreme Court affirmed the constitutionality of restriction on political contributions by civil service workers in *Ex Parte Curtis*, 106 U.S. 371 (1882).
14. MaryAnne Borelli, *The President's Cabinet: Gender, Power, and Representation* (Boulder, CO: Lynne Rienner Publishers, 2002), 2.
15. For an examination of political executives' perspectives on politics within the federal bureaucracy, see Joel D. Aberbach and Bert A. Rockman, *In the Web of Politics: Three Decades of the U.S. Federal Executive* (Washington, D.C.: Brookings Institution, 2000).
16. President George W. Bush initially established the White House Office of Homeland Security by executive order. Congress passed Public Law 107-296 in November 2002, formally establishing it as a cabinet department. It has since undergone subsequent modifications in its organizational structure.
17. The U.S. Armed Forces, which are part of the executive branch, have a different organizational structure, although the secretary of defense and deputy and assistant secretaries are political appointees.
18. Thanks go from author Scott Abernathy to Professor John J. Dilulio Jr., for his thoughts on this topic, learned mostly through an independent study on the bureaucracy at Princeton, to which he was so generous to agree.
19. For a foundational study of the challenges of implementation, see Jeffrey L. Pressman and Aaron Wildavsky, *Implementation: How Great Expectations in Washington Are Dashed in Oakland; or, Why It's Amazing That Federal Programs Work at All, This Being a Saga of the Economic Development Administration as Told by Two Sympathetic Observers Who Seek to Build Morals on a Foundation of Ruined Hopes*, 3rd ed. (Berkeley: University of California Press, 1984).
20. Herbert Kaufman, "Fear of Bureaucracy: A Raging Pandemic," *Public Administration Review* 41, no 1 (1981): 4.
21. Michael Lipsky, *Street-Level Bureaucracy: Dilemmas of the Individual in Public Services* (New York: Russell Sage Foundation, 1980).
22. Cornelius M. Kerwin, *Rulemaking: How Government Agencies Write Laws and Make Policy* (Washington, D.C.: CQ Press, 1994), 4.
23. Kenneth J. Meier, "Representative Bureaucracy: A Theoretical and Empirical Exposition," in *Research in Public Administration*, ed. James Perry (Greenwich, CT: JAI Press, 1993).
24. Sally Coleman Selden, *The Promise of Representative Bureaucracy: Diversity and Responsiveness in a Government Agency* (Armonk, NY: ME Sharpe, 1997).

25. 5 U.S.C. §§ 7321–7326.
26. 107 Stat. 1001.
27. For a classic study of the challenges posed by outside pressures on bureaucrats and how bureaucratic agencies deal with them, see Herbert Kaufman, *The Forest Ranger: A Study in Administrative Behavior* (Washington, D.C.: Resources for the Future, 1960).
28. Joel D. Aberbach, *Keeping a Watchful Eye: The Politics of Congressional Oversight* (Washington, D.C.: Brookings Institution, 1990), 4.
29. The legislative and judicial branches also contain bureaucratic organizations, though these are few in number and small in size compared to the departments, agencies, and bureaus in the executive branch.
30. Saul Pett, "It's No Mickey Mouse War: White House Fights Mice That Roar," *Chicago Tribune*, March 12, 1978, 4, available from ProQuest Historical Newspapers.
31. United States Government Accountability Office, "Preliminary Observations on Hurricane Response," February 1, 2006, GAO-06-365R, http://www.gao.gov/assets/100/94002.pdf.
32. Eric Lipton, "Chertoff Hears Harsh Criticism from Senators," *New York Times*, February 16, 2006, A1, available from Lexis-Nexis Academic.
33. Ibid.
34. Select Bipartisan Committee to Investigate the Preparation for and Response to Hurricane Katrina, *A Failure of Initiative: Final Report of the Select Bipartisan Committee to Investigate the Preparation for and Response to Hurricane Katrina* (Washington, D.C.: U.S. Government Printing Office, 2006), x.
35. Ibid.
36. 576 U.S. __ (2015).
37. 42 U. S. C. § 7412.
38. Michigan v. Environmental Protection Agency, 576 U.S. __ (2015).
39. Walter Lippmann, *The Phantom Public* (New Brunswick, NJ: Transaction Publishers, 2011 [1927]), 55.
40. William Douglas and Steven Thomas, "On Katrina Anniversary, Bush Returns to Gulf Coast," Knight Ridder Washington Bureau, August 28, 2006, available from Lexis-Nexis Academic.
41. Select Bipartisan Committee, *A Failure of Initiative*, 17.
42. Brad DeLong "Katrina Reveals the Presidential Flaws," *Financial Times*, September 7, 2005, 13, available from Lexis-Nexis Academic.
43. Anthony Lonetree, "From the Wreckage of Katrina to the Walls of Local Art Centers: Artwork That Survived or Was Influenced by the Hurricane Makes Its Way Here from Mississippi in Yet Another Step in the Long Recovery," *Minneapolis Star Tribune*, January 11, 2006, 1B, available from Lexis-Nexis Academic.
44. David Hench, "Katrina Response Brings Out the Best, Worst in People," *Portland Press Herald* [Maine], September 15, 2005, available from Lexis-Nexis Academic.
45. "See Katrina's Trail," *Gold Coast Bulletin*, December 17, 2005, 96, available from Lexis-Nexis Academic.
46. The National Academies of Sciences, Engineering and Medicine, September 22,

2015. http://www8.nationalacademies.org/onpinews/newsitem.aspx?RecordID=21803, accessed December 11, 2017.
47. https://www.fda.gov/AnimalVeterinary/ResourcesforYou/ucm268127.htm, accessed December 11, 2017.
48. Harper Neidig and Ali Breland, "Week Ahead in Tech: House to Hold FCC Oversight Hearing," *The Hill*, July 24, 2017.
49. Life's Little Mysteries staff, "Chocolate Allergies Linked to Cockroach Parts," *NBC News*, April 2, 2012.
50. "Overregulated America: The Home of Laissez Faire Is Being Suffocated by Excessive and Badly Written Regulation," *The Economist*, February 28, 2012, http://www.economist.com/node/21547789, accessed December 11, 2017.
51. *PHH Corporation v. Consumer Financial Protection Bureau*, United States Court of Appeals for the District of Columbia Circuit, No. 15-1177, January 31, 2018.
52. Ibid.

Unit 2 Review

1. 557 U.S. 193 (2013).
2. Bruce Walker, "Should We Elect Judges?" *American Thinker*, May 23, 2011.
3. 576 U.S. __ (2015).
4. Kathy Kristof, "Target Selling Fidget Spinners with High Levels of Lead," *CBS Moneywatch*, November 9, 2017, https://www.cbsnews.com/news/target-fidget-spinners-high-levels-lead, accessed March 14, 2018.
5. "How Trump Was Able to Order U.S. Strikes on Syria without Congressional Approval," CBS News, April 7, 2017, https://www.cbsnews.com/news/how-trump-was-able-to-order-u-s-strikes-on-syria-without-congressional-approval, accessed March 14, 2018.

Chapter 8

1. James Bamford, "The Most Wanted Man in the World," *Wired Magazine*, August 2014, http://www.wired.com/2014/08/edward-snowden/, accessed March 8, 2016.
2. Glenn Greenwald, "NSA Whistleblower Edward Snowden: 'I Do Not Expect to See Home Again,'" *The Guardian*, June 9, 2013, available from Lexis-Nexis Academic.
3. Espionage Act of 1917 (amended in 1918), 40 Stat. 2017.
4. Jonah Engel Bromwich, "Snowden Leaks Illegal but Were a 'Public Service,' Eric Holder Says," *New York Times*, May 31, 2016, http://www.nytimes.com/2016/06/01/us/holder-says-snowden-performed-a-public-service.html?_r=0.
5. Catherine Drinker Bowen, *Miracle at Philadelphia: The Story of the Constitutional Convention, May to September 1787* (Boston: Little, Brown and Company, 1985 [1966]), 244.
6. U.S. Const. art. III, § 3.
7. Elbridge Gerry (MA) offered the motion; George Mason (VA) seconded it. Max Farrand, ed., *The Records of the Federal Convention of 1787, Volume II* (New Haven: Yale University Press, 1911), 588–89, http://lcweb2.loc.gov/ammem/amlaw/lwfr.html, accessed July 22, 2014.

8. Farrand, *The Records of the Federal Convention of 1787*, 617–18.

9. Irving Brant, *The Bill of Rights: Its Origin and Meaning* (Indianapolis, IN: Bobbs-Merrill, 1965), 39.

10. Alexander Hamilton, *Federalist No. 84*, in George W. Carey and James McClellan, ed., *The Federalist* (Indianapolis, IN: Liberty Fund, 2001), 447.

11. Ibid., 445.

12. Bowen, *Miracle at Philadelphia*, 245.

13. *Annals of Congress*, House of Representatives, 1st Cong., 1st sess. (June 8, 1789), 440–41, http://memory.loc.gov/ammem/amlaw/lwac.html, accessed July 19, 2014.

14. Two of the proposed twelve did not receive enough votes to secure ratification. The first involved apportionment of seats in the House of Representatives, the second restricted Congress's ability to raise its own pay. This latter amendment was ratified, but not until 1992 (Twenty-Seventh Amendment). Amendments are typically proposed including a date when they expire, but this was not the case for the two unratified, originally proposed amendments.

15. The National Council of the Left Wing, "The Left Wing Manifesto," *The Revolutionary Age: Devoted to the International Communist Struggle* 2, no. 1 (July 5, 1919): 6, 14, 15, https://www.marxists.org/history/usa/pubs/revolutionaryage/v2n01-jul-05-1919.pdf, accessed July 22, 2014.

16. Michael Hannon, "The People v. Benjamin Gitlow (1920)," *University of Minnesota Law Library*, May 2010, http://darrow.law.umn.edu/trialpdfs/Gitlow_Case.pdf, accessed July 22, 2014.

17. Ibid., 14.

18. Gitlow v. New York, 268 U.S. 652 (1925).

19. U.S. Const. amend. XIV.

20. Gitlow v. New York, 268 U.S. 652 (1925).

21. Gitlow v. New York at 666.

22. McDonald v. Chicago, 561 U.S. 742 (2010).

23. West Virginia School Board v. Barnett, 319 U.S. 624 (1943).

24. "Thomas Jefferson to the Danbury Baptists, 1 January 1802," in *Church and State in American History: Key Documents, Decisions, and Commentary from the Past Three Centuries*, 3rd ed., ed. John F. Wilson and Donald L. Drakeman (Cambridge, MA: Westview Press, 2003), 74.

25. Board of Education v. Allen, 392 U.S. 236 (1968). The Court has been similarly divided over the issue of tax relief for tuition reimbursement. See Committee for Public Education v. Nyquist, 413 U.S. 756 (1973) and Mueller v. Allen, 463 U.S. 388 (1983). In *Zobrest v. Catalina Foothills School District*, 509 U.S. 1 (1993), the Court, again divided 5–4, ruled in favor of using taxpayer funds to provide a student in a Catholic high school with a sign language interpreter.

26. Engel v. Vitale, 370 U.S. 423 (1962).

27. Ibid.

28. Ibid.

29. Ibid., 431.

30. Ibid., 450.

31. 347 U.S. 203 (1963).

32. U.S. Department of Education, "Guidance on Constitutionally Protected Prayer in Public Elementary and Secondary Schools," February 7, 2003, http://www2.ed.gov/policy/gen/guid/religionandschools/prayer_guidance.html, accessed July 25, 2014.

33. Lemon v. Kurtzman, 403 U.S. 602 (1971). In creating the test, the Court drew on the logic of *Board of Education v. Allen*, 392 U.S. 236 (1968), and other cases.

34. 406 U.S. 205 (1972).

35. Ibid., 208–9.

36. Ibid., 218.

37. Ibid., 223.

38. Ibid., 245.

39. Employment Division Dept. of Human Resources of Oregon v. Smith, 494 U.S. 872 (1990).

40. Ibid., 878.

41. 505 U.S. 577 (1992).

42. Schenck v. United States, 249 U.S. 47 (1919).

43. Ibid., 52.

44. Ibid.

45. Brandenburg v. Ohio, 395 U.S. 444 (1969).

46. Ibid., 447.

47. Ibid., 449.

48. New York Times Co. v. United States, 403 U.S. 713 (1971).

49. Ibid., 717.

50. Ibid., 721.

51. Ibid., 751.

52. Ibid., 755.

53. Tinker v. Des Moines Independent Community School District, 393 U.S. 503 (1969).

54. Ibid., 514.

55. Ibid., 518.

56. Morse v. Frederick, 551 U.S. 393 (2007).

57. The definitions of legal terms in this section are informed by Bryan A. Garner, ed., *Black's Law Dictionary*, 8th ed. (St. Paul, MN: Thompson/West, 2004).

58. New York Times v. Sullivan, 376 U.S. 254 (1964).

59. Ibid., 280.

60. R.A.V. v. St. Paul, 505 U.S. 377 (1992).

61. Ibid., 392.

62. Roth v. United States, 354 U.S. 476 (1957).

63. Miller v. California, 413 U.S. 15 (1973).

64. Ibid., 30.

65. Reno v. American Civil Liberties Union et al., 521 U.S. 844 (1997).

66. "First Amendment: Freedom of Speech," Cornell Law School, Legal Information Institute, https://www.law.cornell.edu/constitution/first_amendment.

67. De Jonge v. Oregon, 299 U.S. 353 (1937).

68. Ibid. See also *Edwards v. South Carolina*, 372 U.S. 229 (1963).

69. Noting, however, that the process of incorporating these rights has involved the Fourteenth Amendment as well.

70. District of Columbia v. Heller, 554 U.S. 570 (2008).

71. McDonald v. Chicago, 561 U.S. 742. A similar law in Oak Park, a suburb of Chicago, was also overturned.

72. Ibid.

73. Ibid.

74. Ibid., dissenting opinion by Justice Stevens.

75. Ibid., dissenting opinion by Justice Breyer.

76. Snyder v. Phelps, 562 U.S. 443 (2011).

77. U.S. Const. art. I, § 9.

78. John Rawls, *A Theory of Justice* (Cambridge, MA: Belknap Press of Harvard University Press, 1999).

79. See Warden v. Hayden, 387 U.S. 294 (1967).

80. Mapp v. Ohio, 367 U.S. 643 (1961).

81. Ibid., 367 U.S. 643 (1961).

82. United States v. Sokolow, 490 U.S. 1 (1989).

83. Horton v. California, 496 U.S. 128 (1990).

84. Whren v. United States, 517 U.S. 806 (1996).

85. Kyllo v. United States, 533 U.S. 27 (2001).

86. Riley v. California, 573 U.S. __ (2014).

87. Ferguson v. City of Charleston, 532 U.S. 67 (2001).

88. Vernonia School District v. Acton, 515 U.S. 646 (1995).

89. Board of Education of Independent School District No. 92 of Pottawatomie County v. Earls, 536 U.S. 822 (2002).

90. Miranda v. Arizona, 384 U.S. 436 (1966).

91. Ibid., 444. Miranda was retried without the illegally obtained evidence but was convicted based on other evidence, including identification by the victim and the testimony of his girlfriend.

92. Kloppfer v. North Carolina, 386 U.S. 213 (1967).

93. Powell v. Alabama, 287 U.S. 45 (1932).

94. Johnson v. Zerbst, 304 U.S. 458 (1938).

95. Gideon v. Wainwright, 372 U.S. 335 (1963).

96. Ibid., 344.

97. Wiggins v. Smith, 539 U.S. 510 (2003).

98. See, for example, National Research Council, *Deterrence and the Death Penalty*, (Washington, DC: National Academies Press, 2012), https://doi.org/10.17226/13363.

99. 408 U.S. 238.

100. 428 U.S. 153.

101. Atkins v. Virginia, 536 U.S. 304 (2002).

102. Roper v. Simmons, 543 U.S. 551 (2005).

103. Sarah Childress, "Locked Up in America: Why the Death Penalty Is on the Decline," *Frontline*, December 18, 2014.

104. Ibid.

105. Griswold v. Connecticut, 381 U.S. 479 (1965).

106. Ibid., 485.

107. Ibid., 486.

108. Eisenstadt v. Baird, 405 U.S. 438 (1972).

109. Lawrence v. Texas, 539 U.S. 558 (2003). In its ruling, the Court overturned *Bowers v. Hardwick*, 478 U.S. 186 (1986).

110. Lawrence v. Texas, 539 U.S. at 558.

111. Roe v. Wade, 410 U.S. 113 (1973).

112. Ibid., 120.

113. Ibid.

114. Ibid.

115. Ibid., 141–42.

116. Ibid., 165.

117. Ibid., 174.

118. See Webster v. Reproductive Health Services, 492 U.S. 490 (1989); Planned Parenthood v. Casey, 505 U.S. 833 (1992); Stenberg v. Carhart, 530 U.S. 914 (2000); Gonzales v. Carhart, 550 U.S. 124 (2007).

119. Minnesota v. Dickerson, 508 U.S. 366 (1993).

120. Noelle Walker, "Parade Permit Denied for Controversial Arlington MLK Day Parade," *NBC*, January 22, 2018.

121. Bethel School District v. Fraser, 478 U.S. 675 (1986).

122. Christopher Coble, "3 Exceptions to the Miranda Rule," *FindLaw*, December 27, 2017.

123. Rosenberger v. University of Virginia, 515 U.S. 819 (1995).
124. Brandenburg v. Ohio, 395 U.S. 444 (1969).
125. Ibid., 449.
126. John Frank and Alicia Wallace, "Denver 4/20 Rally Organizers Receive 3 Year Ban after Event Left Civic Center Park Trashed," *Denver Post*, May 20, 2017, https://www.denverpost.com/2017/05/20/denver-420-rally-ban/, accessed March 19, 2018.

Chapter 9

1. Judith Heumann, "Justice for All: Advancing Dr. King's Call," *DIPNOTE* (U.S Department of State Official blog), January 18, 2016, https://blogs.state.gov/stories/2016/01/18/justice-all-advancing-dr-king-s-call, accessed March 17, 2016.
2. Team Celebration, "Judith E. Heumann—Woman of Action," A Celebration of Women, July 24, 2012, http://acelebrationofwomen.org/2012/07/judith-e-heumann-woman-of-action/, accessed March 16, 2016.
3. Ibid.
4. "A Look Back at 'Section 504,'" The Minnesota Governor's Council on Developmental Disabilities, April 28, 2002, http://mn.gov/mnddc/ada-legacy/npr-504.html, accessed March 18, 2016. The article was drawn from the transcript of "Disability Rights, Part II," *National Public Radio*, April 28, 2002, http://www.npr.org/templates/story/story.php?storyId=1142485.
5. Michael Irvin, "The 25 Day Siege That Brought Us 504," Independent Living Institute, http://www.independentliving.org/docs4/ervin1986.html, accessed March 17, 2016.
6. 42 U.S.C. § 12101, Pub. L. No. 101-336, 104 Stat. 328 (1990).
7. Americans with Disabilities Act of 1990, Pub. L. No. 101-336, § 1, 104 Stat. 328 (1990).
8. Lanny E. Perkins and Sara D. Perkins, "ADA Update," Multiple Sclerosis Foundation, http://msfocus.org/article-details.aspx?articleID=340, accessed March 16, 2016.
9. American Civil Liberties Union, "Disability Rights—ACLU Position/Briefing Paper," no. 21 (Winter 1999), https://www.aclu.org/disability-rights-aclu-positionbriefing-paper, accessed March 17, 2016.
10. Ibid.
11. Dred Scott v. Sandford, 20 U.S. 393 (1857).
12. Ibid., 407.
13. W. E. B. Du Bois, *Black Reconstruction in America, 1860–1880* (New York: Anthem, 1992), 167.
14. U.S. Const. amend. XIII.
15. U.S. Const. amend. XIV.
16. U.S. Const. amend. XV.
17. Plessy v. Ferguson, 163 U.S. 737 (1896).
18. *Plessy* did not deal with education. In 1899, the Supreme Court approved segregated educational facilities in *Cumming v. Board of Education*, 175 U.S. 528 (1899).
19. Mark V. Tushnet, *The NAACP's Legal Strategy against Segregated Education, 1925–1950* (Chapel Hill: University of North Carolina Press, 1987), 21. The section on the NAACP's strategic decision-making processes draws heavily on Tushnet's analysis and Richard Kluger's historical account.
20. The four states were Kansas (Brown v. Board of Education, 98 F. Supp. 797 [D. Kan. 1951]); South Carolina (Briggs v. Elliot, 103 F. Supp. 920 [E.D.S.C. 1952]); Delaware (Gebhart v. Belton, 33 Del. 145, 91 A.2d. 137 [1952]); and Virginia (Davis v. County School Board of Prince Edward County, Virginia, 103 F. Supp. 337 [E.D. Va. 1952]). The Washington, D.C., case was *Bolling v. Sharpe*, 347 U.S. 497 (1954). Because the District of Columbia is not a state, the case was tried under the due process clause of the Fifth Amendment. Thurgood Marshall argued the South Carolina case before the Supreme Court. His legal team divided the oral arguments.
21. Jack Greenberg, *Crusaders in the Courts: How a Dedicated Band of Lawyers Fought the Civil Rights Revolution* (New York: Basic Books, 1994), 167.
22. Alexander Hamilton, *Federalist* No. 78, in George W. Carey and James McClellan, ed., *The Federalist Papers* (Indianapolis, IN: Liberty Fund, 2001), 402.
23. Richard Kluger, *Simple Justice: The History of* Brown v. Board of Education *and Black America's Struggle for Equality* (New York: Vintage Books, 1977), 706.
24. McLaurin v. Oklahoma State Regents for Higher Education, 339 U.S. 637 (1950).
25. Ibid.
26. Ibid., 395.
27. Brown v. Board of Education of Topeka, 347 U.S. 483 (1954).
28. It was said that Justice Frankfurter told Justice Reed, who was most likely to dissent, that "a dissent is written for the future, but that there was no future for segregation." (Greenberg, *Crusaders in the Courts*, 198.)
29. Quoted in Jennifer Hochschild, *The New American Dilemma: Liberal Democracy and School Desegregation* (New Haven, CT: Yale University Press, 1984), 15.
30. Ibid., 34.
31. Brown v. Board of Education of Topeka, 349 U.S. 294 (1955).
32. See table 7 in Gary Orfield and Chungmae Lee, "Brown at 50: King's Dream or *Plessy*'s Nightmare," Civil Rights Project, Harvard University (2004), www.civilrightsproject.ucla.edu/, accessed March 19, 2018.
33. Swann v. Charlotte-Mecklenburg Board of Education, 401 U.S. 1 (1971).
34. Milliken v. Bradley, 418 U.S. 717 (1974).
35. *Milliken* II, 433 U.S. 267, 281.
36. Regents of the University of California v. Bakke, 438 U.S. 265 (1978).
37. Ibid., 318.
38. Gratz v. Bollinger, 539 U.S. 244 (2003).
39. Grutter v. Bollinger, 539 U.S. 306 (2003).
40. Ibid.
41. Fisher v. University of Texas at Austin, 50 U.S. 215 (2013).
42. Adam Liptak, "Supreme Court Upholds Affirmative Action Program at University of Texas," *New York Times*, June 23, 2016, http://www.nytimes.com/2016/06/24/us/politics/supreme-court-affirmative-action-university-of-texas.html?_r=0.
43. United States v. Scotland Neck City Board of Education, 407 U.S. 484 (1972).
44. Gerald N. Rosenberg, *The Hollow Hope: Can Courts Bring About Social Change?* (Chicago: University of Chicago Press, 1991), 49.
45. Taylor Branch, *Parting the Waters: America in the King Years, 1954–63* (New York: Simon and Schuster, 1988), 129.
46. Ibid., 129.
47. Ibid., 139–40.
48. Gayle v. Browder, 352 U.S. 903 (1956).
49. Martin Luther King, Clayborne Carson, Ralph Luker, and Penny A. Russell, *The Papers of Martin Luther King, Jr., Volume IV: Symbol of the Movement* (University of California Press, 2000).
50. Terry Gross, "The Freedom Riders of 1961," *NPR Fresh Air*, January 12, 2006.
51. Pub. L. 88–352, 78 Stat. 241.
52. Pub. L. 89-110, 79 Stat. 437.
53. Shelby v. Holder, 570 U.S. 2 (2013).
54. Ibid.
55. Betty Friedan, *The Feminine Mystique* (New York: Dell Publishing Co., 1963), 351.
56. Pub. L. No. 92-318, 86 Stat. 235 (June 23, 1972), codified at 20 U.S.C. §§ 1681–1688.
57. Pub. L. 88-352, § 7, 42 U.S.C. § 2000e et seq. (1964).
58. Title IX of the Education Amendments of 1972, Vol. 20, U.S.C. § 1681.
59. Jake Simpson, "How Title IX Sneakily Revolutionized Women's Sports," *The Atlantic*, June 21, 2012.
60. Ibid.
61. Mark R. Daniels and Robert E. Darcy, "As Time Goes By: The Arrested Diffusion of the Equal Rights Amendment," *Publius* 15, no. 4 (Autumn 1985): 51–60.
62. Jane J. Mansbridge, *Why We Lost the ERA* (Chicago: University of Chicago Press, 1986).
63. The distinction originally appeared in a footnote to Justice Harlan Fiske Stone's opinion in *United States v. Carolene Products Co.*, 304 U.S. 144 (1938).
64. Federal Aviation Administration, https://www.faa.gov/jobs/employment_information/benefits/csrs/.
65. Rostker v. Goldberg, 453 U.S. 57 (1981).
66. See Meritor Savings Bank, FSB v. Vinson, 477 U.S. 57 (1986), and Harris v. Forklift Systems, Inc., 510 U.S. 17 (1993).
67. Susan Saulny, "Census Data Presents Rise in Multiracial Population of Youths," *New York Times*, March 24, 2011, http://www.nytimes.com/2011/03/25/us/25race.html, accessed on August 5, 2011.
68. Anna Clark, "Suing for Better Cities: Despite a Robust Complete Streets Movement and a Growing Emphasis on Accessible Design, the Surest Path to ADA Compliance in America Is Still through Legal Threat," *Next City*, June 13, 2016.
69. Parents Involved in Community Schools v. Seattle School District No. 1, 551 U.S. 701 (2007).
70. United States v. Virginia, 518 U.S. 515 (1996).
71. Ibid.

Unit 3 Review

1. Lynch v. Donnelly, 465 U.S. 668 (1984).
2. 418 U.S. 717 (1974).
3. 433 U.S. at 282.

4. 10 U.S.C. § 1251 (2006).
5. Bethel v. Fraser, 478 U.S. 675 (1986).
6. 393 U.S. 503 (1969).

Chapter 10

1. https://www.darrylglennforcongress.com/.
2. https://coffman.house.gov/.
3. Ibid.
4. Statement of Hannah Sievers, December 30, 2017.
5. "Transcript: Donald Trump's Taped Comments about Women," *New York Times*, October 8, 2016.
6. Written statement of Hannah Sievers, December 30, 2017.
7. Ibid.
8. Alexis de Tocqueville, *Democracy in America*, trans. George Lawrence, ed. J. P. Mayer (New York: Business Plus, 2010).
9. Ibid.
10. Ibid.
11. Ibid.
12. Ibid.
13. Ibid.
14. Frederick Jackson Turner, *The Significance of the Frontier in American History* (New York: Readex Microprint, 1966), 221.
15. James Willard Hurst, *Law and the Conditions of Freedom in the Nineteenth-Century United States* (Madison: University of Wisconsin Press, 1956).
16. Bruce Drake, *6 New Findings about Millennials*, Pew Research Center, March 7, 2014.
17. Pew Research Center, Millennials, http://www.pewresearch.org/topics/millennials/.
18. Drake, *6 New Findings about Millennials*.
19. Gallup Poll, September 6, 2017, http://news.gallup.com/poll/27286/government.aspx.
20. Taylor Kate Brown, "How US Welfare Compares around the Globe," BBC, August 26, 2016.
21. Drew DeSilver, "Among Developed Nations, Americans' Tax Bills Are below Average," Pew Research, October 24, 2017.
22. Benjamin Page and Lawrence Jacobs, *Class War?* (Chicago: University of Chicago Press, 2009); see also, Hannah Fingerhut, "Most Americans Say U.S. Economic System Is Unfair, but High-Income Republicans Disagree," Pew Research Center, February 10, 2016, http://www.pewresearch.org/fact-tank/2016/02/10/most-americans-say-u-s-economic-system-is-unfair-but-high-inco.
23. Patient Protection and Affordable Care Act, 42 U.S.C. § 18001 (2010).
24. James Madison, *Federalist* No. 51, February 8, 1788, Avalon Project, Yale Law School.
25. Alexander Hamilton, *Federalist* No. 78, Avalon Project, Yale Law School, http://avalon.law.yale.edu/18th_century/fed78.asp.
26. "What Is the Rule of Law," American Bar Association, https://www.americanbar.org/content/dam/aba/migrated/publiced/features/Part1DialogueROL.authcheckdam.pdf.
27. Freedom of Information Act, 5 U.S.C. 552 (1967).
28. John Locke, *Two Treatises on Government* (London: Printed for R. Butler, etc., 1821), Bartleby.com, 2010.
29. The Declaration of Independence, July 4, 1776, Avalon Project, Yale Law School, http://avalon.law.yale.edu/18th_century/declare.asp.
30. Ibid.
31. U.S. Department of Health and Human Services, 2017 Federal Poverty Level Guidelines.
32. David Rosenbaum, "Welfare: Who Gets It? How Much Does It Cost?" *New York Times*, March 23, 1995, A23.
33. Fred I. Greenstein, "The Benevolent Leader: Children's Images of Political Authority," *American Political Science Review* 54, no. 4 (1960): 934–43; David Easton and Robert D. Hess, "The Child's Political World," *Midwest Journal of Political Science* 6, no. 3 (1962): 229–46. For a more qualified view of the effectiveness of parent-child transmission of political attitudes and values, see M. Kent Jennings and Richard G. Niemi, "The Transmission of Political Values from Parent to Child," *American Political Science Review* 62, no. 1 (1968): 169–84.
34. Christopher H. Achen, "Parental Socialization and Rational Party Identification," *Political Behavior* 24, no. 2 (2002): 151–70.
35. See Kenneth P. Langton and M. Kent Jennings, "Political Socialization and the High School Civics Curriculum in the United States," *American Political Science Review* 62, no. 3 (1968): 852–67.
36. David E. Campbell, *Why We Vote: How Schools and Communities Shape Our Civic Life* (Princeton, NJ: Princeton University Press, 2006).
37. Lee H. Ehman, "The American School in the Political Socialization Process," *Review of Educational Research* 50, no. 1 (1980): 99–119.
38. "Jewish Voting Records (1916-present)," Jewish Virtual Library, American-Israeli Cooperative Enterprise.
39. "How the Faithful Voted: A Preliminary 2016 Analysis," Pew Research Center, November 9, 2016.
40. Ibid.
41. "US Muslims Concerned about Their Place in Society but Continue to Believe in the American Dream," Pew Research: Religion and Public Life, July 26, 2017.
42. Habitat for Humanity Chicago, https://www.habitatchicago.org/.
43. Ibid.
44. Diana Owen, "Political Socialization in the Twenty-First Century: Recommendations for Researchers, Georgetown University," presented at "The Future of Civil Education in the 21st Century," conference cosponsored by the Center for Civic Education and the Bundeszentrale für politische Bildung, James Madison's Montpelier, September 21–26, 2008.
45. "The Whys and Hows of Generations Research," Pew Research Center: U.S. Politics & Policy, September 3, 2015.
46. Ibid.
47. Ibid.
48. Ibid.
49. "Primary vs. Secondary Sources," University Library, American University, Washington DC, https://subjectguides.library.american.edu/primary.
50. Ibid.
51. Julia Glum, "Young Voters Don't Like Hillary Clinton or Donald Trump: What That Means for November," *International Business Times*, March 29, 2016.
52. Ibid.
53. Gillian Flaccus, "Why Some Millennial Voters Are Turning to Trump," *PBS NewsHour*, May 27, 2016.
54. Ibid.
55. Ibid.
56. Beth Ann Bovine, "Why Millennials and the Depression-Era Generation Are More Similar Than You Think," *Fortune*, April 29, 2015.
57. "The Whys and Hows of Generations Research," Pew Research Center: U.S. Politics & Policy, September 3, 2015.
58. Patrick H. O'Neil, Karl Fields, and Don Share, "Globalization and the Future of Comparative Politics," *Essentials of Comparative Politics*, (New York: W.W. Norton & Company, 2015).
59. Daniel Brown, "Russia Seems to Be Intensifying Its New Cold War on the West," *Business Insider*, April 24, 2017.
60. Vincent Trivett, "25 Mega Corporations: Where They Rank If They Were Countries," *Business Insider*, June 27, 2011.
61. Joelle Tanguy, "Controversies around Humanitarian Interventions and the Authority to Intervene," Doctors Without Borders, November 5, 1999.
62. Anup Shah, "Non-Governmental Organizations on Development Issues," *Global Issues*, June 1, 2005, http://www.globalissues.org/article/25/non-governmental-organizations-on-development-issues.
63. Ibid.
64. "List of the Top 10 Non-Governmental Organizations in the United States," Transparent Hands, October 20, 2017, https://www.transparenthands.org/list-of-top-10-non-governmental-organizations-in-usa/.
65. Patrick O'Neil, Karl Fields, and Don Share, *Essentials of Comparative Politics with Cases*, 5th ed. (New York: W.W. Norton, 2015), 218–26.
66. "Members and Observers," World Trade Organization, https://www.wto.org/english/thewto_e/whatis_e/tif_e/org6_e.htm.
67. Ibid., 463.
68. "10 Things the WTO Can Do," World Trade Organization, https://www.wto.org/english/thewto_e/whatis_e/10thi_e/10thi00_e.htm.
69. Aurelie Walker, "The WTO Has Failed Developing Nations," *The Guardian*, November 14, 2011.
70. Sabri Ben-Achour, "Did NAFTA Cost or Create Jobs? Both," *Marketplace*, March 22, 2017, https://www.marketplace.org/2017/03/21/economy/did-nafta-cost-or-create-jobs-both.
71. Ana Swanson, "Trump's Tough Talk on NAFTA Raises Prospects of Pact's Demise," *New York Times*, October 11, 2017.
72. Peter Baker, "Trump Abandons Trans-Pacific Partnership, Obama's Signature Trade Deal," *New York Times*, January 23, 2017.
73. Ayako Hobbs and Sarah Rathke, "Coming to America: Foreign Manufacturers Looking to Produce in the U.S.," Patton Boggs: Global Supply Chain Blog, August 6, 2015.
74. Ben-Achour, "Did NAFTA Cost or Create Jobs?"

75. "Conditions for Membership," European Neighbourhood Policy and Enlargement Negotiations, European Union.

76. Human Rights Watch: About, https://www.hrw.org/about.

77. Michael Anti, "Behind the Great Firewall of China," TED Talk, TEDGlobal 2012.

78. Heather Long, "U.S. Has Lost 5 Million Manufacturing Jobs since 2000," CNN Monday, March 29, 2016.

79. Financial Times/lexicon.

80. "Handmade vs. Factory Made: Comparing Time and Cost," *Industry Week,* January 5, 2017.

81. David Z. Morris, "Leaked Chats Show Charlottesville Marchers Were Planning for Violence," *Fortune*, August 26, 2017, http://fortune.com/2017/08/26/charlottesville-violence-leaked-chats/.

82. J. M. Berger, "How Terrorists Recruit Online (and How to Stop It)," Brookings, November 9, 2015, https://www.brookings.edu/blog/markaz/2015/11/09/how-terrorists-recruit-online-and-how-to-stop-it/.

83. "Massive Blow to Criminal Dark Web after Globally Coordinated Operation," Europol, Press Release, July 20, 2017.

84. "Meeting with the Young People of the Dioceses of Abruzzi and Molise: Address of Pope Francis," The Vatican, July 5, 2014, https://m.vatican.va/content/francesco/en/speeches/2014/july/documents/papa-francesco_20140705_molise-giovani.html.

85. Alexis de Tocqueville, *Democracy in America*, trans. George Lawrence, ed. J. P. Mayer (New York: Business Plus, 2010).

86. Mitt Romney, "Remarks in St. Louis, Missouri: 'A Champion for Free Enterprise,'" July 7, 2012, American Presidency Project, http://www.presidency.ucsb.edu/ws/index.php?pid=101162.

87. James Wilson, *Collected Works of James Wilson*, Vol. 1, eds. Kermit L. Hall and Mark David Hall, with an introduction by Kermit L. Hall, and a bibliographical essay by Mark David Hall, collected by Maynard Garrison (Indianapolis, IN: Liberty Fund, 2007), http://oll.libertyfund.org/titles/2072, accessed March 24, 2018.

88. Larry D. Rosen, "Welcome to the iGeneration!" *Psychology Today*, March 27, 2010.

Chapter 11

1. Christine Byers, "Darren Wilson Resigns from Ferguson Police Department: 'It Is My Hope That My Resignation Will Allow the Community to Heal,'" *St. Louis Post-Dispatch*, November 30, 2014, available from Lexis-Nexis Academic.

2. "Police-Community Reform and the Two Fergusons," Editorial, *St. Louis Post-Dispatch,* December 3, 2014, http://www.stltoday.com/news/opinion/columns/the-platform/editorial-police-community-reform-and-the-two-fergusons/article_c486f098-588a-5951-af85-036d74bd6999.html.

3. "Ferguson Timeline," *St. Louis Post-Dispatch*, August 2, 2015, available from Lexis-Nexis Academic.

4. Tim Barker, "Ferguson-Area Businesses Cope with Aftermath of Weekend Riot," *St. Louis Post-Dispatch*, August 12, 2014, available from Lexis-Nexis Academic.

5. Joe Holleman and Kevin Johnson, "Ferguson Notes Ferguson Police Shooting," *St. Louis Post-Dispatch*, November 22, 2014, available from Lexis-Nexis Academic.

6. "Police-Community Reform and the Two Fergusons."

7. Rick Morin, Kim Parker, Renee Stepler, and Andres Mercer, "Behind the Badge: Amid Protests and Calls for Reform How Police View Their Jobs, Key Issues and Recent Fatal Encounters between Blacks and the Police," Pew Research Center, January 11, 2017.

8. Pew Research Center, "Across Racial Lines, More Say Nation Needs to Make Changes to Achieve Racial Equality," August 5, 2015, http://www.people-press.org/2015/08/05/across-racial-lines-more-say-nation-needs-to-make-changes-to-achieve-racial-equality/; Scott Clement, "A Year after Ferguson, 6 in 10 Americans Say Changes Are Needed to Give Blacks and Whites Equal Rights," *The Washington Post*, August 5, 2015, https://www.washingtonpost.com/news/the-fix/wp/2015/08/05/what-changed-since-ferguson-americans-are-far-more-worried-about-black-rights/.

9. "Colin Kaepernick Protests Anthem over Treatment of Minorities," ESPN.com News Services, August 27, 2016, http://theundefeated.com/features/colin-kaepernick-protests-anthem-over-treatment-of-minorities/.

10. Ibid.

11. Adam Stiles, "Everything You Need to Know about NFL Protests during the National Anthem," SBNation.com, October 19, 2017, https://www.sbnation.com/2017/9/29/16380080/donald-trump-nfl-colin-kaepernick-protests-national-anthem.

12. Ibid.

13. Tom Wolfe, *The Bonfire of the Vanities* (New York: Farrar, Straus & Giroux 1987).

14. Michael Delli Carpini and Scott Keeter, *What Americans Know about Politics and Why It Matters* (New Haven, CT: Yale University Press, 1996).

15. Samuel L. Popkin, *The Reasoning Voter: Communication and Persuasion in Political Campaigns* (Chicago: The University of Chicago Press, 1991), 212.

16. Arthur Lupia and Mathew D. McCubbins, *The Democratic Dilemma: Can Citizens Learn What They Need to Know?* (New York: Cambridge University Press, 1998).

17. Wendy M. Rahn, "The Role of Partisan Stereotypes in Information Processing about Political Candidates," *American Journal of Political Science* 37, no. 2 (1993): 472–96.

18. See James Surowiecki, *The Wisdom of Crowds* (New York: Doubleday, 2004).

19. Benjamin I. Page and Robert Y. Shapiro, *The Rational Public: Fifty Years of Trends in Americans' Policy Preferences* (Chicago: University of Chicago Press, 1992), 14.

20. "Iowa Entrance Polls," *New York Times*, February 1, 2016, https://www.nytimes.com/interactive/2016/02/01/us/elections/iowa-democrat-poll.html.

21. Humphrey Taylor, "The Case for Publishing (Some) Online Polls," *Polling Report*, January 15, 2007.

22. Ibid.

23. James M. Druckman, "The Implications of Framing Effects for Citizen Competence," *Political Behavior* 23, no. 3 (Sept. 2001): 225–56.

24. Pew Research Center, "Questionnaire Design," http://www.pewresearch.org/methodology/u-s-survey-research/questionnaire-design/.

25. Pew Research Center, "Questionnaire Design," http://www.pewresearch.org/methodology/u-ssurvey-research/questionnaire-design/.

26. Darren W. Davis and Brian D. Silver, "Stereotype Threat and Race of Interviewer Effects in a Survey on Political Knowledge," *American Journal of Political Science* 47, no. 1 (2003): 33–45.

27. Andrew Mercer, Claudia Deane, and Kyley McGeeney, "Why 2016 Election Polls Missed the Mark," Pew Research Center, November 9, 2016.

28. Nate Silver, "Why FiveThirtyEight Gave Trump a Better Chance Than Almost Anyone Else," FiveThirtyEight, November 11, 2016, http://fivethirtyeight.com/features/why-fivethirtyeight-gave-trump-a-better-chance-than-almost-anyone-else/.

29. Mercer, Deane, and McGeeney, "Why 2016 Election Polls Missed the Mark."

30. Ibid.

31. Ibid.

32. Nate Silver, "Education, Not Income, Predicted Who Would Vote for Trump," FiveThirtyEight, November 22, 2016, http://fivethirtyeight.com/features/education-not-income-predicted-who-would-vote-for-trump/.

33. Mercer, Deane, and McGeeney, "Why 2016 Election Polls Missed the Mark."

34. Ibid.

35. Ibid.

36. Pew Research Center, "Stark Racial Divisions in Reactions to Ferguson Police Shooting," August 18, 2014, http://www.people-press.org/files/2014/08/8-18-14-Ferguson-Release.pdf.

37. Michael Dawson, *Black Visions: The Roots of Contemporary African American Political Ideologies* (Chicago: University of Chicago Press, 2001).

38. Dennis Chong and Dukhong Kim, "The Experiences and Effects of Economic Status among Racial and Ethnic Minorities," *American Political Science Review* 100, no. 3 (2006): 335–51.

39. Pew Research Center, "Stark Racial Divisions in Reactions to Ferguson Police Shooting."

40. Ben Page, "It's OK for Politicians to Ignore Public Opinion," *The Guardian*, March 25, 2013.

41. Ibid.

42. Dionne and Mann, "Polling & Public Opinion."

43. 110 Stat. 2105.

44. "National Survey of Public Knowledge of Welfare Reform and the Federal Budget," Henry J. Kaiser Foundation, December 30, 1994.

45. Ibid.

46. 10 Stat. 2105.

47. Pub. L. No. 115-97.
48. Frank Newport, "Public Opinion and the Tax Reform Law, Gallup, December 21, 2017, http://news.gallup.com/opinion/polling-matters/224432/public-opinion-tax-reform-law.aspx.
49. Ibid.
50. Ibid.
51. Dylan Scott, "House Republican: My Donors Told Me to Pass the Tax Bill 'or Don't Ever Call Me Again,'" *Vox*, November 7, 2017, https://www.vox.com/policy-and-politics/2017/11/7/16618038/house-republicans-tax-bill-donors-chris-collins.
52. Ibid.
53. "1 Person Shot, Crowd Scatters as Gunshots Ring Out Late Sunday in Ferguson," *St. Louis Post-Dispatch*, August 10, 2015, available from Lexis-Nexis Academic.
54. Mitch Smith, "A Year On, Ferguson Killing Is Recalled," *New York Times*, August 8, 2015, http://www.nytimes.com/2015/08/09/us/a-year-on-ferguson-killing-is-recalled.html?_r=0.
55. Zeeshan Aleem, "The First Democratic Debate Proved That Black Lives Matter Is Making a Difference," Policy.Mic, October 14, 2015, http://mic.com/articles/126730/the-first-democratic-debate-proved-that-black-lives-matter-is-making-a-difference.
56. "Law Enforcement and Violence: The Divide between Black and White Americans," NORC Center for Public Affairs at the University of Chicago, http://www.apnorc.org/projects/Pages/HTML%20Reports/law-enforcement-and-violence-the-divide-between-black-and-white-americans0803-9759.aspx.
57. Lilly Fowler, "Members of the Congressional Black Caucus Arrive in Ferguson to Pledge Their Support," *St. Louis Post-Dispatch*, January 19, 2015, available from Lexis-Nexis Academic.
58. John W. Kingdon, *Agendas, Alternatives, and Public Policies,* 2nd ed. (New York: Longman, 2003), 1.
59. David Zarefsky, "'Public Sentiment Is Everything': Lincoln's View of Political Persuasion," *Journal of the Abraham Lincoln Association* (Summer 1994).
60. Philip Bump, "Why Is National Polling All over the Map?" *Washington Post*, October 27, 2016.

Chapter 12

1. Norm Ornstein, "The Real Story of Obamacare's Birth," *The Atlantic*, July 6, 2015, http://www.theatlantic.com/politics/archive/2015/07/the-real-story-of-obamacares-birth/397742/.
2. "Remarks of President Barack Obama—Address to Joint Session of Congress," The White House, Office of the Press Secretary, February 24, 2009, https://www.whitehouse.gov/the-press-office/remarks-president-barack-obama-address-joint-session-congress.
3. Ibid.
4. Michael McAuliff, "Pelosi's Health Coup: Says Affordable Care for All Is on Horizon as She Unveils the House's 20-Pound Bill," *New York Daily News*, October 30, 2009.
5. Ibid.
6. Patient Protection and Affordable Care Act, 42 U.S.C. § 18001 et seq. (2010).
7. Jonathan Cohn, "The Story of 2 Families and the Real-Life Impact of Obamacare Repeal," The Huffington Post, accessed March, 19, 2017, https://www.huffingtonpost.com/entry/obamacare-repeal-premiums_us_58cc4cc0e4b0be71dcf4dba4.
8. Ibid.
9. Dan Mangan, "Trump Touts Repeal of Key Part in 'Disastrous Obamacare'—the Individual Mandate," CNBC, January 20, 2018.
10. Timothy Cama, "Fracking Divides Red States, Blue States," *The Hill*, June 6, 2015, http://thehill.com/policy/energy/244194-fracking-creates-new-fault-line-between-red-and-blue-states.
11. Ibid.
12. Ibid.
13. Republican National Committee, Press Release, "RNC Statement on the ISIS-Linked Terrorist Attack in California," December 4, 2015, https://gop.com/rnc-statement-on-the-isis-linked-terrorist-attack-in-california/.
14. Jennifer Bendery, "Debbie Wasserman Schultz Campaigns against Republicans Who 'Prefer to Act Like Children,'" The Huffington Post, July 31, 2012, http://www.huffingtonpost.com/2012/07/31/debbie-wasserman-schultz-campaign_n_1726020.html.
15. The World Bank in China, World Bank, http://www.worldbank.org/en/country/china/overview.
16. Labor Force Statistics from the Current Population Survey, Bureau of Labor Statistics, https://www.bls.gov/cps/cps_htgm.htm#concepts.
17. Consumer Price Index, Bureau of Labor Statistics, https://www.bls.gov/cpi/.
18. Ibid.
19. David J. Smyth and Susan Washburn Taylor, "Inflation-Unemployment Trade-Offs of Democrats, Republicans, and Independents: Empirical Evidence on the Partisan Theory," *Journal of Macroeconomics*, Winter 1992.
20. John Maynard Keynes, *The General Theory of Employment, Interest, and Money* (New York: Harcourt, Brace & Company, 1936).
21. Michael D. Shear, "Obama Offers First Look at Massive Public Works Plan to Create 2.5 Million Jobs," *Washington Post*, December 7, 2008.
22. Kamal Ahmed, "Trump Tax Cuts: Here's Why They Matter to Us All," *BBC*, December 20, 2017.
23. Economic Growth and Tax Relief Reconciliation Act of 2001, Pub. L. 107–16, 115 Stat. 38, June 7, 2001; Jobs and Growth Tax Relief Reconciliation Act of 2003, Pub. L. 108–27, 117 Stat. 752.
24. Jarrett Murphy, "Federal Deficit Hits Record $374B," CBS News, August 26, 2003, https://www.cbsnews.com/news/federal-deficit-hits-record-374b/.
25. Jackie Calmes, "Obama Tax Plan Would Ask More of Millionaires," *New York Times*, September 17, 2011, https://www.nytimes.com/2011/09/18/us/politics/obama-tax-plan-would-ask-more-of-millionaires.html.
26. Steven Mufson, "Obama's Final Budget Proposal Calls for $4.15 Trillion in Spending," *Washington Post,* February 9, 2016.
27. Lindsay Dunsmuir, "U.S. Fiscal Year Budget Deficit Widens to $587 Billion," Reuters, October 14, 2016, https://www.reuters.com/article/us-usa-economy-budget/u-s-fiscal-year-budget-deficit-widens-to-587-billion-idUSKBN12E2B5.
28. Stan Collender, "Trump Trillion-Dollar Budget Deficits Officially Begin This Week," *Forbes*, April 8, 2018, https://www.forbes.com/sites/stancollender/2018/04/08/trump-trillion-dollar-budget-deficits-officially-begin-this-week/#499fc2d83365.
29. Stephen Moore, "There Are Zero Excuses to Stand against the Trump Tax Cut," *The Hill,* December 19, 2017.
30. For an excellent treatment of this history, see Adam Fergusson, *When Money Dies: The Nightmare of the Weimar Collapse* (London: Kimber, 1975).
31. Federal Reserve Governor Ben S. Bernanke, "Deflation: Making Sure 'It' Doesn't Happen Here," Board of Governors of the Federal Reserve System, November 21, 2002, https://www.federalreserve.gov/boarddocs/Speeches/2002/20021121/default.htm, accessed August 12, 2016.
32. Milton Friedman, *The Optimum Quantity of Money: And Other Essays* (Chicago: Aldine, 1969), 4–6.
33. Elizabeth Lazarowitz, "Bernanke Missed Signs of Crisis," *Daily News*, January 18, 2013.
34. From "Federal Reserve Governor Powell's Policy Views, in His Own Words," Reuters, November 2, 2017, accessed March 30, 2018, https://www.reuters.com/article/us-usa-trump-powell-quotes/federal-reserve-governor-powells-policy-views-in-his-own-words-idUSKBN1D22OU.
35. Medicare Prescription Drug Improvement and Modernization Act, Pub. L. 108–173, 117 Stat. 2066.
36. The Henry J. Kaiser Family Foundation, "Total Medicaid Spending," 2014, http://kff.org/medicaid/state-indicator/total-medicaid-spending/, accessed March 16, 2018.
37. "Health Care Costs: How the U.S. Compares with Other Countries," PBS, October 22, 2012.
38. Tami Luhby, "The Truth about the Uninsured Rate in America," CNN, March 14, 2017, accessed March 30, 2018, http://money.cnn.com/2017/03/13/news/economy/uninsured-rate-obamacare/index.html.
39. U.S. Department of Health and Human Services, "The Affordable Care Act Is Working," 945:121, June 24, 2015, http://www.hhs.gov/healthcare/facts-and-features/fact-sheets/aca-is-working/index.html#, accessed July 27, 2016.
40. National Federation of Independent Businesses v. Sebelius, 567 U.S. 519 (2012). The Court also upheld portions of the Medicaid expansion, although with limitations.
41. King v. Burwell, 576 U.S. __ (2015).
42. Michael Cooper, "Conservatives Sowed Idea of Health Care Mandate, Only to Spurn It Later," *New York Times,* February 14, 2012, https://www.nytimes.com/2012/02/15/health/policy/health-care-mandate-was-first-backed-by-conservatives.html.

43. "Why Republicans Hate Obamacare," *The Economist*, December 11, 2016.
44. Katherine Stewart, "School Vouchers and the Religious Subversion of Church-State Separation," *The Guardian*, April 12, 2012.
45. Laura Putre, "Hangin' with Mother Hough," *Cleveland Scene,* March 9, 2001, http://www.clevescene.com/cleveland/hangin-with-mother-hough/Content?oid=1476527, accessed July 22, 2014.
46. Gregory B. Bodwell, "Grassroots, Inc.: A Sociopolitical History of the Cleveland School Voucher Battle 1992–2002" (Ph.D. diss., Case Western Reserve University, 2006), 2, https://etd.ohiolink.edu/rws_etd/document/get/case1133366159/inline.
47. 536 U.S. 639 (2002).
48. John F. Kennedy, Address to the Economic Club of New York, December 14, 1962.
49. Sources: Republican Platform (Party A), accessible via https://prod-cdn-static.gop.com/media/documents/DRAFT_12_FINAL[1]-ben_1468872234.pdf. Democratic Platform (Party B) accessible via https://www.democrats.org/party-platform#environment.

Unit 4 Review

1. Gov. Ronald Reagan, Address at Installation of President Robert Hill, Chico State College, May 20, 1967.
2. Donna Brazile, "Lies, Damned Lies, Statistics, and Polls," posted July 3, 2014, at http://www.brazileassociates.com/?p=1127.

Chapter 13

1. James Madison, *Federalist* No. 10, "The Same Subject Continued: The Union as a Safeguard against Domestic Faction and Insurrection," *New York Daily Advertiser,* November 22, 1787.
2. Dan Eggen, "Poll: Large Majority Opposes Supreme Court's Decision on Campaign Financing," *Washington Post*, February 17, 2010.
3. Citizens United v. Federal Election Commission, 558 U.S. 310 (2010).
4. Tillman Act of 1907, 34 Stat. 864 (January 26, 1907).
5. Federal Election Campaign Act of 1971, Pub. L. 92-225, 86 Stat. 3 (1972). In 1974, after the Watergate scandals, the Act was amended to place limits on campaign contributions and expenditures. The 1974 amendments also created the Federal Election Commission (FEC).
6. Ibid.
7. Ibid.
8. Buckley v. Valeo, 424 U.S. 1 (1976).
9. Bipartisan Campaign Reform Act, Pub. L. 107-155, 116 Stat. 81 (2002). It is also known as the McCain-Feingold Act after its key Senate sponsors.
10. McConnell v. Federal Election Commission, 540 U.S. 93 (2003).
11. Cited in Ryan O'Connell, "David Bossie: 5 Fast Facts You Need to Know," June 1, 2015, http://heavy.com/news/2017/06/david-bossie-trump-war-room-russia; Lloyd Grove, "A Firefighter's Blazing Trail," *Washington Post*, November 13, 1997.

12. What We Do, http://www.citizensunited.org/what-we-do.aspx.
13. Adam Winkler, "*Citizens United*, Personhood, and the Corporation in Politics," in Naomi Lamoreaux and William Novak, eds., *Corporations and American Democracy* (Cambridge: Harvard University Press, 2017), 363–64.
14. Citizens United v. Federal Election Commission, 558 U.S. 310 (2010).
15. Citizens United, 58 U.S. 310, 335, citing Buckley v. Valeo, 424 U.S. 1 (1976).
16. 558 U.S. 310, 452–53.
17. 558 U.S. 310, 441.
18. Caperton v. A. T. Massey Coal Co., 556 U.S. 868 (2009).
19. SpeechNow.org v. Federal Election Commission, 599 F.3d 686 (D.C. Cir. 2010).
20. 2012 Top Donors to Outside Spending Groups, Center for Responsive Politics, https://www.opensecrets.org/outsidespending/summ.php?cycle=2012&disp=D.
21. Emily Dalgo and Ashley Balcerzak, "Seven Years Later: Blurred Boundaries, More Money," Center for Responsive Politics, January 19, 2017, https://www.opensecrets.org/news/2017/01/citizens-united-7-years-later/.
22. https://www.opensecrets.org/outsidespending/outvscand.php?cycle=2016.
23. Sidney Verba, Kay Lehman Schlozman, and Henry E. Brady, *Voice and Equality: Civic Voluntarism in American Politics* (Cambridge, MA: Harvard University Press, 1995), 42.
24. Russell J. Dalton, "The Myth of the Disengaged American," *Comparative Study of Electoral Systems (CSES)*, 2005, http://www.cses.org/resources/results/POP_Oct2005_1.htm, accessed May 13, 2016.
25. Donald Ratcliffe, "The Right to Vote and the Rise of Democracy, 1787–1828," *Journal of the Early Republic,* Summer 2013.
26. "Voting Rights Act Timeline," American Civil Liberties Union, March 4, 2005. https://www.aclu.org/news/voting-rights-act.
27. Jose A. DelReal, "Voter Turnout in 2014 Was the Lowest Since WWII," *Washington Post*, November 10, 2014, https://www.washingtonpost.com/news/postpolitics/wp/2014/11/10/voter-turnout-in-2014-was-the-lowest-since-wwii/, accessed February 19, 2016.
28. Raymond E. Wolfinger and Steven J. Rosenstone, *Who Votes?* (New Haven, CT: Yale University Press, 1980).
29. Sean McElwee, "How Unions Boost Democratic Participation," *American Prospect*, September 16, 2015, http://prospect.org/article/how-unions-boost-democratic-participation.
30. See Eric Plutzer, "Becoming a Habitual Voter: Inertia, Resources, and Growth in Young Adulthood," *American Political Science Review* 96, no. 1 (March 2002): 41–56.
31. Symm v. United States, 439 U.S. 1105 (1979).
32. Laura Fitzpatrick, "College Students Still Face Voting Stumbling Blocks," *Time*, October 14, 2008, http://content.time.com/time/nation/article/0,8599,1849906,00.html, accessed February 15, 2016.
33. Center for American Women and Politics, Eagleton Institute of Politics, Rutgers, the State University of New Jersey, "Fact Sheet: Gender

Differences in Voter Turnout," October 2015, http://www.cawp.rutgers.edu/sites/default/files/resources/genderdiff.pdf, accessed June 10, 2016.
34. John Light, "The Link between Mass Incarceration and Voter Turnout," Moyers & Company, May 15, 2013, http://billmoyers.com/2013/05/15/the-link-between-mass-incarceration-and-voter-turnout/.
35. Jens Manuel Krogstad and Mark Hugo Lopez, "Black Voter Turnout Fell in 2016, Even as a Record Number of Americans Cast Ballots," Pew Research Center, May 12, 2017, http://www.pewresearch.org/fact-tank/2017/05/12/black-voter-turnout-fell-in-2016-even-as-a-record-number-of-americans-cast-ballots/.
36. Australian Electoral Commission Site on Rules Governing Compulsory Voting in Federal and State Elections, http://www.aec.gov.au/Voting/Compulsory_Voting.htm.
37. Drew DeSilver, "U.S. Voter Turnout Trails Most Developed Countries," Pew Research Center, May 6, 2015, http://www.pewresearch.org/facttank/2015/05/06/u-s-voter-turnout-trails-mostdeveloped-countries/, accessed February 16, 2016.
38. Christopher Uggen and Sarah Shannon, "State-Level Estimates of Felon Disenfranchisement in the United States, 2010," The Sentencing Project, July 2012, http://sentencingproject.org/doc/publications/fd_State_Level_Estimates_of_Felon_Disen_2010.pdf, accessed February 28, 2016.
39. "Number of People by State Who Cannot Vote Due to a Felony Conviction," ProCon.org, October 4, 2017.
40. Aamna Mohdin, "American Women Voted Overwhelmingly for Clinton, Except the White Ones," *Quartz*, November 9, 2016, https://qz.com/833003/election-2016-all-women-voted-overwhelmingly-for-clinton-except-the-white-ones/.
41. Krogstad and Lopez, "Black Voter Turnout Fell in 2016."
42. Hannah Fingerhut, "What Voters Want in a President Today, and How Their Views Have Changed," Pew Research Center, February 12, 2016, http://www.pewresearch.org/fact-tank/2016/02/12/what-voters-want-in-a-president-today-and-how-their-views-have-changed/.
43. Ibid.
44. Lynne Marks, "Political Elections: How Much Does Image Matter?" London Image Institute, August 15, 2016, http://www.londonimageinstitute.com/politicalimage/.
45. Richard Alleyne, "Attractive candidates really do pick up more votes," *The Telegraph*, September 17, 2012, http://www.londonimageinstitute.com/politicalimage/.
46. Ryan Enos, "No, Good Looks Don't Win Elections," *Washington Post*, November 13, 2013, https://www.washingtonpost.com/news/monkey-cage/wp/2013/11/13/no-good-looks-dont-win-elections/?utm_term=.9b7bfe682270.
47. Ibid.
48. Angus Campbell et al., *The American Voter* (Midway Reprint) (Chicago: University of Chicago Press, 1960).

49. Steven J. Rosenstone and John Mark Hansen, *Mobilization, Participation, and Democracy in America* (New York: Macmillan, 1993).

50. "Disenfranchisement in Other Countries," Human Rights Watch, https://www.hrw.org /legacy/reports98/vote/usvot98o-04.htm.

51. "Automatic Voter Registration," Brennan Center for Justice, April 17, 2018, https://www .brennancenter.org/analysis/automatic -voter-registration.

52. USA.gov, "Voter Registration Deadlines for the General Election by State," https://www.usa .gov/voter-registration-deadlines, accessed February 17, 2016.

53. Pub. L. 103-31, 107 Stat. 77 (1993).

54. Oklahoma had passed a law, which was pending at the time of the writing of the article. National Conference of State Legislatures, "Online Voter Registration," December 6, 2017, http://www.ncsl.org/research/elections -and-campaigns/electronic-or-online-voter -registration.aspx, accessed March 26, 2018.

55. Jack Fitzpatrick, "College Students Face New Voting Barriers," Minnpost, August 16, 2012, https://www.minnpost.com/politics-policy /2012/08/college-students-face-new-voting -barriers, accessed February 19, 2016.

56. U.S. Const. art. I, § 4.

57. The power of states to restrict the rights of convicted felons to vote, which is called felony (or felon) disenfranchisement, is rooted in the Fourteenth Amendment's vague phrase, "or other crime."

58. Anthony Downs, *An Economic Theory of Democracy* (New York: Harper & Row, 1957).

59. Morris P. Fiorina, "When Stakes Are High, Rationality Kicks In," *New York Times,* February 26, 2000.

60. Morris P. Fiorina, *Retrospective Voting in American National Elections* (New Haven, CT: Yale University Press, 1981).

61. "Full Text: Donald Trump Announces Presidential Bid," *Washington Post,* June 16, 2015, https://www.washingtonpost.com /news/post-politics/wp/2015/06/16/full-text -donald-trump-announces-a-presidential -bid/?utm_term=.2cefbde9858f.

62. Christopher Achen and Larry Bartels, *Democracy for Realists* (Princeton: Princeton University Press, 2016), 299.

63. Bryan Caplan, *The Myth of the Rational Voter: Why Democracies Choose Bad Policies* (Princeton, NJ: Princeton University Press, 2007).

64. 1824, 1876, 1888, 1992.

65. "1992 Presidential Election," https:// www.270towin.com/1992_Election/.

66. 1824, 1876, 1888, 2000, and 2016.

67. 2016 Presidential Race, Center for Responsive Politics, https://www.opensecrets.org /pres16.

68. Ibid.

69. S. Ansolabehere and S. Iyengar, *Going Negative: How Political Advertisements Shrink and Polarize the Electorate* (New York: Free Press, 1995).

70. John G. Geer, *In Defense of Negativity: Attack Ads in Presidential Campaigns* (Chicago: University of Chicago Press, 2006), 13.

71. Pub. L. 92–225, 86 Stat. 3, enacted February 7, 1972, 52 U.S.C. § 30101 et seq.

72. Buckley v. Valeo, 424 U.S. 1 (1976).

73. Citizens United v. Federal Election Commission, 558 U.S. 310 (2010).

74. 558 U.S. 310, 339 (2010).

75. 558 U.S. 310, 331.

76. 558 U.S. 310, 350 (2010).

77. Justice Stevens (joined by Justices Ginsberg, Breyer, and Sotomayor), concurring in part and dissenting in part, Citizens United v. Federal Election Commission, 558 U.S. 310, 394 (2010).

78. 558 U.S. 310, 394.

79. 558 U.S. 310, 418 (2010).

80. David Bossie, "I'm Responsible for Citizens United. I'm Not Sorry," *Los Angeles Times*, March 1, 2016.

81. Dan Eggen, "Poll: Large Majority Opposes Supreme Court's Decision on Campaign Financing," *Washington Post*, February 17, 2010.

82. Anthony Dick, "Defending *Citizens United,*" *National Review*, January 25, 2010, https:// www.nationalreview.com/bench-memos /defending-citizens-united-anthony-dick/, accessed March 27, 2018.

83. Bennet Statement on Supreme Court Decision in *Citizens United v. FEC*, January 21, 2010, https://www.bennet.senate.gov /?p+release&id=1030.

84. Katanga Johnson, "'Vote Them Out!'— Thousands Register to Vote at U.S. Gun-Control Marches," Reuters, March 24, 2018, https://www.reuters.com/article/uk-usa -guns-voters/vote-them-out-thousands -register-to-vote-at-u-s-gun-control-marches -idUKKBN1H00S0.

Chapter 14

1. Jonathan Rauch, "The Secret to Saner Elections? Stronger State Parties," *Los Angeles Times*, March 22, 2016, http://www.latimes .com/opinion/op-ed/la-oe-0322- rauch-state -parties-20160322-story.html.

2. "Transcript of the Democratic Presidential Debate in Milwaukee," *New York Times,* February 11, 2016, http://www.nytimes .com/2016/02/12/us/politics/transcript-of -the-democratic-presidential-debate -in-milwaukee.html?_r=0.

3. Michael Cooper Jr., "A Message from Trump's America," *U.S. News & World Report,* March 9, 2016, http://www.usnews.com/news/the -report/articles/2016-03-09/a-message-from -trumps-america.

4. Lee Drutman, "Sanders and Trump Really Are the Candidates of Economic Pessimism," Vox.com, April 1, 2016, http://www.vox.com /polyarchy/2016/4/1/11340264/sanders -trump-economic-pessimism.

5. V. O. Key Jr., *Politics, Parties, and Pressure Groups,* 5th ed. (New York: Cromwell, 1964).

6. Citizens United v. Federal Election Commission, 558 U.S. 310 (2010).

7. Jeffrey M. Jones, "Democratic, Republican Identification near Historical Lows," Gallup, January 11, 2016, http://www.gallup.com /poll/188096/democratic-republican -identification-near-historical-lows.aspx?g _ source=Politics&g_medium=lead&g _campaign=tiles.

8. Lydia Saad, "Government Named Top U.S. Problem for Second Straight Year," Gallup, January 11, 2016, http://www.gallup.com /poll/187979/government-named-top -problem-second-straight-year.aspx.

9. Tom Price, "Polarization in America," *CQ Researcher,* February 28, 2014, http://library .cqpress.com/cqresearcher/document .php?id=cqresrre2014022800.

10. Chris Cillizza, "Ticket Splitting Reached a 92-Year Low in 2012," *Washington Post,* April 22, 2014, https://www.washingtonpost.com /news/the-fix/wp/2014/04/22/ticket-splitting -is-the-lowest-its-been-in-92-years/.

11. Mark Landler, "Pushed by Obama, Democrats Alter Platform over Jerusalem," *New York Times,* September 5, 2012, http://www .nytimes.com/2012/09/06/us/politics /pushed-by-obama-democrats-alter -platform-over-jerusalem.html.

12. Ed O'Keefe, "Republicans Outside of Washington Are Dropping Their Opposition to Gay Marriage. Will the National Party Follow Along?" *Washington Post,* April 22, 2014, https://www.washingtonpost.com/news /the-fix/wp/2014/04/22/republicans-outside -of-washington-are-dropping-their -opposition-to-gay-marriage-will-the-national -party-follow-along/.

13. Zeke J. Miller, "Republican Committee Quietly Rejects Anti-Gay Marriage Resolution," *Time,* August 5, 2015, http://time.com/3986485 /republican-national-committee-gay-marriage/.

14. John Wagner, "Clinton's Data-Driven Campaign Relied Heavily on an Algorithm Named Ada. What Didn't She See?," *Washington Post,* November 9, 2016, https://www.washingtonpost.com/news /post-politics/wp/2016/11/09/clintons-data -driven-campaign-relied-heavily-on-an -algorithm-named-ada-what-didnt-she-see /?noredirect=on&utm_term=.10c119cfbaa5.

15. Ibid.

16. Major Garrett, "Trump Campaign Phased Out Use of Cambridge Analytica Data before Election," CBS News online, March 18, 2018, https://www.cbsnews.com/news/trump -campaign-phased-out-use-of-cambridge -analytica-data-before-election/, accessed May 1, 2018.

17. Jonathan V. Last, "Does the Ground Game Matter?" *Weekly Standard,* September 19, 2016.

18. John H. Aldrich, *Why Parties? The Origin and Transformation of Political Parties in America* (Chicago: University of Chicago Press, 1995), 261. See also V. O. Key Jr., "A Theory of Critical Elections," *Journal of Politics* 17, no. 1 (Feb. 1955): 3–18.

19. Key, "A Theory of Critical Elections," 3–18.

20. Morris P. Fiorina, "An Era of Divided Government," in G. Peele, C. J. Bailey, and B. Cain (eds.), *Developments in American Politics* (London: Palgrave, 1992).

21. Nixon Presidential Library and Museum Collection, "Silent Majority," https://www .nixonlibrary.gov/forresearchers/find/subjects /silent-majority.php.

22. James Hohmann, "The Daily 202: The Reagan Democrats Are No Longer Democrats. Will They Ever Be Again?" *Washington Post,* November 11, 2016, https://www.washingtonpost.com/news/powerpost/paloma/daily-202/2016/11/11/daily-202-the-reagan-democrats-are-no-longer-democrats-will-they-ever-be-again/58252889e9b69b6085905df0/?utm_term=.c8eb9c56c18d.

23. Edmund L. Andrews, "It's the Economy Again, and Some See Similarities to 1992," *New York Times,* February 4, 2008, https://www.nytimes.com/2008/02/04/business/04jobs.html.

24. Napp Nazworth, "Barna: Romney Got Lowest Level of Evangelical Support since Dole," *Christian Post,* December 5, 2012, http://www.christianpost.com/news/barna-romney-got-lowest-level-of-evangelical-support-since-dole-86145/.

25. Popular Votes 1940-2016, The Roper Center, https://ropercenter.cornell.edu/polls/us-elections/popular-vote/.

26. See Stan Luger and Brian Waddell, *What American Government Does* (Baltimore: Johns Hopkins University Press, 2017), chap. 10, "The Bailout State."

27. Vanessa Williamson, Theda Skocpol, and John Coggin, "The Tea Party and the Remaking of American Conservatism," *American Political Science Association Perspectives on Politics 9,* no. 1 (March 2011): 25–43.

28. "2014 Election Turnout Lowest in 70 Years," *PBS News Hour,* November 10, 2014, https://www.pbs.org/newshour/politics/2014-midterm-election-turnout-lowest-in-70-years.

29. Democratic National Committee, "Democratic Victory Task Force Final Report and Action Plan," November 17, 2017, https://uploads.democrats.org/Downloads/DVTF_FinalReport.pdf.

30. Lindsey McPherson and Rema Rahman, "The Right Holds," *CQ Guide to the New Congress,* November 10, 2016, 12.

31. Mara Liasson, "The Democratic Party Got Crushed during the Obama Presidency. Here's Why," NPR, March 4, 2016, http://www.npr.org/2016/03/04/469052020/the-democratic-party-got-crushed-during-the-obama-presidency-heres-why.

32. Russell Berman, "What If the Parties Didn't Run Primaries?," *The Atlantic,* October 19, 2015, http://www.theatlantic.com/politics/archive/2015/10/what-if-the-parties-didnt-run-primaries/411022/.

33. Kevin J. Coleman, "The Presidential Nominating Process and the National Party Conventions, 2016: Frequently Asked Questions," Congressional Research Service, December 30, 2015, https://www.fas.org/sgp/crs/misc/R42533.pdf.

34. Michael P. McDonald, "Iowa's Caucus Turnout and What It Means from Now until November," Huffington Post, February 2, 2016, http://www.huffingtonpost.com/michael-p-mcdonald/iowa-caucus-turnout-what-it-means_b_9141408.html.

35. Drew DeSilver, "So Far, Turnout in This Year's Primaries Rivals 2008 Record," Pew Research Center, March 8, 2016, http://www.pewresearch.org/fact-tank/2016/03/08/so-far-turnout-in-this-years-primaries-rivals-2008-record/.

36. Joanna Weiss, "15 Percent Rule? It's Democratic," *Boston Globe,* March 21, 2014, https://www.bostonglobe.com/opinion/2014/03/21/percent-rule-democratic/xXmONscP6gFog77mOJEKYK/story.html.

37. Robert Hendin, Jennifer Pinto, and Anthony Salvanto, "RNC to Punish Florida, but Says Goal of Primary Rules Has Been Met," CBS News online, September 30, 2011.

38. Republican National Committee, Growth and Opportunity Project, March 2013, http://goproject.gop.com/rnc_growth_opportunity_book_2013.pdf, accessed September 5, 2016.

39. Ibid.

40. Democratic National Committee, "Democratic Victory Task Force Final Report and Action Plan," February 2015, https://uploads.democrats.org/Downloads/DVTF_FinalReport.pdf, accessed September 5, 2016.

41. John H. Aldrich, *Why Parties? The Origin and Transformation of Political Parties in America* (Chicago: University of Chicago Press, 1995), 26.

42. Kristina Nwazota, "Third Parties in the U.S. Political Process," *PBS NewsHour,* July 26, 2004, http://www.pbs.org/newshour/updates/politics-july-dec04-third_parties/.

43. "1968 Presidential Election Results," U.S.ElectionAtlas.org, http://uselectionatlas.org/RESULTS/national.php?year=1968.

44. "1980 Presidential Election Results," U.S.ElectionAtlas.org, http://uselectionatlas.org/RESULTS/national.php?year=1980.

45. "1992 Presidential Election Results," U.S.ElectionAtlas.org, http://uselectionatlas.org/RESULTS/national.php?year=1992.

46. "2000 Presidential Election Results," U.S.ElectionAtlas.org, http://uselectionatlas.org/RESULTS/national.php?year=2000.

47. Johnathan Easley and Ben Kamisar, "Third-Party Candidates Face Uphill Climb to Get a Place on Presidential Debate Stage, *The Hill,* May 12, 2016, http://thehill.com/homenews/campaign/279624-third-party-candidates-face-uphill-climb-to-get-place-on-presidential.

48. Christopher J. Devine and Kyle C. Kopko, "5 Things You Need to Know about How Third-Party Candidates Did in 2016," *Washington Post,* November 15, 2016, https://www.washingtonpost.com/news/monkey-cage/wp/2016/11/15/5-things-you-need-to-know-about-how-third-party-candidates-did-in-2016/, accessed November 20, 2016.

49. Gregg LaGambina, "Interview: Ralph Nader," AV Club, September 24, 2008, https://www.avclub.com/ralph-nader-1798214865.

50. Reeve Hamilton, "The Straight Story," *Texas Tribune,* March 2, 2010.

51. Nate Silver, "Was the Democratic Primary a Close Call or a Landslide? Why It's Easy to Underestimate Both Clinton's and Sanders's Accomplishments," FiveThirtyEight, July 27, 2016.

52. Drew DeSilver, "Turnout Was High in the 2016 Primary Season, but Just Short of 2008 Record," Pew Research Center, June 10, 2016.

53. Sabrina Tavernise and Robert Gebeloff, "They Voted for Obama, Then Went for Trump. Can Democrats Win Them Back?," *New York Times,* May 4, 2018, https://www.nytimes.com/2018/05/04/us/obama-trump-swing-voters.html.

Chapter 15

1. Universal Serv. Report and Order, 12 FCC Rcd. 8776, 7 Comm. Reg. (P & F) 109.

2. Brian Fund, "The FCC's Net Neutrality Rules Are Officially Repealed Today. Here's What That Really Means," *Washington Post,* June 11, 2017.

3. "Net Neutrality: What You Need to Know Now," savetheinternet.com, https://www.savetheinternet.com/net-neutrality-what-you-need-to-know-now.

4. Martin Giles, "Net Neutrality Is Dead. The Battle to Resurrect It Is Just Beginning," *MIT Technology Review,* January 3, 2018, https://www.technologyreview.com/s/609840/net-neutralitys-dead-the-battle-to-resurrect-it-is-just-beginning/.

5. Ibid.

6. James Madison, *Federalist* No. 10, in George W. Carey and James McClellan, ed., *The Federalist Papers* (Indianapolis, IN: Liberty Fund, 2001), 48.

7. Ibid.

8. Madison, *Federalist* No. 10, 44.

9. Charles A. Beard, *An Economic Interpretation of the Constitution of the United States* (New York: Macmillan, 1913).

10. David B. Truman, *The Governmental Process: Political Interests and Public Opinion* (New York: Alfred A. Knopf, 1962), 5.

11. "What Is a Free Rider?" Khan Academy, https://www.khanacademy.org/economics-finance-domain/microeconomics/consumer-producer-surplus/externalities-topic/a/the-role-of-government-in-paying-for-public-goods.

12. Lawrence Hunter, "Why James Madison Was Wrong about a Large Republic," *Forbes,* October 30, 2011.

13. Center for Responsive Politics, "Lobbying Database," OpenSecrets.org, May 10, 2018. Their figures were calculated from data obtained from the Senate Office of Public Records.

14. "Revolving Door: Former Members of the 114th Congress," Open Secrets.org: Center for Responsive Politics, https://www.opensecrets.org/revolving/departing.php?cong=114.

15. Kay Lehman Schlozman and John T. Tierney, *Organized Interests and American Democracy* (New York: Harper & Row, 1986), 148–57.

16. Administrative Procedure Act of 1946.

17. Scott R. Furlong, "Exploring Interest Group Participation in Executive Policymaking," in Herrnson, Shaiko, and Wilcox, eds., *The Interest Group Connection* (Washington, DC: CQ Press, 2005), 282–97.

18. 347 U.S. 483 (1954).

19. Citizens United v. Federal Election Commission, 558 U.S. 477 (2010).

20. National Rifle Association: Political Victory Fund, www.nrapvf.org/grades/.

21. Nathan Nascimento, "The Biggest Threat to Tax Reform," *U.S. News & World Report,* October 24, 2017.

22. Frances Fox Piven and Richard Cloward, *Poor People's Movements: Why They Succeed, How They Fail* (New York: Vintage Books, 1977).

23. Occupy*Posters, Tumblr, http://owsposters.tumblr.com/post/11944143747/if-us-land-mass-were-distributed-like-us, accessed July 3, 2016.

24. Harold Brubaker, "'Occupy Wall Street' Protest Movement Seeks a Philadelphia Foothold," *Philadelphia Inquirer*, October 2, 2011, available from Lexis-Nexis Academic.

25. James C. McKinley Jr., "At the Protests, the Message Lacks a Melody," *New York Times*, October 19, 2011, available from Lexis-Nexis Academic.

26. Letter to the Editor, *New York Times*, November 17, 2011, available from Lexis-Nexis Academic.

27. Gloria Goodale, "Occupy Wall Street: Time to Become More Overtly Political?," *Christian Science Monitor*, November 16, 2011, available from Lexis-Nexis Academic.

28. Fox Piven and Cloward, *Poor People's Movements*.

29. Stephanie Zacharek, Eliana Dockterman, and Haley Sweetland Edwards, "The Silence Breakers," *Time*, December 18, 2017.

30. Shyaam Subramanian, "Advocacy Works: Grassroots Advocacy Helps Protect Access to Healthcare," *Bolder Advocacy*, April 15, 2017.

31. Address to the Senate, September 28, 1987 (updated 1989), in United States Senate, Lobbyists, https://www.senate.gov/legislative/common/briefing/Byrd_History_Lobbying.htm.

32. Dr. Adam Feldman, "The Most Effective Friends of the Court," May 16, 2016, https://empiricalscotus.com/2016/05/11/the-most-effective-friends-of-the-court/.

Chapter 16

1. Harold Lasswell, "The Structure and Function of Communication in Society," in *Mass Communications*, ed. Wilbur Schram (Urbana: University of Illinois Press, 1969), 103, as discussed in Graber, *Mass Media and American Politics*, 5.

2. John D. Stevens, *Sensationalism and the New York Press* (New York: Columbia University Press, 1991).

3. David Protess, *The Journalism of Outrage: Investigative Reporting and Agenda Building in America* (New York: Guilford Press, 1991).

4. Greg Botelho, "The Day Politics and TV Changed Forever," CNN, March 14, 2016, https://www.cnn.com/2016/02/29/politics/jfk-nixon-debate/index.html.

5. Leslie Clark, "Walter Cronkite: Witness to History," PBS, 2016, http://www.pbs.org/wnet/americanmasters/walter-cronkite-about-walter-cronkite/561/.

6. Jeffrey M. Berry and Sarah Sobieraj, *The Outrage Industry: Political Opinion Media and the New Incivility* (New York: Oxford University Press, 2014), 7.

7. Markus Prior, "Media and Political Polarization," *Annual Review of Political Science*, February 2, 2013, 10.1146/annurev-polisci-100711-135242.

8. Amy Mitchell, Jeffrey Gottfried, Jocelyn Kiley, and Katerina Eva Matsa, "Political Polarization and Media Habits," Pew Research Center, October 21, 2014.

9. Annual Report of the Federal Radio Commission to the Congress of the United States for the Fiscal Year Ended June 30, 1927 (Washington, DC: U.S. Government Printing Office, 1927), 1.

10. Radio Act of 1927, 47 U.S.C. §§ 81–119 (Suppl. 1 1925).

11. 47 U.S.C. §§ 151 et seq.

12. New York Times Company v. United States, 403 U.S. 713 (1971).

13. United States Telecom Association v. FCC, No. 15-1063 (D.C. Cir. 2016).

14. Alex Byers, "Court Upholds Obama-Backed Net Neutrality Rules," *Politico*, June 14, 2016, http://www.politico.com/story/2016/06/court-upholds-obama-backed-net-neutrality-rules-224309, accessed June 24, 2016.

15. Gerry Smith, "Why Trump Wants to Toss Obama's Net Neutrality Rules," *Washington Post*, November 29, 2017.

16. The Telecommunications Act of 1996, Pub. L. No. 104-104, Stat. (1996).

17. John Light, "How Media Consolidation Threatens Democracy: 857 Channels (and Nothing On)," *Moyers & Company*, May 12, 2017.

18. United States v. AT&T, Inc., United States District Court for the District of Columbia, Civil Case No. 17-2511, June 12, 2018.

19. Light, "How Media Consolidation Threatens Democracy."

20. "The Overlooked, Under-Reported and Ignored Stories of 2016," *Moyers & Company*, December 28, 2016.

21. Jody Baumgartner and Jonathan S. Morris, "The *Daily Show* Effect: Candidate Evaluations, Efficacy, and American Youth," *American Politics Research* 34, no. 3 (2006): 341–67.

22. Thomas E. Patterson, "Doing Well and Doing Good," Faculty Research Working Paper Series, RWP01-001 (Cambridge, MA: John F. Kennedy School of Government, Harvard University, 2000).

23. See, for example, Bernard Goldberg, *Bias: A CBS Insider Exposes How the Media Distort the News* (New York: Perennial, 2002).

24. D. Domke et al., "The Politics of Conservative Elites and the 'Liberal Media' Argument," *Journal of Communication* 49, no. 4 (1999): 35–58.

25. Larry J. Sabato, *Feeding Frenzy: How Attack Journalism Has Transformed American Politics* (New York: Free Press, 1991).

26. Markus Prior, *Post-Broadcast Democracy: How Media Choice Increases Inequality in Political Involvement and Polarizes Elections* (New York: Cambridge University Press, 2007).

27. Ibid.

28. Aldous Huxley, *Brave New World* (London: Chatto & Windus, 1932).

29. Prior, *Post-Broadcast Democracy*, 142.

30. Andrea Caumont, "Who's Not Online? 5 Factors Tied to the Digital Divide," Pew Research Center, November 8, 2013, http://www.pewresearch.org/fact-tank/2013/11/08/whos-not-online-5-factors-tied-to-the-digital-divide/, accessed Mary 12, 2016.

31. Pew Research Center, "What Americans Know: 1989–2007," April 15, 2007, http://www.people-press.org/files/legacy-pdf/319.pdf.

32. Markus Prior, *Post-Broadcast Democracy*.

33. Theodore Kupfer, "According to Polls, Roy Moore Is Winning," *National Review*, November 29, 2017.

34. F. H. Buckley, "Education in 2018—Three Major Challenges Facing America's Schools and Students," Fox News, December 25, 2017.

35. Letter from Thomas Jefferson to Marie-Joseph-Paul-Yves-Roch-Gilbert du Motier, marquis de Lafayette, 4 November 1823, Founders Early Access, http://rotunda.upress.virginia.edu/founders/default.xqy?keys=FOEA-print-04-02-02-3843.

36. Knight First Amendment Institute at Columbia University v. Donald Trump, U.S. District Court for the Southern District of New York, 17 Civ. 5205 (2018).

Unit 5 Review

1. Andrew Cohen, "How Voter ID Laws Are Being Used to Disenfranchise Minorities and the Poor," *The Atlantic*, March 16, 2012.

2. Ryan Scott, "New Report: Millennials' Political Behavior Will Surprise You," HuffPost, December 12, 2016, https://www.huffingtonpost.com/ryan-scott/new-report-millennials-po_b_10764426.html.

3. Nicholas Lemann, "Conflict of Interests: Does the Wrangling of Interest Groups Corrupt Politics—or Constitute It?" *The New Yorker*, August 11, 2008.

4. Full Transcript: Jill Stein, Politico, September 19, 2016, https://www.politico.com/story/2016/09/full-transcript-jill-stein-228336.

5. 585 U.S. __ (2018).

6. Emily Mongon, "AARP Launches Lawsuit against Provider over Alleged Resident Dumping," *McKnight's Long Term Care News*, November 14, 2017.

7. McCutcheon v. Federal Election Commission, 572 U.S. __, 134 S. Ct. 1434 (2014).

Practice Exam

1. Michael Greshko, Laura Parker, and Brian Howard Clark, "A Running List of How Trump Is Changing the Environment," *National Geographic*, published March 31, 2017. Updated July 5, 2018. Accessed on July 12, 2018 at https://news.nationalgeographic.com/2017/03/how-trump-is-changing-science-environment/.

Index

Note: Page numbers followed by *f* indicate figures, and page numbers followed by *t* indicate tables.

D

DACA (Deferred Action for Childhood Arrivals Program), 174, 331
The Daily Show, 519
Dark money donations, 187
Dark Web, 349
Data
  analyzing, 11, 80, 120, 139, 140–141, 226–227, 495, 522
  analyzing limitations of, 367
  analyzing trends in, 445
  explaining patterns and trends in, 431
  geographic representation of, 470
  interpreting, 305
  polling, 522
  quantitative, analyzing and interpreting, 470–471
Davis, Thomas, 112
Daylight Savings Time, 218
DEA (Drug Enforcement Agency), 65
Death penalty, 281–282
Debt, post-Revolutionary era, 30
Declaration of Independence
  ideals in, 8–9
  importance of, 333
  natural rights and, 272, 338
  preamble to, 9, 292, 335
De facto segregation, 302
Defamation, 275
Defense of Marriage Act (DOMA), 86–87
Defense spending, 133
Deferred Action for Childhood Arrivals Program (DACA), 174, 331
De Jonge v. Oregon, 265t, 276–277
De jure segregation, 302
Delegate, 467, 468–469
Delegate role, 137
Democracy
  ancient Greece, 10
  definition of, 8
  direct, 49
  founders' distrust of, 54–55
  globalization and, 348
  information access in, 356
  participatory, 13, 487
  political participation and, 417
  representative, 10, 16, 418, 425, 447, 454, 486–487
  theories of, 13–15
Democracy in America (Tocqueville), 333–334
Democratic National Convention, 387, 472, 473f
Democratic Party
  Ada algorithm, 461
  economic policy of, 391–392
  ideology of, 385, 385f, 386–387
  modern, 462–464, 465
  national strategy of, 472
  nomination process, 468–469
  political beliefs of, 329
  Sanders and, 455–456
  voter identification with, 459
  women and, 369
Democratic representation
  public opinion and, 369–374
  voting behavior and, 436–438
Demographic characteristics, voter turnout and, 426–428
Department of Agriculture, 219f, 220f
Department of Commerce, 220f

Department of Defense, 219
Department of Education, 220f
Department of Energy, 81, 220f
Department of Health and Human Services, 81, 220f
Department of Homeland Security, 220f, 224
Department of Housing and Urban Development, 220f
Department of Justice, 219, 220f, 223
Department of Labor, 220f
Department of State, 219, 220f
Department of the Interior, 220f, 236
Department of Transportation, 220f
Department of Treasury, 219, 220f
Department of Veterans Affairs, 220f
Department of War, 219, 220f
Deputy secretaries, 224
Deregulation, 515
Descriptive representation, 118, 139–140
Desegregation, 208, 301–302
Devolution, 81
DeVos, Betsy, 158
Digital divide, 521
Dionne, E. J., 371
Diplomacy, by president, 159
Direct democracy, 49
Disability insurance, 77
Disability rights, 79, 293–296
Discharge petition, 129
Discretionary spending, 133
Discrimination
  affirmative action and, 302–303
  gender, 311–313
  laws against, 311
  against people with disabilities, 294
  racial, 297, 357–360, 373f
  reverse, 302–303
  Supreme Court rulings on, 312–313
  workplace, 311
Disenfranchisement, 432, 437
Dissenting opinions, 72, 204
District courts, 44, 105, 190, 192, 193, 200, 201f
District of Columbia v. Heller, 277–278
Divided government, 138
Doctors Without Borders, 346, 346f
Dollar, U.S., 394
"Doll study," 301, 301f
DOMA (Defense of Marriage Act), 86–87
Domestic policy. *See* Public policy
Donors, 372, 488
Double jeopardy, 280–281
Douglas, William, 270, 273–274, 283
Downs, Anthony, 437
Dred Scott v. Sanford, 198, 296
Drinking age, 79
Drone strikes, 131, 176, 177
Drug Enforcement Administration (DEA), 65
Drug testing, 280
Dual federalism, 74–75, 75f
Due process clause, 74, 86, 187, 255, 263, 264
Durant, Paul Skyhorse, 271f

E

EAA (Equal Access Act), 5–7
Earle, Peter, 107, 108f
Earmarks, 112
Eckhardt, Christopher, 274
E-commerce, 485

Economic crises
  Great Depression, 170, 343, 391, 76077
  Great Recession, 343, 391
  post-Revolutionary era, 30
Economic interest groups, 491
Economic policy
  Congress and, 111t
  Federal Reserve System, 393–394
  fiscal policy, 391–392
  Keynesianism, 390–391, 392t, 393
  monetary theory, 392t, 393
  political ideology and, 386–387, 389–393
  supply-side theory and, 391, 392t
  theories of, 390–391
Economic recession, 389
Economy
  command-and-control, 336, 389
  globalized, 347–348
  government role in, 336–337, 389
  gross domestic product, 389
  inflation and, 389–390, 394
  laissez-faire, 336–337, 389
  mixed, 389
  monitoring health of, 389–390
  voting decisions and, 343
Education
  civic, 340–341
  Elementary and Secondary Education Act, 81
  Every Student Succeeds Act, 81
  federal funding of, 80, 81
  No Child Left Behind Act, 81
  per-pupil spending by state, 83f
  political efficacy and, 427
  reform of, 399
  school choice, 399
  segregated, 298–300
  state control over, 81, 83
  student debt, 456
  voter turnout and, 426, 426f
Education policy, 81, 83
Eighth Amendment, 261, 261t, 265t, 281–282
Eisenhower, Dwight David, 235–236, 305
Eisenstadt v. Baird, 284
Elastic clause, 43
Elected representatives. *See also* Political candidates; Representatives, U.S.; Senators, U.S.
  accountability of, 356, 418
  roles of, 137–138, 139–140, 418
  voting decisions by, 137
Election districts, boundaries of, 107–108
Elections. *See also* Presidential elections
  citizen preferences and, 364
  critical, 462
  to House of Representatives, 10, 43
  impact of, 438
  incumbency advantage in, 115, 117, 119
  of judges, 187–188
  money and, 419–421, 443–448
  nomination process, 466–474
  politics of congressional, 114–121
  primary, 439, 467–470, 467f
  to Senate, 10, 43
  state control over, 437
  by state governments, 68
  voter turnout in, 425, 435f
Elector, 440
Electoral College, 44, 55, 168, 195, 436, 439, 440–441, 441f, 475. *See also* Voters and voting process